Atiyah's
ACCIDENTS, COMPENSATION
AND THE LAW

LAW IN CONTEXT

Editors: Robert Stevens (Haverford College, Pennsylvania),
William Twining (University College, London) and
Christopher McCrudden (Lincoln College, Oxford)

ALREADY PUBLISHED

Company Law and Capitalism (Second Edition), Tom Hadden
Karl Llewellyn and the Realist Movement (reissue), William Twining
Cases and Materials on the English Legal System (Fourth Edition), Michael Zander
Computers and the Law, Colin Tapper
Tribunals and Government, J. A. Farmer
Government and Law (Second Edition), T. C. Hartley and J. A. G. Griffith
Lane, Law and Planning, Patrick McAuslan
Landlord and Tenant (Second Edition), Martin Partington
How to do Things with Rules (Second Edition), William Twining and David Miers
Evidence, Proof and Probability (Second Edition), Richard Eggleston
Family Law and Social Policy (Second Edition), John Eekelaar
Consumers and the Law (Second Edition), Ross Cranston
Law and Politics, Robert Stevens
Obscenity, Geoffrey Robertson
Labour Law (Second Edition), Paul Davies and Mark Freedland
Charities, Trusts and Social Welfare, Michael Chesterman
The Law-Making Process (Second Edition), Michael Zander
An Introduction to Law (Second Edition), Phil Harris
Sentencing and Penal Policy, Andrew Ashworth
Law and Administration, Carol Harlow and Richard Rawlings
Legal Foundations of the Welfare State, Ross Cranston
British Government and the Constitution, Colin Turpin
Sexual Divisions in Law, Katherine O'Donovan
The Law of Contract, Hugh Collins

CONTENTS

Table of cases ... x
Preface to the fourth edition ... xix
Abbreviations ... xxi

PART 1 THE ISSUES IN PERSPECTIVE

Chapter 1 Introduction ... 3
1. *Compensation for accidents* ... 3
2. *Mixed systems in a mixed society* ... 7
3. *Some facts and figures* ... 15

PART 2 THE TORT SYSTEM

Chapter 2 Negligence as fault ... 31
1. *The conceptual structure of the law* ... 31
2. *A question of fact?* ... 35
3. *The nature of negligence* ... 39
4. *Foreseeability* ... 44
5. *The magnitude of the harm which may occur* ... 48
6. *The value of the activity being pursued, and the burden of the precautions needed to avoid the harm* ... 49
7. *The purposes of the negligence formula* ... 51
8. *The objective standard of care* ... 53
9. *Negligence in design and negligence in operation* ... 55

Chapter 3 Negligence: the scope of the tort ... 60
1. *The nature of the duty of care* ... 60
2. *Liability for physical damage* ... 63
3. *Mental distress* ... 69

	4 *Economic or pecuniary loss*	73
	5 *Family claims*	75
	6 *Omissions*	80

Chapter 4 Causation and remoteness of damage   94
  1 *Cause in fact*   95
  2 *Legal limits on the liability of causes in fact*   101
  3 *Some practical consequences of need to limit liability for consequences*   111

Chapter 5 The conduct of the plaintiff   116
  1 *Contributory negligence*   117
  2 *Volenti non fit injuria*   126

Chapter 6 Strict liability   133
  1 *Breach of statutory duty*   133
  2 *Contractual duties*   137
  3 RYLANDS v. FLETCHER, *nuisance and animals*   138
  4 *Joint liability*   140
  5 *Vicarious liability*   141
  6 *The nature of strict liability*   142
  7 *Proposals to extend strict liability*   143

Chapter 7 Damages for personal injuries and death   150
  1 *The lump sum*   150
  2 *Full compensation*   162
  3 *Lost earnings*   166
  4 *Full compensation for lost earnings: is it justified?*   169
  5 *Full compensation: the commitment in practice*   175
  6 *Medical and other expenses*   181
  7 *Intangible losses*   183
  8 *Overall maxima*   191

PART 3 THE TORT SYSTEM IN OPERATION

Chapter 8 The plaintiffs   195
  1 *Accident victims and tort claimants*   195
  2 *Claims consciousness*   201
  3 *Road accidents and industrial accidents*   204

Contents vii

Chapter 9	The defendants: part I	210
	1 The individual defendant	210
	2 Employers and corporations	216

Chapter 10	The defendants: part II	223
	1 Insurers	223
	2 The nature of liability insurance	224
	3 First party insurance for the benefit of others	230
	4 The impact of liability insurance on the law	232
	5 The Motor Insurers' Bureau	247
	6 Some problems of liability insurance	252

Chapter 11	The administration of the tort system	256
	1 The importance of settlements	257
	2 Obtaining legal assistance	257
	3 The course of negotiations	261
	4 When negotiations break down	267
	5 The time taken to achieve a settlement	271
	6 The amount of compensation	273

PART 4 OTHER COMPENSATION SYSTEMS

Chapter 12	First party insurance	279
	1 The types of first party insurance	279
	2 First party insurance compared with tort liability	283

Chapter 13	Criminal injuries	291
	1 The justification for the scheme	291
	2 The scope of the scheme	297
	3 Comparison between the scheme and tort liability	303

Chapter 14	The common law and the welfare state	313
	1 Workman's compensation and national insurance	313
	2 The Beveridge Report and the 1946 Acts	319
	3 Developments since 1946	323

viii   Contents

Chapter 15	The industrial injuries system	327
	1 The scope of the system	327
	2 Accidents and diseases	330
	3 Benefits: short-term incapacity	333
	4 Benefits: long-term incapacity	335
	5 Benefits for widows	346
	6 Administration	348
Chapter 16	Social security: sickness and other benefits	355
	1 Benefits for sickness and invalidity	355
	2 Benefits for widows	361
	3 Supplementary benefits	362
	4 Administration	365
	5 The problem of fraud and abuse	366
Chapter 17	Other forms of assistance	369
	1 The taxation system	369
	2 Occupational sick pay and other employment benefits	371
	3 Ad hoc Government schemes	373
	4 The social services	375

PART 5   THE OVERALL PICTURE

Chapter 18	A plethora of systems	387
	1 The inter-relation of the systems	387
	2 The choice of compensation systems	390
	3 Subrogation	393
	4 Tort damages and other compensation	398
	5 Criminal injuries and other compensation	409
Chapter 19	An appraisal of the fault principle	411
	1 The dominance of the fault principle	411
	2 An indictment of the fault principle	415
Chapter 20	The distinction between human and natural causes	437
	1 Society's 'responsibility' for human causes	438
	2 Protecting reasonable expectations	441

	3 Egalitarianism and the problem of drawing the line	442
	4 Drawing the line in practice	445
Chapter 21	The cost of compensation	447
	1 The cost of tort compensation	449
	2 Costs not paid through the tort system	455
	3 The cost of criminal injuries compensation	461

PART 6   OBJECTIVES

Chapter 22	The meaning and purposes of compensation	467
	1 Some preliminary questions	467
	2 Compensation	472
	3 The distribution of losses and the allocation of risks	476
Chapter 23	Retribution and vindication	484
	1 Retribution	484
	2 Vindication or satisfaction	486
Chapter 24	Deterrence and Prevention	489
	1 Rules and standards of behaviour	490
	2 Accident prevention via insurance	499
	3 General deterrence	506

PART 7   THE FUTURE

Chapter 25	Reform	545
	1 Basic issues	545
	2 Proposals and schemes	566
	3 The way ahead	571
	4 Damage to property	576
	5 The role of the insurance industry and the legal profession	577
	Notes	581
	Index	629

TABLE OF CASES

Ackworth v. *Kempe* (1778) 1 Doug. K.B. 40 — 597
Adams v. *Andrews* [1964] 2 Lloyd's Rep. 347 — 249
Adamson v. *Motor Vehicle Insurance Trust* (1957) 58 W.A.L.R. 56 — 617
Albert v. *M.I.B.* [1972] A.C. 301 — 251
Alder v. *Moore* [1961] 2 Q.B. 57 — 602
Allen v. *Burroughs Machines* [1983] C.L.Y. 994 — 593
Allen v. *Distillers Co. (Biochemicals) Ltd* [1974] 2 All E.R. 365 — 590
Allen v. *Sir Alfred McAlpine* [1968] 2 Q.B. 229 — 271
Andrews v. *Grand & Toy Alberta Ltd* (1978) 83 D.L.R. (3d) 452 — 593
Anns v. *Merton L.B.C.* [1978] A.C. 728 — 583, 584, 585
Arenson v. *Arenson* [1977] A.C. 405 — 584
Arnold v. *Teno* (1978) 83 D.L.R. (3d) 609 — 82
Ashton v. *Turner* [1981] Q.B. 137 — 599
Austin v. *Zurich Insurance Co.* [1945] K.B. 250 — 613

Baker v. *Willoughby* [1970] A.C. 476 — 586
Barnett v. *Chelsea Hospital* [1968] 1 All E.R. 1068 — 585, 586
Bernina, The (1888) 13 App. Cas. 1 — 587
Beswick v. *Beswick* [1968] A.C. 58 — 599
Birch v. *Thomas* [1972] 1 All E.R. 905 — 597
Bird v. *Pearce* [1978] R.T.R. 290 — 619
Birkett v. *James* [1978] A.C. 297 — 272
Bishop v. *Cunard White Star* [1950] P. 240 — 591
Blake v. *Richards and Wellington Industries* (1974) K.I.R. 151 — 598
Boardman v. *Sanderson* [1964] 1 W.L.R. 1317 — 584
Bolton v. *Stone* [1951] A.C. 850 — 429–30, 583, 598
Bourhill v. *Young* [1943] A.C. 92 — 584
Bowker v. *Rose* [1978] 2 C.L. §271 — 615
Bradburn v. *G.W. Rly* (1874) L.R. 10 Ex. 1 — 403, 405
Brice v. *Brown* [1984] 1 All E.R. 997 — 587
Broome v. *Cassell* [1972] A.C. 1027 — 484

Table of cases   xi

Brown v. Roberts [1965] 1 Q.B. 1   585, 598
Buckley v. John Allen & Ford Ltd [1967] 2 Q.B. 637   590
Buckley v. Smith Transport [1946] 4 D.L.R. 721   617
Burmah Oil Co. v. Lord Advocate [1965] A.C. 75   100, 617
Burns v. Edman [1970] 2 Q.B. 541   306
Bux v. Slough Metals Ltd [1974] 1 All E.R. 262   98

Caltex Oil (Australia) Pty. Ltd v. The Dredge 'Willemstad' 136 C.L.R. 529
    (1975–6)   584
Carmarthenshire County Council v. Lewis [1955] A.C. 549   422
Carroll v. Hooper [1964] 1 All E.R. 845   615
Cassidy v. Minister of Health [1951] 2 K.B. 343   596
Caswell v. Powell Duffryn Collieries [1940] A.C. 152   586, 587
Cavanagh v. Ulster Weaving Co. [1960] A.C. 145   583
Chadwick v. British Railways [1961] 1 W.L.R. 912   584
Chaplin v. Boys [1971] A.C. 356   242
Charlton v. Forest Printing Ink Co. [1978] I.R.L.R. 559   603
Clarke v. National Insurance Corpn. [1963] 3 All E.R. 375   597
Clarke v. Vedel [1979] R.T.R. 26   599
Cook v. Lewis [1952] 1 D.L.R. 1   98
Cookson v. Knowles [1979] A.C. 556   155–6, 591, 592
Cooper v. M.I.B. [1985] Q.B. 575   599
Cope v. Sharpe [1912] 1 K.B. 496   618
Corfield v. Groves [1950] 1 All E.R. 488   251
Crowes Transport Ltd v. Phoenix Assurance Ltd [1965] 1 All E.R. 596 602
Cunningham v. Harrison [1973] Q.B. 942   585, 592, 615

Davie v. New Merton Board Mills [1959] A.C. 604   233
Davies v. Swan Motor Co. [1949] 2 K.B. 291   587
Davies v. Taylor (No. 2) [1972] 3 All E.R. 836   242, 243, 598, 600
Davies v. Whiteways Cyder [1975] Q.B. 262   163
Davis Contractors Ltd v. Fareham U.D.C. [1956] A.C. 696   582
Deatons Pty. Ltd v. Flew (1949) 79 C.L.R. 370   596
Dennis v. L.P.T.B. [1948] 1 All E.R. 779   615
Deyong v. Shenburn [1946] K.B. 227   585
Dillon v. Twin State Gas & Electric Co. (1932) 163 A. 111   586
Dodd v. McGlashen [1967] A.L.R. 433   588
Dodd v. Wilson [1946] 2 All E.R. 691   588
Dodds v. Dodds [1978] Q.B. 543   122
Donnelly v. Joyce [1974] 1 Q.B. 454   585, 615
Donoghue v. Stevenson [1932] A.C. 562   60, 65–8
Dooley v. Cammell Laird Ltd [1951] 1 Lloyd's Rep. 271   584
Dorset Yacht Co. Ltd v. Home Office [1969] 2 Q.B.   412

xii TABLE OF CASES

Doughty v. *Turner Manufacturing Co.* [1964] 1 Q.B. 518   110, 115
Dunne v. *N W. Gas Board* [1964] 2 Q.B. 806   482

Electrochrome Ltd v. *Welsh Plastics* [1968] 2 All E.R. 205   584
Elliott v. *Liggens* [1902] 2 K.B. 84   613
Elstob v. *Robinson* [1964] 1 All E.R. 848   615
Erie Railroad Co. v. *Tompkins* (1938) 304 U.S. 64   427–9

Fagan v. *Metropolitan Police Commissioner* [1969] 1 Q.B. 439   586
Finlay v. *Railway Executive* [1950] 2 All E.R. 969   600
Fletcher v. *Autocar Ltd* [1968] 2 Q.B. 322   593, 598
Flint v. *Lovell* [1935] 1 K.B. 345   585
Foxley v. *Olton* [1964] 3 All E.R. 248   615
Franklin v. *Franklin* (1975) C.L.Y. 811   587
Froom v. *Butcher* [1979] Q.B. 268   119

Gale v. *Motor Union Insurance Co. Ltd* [1928] 1 K.B. 359   613
Gardner v. *Moore* [1984] A.C. 548   599, 604, 613
Gaskins v. *British Aluminium* [1976] Q.B. 524   600
Re Gillingham Bus Disaster Fund [1959] Ch. 62   614
Goldman v. *Hargrave* [1967] 1 A.C. 645   90–2
Goodburn v. *Thomas Cotton Ltd* [1968] 1 Q.B. 845   590
Gorris v. *Scott* (1874) L.R. 9 Ex. 125   109
Gowar v. *Hales* [1928] 1 K.B. 191   597
Gray v. *Barr* [1970] 2 Q.B. 626   604
Green v. *Russell* [1959] 5 Q.B. 226   597
Gregory v. *Kelly* [1978] R.T.R. 426   588
Groves v. *Wimborne* [1898] 2 Q.B. 402   314, 588
Gurtner v. *Circuit* [1968] 2 Q.B. 587   251, 599

Haigh v. *Ireland* [1974] 1 W.L.R. 43   136
Haley v. *London Electricity Board* [1965] A.C. 778   43
Hall v. *Brooklands Auto Racing Club* [1933] 1 K.B. 205   588
Hambrook v. *Stokes Bros.* [1925] 1 K.B. 141   584
Hammersmith City Rly. v. *Brand* (1896) L.R. 4 H.L. 171   618
Hardy v. *M.I.B.* [1964] 2 Q.B. 745   604
Harman v. *Crilly* [1943] 1 K.B. 168   597
Re Harrington Motor Co. Ltd [1928] Ch. 105   598
Re Harvest Lane Motor Bodies [1969] 1 Ch. 457   241
Haste v. *Sandell Perkins Ltd* [1984] Q.B. 735   615
Hay v. *Hughes* [1975] 1 All E.R. 257   590, 615
Heaps v. *Perrite Ltd* [1937] 2 All E.R. 60   598

Hedley Byrne & Co. v. *Heller & Partners Ltd* [1964] A.C. 465   73, 584
Hepburn v. *Tomlinson* [1966] A.C. 451   597
Hinz v. *Berry* [1970] 2 Q.B. 40   584
Hobbs v. *Marlowe* [1978] A.C. 16   237
Hodges v. *Harland & Wolff* [1965] 1 W.L.R. 235   593
Home Office v. *Dorset Yacht Co.* [1970] A.C. 1004   62, 63, 583, 585
Hood's Trustees v. *Southern Union* [1928] Ch. 793   598
Houghton v. *Hackney B.C.* (1961) 3 K.I.R. 612   603
Housecroft v. *Burnett* [1986] 1 All E.R. 332   593
Hudson v. *Ridge Manufacturing Co.* [1957] 2 Q.B. 348   585
Hultquist v. *Universal Pattern Engineering Co.* [1960] 2 Q.B. 467   601, 616

I.C.I. v. *Shatwell* [1965] A.C. 656   425, 588
I.R.C. v. *Hambrook* [1956] 2 Q.B. 641   613, 615
Ichard v. *Frangoulis* [1977] 2 All E.R. 461   591

Jefford v. *Gee* [1970] 2 Q.B. 130   407, 591
Jenner v. *Allen West & Co.* [1959] 1 W.L.R. 554   615
Jobling v. *Associated Dairies Ltd* [1982] A.C. 794   586
Jones v. *Livox Quarries Ltd* [1952] 2 Q.B. 608   604
Jones v. *Lloyd, The Times,* 22 March, 1967   596
Junior Books Ltd v. *Veitchi Co. Ltd* [1983] 1 A.C. 520   584

Kearns v. *Higgs & Hill* (1968) 4 K.I.R. 393   593
Keppel Bus Co. Ltd v. *Sa'ad Bin Ahmed* [1974] 2 All E.R. 700   596
King v. *Phillips* [1953] 1 Q.B. 429   584
King v. *Spours,* Kemp & Kemp, *The Quantum of Damages,* 11th Suppt.
    London, 1973   589
Kingston v. *Chicago & N.W. Rly* (1927) 211 N.W. 913   586

Lamb v. *Camden L.B.C.* [1981] Q.B. 625   586
Lamb v. *Durham C.C.* [1983] C.L.Y. 1011   593
Lane v. *Holloway* [1968] 1 Q.B. 379   604
Leakey v. *National Trust* [1980] 1 All E.R. 17   92
Lee v. *Lee's Air Farming Ltd* [1961] A.C. 12   607
Leigh and Sillivan Ltd v. *Aliakmon Shipping Co. Ltd* [1986] 2 W.L.R. 906   584
Leversley v. *Thomas Firth* [1953] 1 W.L.R. 1206   588
Lim Poh Choo v. *Camden Health Authority* [1980] A.C. 174   163, 182, 477, 592, 598
Lincoln v. *Hayman* [1982] 1 W.L.R. 488   615
Lister v. *Romford Ice & Cold Storage Co. Ltd* [1957] A.C. 555   242, 597, 613
Liverpool & London War Risks Insurance Association v. *Ocean Steamship Co.*
    Ltd [1947] 2 All E.R. 586   602

TABLE OF CASES

Liverpool Corpn v. *T. & H. R. Roberts* [1964] 3 All E.R. 56   602
Lloyd v. *Grace Smith & Co.* [1912] A.C. 716   597

McCallion v. *Dodd* [1966] N.Z.L.R. 710   614
McDowall v. *G.W. Rly* [1903] 2 K.B. 331   586
McGhee v. *National Coal Board* [1972] 3 All E.R. 1008   96, 98, 100–1
McGuckin v. *Cammell Laird & Co. Ltd* [1962] 1 Lloyd's Rep. 635   601
McHale v. *Watson* (1964) 111 C.L.R. 384   617
McKew v. *Holland and Hannen and Cubitts (Scotland) Ltd* [1969] 3 All E.R. 1621   586
McKinnon v. *Burtakowski* [1969] V.R. 899   586
McLoughlin v. *O'Brian* [1983] 1 A.C. 410   70, 72
McWilliams v. *Sir William Arrol & Co.* [1962] 1 All E.R. 623   97–8, 100
Mallett v. *McMonagle* [1970] A.C. 166   592
Marrison v. *Bell* [1939] 2 K.B. 187   613
Mason v. *Levy Auto Parts* [1967] 2 Q.B. 530   588
Maynard v. *West Midlands R.H.A.* [1984] 1 W.L.R. 634   583
Metzger v. *DHSS* [1978] 1 W.L.R. 1046   606
Midland Bank Trust Co. Ltd v. *Hett, Stubbs and Kemp* [1979] Ch. 384   585
Miller v. *Jackson* [1977] Q.B. 966   519, 618
Miller v. *Tremberth* [1983] C.L.Y. 1011   593
Mitchell (George) Ltd v. *Finney Lock Seeds Ltd* [1983] 2 A.C. 803   588
Mitchell v. *Mulholland* [1971] A.C. 666   153, 154, 592
Monk v. *Warbey* [1953] 1 K.B. 75   246, 251
Moody v. *Newcastle Church High School* [1983] C.L.Y. 1029   593
Ex parte Moore [1965] 1 All E.R. 81   609
Moorgate Mercantile Ltd v. *Twitchings* [1977] A.C. 890   584
Morey v. *Woodfield* [1963] 3 All E.R. 533n   597
Morgan v. *T. Wall Ltd* [1974] 1 Lloyd's Rep. 165   623
Moriarty v. *McCarthy* [1978] 1 W.L.R. 155   592
Morris v. *Ford Motor Co.* [1973] 1 Q.B. 792   598, 613
Morris v. *West Hartlepool Steam Co.* [1965] A.C. 552   494, 583
Mullarky v. *Edmund Nuttall* [1983] C.L.Y. 996   593
Murphy v. *Culhane* [1977] Q.B. 94   304
Murphy v. *Stone Wallwork Ltd* [1969] 2 All E.R. 949   153
Murray v. *Harringay Arena* [1951] 2 K.B. 529   588

Nabi v. *British Leyland (UK) Ltd* [1980] 1 All E.R. 667   615
Nettleship v. *Weston* [1971] 2 Q.B. 691   583, 598
Newton v. *Edgerley* [1959] 1 W.L.R. 1031   585
Nimmo v. *Alexander Cowan & Sons* [1968] A.C. 107   588

Table of cases   xv

Ogopogo, The [1971] 2 Lloyd's Rep. 410   585
Oliver v. *Birmingham & Midland Omnibus Co.* [1933] 1 K.B. 35   587
Olsen v. *Demolition & Construction Co. Ltd* (1957) *Kemp & Kemp*, Vol. 1, p. 361   592
Orman v. *Saville Sportswear* [1960] 3 All E.R. 105   611
Osterlind v. *Hill* (1928) 160 N.E. 301   82
Owens v. *Brimmell* [1977] 2 W.L.R. 943   587, 588

Paris v. *Stepney Borough Council* [1951] A.C. 367   48
Parry v. *Cleaver* [1970] A.C. 1   404, 614
Paterson v. *Chadwick* [1974] 2 All E.R. 772   597
Payne v. *Rly Executive* [1952] 1 K.B. 26   614
Peacock v. *Amusement Equipment Co. Ltd* [1954] 2 Q.B. 347   615
Performance Cars Ltd v. *Abraham* [1961] 3 All E.R.   413, 586
Perry v. *Kendricks Transport Ltd* [1956] 1 W.L.R. 85   588
Persson v. *London Country Buses* [1974] 1 All E.R. 1251   599
Pettersson v. *Royal Oak Hotel Ltd* [1948] N.Z.L.R. 136   596
Phillips v. *Britannia Hygiene Laundry* [1923] 2 K.B. 832   588
Phillips v. *L. & S.W. Rly Co.* (1879) 5 C.P.D. 280   593
Photo Production Ltd v. *Securicor Transport Ltd* [1980] A.C. 827   588
Pickett v. *British Rail* [1980] A.C. 136   591
Pigney v. *Pointer's Transport Ltd* [1957] 1 W.L.R. 1121   589
Re Polemis [1921] 3 K.B. 560   111
Pope v. *Murphy & Son Ltd* [1961] 1 Q.B. 222   591

Randall v. *M.I.B.* [1968] 1 W.L.R. 1900   599
Read v. *Lyons* [1947] A.C. 156   412, 588
Redpath v. *Belfast & Co. Down Rly* [1947] N.I. 167   615
Reffell v. *Surrey County Council* [1964] 1 W.L.R. 358   494
R v. *CICB, ex parte Clowes* [1977] 1 W.L.R. 1353   298
R v. *CICB, ex parte Ince* [1973] 3 All E.R. 808   305, 604
R v. *CICB, ex parte Lain* [1967] 2 Q.B. 864   603
R v. *CICB, ex parte Schofield* [1971] 2 All E.R. 1011   604
R v. *CICB, ex parte Thompstone* [1984] 1 W.L.R. 1234   305
R v. *CICB, ex parte Webb* [1986] Q.B. 184 (D.C.)   603
R v. *CICB, ex parte Webb* [1986] 3 W.L.R. 251 (C.A.)   603
R v. *Daly* [1974] 1 All E.R. 290   596, 602
R v. *Deputy Industrial Injuries Commissioner* [1967] 1 A.C. 725   609
R v. *Industrial Injuries Commissioner* [1966] 2 Q.B. 31   607
R v. *Industrial Injuries Commissioner, ex parte Humphreys* [1965] 3 All E.R. 885   608
R v. *Industrial Injuries Commissioner, ex parte Mellors* [1971] 2 Q.B. 401   608

TABLE OF CASES

R v. *National Insurance Commissioner, ex parte Viscusi* [1974] 2 All E.R. 724	610
Regan v. *Williamson* [1976] 1 W.L.R. 305	590
Reincke v. *Gray* [1964] 1 W.L.R. 832	608
Rivtow Marine Ltd v. *Washington Ironworks* (1973) 40 D.L.R. (3d) 530	584
Roberts v. *Dorothea Slate Quarries* [1948] 2 All E.R. 201	607
Roberts v. *Ramsbottom* [1980] 1 All E.R. 7	583, 617
Robinson v. *Post Office* [1974] 2 All E.R. 737	115, 598
Re *Roehampton Swimming Pool* [1968] 1 W.L.R. 1693	598
Romney Marsh v. *Trinity House* (1870) L.R. 5 Ex. 204	618
Rookes v. *Barnard* [1964] A.C. 1129	484
Rootes v. *Shelton* (1967) 116 C.L.R. 383	588
Rowden v. *Clarke Chapman & Co. Ltd* [1967] 3 All E.R. 608	152
Rowlands (Mark) Ltd v. *Berni Inns Ltd* [1985] 3 W.L.R. 964	614
Ryan v. *New York Central Rly Co.* (1866) 35 N.Y. 210	586
Rylands v. *Fletcher* (1868) L.R. 3 H.L. 330	133, 138, 482
S.C.M. (United Kingdom) Ltd v. *W. J. Whittall & Son, Ltd* [1971] 1 Q.B. 337	584
St Helen's Colliery Ltd v. *Hewitson* [1924] A.C. 59	328
Saltpetre, Case of, 12 Co. Rep. 12	618
Sayers v. *Perrin* (1966) Q.L.R. 89	587
Schuster v. *New York* (1958) 154 N.E. 2d. 534	583
Scottish Omnibuses v. *Wyngrove, The Times,* 24 June, 1966	583
Selfe v. *Ilford & District Hospital Management Committee, The Times,* 26 November, 1970	585
Shiels v. *Cruikshank* [1953] 1 W.L.R. 533	591
Smith v. *B.E.A.* [1951] 2 K.B. 893	597
Smith v. *Baker* [1891] A.C. 325	314, 588
Smith v. *Leech Brain* [1962] 2 Q.B. 405	586, 587
Smith v. *W. H. Smith & Son Ltd* [1952] 1 All E.R. 528	236
Southport Corpn v. *Esso Petroleum* [1956] A.C. 218	617
Spartan Steel & Alloys Ltd v. *Martin & Co. (Contractors) Ltd* [1973] 1 Q.B. 27	584
Stapley v. *Gypsum Mines* [1953] A.C. 663	587
Staveley Iron & Chemical Co. v. *Jones* [1956] A.C. 627	587
Sturges v. *Bridgman* (1879) 11 Ch.D. 852	516
Tan Chye Choo v. *Chong Kew Moi* [1970] 1 All E.R. 266	588
Taylor v. *Bristol Omnibus Co.* [1975] 2 All E.R. 1107	78
Taylor v. *O'Connor* [1971] A.C. 115	592
Thomas v. *Quartermaine* (1887) 18 Q.B.D. 685	587

Thomas v. *Wignall, The Times*, 20 December, 1985 — 594
Thompson v. *Price* [1973] Q.B. 838 — 590
Thornton v. *Board of School Trustees* (1978) 83 D.L.R. (3d) 480 — 593
Thornton v. *Kirklees M.B.C.* [1979] 2 All E.R. 349 — 612
Thurston v. *Todd* (1966–67) 84 W.N. (N.S.W.) Pt. 1, 231 — 178
Trew v. *Rly Passengers' Assurance Co.* (1861) 6 H. & N. 839 — 602

U.S. v. *Carroll Towing Co.* (1947) 159 F. 2d. 169 — 583

Vaughan v. *Taff Vale Rly* (1860) 5 H. & N. 679 — 618
Versic v. *Connors* (1969) 90 W.N. (N.S.W.) (Pt. 1) 33 — 587
Videan v. *British Transport Commission* [1963] 2 Q.B. 650 — 425
Vincent v. *Lake Erie Transportation Co.* (1910) 124 N.W. 221 — 427–9

Wagman v. *Vare Motors* [1959] 1 W.L.R. 853 — 601
The Wagon Mound (No. 1) [1961] A.C. 388 — 111, 412
The Wagon Mound (No. 2) [1967] 1 A.C. 617 — 583
Waite v. *N.E. Rly* (1858) E.B. & E. 719 — 587
Walker v. *John McLean & Sons Ltd* [1979] 2 All E.R. 965 — 593
Walton v. *British Leyland, The Times*, 13 July, 1978 — 93
Ward v. *James* [1966] 1 Q.B. 273 — 593
Warren v. *Henley's* [1948] 2 All E.R. 935 — 596
Warren v. *King* [1963] 3 All E.R. 993n — 590
Warren v. *Scruttons* [1962] 1 Lloyd's Rep. 947 — 587
Watson v. *Powles* [1968] 1 Q.B. 596 — 591
Waugh v. *James Allan Ltd* [1964] 2 Lloyd's Rep. 1 — 619
West (H.) & Sons Ltd v. *Shephard* [1964] A.C. 326 — 188
White v. *Blackmore* [1972] 3 All E.R. 158 — 598
Wilkinson v. *Downton* [1827] 2 Q.B. 57 — 622
Williams v. *Grimshaw* (1967) 3 K.I.R. 610 — 603
Wise v. *Kaye* [1962] 1 Q.B. 638 — 188, 593
Withers v. *Perry Chain Co.* [1961] 1 W.L.R. 1314 — 588
Woolfall & Rimmer v. *Moyle* [1942] 1 K.B. 66 — 602
Wooldridge v. *Sumner* [1963] 2 Q.B. 43 — 588, 598
Wringe v. *Cohen* [1940] 1 K.B. 229 — 589
Wright v. *British Railways Board* [1983] 2 A.C. 773 — 591, 592
Wulfson v. *Switzerland General Insurance Co. Ltd* [1940] 3 All E.R. 221 — 602
Wyatt v. *Hillingdon L.B.C.* (1978) L.G.R. 727 — 612

PREFACE TO THE FOURTH EDITION

The task of preparing a new edition of a major work by a distinguished scholar is both exciting and daunting. When left as free to pursue one's own course as I have been left by Professor Atiyah, decisions are having to be made constantly about whether merely to update a particular section or to attempt some more radical revision. In making such decisions I have been somewhat influenced by the publisher's desire to produce the book before the last edition became too out of date. It is no easy task to absorb, let alone revise, the many details of a book of the breadth of this one. Nevertheless, with Professor Atiyah's encouragement, I have not only considerably revised many sections of the text to bring them into line with recent developments, but also I have made quite a few stylistic changes and, in some places, rewritten passages which seemed to me unclear or misleading. I should add immediately, however, that I make the nature of my revisions clear only for the purpose of alerting readers to the fact that much in this edition is not the work of the original author, and is in no way his responsibility. At the same time, I must say that Professor Atiyah has been unstinting in his support and advice. He has read the whole manuscript with meticulous care and made penetrating comments which have saved me from some bad blunders. One could not imagine or wish for a more helpful and encouraging mentor.

The major structural alterations in this edition are the addition of much new material in Chapter 25 on no-fault compensation schemes; and the redistribution of material between Chapters 23 and 24. Throughout the book, but in particular in Chapter 20, I have made a start on coming to terms with Dr Jane Stapleton's important book, *Disease and the Compensation Debate* (Oxford, 1986). Much more will need to be done in the next edition to give proper emphasis to the distinction (to which her work alerts us) between accidents and diseases.

Even though there has been no single development since the last edition to approach in any way the importance of the Pearson Commission Report, there has been no shortage of relevant changes in the law. Particularly significant have been changes in the law relating to the assessment of damages, the adoption of an E. C. Directive on Liability for Defective Products, and the 1979 amendments to the Criminal Injuries Compensation Scheme (mentioned in the Preface to the last edition). There have also been (as always) a myriad of alterations, both major and minor, to the social security system. In fact, the law of social security was, at the time of writing, in such a state of flux and uncertainty (the White Paper had not been published) that much had to be left in a tentative state.

As things have turned out, the State earnings-related pension scheme has not been scrapped (see p. 345), but it has been somewhat modified. The changes to widows' benefits mentioned on pp. 348 and 362, and the changes to supplementary benefits mentioned on pp. 365–6, are contained in the Social Security Act 1986. Special hardship allowance (see pp. 343–4) has been replaced by a reduced earnings allowance at a maximum rate of 40% of the maximum rate of disablement benefit. The most important change contained in the 1986 Act but not foreshadowed in the text is the abolition of disablement gratuities for disablement assessed at less than 14% (see p. 335) except in the case of certain industrial diseases. Degrees of disablement between 14% and 19% will now qualify for a 20% pension. The former change seems desirable, while the latter is open to criticism (see p. 337).

In other respects, I have attempted to take account of developments up to the end of 1985, except that the social security benefit rates are those operating from 31st July, 1986.

October 1986   Peter Cane

ABBREVIATIONS

Australian Committee Report	*Compensation and Rehabilitation in Australia, Report of the National Committee of Inquiry* (Australian Government Publishing Service, Canberra, 1974)
Beveridge Report	*Social Insurance and Allied Services, Report by Sir William Beveridge* (Cmd. 6404, 1942)
Cantley Committee Report	*Report of the Personal Injuries Litigation Procedure Working Party* (Cmnd. 7476, 1979)
Conard	A. F. Conard and others, *Automobile Accident Costs and Payments* (University of Michigan Press, 1964)
Crisis in Car Insurance	ed. Keeton, O'Connell and McCord (University of Illinois Press, 1968)
Dollars, Delay and the Automobile Victim	*Studies in Reparation for Highway Injuries and Related Court Problems.* Supported by the Walter E. Meyer Research Institute for Law (Bobbs-Merril, 1968)
Finer Committee Report	*Report of the Committee on One-Parent Families* (Cmnd. 5629, 1974)
Fisher Committee Report	*Report of the Committee on the Abuse of Social Security Benefits* (Cmnd. 5228, 1973)
George	*Social Security: Beveridge and After* (Routledge & Kegan Paul, London, 1968)
Harris Survey	Report of a Pilot Survey of the Financial Consequences of Personal Injuries Suffered in Road Accidents in the City of Oxford During 1965, by D. R. Harris with the assistance of S. J. Hertz (unpublished, but for a summary see 119 *New Law Journal* 492)

Abbreviations

Harris 1984 Survey	D. R. Harris & Others, *Compensation and Support for Illness and Injury* (Oxford, 1984)
Ison	T. G. Ison, *The Forensic Lottery* (Staples Press, London, 1967)
Osgoode Hall Study	Linden, *Report of the Osgoode Hall Study on Compensation for Victims of Automobile Accidents* (Toronto, 1965)
Osgoode Hall Study (Victims of Crime)	Linden, *Report of the Osgoode Hall Study on Compensation for Victims of Crime* (Toronto, 1968)
Ogus and Barendt	*The Law of Social Security*, 2nd edn (London, 1982)
Pearson Report	*The Report of the Royal Commission on Civil Liability and Compensation for Personal Injury* (Cmnd. 7054, 1978, 3 volumes)
Piercy Committee Report	*Report of the Committee of Inquiry on the Rehabilitation, Training and Resettlement of Disabled Persons* (Cmd. 9883, 1956)
Reports (in Chapter 13)	*Reports of the Criminal Injuries Compensation Board: First Report* (Cmnd. 2782, 1965); *Second Report* (Cmnd. 3117, 1966); *Third Report* (Cmnd. 3427, 1967); *Fourth Report* (Cmnd. 3814, 1968); *Fifth Report* (Cmnd. 4179, 1969); *Sixth Report* (Cmnd. 4494, 1970); *Seventh Report* (Cmnd. 4812, 1971); *Eighth Report* (Cmnd. 5127, 1972); *Ninth Report* (Cmnd. 5468, 1973); *Tenth Report* (Cmnd. 5791, 1974); *Eleventh Report* (Cmnd. 6291, 1975); *Twelfth Report* (Cmnd. 6656, 1976); *Thirteenth Report* (Cmnd. 7022, 1977); *Fourteenth Report* (Cmnd. 7396, 1978); *Fifteenth Report* (Cmnd. 7752, 1979); *Sixteenth Report* (Cmnd. 8081, 1980); *Seventeenth Report* (Cmnd. 8401, 1981); *Eighteenth Report* (Cmnd. 8752, 1982); *Nineteenth Report* (Cmnd. 9093, 1983); *Twentieth Report* (Cmnd. 9399, 1984); *Twenty-First Report* (Cmnd. 9684, 1985)
Robens Committee Report	*Report of the Committee into Safety and Health at Work* (Cmnd. 5304, 1972)
Seebohm Report	*Report of the Committee on Local Authority and Allied Personal Social Services* (Cmnd. 3703, 1968)
Winn Committee Report	*Report of the Committee on Personal Injuries Litigation* (Cmnd. 3691, 1968)

| Woodhouse Report | *Report of the Royal Commission of Injury on Compensation for Personal Injuries in New Zealand* (Government Printer, New Zealand, 1967) |

PART ONE
The Issues in Perspective

1
Introduction

1 COMPENSATION FOR ACCIDENTS

This book deals with certain kinds of misfortune, and in particular with injury and damage arising from accidents. Although the term 'accident' is a convenient one, its meaning is not straightforward, and some further explanation of the way it is used in this book is necessary. First, we shall use the word 'accident' to cover injury and damage inflicted intentionally (as when, for example, one person deliberately assaults another), even though neither the inflicter nor the victim may consider the injury to be 'accidental' in the normal sense. Secondly, our use of the term is not confined to the technical legal sense – in this sense, injury or damage would be accidental only if it was not a foreseeable consequence of a deliberate or negligent act.

Thirdly, we are sometimes reluctant to refer to injury or damage resulting from natural causes as accidental: we might hesitate to say that a house, the roof of which was blown off by a hurricane, was damaged 'by accident' (although we might say that a person hit by the debris suffered an accident); or we might hesitate to say of a person who died of leukemia, that he died accidentally (although, of course, if a person, while on holiday, contracts a rare viral disease and dies soon after, we might call his death an accident). Fourthly, the term 'accident' is often used to refer to injury and damage which is caused by a sudden, non-repetitive, traumatic occurrence; in this sense it is contrasted with illness or disease, which often develops gradually, and often has no easily identifiable starting point. This is the sense in which it is most frequently used in this book. The distinction between 'traumatic' accidents and 'non-traumatic' diseases is, as has recently been pointed out,[1] of considerable practical and theoretical importance in the law, and it will be mentioned at various points, although the discussion in several parts of the book is concerned more specifically with 'traumatic' occurrences, such as road and industrial accidents, than with diseases.

The scope of this book is not limited to any of these narrower senses of the word 'accident', although its primary focus is on injury and damage for which the law provides some compensation. As we will see, the law distinguishes in many ways, not only between injury and damage resulting from natural causes, on the one hand, and human activity, on the other; but also between injury and damage of the latter type according to whether the person responsible for it was in some sense at fault. We will be considering to what extent these distinctions are justified. The ultimate questions with which we are concerned are: for what injuries and damage ought the law to provide compensation; what form should that compensation take; how should it be assessed; and who should pay for it? Important related issues include how compensation systems are administered and how the law seeks to reduce the amount of injury and damage inflicted.

This book is principally concerned with personal injuries and death, and only secondarily with damage to property. The principal reason for including some discussion of property damage questions is that it enables illuminating contrasts to be drawn between different possible ways in which a compensation system can operate. The comparison, for instance, between the way in which tort law works in relation to personal injuries and the way fire insurance works in relation to damage to houses is so significant that it would be wrong to exclude all reference to property damage. However, this book is not primarily concerned with property damage, and it does not deal, for example, with damage resulting from collisions or natural perils at sea. Shipping laws and practices are a matter of international concern and they therefore raise issues in many ways different from those raised by personal injury or even by other forms of property damage. For the same reason questions arising from aircraft accidents are not specifically dealt with. On the other hand, the general discussion of accidental personal injury and fatal accidents is partly, at least, relevant to shipping and aircraft accidents as to all others.

Just as the word 'accident' has a complex set of meanings, so the meaning of the term 'compensation' is also far from straightforward. We will consider the meanings of the word and the purposes of giving compensation in detail later. Here it is sufficient to note that the lawyer generally thinks of compensation as a method of making good a 'loss', of replacing something of which a person has been deprived. But the lawyer uses the word 'loss' in a rather strange way to include many things which are not losses in a literal sense. But in the context of personal injury and death, and accidental damage to property, it is at least reasonably clear that compensation has two major purposes. First, it is designed to make good measurable financial losses such as out-of-pocket expenses, income which has been 'lost' in the sense that it can no longer be earned, and property which has been physically damaged and must be repaired or replaced. Secondly it is designed to make amends for disabilities or loss of faculty, pain and suffering or death of a close relative. Here also the lawyer thinks mainly of compensating in financial terms: even though the 'loss' has no measurable financial value, compensation in money can be, and is, given.

Another question closely related to these is whether, as a society, we are making the most sensible use of the resources we devote to compensation for injury and damage. Without even beginning to embark on the controversial question whether we should not contribute a larger share of national resources to the old, the sick and the disabled, we cannot fail to ask whether the proportion of national resources which is already distributed to these groups is being sensibly allocated. Do we over-compensate some and under-compensate others? Is there any justification for compensating some people twice over and others not at all for basically similar misfortunes?

The answers to these questions cannot be found by looking at any one segment of the law. It is true that one large chapter of private law – the law of torts – appears to be central to the questions we have posed, and a large part of this book is in fact concerned with the law of torts. But to concentrate on this segment of private law to the exclusion of all else is to get a very distorted view of the way in which the problem of compensation for misfortunes is dealt with in our society. There are many other methods of compensation, such as the social security system and the criminal injuries compensation system, which deal with sickness and bodily injuries; then there is personal accident insurance, which operates principally, though by no means exclusively, in the field of damage to property.

But besides being only a part of the picture, the law of torts has come in practice to operate in a way which is very different from the way a simple statement of the relevant legal rules would suggest. The development of liability insurance has altered administration and financing of the tort system out of all recognition. Despite this, a book on the law of torts today does not look so very different from a similar book fifty years ago. There is surprisingly little difference in general form and structure between the first edition of Salmond on *Torts* published in 1907 and the 18th edition published in 1981. This is largely because it has been traditional in England and other common law countries to assume that law is largely, if not entirely, concerned with what goes on in courts and particularly appellate courts. What the Court of Appeal or the House of Lords decide is, in a very real sense, the law. What the courts decide is, of course, important, but it is necessary to place this part of the law in perspective, and that involves looking at things which go on outside the courts.

For example, since the vast majority of tort claims are settled out of court, the behaviour of insurance companies is at least as important as what lawyers and courts do, to an understanding of the way the tort system is administered in practice. Again, reading a book on the law of torts might well lead one to think that people who commit torts are constantly being called upon to pay damages or compensation for what they have done. Nothing could be farther from the truth. People who commit torts very rarely pay compensation to anyone although the courts certainly seem largely to ignore this fact. When tortfeasors *did* pay damages, lawyers were very concerned to justify this result. But now that they do not generally do so, most lawyers seem to have little interest in the question of financing. Yet there are very important questions at stake here. If the person who causes bodily injury to another is not to pay him compensation, then who *is* to pay it? Furthermore, once it is conceded that tortfeasors do not generally pay for the damage they have caused, all sorts of other hidden questions come to the surface. For example, should the way in which we assess compensation be different depending on who will pay it? Again, if the party at fault does not pay the compensation why should people be entitled to compensation only if they can find a person at fault? Moreover, recognition that tortfeasors do not pay damages must be accompanied by recognition that these damages are largely paid for by society as a whole. But recognition of *this* fact carries in its wake many other puzzles. In particular, it raises the question of the relationship between the welfare state and the tort system. *Society's* duty to the sick, the injured and the disabled is, it might be thought, discharged by the provision of social security benefits, the national health service and personal health and welfare services. What, then, is the place of the tort system in all this?

In addition to questions of this kind which arise from the changes in the practical operation of the tort system, all sorts of complex problems arise from the interrelation of the many systems of compensation operating simultaneously today. Should an injured person get his compensation through one system or another? Should he be compensated twice over? Should one compensation fund be entitled, having paid out compensation to an injured person, to recoupment from another fund? These questions have been dealt with to some extent by the courts in relation to the tort system. But they also arise in relation to compensation systems which are rarely the subject of court proceedings. In order to see these issues in perspective and to discuss them rationally it is necessary to look beyond what the courts do.

This book is primarily concerned with compensation for injury and damage, but it is impossible to overlook completely the question of accident prevention. Compensation is nearly always second best; prevention is usually the first aim. Law can play only a limited part in preventing injury and damage: the skills of mechanics, engineers, psychologists and so on are probably much more relevant. But even when the law is invoked to prevent (or reduce) accidents is is usually the criminal law which is used; and in our legal system the criminal law has very little to do with compensating people. This book does not profess to deal at length with the role of the criminal law in injury prevention, but the claim is often made for compensation systems that they also perform the incidental role of reducing or preventing accidents, and this subject is dealt with at length in Chapter 24.

2 MIXED SYSTEMS IN A MIXED SOCIETY

We live in a society which is based on a mixture of political and economic principles. It is a society in which many aspects of our lives are regulated by the State, and in which much of our money is spent for us by the State. But it is also a society in which we are entitled, within fairly broad margins, to spend the rest of our money on what we like and to arrange our affairs as we wish. It is a society in which, in principle, the prices of goods and services are fixed by supply and demand, so that prices reflect consumer preference; but it is also a society in which taxes and subsidies at every turn deflect consumer preferences from the directions they would take entirely unaided by the State's interference. It is a society in which there are great inequalities of income and wealth, and in which a substantial degree of inequality appears to be acceptable to the public; but it is also a society in which some of the most extreme and glaring forms of inequality of income are reduced by the taxation system.

In a society of this nature it is not surprising that we have a mixed collection of regimes for dealing with the problem of compensation for misfortune. Some misfortunes are so trivial that they are simply accepted as routine ups and downs of life; others are less trivial but are still regarded as a matter for the private individual to protect himself against if he wishes by private insurance; others are seen as sufficiently important to justify the State instituting a coercive system to ensure that compensation is paid to the victim by some other person; still others are so important that the State takes upon itself the burden of raising money to provide compensation or to assist victims with benefits in kind.

Obviously the choice of one system rather than another raises fundamental political, economic and social issues. For instance, how far is society justified, by the use of coercive power, in requiring people to protect *themselves* against misfortune? Or to put the question in another way, is society justified in instituting a system of compulsory insurance against certain misfortunes? If so, what provides this justification?

Again, if society regards some misfortunes as so serious and so deserving of the interference of the State that it is willing to shoulder the burden of paying compensation, how is the money to be raised for this compensation? Should it be raised by an insurance system in which premiums vary according to the risk insured against? Or by a system of flat-rate premiums? Or should the whole system be financed out of taxation? These questions in turn raise important issues about income redistribution.

As for the good of preventing or reducing injuries, it might seem at first sight that it raises no fundamental political problems. Surely everything possible should be done to prevent at any rate those accidents which cause personal injuries. But on further reflection it will be seen that this is not so. Society never tries to prevent all accidents, even those which cause personal injury. As a society we often have choices to make between objectives: shall we permit such and such an activity even though we know it will cause injuries? In making choices of this nature, there is plenty of room for disagreement on fundamental political grounds. For instance, we may decide to prohibit or regulate certain types of activity by statutory or administrative machinery: alternatively, we may decide to leave them to be regulated by the operation of a free market. For example we know that young drivers cause more accidents than older ones, and we may want to reduce the number of these accidents. How shall we do this? One way is to fix an age below which people are not allowed to drive – this is sixteen for a motor cycle, and seventeen for a car. Another way is to use the law to require drivers to insure, but to let the market provide the insurance. In this way, young drivers will have to pay higher premiums because, as a group, they cause more accidents than older people, and the costs of road accidents are mostly paid for out of premiums fixed by normal insurance principles. In fact, of course, we use both methods: statutory regulation (fixed age limits) and the market (variable insurance rates), but the precise combination of these two methods is largely arbitrary. Why sixteen or seventeen as the appropriate age limits? And are the extra premiums for young people really 'fair'? If a young person is allowed to drive at all, might it not be urged that all should be treated alike?

The distinction between an individualistic political philosophy and a more socialist philosophy affects the choice of compensation systems in many ways. Socialists tend to favour active state participation in the provision of help and care to those in need, whereas individualists often advocate that the state should just provide a coercive mechanism for enabling injured persons to obtain compensation from their injurers if they choose to. Individualists often favour providing assistance in cash, which the recipient can then use as he chooses, rather than assistance in kind.

The types and level of compensation available to members of a particular society will also depend to a great extent on the wealth of that society. In a society which has ceased to depend on subsistence agriculture it is clear that the first need of an individual is an income, and that the loss of income is the loss which ranks highest for compensation purposes; although even in wealthy countries there is room for argument about whether income should be replaced in full, irrespective of the size of the income. If society can afford it, other 'losses' may also be recognized as worthy of compensation such as loss of bodily function, pain and suffering, and perhaps at the end of the scale, mental distress from insult or indignity.

In modern Britain we can in practice distinguish broadly between three different compensation systems according to the State's involvement. First, there is personal accident insurance which the individual can buy if he wishes to protect himself against particular misfortunes. In practice – and this must be emphasized – the field of damage to property is almost entirely looked after by this form of compensation. People commonly insure against destruction of their houses by fire. Motor vehicles, too, are often insured comprehensively, which means that the owner will be compensated by his insurer for loss of or damage to the vehicle. Property which is used in the earning of profit, such as a factory or an office, or plant and machinery, is often insured, not only for its own replacement value, but also for loss of profit which might result from its being damaged or destroyed. Personal accident insurance can also be bought to provide protection against the risk of personal injury, but this is relatively uncommon. But the State does not force people to take out such insurances, however prudent it would be to do so. However, despite the lack of direct state involvement in this area, the State does intervene indirectly in various ways. First, it provides the legal framework within which people can make insurance contracts and enforce them in the courts. Secondly, there are statutory provisions regulating the activities of insurance companies. Many people depend greatly on insurance companies in arranging their affairs, and would suffer great loss and misfortune if an insurance company failed. So there is a great public interest in the solvency of insurance companies, although in this country, by contrast with the United States, statutory provisions are concerned only with the solvency of insurance companies, and not with the way they fix their premiums.

Secondly, we must consider the compensation system based on tort liability and liability insurance. This system is concerned primarily (although by no means exclusively) with providing protection against the risk of personal injury and consequent loss of income, pain and suffering, and permanent or partial disability; against the risk of the death of a breadwinner, causing loss of support to dependants; and against the risk of the death of a spouse or a child who did not support anyone, but whose death causes grief and anguish. Here, once again, the State provides the legal framework of rights and obligations, and the system of courts to enforce these rights and obligations. But, in addition, in important areas the State has used its coercive power to require potential tortfeasors to take out insurance against the risk of their being held liable. Users of motor vehicles must insure against liability for personal injury caused by their cars, and employers must insure against liability to their employees for injuries suffered at work. The function of compulsory insurance is not really to protect the insured against the cost of liability, but to ensure that the victim receives adequate compensation.

Tort compensation is, in theory, usually available only if the injury or damage was caused by someone's 'fault' – a very complex notion which we will examine later. In practice, tort liability is further restricted: most successful tort actions arise out of road or industrial accidents. In fact, only a very small proportion of injury victims receive any tort compensation.

The third compensation system consists of schemes operated directly by the State. The national insurance system primarily protects workers against income loss, and provides for various needs resulting from illness and unemployment; the industrial injuries scheme deals with injuries suffered and diseases contracted at work; the criminal injuries compensation scheme compensates the victims of criminal violence to the person. The supplementary benefits scheme provides basic assistance to persons in need who do not qualify for other benefits. In addition to cash benefits, the welfare state provides a wide range of personal social services useful to those who suffer personal injury – the national health service, rehabilitation and employment training centres, residential accommodation and day centres, home helps, and so on. Some groups of the disabled, especially blind people, receive special tax reliefs. Most social security benefits are available to those with the relevant need, regardless of whether the need was the result of natural causes or human conduct. And, unlike tort compensation, entitlement to social welfare benefits does not depend on proof that the need was the result of someone's *fault*.

This social welfare system has very little contact with the tort system or with private insurance systems, although some problems have arisen in connection principally with the question of double compensation. Should a person be able to claim both tort compensation and social security benefits? Suppose he receives free medical treatment; can he recover in a tort claim what it would have cost to have private treatment? Or suppose he has private treatment when he could have had free treatment; can this cost be recovered in a tort claim? And suppose he has private treatment paid for by private insurance; can he recover the cost of the treatment in a tort claim? All these problems are dealt with fully later. Here we are concerned to point out how little the tort system and the welfare state have influenced each other. They are utterly different from each other in structure, philosophy and execution. Tort offers 'full compensation', social security a good deal less. Tort pays compensation for pain and suffering; social security does not – though it does pay something for some disabilities. Tort compensates in money alone; social security provides a wide variety of welfare benefits as well as money. Tort pays lump sum compensation; social security payments are nearly all made periodically. Tort depends in practice on liability insurance; social security is financed by a mixture of personal (but compulsory) insurance and taxation – though the insurance element is becoming somewhat attenuated. Tort claims are mainly dealt with by private institutions, the insurance companies; social security is administered by the State. The tort system is vastly more expensive to operate than the social security system. Above all, tort claims are in the main confined to cases in which fault can be proved against someone covered by liability insurance; in the social security systems fault is utterly irrelevant.

In general, practising and academic lawyers alike have tended to ignore the social welfare system, particularly the 'personal social services' (i.e. the non-cash welfare services), and to devote all their attention to the tort system; and it has not yet become customary in English universities to teach the law relating to compensation for personal injury as a whole. This no doubt partially explains why reforms and change are rarely discussed against the background of *both* systems, except when discussion actually revolves around the points of contact. Changes in the tort system are continuously advocated by those who wish to reform it without paying the slightest attention to the social security system; and changes in the social security system are often advocated, and made, with no regard to their possible impact – indirect though it usually is – on the tort system.

The Pearson Royal Commission paid lip-service to the need to plan reforms in the light of both the tort and the social security systems. 'It is clear to us [the Report says] that the two systems have for too long been permitted to develop in isolation from each other, without regard to the fact that, between them, they meet many needs twice over and others not at all'.[2] Unfortunately, as is explained more fully later, the Report does not seriously and systematically face up to the problems of integrating the two systems.

Fundamental questions of priorities arise both within the existing compensation systems, and as between the existing systems and other forms of public expenditure. As an example of the latter, should more money be spent on compensating the sick and the injured and less (say) on schools or roads? This is a political question, the answer to which may well depend to a substantial extent on the economic development of the society asking it. In an under-developed country, for example, it may well be that compensation of the sick and injured is a low priority compared with the need for massive investment in industry or public education. In a more advanced country, on the other hand, it may well be right to devote a larger share of national resources to compensation for the disabled. Although lawyers must not ignore such issues, they are not legal questions and are not dealt with in this book. More important for the lawyer is the question of whether society strikes the right balance between accident prevention and compensation for accidents. Would it be wiser (or more economic) to devote a greater part of our resources to accident prevention, even at the expense of what we devote to compensation? If we spent more money on roads would this enable us to save more than it costs in compensation for road accidents? Questions like this are more likely to be asked by the economist engaged in cost-benefit analysis, or by the road-traffic engineer, than by the lawyer; but if the lawyer is to understand his own job properly it may well be necessary for him to look into questions of this kind, and they are touched on in parts of this book, though considerations of space, if nothing else, preclude fuller discussion.

The lawyer should be much more concerned, however, with issues concerning priorities within the existing systems. For example, should tort compensation continue to be 'full' when social security benefits are relatively low? Should a young childless widow be entitled to be maintained out of tort compensation if her husband is killed by fault, while the social security system expects a childless widow of thirty-nine to earn her living if her husband dies a natural death? Should tort benefits continue to be paid for 'pain and suffering' when social security benefits for permanent disability are still confined to industrial accidents? Should we continue to allow people to recover compensation from more than one compensation system when so many people receive so little, if anything, under any system? Is there any justification for paying higher compensation for accidents at work than for other accidents, as the social security system – but not the tort system – continues to do? Is there any justification for reducing the compensation payable to a claimant when his loss is partly his own fault – which the tort system does regularly but the social security system very rarely? Should we concentrate more help on benefits in kind and less on financial assistance? How should the cost of compensation systems be borne? Should the long-term disabled be treated more generously than those whose disabilities are short-lived? Should those whose injuries result from someone's fault be treated more generously than others? These and many other questions must be answered if our compensation systems are to operate rationally.

A few years ago it seemed probable that the steady development of the welfare state might well supplant the entire tort system in the foreseeable future. New Zealand led the way with the total abolition of the tort action for damages for personal injuries caused by accidents, and its replacement by a national accident insurance scheme.[3] An Australian committee of inquiry advocated a still more comprehensive scheme which would have brought accidental injuries and diseases under one national insurance system.[4] However, these proposals were never acted upon, and are unlikely to be revived in their original form in the foreseeable future.

In this country public dissatisfaction with the tort system as a means of compensating accident victims began to be expressed in the 1960s. After an abortive attempt by the Law Commission to conduct an inquiry into the principles of liability for personal injury, an attempt was made in 1969 to persuade the Lord Chancellor to establish a Royal Commission to explore the whole question.[5] The proposal excited some interest among lawyers, and it was subsequently supported by the Robens Committee into Safety and Health at Work,[6] but there was at first insufficient public interest in the question. However, the eruption in 1972 of the thalidomide cases indicated the strength of public dissatisfaction with the existing compensation laws, and the result was the establishment in March 1973 of the Royal Commission on Civil Liability and Compensation for Personal Injury, under the Chairmanship of Lord Pearson. The Commission duly reported in March 1978, but it rapidly became clear that the Report would not provide the basis for any wide-ranging reforms acceptabe to the Government or public. The Report does not offer anything in the way of a blueprint for a future integrated compensation system, nor even any serious strategy for developing the different systems in a seriously co-ordinated fashion. There are a very large number of recommendations, some of which would indeed be of considerable value, and some of which would have quite dramatic effects on the number of tort claims (for example, in minor injury cases); there is also a great deal of exceptionally valuable data, mainly in Volume 2 of the Report, much of which will be referred to in the relevant places in this book. But is now clear that, at any rate for the foreseeable future, the basic structure of the different compensation systems is likely to remain unchanged. Quite apart from the relatively unadventurous nature of the Pearson Report, the political climate is unpropitious for any extension of the welfare state sufficient to render acceptable the radical reform or abolition of the tort system.

3 SOME FACTS AND FIGURES

Before we proceed to examine in detail the various compensation systems in operation, it is worth devoting some attention to the factual problems we have to deal with. Who, in fact, is in need of compensation? How much money is actually being devoted to compensation? Unfortunately it is not easy to find comprehensive statistical information on questions of this kind, though it has been

Accidents causing personal injury or death

There are some 20,000 deaths from accidental injury each year in the whole of the United Kingdom.[7] The number of injuries depends, of course, on the definition of injury which is adopted; obviously, if all minor and trivial cuts and scratches are included, a considerable proportion of the population would be included in any estimate of those who suffer injury every year. The Pearson Report adopted a definition of injury which included only those injuries which resulted in an absence from work of four days or more; and for those not at work, an injury of comparable severity. This is a convenient working definition because it fits in with the provisions of the social security system which, in general, only provides cash benefits for those off work for more than three days. On this basis the Pearson Report found that there are something like three million injuries each year.[8] Table 1 gives some indication (based on figures drawn from the Pearson Report) of the sources of these accidents.

Many accidents are suffered on the roads and at work; but a very large number are not. Relatively little is known about these other accidents. From information contained in the Pearson Report it appears that as many as 27% of all injuries take place in the home, and that a considerable proportion of injuries (over 9%) are suffered by children playing together, or fighting, or when under some super-

TABLE 1
PERSONAL INJURY AND FATAL ACCIDENTS
IN THE UK – AVERAGE 1973-75

	Killed	Injured
Road accidents	7,696	403,000
Railway accidents	182	not known
Aircraft accidents	94	not known
Water transport accidents	158	not known
Accidents at work:		
Employees	1,300	680,000
Self-employed	not known	40,000
Crimes of violence	720	55,000

vision at school.⁹ The Commission estimated that one-third of all injuries were not caused by the act or omission of any person other than the injured party himself.¹⁰ These are therefore cases which will inevitably fall outside the tort system, no matter how far it may be extended in the future. A recent White Paper on the Safety of Goods¹¹ estimated that 7,000 people in Great Britain die each year in home accidents.

Of this very large number of injuries (even as defined by the Pearson Commission) it is clear that the greater number are of a relatively minor character. Nearly 46% of those who claimed national insurance benefits following an injury in 1972–75 were back at work after two weeks, nearly 90% were back at work within eight weeks, and only 5% were still away from work after three months.¹² Of course there are, in aggregate, large numbers of persons who do suffer permanent and incapacitating injury. The number of more serious cases of injury falling within the industrial injuries scheme may be gauged from the fact that there were in 1982 over 140,000 initial assessments for disablement benefit – which until 1983 was usually only payable for injuries lasting more than six months, now three months.¹³ Over 12,000 disablement pensions were awarded to these claimants,¹⁴ and as these are only awarded where the disability is assessed at 20% or over, this also gives some indication of the number of serious injuries occurring to people at work. There were in 1984 nearly 190,000 disablement pensions being paid under the industrial injuries scheme,¹⁵ representing a toll of many years' injuries to people permanently disabled by injury at work. Even among these cases of permanent disability it would be a mistake to assume that all are cases of the greatest seriousness. Most of these had disabilities assessed at 20%, 30% or 40%, and relatively few had more serious disabilities. Less than 5% were assessed as between 85% and 100% disabled, and (as we shall see later) even 100% disablement is far from representing complete helplessness.¹⁶ Moreover, even these relatively long-term incapacities are not necessarily permanent. Thus, of these disablement pensions, most are paid for under a year; only about 30% are still being paid three and more years after they are awarded.¹⁷

Disease and disability

In order to keep the problem of accidental injury in perspective, it is necessary to appreciate that disabilities from diseases and birth defects due both to natural causes and the result of human activity (diseases caused by exposure to asbestos and deformity caused by Thalidomide are examples of the latter) are very much more widespread than those from accidents. For example, about 80,000 die each year in Britain as a result of cigarette smoking and many thousands more suffer ill-health. Indeed, it is probable that only about 10% of the permanently disabled and handicapped owe their disabilities to accidental injury.[18] A great deal of information about the extent of disabilities and impairment in Great Britain became available as a result of a major Government social survey the results of which were published in 1971–72.[19] This survey estimated that some three million men and women over the age of 16, living in private households, suffered from some impairment.[20] This figure, however, is of little practical significance since it includes very large numbers of people who are not significantly handicapped by their impairments – a term which was very widely interpreted by the survey. Moreover, a very large proportion of the impaired are over normal retiring age, and for the purpose of this book, which is mainly concerned with lost incomes, figures relating to those of normal working age are more important. The survey classified the impaired into four categories, namely those suffering no, or only minor handicaps from their impairment, those appreciably handicapped, those severely handicapped, and those very severely handicapped.[21] On this basis, Table 2 shows the number of those suffering appreciable, severe or very severe handicaps in Great Britain. In addition, it was estimated by

TABLE 2[22]
NUMBERS OF APPRECIABLY, SEVERELY, AND VERY SEVERELY HANDICAPPED PERSONS IN GREAT BRITAIN OF NORMAL WORKING AGE

Age group	Appreciably handicapped	Severely handicapped	Very severely handicapped
16–29	11,000	4,000	5,000
30–49	55,000	30,000	12,000
50–64	162,000	94,000	26,000
Total ages 16–64	228,000	128,000	43,000

the Pearson Commission that there may be as many as 100,000 children under the age of 16 living at home who suffer from severe disability, of a kind which would entitle them to assistance from the Family Fund – a Government-sponsored charity administered by the Joseph Rowntree Memorial Trust. Of this number, it was estimated that not more than one or two thousand were disabled by injury, by far the greater number having been disabled from birth, and rather under 10% having been disabled by disease.[23]

The effect of handicaps on income and earnings is shown by the fact that a large proportion of the more severely handicapped are quite incapable of employment. Some 85% of the very severely handicapped of normal working age were estimated to be permanently disabled and unable to work, and 55% of the severely handicapped were prematurely retired and unable to work again.[24] Of those who are able to work, some 10% are likely at any given time to be temporarily off work as a result of sickness. Of those with appreciable handicaps, half are in ordinary employment, but a third are prematurely retired and unable to work again.[25]

Another source of information about the numbers of disabled persons are the Registers maintained by local authorities under section 1 of the Chronically Sick and Disabled Persons Act, 1970. Over 900,000 persons were on these registers in 1977, as shown in Table 3 (although perhaps as many as two-thirds of these would be over normal retiring age).

The social survey referred to above confined its attention to those living in private households. Plainly this must exclude a significant number of those who are seriously disabled, because many of these live permanently in hospitals or institutions. Although there do not appear to be any statistics showing the number of physically handicapped persons who live permanently in institutions, there were

TABLE 3
DISABLED ON LOCAL AUTHORITY REGISTERS 1977[26]

Blind	103,000
Partially sighted	45,000
Deaf	55,000
Others	714,000

over 9,700 handicapped persons under the age of 65 living in local authority institutions in 1981,[27] and in 1982 there were over 35,000 mentally handicapped persons of normal working age in mental hospitals and units, of whom a large proportion had been resident for more than five years.[28]

As has been said, accidental injury accounts for a very low proportion of the cases of disablement. Even among amputees, for instance, disease accounts for 77% of the cases, and accidents for only 18%.[29] In another government survey in 1973, out of 201 persons in every 1,000 who claimed to suffer from some long-standing illness or disability, only 15·8 (i.e. under 8%) gave injury as the cause.[30] On the other hand, disablement among those of working age is much more likely to be caused by accident, because a substantial proportion of the permanently disabled are also the old. Thus at least two-thirds of the blind are over sixty-five years of age, and the same is true of amputees. Comparison of the figures published by the Department of Health and Social Security for time off work shows that in 1976–77 about 229 million days were lost due to sickness and 40 million due to accident.[31] It is true that the average time off work due to accident was greater than the average time off due to sickness; but despite this, it is clear that accidental personal injury is, both in the less serious and in the more serious cases, far less significant quantitatively than disablement caused by disease. In financial terms, it is clear that the cost to the individuals concerned (in the form of lost income), arising from illness and disease, is much greater than the cost of accidents.

The position with regard to accidental deaths is not quite the same. As is to be expected, accidental death is more common than death from disease in the lower age groups. And although the cost is affected by the fact that the lower age groups are less likely to leave so many dependants as the higher age groups, dependants of persons in the lower age groups have to be maintained for much longer periods. Therefore the amount of compensation for lost income which is required to maintain widows and children is proportionally less for cases of death from illness and disease than for cases of accidental death.[32] But in all age groups there are far fewer cases of accidental death than of death from illness or disease, so the overall cost of the latter is far greater.

Distribution and sources of compensation

The Pearson Report gives us reasonably firm estimates of the number

TABLE 4[33]
NUMBERS OBTAINING COMPENSATION FROM DIFFERENT SOURCES

Source of compensation	Number of new beneficiaries per annum (thousands)
Social security	1,550
Tort	215
Occupational sick pay	1,000
Occupational pensions	4
Private insurance (excluding life insurance)	200
Criminal injuries compensation	18
Other forms of compensation	150
All forms of compensation	1,700

of injured persons who received compensation from various sources, and of the relative proportions of society's total provision for the injured which was attributable to the different compensation systems. Of the total number of some three million persons suffering an injury (as defined by the Commission), only some 1.7 million, or about 55%, were estimated to receive any financial assistance at all. Some of these received compensation from more than one source, as set out in Table 4.

Thus, of the 3 million persons suffering some injury in each year, only some 215,000 (approximately 6½%) received any compensation in the form of tort damages. However, the total value of the damages paid to this 6½% was almost half of the total value of the social security payments made to the million and a half recipients of those payments. When account is then taken of the administrative costs of the differing compensation systems, the position is even more striking, because the tort system is much more expensive to administer. The figures are set out in Table 5, from which it will be seen that of the total cost of compensation paid (on average in each of the years 1971–76) of some £827 million, the tort system accounted for no less than £379 million. Thus 6½% of the accident victims accounted for some 45% of the total cost of the compensation paid out. It must be pointed out at once that the 6½% who received tort damages certainly included a quite disproportionate number of the more seriously injured, so that one would not expect the tort victims to

TABLE 5[35]

COST OF COMPENSATION PAID FROM DIFFERENT SOURCES TO INJURED PERSONS AND ADMINISTRATIVE COSTS OF PAYMENTS, AVERAGE OVER 1971–76 (1977 prices)

Source of compensation	Annual Payments	Administrative costs p.a. (£s)
Social security	421 million	47 million
Tort	202 million	175 million
Occupational sick pay	125 million	*
Occupational pensions	5 million	*
Private insurance (excluding life insurance)	51 million	*
Criminal injuries compensation	10 million	1·2 million†
Other forms of compensation	6 million	*

* No estimates provided by the Pearson Commission.
† Figure derived from the latest Report of the Criminal Injuries Compensation Board.

receive only the same proportion of payments as their number bears to the whole; nevertheless, it is apparent that, even allowing for this fact, the beneficiaries of the tort action come off remarkably well compared to all the other injured. Indeed, their position is even better than is indicated by this Table because many of those who obtained payment of tort damages would also have been beneficiaries under one or more of the other compensation systems. For example, about three-quarters of those who received tort damages would also have received social security payments, and many of these would also have received occupational sick pay.[34]

Furthermore, the vast majority of those who receive tort compensation are the victims of accidental injury. Only a tiny number of those disabled from birth or by illness or disease receive tort damages, not only because very many such disabilities are the result of natural causes but also because, even if a particular victim's disability was the result of intentional or negligent human action, it will often be very difficult or impossible for him to prove this with the degree of certainty the law requires. So we have a situation in which a very small proportion of the disabled receive about half of total compensation payments. Most people disabled by illness or disease must rely on the sickness and invalidity benefits paid under the Social

Security Act. But there are many permanently disabled and unemployable people who cannot claim even these benefits because they do not satisfy the contribution conditions laid down by the Social Security Act. Those who have never worked because they are congenitally disabled, or have suffered from crippling disease since childhood, will never qualify for contributory benefits and must rely primarily on the supplementary benefits provided under the Supplementary Benefits Act 1976. Nobody knows how many persons fall into this category, but in 1982, sick and disabled supplementary benefit recipients under pensionable age numbered nearly 240,000.[36] As we shall see later, there has recently been some amelioration in the position of this class with the introduction of some new non-contributory benefits. There has been a fall in the past ten years in the total number of sick and disabled in receipt of supplementary benefits from nearly 300,000 to the figure of 240,000 already mentioned. But it is still the case that chronic sickness and disablement is one of the major causes of poverty in modern Britain.

But preferential treatment of certain groups of the disabled does not end here. In addition to compensation for loss of income, those fortunate enough to be compensated under the tort system, the criminal injuries compensation system (although this is of little quantitative importance), or the industrial injuries scheme, can also be paid compensation for 'loss of faculty', or the disability as such, regardless of whether it causes any loss of income. For example, a person who loses an eye may receive up to £11,000 if he has a tort claim, and a disablement pension of £18.96 per week if he qualifies under the industrial injuries scheme, even if his earning power is quite unimpaired. But a disabled person who cannot claim under any of these schemes will not receive any compensation for disability as such, even if he receives some compensation for loss of earning power. We will meet such distinctions between different groups of the disabled time and again, and we will be forced to ask whether there is any justification for them.

The more serious and less serious

It is plain that long-term disability and chronic sickness raise social and financial problems for the victim and his family which are different in kind from those raised by short-term sickness or minor injuries. Many (but by no means all) families can weather a short period of lost income, or of reduced income, without great hardship. Savings can be used; borrowing can be relied on; payment of bills deferred; expenditure can be cut down for short periods. So also minor disabilities which do not affect earning power can be tolerated and lived with, even though they may be permanent or long lived. But long-term or permanent income loss or reduction, or permanent disabilities, are far more serious. Now it is clear that less serious injuries and disabilities greatly outnumber more serious. Most of the figures relate to accidents, but a similar pattern is certainly true of natural diseases. For every person who is off work for months, hundreds are off work for weeks, and for every one off for weeks scores are off for days. For every one who loses a leg or an arm or an eye, hundreds of others suffer nothing worse than scratches and bruises.

Translate bodily injuries to financial losses and the position is the same. For everyone who counts his losses in thousands of pounds there are hundreds who count their losses in tens and twenties. One survey among those who recovered damages in respect of industrial injuries found that 20% received less than £100 each, another 25% recovered between £100 and £249, while only 19% obtained more than £1,000.[37] The Pearson Commission's own survey among 3,302 injured persons showed that fully 19% had no income loss at all (after allowing for sick pay), that 67% incurred income loss of under £100 (1973 prices), some 3·7% had losses of between £500 and £999, and only 2·2% had losses exceeding £1,000.[38] A study of insurance company payments, also made for the Pearson Commission, showed that in the month of November, 1973, nearly half the payments were of less than £200, and only 1% exceeded £5,000.[39] The 1984 Harris Survey (based on data collected in 1976–7 from 169 persons who received tort damages) found that the mean amount of damages was £1,135 while half of the respondents received less than £500.[40]

The same pattern is revealed by the figures relating to disablement pensions under the industrial injuries scheme. Of the 192,000 pensioners being paid in 1982 only 11,000 were receiving pensions for disabilities assessed at 65% or above, and over 94,000 were receiving pensions for disabilities assessed at 25% or less.[41] Similarly, of the 19,771 persons who received awards from the Criminal Injuries Compensation Board in 1984–5, 24·2% received under £500, 83·6% received less than £2,000, while almost 98% received less than £10,000.[42]

On the other hand, it will also be found that although a very small proportion of accident victims suffer serious injury or heavy financial loss, they receive a very considerable proportion of total payments of compensation. The Pearson Commission's study of insurance payments, for instance, found that 1% of payments accounted for no less than 23% of the sums paid.[43] And among the recipients of criminal injury awards in 1977–78, rather under 2% (or 261 out of 14,052) received approximately £3 million, or 29.6% of the total sum paid out under the criminal injuries scheme during that year.[44] Again, it has recently been estimated that one-third of all days of incapacity for work are due to those who have been unable to work for more than 12 months.[45]

One conclusion of vital importance can be drawn from these facts, namely that insistence on equal treatment for all cases is likely to prejudice satisfactory treatment of the more serious cases. It is also of the first importance to any satisfactory compensation system to achieve a proper financial balance between treatment of the more serious cases and treatment of the less serious. If we attempt to treat *all* cases alike, the paradoxical result is that we end up in practice by treating the more serious and deserving cases less generously. If one person is off work for six months and loses £1,000 in wages, and another person is off work for two days and loses £20 in wages, and we cannot afford to compensate them both in full, equality of treatment might suggest that we pay the first person £500 in compensation and the second person £10 in compensation. Yet it is clear that this would cause much greater hardship to the first person than the second. Moreover, we know that large sums can be saved by eliminating the smallest claims altogether. Although the smallest claims may not in aggregate be as great as the few much larger claims, they still represent a substantial proportion of the total sums paid out. They also account for an enormous proportion of the administrative costs of any compensation scheme, since these costs are proportionate to the number of claims as well as to the size of the claims. Administratively it costs far more to process 100 claims for £10 each than one claim for £1,000; and this is true whether the administration is in the hands of courts, insurance companies, the Department of Health and Social Security or anyone else. Thus by refusing to pay any compensation to the person who has lost £20 we may be able to afford to pay very much more to the person who has lost £1,000, because for every one who has lost £1,000 there will be scores if not hundreds who have lost only £20. In America it has been calculated that the cost of workmen's compensation programmes can be reduced by no less than 17% by the simple expedient of denying benefits for the first 7 days of incapacity, unless the incapacity lasts more than 28 days.[46]

We shall see later that virtually every one of the compensation systems in operation today, except the tort system, goes some way to meet the point being made here by eliminating the smallest claims. Only the tort system clings to the principle of full compensation. Even so, the question is whether the elimination of small claims is sufficient. There is an overwhelming case for increasing the *proportion* of compensation payable in cases of more serious or more prolonged injury, and the social security system shows an increasing tendency to implement this principle. Since the tort system professes to make full compensation for *all* injuries, it could hardly acknowledge the need for better compensation for the more gravely injured. In practice, as we shall see fully later, the tort system, too, treats those with minor injuries far more generously than those with grave injuries. Sick pay schemes, also, quite naturally, tend to be more generous to those off work for short periods, than to those with chronic disability. In short, all existing compensation systems appear to be relatively more generous to the great mass of those suffering minor injury, as compared with the really seriously disabled. This raises some very fundamental questions for the future development of compensation systems.

Another vital question, arising from these considerations, concerns the strategy for future improvement. There seems no doubt that in the long run society will, within the limits of its resources, gradually improve the provision it makes for the accident victim, the disabled and the sick. This has been happening for many years, and there is every reason to expect the process to continue. The crucial question, however, is whether the process is to continue along a broad front, with steady, but necessarily slow improvement in the position of all those similarly placed; or alternatively, whether some more fortunate groups among the afflicted are to be permitted to advance far ahead of others similarly placed. For example, are tort victims to be permitted to continue reaping the great advantages of the tort action, as compared with those unable to recover damages? And if so, is the value of tort damages to continue to be improved, as has been happening in many cases, so that the disparity in treatment becomes even greater? Are accident victims to be continued their favoured treatment over the victims of disease? Or alternatively, are all those unable to earn an income because of incapacity to be treated equally, and perhaps not very generously at the outset, so that improvement will come gradually for all? Are tort-type benefits to be provided for new classes of victims, unable to prove fault? And if so, on what principle are these new classes to be selected if indeed there is to be any principle at all other than that of giving most to those who shout loudest? These are difficult questions indeed.

PART TWO
The Tort System

2
Negligence as fault

1 THE CONCEPTUAL STRUCTURE OF THE LAW

The boundaries of a legal subject are not set by divine prescript but by the custom of lawyers, and more particularly, by those lawyers whose business it is to expound the law, and for whom classification, division and sub-division are therefore necessities. Hence during the past hundred years or so, when academic lawyers in England have begun to treat the law as a serious subject for study, it has become customary to draw firm lines between the segments of the law and attach to them the labels, 'tort', 'contract', 'criminal law' or whatever. In course of time, as textbooks have multiplied and university law courses have been built around the textbooks, the boundaries of the subjects have taken on the appearance of being almost immutably fixed. The perspective of time shows this appearance to be an illusion.

During the first few centuries of the common law, nothing comparable to the modern law of tort existed at all. The King's courts were concerned above all with two things: first and foremost, they were concerned to keep the peace and to prevent outbreaks of disorder and the use of violence, and secondly, they were concerned with the protection of rights of property – which in those days chiefly meant land. With respect to the maintenance of peace, no clear distinction existed between what we now call civil and criminal law. The writ of trespass, which was at first a complaint based on the use of force against person or property, originated during this period, and is the ancestor of most of the law of torts, and the law of contract as well. The protection of rights of property centred on interests in land, land being the main form of valuable property and itself a source of disputes and violence. Other forms of physical property were also protected from the earliest times, but the development of legal protection against the infliction of intangible economic loss through what we would now call tort law was a somewhat later phenomenon. At different periods of history different interests have needed protection by the law. So, for instance, the protection of personal liberty through the medium of tort law (as well as through the writ of *habeas corpus*) was particularly important during the constitutional struggles of the seventeenth century when parliament and the common lawyers united against the arbitrary power of the crown. The protection afforded a plaintiff against some forms of conduct has declined with the passage of time; for instance protection against 'malicious prosecution' was more needful when false accusations were more easily made than they are today, when the ascertainment of facts was not the strongest point in the judicial process, and when punishments were severe, not to say barbarous. Today, though the action for malicious prosecution remains available, it is rarely successful, and it is clear that the judiciary have actively discouraged its use in the belief that it is less needed, particularly since the development of the modern police force.

The law of torts, as it is thought of today, deals with a variety of social and economic problems which may be classified in a variety of different ways. For instance, the problems may be classified by looking at the interest of the plaintiff who complains of some injury. What exactly is he complaining of? Deprivation of liberty? Injury to his person or his feelings? Damage to his property, or the invasion of his land? Damage to his reputation or the invasion of his privacy? Injury to his domestic relations with his wife or family? Damage to his trade or business? Alternatively, problems may be looked at in terms of the cause of the injury. Who caused it? Was it caused intentionally, maliciously, negligently or altogether without 'fault' on the part of anyone? Did the plaintiff himself play a part in the cause of his injuries? A third way of classifying problems is according to the relationship between the plaintiff and the defendant. For example, the liability of an employer to his employees could be isolated as a subject for legal treatment on its own, and so also could the liability of a manufacturer of products to a consumer injured by the use of the product; similarly, the liability of a landowner to his neighbours, and the liability of one road user to another, could be, and to a limited extent are, studied as separate parts of the law of torts. What precisely is to be treated as part of the law of torts and what is to mark off tort liability from other forms of liability is (as we have suggested) largely a matter of convention, and might in any event differ according to which of these three ways of looking at a problem is chosen as the most convenient. For instance, if a problem is classified according to the relationship between the parties, it would be necessary to examine some aspects of what is usually known as contract law, insofar as it may bear on that relationship. In general it has not been customary for English lawyers to classify problems according to the nature of the relationship between the parties, though this is done sometimes, as in the case of liability between neighbours. More usually problems are classified partly according to the nature of the plaintiff's interest, and partly according to the way in which the injury was caused, whether intentionally, maliciously, negligently or without fault.

The result of all this is that the conceptual structure of tort law is a disorganized and ramshackle affair. On the one hand we have the tort of negligence, which is based on the blameworthy nature of the defendant's conduct and which today covers not only injury to the person and damage to property, but is also, and increasingly, intangible financial loss. On the other hand, we have a collection of 'specific' torts. Some of these are based on the interest they protect (e.g. defamation, malicious prosecution and wrongful imprisonment), others on the relationship between the parties (e.g. some types of nuisance, and the form of liability known as the rule in *Rylands* v. *Fletcher*), and yet others on a combination of the two (as with the economic torts such as intimidation or interference with contractual relations).

The structure of the law is made still more confusing by the fact that lawyers today insist that negligence itself is also a 'distinct' tort. The very notion of a 'distinct' tort is puzzling, and perhaps meaningless; whether a particular type of conduct is dignified with the status of a distinct tort depends largely on accidents of history. For instance, to strike a man intentionally is (in the absence of any justification or excuse) a 'distinct' tort (an assault), whereas to strike a man negligently is not a distinct tort but merely one way of committing the tort of negligence. To assert that negligence itself is a distinct tort, therefore, means that damage caused by negligent conduct is generally actionable, irrespective of the kind of activity in question. The tort of negligence thus extends over the whole sphere of human activity and is not confined, as most other torts are, to particular types of conduct or activity. It concerns the way in which activities are carried out, and not any particular activity.

Having said this, it is necessary to observe that in practice the law of negligence is very largely concerned with certain consequences of two particular activities, that is, with bodily injury, and to a lesser extent, damage to property, resulting from road and industrial accidents. Indeed, actions for damages for personal injuries (which except in rare cases must be based on negligence) constitute a very large proportion of all civil litigation in this country at the present day. We must not, of course, make the mistake of supposing that the importance of a tort or a branch of the law can be measured solely by what happens in courts; the torts of false imprisonment and defamation, for instance (despite the small number of such cases which are litigated), probably have more influence on people's conduct than the tort of negligence. And since the tort of false imprisonment is of prime importance in protecting personal liberty, it deals with a subject matter which may be thought even more vital than personal injury.

But we know that for every action for damages for personal injuries which comes up for trial in court, another 99 claims are settled by negotiation. It also seems likely that the total amount of money which changes hands as a result of negligence cases (including settlements) is greater than that involved in any other single class of litigation. It was estimated at some £200 million per annum (at 1977 prices) by the Pearson Commission. It is true (as we shall see) that the maximum amount involved in a single negligence claim, especially a personal injury claim or a fatal accidents claim, is relatively small compared to the maximum which may be involved in a single commercial claim arising out of an important contract, but the total amounts involved in these classes of litigation is a different matter. It is, then, clear that in quantitative terms, the tort of negligence is of great importance today in the process of compensating people for accidental personal injury; and it is on this tort, therefore, that this part of this book mainly concentrates.

The tort of negligence is said to consist of three essential elements; first, a duty to take care, secondly, a breach of that duty, and thirdly, damage to the plaintiff caused by that breach of duty. This third element can be subdivided into two further elements, namely that the defendant's conduct must have been the 'cause in fact' of the damage; and secondly that it must have been the 'legal cause' of the damage. It is customary in expositions of English law to start with the 'duty of care', and not with the second element of the tort which concerns the definition of negligent conduct. Thus generations of English law students have attempted to understand when a defendant is liable for negligence, before they have studied the definition and nature of negligence itself. This approach tends to obscure the fact that the duty of care concept has more often been used for the purpose of restricting liability for cases of proved fault, rather than as a means of expanding liability. This point is elaborated in the next chapter. The remainder of this chapter examines the nature of negligence as a species of fault.

2 A QUESTION OF FACT?

The first requirement of success in a negligence action is proof that the defendant was negligent; that he failed to take that degree of care which was reasonable in all the circumstances of the case; or that he failed to act as a reasonable man would have acted. Then, if the defendant did 'owe a duty of care' we can call his negligence a breach of that duty. Very often the breach of duty is itself talked of as though it were 'negligence', while leaving aside the other requirements of the tort. For instance, a judge faced with a case in which there is doubt about the existence of the duty of care may start by deciding whether 'assuming the defendant owes a duty' he was negligent. This is often condemned as inaccurate, and no doubt it is if we start by assuming that the only correct use of the word 'negligence' is to describe a situation in which all the ingredients of legal liability exist. But, as we shall see, the duty of care to avoid physical injury or damage by affirmative conduct is so universal that in the vast majority of cases of negligence which arise in practice, it can be assumed to exist, and the principal question is whether the defendant was negligent in the sense that he has breached the duty of care.

This question is often said to be a 'question of fact', but this is itself a misleading expression. In the first place it is necessary to distinguish between primary facts and inferences or evaluations. What actually happened is a question of primary fact. How an accident occurred, whether the plaintiff did thus and thus, or the defendant did so and so, what part was played by third parties, and so forth, all these are questions of primary fact. Usually the judge decides what he thinks actually happened, or what the primary facts of the case are, after hearing the evidence. Sometimes there is no dispute about the primary facts: everyone agrees that this is what happened. Sometimes, unfortunately, it is not possible for the judge to reach any satisfactory conclusion about the primary facts because the evidence is fragmentary – perhaps the parties were killed in the accident – or because the defendant is the only person who knows what happened, and he takes refuge in silence, or for some other reason. In these circumstances the judge is still bound to make 'findings of fact'; that is, to determine, in accordance with certain rules of law and procedure and evidence, what facts shall be assumed to be the primary facts. The judge may assume them because the contrary has not been proved; or because of some legal presumption; or because they are reasonable inferences from what has been proved, and so on. When all findings of fact which are necessary or relevant have been made, inferred or presumed, the judge will proceed to the second stage of the negligence inquiry, which is that of making a judgment. These being (or being assumed to be) the facts, was the defendant negligent? Although this is also often referred to as a question of fact, this is a somewhat unfortunate usage. It arose when actions of this nature were usually tried with juries and the judge's task was to decide on the law, while the jury's task was to decide on the facts. Since the jury had the task of saying whether they thought the defendant's conduct amounted to negligence, this question was regarded as one of fact. It is quite true that there are still certain ways in which such a question is treated – for the purpose of various legal rules – in the same way as a question of fact; for instance, a decision of this kind cannot technically constitute a precedent. But in many other respects a finding of negligence is treated rather like a decision on a question of law. For example, appeal courts are prepared to reverse such findings, while they are still very reluctant to disagree with a trial court's findings of primary fact. It will be observed that one cannot *prove* that a person was negligent any more than one can prove a rule of law. One can merely *argue* that he was negligent and hope to persuade the judge by argument.

At all events, it is clear that a finding that a defendant was negligent involves making a judgment on his conduct; and it is therefore necessary to what criteria are employed in the process of making this judgment. At one time the conventional answer to this question invoked that somewhat mystical, and certainly much misunderstood, figure, the reasonable man. A person is negligent if he fails to take the degree of care which a reasonable man would or does take. A vast amount has been written about the reasonable man. He is the 'man on the Clapham omnibus', the 'average man', the 'average juryman', the 'man who comes home from work, rolls up his shirt sleeves and mows the lawn'; he is (according to Sir Alan Herbert) never a woman; he is, according to some, an odious and insufferable creature who never makes a mistake; he is even (according to a letter published in an English periodical some years ago) an absurd myth of the imagination of the legal profession, which refuses to admit that he does not really exist. He is merely a conception, an abstraction, or as Lord Radcliffe has put it, 'the anthropomorphic conception of justice'.[1] But if Lord Radcliffe is right, the reasonable man can hardly tell us what negligence consists of. To translate the conventional 'reasonable man test' of negligence into modern terms, recognizing the creature for what he is – according to Lord Radcliffe – we get something like this: a person is negligent if he fails to take that degree of care which justice requires that he should take.

This may be illuminating as to the nature of the issue, but it does not assist the process of making the decision. Does any more help lie in the concept of the 'average man' with whom the reasonable man is so often equated? He also, of course, is an abstraction, but at least he is an abstraction with rather more meaning. True, perhaps, the statistician would reject the idea that there is such a person as the 'average person',[2] but there is no insuperable problem in finding out how people generally behave or react to given situations. Suppose, for instance, that an employee is injured by a machine in a factory, and alleges that it was negligent of his employer to use the machine without taking certain precautions; is it any help to find out whether other employers do the same? Suppose we find that the great majority of employers who use this machine also do not take the allegedly required precautions? Is this not evidence that at least the 'average employer' would not regard it as necessary? The answer is that it is, and that the courts pay great weight to the practice of businessmen in this respect. In fact the courts pay great weight to the practice of mankind generally, and particularly to the practice of professional and business people, in arriving at decisions on questions of negligence. To some extent decisions of this kind are probably based on the feeling that a person should not be blamed for doing what everybody else does, and the judge may be reluctant to open the issue as to whether the common practice was in fact negligent. But to some extent also, a decision of this kind may be based on acceptance by the judge of the standards of the community, so that although he may personally feel that the common practice is unsatisfactory he may subordinate his own views to those of the community. In this way the reasonable man – at least if he is taken to mean the average man – may be of assistance to the courts in helping to set the standard of care in particular circumstances.

But this does not mean that we can equate the reasonable man with the average man in all circumstances; nor does it mean that negligence consists simply of the failure to observe the normal or usual precautions in a given situation, or conversely, that observance of the normal or usual precautions cannot amount to negligence. The courts have never accepted that they are precluded from finding negligence even in the face of unanimous and long-standing practice.[3] If the practice of businessmen is not conclusive on the issue of negligence, still less is the practice of private individuals – for example drivers. If it were alleged that a driver was negligent in driving across a road junction without stopping, it would not advance his case much to prove that he had observed the crossing in question and ascertained that 90% of drivers did the same. On the other hand where professional negligence is alleged, for example against a doctor, the fact that the defendant observed the care or precautions customarily enjoined by his professional colleagues will usually lead a court to hold that there has been no negligence.

But if the concept of the reasonable man is sometimes of assistance in solving a particular case, it can also obscure the way in which negligence decisions are arrived. Let us look first at the way the use of the concept appears to turn what is a judgment into a finding of primary fact. What is negligence? It is the failure to do what the reasonable man does. These words give the appearance of being a statement of fact. We first assume that the reasonable man exists; then we assume that he actually behaved in a certain way; then we measure the defendant's behaviour against his. But this hides the element of judgment; it hides the fact that the judge decides not merely how the defendant behaved but whether he *ought* not to have behaved differently. In deciding that question the judge is not merely comparing the defendant's behaviour against the behaviour of the reasonable man – in the absence of common practice, there is no such man and no such behaviour *in fact*. The standard of behaviour against which the defendant's conduct is thus measured is a standard decided on, and inevitably decided on, by the judge himself.

It is not suggested that all this has never been appreciated before; far from it, it is well known to those acquainted with the law's methods and techniques. But it would probably be going too far to suggest as Sir Carleton Allen did some years ago, that 'Nobody is deceived by the fiction that the judge is stating, not what he himself thinks, but what he thinks an average reasonable man might think.'[4] If nobody were deceived by the fiction it is hard to see why it should have survived so long. The fact is that – like many other fictions designed to serve the same purpose – it tends to obscure the role of the judge as a policymaker. Judges in this country have traditionally eschewed the role of policy-maker: they continue to proclaim that they are not concerned with policy but only with law, and it is possible that the public prefers it that way. To many people 'impartial justice' means justice without policy. If a judge were to say to a defendant: 'You have failed to do what I think you should have done and that amounts to negligence', the defendant may come away thinking of the judge, 'Who does he think he is?' But if the judge says: 'You have failed to do what the reasonable man would have done, and that amounts to negligence', the defendant may come away with more respect for the judge and the law. Different views are perhaps possible on whether there is any substance in this, and on whether it might not be possible to educate the public to understand the legal process better. But what is surely incontestable is the desirability of the judges themselves appreciating the nature of the task they are performing.

3 THE NATURE OF NEGLIGENCE

If we can finally exorcize the reasonable man from this branch of the law, it should be possible to go on to state with some confidence the nature of a decision on a question of negligence. What is involved is, first, putting oneself in the position in which the defendant found himself immediately before the challenged conduct; and secondly, deciding on the desirability of his conduct having regard to the interests of the defendant and of such other persons as might appear to be affected by it. We have deliberately used the word 'desirability' where most lawyers would have used the word 'reasonableness' because it emphasizes the policy nature of the decision; little different in fact from policy decisions which public officials are continuously having to make. The judge's decision is, indeed, usually a far less momentous decision, because in most circumstances it involves a microscopic analysis of conduct in a bare moment of time. But this is not always so, and there are certainly occasions on which a judge will be required to pronounce whether a decision taken 'on grounds of public policy' or the 'public interest' is 'reasonable' – i.e. on whether he agreed with the policy makers. For instance, a few years ago British Railways and the Ministry of Transport spent a great deal of time debating the desirability of replacing manually operated level crossings by automatically operated barriers which are now familiar to road users. They took into account the savings in money which would result, and the risk of possible accidents, and they decided on balance the changeover was desirable. Subsequently an accident occurred at one of these crossings which formed the subject of a Public Inquiry by a Queen's Counsel.[5] Had legal proceedings been brought, the judge would have had to determine a similar question to that which the Railway authorities and the Ministry had already determined, though he would have couched it in the language of 'negligence'.

Now as has been said, most decisions on questions of negligence are far less momentous; and the great majority are answered quickly and easily by the judge once the facts are found. Issues of negligence in road accidents, and even in industrial accidents, rarely give rise to much difficulty once the actual facts are known. The reasons for this will be more apparent later.

If the issue of negligence is often nothing more nor less than the issue of 'desirability in the public interest', it does not follow that in making his decision a judge will take into account all those factors which a public official or a Minister may take into account. A Minister may, for example, decide that a certain course is likely to win votes for his party and that this consideration outweighs all others; a judge, needless to say, would not be influenced by such consideration.

But even leaving aside pure party politics, a Minister could well be influenced by considerations of the public interest which a judge would probably disregard. Suppose, to return to our discussion about the level crossing barriers, it were found that these barriers required the importation of machinery or equipment from abroad; a public official could take into account the fact that foreign currency might be needed for the change whereas a judge probably would not. In fact a judge is likely to take into account a strictly limited number of considerations, which in the great majority of cases can be reduced to four.[6] First, the degree of probability that damage will be done by the conduct which is challenged; secondly, the magnitude of the harm which is likely to be done if the risk materializes; thirdly, the value or utility of the object to be achieved by the conduct in question; and fourthly, the burden in terms of cost, time and trouble, of taking precautions against the risk of damage.

A famous American judge, Learned Hand, once declared that negligence was a function of three variables;[7] but he did not specifically take account of the third factor stated above. If the third factor can be assumed to be implicit within the others, we can say with Judge Learned Hand, that negligence is shown where the burden of the precautions needed to avoid the risk is less than the product of the magnitude of the damage and the probability that the damage will occur. In recent times it has been argued that this is fundamentally an economic test.[8] If it can be shown that the expenditure of £X on avoiding or minimizing the risk of an accident will prevent accident costs of £X + Y, then it is clearly desirable that the £X should be spent. On the other hand, there is no point in spending £X to prevent accident costs which are less than £X. In some situations this is a useful perspective, and sometimes it may even be possible to put actual figures on the probability of an accident occurring and the likely damage which will be caused if an accident does happen. But any attempt to reduce the whole law of negligence to the form of an algebraic equation must be dismissed because we are not dealing with precisely measurable values. What value do we place on the object to be achieved? Plainly this cannot be reduced to terms of cash in most instances. The value of this or that object requires a subjective decision. Perhaps the object to be achieved is the saving of a life. Perhaps it is the playing of a game of cricket. How do we value such things? Then again the degree of probability of harm is not usually mathematically calculable since it depends on such an immense variety of factors. If an ambulance driver is taking a seriously injured person to hospital and is driving faster than usual in order to arrive sooner and so give the injured person a better chance of survival, the factors that have to be balanced are: the degree of probability that the extra speed may save the patient's life; and the value of the life of the patient against the value of the lives which may be lost in an accident. These things can only be the subject of a delicate judgment; they cannot be calculated by a computer. Inevitably, therefore, people will differ in making such a judgment.

The point is even stronger where, as often happens, the court is required to weigh, not similar but dissimilar things. Suppose a court is asked to say whether it is negligence to organize cricket in a ground without the protection of a fence, so that balls occasionally get hit into the street. Here the judge is required to balance the degree of probability that an injury will occur; the 'cost' of the injury which may occur; the cost of building a fence around the ground; and the value of cricket as a pastime. Findings about the first of these – the probability question – can be reduced to something approximating a question of fact since it may be possible to show that balls get hit out of the ground only so many times a year, and so on. It would also be possible to ascertain without great difficulty what the cost of the precautions (in this case, building a fence) would be – though this is by no means always so, since (for example) great difficult may arise in attempting to decide whether a drug company has adequately tested a drug, what alternative precautions could have been taken, what the repercussions of these alternatives might have been, and the total cost. But in any case the difficulties over these matters pale into insignificance beside the problems raised by the other two factors, which require the judge to weigh in the balance the 'cost' of injuries to a person and the value of cricket as a pastime.

At this stage it might be thought that we reach the realm of what is purely subjective judgement, but this is not entirely so. The judge does not reach his decision on the basis of what *he* thinks are the correct values to place on human injury or the game of cricket. He may be a stoic who bears pain and injury with great fortitude; or he may detest the game of cricket; but a judge, certainly a good judge, tries to take his values in general from the community, and we have seen how the concept of the reasonable man may help him to do so. If he finds that the community has a high regard for the game of cricket he is right to place a high value on it in weighing it against the possibility of personal injury, and to disregard his own personal and possibly idiosyncratic feelings about cricket. Of course, there may be occasions on which the courts feel very strongly that the community's values are wrong or misguided, and judges may then make a determined attempt to change the community's values; to apply their own values and to stress in their judgments why they place such a high value on such and such, and so low a value on this or that. By these means the courts themselves may help to mould opinion, and change the community's sense of values. There may also be times when the judges get very out of touch with the community's sense of values. If the bench consists largely of judges drawn from one segment of society, and almost entirely from the older generations, judges may lose touch with popular opinions and feelings; and there can be no doubt that this has sometimes happened in the past.

In making a finding of negligence – in balancing the various factors that weigh on a negligence decision – the courts do not generally rely on factual or statistical or expert knowledge, at least where the facts do not clearly fall within the realm of scientific knowledge. Obviously where allegations of professional negligence are made (say) against a doctor the courts must rely on expert medical witnesses to tell them what is sound practice and what is not. But in areas which do not clearly fall within the realm of the expert the courts tend to rely almost entirely on common experience or hunch or instinct. Thus the 'foreseeability' of an event is almost invariably decided without the assistance of statistical evidence; and the assessment of the amount of damage likely to be done and the burden of precautions is rarely reduced to arithmetical calculations. Of course, as we have pointed out, since non-measurable values are often involved in these assessments, precise calculations would often present insuperable difficulties, unless certain arbitrary assumptions were made as to the method by which these values were to be ascertained. But even if we confine our attention to cases in which hard facts could be adduced and measured, courts appear in general to prefer to rely on a minimum of empirical evidence. In short what is known in America as the 'Brandeis Brief' is unknown in this country. This is not to say that statistical data never plays a part in negligence actions. In *Haley* v. *London Electricity Board*[9] the question at issue was whether the defendants ought to have guarded against the possibility of a blind man falling into an excavation in a London pavement. The trial judge and the Court of Appeal held that the risk was 'too remote', but the House of Lords was impressed by the statistics of the number of blind persons in London which had not been given in evidence, and found for the plaintiff. But even in this case no serious attempt was made to assess the statistical chance that a blind person would walk along the pavement in question in a given period, and indeed, the difficulty of gathering the information (assuming it was available at all) and making the calculations necessary for this purpose would probably have been quite disproportionate to the issue at stake.

4 FORESEEABILITY

The concept of foreseeability is one of the dominant concepts of the law of negligence, and it also plays a substantial role in quite different branches of the law, such as the law of contract. We shall see later how, in theory, foreseeability plays a role in determining whether a duty of care exists in law, though we shall find that in practice its role is almost negligible in that sphere. Some writers also claim that foreseeability is a chimera as it applies to the question of whether the defendant's conduct was negligent. Among American academic lawyers it is fashionable to regard the whole concept of foreseeability as meaningless – or, perhaps, more accurately, as meaning whatever it is desired to make it mean. It is thought to be one of those pliable formulae which can be used by the judge to hide what he is really doing. Certainly this is the case when one deals with foreseeability as part of the 'duty of care' concept. The use made of the notion by the courts in cases of mental distress is ample illustration of the point, for there the judges have simply said that the distress was or was not foreseeable, according as they desired to impose liability or not; and there is no gainsaying them because serious mental distress is not so much a part of common experience as to enable us to say when it is likely to occur.

But the attack on the role of foreseeability in deciding whether a defendant's conduct was negligent takes a different form. Here it is stressed that foreseeability is a relative conception, and this is undoubtedly a fundamental truth which is recognized by the law, though it is all too often forgotten and not only by students. We cannot simply say that such and such an event is or is not foreseeable. The truth is that all sorts of events are foreseeable – with a greater or lesser degree of probability. Some events are foreseeable with substantial certainty, or at least with such a degree of certainty that there would be no point in conducting one's life except on the assumption that the event will take place – for example, that the earth will continue to spin on its axis in its accustomed orbit round the sun.[10] Other events may be such remote possibilities that nobody would adjust his conduct because of them – for instance, that an earthquake may occur in this country. But in between these extremes there are an infinite number of gradations, and these degrees of probability or foreseeability are constantly reflected in the language of the courts. There are events which are 'very probable', 'highly probable', 'quite likely', 'not unlikely'; there are events which may be said, after they have happened, to have been 'remarkable' or 'extraordinary'; there are risks which before the event may be stigmatized as 'remote' or 'fantastic possibilities'. Now it is essential to grasp that there is no fixed point on the graph at which the law requires people to take account of a possibility. The point is a moving one, because as we have already seen, negligence is a function of several variables. In other words, it may be negligent to disregard a very remote chance in one situation; and not negligent to disregard a much greater chance in another situation. We must consider alongside foreseeability the other factors mentioned above – the utility of the conduct in question, the magnitude of the damage which may be done; and the burden of the precautions required to avoid the damage. So, for example, it is certainly foreseeable that a cricket ball may be struck out of a ground and hit someone in the street, but when one sets against this the fact that the chance of its happening is quite small, the amount of damage it is likely to do – if it does any – will be limited, and the fact that one can't play cricket without running such risks, short of building a high and costly fence, the balance is in favour of no liability.[11] On the other hand, the chance that oil accidentally discharged from a vessel in a harbour may ignite on the surface of the water is very remote indeed. But set against this extreme improbability the fact that, if it does ignite, very considerable damage may be done, the fact that a discharge of oil serves no useful purpose and that the only precaution required to avoid it is that of turning a tap off, and the balance is in favour of liability.[12] When the installation of automatic level crossings was under consideration the possibility of a vehicle stalling across the railway lines when a train was due was not merely foreseeable but was actually foreseen; but it was dismissed as too remote a possibility to be worth troubling with.[13] In the event, the risk materialized, but those responsible for the decision were not necessarily negligent since other factors may have outweighed the risks involved.

The fact that the degree of probability of an event which justifies a finding of negligence is not always the same, has often been disguised by speaking of 'reasonable foreseeability'. It is not enough, it will sometimes be said, that harm was foreseeable as a possibility or a remote chance; it must have been 'reasonably foreseeable'. But this phrase is ambiguous in the extreme. It may mean 'foreseeable by someone with a reasonable degree of knowledge, skill or understanding.' So, for example, we may say that a doctor ought 'reasonably to have foreseen' that a certain course of treatment would be unsatisfactory, meaning thereby, not that unsatisfactory results were 'reasonably likely' to follow (they may have been virtually certain to follow), but that a 'reasonable' doctor would have known that they would follow. But more often 'reasonably foreseeable' is an extremly elliptical phrase meaning 'foreseeable as so probable or likely as to make it unreasonable not to take certain precautions to avoid it.' If the phrase is used to refer to the degree of probability of an event there is nothing else that it can mean, because we cannot meaningfully talk of a 'reasonable probability' or a 'reasonable statistical chance' except in relation to a proposed course of conduct; it is reasonable to take this or that risk, it is reasonable to take this or that precaution, and so on.

There is, however, another sense in which foreseeability may be said to be a relative concept. An event may be said to be more or less foreseeable according to the detail in which the event is described. The fact that most houses are insured against fire is testimony to the foreseeability of the possibility of damage or destruction of a house by fire; but it would be a very different matter to say, after a fire has occurred, that anyone should or could have foreseen when, where and how it might break out. Once again there is no fixed point on the scale to which we can point and say: this amount of detail needs to be foreseeable before we can condemn failure to foresee it, or act on it, as negligence. But this does not mean, as some American writers have asserted, that the whole concept of foreseeability is meaningless. We must remember that the object of bringing foreseeability into the equation is to help in deciding whether the party in question acted 'reasonably', that is, whether he took the correct decision; and the detail in which a possibility is foreseeable must be related to the conduct we are considering. For example, a manager of a factory who omits to insure it against fire may well be condemned by the company's board of directors for having been 'negligent' in failing to foresee that the possibility of fire is sufficiently serious to require a certain precaution to be taken, i.e. fire insurance. But this degree of foreseeability could not possibly justify a court in holding the manager 'negligent' in failing to prevent a fire from actually breaking out (say) by a leak of gas igniting in some unusual or extraordinary way. To condemn the manager as negligent for failure to guard against this it would have to be shown that it was sufficiently foreseeable that there would be a leak of gas to require precautions to be taken against fire *caused by a leak of gas*. Thus the degree of detail which must be foreseeable varies according to the type of precaution which it is suggested ought to have been taken.

There is yet a third sense in which foreseeability is relative, because foreseeability may depend on knowledge. What is foreseeable to one person as only a remote possibility may be foreseeable to another as highly probable because the latter may know more about the circumstances than the former. The chances of a vessel being consumed by fire may in general be very remote; but it is foreseeable as quite probable if it is known that the vessel is full of petrol vapour. Moreover, foreseeability may depend, not only on knowledge of the actual circumstances in question, but also on scientific knowledge, knowledge about the way things behave. Whose knowledge, then, is to be taken into account in deciding whether negligence is proved? The answer is, first, that knowledge which the party responsible actually had; and secondly, that knowledge which he *ought* to have had. To say that a person 'ought to have known' something, of course, brings in once again a standard of behaviour, and the same standard (i.e. reasonableness in the sense of desirability judged in policy terms) is used for this purpose too.

5 THE MAGNITUDE OF THE HARM WHICH MAY OCCUR

This is the second factor which must be taken into account in deciding a negligence issue, and it may in many cases turn the scales. The point is nicely illustrated by the decision of the House of Lords in *Paris* v. *Stepney Borough Council*,[14] in which it was held that an employer who knows that one of his workmen has only one sound eye may be negligent if he fails to supply that man with goggles for work involving a slight risk to the eyes, even though the risk is so remote that the employer must be justified in disregarding it in the case of a normally sighted workman.

It is interesting to note that there is some empirical evidence to suggest that people do behave in the way in which the House of Lords said they should behave. In an experiment conducted by the Road Research Laboratory in 1961[15] a group of motorists were asked to drive through three narrow gateways, the pillars of which appeared to be made of plastic, wood and concrete respectively. It was found that they drove at the lowest speed and took the greatest care when the pillars were concrete, at the highest speed and least care when the pillars were plastic. Unfortunately there was insufficient evidence to show whether lower speeds and greater care actually made any material difference to the accident rate, but the experiment does at least confirm that people do take into account the magnitude of the damage which their conduct may cause in determining the degree of care with which they will perform some task.

In order to determine the magnitude of the harm it may be necessary to make judgments based on community values. Is the death of one individual harm of 'greater magnitude' than the injury of a dozen others; or than the physical destruction of thousands of pounds worth of property? Can the death of one individual ever be regarded as harm of greater magnitude than that of another or are all men (and children) equal for this purpose? These are difficult questions which are never openly discussed by courts or lawyers; and it may very well be that society's sense of values on such matters is not always wholly rational. For example, it is not always easy to find a rational explanation for the values apparently placed by society in varying situations. In general society is so regulated that many risks are constantly run which could be avoided at manageable cost. Cars, for example, could be made safer if society were prepared to spend more money on them; roads could certainly be much safer, and many lives could be saved if more money was spent on them, or if cars travelled slower. Vast numbers of accidents could be avoided every year – at a cost which society is evidently not prepared to pay. But it is noticeable that, if a known identifiable person is in actual and immediate peril, the amount society is prepared to save his life becomes at once very large indeed, if not actually infinite. There is a real limit to the amount which (for instance) will be expended to avoid accidents in coal mines, but there is virtually no limit to the amount which would be expended in trying to rescue miners actually trapped underground. If it is hard to find any rational basis for this[16] it is also hard to dissent from the way in which society reacts to these situations.

6 THE VALUE OF THE ACTIVITY BEING PURSUED, AND THE BURDEN OF THE PRECAUTIONS NEEDED TO AVOID THE HARM

The negligence formula requires the court to compare the harm which may be caused by the conduct, with the benefits that come from that conduct; or, to put it another way, to compare the harm which may be caused by the conduct, with the harm or loss which would occur if the conduct did not take place; or if it only took place subject to precautions which prevented the former harm from occurring. So, for instance, in the cricket ball case the court must decide whether the risk of injury to passers-by in the street is (given its likelihood and magnitude) more serious or more costly than the value (objectively judged by the court), not of the playing of cricket, but of the playing of cricket without an adequate protective fence (given the cost of building a fence). Whether, if the activity is made to pay for the harm that it causes, the result will be a cessation of the activity or the taking of precautions against the harm, obviously depends on the cost of possible precautions relative to the value of the activity to those who participate in it. If erecting a fence around a cricket club would cost so much that the cost of playing cricket on the ground became prohibitive, in the sense that people would not be prepared to pay the entrance fees or membership fees, then the result of making the club pay for the damage it causes might be to close it down. If however the club could pay for a fence to prevent the damage it causes and still carry on, then the result of making them pay for the harm they do might be the erection of the fence. Another possibility might be for the club to avoid causing damage, not by erecting a fence around the ground, but by persuading its neighbours to move out, or buying the adjoining land. Which of these actual results ensues depends upon their cost, but this does not affect the comparison which has to be made for the purposes of the negligence formula.

Of course there are occasions when no precautions are possible so that if pursuit of the activity is alleged to be negligent (e.g. use of a very dangerous type of machinery) the question of precautions may be dismissed altogether, and the only question is whether the gain from using the machinery is worth more than the loss or harm that it causes. There are also occasions when the precautions required to avoid harm are so elementary and trouble free that it is almost certain that the court will find that failure to take the precautions amounts to negligence. For instance, the precautions required to avoid most road accidents are very simple – driving more slowly, giving a signal, blowing a horn, waiting for the next straight stretch of road before overtaking, and so on. This is probably why questions of foreseeability so rarely arise in relation to road accidents. However unusual the consequence of an accident may be, the magnitude of the harm likely to occur is so great and the avoidance of the accident is so easy, that liability for negligence will almost certainly be imposed.

We cannot measure the value of an activity without first defining it, and there are difficulties inherent in the concept of the 'activity' which causes the accident. For instance, in a road traffic accident caused by overtaking on a corner, is the activity which causes the accident that of 'motoring', or that of 'overtaking on a corner'? If we say that the activity is 'motoring', then we have to argue that the whole activity of motoring is of such little value compared with lives it takes, that it is negligent to drive a car at all. Plainly this would be an unacceptable conclusion, so we are reduced to saying that it was overtaking on a corner which was the activity in question. *This* activity has little value when compared with the risk: the only value it has is the slight gain in time it may give to the overtaking driver, and (conceivably) some slight satisfaction in the thrill of taking the risk of overtaking on a corner. Clearly, these gains do not outweigh the risks involved, so we say the act of overtaking on a corner is negligent. Of course if it could be shown that the gain in time as a result of overtaking on a corner was a matter of vital importance for this or that purpose – e.g. because the driver was taking some desperately ill person to hospital – we might then say that the 'activity' in question was that of taking a person to hospital.

But in practice the activity being pursued is irrelevant in the great majority of cases of personal injury or property damage. The courts are not, save in very exceptional cases, prepared to acquit someone of negligence because he was doing something very useful, nor conversely are they prepared to convict someone of negligence because he is doing something useless or even anti-social. A gang of robbers driving a get-away car might in theory be said to be doing something negligent in the mere act of driving the car, even if they drive with all 'due care,' because it could be said that the risk of damage even when the car is carefully driven outweighs the social value of their journey, which would be a minus quantity. But no court would so hold. And conversely, except in the extreme cases where a car is being driven specially fast in order to save life or in some other emergency, a court would not acquit the driver of negligence because of the utility of his journey.

7 THE PURPOSES OF THE NEGLIGENCE FORMULA

We have seen that the function of the court in deciding whether a person has been negligent is not very different from the function of any person who has to make a decision as to a course of conduct: namely, it has to decide whether the advantages of the conduct outweigh the disadvantages. Now that we have examined the ingredients of the negligence formula, this can be seen even more clearly. The allegation in a negligence action is basically that the defendant has paid insufficient attention to the interests of others, and has pursued his own objectives at the risk of the safety of other persons' lives and property. This is perhaps the foundation for the view that negligence is a moral fault. But whereas the individual looks at the matter primarily from his own point of view, the judge looks at the matter from the point of view of the public interest, and the need to balance the interest of different persons. We are entitled to pursue our own interests and objectives even if by doing so we may discomfort or annoy our neighbours to some degree; and even though we may endanger their property or persons to some degree. But there are limits to the extent to which we may do this, and the judge's task is to define those limits with the aid of the negligence formula. I may drive my car at a 'reasonable' speed because the gain to me and the public from my being allowed to drive my car at a 'reasonable' speed outweighs the risk of the loss such driving may cause; but I am not allowed to drive my car at an 'excessive' speed because the additional gain that it brings to me does not outweigh the additional risk that it imposes on others.

There is another fundamental difference between the judge's task and that of anyone else who is called upon to decide between different courses of conduct; and that is the purpose for which the decision is to be made. Most people who are called to decide whether conduct A is better than B in their (or the public) interest have to make the decision as a prelude to action, as a necessary prelude to actually doing A or B. The employer, for instance, who weighs up the advantages and risks of installing some dangerous machine does so in order to decide whether to install the machine or not; and having made his decision he acts accordingly. Similarly, public bodies or officials who may have to determine whether this or that is desirable in the public interest, whether the advantages outweigh the disadvantages, do so with a view to implementation of their decision. Not so with the judge. The purpose of his decision is quite different. It is always retrospective: he is never called on to decide what *should be done* in the future, but what *should have been done* in the past. And the purpose of this enquiry is to decide whether compensation should be paid to those who have suffered injury or damage as a result of the decision which was taken by the person responsible for carrying it out.

At first sight it may be hard, from this perspective, to see the relevance of the negligence formula. There is a very obvious connection between determining whether course A or B is more advantageous, and actually carrying out A or B. There is not such an obvious connection between determining whether course A or B *was* more advantageous and awarding compensation to Z. There appear to be only two ways of defending the rationality of this procedure. The first depends on the assumption that a moral basis can be found for the fault principle. If negligent conduct can be stigmatized as morally blameworthy, and if it then follows that morally a negligent defendant ought to compensate an innocent plaintiff for his injuries, then of course there is a good reason for a retrospective inquiry into the defendant's conduct.

The second possible justification for these retrospective inquiries depends on the assumption that the law can operate as a deterrent to future negligent conduct. To hold *past* conduct to have been negligent cannot stop what has already happened, though it might have some deterrent effect on future behaviour. If, for example, a court were to hold that a cricket club had been negligent in not building a fence around its ground, this might have some influence on the future behaviour of that and other clubs. The assumption that the law can operate as a deterrent is, in theory, capable of being empirically tested, and if it proved unfounded then this second justification would collapse. It is interesting to note in this connection that recent economic literature about the law of negligence assumes that the *only* relevant function of the law is the deterrent function. Once the negligent act has occurred, the damage that has been caused is a 'sunk cost', and nothing can call it back. An order to pay damages is, from an economic point of view, merely an order to transfer money from one person to another, something of little economic significance. It is paradoxical that this argument should come to the fore at the very time when the courts are being most insistent that the function of tort law is to compensate and not to punish or to deter.

It seems, then, that defence of the negligence inquiry must depend on the validity of one or other, or both, of these views about the moral basis and the deterrent effect of the fault doctrine. These views are discussed extensively later in this work.[17]

8 THE OBJECTIVE STANDARD OF CARE

We have seen how the negligence formula leaves a very great deal to what we may call, for want of a better word, 'judgment'. It involves balancing things which cannot be balanced, it involves measuring incommensurables. At the end of the process the judge has to say whether he thinks the defendant should have behaved in a certain way or not. It will be seen that this approach simply eliminates the personal element. The judge's decision is not dependent on the question whether the defendant personally could have foreseen the harm or could have avoided it. The defendant may be stupid, slow-witted, clumsy, or accident prone; he may be disabled or sick; all this is irrelevant. The judge is saying what should have been done, not what could have been done, by this defendant. One reason for disregarding these matters is probably that the difficulty of investigating them would not be worth the benefits such investigation might bring. It is likely that in most cases the result would be the same anyway, since most people can probably conform to the standards of behaviour required by the law;[18] but in a small number of cases it might be found that a person could not have conformed because of his personal characteristics. However, in order to identify these cases, *all* cases would require investigation of the defendant's capacity to conform to the required standard. This investigation would be difficult if not impossible; how is one to determine if a slow-witted, clumsy or accident prone individual could personally have avoided an accident after the event?

But naturally, the judge must pay some attention to what *could* have been done, because he can hardly say that something should have been done by the defendant if it could not have been done by anybody. Conversely if the judge is dealing with a person claiming special skill, such as a doctor or other professional man, who is accused of negligence, he will, in applying the negligence formula – in deciding what should have been foreseen, or what precautions should have been taken – take into account the standard that can be attained by people possessed of that skill, or members of that profession.

This is really all that is involved in the notion that the standard of care required by the law is an 'objective' standard. If the law is discussed in terms of the 'reasonable man', the concept of an objective standard of care is of course incorporated in the characteristics of that mythical figure. But if the law is stated without reference to the reasonable man – as I have tried to state it, as involving a balancing of risks and advantages – we must recognize that the whole process of deciding what 'should' have been done requires the judge to decide on the relevance of personal considerations. It is not so much that the law adopts an objective standard of care, or follows the activities of a wholly mythical creature, as that the courts treat certain personal characteristics of the defendant as irrelevant. Generally, this involves rejecting the defendant's individual characteristics as irrelevant. For example a learner-driver will be held negligent if he fails to conform to the standard of care and skill of a qualified driver.[19] It seems that physical disabilities would be ignored in judging whether a driver had been negligent.[20] But there may still be doubts about the extent to which the courts would take account of special skills. Clearly a specialist medical practitioner, for example, is required to exercise his special skill.[21] But would a general practitioner, for example, be able to plead that he was not negligent in failing to diagnose some illness on the ground that he does not profess the skill of a specialist?

Problems of this kind result from uncertainty about the purposes for which the negligence formula is used. If the object were simply to condemn the defendant for paying insufficient attention to the interests of others, for 'fault' or immoral conduct, then there would plainly be a justification for subjectivizing the standard care. It is unfair, for example, for an inexperienced person to be condemned for failing to observe that degree of skill which a more experienced person could exercise. But if the ultimate purpose of applying to negligence formula is to decide if compensation should be paid to an innocent plaintiff, the merits of whose claim may have little to do with the demerits of the defendant, there is justification for imposing high standards of care even on the inexperienced. This tendency is greatly strengthened by the fact (as we shall see) that the damages are almost certain to be paid by an insurance company anyway; thus the defendant will not personally have to pay for his 'no-fault' negligence.

9 NEGLIGENCE IN DESIGN AND NEGLIGENCE IN OPERATION

In practice, although not in legal theory, there is an important difference between negligence in the operation of an object or an activity and negligence in the design of an object or activity. The distinction is not always easy to draw, but in general terms it is much easier to establish negligence in operation than negligence in design.

This is especially noticeable in the case of road accidents. There is no reason in theory why an injured plaintiff should not sue a motor manufacturer for the negligent design of a vehicle, or a highway authority for negligent design of a road junction or a roundabout, but in practice such actions would be unlikely to succeed. Bad vehicle design is undoubtedly a factor in the causation of many injuries, and in America it has already been the source of much negligence litigation. But so far in Britain no judgment in favour of a plaintiff in a car accident case has been based on bad vehicle design. One hardy litigant sued the manufacturers of a bus alleging that the failure to provide a central pillar on the platform was negligence, but the action failed in the House of Lords.[22] English courts are unwilling to decide cases on design issues and tend to base their judgments on other grounds. This unwillingness appears also to be a feature of cases involving injuries caused by defective products in which negligent design is alleged: courts tend to decide such cases on the issue of failure to control the hazard rather than on that of negligent creation of the hazard.[23] In general there is a strong tendency to attribute injuries to some act or omission occurring close in time to the event causing injuries (such as speeding or failure to protect a worker from some health hazard) rather than to some design feature of the environment in which the act or omission occurs (such as the state of the road or the design of equipment).

A number of factors account for the lack of litigation on design issues. First, the fact that *most* cars are still designed with the same basic defects might help manufacturers in that it would enable them to argue that they built all the customary safety features into their cars and that there is no reason why they should be required to do more. But, as we have seen, the courts have never accepted customary practice as completely precluding a finding of negligence, and there is nothing in law which would prevent them holding that customary design was negligent.

Another factor is that a decision by a court that a vehicle was badly designed, though technically on a 'question of fact', would be virtually a legislative act. If there has been negligence in the design of an article then there must have been negligence in the manufacture of all other articles made to the same design. When dealing with motor vehicles a court would doubtless be reluctant to make a decision of this kind, because in doing so it would be competing with the statutory powers of the appropriate Minister to make regulations prescribing requirements in regard to the construction of vehicles. There is certainly no legal reason why a court should not declare a design to be negligent, even though the Minister has not proscribed that aspect of the design alleged to be faulty. But there are some grounds for regarding the legislative powers of the Minister as a more appropriate way of dealing with this sort of problem; partly because the Minister could take into account wider issues of public interest which would be ignored in the courts, such as, for instance, the effect of particular design requirements on the export trade, and the need to give the makers time to change their designs.[24] Similarly, if the courts were to hold that it is negligent of the Home Office to maintain 'open' Borstal institutions from which the inmates can easily escape and do damage, they would be pronouncing on complex and politically sensitive issues about the design of the penal system which are more appropriately decided by the Executive and the Legislature.[25] But there would be no such difficulty in a finding that Borstal officers had performed their custodial task negligently.

A third factor militating against judicial resolution of design issue arises from doubts as to whether courts are able to weigh the social costs and benefits of different design and whether they ought to do so. If it costs £X to install a new safety device in all cars, are the judges the right people to decide that everybody should pay £X more for their cars? Is a court the right body to decide how much money a highway authority should spend on road works? Again, for example, in the Report of the Chief Inspector of Accidents for 1966, attention is drawn to the design of a new kind of crane – the 'small tower cranes' used at building sites:

In meeting the demands for such cranes at prices which will attract small builders, the makers have sometimes made such structural and mechanical economies in their designs as to make the machines potentially dangerous, unless handled and maintained with special care – which is less likely to be the case on a small site.[26]

The problem of balancing risks against gains in a case of this kind is very difficult indeed, and probably beyond the resources of the courts. It would involve an assessment of the risk of accident – which is not so difficult, perhaps – but it would also involve consideration of how much the public gains through the use of such cranes. Are builders who could not buy safer and more expensive cranes enabled thereby to use cranes? Does this enable builders to do their work more cheaply? What does this mean in practice? Will it lower the cost of housing? And so on.

A fourth relevant factor is one of cost – litigation which considers design issues is likely to be much more complex, lengthy and costly than litigation which concentrates on specific acts or omissions.

The question of whether the courts ought to be making decisions in 'design' cases that certain precautions to avoid loss or damage ought to have been taken is of particular importance in relation to actions against public bodies. Suppose, for example, that a local authority is sued in respect of a road accident on the ground that it should have installed traffic lights at a dangerous intersection; or in respect of someone's death by drowning at a dangerous beach because it neglected to provide warning flags or a life-saver. Installing lights or providing life-savers costs money. And a decision that lights ought to have been installed at one intersection or a life-saver provided on one beach might lead this and other local authorities to feel that in order to avoid liability in negligence it would be necessary to install lights at many dangerous intersections or to provide lifesavers on many dangerous beaches. To meet the cost of such precautions other public projects, such as the provision of new hospitals or extensions to schools, might have to be starved of funds if extra revenue cannot be raised. As a matter of constitutional theory it is widely accepted that such policy choices between safer roads, better schools and more hospitals ought to be made by elected representatives of the people and not by judges.

Another interesting example of this problem relates to the prevention of crime. Criminal attacks on individuals are sometimes the result of inefficient police patrols; or of a refusal by the police to protect someone who has been threatened by thugs or a vital witness in a case against a well organized gang of criminals.[27] In England a court would be very unwilling to find negligence against the police for failure to take adequate steps to prevent this or that crime, because questions about expenditure on the prevention of crime and about the level of policing are left to the police or their political masters. (The existence of a scheme, entirely divorced from the law of negligence, for the compensation of the victims of criminal injuries means that in this country such issues are unlikely to arise before a court except, perhaps, in relation to theft, robbery and the like).

'Design' cases against public bodies will, then, often raise difficult policy questions about the expenditure of limited public resources. In such cases English courts would not even entertain an allegation of negligence against a public body unless the body had acted so unreasonably that it could be said to have acted *ultra vires* (that is, unlawfully in the public law sense).[28]

In summary, therefore, we can say that some problems about

negligent design are best left to legislation because they affect many cases, not just one; and others are, for policy reasons, best left to public administrative bodies which are directly or indirectly responsible to Parliament or the electorate.

3
Negligence: the scope of the tort

1 THE NATURE OF THE DUTY OF CARE

Negligence, it is said, cannot be committed 'in the air'. A person may be as negligent as he pleases so long as he owes no duty to take care; and the function of the law is to decide when a person owes a duty of care to another. Such duties, although today very widespread, are by no means universal, and it is therefore necessary to discover what criteria, if any, exist for determining when a person owes a duty to take care. The basic criterion for this purpose is often said to be that of 'foreseeability' of injury. Thus, in general, we can say that a person who ought to foresee that his conduct may cause injury to another if he fails to take reasonable care, is under a duty to take care. This general principle is derived from the famous case of *Donoghue* v. *Stevenson*,[1] in which the House of Lords held that the manufacturer of a product owes a duty to take care that the product is not so defective that it may cause injury to those who may be expected to use it in the ordinary course. Until that case, there was no general principle governing the existence of duties of care; there were merely cases in which it had been decided that there was a duty to take care, and there were other cases in which it had been decided that there was no duty to take care.

In addition, it is said, the duty to take care is a relative concept. A person may be able to foresee damage to one person but not to another, in any given situation, and in this event he may owe a duty to be careful to one person and not the other. If he breaks that duty the first party can sue him, but not the second, even though the second suffers damage. A person must build his cause of action on a breach of duty owed to himself and not to another.

The foreseeability criterion is not, however, a complete test of whether a duty of care exists. Even if the defendant ought to have foreseen that the plaintiff might suffer injury if he did not take care he may, for some policy reason, be under no duty of care or his duty may be in some way limited or restricted.[2] For example, for policy reasons barristers owe no duty of care to their clients in respect of work done in court even though it is quite foreseeable that if a barrister conducts a case negligently his client may suffer loss.

This is, broadly and somewhat crudely, the formal legal account of the duty of care. But it is a rather misleading account. We may, in the first place, note that the concept of the duty of care adds nothing to the concept of the tort of negligence itself.[3] There are some circumstances in which a person is liable for negligently causing damage to another, and there are some circumstances in which a person is not so liable. If his conduct falls within the first category we say that he owes a duty of care and has committed the tort of negligence; if his conduct falls within the second category we say he owes no duty of care and has not committed the tort. So the concept of the duty of care is simply co-extensive with the boundaries of liability for damage caused by negligent conduct. We might just as well say that no person can be guilty of the tort of defamation unless he owes 'a duty not to defame' and that this duty only exists in certain circumstances. Once we have stated the circumstances in which a person is liable in the tort of defamation, we add nothing but an unnecessary complexity to the law by saying that in those circumstances that person owes 'a duty not to defame'. Indeed, none of the other torts are constructed on the same conceptual framework as the tort of negligence, with its duty to take care. If we are faced with a problem in the law of nuisance we never, as lawyers, ask, 'Does the defendant owe a duty not to commit a nuisance?' We merely ask what in law are the boundaries of the tort of nuisance. There is no logical reason why we should not do the same in the law of negligence. There is no reason why the law should not (without changing its substance) simply declare that in circumstances A, B, C, a person is liable for negligently causing damage, and in circumstances X, Y, Z, a person is not liable for negligently causing damage. The duty of care concept is, therefore, an unnecessary abstraction which adds nothing to the substance of the law.

The same point can perhaps be made by noting that a breach of the duty of care is not actionable in tort unless actionable damage actually occurs as a result. A plaintiff will not recover damages for a breach of a duty of care unless he has actually suffered some damage in consequence. Whenever someone drives negligently on the highway he is breaking the duty of care which he owes to all other road users, but he will not be liable in tort unless his breach causes damage. Once damage occurs, however, the picture changes. Now, if negligence can be proved, and if a duty exists, legal liability will follow. It would seem, then, more accurate to recognize that so far as the law is concerned the duty is not a 'duty to take care' but a 'duty to avoid causing damage by lack of care'. But once this stage in the argument has been reached, it seems simpler still to recognize that this 'duty' is merely the logical equivalent of actual legal liability for damage caused by negligence. Thus, to say that a person owes a duty of care in a particular situation *means* (and means only) that he will be liable for causing damage by negligence in that situation.

Thus discussion of the duty of care resolves itself into discussion of the extent of legal liability for negligence: and the extent of liability for negligence is a legal-policy question to be settled by the courts. That this is the correct view, is now coming to be recognized by the courts themselves. For example, in the *Dorset Yacht* case Lord Denning (in the Court of Appeal) said:

It is, I think, at bottom a matter of public policy which we, as judges, must resolve. This talk of 'duty' or 'no duty' is simply a way of limiting the range of liability for negligence.[4]

Lord Diplock explicitly agreed with this dictum when the case reached the House of Lords.[5] Furthermore, the principle that a duty of care based on foreseeability can be excluded or limited for policy reasons is having the effect that judicial discussion of the duty of care tends to concentrate on cases in which, for policy reasons, it is argued that there is or ought to be no liability for negligently inflicted damage.

Once it is appreciated that the duty of care concept is no more than a 'control device' for setting limits on liability for negligently inflicted damage, certain lines of reasoning can be seen to be fallacious. Two examples may be given. First, it is wrong to think that because a person is under no *legal* duty of care he therefore has no *moral* duty to take care.[6] It is quite logical to say that a person ought morally to take care but that he cannot be made legally liable for causing damage by failure to do so. The second example concerns liability for negligently causing damage to an unborn child. The matter is now dealt with by the Congenital Disabilities (Civil liability) Act 1976; but before this Act there was real doubt as to whether a duty to take care not to injure an unborn child could exist. This was because, so far as the common law was concerned, human existence began only at birth; and it was argued that no *legal* duty could be owed to a foetus which was not a *legal* person. The supposed logical problem disappears when it is realized that the real question is simply whether, as a matter of policy, a child born with injuries as a result of negligent acts or omissions done before its birth (or conception) should be allowed to recover damages. To that policy question it was never suggested that the answer should be other than affirmative.

2 LIABILITY FOR PHYSICAL DAMAGE

Because of the emphasis placed on the concept of duty of care, and on the part played by foreseeability in determining the existence of the duty, the conventional exposition of the tort of negligence appears to suggest that the tort is mainly concerned with problems relating to unforeseeable plaintiffs, unforeseeable damage, and unforeseeable events. The absurdity of this analysis is perhaps best demonstrated by stating what appears to be a principle of the law of negligence of quite fundamental importance, yet a principle which was not found in the books or the cases prior to 1970 because its existence was hidden by the confusion which surrounds the duty of care. This principle, which was stated by Lord Reid, in the *Dorset Yacht*[7] case, is that with very few exceptions, a person is guilty of the tort of negligence, and therefore liable to pay compensation, for *physical* damage to the person or property of another, caused by *affirmative* negligent conduct on his part. The doubtful areas in the law are nearly all concerned with two principal questions: first, the extent of liability for damage of a kind other than physical injury, for instance, mental distress or pecuniary loss; secondly, the extent of liability for omissions as opposed to affirmative conduct.[8]

The present position is the culmination of many years of legal development during the course of which liability for physical damage or injury in negligence cases has been steadily widened. In order to appreciate the present position more clearly it is desirable to examine three main areas of liability separately, namely that relating to road accidents, that relating to industrial accidents, and a third miscellaneous group of cases covering a wide variety of situations.

Road accident cases

The majority of negligence actions arise out of road accidents. Legal liability for negligence in respect of such accidents has been recognized certainly since the seventeenth century and perhaps earlier. There has never been any doubt that those using the highways are under a duty of care in so doing, and the legal position today is quite plain: any person using the roads, whether as a motorist, pedestrian or cyclist, will be liable if, by his positive action, he negligently causes physical injury to anybody else. We can, if we choose, rationalize this in terms of the duty concept by saying that it is so obvious that negligent conduct may cause physical injury on the road that everybody must foresee such injury if he acts negligently, and accordingly that every road user owes a duty to take care to avoid physical injury to all other road users. But there seems little purpose to this rationalization and, indeed, a lawyer would scarcely ever waste time in an ordinary accident case by enquiring whether the defendant owed a duty of care to the plaintiff. This would simply be taken for granted.

Industrial accidents

The general principle also holds good for positive negligent action in industrial injury cases. It is indeed hard to visualize any room for doubt about the existence of a duty of care in circumstances in which personal injury results from a positive act of negligence by an employer or a fellow servant. But although the position today is clear enough, it is only in comparatively recent years (indeed, since 1948) that those injured in industrial accidents have had much prospect of success in a negligence action. The main reason for this until 1897 was not the absence of a duty of care, but the use made by the courts of a number of other 'control devices' which served a similar purpose. There were three such devices, namely the 'doctrine of common employment', under which an employer was not liable to one servant for the negligence of another; the defence of contributory negligence, under which the employer was not liable if the servant was himself partly to blame for the accident; and the defence of *volenti non fit injuria*, under which the employer was held not liable for injuries flowing from a known and obvious risk. As we shall see later, these 'control devices' were abolished or gradually whittled down, but between 1897 and 1948 another major obstacle existed to actions for negligence arising from industrial accidents. This was the provision in the Workmen's Compensation Acts requiring the workman to 'elect' between his statutory rights to compensation and his common law right to damages.

Miscellaneous cases: Donoghue v. Stevenson

Perhaps the most important area of liability in this miscellaneous category is that of manufacturers for defective products. The famous and leading case is that of *Donoghue* v. *Stevenson*[9], to which we have already briefly referred. In this case the plaintiff allegedly suffered injuries – gastroenteritis and shock – as a result of drinking a bottle of ginger-beer which was said to have contained the remains of a decomposed snail. The question at issue was whether, assuming that the presence of the snail was due to the lack of reasonable care by the defendants or their servants, the defendants would be liable to the plaintiff. To us, it may seem astonishing that the answer could ever have been in doubt, since every consideration so clearly points in favour of liability in such circumstances – the desire to compensate the plaintiff for injuries; the fact (or assumption) that the injuries were due to the fault of the defendants; the need to induce manufacturers producing food and drink for the public to take precautions against such events; and finally the fact that the manufacturer is so much the better 'loss distributor', i.e. is so much better able than the consumer to bear the loss and distribute it through the costs of his enterprise. However, despite all this, liability was very much doubted in *Donoghue* v. *Stevenson*, and it is generally agreed that the majority in the House of Lords in favour of the plaintiff made 'new law', in the sense that before this famous decision the precedents suggested that there would be no liability on such facts.

The strange thing about this case is that although everybody agrees that it was of considerable importance in the law of torts, there is considerable disagreement as to why the case should be regarded as so important. At first sight its importance appears to lie in some famous remarks of Lord Atkin in which he attempted to find some general principle underlying the circumstances in which a duty of care may be held to exist in the law. These remarks must now be ranked as probably the most famous dicta in all English (and indeed perhaps also Commonwealth and American) case law. Yet Lord Atkin did not really say very much in this dictum. All that he said was that there must be some underlying principle common to all cases in which a duty of care exists, and that this principle could be found in what is called the 'neighbour principle': you must take care not to injure your neighbour, and your neighbour is anyone who is so closely and directly affected by your act that you ought to have him in contemplation when acting. This is just the foreseeability principle: if you can foresee that your acts will injure someone, you owe them a duty to be careful that you do not injure them. But the dictum has produced much argument and discussion. Lord Atkin could not, it is said, have meant his statement as a general principle covering all circumstances. The existence of a duty to take care in new circumstances must still be treated as raising a new point, and one to be decided on policy grounds. Lord Atkin's dictum says that new duties of care *may* be recognized despite the absence of precedent, but not that they must be recognized. Some have objected that 'As a formula this [dictum] is so vague as to have little meaning, and as a guide to decision it has had no value at all.'[10] Others have argued that Lord Atkin could not have meant his dictum to apply to omissions, nor to cases of purely pecuniary damage. Some have indeed wondered whether Lord Atkin's dictum, or the case as a whole, has really been as influential on the subsequent development of the law as most lawyers appear to believe.[11]

It is, however, generally agreed that one of the most important aspects of the decision in *Donoghue* v. *Stevenson* was the elimination of the privity of contract restriction on liability in negligence, that is, recognition that liability could exist for negligence between parties who are not in a contractual relationship. Although liability for negligent acts was well established in some areas even in the absence of any contractual relationship long before this case – as in the road accidents field – there is no doubt that the privity of contract principle had become a severe limitation on the extension of the law of negligence, and that it had been used by the courts in the nineteenth century exactly in order to *restrict* liability for negligent acts. This may have been partly because, their judgment unclouded by the existence of liability insurance (the presence of which we so often take for granted today), the judges of this period did not find it just to impose liabilities on defendants for trifling acts of negligence; or because, as many American scholars think, the judges did not want to stifle initiative, and particularly did not want to cripple the emerging industries on which the country's wealth depended.[12] The fact that defendants were most likely to be members of the upper or middle classes while plaintiffs were likely to be workmen may have played some part in motivating the judges; or they may have feared that an expansion of liability would bring in more business than the courts were equipped to handle.[13] Whatever their motives, it is clear that the courts wanted to limit liability for negligence during this period, and one very effective way of doing this was by denying the liability of a defendant to a plaintiff with whom he had no contractual relations. In this way, the number of potential plaintiffs was confined within very narrow bounds. Many people may be injured by the negligence of, for example, manufacturers, builders, repairers, and so on. But if liability was restricted to those with contractual relations with the manufacturer, etc, there would normally be only one potential plaintiff, and at worst the number of plaintiffs would be confined within finite bounds.

Donoghue v. *Stevenson* finally removed this restriction on liability for negligence, and this began a movement towards a general liability for physical damage caused by affirmative negligent conduct which has been going on ever since. And it has become clear since *Donoghue* v. *Stevenson* that the number of cases of accidental personal injury has not put undue strain on the courts; although delay in getting cases heard is a problem despite the fact that even today only a small proportion of all cases of accidental personal injury result in a tort claim, and only a minute proportion even of these cases get into court. On the other hand, the great majority of tort claims still arise out of road accidents (where the privity restriction never prevented liability being imposed on negligent drivers) and industrial accidents (where the privity requirement was normally satisfied). The removal of the privity restriction has thus only affected a relatively small number of cases compared with the great numbers arising from road and industrial accidents.

It is, then, suggested that the real importance of *Donoghue* v. *Stevenson* lay in the removal of the privity of contract restriction. It was left to later courts to decide to what extent liability for negligent conduct was to be extended once this barrier was gone. And liability for physical damage caused by affirmative negligent conduct has now become very general indeed. Indeed, one of the most notable developments of recent years has been the gradual reversal of older precedents denying liability for negligence in various situations. This gradual elimination of what now seem anomalous or exceptional 'no-duty' situations has greatly assisted the tendency towards creation of liability for negligence in new situations.

Elimination of 'limited duty' or 'no duty' situations

In a work of this kind it is unnecessary to trace these developments in any great detail. It is enough to point out that before about 1950 the courts had recognized a number of situations in which there was either no liability for negligence ('no duty' situations), or only some limited form of liability ('limited duty' situations), and that during the past quarter century or so, most of these cases have been reversed either by the courts themselves or by statute. At first, most of the changes related to cases of physical injury or damage, but recently there has been significant development in cases involving purely pecuniary loss.[14] It is only necessary to refer briefly to the more important of these situations.

The law relating to the liability of an occupier of premises to someone injured on those premises, or to someone whose property is damaged on those premises, was for long subject to special rules, as a result of which liability for negligence was not always recognized. These rules were radically overhauled by the Occupiers Liability Act 1957 and it is unnecessary for our purposes to look at the law which was abrogated by this Act. Broadly speaking, visitors are divided into two classes, namely lawful visitors and trespassers. The liability of an occupier to lawful visitors has been very largely assimilated to that of ordinary liability in negligence, so that the occupier now owes to his lawful visitors a 'common duty of care' – which is for all practical purposes indistinguishable from the ordinary duty of care which governs most common law actions for negligence. Nothing here need detain us because it is plain that the occupier always owes his lawful visitors a duty to take care, and is therefore liable for causing them physical injury by his negligence – indeed he is liable whether his negligence consists of misfeasance or nonfeasance.

Liability to trespassers continued to be governed by the common law until the enactment of the Occupiers Liability Act 1984, which imposes on occupiers a duty to take such care as is reasonable considering, in particular, that the trespasser has forced his presence on the occupier without the latter's consent.

Another exceptional case, which was formerly a 'no duty' situation, concerned the liability of the landlord or vendor of defective premises. Because this was a contractual situation in which the traditional common law approach was *caveat emptor*, the courts generally held that the landlord or vendor of dangerous premises was not liable, even where the danger was created by his own negligence. Most of these immunities have now been abolished, both at common law by the courts and by the Defective Premises Act 1972. Another example is to be found in the Animals Act 1971, which largely (though not quite entirely) removes the former immunity from liability of the owner of an animal which strays onto a highway causing injury or damage. Other examples of statutory extensions of liability for negligence, reversing former 'no duty' situations, are the Highways (Miscellaneous Provisions) Act 1961, imposing liability on highway authorities, for – in effect – negligently failing to repair a highway; and the Law Reform (Husband and Wife) Act 1962, enabling husbands and wives to sue each other for negligence (with a view to obtaining damages from insurance companies). The Congenital Disabilities (Civil Liability) Act 1976 also eliminates any doubts about another possible no-duty situation by making it clear that, in general, legal liability will exist for negligently inflicting injuries on an unborn child.

3 MENTAL DISTRESS

We now turn to consider cases in which, in practice, doubt may arise about the existence of a legal duty of care where there has been active negligence. There are, as suggested earlier, two principal situations in which this may occur, namely cases of mental distress, and cases of purely pecuniary loss. It must be stressed at the outset that no difficulty arises about awarding damages to a person for mental distress or pecuniary loss where these follow from the infliction of physical injuries on him. A person who is run over in a motor accident may recover damages for mental distress, e.g. pain and suffering; knowledge that he has a shortened expectation of life; discomfort and inconvenience arising from confinement to bed or hospital or wheelchair. And he may recover damages for pecuniary loss, in particular, of course, for lost income which he is no longer able to earn. The recovery of damages for mental distress and pecuniary loss in such cases is an everyday matter; and indeed the bulk of damages awarded in personal injury actions *is* for mental distress and pecuniary loss. The extent to which such damages may be awarded where physical injury is proved has never been treated as raising a problem involving the duty of care, but merely as involving a problem in the assessment of damages. That aspect of the problem is dealt with fully in Chapter 7.

Let us now look a little more closely at cases of mental distress not caused by physical injury. Although there is a general rule that a person who negligently inflicts foreseeable physical injuries on another is liable for them, the existence of such a rule in relation to mental distress is a matter of uncertainty and doubt. In the recent case of *McLoughlin* v. *O'Brian*[15] a woman suffered severe depression and a personality change as a result of learning that her daughter had been killed, and her husband and other three children injured in a car accident (which occurred several miles from their home, where the woman was at the time); and as a result of visiting the hospital soon afterwards and witnessing the nature and extent of the injuries suffered. The members of the House of Lords agreed that the plaintiff should recover damages, but various different reasons for the decision were given. Lord Wilberforce took the view that mental distress ought to be treated differently from physical injury, in the sense that special and more restrictive rules ought to govern liability for the former.

Several arguments have traditionally been put forward in favour of such an approach. One is that mental distress which has no physical symptoms, or only psychosomatic symptoms, is relatively difficult to prove. The law attempts to deal with this problem by providing that mental distress is only compensatable if it amounts to some 'recognizable psychiatric illness'[16] – usually referred to, rather inaccurately, as 'mental shock'. Thus, expert medical evidence will normally be necessary to establish that the plaintiff has suffered nervous shock in this sense. Mere grief, anguish, fear, unhappiness, humiliation, outrage, and so on, however distressing they may be, are only compensatable if they are the result of physical injury to the person experiencing any of these feelings.

But even though a judge may, with the aid of expert evidence, not have too much difficulty in distinguishing a real psychiatric illness from less serious mental disturbance, this may not justify drawing a sharp line between the two, because at least some psychiatric disorders (e.g. depression) are just extreme versions of commonplace emotional states. Moreover, it is difficult to assess how big a problem the need to draw this line creates in cases which do not go to court, but are settled out of court simply on the basis of written medical reports and without the benefit of cross-examination of expert witnesses. It may well be that, in practice, much more will turn, in settled cases, on the effect of the symptoms on the plaintiff's lifestyle (e.g. is he confined to bed, unable to work, and so on), rather than on whether the symptoms amount to a recognized psychiatric illness, especially in cases where the claim is accompanied by claims for physical injury by other members of the plaintiff's family. Furthermore, it may be that, in reality, damages for nervous shock are most often awarded to a family member who suffers shock as a result of injuries to other family members, and that such damages are only rarely awarded to persons who are not related to the physically injured person.

Another reason for the restrictive approach to mental distress is the so-called 'floodgates argument': if recovery for mental distress were allowed simply on the basis that it was foreseeable, there might well be a flood of claims which would clog up the court system and divert too many of society's resources into compensating the victims of nervous shock at the expense of the many who presently receive little or no compensation, even for physical injuries suffered as a result of negligent conduct. The force of the floodgates argument is disputed by judges and commentators. On the other hand, given the large number of serious road accidents each year, and the fact that a person may suffer mental distress even if he is in no physical danger himself, it might be expected that many people would suffer some sort of mental distress as a result of witnessing harrowing events. But it must also be remembered that the narrow definition of nervous shock would probably rule out very many, if not most, of such cases.

Nevertheless, the law has not traditionally allowed recovery for nervous shock as freely as it has allowed recovery for physical injury. It has not been sufficient for the plaintiff to establish that the nervous shock was a foreseeable result of the defendant's negligence. In one case, recovery was denied partly on the basis that the plaintiff was not herself put in *physical* danger by the defendant's conduct;[17] but more recent cases make it clear that this restriction is no longer valid. In some cases the physical proximity of the plaintiff to the scene of the accident has been treated as important,[18] although it is clearly not crucial, as *McLoughlin* v. *O'Brian* shows.[19] It used to be thought that a plaintiff could only recover if he or she had witnessed the accident itself with his or her own unaided senses; but *McLoughlin* v. *O'Brian* shows that it may be sufficient for the plaintiff to witness the *immediate aftermath* of the accident. It is not clear whether a plaintiff who, for example, sees distressing events on television, could recover. A firm line has always been drawn between those who suffer shock merely as a result of being *told* of events which may cause them distress (e.g. the death of a husband or child), and those who actually witness the event (or its aftermath) – the former could not recover.[20] The status of this restriction since *McLoughlin* v. *O'Brian* is unclear. Finally, the relationship between the plaintiff and the person killed or injured is sometimes relevant, but not always – for example, in one case a volunteer who helped victims of a tube crash at the scene of the accident recovered damages for nervous distress suffered as a result.[21] In another case, a crane driver recovered damages for shock suffered as a result of fear for the safety of his fellow workmen when the load fell off his crane.[22]

Two views are possible of the status of these restrictions on liability. One is that they are legal limits imposed, independently of and additionally to the requirement of foreseeability, to meet the floodgates argument, and as a recognition of the relative unimportance of compensating for mental distress as opposed to physical injury. The other view, which seems to have attracted majority support in *McLoughlin* v. *O'Brian*,[23] is that these restrictions are, at most, factors to be taken into account in deciding whether the plaintiff's injury was foreseeable or not. Because the relative susceptibility of particular individuals to suffer nervous shock varies more widely than does susceptibility to physical injury, the factors which are likely to render some people more susceptible to shock than others need to be spelt out, and this the restrictive considerations are designed to do.

It is clear that, in some cases, this difference of approach may produce different results. For example, it may be foreseeable that a person might suffer shock if told in sufficient detail of horrific injuries to a loved one; but if there is a rule of law that merely being told of an accident does not generate liability, then the fact that the shock was forseeable in the particular case would be irrelevant. If the main argument in favour of rigid legal restrictions is fear of a flood of litigation, Australian experience suggests that such restrictions are unnecessary. Statutory provisions in New South Wales,[24] for example, give a remedy to a parent or spouse who suffers nervous shock as a result of the death of or injury to a child or spouse, even where the plaintiff has not witnessed the accident or injuries. No flood of litigation has followed this provision.

4 ECONOMIC OR PECUNIARY LOSS

As with mental distress, damages for economic loss are recoverable when the loss is a consequence of physical injury (for example loss of earnings following physical injury in a road accident); and damages are also sometimes recoverable when the loss is intentionally inflicted; but damages are not generally recoverable when the loss is negligently inflicted and is not the consequence of any physical injury.

In practice, economic loss which does not arise from direct physical damage to the person or property is likely to arise in three principal ways. First, it may result from commercial transactions of one kind or another; whether losses of this kind should be compensated for, or whether they should be regarded as the risk of the person incurring the loss, has traditionally been the concern of the law of contract. But in recent years the courts have recognized a new species of liability for financial loss in the law of tort, which bears a distinct resemblance to the kind of liability which is normally treated as the subject of a contractual action. This type of liability, first recognized by the House of Lords in the famous *Hedley Byrne* case[25] in 1964, enables a person to claim damages for financial loss incurred as a result of negligently given advice, even though the advice is given gratuitously and not in performance of a contract. More recently, the House has held that a factory owner, in whose factory a defective floor was laid, could sue the sub-contractor who had laid the floor for the cost of relaying it and financial loss suffered while this was being done, despite the fact that the plaintiff had no contract with the sub-contractor, but only with the head contractor who had employed the defendant.[26] The cases are, at bottom, concerned with commercial relations, and with financial losses which arise from contracts, investments and other business activities, rather than with financial losses incurred by individuals as a result of being deprived of their incomes. This does not mean that this is not a very important branch of the law. But the social problems raised by financial loss related to breaches of contract, commercial relationships, bad investments, bad advice, or pressure of competition, are very different from the social problems produced by accidents and disease, with which we are principally concerned in this book.

Secondly, economic losses may result from physical injury to the person or property of another, on whom the first person is dependent, or with whom he is associated in some way. Here we may (as the law does) distinguish between domestic dependency or association, and commercial dependency or association. Domestic dependency or association is illustrated by cases within the family circle: injury to a wife or a child causes pecuniary loss to husband or father; death of the breadwinner causes pecuniary loss to those who depend on his support. On the other hand, there has so far been no tendency to expand the law of tort to cover those cases of economic loss which arise from physical damage to the property of another, with whom the first is associated in some commercial relationship – for example, where a factory is deprived of its water supply because someone has negligently damaged a water hydrant or electric cable in the road,[27] or where an enterprise loses orders because its customer's premises are destroyed by a negligently caused fire.

Losses of this kind have never figured in the law of torts in the past, probably because they were accepted risks in the use of capital. It would never have occurred to a nineteenth-century businessman whose factory was (say) temporarily deprived of its water supply by the negligence of a third party, to regard the risk as other than one of the risks of business. Today businessmen prefer to guard or hedge against risks of this kind if they possibly can. Of course, many risks are inherent in any form of business, and the essence of a capitalist society is that businessmen pit their wits against each other in assessing these risks; but they prefer to avoid certain types of risk if they can, partly at least because no amount of business acumen can guard against them. In general, a businessman has to learn to live with the risk that the terms of trade may turn against him; that currencies may be devalued; that import or export controls may be introduced; that he may have strike troubles with his labour force, and so on. But he can insure against some risks. For example, the risk that a major customer or supplier may suffer fire damage, with consequential loss of profits to the company, is today a well recognized species of insurable risk.[28] Insurance is also now readily available for loss of profits arising from deprivation of water, electric or gas supplies.[29] We shall see later that, although in theory damage by fire is (if negligently caused) within the scope of the tort system, in practice this type of damage is almost invariably compensated by insurance taken out by the property owner. It is, therefore, not surprising that as consequential loss has come to be regarded as a normal insurable risk, the courts have resisted all invitations to extend tort liability for this kind of loss. Nevertheless, the pressure to expand tort liability into these new areas is considerable, especially for a judiciary so imbued with the basic moral idea that a person who suffers loss through another's negligence is entitled to damages for that negligence. Recent decisions in Australia[30] and Canada[31] show some signs of a willingness to expand the frontiers of the law here, though so far the English courts have seemed more hesitant.[32]

Whatever motives have actuated the courts, there seems no doubt that their instincts have been sound. If tort liability for this sort of loss were to be imposed, the result could only be a demand for third-party liability insurance on the part of those liable to cause such loss. And the whole trend in the fire-damage field towards personal insurance by the property-owner – with conspicuous success in almost every way – is a warning against any attempt to introduce tort law into this area, which is so far exclusively tenanted by the insurance companies.

5 FAMILY CLAIMS

The law's relative unwillingness to compensate for mental distress and economic loss creates particular problems in the context of claims arising out of injury to or the death of members of a family which causes consequential loss to other members of the family.

Bereavement

Considering mental distress first, we have seen that mere grief, anguish or unhappiness does not amount to compensatable nervous shock. But in the context of claims arising out of the death of a family member, there is a limited statutory exception to this rule. Under the Fatal Accidents Act 1976[33] (as amended by the Administration of Justice Act 1982), an award of a fixed sum of £3,500 (called damages for bereavement) may be made to a husband or wife in respect of the death of his or her spouse or to parents in respect of the death of an unmarried minor child. These damages are meant as a solatium (or solace) for the grief caused by the spouse's or child's death (so they cannot be recovered by the estate of a deceased spouse or parent). This head of damages also constitutes an exception to the principle laid down by the courts that damages under the Fatal Accidents Act (which, loosely, allows members of the close family of a deceased person to recover damages in respect of that person's death if it was wrongfully caused) are meant to compensate for financial loss only.

Damages for bereavement were designed partially to replace damages for loss of expectation of life, which were abolished by the 1982 Act.[34] This latter head of damages (which never exceeded about £2,000) was awarded to victims of personal injuries in cases where the person's life expectancy had been reduced by the accident in order to compensate him for the 'lost years'. Sometimes, however, the award went not to the injured person but to the beneficiaries of his estate. This came about in the following way. Until the enactment of the Law Reform (Miscellaneous Provisions) Act 1934 it was not possible to sue the estate of a person who had negligently caused an accident. When compulsory third party insurance for road accidents was introduced in 1930 this rule became intolerable because if, as not infrequently happened, the tortfeasor was killed in the accident, his estate was not liable and so neither was his insurance company. So the rule was reversed by the 1934 Act.

At the same time the Act also reversed the companion rule that the estate of a dead person could not sue the tortfeasor responsible for the death. This, broadly, enabled the victim's estate to recover heads of damages which the victim could have recovered had he not died. These heads included, from 1935, damages for loss of expectation of life.[35] This provision of the Act had two probably unanticipated consequences. First, by allowing beneficiaries of the estate to recover, via the estate, damages for loss of expectation of life it created what was, in effect, an award for the intangible loss inflicted by the deceased's death. Secondly, it allowed beneficiaries who had not suffered any financial loss as a result of the death to recover damages in respect of the death. This happened most commonly where the deceased was a child and the beneficiaries were its parents. This consequence became particularly important when it was decided in 1980 that the estate could recover damages for loss of earnings which the deceased would have earned had he not been killed (before this damages could only be recovered for earnings lost up until the death). This decision has, however, been reversed by statute.[36] This is discussed further in Chapter 7.

These two unanticipated consequences of the 1934 Act ran counter to two basic principles underlying the Fatal Accidents Act, namely that the only losses resulting from death for which compensation could be given were financial losses; and that only persons who had actually suffered loss as a result of a death could be awarded compensation for the death. However, the right of the estate of a deceased person to recover damages for loss of the deceased's expectation of life became so entrenched that when the Law Commission reviewed the law of damages in 1973 it thought that people would object if damages for loss of expectation of life were abolished and no alternative compensation for the loss caused by bereavement were put in its place.[37] Hence damages for bereavement. There is a similar provision for damages for 'loss of society' in Scotland under the Damages (Scotland) Act 1976 but, unlike in England, there is no statutory limit to the award.

Naturally the death of a close relative in an accident must give rise to sympathy for the survivors, but these provisions are nevertheless highly objectionable. There are two main objections to all awards by way of *solatium*. The first is that they tend to be sought by vindictive survivors, either as a way of penalizing the party thought to be responsible (although it is of course the insurers who will pay), or as a form of distasteful gold-digging. The second main objection is that it seems so very arbitrary to select the death of a close relative as the criterion for paying what is still to many people a substantial sum of money. It must be remembered that the relatives of a person who is very severely injured in an accident may well suffer much greater mental suffering than the relatives of someone who is killed. For one thing, the suffering is continuous and may be prolonged in such cases for many years. The anguish of parents whose young child was seriously injured in an accident was well expressed by Lord Denning in *Taylor* v. *Bristol Omnibus Co.*:[38]

Before this accident they [the parents] could have looked forward to a future of happiness, bringing up their baby son with the joy it brings, seeing him through his schooldays, marrying and having children of his own, and then his caring for them in their old age. Now, in consequence of this accident, they are deprived of it all. They have nursed him day and night. They have watched over him. They have carried him everywhere. They have taught him to do little things for himself. They have devoted their lives to him and will continue to do so. Yet they are not entitled to recover any damages for all their grief and suffering. Not a penny. Nor would they ask it.

It does not seem right that, when nothing is awarded in such a case, damages should nevertheless be awarded for the death of a child.

In addition, the fact that the sum to be awarded is fixed by statute means that the same sum would be awarded in a very wide variety of situations, e.g. to a mother for the death of a newly born child; to parents of an older child irrespective of whether he was a comfort or a trial to his parents; and to a spouse irrespective of the age, state of health, or even relationship to the other spouse. The same sum would, indeed, be payable to a wife whose husband has deserted and refused to maintain her, as to a devoted and faithful husband still living with her – though in this latter case there would of course be a substantial difference in the sums awarded for financial loss under the Fatal Accidents Acts. Apart from all these criticisms, there is a further fundamental point that damages by way of *solatium* ought to be a very low priority in any legal system which still denies adequate compensation for loss of income to so many of those injured in accidents or crippled by disabling illness.

Financial loss

The law deals in a rather complex way with financial losses suffered by one person as a result of the death of or injury to another caused by a wrongful act or omission. First, under the Fatal Accidents Act 1976 a dependant, such as a wife or child of a breadwinner, has a statutory right of action for the financial loss incurred as a result of the breadwinner's death. This statutory cause of action dates back to

1846, by which time the common law's total refusal to recognize any right of action in a dependant of a breadwinner was producing intolerable hardship as a result of the increasing frequency of railway and industrial accidents. But its age means that it predates the present conceptual structure of the law of negligence. It is unnecessary to show that the dependant was personally owed a duty of care, or that his existence was known to or foreseeable by the negligent party; he (or more usually she) is simply given a right of action as a result of a breach of duty owed to the deceased himself.

We have already seen how the law also allows the estate of a deceased person to recover damages which will go to the beneficiaries of that estate. In the great majority of cases the beneficiaries will be the same persons as the dependants, that is normally the spouse and children of the deceased. In practice, this means that the surviving dependants can both inherit the deceased's property under his will and any sums paid as damages to the estate, and also recover damages for loss of support under the Fatal Accidents Act. In most cases the damages awarded to the estate will be small – mainly the deceased's out of pocket expenses and lost earnings between the accident and his death. The justification for allowing the dependants both to inherit and recover damages for loss of support is that they would have benefited from the inheritance sooner of later even if the deceased had not been tortiously killed.

The Fatal Accidents Act is concerned, of course, with cases in which the injured person dies as a result of the tort. But the law, also deals to some extent with cases where a family suffers loss consequential upon mere injury to one of its members. For example, if a spouse who stays at home and looks after house and family is injured and disabled from doing housework then usually either the earning spouse will employ someone to do the work or the able-bodied members of the family will do it themselves. The law's response to this used to be to allow a husband whose wife was injured to recover damages for loss of her domestic services. It did not, however, give the wife a right to such damages because the theory underlying the action was that the husband had a sort of right of property in his wife's services. This action – the *actio per quod consortium amisit* – has now been abolished,[39] and instead the injured housekeeper is entitled to recover damages for loss of the ability to keep house.[40] This is more in line with modern views of marriage. It does not have to be shown that anything will actually be spent on hiring a housekeeper, probably because it is thought that damages ought to be awarded even if the family decides to cope with the situation by doing more around the house themselves.

An analogous situation arises where one member of a family renders gratuitous services to another member who has been tortiously injured. The injured person would normally be entitled to recover damages to cover the cost of engaging professional assistance – e.g. a nurse. But if the services have been rendered gratuitously, say by the injured person's wife or mother, the injured person will have suffered no financial loss (although the person rendering the services may have). Nevertheless, the damages recovered by the victim will cover the reasonable value of the gratuitous services.

There is not space in this book to deal fully with the whole problem of the family within the present tort system.[41] It is sufficient to observe that it is, in most cases, unreal to treat the family as a group of separate individuals, since injury to one of them may cause financial loss to another. Clearly the problems arising in these cases are entirely different from those which arise where (say) damage to one company's factory produces financial loss to another which is a customer of the first.

Finally, it is worth noting (although it is not strictly relevant in this context) that an employer used to be able to claim damages for the loss of the services of certain 'servants' if the servant had been tortiously injured and disabled from work. This action (the *actio per quod servitium amisit*) has now been abolished.[42] It was, at all events, very rarely used. Most people regard a right of action for damages as a very inferior way of protecting themselves against financial loss. If employers do wish to secure themselves against the loss caused by making sick payments to a workman injured by negligence (and many do not bother) there are simpler ways of doing so, as we shall see later.[43]

6 OMISSIONS

So far we have suggested that the conventional conceptual picture of the law of negligence is misleading, in that it fails to recognize that with very few exceptions there is, today, liability for negligently caused physical damage or injury where the negligence takes the form of affirmative conduct. We now turn to some of the difficulties raised by the concept of affirmative conduct, and to the way in which liability for nonfeasance has been gradually extended by the law. It must be admitted at the outset that there are many situations in which it is impossible to draw any logical line between affirmative and negative conduct, or between misfeasance and nonfeasance. A solicitor instructed to make a will allows it to be wrongly witnessed so that it is invalid: this may be seen as misfeasance in making the will or as failure to ensure that it was properly witnessed. A person digs a hole on his land and a visitor falls into it: this may be seen as the affirmative conduct in digging the hole or as mere nonfeasance in failing to fence the hole or give a warning. A person drives across a line of traffic without signalling: this is either positive bad driving or a mere failure to signal. More generally, whether failure to act is viewed as nonfeasance or misfeasance depends largely on whether we view the failure in isolation or as part of a larger activity. Nevertheless, despite the difficulty of the distinction, the law recognizes and acts on it. It is, after all, at the root of the distinction between tort and contract. A person is not generally bound to *act* unless he has agreed to do so, and is paid for doing so; but he is in general bound to *abstain* from causing damage by his negligence, whether or not he has agreed to do so, or is paid for doing so.

Problems of nonfeasance are peculiarly suited to discussion in terms of the duty concept, because in relation to nonfeasance not only can we ask was the defendant under a duty to take care? but also: was the defendant under a duty to do anything at all? It was suggested earlier that in strict logic the duty concept adds nothing to the law of negligence; and this is just as true of liability for nonfeasance as for misfeasance. But it is much more natural to think in terms of duty in dealing with cases of nonfeasance. Furthermore, in this context the concept of duty may act as a cloak for development of the law. We may easily start by using the term 'duty' in the sense of a moral or social duty, and then convert this into a legal duty; and this process is probably easier with nonfeasance than with misfeasance. For instance, we may say that a person is under a duty (sc. moral or social duty) to control his young children; we may then go on to say that he therefore owes his neighbour a duty (sc. legal duty) to take care that his children cause no damage to the neighbour's property.

It must be stressed at the outset that there is no clear answer to many problems which arise in this field. Indeed, many of the propositions put forward below can only be supported from American case law, and it is not certain how an English court would react to them. The main reason for this is the failure to identify and appreciate the significance of the problem of nonfeasance in the law of negligence. This means that there is virtually no discussion in the case law of the principles or policies on which liability for nonfeasance turns; there is indeed, scarcely any recognition that the problem exists at all.

Policy

What lies behind the policy of distinguishing between nonfeasance and misfeasance? Why does the law – which in some ways appears to be based on the moral principle of liability for fault – almost completely abandon all connection with morality at this point? How can we regard a momentary aberration while driving a motor vehicle as something more reprehensible than walking by while a child is drowning in a few feet of water? This is the stock example of a clear case of immunity from liability for negligence (and indeed in the criminal law), but circumstances very close to this have happened in a real life. In *Osterlind* v. *Hill*,[44] the defendant rented a canoe to an intoxicated man who was obviously unfit to manage it safely. The man paddled out into the lake, then overturned, and clung to the canoe for half an hour calling for help. The defendant heard the cries, perceived the man's plight but did nothing whatever to assist him; and the man drowned. The defendant was held not liable by a Massachusetts court. Perhaps an English court would have avoided this result by 'praying in aid' the blessed elasticity of the contractual 'implied term'. It could, perhaps, have been successfully argued that it was an 'implied term' of the contract for the renting of the canoe that the defendant would summon aid if he saw the hirer in distress. Some support for such an approach is to be found in the decision of the Supreme Court of Canada in *Arnold* v. *Teno*,[45] where an ice-cream vendor was held liable to a child who dashed into the road after buying an ice cream on the ground that the vendor should have warned the child of an approaching vehicle. And we shall see below that the law of contract may often be called in to supplement the deficiencies in the law of torts in this field. But none of this helps in cases where there is nothing but tort to fall back on; nor does it begin to explain what policy considerations underlie the distinction between nonfeasance and misfeasance.

In looking for rational policy considerations it is necessary first to remember that we are discussing cases of physical damage and injury. We are not, therefore, challenging the whole distinction between contract and tort or suggesting that a man should be held liable for a nonfeasance which produces only financial loss where he has not undertaken to do the thing in question. The question to be answered is why a man should be immune from liability for nonfeasance causing physical damage or injury.

The first possible consideration is that the imposition of affirmative duties is often more burdensome than the imposition of negative duties. In its main spheres of practical operation the law of negligence tends to prescribe not what we are to do, but only how we are to do it. Thus I am generally quite free to drive my car when and where I want to on the roads; and it is not particularly burdensome to be required to drive it carefully. This does not prevent me going where I want to and when I want to, though it may force me to go a little more slowly than I might have wanted to. There is no doubt that the law imposes negative obligations on us much more readily than affirmative ones. 'Thou shalt not' is the typical form of the law's requirements, and not, 'thou shalt'. And even when the law does impose affirmative obligations they are frequently of a kind which do not involve much expenditure of time and effort.

Requiring someone to render positive assistance to persons in danger may be burdensome not only in that it takes time and effort. Rendering assistance may cost money and involve risks. In 1967 an (unsuccessful) operation launched by a 'rescue team' to rescue six young potholers trapped by floodwater cost the team £500 and threatened them with bankruptcy. They were obliged to launch a public appeal to pay for the cost of the rescue attempt.[46] If a man may be required to drive someone to hospital merely because he finds him lying injured in the road, who is to pay for the cost of doing so – not merely the few pence for petrol and depreciation, but perhaps also wages forgone? And suppose there is an element of risk in rendering assistance, and the risk eventuates: who is going to pay compensation for this? Suppose a man sees a child struggling in a river and he is not a swimmer himself; an attempt to rescue the child may cost him his own life. Who is then going to maintain the rescuer's own wife and children? English law does not generally recognize any right to reward for rescue. If some third party (or the rescued person himself) was, by his negligence, responsible for creating the dangerous situation, then the rescuer may have an action against the third party or the rescued person for his injuries. It should be noted, however, that an action against the rescued person would rarely be covered by insurance, which probably explains the rarity of such actions.

Another reason why it may be felt desirable to distinguish between misfeasance and nonfeasance is that in the case of misfeasance the defendant normally identifies himself, in the sense that some affirmative conduct of his has resulted in damage to the plaintiff. On the other hand, the defendant accused of nonfeasance is likely to feel, 'Why pick on me? I didn't do anything.' This sort of defence may take one of two forms. First, the defendant may be asserting that he is merely one of hundreds, and that it is unfair to pick on him while leaving all the others alone. If, for instance, a driver knocks down and injures a pedestrian by his negligence, it is easy enough to fasten liability on the driver for misfeasance. But if the unfortunate pedestrian is left bleeding in the road and a dozen or a hundred other motorists drive by without stopping to render assistance, there would be no justification for imposing liability for nonfeasance on any one rather than another. In this type of situation the defendant is unlikely to deny that he *ought* to have stopped to render assistance: his complaint is that so ought many others.

But the defence may take a second form which raises rather different issues. The defendant may be asserting that it was not up to *him* to do something, that the burden of taking the desired precautions was really someone else's, perhaps the plaintiff's, perhaps a third party's, but in any case not his. For instance, suppose that a window cleaner sent by his employer to clean the windows at a block of offices is injured in a fall resulting from defective belt-hooks, or the like. If he sues his employer, his complaint against him will be one of nonfeasance since it may be assumed the employer did not install the defective belt-hooks; that is, he will be complaining that the employer ought to have checked the belt-hooks, or ought to have supplied safer means of cleaning windows which did not depend on possibly unsafe belt-hooks. In this situation the employer's defence will probably be: 'It was not *my* responsibility to check the belt-hooks. The occupiers of the offices should have seen that the belt-hooks were safe; it was their responsibility, not mine.' In some cases the employer might argue that it was the plaintiff's own responsibility to take the necessary precautions. For instance, suppose the plaintiff's belongings are stolen at his place of work.[47] Whose business is it to take precautions against this possibility: the plaintiff's or his employer's?

A third possible ground for distinguishing between nonfeasance and misfeasance is based on notions of causation. In some cases at least a person guilty of nonfeasance does not *cause* damage; he simply fails to act to prevent damage being caused by someone or something else. A person who fails to render assistance to a person put in peril by the negligence of the person in peril or of some third party has not in any real sense caused damage to the person in peril.

But it must be said that these arguments really amount to very little. The first point – the possible burdensomeness of affirmative obligations – can easily be met. For one thing, the immunity from liability for nonfeasance does not apply only where it would be burdensome to require affirmative conduct. It applies even, for instance, where all that a person has to do is shout a warning, or make a telephone call. A man sees his neighbour's house on fire: how burdensome would it be to require him to telephone for the fire brigade? A pedestrian can watch a blind man walk straight into a hole in the road without liability in tort, or any other branch of the law. What burden would it be to require him to shout a warning? Even if an affirmative duty would in some cases involve a real burden, there seems no reason why the law should be incapable of balancing the burdensomeness of the duty sought to be imposed against the end sought to be achieved. If the burden seems disproportionate to the end, then no duty need be imposed. Such an exercise would simply involve applying to cases of nonfeasance the negligence formula used when determining liability for misfeasance. No doubt it would be advisable to move cautiously here so that the standard of what it is reasonable to expect by way of positive action is not pitched too high.

The second argument, that there is difficulty in identifying the person liable for nonfeasance, and that to impose liability would often be to fasten onto the nearest convenient defendant, can be rebutted by observing that the law does this even where misfeasance is in issue. For example, bad road design contributes to many motor vehicle accidents but road authorities are rarely sued because the negligent driver is a much more convenient target. And the fact that he may be less or no more culpable than the road designer is not of much importance given that the driver will always be insured and so will not himself pay the damages. So the question is not whether there are others more or equally culpable but whether this defendant was himself at fault.

As for the third (causal) argument, it does often seem easier to hold someone responsible for an occurrence which he has 'caused' by his affirmative conduct, and we may have doubts about treating nonfeasance as a cause at all. We examine later some of the intricacies of the notion of 'cause' but it is enough here to say that many people feel instinctively, if irrationally, that one can only treat nonfeasance as a 'cause' if one first starts by assuming that there was a *duty* to act.[48] Take the following example:[49] suppose a passenger on a small pleasure boat falls overboard through his own carelessness into ice-cold waters and eventually drowns. We might well want to say that a fellow-passenger could not be held in any way responsible for the death, that he did not 'cause' the death by failing to jump in and attempt a rescue, because he was under no duty to take such action. But we might feel differently if the owner of the boat failed to attempt to manoeuvre it into a position where a lifeline could be thrown to the drowning man. The owner could more easily be said to be a cause of the death because under the circumstances he surely had a duty to take advantage of his control over the vessel to help the passenger.

There is, however, a basic objection to this causal argument. At first sight to say that the defendant's nonfeasance did not cause the plaintiff's loss seems to provide a sort of objective criterion for not imposing liability. But the way we view the causation issue depends, as we have seen, on whether we think that the defendant *ought* morally to have done something and whether we think that this moral duty ought to be translated into a legal duty. This is a matter of legal policy and does not depend on any objective distinction between misfeasance and nonfeasance. In other words, the language of causation in this context simply provides a way of expressing a judgment about the proper limits of liability for negligent failure to act.[50]

The truth appears to be that there is no really satisfactory way of, or reason for, distinguishing between misfeasance and nonfeasance. The extent of liability for failure to act is a legal policy issue and each of the three arguments we have examined can explain some cases in which it does not seem right to impose liability.

Undertakings

A person who contracts to do something incurs liability for not doing it; but there is also a somewhat hazy and undeveloped part of the law dealing with voluntary undertakings without contract. Even contractual undertakings are relevant to the problem of liability for nonfeasance in tort, because the person injured may not be the other contracting party.[51] For example: A contracts with B that he will clear the snow of B's doorstep during winter snowfalls. One day he fails to do so and C, a visitor to B's house, slips on the snow and is injured. Is A liable to C in tort for failing to take reasonable care? A has not created the danger, and although he was under a duty towards B to remove it, can C rely on that duty? In this kind of case there is much to be said for imposing liability, and a court would probably do so. Since the contractual obligation already exists, the natural reluctance to force people to do things, which imposing liability for nonfeasance usually involves, simply does not arise. Furthermore, in many cases of this kind the undertaking leads other people to rely on it and so create dangers which would not have arisen without it. For example, a man takes his car to a garage and asks them to repair the brakes. They omit to do so altogether, but the owner thinks they have done the repair. Here the car owner is induced by reliance on the garage to continue driving the car, thereby creating dangers to third parties on the road. By their undertaking and failure to carry it out, the garage has made a positive contribution to the danger.

Cases involving voluntary undertakings without contract raise more complex issues. Suppose a doctor sees a man injured in a car accident lying on the road. He could probably not be held liable for failing to stop and help. But suppose he does render assistance and fails to take some action required by reasonable care and skill (such as applying a tourniquet) which would have saved the victim's life; or that he treats him negligently with the result that he dies. Could the doctor be held liable for his negligence? It is unlikely, even in the first case, that the law would treat the doctor's negligence as nonfeasance, though we might want to say that the doctor's negligence did not *cause* the death but only failed to prevent it. But there is a policy argument against imposing liability in such cases: the imposition of liability might make people less willing to render gratuitous assistance if thereby they risk liability for negligence in so doing. In America it is well known that doctors will not render assistance to people injured in road accidents for this very reason, and in some States legislation has relieved them of liability to remove the discouragement to voluntary help. On the other hand there is no reason in principle why even a voluntary 'rescuer' should not be subject to legal liability if he acts negligently. This seems reasonable if the rescuer actually makes things worse by his intervention. The liability would not be based on a voluntary undertaking to exercise care or skill in rescue but simply on doing a job negligently and thus injuring another. But since the rescuer acts under pressure of emergency the courts would be unlikely to impose a very high standard of care.

The imposition of liability seems less justifiable where, as in the examples above, the rescuer does not make matters worse but only fails to make them better. However, it has been held that a local authority whose inspector, in exercise of statutory powers, inspects the foundations of a building but negligently fails to notice that they do not comply with building regulations can be held liable to a purchaser of the building who suffers loss when the building subsides and becomes dangerous.[52] Here the inspector's negligence did not cause any damage but only failed to prevent it occurring. But there is an important difference between this case and ours: in theory at least the local authority can in certain circumstances be liable in negligence for failure to inspect, and so liability for negligence in inspecting will not in this case have the same disincentive effect as in ours.[53] Nevertheless on balance, provided the required standard of care is not pitched too high, the arguments in favour of liability in our case would seem to outweigh those against.

What about cases which more clearly involve gratuitous undertakings? Suppose the doctor decides there is not much he can do and tells the victim he will call an ambulance but then fails to do so. This would seem a strong case for liability, especially if, in reliance on the undertaking, the victim had declined help from someone else. Or suppose an altruistic citizen who regularly frequents an isolated beach and is trained as a lifesaver offers his services to those using the beach as a voluntary lifesaver. This might justify imposition of liability on him if he makes no attempt to rescue someone who relied on his offer in using the beach.

Control of the conduct of others

One very common type of liability for nonfeasance is to be found in liability for failing to control the conduct of a person over whom the defendant has powers of control. For example, a person must control the behaviour of his children, and is liable for pure nonfeasance in failing to control them. If a child, for instance, is given a gun by a third party, and is known by the parent to have a gun, the parent becomes responsible for seeing that the child is old enough and sensible enough to be allowed to have the gun; for instructing the child in how to use if safely, and so on. If the parent does nothing at all, and if it is shown to be negligent to do nothing, he will be liable for injuries caused by his child.[54] Similarly, an employer is under a duty to control his staff and is liable for nonfeasance in failing to take reasonable care to control them. This application of the principle is not of great practical importance, because an employer is vicariously liable for the negligence of his employees whether he is himself negligent or not; but there are a few cases in which the employer may be liable for personal nonfeasance though he is not vicariously liable, e.g. because the servant was not acting in the course of his employment.[55]

A similar liability for nonfeasance rests on those in charge of a hotel, bar, restaurant, jail or school, to exercise some degree of control over the customers or inmates. A man who sees someone being criminally assaulted and beaten up in the streets may walk on without assisting, but a hotel proprietor who saw someone in danger of being attacked by a guest in his hotel might well be liable if he failed to take some reasonable steps to protect the victim. Those in charge of public transport vehicles or vessels would also have some duty to control passengers. The same might also apply to private vehicles; for example a car driver might be held liable to an injured cyclist if he sat and watched a passenger negligently opening the offside door of his car in the way of approaching traffic, at least if he were in a position to stop him.[56] So also it is now clear that the Home Office is liable for negligently failing to prevent the escape of a Borstal boy, though it is also clear that this liability only extends to damage done in the immediate vicinity and aftermath of the escape.[57]

Control over another is frequently a ground for imposing liability for nonfeasance in failing to prevent that other from causing damage; but such control is also often a ground for imposing liability for failure to protect the person under control. For example a hospital has been held liable to a known 'psychiatric and suicide risk' who seriously injured himself when he jumped out of a window.[58] Similarly, a person would be liable for neglecting to summon a doctor to treat his young child, or indeed any other occupant or guest in his house, who becomes helpless through disease or accident.

Furthermore, there seems little doubt that occupiers of business premises such as hotels, restaurants, shops and even offices, would be held liable if they failed to take reasonable steps to summon medical help in an emergency due to sudden illness to a visitor to the premises. Related to these instances are the duties of employers towards their employees to provide a safe work-place, safe tools and a safe system of work. These duties often require the employer to take positive steps to ensure that his employees are safe in their work, because he has control over what they do and where they do it.

Control over property

Another ground on which liability for nonfeasance may sometimes be imposed is that the defendant was in control of some property from which, or by means of which, the damage was done. An interesting and striking recent example of this kind of liability is to be found in the Privy Council decision of *Goldman* v. *Hargrave*,[59] an appeal from Australia. In this case a tree on the defendant's land was struck by lightning and caught fire. The defendant took some, but (it was found) negligent and ineffectual, steps to put the fire out and it spread to the plaintiff's property, causing damage there. Here, it will be observed, the complaint against the defendant was simply that he had failed to take reasonable steps to put out the fire. He had not started it, nor even created any conditions on his land which could be said to have contributed to the risk of the fire. The argument in favour of such liability is that the ownership of land should entail responsibilities as well as rights.

One important aspect of *Goldman* v. *Hargrave* is that the court attempted to 'subjectivize' the standard of care required. As we have already seen, the standard of care required by the law of negligence is generally an objective standard, which takes no account of the defendants's personal characteristics. But in this case the Privy Council evidently had doubts about applying so objective a standard to cases of nonfeasance. In particular, they thought that the 'reasonable' steps which an occupier of land must take to prevent his land being a source of danger to others, must take account of the wealth and capacities of the occupier: what is reasonable for the individual landowner may not be reasonable for the large company.

In relation to the capacity of the landowner, this approach may not in practice make a great deal of difference, because if the occupier is unable to do something himself he will usually be able to secure outside assistance. The principle that the wealth of the occupier may be taken into account in determining what is reasonable raises some wide issues. As we shall see later, the law does not generally take into account the defendant's capacity to pay in determining his legal liabilities, nor in determining the level of damages to be awarded where liability is clear. Why, then, should it sometimes be taken into account in determining the standard of care required of a defendant? In the great majority of cases, the cost facing the occupier of land is not really the cost of taking precautions against his land being a danger to his neighbours, but the cost of insuring against this; and it is perfectly reasonable to regard this insurance cost as an essential part of the cost of using land, so that if the occupier cannot afford it he should not be occupying the land at all, or at least, using it for the purpose in question. For instance, it may be doubted whether a poor cricket club which fails to erect a fence around its ground to protect passers-by in the streets from being hit by stray cricket balls, should be any better off than a wealthy cricket club. The real effect of imposing liability in such a case would not be to force clubs to build fences, but to force them to buy insurance; and a club which could not afford the insurance premium has no business to be playing at all – any more than a club which could not afford to pay rates.

In the particular circumstances of *Goldman* v. *Hargrave* itself – liability for fire – the Privy Council may have been wise in restricting the extent of liability. As will be seen below, it is very doubtful whether any good purpose is served by extending liability in tort for damage caused by fire, at all events in this country; the position in Australia may be affected by special considerations, such as the great danger of bush fires and the importance of providing every inducement to landowners to take precautions against fire. But the means chosen to restrict liability – that is by subjectivizing the standard of care – are not desirable. In the wider context of liability for personal injury arising from the use of land it would be even more unsatisfactory to use a subjective test of standard of care. Admittedly, the 'subjective' standard of care for nonfeasance may make it more likely that liability for nonfeasance will be expanded in the future. But not only is the distinction thus drawn between misfeasance and nonfeasance of doubtful value; also, to consider the wealth of the defendant without regard to whether he is or ought to be insured is difficult to justify.

It was at one time held that an occupier of land was likewise not liable for a nuisance if the nuisance was the result of natural occurrences and not due to any act of the occupier himself. This is another way of saying that the occupier may not be liable for pure nonfeasance. Since *Goldman* v. *Hargrave*, however, the older authorities have been abandoned. In *Leakey* v. *National Trust*[60] it was held that the Trust was liable for a fall of earth from a large mound which abutted onto the plaintiff's house, even though the fall was entirely due to natural causes. In this kind of situation the moral issue posed by liability for nonfeasance is particularly difficult. The Trust had offered the plaintiff permission to enter their land to abate the danger when it had first become apparent; so it could not be argued that liability had to be imposed on the occupier because he was the only person able to prevent the damage. In the last analysis, it seems that liability is imposed in such a case because it is felt that the occupation of land is a benefit and that the occupier should accept the corresponding burdens.

The other main context in which control over land provides a justification for imposing liability for nonfeasance is that of occupiers of land to visitors to the land. The law in many instances requires occupiers to take positive steps to remove or warn of dangers on their land even if not created by the occupier.

Other cases

In the cases where liability for nonfeasance is or might be imposed on the basis of an undertaking or the fact that the defendant has voluntarily rendered assistance or is in control of a situation, any initial reluctance to impose liability is overcome because there is a good reason why the defendant ought to have taken positive action. Another case of some interest is that in which the defendant has – without fault – caused an accident in which the plaintiff is injured. So far the defendant is plainly exonerated from liability by his lack of fault. But suppose now that he fails to take reasonable steps, such as summoning aid. Can he be rendered liable for additional injury suffered by the plaintiff? A motorist drives his car without negligence onto the plaintiff's foot; negligently he fails to drive it off again with sufficient dispatch. Is he liable for the injuries caused by the delay?[61] There is no reason why we should hesitate to impose liability here. The burden is trivial in comparison with the danger sought to be avoided; and it is clear that the *defendant* ought to have done something.[62] A similar case is *Walton* v. *British Leyland*,[63] decided in 1978 but apparently unreported. The plaintiff was injured in a road accident when a rear wheel flew off an Austin Allegro made by the defendants. It seems, from the brief report, that the plaintiff did not allege that the car was negligently designed in the first place, but she complained that the defendants failed to recall the cars when they had mounting evidence of similar failures in many other cases. There is nothing in the report to indicate whether it was appreciated that a novel point of law was involved, in that this was an allegation of negligence based on nonfeasance, but in any event, the defendants were held liable.

4
Causation and remoteness of damage

The third requirement of a negligence action is commonly expressed by saying that the plaintiff must have suffered damage as a result of the defendant's negligence. This deceptively simple statement raises many complex questions, which can best be divided into three main heads. First, there is the question whether indeed the plaintiff's damage *was* 'the result' of the defendant's negligence; whether, in other words the defendant *in fact caused the damage*. This is referred to by American lawyers as the problem of 'Cause in Fact', and we propose to follow this usage. Secondly, there are a number of further attempts to impose restrictions on liability for negligence. In the last chapter we saw how the 'duty of care' concept has been used as a 'control device' to limit liability where, for a variety of policy reasons, the courts have felt this to be desirable. In this chapter yet other restrictions on liability will be examined. These restrictions are expressed by the courts in an extraordinary variety of ways: sometimes by saying that the damage is not foreseeable; sometimes by saying it is too 'remote'; sometimes by saying it is damage of a kind not recognized by the law; sometimes by saying that the defendant's negligence was not the 'real' or 'proximate' cause of the damage. English lawyers generally discuss these questions under the heading 'Remoteness of Damage', though many are also discussed under the 'duty of care' concept. American lawyers generally talk of 'proximate cause', though they are now nearly unanimous in thinking that this has nothing to do with 'cause in fact'. The third type of problem which must be considered is that of assessing the damages, a problem which has thrust itself to the forefront of the law of negligence in recent years, and which now probably consumes more appellate judicial time than questions of legal liability; this problem is left for Chapter 7.

1 CAUSE IN FACT

Generally speaking nobody is liable in the tort of negligence unless his conduct in fact caused, or at least contributed to, the plaintiff's damage. If a dozen cars speed round a bend without due regard for the safety of a pedestrian on the road, each one of the drivers will owe a duty of care to the plaintiff and may be guilty of negligence. But liability will only be imposed on a driver whose conduct was a cause of the plaintiff's injuries. This does not necessarily mean that liability can only be imposed on the driver whose car actually runs into the pedestrian. Other drivers may also contribute to the accident. But what it does mean is that a person may owe a duty of care, and may be negligent towards a plaintiff who is in fact injured, but may not be liable because the plaintiff's injuries were in no way caused by him.

In the great majority of cases, this requirement of the tort of negligence gives rise to no practical difficulties. Indeed, cause in fact is usually much more obvious than negligence. In practice, a plaintiff who is looking for a defendant to sue will normally find him pointed out by 'cause in fact' rather than negligence. A man who is run over in the road will normally start by 'blaming' the driver of the car which injured him: the driver was obviously a cause of the accident. Whether he was also at fault is a different and often more difficult question. Sometimes, however, accidents occur and the cause is not apparent at once. An explosion takes place and wrecks a house, killing the occupants. What was the cause of the explosion? In most cases this is a purely factual inquiry. Sometimes, though perhaps more rarely, we may even know that there has been negligence, but be uncertain at first whether the damage was contributed to by the person guilty of negligence. A workman, for example, is found dead near some machinery which has been negligently maintained in a dangerous manner by his employer. The employer is guilty of negligence; but has he caused or contributed to the workman's death?[1] Until we have tried to reconstruct the events which led to his death, and can form some conclusions as to the way in which this probably occurred, we cannot say. In some cases a prolonged scientific investigation may be required before it is possible to say what caused the damage. Such an investigation would obviously be a formidable burden for a prospective plaintiff to have to arrange, let alone finance, but fortunately such a burden would rarely have to be borne by a plaintiff in practice. Investigations of this sort would most commonly be needed in connection with serious disasters such as railway or aircraft accidents, in which case public inquiries are invariably held under statutory powers to investigate the causes of the accident. In cases of industrial accidents there is the possibility of assistance from the factory inspectorate, though this would not always be available. Sometimes, too, the plaintiff may be helped by a legal doctrine (known by a Latin tag *res ipsa loquitur*) which says that where an accident results from a situation or thing under the exclusive control of the defendant or persons for whom he is responsible; and where, further, the accident is such that, in the ordinary course of events it would not occur without negligence on the part of the defendant, it is for the defendant to explain how it happened and to show that he was not negligent.

It has recently been pointed out[2] that problems of factual causation are much more difficult in many cases involving disabilities, diseases or illnesses as opposed to accidents causing traumatic injuries. Sometimes these problems arise from the fact that medical knowledge about the causation of many conditions is quite limited; in other cases it may be possible to say that conduct of the allegedly negligent kind is a cause of a particular condition in a certain percentage of cases but it may not be possible to say whether it caused the condition in *this* case. The first source of difficulty becomes less acute as medical science advances. For example, much more is known today about the causes of heart disease or cancer than was known thirty years ago. But the second source of difficulty is impossible to eradicate in many cases because many conditions can be caused by more than one factor.

These difficulties of proof are to some extent ameliorated by the fact that the law only requires the plaintiff to prove that his injury or damage was 'more probably than not' caused by the defendant's negligence. In *McGhee* v. *National Coal Board*[3] the House of Lords went further and held that a plaintiff could recover damages in respect of a skin condition even though the defendant's negligence only 'increased the risk' (albeit substantially) that the plaintiff would contract the condition. A major problem with this approach is that a defendant responsible for a disease-causing process (e.g. one involving the use of some carcinogen) or product may have to pay damages to a large number of people, many of whom contracted their disease from some other source than the defendant's careless conduct.

When the actual sequence of events has been ascertained, or is sufficiently known, the question of cause in fact is most commonly and simply answered by the 'but for' test. Would the damage have occurred 'but for' the defendant's conduct? Here again, in most cases the question is simply enough answered. *Of course*, the road accident in which A's car collided with the pedestrian would not have occurred but for the motorist's presence on the road; *of course*, the plaintiff hit on the head by the cricket ball would not have suffered these injuries but for the use of the ground as a cricket club; *of course*, this industrial accident would not have happened but for the fact that this piece of dangerous machinery was unfenced. But there are cases in which the 'but for' test does lead to difficulties. We may note two main types of case in which these difficulties arise.

Omissions

Suppose that an employer negligently omits to provide safety belts for his workmen who are working at such dangerous heights that belts should be worn. A workman falls and is killed; if he had been wearing a safety belt he would not have fallen. Is the employer's omission to supply the safety belt a 'cause in fact' of the workman's death? In order to decide this question we must ask whether 'but for' the omission, the workman would have died; but we cannot answer that question unless we know whether the workman would in fact have worn the belt if it had been provided. Because of the hypothetical nature of this latter question (it is not about what happened but about what *might have* happened), it may in many cases be extremely difficult to answer with confidence. As a result, the outcome of a case which raises such a question may in the end depend on whether the court requires the plaintiff to prove that he would have taken the precaution or the defendant to prove that he would not have. In *McWilliams* v. *Sir William Arrol & Co.*[4] the House of Lords held that the normal rule – that the plaintiff must prove his case – applied in such a case.

In policy terms this approach is arguably unsatisfactory because it gives employers inadequate incentives to perform their duty to provide safety precautions and to see that they are used. This seems to have been appreciated in *Bux* v. *Slough Metals Ltd*[5] where defendants were held liable for the plaintiff's failure to wear safety goggles, on the ground that he probably would have worn them if there had been adequate instruction and supervision. More recently, there are signs that the House of Lords has moved yet further away from *McWilliams* v. *Arrol*. In *McGhee* v. *National Coal Board* (mentioned earlier) it seems to have been held that if the defendant has exposed the plaintiff to an increased risk of injury as a result of his negligence, and if the plaintiff has in fact suffered an injury which may have been a result of that risk, the burden of proof will then pass to the defendant to show that it was not his negligence which caused the injuries. This approach might well have led to a different result in *McWilliams* v. *Arrol*; and the *McGhee* case has for that reason been hailed as a major advance in the law of factual causation.[6] This it may yet prove to be, but it is not clear that the House itself was conscious of making any such advance. Even if it is not accepted that tort liability can make a significant contribution to increased safety[7] it is clear from the above discussion that issues of but-for causation in this type of case have important policy ramifications.

The issue of where the burden of proof lies is also important where it is not apparent which of two parties has caused the plaintiff's injuries. For instance, in *Cook* v. *Lewis*[8] the plaintiff was injured by a stray shot from the gun of someone who was out hunting. It was proved that the shot must have been from the gun of either A or B, both of whom had fired more or less simultaneously in the direction of the plaintiff, and both of whom had (as the judge found) negligently failed to take due precaution. It was held in the Canadian Supreme Court that both A and B were liable, on the ground that the burden of proof lay on them to disprove that their negligence had caused the plaintiff's injuries. Since both of them had been negligent, and one of them was certainly the cause of the plaintiff's injuries, this result may seem better than the only alternative possible result, namely to acquit both A and B of responsibility altogether. It seems possible that an English Court might arrive at a similar decision on the basis of the *McGhee* case, but it is uncertain how far this principle can be taken. Suppose several drug manufacturers are sued by a number of plaintiffs who claim to have suffered adverse long-term side effects of taking a drug produced by each of the manufacturers; and suppose that so many years have elapsed since the drugs were taken that it is not possible to say which manufacturer produced the particular drugs taken by each plaintiff. Once again the just approach might appear to be to place the burden of disproving responsibility on the defendants – this would result in their all being held liable. But the problem here is complicated by the number of defendants: if the plaintiffs obtain judgment against all but enforce the judgment against only one, will that one be entitled to contribution from the others and if so, on what basis? The Californian Supreme Court has recently held that liability ought to be imposed on each manufacturer in proportion to the share of the market for the drug enjoyed by that producer; but this decision has generated considerable controversy. The complexity of the issues in such cases may suggest that cases of this kind reach the limits of the practical utility of tort law as a system of compensating victims of personal injury.

Multiple causal factors

A second type of case in which the 'but for' test raises difficulty concerns multiple causal factors. The standard example is that of two fires, independently started by A and B respectively, which unite and spread to C's house which is destroyed.[9] If we ask whether A or B caused the damage in fact, the 'but for' test would seem to acquit both A and B of liability. The damage would have occurred even without A's conduct and also without B's conduct, but it is generally conceded to be unfair to let both parties escape liability. A similar conundrum is raised by consecutive causal factors, either of which would be sufficient on its own to bring about the result in question. A runs over X, wounding him in the leg; later B shoots at X, inflicting a wound which necessitates immediate amputation of the leg, and would have done so even if there had been no earlier wound.[10] Here again we cannot say that 'but for' A's negligence, or B's shot, X would have had an uninjured leg. But again it would be unfair to acquit both A and B of having caused the injury.

A slightly different type of case occurs where one of the causal factors is hypothetical. Suppose, for instance, that the plaintiff is killed in a car accident while being driven to an airport to catch a plane. Now if it had not been for the defendant's conduct, the plaintiff would not have been killed in the car accident: but suppose that the plane the plaintiff intended to catch, subsequently crashes with the loss of all on board. Are we to say that the plaintiff would still have been killed, 'but for' the defendant's conduct? In a famous American case,[11] a boy fell from a bridge to what was certain death or grave injury below, but in his fall he came into contact with some high tension wires negligently maintained by the defendants and was electrocuted. Was the defendant's conduct a 'cause in fact' of the boy's death?

In the first type of case the outcome often depends on whether or not the causal factors operated more or less contemporaneously: if so, both will be held responsible; if not, the first in time will be held liable.[12] Similarly, in the second case where there is any real interval of time between the occurrence of the damage, as things actually turned out, and its probable occurrence as things might have turned out, the courts are apt to treat causal connection as made out. In *Burmah Oil Co.* v. *Lord Advocate*,[13] for instance, where the British armed forces had destroyed oil installations in Burmah to prevent their falling into Japanese hands, it was not questioned that the acts of the armed forces were the 'cause' of the plaintiff's losses.

But an alternative way of dealing with these cases is to by-pass the causal question and treat them as raising a question about the assessment of damages. Thus, in the American case it was held that the defendants did cause the boy's death, but that the damages awarded must be calculated on the footing that the boy probably had only a few seconds to live – or at best would be gravely injured. Similarly, in the *Burmah Oil* case, it is probable that any compensation awarded would have taken account of the fact that the installations were about to fall into the hands of an invading enemy army when they were destroyed.[14] In assessing damages for future economic loss the courts regularly speculate about the likely occurrence of events which would increase or reduce that loss and award damages proportional to the likelihood.

This assessment-of-damages approach seems an obvious and commonsense solution. But what is not so obvious is why, in most cases, we rely on the probabilities (on the balance of probabilities, did the defendant's act cause the plaintiff's loss?) as determining liability and not merely as affecting the assessment of damages. Why, for instance, in *McWilliams* v. *Arrol* should the plaintiff not receive damages calculated according to the chance that he might not have used the safety belt? And, conversely, why in the *McGhee* case should the plaintiff be awarded damages in full rather than have them discounted to reflect the probability that it was not the defendant's negligence which caused the plaintiff's injuries? Or why, when a hospital wrongfully refuses treatment to an emergency patient, is the fact that he would probably have died in any event, treated as a ground for rejecting liability altogether and not merely for reducing damages?[15]

In cases of the first type discussed above a similar result is reached by applying the so-called 'vicissitudes' principle, which says that where events relevant to the assessment of damages occur before the trial the court will take those into account. For example, suppose a worker sustains a back injury at work through the negligence of his employer and later contracts a condition which would in any event have incapacitated him at least as badly as the injury. In such a case the employer would not be required to pay damages for the period after the onset of the condition.[16] Again, in the case of the man run over and then shot, the fact that he was shot and that he could have sought compensation under the Criminal Injuries Compensation Scheme in respect of the shooting would be relevant in assessing the damages, if any, payable by the first tortfeasor.

Why, on the whole, does the law require proof on the balance of probabilities that the defendant's conduct caused loss to the plaintiff before it will award damages which reflect the chance that if he had not been injured he would have suffered loss anyway? The answer may be that the courts wish to discourage litigation in cases where the defendant's contribution to the plaintiff's loss is a matter for great speculation. This rationale will not, however, explain *McGhee's* case, which is accounted for by the special difficulties in proving the cause of dermatitis due to lack of scientific knowledge about the aetiology of the condition. If that case came to be seen as laying down a general principle that liability could be imposed even if the chance that the defendant's negligence caused the plaintiff's injury was less than even, more thought would have to be given as to how a flood of speculative actions might be avoided.

2   LEGAL LIMITS ON THE LIABILITY
    OF CAUSES IN FACT

Even where it is clear that the defendant's conduct was a 'cause in fact' of the plaintiff's damage, and also that the defendant was negligent, the defendant may be held not liable for damage which has occurred in an unexpected or unusual or unforeseeable way. This limitation on liability covers two somewhat different situations. First, it prevents a person being held liable for the consequences of his negligence where these are 'too remote' in time and space from his conduct, and in particular, where some other event intervenes between the defendant's conduct and the occurrence of the injury or damage; for example, where the defendant injures the plaintiff in a road accident and the plaintiff is injured again in a further accident while being taken to hospital. Once a person has been injured by the negligence of another, he may in time to come suffer many further injuries or accidents which might not have occurred at all 'but for' the original negligence, but it is generally felt that it would be absurd to hold the defendant liable for all such consequences. Secondly, this limitation on liability saves a person from liability even for damage which follows his negligent conduct closely in time and space, but where the damage occurs in an unusual or freakish way; for example where a plank dropped into a ship's hold starts a conflagration which destroys the whole ship.

Although the actual policy of denying liability in cases of this kind is clearly discernible, the technical or 'conceptual' shape of this part of the law is a morass. At least three reasons are given for denying liability in cases of this kind. These are, first, that the defendant or the defendant's negligence was not the 'cause' of the damage; secondly, that the damage was not within the risk required to be guarded against; and thirdly, that the damage was not foreseeable.

(a) Legal causation

The but-for test is very indiscriminate in that it will identify as causes many factors which are of little interest because they are merely necessary conditions of the plaintiff's loss. Indeed, the cause-in-fact issue is sometimes referred to as 'Adam and Eve' causation because the preconditions of any event can be traced back almost indefinitely. But most of these necessary causal factors are of no interest for practical purposes. In legal terms this is often put by saying that the court is looking for *the* cause of the damage, or the 'real' or 'effective' cause, or the 'proximate' cause, or the *causa causans*, and not just a *causa sine qua non*. In other words, the court must select one or more out of all the factors 'but for' which the damage would not have occurred. All of these factors are causes in fact, but this approach involves selecting one or more of them as a 'cause in law'. Because the issue of causation is relevant to deciding whether the defendant will be liable at all, the legal causation approach is a way of relieving a party of responsibility for all and any of the consequences flowing from his negligence. By contrast, the third approach (was the damage foreseeable?) and in some cases the second approach (was the damage within the risk?) enable a court to impose on a party liability for some but not other consequences of his negligence.

What is actually meant by saying that A's conduct was *the cause* of this or that event? The first thing to note is that this type of causal inquiry may be made for at least two different reasons: the inquirer may be seeking an *explanation* of what happened and of how it happened; or he may be asking a question about who ought to be held responsible for what happened. Even when making an explanatory inquiry we will be selective in picking a 'cause'.[17] The purpose of the inquiry will influence the choice of 'causes in fact' to explain the event in question. Take a road accident, for example. The highway authority which is responsible for seeing that road surfaces are not excessively skid-prone, may be more interested in one factor; the motor manufacturer who wants to make cars which do not overturn too easily, will be more interested in another factor; the driver who wants to learn how to drive without overturning his car, in another, and so on. Sometimes the purpose of the inquiry may be merely to satisfy curiosity, as for instance, when someone sees a drum fall out of a warehouse window and asks: 'What made it fall?' But even here selection will be at work in making an appropriate answer. At the least the person answering the inquiry will not wish to burden the questioner with facts which are obvious, so he will not, for instance, answer: 'The force of gravity', but will pick on some more informative fact.

The legal causation issue is not concerned with *explaining* what happened or what caused what but with an attributive question: should we 'attribute' this consequence to that cause? If A injures B and B is killed while in an ambulance being driven to hospital, the legal causation question is: *should* A be held responsible for B's death? And this question is incapable of being answered except by reference to some standard or criterion. There appear to be two possible criteria. First, the standard may be that supplied by *the usages of speech*. If it is thought that according to the standards of correct speech A would be said to be the cause of B's death, then indeed we *should* attribute B's death to A. The second possible criterion is policy: 'Yes (or no) the law should (or should not) attribute B's death to A because it would (or would not) be fair, just or equitable for this or that policy reason'. Given the moral basis of so much of the law, this means that causal inquiries of this nature often have a strong ethical basis. In theory at least the law tends to treat one person as the cause of some damage when that person can be said to be morally responsible for it, because it is felt that as a matter of policy the law ought to reflect morality.

The main proponents of the 'ordinary usage' criterion are Hart and Honoré, the authors of the only serious study of causal problems in English law.[18] They do not dispute that there may in some circumstances be good policy reasons for extending liability beyond cases where common speech would attribute causal responsibility to the defendant; nor that there may be good policy reasons, in some circumstances, for restricting liability even in cases where common speech would attribute causal responsibility to the defendant. But they argue that in most cases the usages of ordinary speech provide a suitable criterion for deciding the issue of legal causation. This may be because the usages of speech are not themselves entirely arbitrary but probably derive from deeply-rooted notions about the ascription of responsibility. A person is thought to be responsible for what he does; he should not be held responsible for the actions of others, or for natural disasters, or even for freakish and bizarre events which (we may feel) he did not 'really' cause; and usages of speech reflect these ideas. If this is right, it follows that the usages of speech supply a criterion which is related to widely held feelings of what justice demands.

It would, however, be a mistake to assume that the use of causal concepts in ordinary speech always rests on intuitive ideas of justice derived from notions about the ascription of responsibility for events. There can be little doubt that there are many circumstances in which the ordinary use of causal concepts in attributive inquiries is derived from explanatory contexts. That is to say, when an ordinary man says that X was the cause of Y in an attributive inquiry, he will often do so *because*, faced with an explanatory inquiry into the same facts, he would normally pick on X as the most useful factor to mention. This point can be illustrated by taking a simple example of a road accident in which – *without fault on either side* – a motorist collides with and injures a pedestrian. Now in this situation we would, in an explanatory inquiry, normally start with the pedestrian; we would want to know how he came by his injuries, and the obvious explanation would be: 'A car ran into him.' We would therefore tend to say that the car or the motorist was the cause of the injuries. But if we now pass to the attributive stage of the inquiry, and, knowing exactly *how* the accident happened, we ask: 'Who caused the accident?' there is no more reason for saying that this was caused by the motorist than that it was caused by the pedestrian. This may well be a hard fact to grasp. We are so imbued with the metaphorical idea of cause as a 'force', that it is difficult at first sight to appreciate that there is no logical reason for treating a moving object, rather than a stationary object, as the cause of the collision.[19] There is, in fact, only one reason for doing this; and that is, that in *explaining* the collision it will usually (though by no means always) be more informative to treat the moving object as the cause. It must be remembered that the ordinary man rarely has the same need as the lawyer to ascribe responsibility for events. The ordinary man may often want to know what has happened, or how or why something happened, but when he knows all these things he would not often have any interest in an attributive causal inquiry.

But this is not all. We have already mentioned how, in an explanatory inquiry, we tend to pick on different factors as 'causes' according to the purposes of the inquiry. Given this choice of possible causes, which are we to select in an attributive inquiry? If there is no logical reason for saying that a motorist rather than a pedestrian is the cause of a collision between the two, why should we even confine our attention to these two, when, if we were involved in explaining the facts to some outsider, we might select some entirely different cause, according to whether the outsider was a motor manufacturer, a highway authority, or a psychiatrist. Further, since the purpose of an attributive inquiry is different from the purpose of *any* explanatory inquiry, it is not clear why any explanatory use of the word 'cause' should be thought relevant in an attributive inquiry.

The ordinary running down action is designed to discover which of these two parties was to blame (or more to blame) for this particular accident. It is not designed to answer the question: 'How can this sort of accident best be prevented?' Nor is it designed to answer the question whether some third party, not represented in the case at all, may be responsible as a part-causer of the accident; for example, the vehicle manufacturer, the road designer or even the alcohol distributor who may be in some sense responsible for the condition of the driver or pedestrian. The courts therefore tend to be more interested in human conduct as a cause, and less in other factors. Hence, while we might sometimes explain an accident as due to the state of the road, or the weather, or the poor qualities of the vehicle, a court is much more likely to find the cause in the conduct of one of the parties directly involved. Of course, the condition of the road or the vehicle may also be due to human conduct, but we have already seen in an earlier chapter that there are powerful factors tending to exclude these from consideration in a fault inquiry, and these factors probably carry over into the causal field.

Further doubt is thrown on the assertion that there is a link between the ordinary usage of causal language and widely held notions of justice and responsibility by recent empirical research[20] which suggests that considering someone to be 'at fault' and responsible for an event by no means always involves holding that person to be morally blameworthy. Even more doubt is thrown by this research on the idea that ordinary-language attributions of responsibility and causation provide an appropriate criterion for legal attributions of causal responsibility. It appears that personal injury victims may often sue a person whom they do not consider responsible for their injuries; and for a variety of reasons a person considered responsible may not be sued – for example, because the victim would feel this to be an unjustifiably aggressive act. People, it seems, often make tort claims for reasons which have little to do with notions of cause or responsibility and then *justify* their action by use of such ideas. Furthermore, the decision to sue and, later, the attribution of responsibility often seem to reflect current legal rules and the pattern of effective tort liability rather than being reflected by the law. In other words, people often sue because they think they have a good chance of success and they justify this decision in terms of the language and concepts *of the law*.

It does not follow from these findings that legal attributions of responsibility are not based on morality or on ideas of justice. But the research does suggest that this morality is one worked out by the judges rather than one taken by the law from the reflections of the common man on the sort of situations which give rise to tort liability.

All of this suggests that the standards of ordinary speech may not provide a suitable criterion for settling issues of 'attributive causation'. But there are other reasons too, for rejecting causal conceptions based on the standards or usages of speech as satisfactory grounds for decision. First, because they are extraordinarily difficult to formulate and apply. Secondly, because there are other important policy considerations which tend to be obscured by causal treatment in terms of language, and which ought to be articulated and debated as the ground for decision. These considerations require amplification.

Difficulty of formulation

The courts have for years floundered around in attributive causal inquiries. Their language has tended to be full of obscure and unhelpful metaphors: 'breaking the chain of causation'; 'intervening forces'; 'a new force'; a *novus actus interveniens*; 'conduit pipes' and sundry other expressions. Undoubtedly the ordinary man would use many of these metaphors in describing causal problems. But they do not provide any intelligible principle which can be used as a basis for prediction by legal advisers, nor as a basis for decision by a judge. This doubtless explains why, in more recent times, courts have tended to treat attributive causation as raising questions which can only be answered in the circumstances of each case.

Hart and Honoré take the view that in using the standard of ordinary language the courts have generally applied the notion that an act is the cause of harm 'if it is an intervention in the course of affairs which is sufficient to produce the harm without the cooperation of the voluntary action of others or abnormal conjunctions of events.'[21]

Other policy factors become obscured by causal inquiries

The second reason why it seems unsatisfactory to treat attributive causal inquiries as turning on the ordinary usages of speech, is that there are many policy issues which may be obscured by treating the causal discussion as if it turned solely on the meanings of words.

Take, for example, the modern policy argument that loss ought to be borne by the person best able to insure against the risk of its occurring. Suppose a person negligently starts a fire which burns down half a town; ought there to be any limit on his liability to owners of destroyed houses? Because the law professes to award 'full compensation' if a tort is proved, it is necessary, in order to impose a limit on liability, to say something like, 'the defendant did not "cause" all the damage'.[22] But a better reason for limiting the liability would be that it is much more sensible for houseowners to take out insurance against fire damage to their own property.

Or suppose that a motorist leaves his car in a position where it is tampered with by children with resultant damage to an innocent plaintiff. Causal principles might point to the children as being liable whereas it would be much more sensible to impose liability on the car owner who is (and indeed must be) insured against the harm for which he is liable through the use of his vehicle.[23] Similar considerations would apply where damage is done by the escape of dangerous things from a person's land. These are in theory instances of strict liability in the law, but in practice the liability is scarcely any stricter than that imposed by negligence, because the courts hold the defendant not liable where the escape is 'caused' by some third party's act, or by some unforeseeable natural event. This is unfortunate because it obscures the important policy considerations which suggest that the owner of property is the right person to bear and insure against liability arising form injury to the person caused by anything escaping from his property. Conversely, there are policy considerations tending against imposing such liability in respect of damage to other property (viz., that this form of damage is much better compensated by personal insurance); but these also would be buried in the discussion of causal conceptions.

The fact appears to be that the concept of cause as used in the law is very closely tied to the idea that the function of the law is to compensate for losses on the basis of attribution of personal responsibility for those losses. Causal reasoning does not give effect to more modern ideas about the functions of tort liability such as efficient loss-spreading by means of insurance or accident prevention. It is plausible to believe, for instance, that the number of road accidents is more likely to be reduced by improvements in vehicle design and engineering and by the elimination of dangerous road features than by imposing liability on bad or careless drivers.

The criticism of the notion of causation being currently considered is, therefore, part of the wider critique of the tort system developed later in this book which rejects notions of fault and individual moral responsibility as inappropriate grounds for deciding how personal injuries should be compensated for.

This general point prompts some comments on the idea that the legal causation issue is a question of policy. The discussion so far has implied that the legal policy here is that legal liability ought to reflect moral responsibility and that the concept of cause in law gives effect to notions of moral responsibility. This suggests (as is indeed borne out by an examination of the case law) that in the vast majority of personal injury actions, once the court has decided that the defendant was negligent, that negligence will be held to be the legal cause of the injuries. In other words, in most cases being negligent and being the legal cause coincide because both rest on ideas of moral responsibility. On this view, the only advantage of the 'legal policy' view of causation over the 'ordinary language' view is that the former recognizes that the morality reflected in the law is the product of judicial policy, not of everyday notions of right and wrong. But it is no easier for policy considerations such as those relating to insurance to be fitted into the 'legal policy' account than into the 'ordinary language' account.

(b) Damage not within the risk

The second 'conceptual' way in which liability may be restricted for remote or unusual or unforeseeable damage may be formulated as follows: liability for breach of a rule only extends to consequences the risk of which that rule is 'designed' to guard against. This principle is a well accepted one in English law in connection with actions for breach of statutory duty, though it is only recently that attempts have been made to apply the same idea to cases of negligence. In the action for breach of statutory duty, the leading case of *Gorris* v. *Scott*[24] established this principle many years ago. In this case the defendants, shipowners, were required by statute to provide pens for all animals carried on board ship. When the plaintiff's animals were swept overboard in a storm he sued the defendants, on the ground that they had failed to provide pens which would have prevented this disaster. It was held that they were not liable, because the 'purpose' of the statute was not to protect the animals against perils of the sea but against the spread of infection.

Application of the same notion to cases of negligence may be illustrated by reference to the decision of the Court of Appeal in *Doughty* v. *Turner Manufacturing Co.*,[25] in which the defendants were manufacturers who used vats of extremely hot liquid chemicals in their processes. These vats were protected by asbestos covers, and a servant of the defendants replaced one of these covers carelessly so that it fell into the vat. Unknown to the defendants – or indeed anyone – the asbestos was liable, in conjunction with the heated chemicals, to produce a violent explosion; and this is in fact occurred and injured the plaintiff. Since nobody knew of the dangerous nature of the asbestos in conjunction with the chemicals, the plaintiff could not argue that the defendants (or the servant in question) should have foreseen the possibility of an *explosion*; but he contended that the servant should have foreseen the possibility of some of the hot chemicals *splashing out* and injuring him; that accordingly dropping the asbestos lid into the vat was a negligent act, and that the defendants were liable for his injuries. But the defendants were held not liable; the risk of explosion, being unforeseeable, was not a risk which the defendants' servant ought to have taken precautions against when the lid was replaced on the vat.

One way of stating the ground of decision in *Doughty* is to say that the defendant was not negligent *in relation* to the risk of explosion. In other words, on the approach currently being considered, the defendant is only liable for consequences the risk of which he ought to have taken precautions against. The risks relevant to determining whether the defendant was negligent and therefore liable at all are also the risks which define the *extent* of his liability. Liability only extends as far as the concept of negligence itself. Thus the 'damage not within the risk' formulation only explains some cases because, as we will see in a minute, a defendant can be held liable for consequences which were not reasonably foreseeable and against which he could not be required to take precautions.

(c) Foreseeability again

The third method of approach to limiting liability for the consequences of negligent action is to invoke foreseeability yet again. If the consequence is a very unusual one, or very remote from the defendant's conduct, it can be said that the damage was unforeseeable, and that the defendant is not liable for unforeseeable damage. This course was adopted in English law by the Privy Council opinion in the famous *Wagon Mound (No 1) Case*,[26] dissenting from the equally famous Court of Appeal decision in *Re Polemis*.[27] Although the Privy Council appeared to think that by their decision in *Wagon Mound* they were laying down a similar test for the extent of liability as had already been laid down for the existence of liability, it is now clear that the two tests are different.[28] The negligence formula does not rely on foreseeability alone as a test of liability, but on a complex balance of factors already fully discussed. Furthermore, a defendant can be held liable for consequences of his negligence which are a direct result of foreseeable consequences but were not themselves foreseeable.[29] Conversely, a defendant may not be liable for consequences of his negligence, even though foreseeable, if they are the result of the (foreseeable) intervention of a human agent.[30] These departures from the foreseeability formula are based on a variety of policy considerations about the proper extent of liability once it is established that the defendant ought to be held liable for some, at least, of the plaintiff's loss.

3 SOME PRACTICAL CONSEQUENCES OF NEED TO LIMIT LIABILITY FOR CONSEQUENCES

In considering the possible practical implications of rules limiting liability for the consequences of negligent action, however they may be conceptualized or formulated, it is necessary to bear in mind the distinction between the two types of case suggested earlier; namely, where the damage is 'remote' in time and space from the defendant's conduct, and where it is not remote, but occurs in an unusual or extraordinary or quite unforeseeable way.

Remoteness in time and space

Remoteness in time and space does not itself prevent a defendant being held liable in law. For example, a manufacturer who negligently made some defective or dangerous product could be liable to someone injured by the defects years later and continents away. But separation of time and space does make it probable that some other damage-causing factor (such as normal deterioration of the product or tampering by a third party) will intervene before the damage occurs and render the defendant's negligence causally irrelevant. We may say that such new intervening factors – especially if these involve voluntary human conduct – sever causal connection. Alternatively, we may say that the damage was not within the risk to be guarded against, or was unforeseeable.

Another consequence of separation in time between tort and damage is that it may become difficult to prove that the tort was a cause in fact of the damage which would not have occurred but for the tort. Suppose that a person is seriously injured in an accident caused by the negligence of the defendant, but makes a complete recovery. In consequence of the accident he changes his job and five years later is injured at work. At one level the second accident would not have occurred but for the first because the first led the person to change his job. But this reasoning is troublesome for two reasons: it seems to introduce a large element of chance into the law by imposing liability for events over which the defendant could have no control. But also, the longer the time gap between tort and damage the harder it becomes to say what might have happened to the person if the first accident had not occurred. He might have been injured in some other accident anyway and so have been just as badly off. Indeed, on balance (weighing up all the gains and losses) he might be better off having suffered the first accident than if it had never happened.

In practice, however, liability for events happening long after an act of negligence would not be as onerous as might appear at first sight because of the rule that an action for personal injuries resulting from a tortious act must be brought within three years of the act.

Extraordinay damage, or damage occurring in an extraordinary way

Where there is little separation in time and space between the defendant's conduct and the damage, but the damage is of an extraordinary kind, or occurs in a freakish or bizarre manner, there would not usually be any problem about 'cause in fact', but the element of 'chanciness' in the extent of liability would still remain.

There is, in this type of case, sometimes an additional factor, which is the desire to restrict the magnitude of the total liability which may be imposed on a single defendant. At one time the reason for this was largely the desire to avoid imposing crushing liabilities on a single wealthy individual or a small company which would have meant the ruin of the individual or the bankruptcy of the company. This risk was not a very serious one where personal injuries were concerned, until the arrival of mechanical power and devices which were capable of killing or maiming large numbers of people in a single disaster. And when disasters of this kind began to occur they usually occurred within the confines of a single workplace – for instance a mine might be flooded killing a large number of miners, or an explosion might occur in a factory, killing or maiming many workmen. In cases of this kind, employers were generally protected from liability by the doctrine of 'common employment', invented by the courts around 1837 – a doctrine which was later found to be irrational and indefensible in England, and was finally abrogated by Statute in 1948.

Much more serious in early tort law was the possibility of being held liable for certain types of property damage, which might be quite ruinous – for example, damage caused by a serious fire, or negligence causing the destruction of a ship with her cargo. It is interesting to observe that in both these spheres limitations on liability were devised. So far as disasters at sea were concerned, there has long been a very serious limitation on liability, which takes the form of restricting the liability for damage done by a vessel in proportion to the size of that vessel. Thus the maximum liability which a shipowner may incur (unless there has been 'actual fault or privity' on his part) is limited by the size of his own ships. So if a small ship collided with and sank some large liner, the liability would be only a small fraction of the value of the liner. As to fires, we find a Statute passed in 1774 (re-enacting an earlier one) which restricts liability for 'accidental' fires, and though the courts later interpreted the Act as not applying to negligently caused fires, it is far from clear that this was what Parliament had in mind.[31]

In modern times the widespread growth of all forms of insurance has to some extent rendered obsolete the desire to restrict liability on grounds of the sheer magnitude of the damage. This is certainly the case with most forms of personal injury, but it is less so with damage to property; and there is more to be said for restricting liability for purely financial losses because insurance against this kind of liability is neither so widespread nor so easy to obtain – particularly with unlimited cover. Nevertheless, the desire to restrict liability where the damage appears likely to be very great is still apparent in some cases, and it is still true that this is more likely to be important in cases of property damage than in cases of personal injury. Given the scale of damages awarded in personal injury cases, it is still much easier to cause vast losses (in terms of money) by damaging property than by injuring or killing people. A single ship, worth several millions, may be sunk by a momentary act of negligence; a fire in this country may cause hundreds of thousands of pounds in damage, and in other countries (such as Australia, or parts of the Western United States) the damage can easily run into millions; an explosion can destroy whole buildings; an oil spillage over the beaches of fishing or holiday resorts may cost millions to put right. But it would be a very unusual disaster which caused anything like this liability in terms of personal injury or death. It is thus not surprising that the two leading cases in English law about 'remoteness of damage' – about extraordinary and freakish occurrences – should concern damage to property caused by fire, and that different rules still appear to apply as between personal injury and damage to property.

The rule that the damage must not itself be a very unusual or unforeseeable consequence of the negligence, only applies to personal injury cases in a very attenuated form. Accidental personal injuries may produce all sorts of unusual or unexpected or strange results, but no one doubts that liability will be imposed. A burn on the lip may lead to cancer and so death, and the person responsible for the burn will be liable for the death;[32] an electric shock may stimulate a latent polio virus, and if the defendant is responsible for the shock, he will also have to pay for the effects of the polio;[33] injuries may lead to melancholia and suicide, and the defendant liable for the injuries will also be liable for the death.[34] In this way many injuries or diseases which are in a sense merely 'triggered off' by the original negligently caused accident, are brought within the scope of the tort system, and so compensable in damages. Results of this kind – since they would not generally be the same in analogous cases of property damage – can no doubt be explained by the overriding object of compensating people for tragic misfortunes; and no difficulty usually arises from the sheer magnitude of the damages recoverable. But the element of chance or luck is very obvious in these cases. Many people die of cancer every year; many others commit suicide; many contract polio or other crippling diseases. Why should the majority go unaided by the tort system while a handful, who are able to latch their disease onto some fortuitous negligently caused injury, be so generously treated? In some of these cases it is utterly unreal to treat the plaintiff's injuries as 'due' in any real sense to the defendant's negligence, yet large sums may be awarded. For example, in *Robinson* v. *Post Office*[35] the plaintiff suffered a minor graze through slipping on steps which had been negligently covered with oil. Unfortunately he suffered a freak reaction to an anti-tetanus injection, with very serious results. He was awarded damages of over £30,000 – yet the only negligence consisted of leaving some oil on a step ladder. There seems little to choose between this case and *Doughty* v. *Turner Manufacturing Co.*,[36] where minor negligence was also followed by unforeseeable injuries of great seriousness. Cases of this kind involve, in a sense, a bridgehead between liability for fault and strict liability. While initial negligence must be proved, the plaintiff recovers damages for what most people would regard as nothing but an accident. Because of their very tenuous connection with the element of fault, such cases seem especially anomalous.

5
The conduct of the plaintiff

Even where the defendant has been negligent and his conduct has been a 'cause in fact' of the plaintiff's damage or injuries, there are many circumstances in which the plaintiff may be deprived of part or all of his damages because of his own conduct. Most of these cases involve conduct which would make the layman say that in a broad sense the plaintiff's injuries were 'his own fault', or at least partly 'his own fault'; and this notion is recognized by the law in the defence of contributory negligence. But there are many other 'conceptual' ways in which the same or a similar result can be arrived at. For instance, there is the defence of *volenti non fit injuria* (or as it is sometimes termed, 'assumption of risk') which in negligence cases is frequently simply another name for contributory negligence – though a name with practical importance since the law today differentiates in one important respect between the two defences: contributory negligence is no longer a complete defence to an action, while *volenti non fit injuria* is. Since the Law Reform (Contributory Negligence) Act 1945, the rule in cases of contributory negligence has been that the plaintiff's damages are to be reduced by the court to such a degree as appears just and equitable, having regard to the plaintiff's share of the responsibility for what has happened. But other conceptual means are also at hand for denying the plaintiff some, or all, of his damages. For instance, it might be possible in some rare cases to deny the existence of a duty of care to a plaintiff where he has placed himself in so unusual or extraordinary a position that he may be classed as an 'unforeseeable plaintiff'. Or again, it is possible to argue in some cases that the plaintiff has 'caused' his own injuries and the defendant's conduct, though a cause in fact, is not a 'cause in law'. Or it may be that the plaintiff has aggravated the damage by failing to take reasonable steps to reduce or mitigate the effect of his injuries, so that the defendant may be said to be responsible for only a part of the damage.

1 CONTRIBUTORY NEGLIGENCE

Until 1945 contributory negligence was a complete defence to an action in tort, and a vast amount of case law developed around this defence. There can be little doubt that this defence was originally based on the same moral sentiments that led to the creation of liability for negligence, i.e. the feeling that a plaintiff guilty of contributory negligence was himself 'at fault' or 'to blame' for his injuries, though the legal justification for the doctrine was expressed in terms of 'cause'.[1] It may also have been partly based, as the law of negligence itself was, on some idea of deterrence. A person should be encouraged to take care for his own safety, even though he was imperilled by someone else's negligence. But, it has been pointed out,[2] neither of these rationales is very satisfying. In the first place, the kind of 'fault' in question is not the same in the two cases. The 'fault' of a defendant can, in a broad sort of way, be treated (anyway in many cases) as being immoral, in that it involves egotistical or unsocial risk-taking at the expense of others. But the plaintiff's 'fault' is not of this kind: his fault is not so much selfish or immoral, as just foolish, and it is not clear that one can equate, or even compare, foolishness with selfishness. The second rationale is looked at in some detail later[3] and it is enough to say here, that the instinct for self-preservation is likely (in most circumstances) to be quite a sufficient deterrent against taking risks with one's own personal safety. It is, therefore, not at all evident that the deterrent function of the doctrine of contributory negligence is of any real value.

Whatever the reason, the injustice of denying all remedy to a plaintiff who was only partly or perhaps slightly to blame, against a defendant who was seriously to blame, eventually led the courts to all sorts of devices to mitigate the effects of the doctrine. These devices took the form of denying the causal relevance of the plaintiff's contributory negligence, and insisting that the defendant's negligence was the 'sole' cause of the damage. Since there was never any doubt that the plaintiff's conduct was at least a 'cause in fact' of the damage, this merely meant that the defendant's conduct should be regarded as the 'sole' cause in law.

In our discussion of 'cause' we saw how there were two standards which might be used by the courts in attempting to decide whether a consequence should be attributed to a person's conduct, i.e. the standards of ordinary speech, and policy standards invented or devised by the law itself. The misfortune of the doctrine of contributory negligence was that the courts could never make up their minds which of these standards they wanted to adopt. To some extent they departed from the standards of ordinary speech, and found defendants 'solely' responsible for accidents which would certainly have been said in ordinary speech to have been partly caused by the plaintiff. This was largely done by the device of the famous 'last opportunity rule', i.e. the rule that the person who had the last opportunity to avoid the accident should be treated as the sole cause.[4] But the courts were never very happy with this rule, partly because it did violence to ordinary speech, and partly because it seemed such a crude method of mitigating the harshness of the contributory negligence rule. Furthermore, the attempt to find a 'sole' cause, whether by use of standards of ordinary speech or by legal and policy devices, became impractical when industrial and road accidents began to form the typical action for negligence. In these cases the accident usually happens in a very short space of time, and the attempt to find one sole cause, or the person with the last opportunity to avoid the accident, simply broke down in practice. The result was constant wavering by the courts and the growth of intolerable subtlety and complexity in the law, until it became well nigh impossible to direct a jury in intelligible terms – and cases were still being tried by juries when these difficulties were at their peak.

Then in 1945 came the Law Reform Act, which enabled the courts to apportion the responsibility for an accident and so to reduce the plaintiff's damages where he had been guilty of contributory negligence, while not denying him a remedy altogether. At first there were extraordinary difficulties, because it was suggested by some pedants that the Act did not alter the 'rules of causation'[5] (when one of the principal difficulties was the failure of the courts to find any rules of causation!). Thus, it was suggested, that in any case where before 1945 the plaintiff or the defendant would have been treated as the 'sole' cause of the accident, that result should remain after the Act, and there could be no apportionment. On this view, only where before 1945 both parties had been treated as part 'cause' of the accident, should apportionment be allowed. Fortunately this argument failed; not because it was ever met head on and rejected by the courts, but simply because it withered away in practice.

In practice the Act of 1945 has changed the question of the effect of contributory negligence from a very difficult and complex question of law into a question which is treated as one of 'fact'; in the sense that each case tends to be dealt with ad hoc. There is little 'law' left in contributory negligence cases today, although occasionally difficult problems have presented themselves, such as that of joint negligent conduct. One of the few points of principle to emerge in recent times has involved the application of contributory negligence rules to passengers in cars. Thus in *Froom* v. *Butcher*,[6] it was held by the Court of Appeal that a passenger who fails to use an available seat belt must bear some share of responsibility for his injuries if he is involved in an accident, and it can be shown that his injuries (or some of them) would not have occurred, or would have been less serious, if he had worn a seat belt. It was laid down as a general guide that 25% of the damages should be lost where the injuries would have been prevented altogether, and 15% where they would have been less severe. More recently, it has also been held that a passenger who allows himself to be driven by a driver clearly the worse for alcohol, may also have his damages reduced for contributory negligence.[7]

But points of difficulty of this kind have been rare. In general, the Act of 1945 appears to have been successful in simplifying the law, and removing a source of injustice. Judging from the reported cases, it appears to work smoothly in practice and few difficulties have been encountered in its application.[8] Nevertheless, there are important questions about the whole doctrine of contributory negligence, and the relationship between the doctrine and liability insurance to which attention should be drawn.

The difference between negligence and contributory negligence

In the first place, the relationship between negligence and contributory negligence in practice is not always fully appreciated. At first sight contributory negligence appears to be a sort of mirror image of negligence itself. There is an apparently satisfying balance in the idea of the negligence of the defendant being counterpoised by the negligence of the plaintiff. But the effect of a finding of contributory negligence is very different from the effect of a finding of negligence. To find a defendant guilty of negligence shifts a loss away from the plaintiff, and spreads it by means of insurance or other processes. But a finding of contributory negligence has precisely the opposite effect: its effect is to leave part or all of the loss on the plaintiff. Thus, contributory negligence falls much more heavily on the plaintiff than negligence falls on the defendant. Negligent people do not pay for the consequences of their negligence in practice; but contributorily negligent people *do* pay for the consequences of their contributory negligence. It is not too much to say that the only significant group of people who are called upon to pay for the consequences of their negligence are accident victims themselves.[9]

This difference between the effect of a finding of negligence and the effect of a finding of contributory negligence, may have influenced the courts in recognizing a very important distinction between negligence and contributory negligence in law. As we have seen, the test of negligence is very largely an objective test; to acquit a person of liability for negligence on the ground that he personally could not have avoided the accident would be to deprive the plaintiff of compensation. But to acquit a plaintiff of contributory negligence, increases the amount of compensation he receives. This may explain the greater subjectivity in the test of contributory negligence; in particular the age of the plaintiff is taken into account in determining negligence. A young person is only expected to show the degree of care which a person of that age should exercise, and the same is true of an elderly person. The importance of this in practice can be gauged from the fact that young children and old people form a disproportionate number of the pedestrians killed and seriously injured in road accidents. In 1983 for example, the casualty rate for pedestrians killed and seriously injured in road accidents was 15.4 per 100,000 for persons aged 30 to 39, but was 80.9 for children aged 5–9, and 55 for those aged over 70.[10] The Pearson Report recommended that contributory negligence should no longer be available as a defence in road accident cases where the injured person is a child under the age of 12.[11] This would make very little difference to the practical position at present, though it is impossible to understand why this proposal should be limited to road accident cases.

There is good ground for believing that in practice the standard of care applied by the courts is higher when dealing with negligence than contributory negligence. At one time there was support for recognizing such a distinction as a matter of law, and though there are authoritative dicta rejecting this approach,[12] nobody familiar with the law reports can have any doubt that judges often find conduct to be negligent which they would hesitate to stigmatize as contributory negligence.

Contributory negligence and family cases

At one time in the nineteenth century there was support for a doctrine of 'identification' under which one person might be so identified with the contributory negligence of another as to preclude the former from recovering damages even though he might have been personally free from fault. For example, a child who was accompanying his grandmother was severely injured at a station when his grandmother crossed the lines and both were struck by a passing train. It was held that as the grandmother had been found to be contributorily negligent the child could not recover.[13] Some such idea applies in Fatal Accident claims where it is settled that the claimant's damages must be reduced proportionately to any negligence on the part of the deceased contributing to his death. And there is a statutory example of the idea in the Congenital Disabilities (Civil Liability) Act 1976, under a provision of which the claim of an unborn child injured before birth can be met with defences available to the defendant against its mother. In general, however, the doctrine was thought unjust, and was rejected in 1888 by the House of Lords which held that a person was not to be affected by the contributory negligence of another unless he was legally liable for that other's acts; for example, if the latter were the former's servant acting in the course of his employment.[14]

But there are cases in which the lack of some such doctrine produces extraordinary and anomalous results in cases involving members of one family. One starts with the basic position that a plaintiff's damages can be reduced or wiped out entirely on account of contributory negligence, on the basis that a person ought not to 'benefit' from his own carelessness. But suppose that a person is injured by the negligent driving of his or her spouse; the injured spouse can recover damages from the other (in reality, from the insurer). The family as a whole will 'gain' from the award of damages and the negligent spouse may well share in these gains. For example, in a case in 1975 a wife recovered damages of £72,500 against her husband for injuries due to his negligent driving.[15]

Suppose, next, that one of the spouses is killed through the negligence of the other. In *Dodds* v. *Dodds*[16] a man was killed in an accident caused by his wife's negligent driving. Plainly the wife could not obtain damages for the loss of her husband. But it was held that their eight and a half year old son was entitled to damages against his mother for causing his father's death, and he was awarded £17,000, paid, of course, by the insurers. In such a case the bulk of the capital would probably be retained under the control of the court until the child reached majority, but the income would probably be paid to the mother for the maintenance and education of the child. So in reality the negligent spouse would share the benefit of the award.

On the assumption that the fault system has a moral basis these results seem remarkable. On the other hand, if emphasis is put on tort as a mechanism for *compensating* rather than for *compensating on the basis of responsibility*, then the cases seem less strange (and the position under the Fatal Accidents Act seems the one which is out of line). There is no particular reason to deprive one family member of compensation on the ground that another faulty one will indirectly benefit thereby when the damages will be paid by an insurer and when the real sufferer if damages are not awarded will be the innocent victim.

The assessment of contributory negligence: relative fault

Even though the principle of reducing damages for contributory negligence may appear to be based on a simple moral idea, the principle according to which the plaintiff's damages are reduced is far from obvious or straightforward. The plaintiff's damages will be reduced, having regard not just to the degree of his fault, not just according to whether he has been slightly or grossly at fault, but according to his fault *relative* to that of the defendant. In addition, just as the amount of compensation which a negligent defendant must pay bears no relation to the degree of his fault where he alone is to blame, so also, the amount of his loss which the plaintiff must bear where he is partly to blame depends not just on the extent of his fault, but also on the extent of the loss itself. Let us consider how all this works with a few simple illustrations.

First: a plaintiff who is 50% to blame for an accident in which he suffers a loss assessed at £100, will lose £50 as a result of his negligence. But a plaintiff who is a mere 10% to blame for an accident in which his loss is assessed at £10,000 will lose £1,000 as a result of his negligence.

Second: a motorist who commits a trivial act of negligence and whose loss is assessed at, say, £1,000 will be held perhaps 10% to blame, and so recover £900 if he collides with a defendant who is driving with gross negligence; while he may be held 50% to blame and so recover only £500 if he collides with a motorist who has merely committed the same mistake as he himself. Yet his own act of negligence is precisely the same in the two cases.

Third: equally, a motorist who is driving with gross negligence, perhaps in a drunken state, will certainly be held very largely responsible and so recover very little if he is involved in an accident partly due (say) to the negligence of a pedestrian who crosses the road in front of him; but if he is fortunate enough to collide with another drunken, reckless motorist he will probably recover 50% of his loss.

Fourth: the last illustration shows that two reckless motorists driving with great negligence will each recover 50% of their loss, assuming their negligence to be of a similar degree; but if *three* negligent motorists all collide simultaneously due to the same degree of negligence, the responsibility of each will be assessed at 33⅓%, so each will recover two-thirds of his loss.

Contributory negligence and the fault system

Finally, and perhaps most serious of all, the combination of the contributory negligence principle with the 'no liability without fault' principle, produces the result that a person injured without fault on the part of anyone receives no tort compensation, whereas a person who may be very largely to blame for his own injuries, can receive some tort compensation. Two workmen may be working side by side in the factory and both may be severely injured, with losses assessed at, say, £100,000 each. Workman A is injured by gross negligence on his own part, and slight negligence on the part of a colleague working with him. He recovers perhaps 20% of his loss i.e. £20,000, not of course from the negligent man, but from his employer, or his employers' insurers. Workman B, on the other hand, is injured entirely by 'accident'. He receives not a penny in tort compensation.

Nobody knows quite what is the quantitative effect of the law of contributory negligence,[17] but in Scandinavia, where apportionment is permitted much as it is in England, it has been estimated that abolition of the defence would increase the cost of motor insurance by at least 7½%.[18] In the survey of insurance claims handled in November 1973, conducted for the Pearson Commission, it was found that 26% of claims settled were disposed of on the basis of partial liability;[19] but this included cases settled without any payment at all. The cases settled with a partial admission of liability comprised about 31% of the number of cases in which some payment was made. But this does not tell us anything about the size of the discount allowed for in cases settled on the basis of partial liability. In Australia it was found that 39% of damages are lost to the plaintiffs where contributory negligence has been found,[20] but this does not tell us what proportion this bears to all tort recoveries. This sum is not, of course, paid out as compensation to victims of accidents caused by no-one's fault, but simply represents a saving, mainly to insurance premium payers. We shall also see, when we look at other compensation systems, that there are many situations in which the aim of compensating victims of injury and damage is so paramount that it is thought unjustifiable to reduce the compensation because of fault on the part of the victim. Life insurance or fire insurance or comprehensive motor insurance would not be such attractive propositions if they did not provide protection against risks which included the negligence of the victim himself.

The usefulness of the doctrine

Does the doctrine of contributory negligence serve any useful purpose today? From one point of view the answer must be 'no', at least in the law relating to personal injuries. The doctrine is no longer needed (if it ever was) to spare an individual defendant the injustice of being made to compensate a plaintiff who was partly to blame for his own injuries. It operates, in fact, as a frankly penal device: the contributorily negligent plaintiff is simply punished by being deprived of some of the compensation to which he would otherwise be entitled, and the extent of the penalty is largely regulated by quite fortuitous factors. In addition to doubts about how the doctrine works, there are thus doubts about its objective. Today penal laws are invariably justified on the grounds of their deterrent value, but it is very doubtful if the doctrine of contributory negligence has any deterrent value at all in personal injury cases, or whether indeed, any legal deterrent is needed to prevent people from injuring themselves. It is true that (as has been argued)[21] the sense of fairness may still seem to demand that if the plaintiff complains of the defendant's negligence, he must be prepared to bring his own conduct into the scales. But the answer to this point surely lies in the effect of current insurance practice, as has been previously pointed out. When this is taken into account the result surely seems less unjust: the plaintiff is, after all uninsured, the defendant insured. The negligent defendant will not pay for his negligence: the negligent plaintiff will, if his damages are reduced for contributory negligence, pay for his own negligence.

There is, however, a pragmatic argument which may favour the retention of the doctrine of contributory negligence in personal injury cases. If attention is confined exclusively to the tort system the case for abolition appears to remain strong; but when the whole scene is surveyed, the case weakens. For it then becomes apparent that a plaintiff who recovers *any* damages is in a sense very fortunate compared with most other victims of accident and disease. As we have previously observed, we are here talking of some 6½% of accident victims, and a very much smaller proportion of those who suffer illness or disabilities from other causes. The financial provision made for this very small proportion of the disabled and injured is already generous by comparison with what is available to the others. It would seem wrong to improve it still further, even by abolishing doctrines unjust in themselves.

Certainly, so long as the tort system retains anything like its present structure, it would be undesirable to abrogate the defence of contributory negligence in relation to property damage. If the doctrine were swept away altogether it would mean that in many road accidents in which two motorists cause damage to their vehicles by their combined negligence, each would be entitled to claim in full from the other. Such a result might be acceptable in a personal injury claim, but if applied to all cases of damage to the vehicles themselves, it would result in a considerable and wasteful use of tort liability and liability insurance, rather than the personal accident insurance of the vehicle owner. With damage-only accidents some six or seven times as frequent as personal injury accidents,[22] this would undoubtedly increase the cost of motor insurance by adding to the administrative cost.

2 VOLENTI NON FIT INJURIA

The defence of *volenti non fit injuria* is also sometimes referred to as the defence of 'assumption of risk'. Its use in the common law has been characterized by a conspicuous imprecision of thought, which has obscured the fact that in some (though not all) cases the defence is nothing else than the doctrine of contributory negligence under another name – except that it is used to deny liability altogether, instead of as a ground for apportioning damages. If we can forget all legal classification for a moment, it would seem that there are three possible reasons why the plaintiff's own conduct should deprive him of a right of action against a negligent defendant. One is that the plaintiff may have *agreed* that the defendant was not to be liable. The second is that the plaintiff may have been to blame, or at fault, or responsible in whole or in part, for his own injury. The third is that the plaintiff may have agreed to the defendant conforming with a standard of conduct which is lower than that normally required by the law. The trouble stems from the fact that these three factors have never been adequately distinguished, and that the defence of *volenti* or 'assumption of risk' has been rested sometimes on one and sometimes on another of these ideas – and sometimes perhaps on a confusion between them.

Volenti as actual agreement to exonerate the defendant

Express agreement to exonerate a defendant from liability is undoubtedly a possibility where the plaintiff and defendant are in some contractual or similar relationship. And it was formerly common in many consumer contracts to include clauses which had the effect of depriving the consumer of any redress in the event of an accident causing personal injury, even if the other party was responsible for the accident. But under Sect. 2(1) of the Unfair Contract Terms Act 1977 these clauses are now altogether banned, at least where there has been negligence. In other cases, where there might be some liability even in the absence of negligence, the exclusion of liability for personal injury is not wholly prohibited, but it is subject to severe controls; and it is completely ruled out in the most common type of case, viz. where liability is based on defective goods bought by a consumer from the defendant. The reasons for prohibiting people from expressly agreeing to give up their rights to sue for personal injuries caused by negligence, are basically an extension of the reasons for creating the right of action in the first place, and a recognition of the fact that this kind of 'express agreement' is usually nothing of the kind in practice.

On the other hand, the position with regard to damage to goods is quite different. Here, we shall see later, the law of torts plays second fiddle to first party insurance, so that there is less reason for insisting on tort liability being maintained and less reason for refusing to allow people to give up these rights by express agreement. Moreover, in practice, the agreement in the case of goods is more likely to be a real agreement, because it will often concern businessmen who may be expected to understand the nature of the agreement, the element of risk and the desirability of insurance. The Unfair Contract Terms Act therefore does not prohibit the use of such exclusion clauses in cases of damage to property, but again it does impose severe controls on their use. In general, such clauses will now be permissible only where they are held to be reasonable, having regard to all the circumstances. And it now seems clear, at least in relation to contracts between business concerns, that the availability of insurance will be an important factor in deciding the issue of reasonableness.[23] It is not clear, however, to what extent the insurance factor will be held relevant in other cases. For example, will the courts hold that car parking concerns may reasonably exempt themselves from liability for negligent damage to cars, on the ground that the owners can insure themselves and that many do so? There is a good deal to be said for the view that such an exclusion would not be unreasonable (at least if it did not extend to the first £50 or £100 of damage), otherwise prudent (insured) owners will be paying for the damage to the less prudent (uninsured) owners.

In addition to clearly contractual cases, people may also expressly agree to things being done which would amount to torts in the absence of such agreement. Obvious examples are agreement to allow a person onto one's land, so preventing his conduct from being a trespass; agreement to bodily contact, or even to being hit, as in sports, where the agreement prevents the conduct amounting to assault. And so on. These are simple and plain cases in which consent or agreement is a perfectly good defence to conduct which would otherwise be tortious.

But the defence of *volenti* or assumption of risk is not confined to cases of actual agreement. The defence extends to cases where the defendant is treated as *volens*, or as having assumed a risk merely by reason of his conduct.

Volenti as another name for contributory negligence

It is sometimes argued that a person may be treated as having *impliedly* agreed to 'assume a risk', from the mere fact that he has done something presenting a great risk – or an unjustified risk – such as taking a ride in a car driven by a drunk, or testing an explosive device without taking shelter. But this involves a serious confusion of thought. Taking a great risk may certainly entail that the plaintiff is willing that the risk should occur, even though this is merely a choice between evils and he does not *want* the risk to occur. But this degree of 'agreement' to the risk has nothing whatever to do with agreeing to abandon the right to sue for damages should the risk occur. A pedestrian who crosses the road certainly 'takes his chance' that he may be injured, and is willing that he should be injured in the sense that he prefers to take that chance than to stay permanently on one side of the road. But willingness to run this risk is no conceivable justification for 'inferring' an agreement not to sue the negligent motorist who actually runs him down. What additional fact then is necessary, besides conduct which actually involves a risk, in order to invoke the defence? Knowledge of the risk? But this too is not enough, for the House of Lords decided at the end of the last century that knowing of a risk did not mean that a person had agreed to bear it.[24] Perhaps the additional factor is that the risk must be a very great one. A person who does something which involves a strong probability of being injured may be said to 'assume the risk' in this sense. But this will not do either, because in some circumstances – and particularly where rescue of those in distress or danger is involved – the taking of great risks is justified, and a person who takes such a risk to effect a rescue is not held to have 'assumed the risk' in the relevant sense. It seems then that the only remaining possibility is to treat the defence as confined to those cases in which the plaintiff ran a risk *which was unjustified and unreasonable having regard to the circumstances*. But this is the classic statement of the defence of contributory negligence. In this type of case, therefore, the two defences seem to overlap completely.

But, it may be asked, if this is so, why is it that the courts fall back on this defence when contributory negligence allows them so much scope in reducing the damages? A court can reduce the damages awarded to the plaintiff by such proportion as they think fit, and it is even possible for a court to admit that a defendant was technically and trivially at fault, but to assess the plaintiff's share of the responsibility at 100%. Why then is this not sufficient to enable them to do justice? In the great majority of cases this discretion enables the court to achieve what it regards as a just solution, and consequently the defence of *volenti* is rarely upheld in this sort of case today. But in some rare cases the apportionment system appears to restrict the court's powers to arrive at what it regards as a just solution. This is because apportionment has to be carried out according to the relative degree of negligence of the two parties; and cases occur in which the plaintiff has been very negligent indeed – has done something which the courts regard as so foolish that they wish to deprive him of all or nearly all his damages – but in which the defendant has been equally or even more negligent. For instance, the passenger who allows himself to be driven by a driver in a seriously drunken state, is doing something very foolish indeed, and evidently some courts (at least some Commonwealth courts)[25] feel that he should be deprived of all damages for doing this. But if the plaintiff has been negligent, what are we to make of the defendant, who actually *drove* the car in this drunken state? The court can hardly assess his share of the responsibility as less than that of the plaintiff, so that the court's power to reduce the damages the plaintiff will receive is very limited in this kind of case. Indeed, when this issue recently arose in court in England, it was held that the damages should only be reduced by 20%, in view of the fact that the driver must be regarded as more responsible than the passenger.[26] In this case, the court evidently did not wish to deprive the plaintiff of a high proportion of his damages; but if the court does feel inclined to do this, it is faced with the difficulty that the assessment must be based on relative fault. The damages cannot be reduced by more than 50%. The same is true of cases of joint negligent action, for example, where two workmen do something very negligent together and injuries occur to one or both. In such a case the House of Lords recently revived the defence of *volenti*[27] – which had not been much used of late – though the only logical purpose of doing so was to evade the need to give the plaintiff any damages at all, as would have been the result of applying the defence of contributory negligence.

But this is hardly satisfactory. The truth is that decisions of this kind fly in the teeth of the relevant statutory provisions, which declare that the plaintiff's claim is not to be defeated where he has been injured partly by his own fault and partly by the fault of the defendant. If it is desired that the plaintiff should have no damages, or should have his damages very much reduced where he has been guilty of gross contributory negligence, and that this result should be wholly independent of the degree of the negligence of the defendant, then this result should be arrived at without fictitious 'agreements' or 'assumptions of risk'. After all, this approach cannot meet the simplest possible case of two grossly negligent motorists colliding with each other; to take the stock case of the undeserving plaintiff, where two 'fleeing felons' both driving getaway cars collide with each other and injure each other. There is no possibility of invoking the defence of *volenti* or assumption of risk here, because it is impossible to construct a fictitious agreement out of these events, so the courts will perforce have to fall back on contributory negligence, and each plaintiff will receive a substantial sum in damages.

The main reason for these difficulties is undoubtedly the prevalence of liability insurance, for the process of apportioning damages according to the relative degrees of fault of plaintiff and defendant is obviously less satisfactory when the damages will not be paid by the defendant. It may well be thought, for instance, that *as between* a drunken driver and a willing passenger, the main responsibility for injuries to the passenger rests on the driver. But as between the willing passenger and some third party – an insurance company, or an employer vicariously liable, or the State – the passenger's responsibility may be thought to be great enough to justify depriving him of all, or most, of his damages. This is yet one more illustration of the difficulty which the law has encountered in trying to come to terms with liability insurance. The courts are in fact only able to achieve what appears to them to be a just result – if at all – by falling back on the doctrinally suspect defence of *volenti non fit injuria*.

Volenti as affecting standard of care

There is yet a third type of case in which the defence of *volenti*, or assumption of risk, may be involved, and that is where in addition to doing something which involves a risk, the plaintiff agrees to the defendant imposing the risk on him. This is *not* the same as agreeing to acquit the defendant of liability should injury occur. The classic example of this type of case, is that in which the plaintiff is injured while watching some sporting event – for example, by a flying puck at an ice hockey match;[28] or a horse at a show jumping contest;[29] or a car at a race track.[30] Here again it is easy to say glibly that the plaintiff has 'assumed the risk' of injury. What do we mean by that treacherous phrase in this context? What we have here, surely, is an agreement by the plaintiff to conduct which would or might be negligent in a different place, or in a different context. The only relevance of the plaintiff's conduct or 'agreement' here, is that it helps to define the limits of negligence. Whether the defendants have failed to take reasonable care depends in part on whether they have a captive or a voluntary audience. A driver who races round a race track at 100 mph in front of the spectators is not driving negligently just because of his speed; he would be if he drove at the same speed in the High Street.

But whether the consent or agreement of the plaintiff *should* affect the limits of permissible conduct, whether it *should* be allowed to affect the standard of care required, is a question of law and of policy. It must not be assumed that because, for instance, the organizers of a popular sport are allowed to take risks at the expense of the spectators, therefore it follows that agreement to dangerous conduct is always of legal significance. The question is whether the spectator's voluntary presence at a dangerous sport affects the standard of care required of the organizers. The answer to this is that it may do so, but whether it does so or not is a policy question. The answer to this question may certainly be influenced by the fact that the plaintiff has voluntarily 'come to the risk' as it were. In the sport cases it is not unreasonable to say that the fact that people come quite voluntarily to watch the spectacle affects what precautions the organizers ought to take to avoid accidents. But the answer may differ in other cases where the degree of risk is high and the value of the objective small.

A simpler case is that of a girl who asked for employment knowing that she was allergic to some substance with which the employers operated, but not anticipating the extent of the risk she thereby faced.[31] Since the employer also knew of the allergic condition, the issue which arose was whether the employers *should* have employed the girl, assuming no precautions were possible. This question was affected by the girl's voluntary conduct in asking for her job, but this factor was not necessarily conclusive. Whether it should have been treated as conclusive depends on the relative weight to be given to the value of individual freedom of choice on the one hand, and that of paternalism on the other. This is a value judgment: not surprisingly in view of the whole tradition of the common law, the court in fact held that there was no liability in this case.

Cases of this kind really have little to do with the other cases which are discussed under the heading of *volenti*, or assumption of risk. They concern the standard of care required of people; the definition of negligence. Their only connection with the cases discussed in this section is that they both have something to do with the plaintiff's own conduct.

6
Strict liability

Our discussion so far has been entirely in terms of the law of negligence. We must now turn our attention briefly to that form of liability which lawyers call 'strict' or sometimes 'absolute' liability. The most famous species of strict liability is that falling under the rule in *Rylands* v. *Fletcher*, but it is doubtful if this rule has much practical importance at the present day; it is certainly unlikely to be of much assistance in action for personal injuries,[1] and it is accordingly dealt with very briefly below.

1   BREACH OF STATUTORY DUTY

Actions for breach of statutory duty are often (in theory at least) 'strict', in the sense that no lack of due care need be proved; but they are by no means always so in practice, and sometimes not even so in theory. Much, of course, depends on the wording of the statute in question. Some prescribe a result to be attained, the most famous and important being section 14 of the Factories Act 1961 which declares that 'every dangerous part of any machinery ... shall be securely fenced'. In such a case it is not defence to plead that all reasonable care has been taken to fence the machinery; or that the machine is unworkable if completely fenced. But other duties may be stated in forms which do not differ greatly from the standard of care required by the law of negligence though the actual requirements of due care will usually be specified in much more detail than at common law. But, for example, a statute may simply require precautions to be taken 'so far as practicable', or words to that effect.

Furthermore, the courts tend to interpret even detailed provisions of industrial legislation in the light of common law notions of fault. For example, 'dangerous machinery' may be held to mean: 'machinery which is capable of causing injury if not carefully operated.' Hence a requirement to fence dangerous machinery, though not expressed in terms of due care at all, may not in fact impose much of a burden over and above that of taking the due care.[2] Obviously, if machinery is only dangerous when injury from its use can be foreseen, it would not be a breach of the statute to omit to fence machinery which was not a foreseeable source of danger – and this is not very different from the ordinary requirements of the law of negligence. For another thing, contributory negligence and principles of remoteness of damage remain as limitations on liability for breach of statutory duty.

Moreover, many of the requirements imposed by statute or regulations are in fact no more than what reasonable care would require if only as much was known about accident causation by the reasonable man (or the courts) as by the appropriate government department. Industrial legislation imposing this or that requirement may not always appear to require only what is reasonable care: it may appear unnecessarily solicitous or 'fussy'. But this is often because the court or the reasonable man does not know how many accidents are caused by the omission to take the required precautions. The statutory requirements are often drawn up as a direct response to a serious accident rate in this or that area of industry.[3] Sometimes the main purpose of detailed legislation is to give the employer greater guidance as to what is required of him in the way of reasonable care; clearly in this event, the object is not to impose strict liability.

Whether an action for damages lies for breach of a statutory duty depends in theory on whether Parliament intended to confer a civil remedy when it created the duty. But this is pure theory, because it is only in very recent times that Parliament has ever paused to consider whether it wishes to confer such a remedy. In practice, the action for breach of statutory duty is almost entirely confined to industrial accidents. Factory legislation and mines legislation have long been held to confer an action for breach. This dates back to the last years of the last century when the first Workmen's Compensation Act was passed, and the whole question of industrial safety was a prominent subject of discussion.[4] There was little confidence at that time that the legislation was being adequately enforced, or could be adequately enforced by the government inspectors appointed under the Factories Act, and it may well be that these factors influenced the courts in their decision to impose civil liability for breach of duties of this nature.

Attempts to extend the action for breach of statutory duty to other situations have almost invariably been rebuffed. In particular, in 1923 the Court of Appeal refused to allow an action for breach of statutory duty for breach of the Ministry of Transport regulations relating to the construction and use of motor vehicles.[5] If a motorist takes reasonable care to maintain his vehicle – for example by having it regularly attended to by a reputable garage – and the vehicle develops some sudden failure of the brakes for instance, the motorist will not be guilty of negligence, though he may well be guilty of an offence under the regulations. The court refused to impose strict liability for breach of the statutory duty on the ostensible ground that Parliament did not 'intend' to confer a civil remedy. Perhaps the Court was influenced – consciously or unconsciously – by that fact that in 1923 it was still not compulsory to insure against third party liability, and the Court may have shrunk from imposing a form of liability without fault on individual motorists who might not have had the resources to meet a judgment for damages. Had this problem arisen after compulsory insurance was introduced in 1930 the result might have been different.

Much of the time spent by appellate courts in deciding on the proper interpretation of detailed provisions in industrial safety legislation is a waste, because the search for the correct interpretation assumes that small differences in wording between different provisions were intended by the legislator to reflect important considerations of policy, which they rarely, if ever, do.[6] More often they reflect either poor draftsmanship or a desire to cover every possible contingency.[7] The problem is exacerbated when provisions are held to concern not only safety standards but also entitlement to monetary compensation, because this encourages courts to search for an interpretation which allows compensation to be awarded in the particular case. A fresh approach is found in the Health and Safety at Work Act 1974. Under this Act broad statutory criteria will gradually replace the accumulated mass of detailed legislation currently in force.

But even if the courts were to look for policy considerations to guide their decisions as to whether compensation ought to be given in particular cases it would not be easy to find a rational legislative approach. The problem lies principally in the fact that the primary justification for strict liability for industrial accidents was to a large extent removed by the introduction of the industrial injuries system in 1948. The main justification for strict liability for industrial accidents is (in effect) that this is a form of insurance for the benefit of the workman at the expense of the employer, rather than that (as in theory with liability for negligence) the employer is in some way to blame or 'at fault' for the accident. An excellent case can be made for saying that workmen should be insured against industrial accidents, and that this should be wholly or partly paid for by employers; but this is precisely the rationale of the industrial injuries system. It is difficult enough to justify the continued existence of liability based on fault in industrial accidents, despite the existence of the industrial injuries system; but it is almost impossible to justify the continued existence of strict liability. This is why in 1946 the Monckton Committee on Alternative Remedies recommended (in effect) that, with the enactment of the Industrial Injuries Act of 1946, actions for breach of statutory duty should cease to be 'strict'. But this recommendation was never implemented by Parliament, and in consequence, the courts have had to approach the problem of interpreting industrial legislation against the background of an indefensible policy decision. Small wonder, then, that the courts have failed to evolve any consistent approach to the problem based on a clear and intelligible policy. A recent judicial pronouncement, by Lord Diplock in *Haigh* v. *Ireland*[9] suggests that the courts are now beginning to appreciate the true situation more clearly. In this case, Lord Diplock declared that the courts must resist the temptation to stretch the interpretation of industrial legislation in order to ensure the compensation of injured workmen. Compensation without fault, as he pointed out, is available under the industrial injuries system to all workmen injured in the course of their employment. Statutory provisions should, therefore, be interpreted without any bias in favour of injured workmen.

In relation to industrial injuries the action for breach of statutory duty would appear to be of great importance if one judged solely by the number of statutory duties imposed on employers in factories and mines and by the number of reported cases. We have seen that a very large proportion of all litigation is personal injury litigation, and that over half of this is industrial in origin (much depending on breach of statutory duty). Nevertheless, in practice the great bulk of employees suffering injury still appear to have no right of action at law; at any rate they do not in fact make claims for common law damages.[10] It is also noticeable that although there are so many 'strict' duties under industrial legislation, and very few under road safety legislation, a much greater proportion of road accident victims than industrial accident victims actually succeeds in recovering some tort damages.[10]

2 CONTRACTUAL DUTIES

The law of contract is primarily concerned with financial losses and not with physical damage or personal injury. But sometimes liability for such damage or injury can be established in a contractual suit. For example, the liability of a seller for injuries caused by dangerous goods does not depend on negligence, but on breach of contractual warranty. A seller of goods is generally held to 'warrant' that the goods he sells are neither dangerous nor defective. If they cause injury to the purchaser he can sue the seller without having to establish that the seller was negligent himself. And in modern retailing conditions it would often be very difficult to establish that a seller was negligent, because he merely acts as a distributor of goods which he could not examine because they are packed in sealed containers such as tins or bottles. And in other cases he could not hope to do more than satisfy himself of the good repute of the maker whose goods he buys, for they may be technical products of which the retailer may have no skilled or personal knowledge, such as electrical equipment. Even if he was skilled enough to examine the goods, it would often be impossible for him to do so in practice. Thus the liability imposed on the retail seller is in fact a fairly strict one – much stricter than that of the employer under most industrial legislation. If the goods actually cause damage or injury to the buyer, the seller can only escape liability in law by showing that the goods were not defective, or that it was the buyer's 'fault' that the accident occurred. Contributory negligence, as such, probably does not apply here, for it is a tort doctrine; but if the plaintiff's conduct was sufficiently foolhardy a court would probably reject his claim on the ground that he 'caused' his own injuries.

Why should a seller of goods be strictly liable for defects when the manufacturer is only liable to the consumer for negligence? At first sight this is an important question because only the actual *buyer* can sue the seller for breach of warranty; if the injury is caused to his wife, or child, or to a friend to whom he has made a gift of the goods, no such action can be brought, so that many users may be reduced to suing the manufacturer. However, in practice, the distinction may not be as important as it seems at first sight, because it is not easy to believe that a manufacturer could often escape liability for negligence in respect of damage done by a defective product[11] at any rate if the defect is one in the manufacture rather than the design of the product.[12] Defects are themselves fairly good evidence of negligence, though they may sometimes be explained away, and they may sometimes be due to components purchased from other manufacturers. If manufacturers are rendered strictly liable for damage caused by 'defects' in products, the definition of a 'defect' becomes crucial. If 'defective' is defined to mean 'unreasonably unsafe' then the liability is similar to negligence liability. At the other extreme, products could be defined as defective if they caused any damage. As we shall see below, so-called strict liability for defective products is about to be introduced in Britain.

3 RYLANDS *v.* FLETCHER, NUISANCE AND ANIMALS

Considerations of space forbid any attempt at detailed treatment of this part of the law of torts. It is enough here to note that liability for damage done by things escaping from land, or by dangerous animals, may occasionally be 'strict', in the sense that negligence need not be shown. But in practice the courts in England have emasculated these torts as torts of strict liability for damage to person or property. If one may judge from the dearth of reported cases, liability under the rule in *Rylands* v. *Fletcher* is almost obsolete in practice.[13] This is not surprising, because the restrictions on the application of the basic rule are so great, and the exceptions to the rule as conventionally formulated are so wide, that this form of liability is likely to be very rare in the absence of negligence. This is not to say, however, that strict liability for the escape of dangerous things might not be socially desirable. Witness the Bhopal disaster in India in 1984.

Nuisance, of course, is of considerable importance as a tort of 'strict' liability in the sense that interference with the comfort of neighbours may be a nuisance, even if all due care is taken to prevent that interference. Even here, however, the defendant may in a sense have been negligent if the concept of negligence is regarded as applying to the whole activity and not merely to the way it is carried out. When a court says that use of a particular piece of machinery, for example, is so noisy as to constitute a nuisance even though every care has been taken to minimize the noise, this is not necessarily an admission that liability in nuisance is 'strict'. Such a decision amounts to holding that the machinery is so inherently noisy that it must not be used at all – that is unreasonable to use it having regard to the harm it caused to the neighbours, nowithstanding the gain to the person using it. This does not look very different from the ordinary negligence formula. The only difference is that it involves application of that formula to the activity itself, and not to the way it is carried out. As we saw in a previous chapter the law of negligence, though in theory capable of being applied to negligence in the whole conduct of an activity – negligence in design as it were – is usually confined to negligence in operation. The peculiarity of the law of nuisance is that the law is concerned just as much with *what* a man does on his land, as with *how* he does it. Be this as it may, nuisance as a source of liability for damage *to person or property* is almost completely coincidental with negligence at the present day. The solitary survival of strict liability is the rule that an occupier may be liable for physical damage caused by non-repair of premises even though he neither knew nor had means of knowing that they were in disrepair.[14] But even here liability is rarely likely to be strict in practice; non-repair will normally connote negligence.

As to animals, the common law rules of strict liability were so drawn as to exclude the main forms of damage which animals actually cause, and the new Animals Act 1971 has not made much difference in this respect. No doubt the owner of a zoo from which a lion escapes will be liable for the damage it inflicts; and no doubt also, the owner of cattle which trespass on his neighbour's garden or crops will be liable even if no negligence is proved. But far more accidents resulting in personal injury are caused by dogs or other domestic animals on the roads[15] than by escaping lions, and here there is no liability without, and often not even with, negligence. And although trespassing cattle may well do a certain amount of damage to crops and such like every year, it will not often be the case that cattle trespass on another's land without negligence on the part of the owner. There are certainly quite a number of accidents involving bulls, mostly to those employed on farms, but the effect of the Animals Act 1971 on liability for such animals is obscure.[16]

4 JOINT LIABILITY

An instance of liability which in one sense may be said to be 'strict', and which is certainly of more practical importance than the strict liability of animal keepers, is to be found in the rules relating to 'joint liability'. This is a technical term, but we are using it in a non-technical sense to include all cases in which more than one person is liable for the same damage. The law on this subject has not received much attention from theorists, but it is of some interest. Briefly, it provides, first that all those responsible for committing a tort in concert are liable for *all* the damage, even though it may be possible to identify the contributions of each to the ultimate damage. And secondly, it provides that all those who by their negligence or other fault produce damage in combination (though not acting in concert), will be liable for all the damage, insofar as it is not possible to separate the contributions of each party.

The first principle applies, not only to those actually acting in concert, but also to cases in which one person assists or encourages another to commit the tort. If two people agree to beat up a third, then they are both liable in full for the injuries suffered by the plaintiff, even though it may be possible to identify one assailant as solely responsible for some of the injuries and the other as responsible for different injuries. This kind of liability is 'strict' in the sense that the defendant is held liable for damage which he may not even have caused 'in fact', since the damage may well have occurred 'but for' his assistance. Probably no other form of tort liability is as 'strict' as this.

The second principle covers the situation where two persons combine without design to produce damage; where, for example, two motorists by their negligence cause an accident in which a pedestrian is injured. It is impossible in this sort of case to quantify the damage done by each of the negligent motorists, and at common law there was no procedure at all whereby the responsibility could be shared between the motorists. The only difference between cases of acting in concert and cases of accidental combinations is that in the second case joint liability is not imposed if it is possible to separate the damage done by the different parties.

In both types of case the common law simply provided that both defendants were liable in full to the plaintiff, but whether he chose to sue one or the other, or both, was left to him; and likewise, if he obtained judgment against both, it was left to him to decide whether to enforce the judgment against one or other, or both. The law was changed by statute in 1935 (now replaced by the Civil Liability, (Contribution) Act 1978), so that it is now possible for one tortfeasor to claim contribution from another tortfeasor liable for the same damage. The amount of contribution is to be assessed by the court according to the share of the responsibility of the two parties. Despite this change in the law, no suggestion was ever made that the change could affect the *plaintiff's* position. He is still entitled to sue both parties, to obtain judgment in full against both and to enforce judgment against either or both, so long as he does not recover more than one amount by his judgment.

5 VICARIOUS LIABILITY

The type of liability we have just mentioned is not essentially dissimilar to vicarious liability – the liability of an employer for the negligence of his employees committed in the course of their employment. This is certainly 'strict', in the sense that the employer is liable however careful *he* may have been, though the liability requires the plaintiff to prove that he was injured by a tort committed by the workman. I defer further examination of this subject until a later chapter [17] because it is better understood as a loss distribution device than as a part of the traditional law of torts.

6 THE NATURE OF STRICT LIABILITY

Lawyers often talk as though 'strict liability' is an alternative to liability for fault, or negligence liability. The contrast seems so simple: liability for fault, liability without fault. And many discussions about law reform today centre around the desirability of extending 'strict liability'. But in order to understand the issues which arise in any discussion of the relative merits of negligence and strict liability, it is necessary to realize that 'strict liability' is *not* an alternative to negligence at all. 'Liability for fault' is an intelligible slogan, which is used to indicate that fault should generally be a necessary condition of liability. But 'liability without fault' merely eliminates fault as a necessary condition of liability; it does not put anything else in its place. Thus strict liability is not one possible alternative to liability for fault, but a collection of such alternatives.

The reason why this is not generally appreciated is that most people take it for granted that strict liability either is, or if extended into other fields, would be, based on 'cause in law'. For example, most people who advocate extending strict liability to motorists simply assume that a motorist would be held to have 'caused' an accident if he collided with a pedestrian, even without fault, and that he would therefore be liable under a strict liability régime. Similarly, a gas undertaking might be thought to 'cause' accidents arising through leaks from their pipes, and strict liability would simply make the gas undertaking liable for such accidents. This faith in the possibility of replacing fault by 'cause in law' overlooks the fact that few if any existing forms of strict liability are based on 'cause in law', if the standards of 'cause in law' are taken from the usages of ordinary speech. A zoo keeper whose lion escapes, despite all due care, is strictly liable for the damage it does, but he would not be said to have 'caused' the death of someone killed by the lion. Moreover, we have already seen that there are considerable difficulties in formulating principles of causation based on ordinary speech and in justifying legal liability on the basis of these principles.[18]

This is not to say that the concept of 'cause' may not in many cases identify the party who, as a matter of sound policy, ought to be made liable – as in the cases of the road accident or the gas leak mentioned above. But a possible criterion of liability which would cover both of these cases and that of the zoo keeper, and which expresses a sound policy, would be to ask which party could more easily bear and distribute (by insurance or other means) the losses caused by the accident. Clearly, for example, not only could the driver more easily insure against the risk than the pedestrian but also it is much easier to enforce compulsory insurance against motorists than it would be against pedestrians.

The line of reasoning, however, has important practical implications. It is true, for example, that a scheme imposing strict liability for road accidents caused without fault[19] would entitle more personal injury victims to claim compensation, but only if there were another motorist involved who could be held strictly liable. But many road accidents involve only one driver, for example where his car veers off the road and collides with a tree or perhaps another (stationary) car. Motorists as a group are just as able, via insurance, to bear and distribute the costs of such accidents as those of accidents involving more than one driver. It is arguments such as these which have led reformers towards 'no fault' compensation schemes under which entitlement to compensation depends on being injured and not on being able to find someone to sue.

Of course, the search for the best 'risk bearer' is not the only reason for extending strict liability. Another possible reason may be that placing the risk on one person rather than another, promotes the policy of reducing accidents. Full examination of all these objectives is deferred to Part 6 of this book. All that needs to be stressed at this stage is that extending 'strict liability' is not a positive programme for reform on its own. Nevertheless, there are a number of current proposals for extending strict liability, mostly emanating from the Pearson Report, and some of these deserve a mention.

7 PROPOSALS TO EXTEND STRICT LIABILITY

Dangerous things and activities

Under the guise of rationalizing and tidying up the present somewhat arbitrary and haphazard law of strict liability, the Pearson Commission made a set of proposals (in Chapter 31 of the Report) which, if implemented, would very greatly extend strict liability. The Commission proposed that there should be two new categories of strict liability introduced. First, the controllers of things or operations which, 'by their unusually hazardous nature require close, careful and skilled supervision' if the risk of personal injury is to be avoided, should be strictly liable. Secondly, the controllers of things or activities which, although normally perfectly safe, are likely 'if they do go wrong, to cause serious and extensive casualties', should also be strictly liable, not merely if there are in fact serious and extensive casualties, but if there is any injury caused which falls within the risk to be guarded against. The first category is designed to cover such things as explosives, imflammable gases and liquids; and the second, such things as large public bridges, dams, major stores and stadiums, and 'other buildings where large numbers of people may congregate'.

Unfortunately, the Commission appears to have paid inadequate attention to the implications of these proposals, nor did it really attempt any serious justification of them in principle. It seems clear that the Commission thought they were of rather minor importance, whereas in practice, their implementation would surely trigger off a huge amount of case-law. Either the limits of the proposals would be left to the courts to settle piecemeal, or they would have to be defined by statute or statutory instrument in a somewhat arbitrary fashion. But one is struck by some limitations inherent in the proposals. Why, for instance, does the second category cover only persons injured on 'large' public bridges, dams and so forth? What conceivable difference does it make to any rational being what size the bridge was which collapsed on top of him, or underneath him? Another difficulty arises from the proposal to cover buildings where large numbers of people may congregate, for this must surely include many factories and other work places. Yet it is clear that the Commission did not intend to introduce any new scheme of strict liability for industrial accidents. But the strongest argument against any attempt to rationalize the law along these lines is the impossibility of providing any rational criterion for deciding what things or activities are 'dangerous'. The problem is that by far the greatest number of accidents are not caused by things normally thought of as 'dangerous' at all, but by everyday things and activities, in particular, motoring. Really 'dangerous' things and activities in fact cause far fewer accidents, no doubt because they are generally strictly controlled by regulatory statutes and other precautions. It is also exceedingly difficult to provide any general criterion of dangerousness, because one cannot measure how dangerous a thing or activity is without some agreed exposure rate; and it is not easy to compare exposure rates for different activities and things. How, for instance, can one compare the dangerousness of (say) petrol, with that of motor cars?

The truth is that these proposals of the Commission were ill-thought out and are unlikely to be implemented.

Products liability

The area in which proposals for strict liability have borne most fruit is that of defective and dangerous products. Both the Law Commission[20] and the Pearson Commission[21] proposed an extension of strict liability in this field. In July 1985, the Council of the European Communities adopted a Directive[22] (which Member States have three years to implement) along similar lines to the proposals of the UK bodies. As indicated earlier, the basic stimulus to reform here has been the anomalous distinction between the contractual rights of the buyer against the seller (which already impose strict liability), and the rights, in tort, of the buyer or other third parties, against the seller or manufacturer (which depend on negligence). It is widely felt that manufacturers should be taken to warrant the safety of their products simply by putting them into circulation, and that a person injured by some dangerous product should not be required to prove negligence. A further stimulus to reform was provided by the Thalidomide tragedy, which highlighted the difficulty facing consumers in cases where (as in that case) they are required to prove that the manufactuer was negligent in testing or marketing the drug.

It is, at this stage, very unclear how important this change in the law will prove to be. First, the Directive provides that a product is defective

when it does not provide the safety which a person is entitled to expect, taking all circumstances into account, including: (a) the presentation of the product; (b) the use to which it could reasonably be expected that the product would be put; (c) the time when the product was put into circulation.

Under the present law, it would usually be negligent to market a product which was defective in this sense. Secondly, the Directive preserves the defence of contributory negligence. Thirdly, the Directive allows the producer to plead 'that the state of scientific and technical knowledge ["the state of the art"] at the time when he put the product into circulation was not such as to enable the defect to be discovered [*query*, by reasonable efforts].' This provision is designed to protect drug manufacturers, for example, by relieving them of liability for so-called 'development risks'. Since it was the very existence of the development risk defence which cast most doubt over the claims of the Thalidomide victims, little progress appears to have been made.

Fourthly, although it is clear that the new regime covers defects in the design of products as well as in their manufacture, it does not follow that the courts will be any more willing to entertain (and, therefore, that litigants will be any more inclined to present) arguments that a product was defective in design, than they are at present. Manufacturers who have opposed the new regime have been influenced by the position in the United States, where 'strict liability' is the rule in most jurisdictions and where, in recent years, the cost of products liability and liability insurance has become very high, and allegedly insupportable for many businesses. But this appears to be the result not so much of the rules of liability, but more of the very high level of litigation (which also affects areas, such as medical malpractice, which are based on negligence), of the size of jury awards, and of greater willingness of US courts to decide design issues. According to the Pearson Commission, some 30,000 to 40,000 persons are injured each year in Britain as a result of defects in products (other than drugs). At present, some 5% of these may recover some tort compensation.[23] Clearly, if the remaining 95% claimed as well, the costs of product liability would soar. But it is unlikely that the new regime will generate a large volume of claims.

Assuming that the new liability is more strict than the present law, the change, viewed within the present framework of tort law, might be thought justifiable and desirable. It might assist a small number of injured persons to obtain compensation who cannot at present do so. But in a wider context of assisting victims of personal injury, it is not clear that such extensions of tort liability are really desirable. As the Pearson Commission itself pointed out, the total number of product-caused injuries accounts for some 1% of all accidental injuries.[24] Even if every victim of product-caused injury were given tort rights, this would not help the remaining 99% of these injury victims, very few of whom recover tort damages. Whether it is desirable to reform the law by giving generous tort rights to small numbers of additional victims, rather than by better social and overall provision for all the disabled, is a question dealt with in some detail in Chapter 25.

Railway accidents

The Pearson Commission have proposed a modest extension of strict liability for railway accidents. Their proposal is that railway undertakings should be strictly liable in tort for death or personal injury caused wholly or partly by the movement of rolling stock.[25] Virtually no justification is given for these proposals, other than the statement that certain aspects of the operation of railways can be characterized as inherently hazardous. This argument seems to echo those relating to exceptional risks in general, and it is open to many of the same criticisms. One starts with the paradox that the movement of rolling stock only causes a minority of the accidents; most railway accidents arise from activities not normally thought of as hazardous at all, such as lifting or moving goods (among railway staff), slipping, or tripping on railway steps (among passengers and staff).[26] It is not obvious why a minority of accident victims should be better treated in the matter of compensation, on the ground that they have been injured by more hazardous activities, when in fact it seems that these more hazardous activities actually account for fewer accidents than the less hazardous ones. It is also to be noted that more than half of the injuries incurred on railway lines are suffered by railway staff,[27] who are, of course, entitled to the benefit of the industrial injury side of the social security scheme. Why should these workers also be entitled to the protection of a strict liability regime, merely because railways are hazardous, when other factory and industrial workers, who also often work with dangerous machinery, are not? On what possible principle can one justify strict liability for railway workers but not (say) for coal miners?

Vaccine damage

In recent years there has been some evidence that children very occasionally suffer severe brain damage as a result of a vaccination, in particular, vaccination against whooping cough. It is difficult to establish causation with any certainty in such cases because, as a medical committee has pointed out,[28] small children not infrequently develop convulsions for the first time in the first two years of life, and by chance some of these attacks will follow routine vaccinations. An Association of Parents of Vaccine Damaged Children was set up some years ago, which told the Pearson Commission that it had registered 356 cases of vaccine-damaged children. The Association pleaded for some form of strict tort liability to be introduced to help such children, mainly on the ground that child vaccination has for many years been recommended by the Government. Moreover, vaccination is a classic case of the 'free-rider' problem much discussed by economists. The benefit to each individual child of being vaccinated may not be very great in view of the fact that most other children are likely to be vaccinated, and that the risk of infection has been thus greatly reduced; yet if the parents of all children reasoned in this way, vaccination would decline and the diseases would spread more widely again, with greater risk to all. Further (although the Pearson Commission failed to make this point), the main beneficiary from vaccination is often not the child himself, but a baby brother or sister. The point is that whooping cough is most dangerous for very young babies, prior to the normal age for vaccination; by the time a child is vaccinated it is normally past the age at which the disease could prove fatal. There is thus a strong emotional and moral case for arguing that young children who are vaccinated before they are old enough to understand the issues are being used for the benefit of others.

The imposition of strict liability on drug manufacturers would not meet the problem, because it is not clear that the product itself is defective. In the result, the Pearson Commission proposed that there should be strict liability in tort on the Government or local authority where a vaccine was given following a recommended programme for which the Government or local authority was responsible. However, the political pressure on this issue was so great that the Government felt forced to announce some concession even before the Commission reported, and it promised a lump sum payment of £10,000 to any child who could be shown to have suffered severe injury as a result of a vaccination against any one of a large number of ailments. Effect was given to this promise in the Vaccine Damage Payments Act 1979, though this was treated as an interim measure without prejudice to the possible acceptance of full Government liability in tort. The introduction of such liability now seems unlikely, and in 1985 the Secretary of State was empowered by legislation to increase the amount of the lump sum payment.[29] It has been increased to £20,000.

Once again, the adoption of a form of strict liability might seem acceptable within the framework of the tort system, though this is an unusual case in that the Government's responsibility is somewhat marginal. But why should children disabled in this particular way be treated so generously in a financial sense, as compared with other disabled children? The Pearson Commission estimated that there were some 100,000 severely disabled children in the country, of whom probably 90% were suffering from congenital defects. Why do 356 vaccine-damaged children have a better claim to financial support than other disabled children? In the Pearson Report, the following two paragraphs raise more questions than they answer:

1406. ... The overriding need is that, where there is serious damage, there

should be prompt recognition that some form of compensation should be payable. We do not think it is right to try to distinguish one severely disabled child from another, and to produce a situation where two children have the same needs, but one is compensated and the other is not. We decided, therefore, that vaccine-damaged children should be considered with other severely disabled children, irrespective of the cause of disablement . . .
1407. For those children who can be shown to have been victims of vaccine damage, we consider that there is a case for an additional remedy in the field of tort.

Later in the Report, there is a proposal for a general social security benefit for disabled children. One is left with the uncomfortable feeling that vaccine-damaged children are to be given more generous financial treatment because their parents have been able to mount an effective campaign, and for no other reason. There are signs that this sort of disturbing ad hoc, politically-motivated approach to compensation issues, is common.[30]

7 Damages for personal injuries and death

1 THE LUMP SUM

Predicting the future

Damages in a tort action are awarded in a lump sum. The award is made once for all, and there is – except in very rare cases – no possibility of increasing it or decreasing it later because of changes in the situation. In the great majority of cases where the injuries are relatively minor this raises no real problem. In these cases the plaintiff is likely to be completely recovered and back at work long before the damages are assessed, and the whole episode is by then past history. But the lump sum remedy does raise acute problems wherever serious injuries – whose effects may still be felt long after the damages are assessed – are suffered. The Pearson Commission estimated that about 7½% of all tort claims (including claims in fatal cases) involved future earnings losses after the trial or settlement of the claim;[1] and these are the claims which raise problems with lump sums. In cases of this nature the judge has to make two wholly different sets of predictions at the date of trial in order to calculate an appropriate sum. First, he has to predict *what would have happened* to the plaintiff if he had not been injured, a prediction which obviously cannot be verified or falsified by subsequent events. Secondly, the judge has to predict what is now likely to happen to the plaintiff. For example, he may have to make a prognosis as to the probable outcome of the plaintiff's injuries: will the plaintiff make a complete recovery? If so, how long will it take? If not, what residual degree of disability may there be? How will this affect the plaintiff's earning capacity? Will the plaintiff suffer further pain and discomfort? Will he die sooner than he might have done otherwise? In the case of certain types of injury there is always a risk of complications in the future, e.g. epilepsy is almost always a risk in brain damage cases, and arthritis is a common risk wherever bones are severely fractured. These risks are often low (e.g. the risk of epilepsy following brain damage is often put at one in ten), but lump-sum damage awards must take account of the risk. This means that the judge must calculate what sum would be appropriate if the risk materialized, and then award a fraction of this sum proportional to the risk occurring. Obviously the task of predicting the future is extremely difficult, and nobody can blame the judges if they often go wrong in their predictions – though nobody knows how accurate their predictions are because no research has ever been done into this problem.[2] But it is highly unsatisfactory that, given the extreme difficulty of the task, there is hardly ever any opportunity for making a subsequent correction. If a judge thinks the plaintiff will make a complete recovery and he is proved wrong, the plaintiff simply gets less damages that he should have got. Conversely, he may get far more. In 'chance' cases (such as those involving risk of epilepsy) the problem is, if anything, even worse, because the lump-sum award is bound to be wrong. If the risk eventuates, the amount awarded will be too little; if it does not, too much. There is no possibility here of the judge making an inspired guess and hitting the right sum.

These difficulties are sometimes aggravated by the phenomenon of 'compensation neurosis'. This well authenticated and not uncommon medical condition – which must be distinguished from conscious malingering – tends to prolong the period of rehabilitation and convalescence until after trial or settlement of a tort claim. Anxiety over the damages which may be recovered is so great as to postpone complete recovery. The same phenomenon has been observed in connection with claims for compensation from the Criminal Injuries Compensation Board.[3] Apart from being a deplorable by-product of the once-for-all lump-sum damages award, this condition can cause great problems for assessing damages. If the judge assumes certain disabilities to be permanent and they vanish overnight, the plaintiff will have been over-compensated; if conversely the judge thinks the case is one of 'compensation neurosis' and wrongly assumes the disability will become better after the trial, the plaintiff may be undercompensated.[4]

To some extent these difficulties of prediction can be, and are, mitigated by postponing the trial of the action until a prediction about the ultimate outcome can be made with greater confidence. Indeed, in many cases of serious injury it is essential to do this because *no* satisfactory predictions can be made at all until many months at least after the injuries were incurred. But postponing the trial (or settlement) of cases has its own evils; indeed, the delay in actually securing payment under the tort system is one of the major causes of dissatisfaction with it. It may be possible to reduce these delays in ways which will be considered later, but plainly the delay cannot be reduced to a point at which the exact nature and extent of the plaintiff's injuries cannot be predicted at all.

Postponement of the trial or settlement of the claim will not, in any event, solve many of the problems which arise. For example, there are many cases in which even when a reasonably firm medical prognosis can be given, the effect of a man's injuries on his future working prospects must remain problematical until long after the time at which a settlement or trial of his claim must be reached. Take a random example from the Law Reports, *Rowden* v. *Clarke Chapman & Co. Ltd*.[5] The plaintiff had been a steel erector before the injury which cost him the little finger of his right hand, and weakened the grip of the hand as a whole. He was unable to follow his normal employment and decided to retrain as a welder. At the time of trial he was awaiting a vacancy at a government retraining centre. About a fifth of those took this course failed to complete it. The judge was therefore obliged to predict, first, if the plaintiff would complete this course, and secondly, what he could hope to earn in a new trade which he had never practised before. The evidence as to the average earnings of a welder was not very helpful because it merely confirmed what one would expect, that conditions and wages varied widely from place to place, and that special 'plum' jobs were available which the plaintiff might secure. Naturally, the attempt to calculate what the plaintiff was likely to lose was not easy. It took a High Court Judge and two experienced counsel the better part of three days in court to deal with this case (though it would be unusual to spend so much time on quantum alone), and this takes no account of the considerable expense which must have been incurred by both parties to the litigation before the trial even started.

To some extent the courts have tried to get over the difficulties caused by the need to make predictions in the assessment of damages. Although in strict law the assessment of damages in most cases should be related to the time of injury, because that is when the 'cause of action' vests in the plaintiff, the courts have always very sensibly insisted that what happens between the date of the accident and the date of the trial must be taken into account in assessing the damages. Thus, lost earnings suffered between the accident and the trial will be calculated, not guessed. And increases in wage rates during this period will become the basis of the assessment of damages for expected future earnings losses.

Variation of awards after trial

Very occasionally, it may be possible to vary an award as a result of changes in circumstances occurring after the trial – at least where they occur soon after the trial. Since the facts are looked at as at the date of the trial, appellate courts have not shrunk from saying that, in the event of an appeal, the facts must be looked at as at the date of the appeal. But notice of appeal must normally be given within a specified time – usually six weeks in a High Court case, twenty-one days in the County Court – and there is therefore little opportunity in the ordinary case for taking new facts into account on appeal. However, the Court of Appeal does have power to extend the time within which an appeal may be entered by granting 'leave to appeal out of time'. This power is discretionary and is not often exercised, but it can be used to increase an award of damages where new facts come to light very soon after the trial. For example, in *Murphy* v. *Stone Wallwork Ltd*[6] where damages had been assessed on the assumption that the plaintiff was still capable of continuing in his former employment, the award was re-opened and increased, when the plaintiff was dismissed as soon as the case was over. Similarly, in *Mitchell* v. *Mulholland*[7] the House of Lords allowed evidence to be given that shortly after the trial it became clear that the plaintiff would have to be maintained in a nursing home, at substantial cost; the assessment of damages at the trial had been made on the assumption that the plaintiff would remain at home.

Of greater potential importance is a new provision in the Supreme

Court Act 1981 (Section 32A) which is designed to deal with the 'chance' cases mentioned above. The provision deals with cases in which 'there is proved or admitted to be a chance that at some definite or indefinite time in the future the injured person will ... develop some disease or suffer some deterioration in his physical or mental condition'. It applies to both the High Court and the County Court, and allows rules of court to be made enabling damages to be awarded in the first instance on the assumption that the plaintiff will not develop the disease or suffer the deterioration, and allowing further damages to be awarded at a later date if the disease or deterioration occurs. It is unclear what the impact of this provision will be. The Lord Chancellor said in Parliament that he did not imagine that the provision would be used very often, and then only if the plaintiff wanted it and it would not cause serious prejudice to the defendant.[8] In *Mitchell* v. *Mulholland* the House of Lords stressed the need for finality in litigation and the undesirability of reopening awards of damages save in very exceptional cases. Furthermore, the provision is unlikely to have much effect on the vast majority of cases which are settled out of court. It is unlikely that insurance companies would settle a case except on the basis that the settlement was final.

It will be noted that this provision only allows awards to be increased, not decreased. This asymmetry in favour of the plaintiff is usually thought of as required by considerations of fairness. In practice, too, it would be very difficult to secure repayment of part of the lump sum if the plaintiff had spent it or invested it in a fixed asset such as a house or a business; but if repayment were only required if he had invested in liquid assets such as shares, plaintiffs would have a strong incentive to deal with their damages in other (and perhaps less prudent) ways.

It can be seen, then, that such techniques as the above are of limited value in dealing even with cases of change in the plaintiff's medical condition; and they do not deal at all with other sources of difficulty in assessing the lump sum.

Fatal cases

There are two quite different types of actions which may be brought in respect of the death of a person as the result of some tortious act of the defendant. The oldest type is the dependency[9] action which lies under the Fatal Accidents Act 1976 (a descendant of the original Act of

1846). This action is primarily designed to provide compensation for the lost income of a breadwinner who was formerly maintaining members of his family, normally a wife and children. An action of this kind is brought by the dependants in their own name, in respect of their own loss of financial support resulting from the death. It is still necessary for the dependants to prove that the deceased died as a result of a tort, and any damages awarded will be reduced if the deceased himself was guilty of contributory negligence. The action provides compensation not only for an actual dependant, but also for a prospective dependant, so long as he falls within the list of persons entitled to sue under the Act. Thus, a parent may be able to sue in respect of the death (say) of a son of 16 who has not yet contributed anything to his parent's support but who might have been expected to do so in future. But not everybody has dependants, and no claim can be brought under the Fatal Accidents Act except by an actual or a prospective dependant.

The second type of claim is one which lies under the Law Reform (Miscellaneous Provisions) Act 1934, which was discussed earlier in connection with the topic of mental distress. Under this Act a claim for damages lies on behalf of the estate of a person killed, and such a claim may be brought whether or not the deceased had any dependants. The only damages recoverable in such an action are for pecuniary and non-pecuniary losses suffered by the deceased between the accident and death, plus funeral expenses. In most cases such an action would be brought concurrently with an action under the Fatal Accidents Act, since the dependants of the deceased and the beneficiaries under his will will usually be the same people.

The mode of assessment for damages in claims under the Fatal Accidents Act was recently reviewed by the House of Lords in *Cookson v. Knowles*[10] where it was held that the award of damages for loss of support should be made in two parts, the first covering the period from the date of death to the trial, and the second, from the date of trial into the future. The first part of the award will normally be based on the actual earnings which would have been received by the deceased during the pre-trial period. A proportion of this sum is awarded representing the amount the deceased would have spent on supporting others.

The second part of the award is harder to calculate. Assessment of compensation in fatal cases involves the same two sets of predictions as must be made in cases of long-term injuries. It is necessary to start by predicting what would have happened to the deceased if he had not been killed. In particular an assessment must be made of what his earnings prospects were. As Lord Diplock said in *Cookson* v. *Knowles*, the court is required to make assumptions 'as to the hypothetical degree of likelihood that all sorts of things might happen in an imaginary future in which the decease lived on and did not die. What in the event would have been the likelihood of his continuing in work until the usual retiring age? Would his earnings have been terminated by death or disability before the usual retiring age or interrupted by unemployment or ill-health? Would they have increased, and if so, when and by how much? To what extent, if any, would he have passed on the benefit of any increases to his wife and dependent children? Would she have have gone to work when the children had grown older and made her own contribution to the family expenses in relief of his?' And so on.

The second set of predictions (i.e. about what will now happen in the future) generally causes less difficulty in fatal cases, apart from one very troublesome point. Obviously a lot of predictions required about the prospects of a living plaintiff are not relevant in a fatal accident claim. But there has been a great deal of difficulty about the problem of remarriage by a widow. Most fatal accident claims are brought by widows, with or without additional claims by dependent children. Prior to 1971 it was the accepted rule that the damages had to be reduced to take account of the re-marriage prospects of the widow[11]; and, *a fortiori*, they had to be reduced where (as is by no means uncommon) the widow had actually remarried before the trial of her action. The application of this rule had considerable effect on claims by young widows, especially widows without children, but much less effect on the claims of older widows, especially those with several children. The rule was based on the simple idea that damages in a fatal accident case, as in all other tort claims, are designed to compensate for a *loss*. The damages given to a widow are designed to replace the share of the income of her former husband which was devoted to her maintenance. When the widow remarries she will often make good her loss, and accordingly, the fact or prospect of remarriage must be taken into account in reducing the damages.

However, many people found the rule distasteful.[12] Women's organizations argued that there was a 'cattle market' element in the valuation of remarriage prospects,[13] and in 1971 a provision was passed to the effect that the fact or prospects of remarriage of a widow in a fatal accidents claim are now to be wholly ignored.[14] This must be one of the most irrational pieces of law 'reform' ever passed by Parliament. It would be as sensible to require a divorced husband to maintain his wife after she has remarried, or for the State to pay widows' pensions after remarriage. An extreme example of the situation this created occurred in 1974, when a young widow of 25 who had remarried an 'oil man with a five figure salary' was awarded £65,000 in damages for the death of her first husband two years earlier.[15] It is hard to see what purpose an award of damages has at all in a case of this kind, except possibly to cover some short period after the husband's death. The real complaint against this kind of piecemeal law reform is that it involves extraordinary generosity to one group of accident victims without regard to the needs of others. In the case referred to above, for example, the deceased man was killed in a motor collision with a car driven by another man who was also killed. Since the latter was clearly at fault his dependants (if any) would have recovered no damages at all, though they would probably have been in much greater need than the plaintiff.

The proper answer to the problems raised by remarriage of widows is to pay them compensation in the form of periodical payments rather than a lump sum. The payments can then be reviewed as circumstances change, and can be ended if the widow remarries.[16] But even this does not wholly dispose of the problems arising from the remarriage of widows. Obviously, if widows' compensation takes the form of periodical payments which come to an end on remarriage, there is a temptation for widows to avoid remarriage and enter into less formal relationships. Consequently, the social security legislation (where analogous problems have to be dealt with) meets this danger by providing that widows' pensions also end on cohabitation; and the cohabitation rule has been much vilified as involving an intrusion into the private lives of widows. The best solution to the problem is found in the industrial injuries scheme, which provides for a lump sum (a 'widow's dowry') to be paid on the widow's remarriage. This provides an incentive to the widow to remarry rather than to indulge in 'cohabitation', and removes the element of harshness which might be thought to be involved in abrupt termination of the pension. It is a sad commentary on the ignorance of many lawyers of the social security system that in the House of Commons debate on the Pearson Report in November 1978, some members criticized the references to the possibility of awarding a widow's dowry on the ground that the reference to a dowry showed how old-fashioned the Commission was.[17] They clearly had no notion that both the concept and the term are widely used in the social security system.

One of the strangest features about the difficulties encountered by the law in dealing with compensation for widows is that the law is already perfectly well acquainted with the system of periodical payments in matrimonial cases. One of the most striking features of the matrimonial jurisdiction is that the amounts payable can be varied as the situations of the parties change. If the wife remarries, or if she secures a better job, or inherits a large fortune from her father, the amount of maintenance payable by a husband or ex-husband, can be reduced; conversely if the husband's income goes up, it can be increased. There is no need for the court to guess or make predictions about the future.

Death of her husband may not only make it possible for a woman to remarry but also to go (back) to work. The law requires 'gains' resulting from the death to be set off against losses, but it is not clear in England to what extent actual earnings or the prospect of earnings are in practice set off against the damages awarded. In Australia the courts take the view that the death of a husband does not revive the wife's ability to work since marriage does not prevent a wife working. And if the fact that there were children prevented the wife working, the death of the husband does not alter this. So neither actual nor potential post-death earnings are taken into account in assessing the widow's damages.[18] This approach, too, can clearly be attacked as overly generous although the disincentive to work which would be generated by the opposite approach might be thought undesirable (even in times of high unemployment) and harder to overcome than the disincentive to remarriage.

It is worth noting that damages under the Fatal Accidents Act can include compensation for the value of the household services of a person killed by tortious conduct. Thus a husband may obtain damages for the value of his wife's lost services,[19] and similarly, a child whose mother is killed may obtain damages for the value of her services to him;[20] so even though she may not have been in employment, the death of a wife and mother can now give rise to quite large claims for damages. It has been held that it is the wife's services which must be valued, excluding any element of emotional or loving support; but on the other hand, account must be taken of the fact that a wife and mother's services may be available twenty-four hours a day to her own family.[21] There has been a certain amount of discussion of how to value such household services.[22] Two possible measures suggest themselves: replacement cost (that is, the cost of hiring someone to perform the services) and opportunity cost (that is, the amount the housekeeper could have earned in paid employment). Neither measure is entirely satisfactory. In some respects a paid domestic helper can never replace a mother, for example. If the person who performed the services has been out of the workforce for a long time, or is unskilled, the opportunity cost measure might not be very useful, and will, at all events, only establish a minimum value for the services. The courts appear not to have adopted either measure as an invariable rule, but rather seek to assess the 'reasonable value of the services'. But, in the absence of any objective price-fixing mechanism, this approach is essentially arbitrary.

Suitability of lump sums

Quite apart from the possibility of varying the amounts payable, there is the additional question whether a lump sum is an appropriate method of compensation for lost earnings – whatever the arguments may be about other heads of damage, such as pain and suffering and loss of 'amenities'. It is true that if the trial or settlement is delayed long enough, all the lost earnings may be a matter of past history and a lump sum award may be quite appropriate; but where lost earnings are still to be anticipated, or where the action is brought by dependants of someone killed in an accident, a large part of the award is for future loss, and it is hard to see that it is appropriate to compensate for this by a lump-sum payment. A lump sum could, of course, be invested to provide an income or used to purchase an annuity, but in practice the sums awarded for lost earnings, even if invested wisely and successfully, would often, especially in times of high inflation, be insufficient to provide an income of the order of that which has been lost. In any event, the recipients may be quite inexperienced in the handling of large sums of money, and they may dissipate or mismanage the money, or fall a prey to confidence tricksters or invest it in reckless and hopeless enterprises. They are, of course, 'entitled' to do this if they wish, but since the money is largely found by society, and since society will have to bear the burden – or some of the burden – of maintaining these people if they should be reduced to utter proverty again, society has some right to say how the compensation should be paid. It is noticeable that nearly all social security payments are made in the form of periodical weekly sums, even though no question arises in most of these cases of an increase or a decrease in the amount as a result of a change of circumstances.

There is in fact very little evidence as to how wisely or unwisely, successfully or unsuccessfully, large awards of damages are actually used or invested by the recipients. The Criminal Injuries Compensation Board has noted that where it makes an interim award, it not infrequently finds that the award is all gone by the time a final award is due.[23] The Pearson Commission found that only about 20% of recipients made any attempt to use their damages for investment, or treated it as capital; most spent the money on current expenses.[24] On the other hand, most of these sums were fairly small (the average was around £250) so this would not necessarily have been a profligate use of the damages. Overseas experience of similar problems is not very encouraging.[25]

Research recently conducted for the New South Wales Law Reform Commission confirms that a significant number of recipients of lump sums have inadequate income from their awards to meet their expenses. In some cases this is the result of mismanagement of the lump sum award by the recipient or unwise investment (e.g. in a house which generates no income, or in low-yield riskless securities). But in other cases it is due to factors entirely outside the recipient's control, such as inflation or an unexpected deterioration in his medical condition. One survey concluded that recipients of high awards who had managed to re-establish themselves in a comfortable and secure fashion had typically benefited from some combination of personal skill and enterprise, good fortune, good advice, and support from family and friends. In cases under the Fatal Accident Act brought on behalf of a widow or dependent children, neither the income nor the capital of damages awarded for the children will normally be paid out of court to the widow except where this is shown to be necessary for the children's own benefit, e.g. to defray school fees, etc. Awards to children are generally paid out to them as soon as they come of age, but in extreme cases the court may press the infant to agree to settle the money on trust.[26] No stranger example could be found of the fundamentally inconsistent philosophies which underlie the social security system and the tort system, and which have somehow managed to co-exist for twenty years. As long ago as 1944, the government declared that they did 'not regard lump sum payments even if administered under strict control as a satisfactory method of assuring an income',[27] and this has remained one of the basic features of the modern welfare state.

Periodical payments under tort law?

There are formidable difficulties in any attempt to alter the law so that damages could be awarded in the form of periodical payments. Even if such an alteration was confined to awards above a certain figure, so that smaller sums could still be paid outright, as is done with minor disability payments under the industrial injuries scheme, the real difficulty would be that of dealing with settlements rather than with trial court awards. To deal with the latter, and ignore the former, would be to deal with only a small fraction of the cases. To deal with settlements as well, however, would involve interference with freedom of contract, as well as requiring some machinery for cases which at present never come into court at all, and which might swamp the courts if they did. The Law Commission, after a full inquiry, came to the conclusion that a system of periodical payments could not be fitted into the existing tort framework.[28] Nevertheless, the majority of the Pearson Commission recommended that a system of damages to be paid by periodical payments should be introduced for serious cases and fatal cases.[29] The Commission proposed that the courts should have power to award damages either as a lump sum, or in the form of periodical payments; and that in the latter case, the amounts should be inflation-proofed and variable if the plaintiff's medical condition subsequently changed. But they refrained from insisting that all settlements of fatal and serious cases should be in this form. Parties would remain free to settle for lump sums, though the Commission thought that plaintiffs might increasingly become aware of the desirability of settling for periodical payments.

One thing which emerges clearly from the Pearson Report is that there are very few cases which would be affected by a change in the law such as they recommend. Of the 215,000 cases per annum in which some tort compensation is payable the Report suggests that only some 2,200, or under 1% are actually tried,[30] though no doubt a substantial proportion of these are serious and fatal cases. Moreover, the insurance survey carried out for the Commission showed that in November 1973 some 98·7% of all tort claimants received under £5,000 in damages, and 95·4% received under £2,000.[31] Allowing for inflation since 1973, it would still seem that only just over 1% of claimants receive damages in excess of £12,000 and that less than 5% receive more than about £4,000. Further, a substantial proportion of these sums would not be compensation for loss of earnings but would be in respect of non-pecuniary loss; and it is generally recognized that there is no case for periodical payments for damages of this character.[32] It is unlikely that it would be felt worth while to award damages by way of periodical payments, in lieu of lump sums, unless the lump-sum equivalent would be at least £6,000. But on these figures, it seems that there are only about 2,000 cases a year all told in which damages are awarded for loss of earnings exceeding £6,000;[33] and of these the great majority will continue to be settled. Judging from the Pearson Report, it would seem that perhaps one quarter of these cases might actually be tried.[34] Thus, the whole of this proposed change in the law would, it seems, affect at most perhaps 600 claimants per annum; though this would be a cumulative figure, so that after 20 years, some 12,000 persons might be in receipt of tort periodical payments. In the light of these figures, it does seem much more questionable whether the proposed change is worth the great cost and complexity which would undoubtedly be entailed.

2 FULL COMPENSATION

The tort system is perhaps the only compensation system which professes to make 'full compensation'. All losses – all pecuniary losses, anyway – must be compensated for in full. 'Full compensation' – but only for those who can prove a tort. Thus runs the conventional doctrine of tort law. A wife who was dependent on her husband is entitled to compensation for the lost dependency – irrespective of whether she can now go out to work. A man who has lost wages is entitled to those lost wages – even though he has not had to earn them. An injured person is entitled to be compensated for everything he has suffered – lost earnings, pain, lost pleasures (past and future), out of pocket expenses, and so on. He must also be compensated for all possible ill-effects of the injury; for example, the risk of subsequent medical complications, possible reduction in marriage prospects, possible loss of employment prospects, and so on. From time to time, it has been said that 'full compensation' does not mean 'perfect' or 'absolute' compensation; and that the compensation must only be 'fair' or 'reasonable'. But it seems that these remarks have been directed to the question of assessing compensation for non-pecuniary losses where 'full compensation' would be meaningless; they are not intended to suggest any qualification of the principle that the plaintiff is entitled to full compensation for all his pecuniary losses. Indeed, in *Lim Poh Choo* v. *Camden Health Authority*,[35] in which record damages of £250,000 were awarded, the majority of the Court of Appeal and, on appeal, the House of Lords, specifically rejected Lord Denning's argument that it would be unfair and unreasonable to award damages for loss of earnings if the plaintiff was in no position to benefit from them (because she was unconscious), had no dependants to support, and had been awarded adequate damages to cover the cost of caring for her.

An extreme example of the 'full compensation' principle at work is *Davies* v. *Whiteways Cyder*,[36] which was an action under the Fatal Accidents Act. The deceased in this case was a wealthy man who had made gifts of some £40,000 to a child; his death within seven years of the gift meant that estate duty of some £17,000 became payable. It was held that this was recoverable as an additional item of damages. The decision becomes even more remarkable when it is noted that a risk of this nature is commonly insured against by persons who have made substantial capital donations in their lifetime, but that if in this case there had been any insurance to cover the contingency, it would not have been deducted from the damages. The Fatal Accidents Act specifically provides that no account is to be taken of any life insurance proceeds in the assessment of damages.[37]

Davies v. *Whiteways Cyder* is, no doubt, an exceptional case, but the principle for which it stands – that injured plaintiffs are in general entitled to be fully compensated for their losses – is applied generally throughout the law of tort and contract, and is seen by common lawyers as a corollary of the fault principle. This principle requires a detailed examination of the particular situation of the individual plaintiff. It is often claimed as an advantage of the tort system that it deals uniquely with the individual plaintiff, though it is somewhat paradoxical that many of those dissatisfied with it complain about its inadequacy to deal with the individual case.[38] But more important than this is the overall context, because (as we shall see) although there are many other ways besides tort of compensating personal injury victims, no other system professes to make full compensation. Thus, every tort victim who actually succeeds in obtaining damages is – as compared with the great majority of injured and disabled persons – exceptionally fortunately placed in a financial sense. It is against this background that one has to judge the desirability of maintaining the integrity of the 'full compensation' principle. And it is also against this background that proposals for the extension of the tort remedy (for example, by expansion of strict liability) have to be considered. Every extension of the tort system means a small increase in the proportion of personal injury victims obtaining 'full compensation' (estimated at some 6½% by the Pearson Commission). There will thus be a few more winners in the forensic lottery; but for the losers these extensions of tort liability will, of course, do nothing.

Damages are customarily awarded under two heads: 'special damages' and 'general damages'. This distinction is based on the difference between losses which are precisely measurable and quantifiable, and those which are not. Special damages are thus confined to out of pocket expenses and loss of earnings incurred before the trial. Damages for loss of earnings likely to be incurred in the future, plus damages for non-pecuniary losses – whether incurred before or after the trial – such as pain and suffering and loss of amenities, are awarded together as general damages. It was formerly customary to award a global figure for general damages so that it was usually impossible to say how much was intended for future loss of earnings, and how much for pain and suffering and loss of amenities.[39] But in recent years, the practice of itemization of the damages has increased, particularly in serious cases. It is now necessary for the court to itemize the sums it awards under the principal headings recognized by the law, especially as between damages for future loss of earnings, and damages for pain and suffering and loss of amenity. But in the most serious cases, it is now quite common for the judges to break the damages down into small sub-headings. For example, specific sums may be awarded for past earnings (that has always been the practice), for estimated losses of future earnings, for estimated losses of pension rights, and for the possible contingency that the plaintiff may wholly lose his employment and suffer yet further income losses. Moreover, on the expenses side, it has also become quite common to itemize the different subheadings under which the damages are assessed; for instance, so much for nursing care, so much for home adaptations, so much for other extra expenses, and so on.

Interest

Since the Administration of Justice Act 1969, the plaintiff's entitlement to full compensation has been yet further enhanced by new provisions as to interest. Unless there are specific reasons to the contrary, the court is now obliged to order the payment of interest on damages in personal injury and fatal cases. The practice has varied since 1969, but the present position is as follows.[40] In actions brought by living plaintiffs, the damages for losses and expenses incurred before the trial (that is the 'special damages') carry interest at half the usual short-term interest rate. Interest is payable because in theory the plaintiff's entitlement to damages arises at the date of his injuries or, at least, the date he issues a writ. Interest is awarded at half rate because special damages represent sums which have been lost over the whole period between injury and the trial, some closer to the date of injury and some closer to the date of trial. A rough and ready approximation is arrived at by taking half the usual interest rate. Damages for pain and suffering and loss of amenity also attract interest, currently at a rate of 2%.[41] The reason why this figure is so low is that, unlike damages for pre-trial pecuniary loss, damages for pre-trial non-pecuniary losses are calculated in currency values current at the date of judgment. This means that inflation between the date of injury and the date of judgment has been taken into account at the basic award, and the interest rate need not include allowance for inflation, as commercial interest rates do. Nevertheless, the figure of 2% is rather low – when inflation is less than 8 or 10 per cent, interest rates tend to be more than 2% above the inflation rate, even allowing for taxation.

The award of interest acts as a discouragement to delay on the part of defendants, especially in cases which are settled out of court. Damages for loss of future earnings and for future expenses do not carry interest since, by definition, these are designed to compensate for losses which have not yet been incurred. In fatal cases the position is much the same. Damages for pre-trial losses carry interest at half the usual rate, damages for bereavement would probably carry interest at 2%, and no interest is payable on damages for future pecuniary loss.

3 LOST EARNINGS

We have already seen how many predictions and guesses have to be made in assessing damages for loss of future earnings (in a personal injuries claim) or future loss of support (in a fatal accident claim). The first step for the judge in a personal injury or death claim is to assess this probable continuing income loss, i.e. the £X per annum of earnings or support which the plaintiff would have received but for the accident. This sum is then multiplied by a 'multiplier' (usually somewhere between 8 and 15), which is a figure somewhat less than the number of years for which the judge thinks the loss will be suffered. The judge usually takes as his starting point the number of years for which the loss is likely to continue – i.e. in a personal injury action until the plaintiff's injuries cease to affect his earnings or he dies or retires, and in a fatal accident claim until the claimants would have ceased to receive support from the deceased. This figure is then reduced partly because of 'contingencies' (i.e. that the plaintiff might not have lived or worked so long or might have lost earnings even if the accident had not occurred), and partly because he is going to receive a capital sum and not an income. For example, in a recent case a 26-year-old miner with engineering training and good prospects of promotion to pit boss was awarded £132,608 for future loss of earnings – this figure was produced by applying a multiplier of 16 to an annual earnings loss of £8,288. The multiplier is not the product of precise calculation but of estimation in the light of the facts of the particular case and of other comparable cases. In some cases where the calculation of damages for loss of earnings requires a more than usual amount of speculation (e.g. if the plaintiff is a young child) the judge may not use the 'multiplier method' but may decide directly on a lump sum.

Methods of this kind can produce wide variations in the pattern of awards. The Court of Appeal does what it can to iron out the grosser deviations from the norm, but it will not interfere with awards unless they are much too high or much too low; appeals are often dismissed with the comment that the damages were on the high side or the low side, and that the members of the Court of Appeal would themselves have awarded more or less, but that the award was not so far from the norm that the Court should interfere. It may be necessary for the Court of Appeal to take this line, for otherwise there would be an incentive to fight an appeal in every case, since there is always room for differences of opinion on matters of this kind. But this does not mean the result is satisfactory to the individual litigants, who are bound to feel aggrieved; nor for the public as a whole whose faith in the administration of even-handed justice may be shaken by such an appearance of chance in the system.

Where the action is a dependency action (i.e. it is brought under the Fatal Accidents Act) a similar process is followed, except that the judge must first assess the extent of the dependency. In other words, if a person earning £8,000 a year is killed, and the judge finds that he spent some £2,500 a year on himself and the rest on his family, the dependency would be £5,500 per annum. This is the figure which must then be multiplied by the magic 'multiplier'. Where there are several dependants – typically, a widow and children – the damages must be apportioned among the dependants by the court. In practice, the lion's share of the award tends to be given to the widow and relatively small shares to dependent children. This is because it is assumed that the widow will in fact maintain the children and she may therefore need the income (if not indeed the capital) of all or nearly all the damages for this purpose. It has, however, been objected that if this is the justification, there is no reason why anything should be given to the children at all.[42] One may perhaps counter this objection by treating the question seriously, and not rhetorically. Why indeed? The social security system does not give grants or payments direct to dependent children; the payments are made to the parent or person having the care of the children, in the belief that most parents will spend the money on the child's maintenance. But of course these payments are not lump sums of capital.

Particular problems have arisen in providing a consistent set of rules applying equally to actions brought by living plaintiffs and actions under the Fatal Accidents Act and the 1934 Act. If the plaintiff's life expectancy is reduced by his injuries he is entitled to recover damages for loss of earnings not only up to the date of his expected death but also in respect of the years when, but for his injuries, he would have been alive and earning (the 'lost years'). But since, by definition, the plaintiff will have no personal living expenses in the lost years, these are deducted from the award.[43] The theoretical justification for this rule is the full compensation principle, but the main function of the lost years award is to provide support for dependants of the plaintiff after his death. For this reason the estate of a deceased person cannot recover lost years damages under the 1934 Act – the dependants can recover for loss of support under the Fatal Accidents Act and non-dependent beneficiaries of the estate do not *need* the award (this is sometimes put by saying that such an award would provide a 'windfall' to non-dependent beneficiaries).

The law, therefore, does in this case recognize that commitment to the full compensation principle does potentially *over*compensate. But this recognition has so far only affected the rules governing fatal cases. The living plaintiff can still recover substantial lost years damages even if he has no dependants (although in such a case the amount deducted for living expenses will be considerably higher than in the case where there are dependants); and a plaintiff who has been reduced to a state of 'living death' can recover full damages for loss of earnings for the rest of his life even where he has no dependants, despite the fact that he can make no use of the award himself (the cost of caring for him will constitute a separate head of damages) and the award will eventually accrue as a windfall to the non-dependent beneficiaries of his estate.[44]

The full compensation principle is seen as a corollary of the basis of tort liability – that the defendant is a 'wrongdoer'. It is not based on any notion of the purposes for which damages are being awarded. By contrast, the idea that an award can constitute a 'windfall' to those who benefit from it is based firmly on the idea that damages serve the purpose of meeting financial needs. Both of these lines of reasoning are present in the law, but the relationship between them is yet to be worked out consistently. It seems undeniable that the purposive approach is much more in line with modern ideas about the role of tort law in the welfare state. As it is, tort law provides very generous financial benefits to a very few injured and disabled persons who can prove fault. There is absolutely no justification for extending those benefits to persons who have suffered no physical or financial loss as a result of the fault.

4 FULL COMPENSATION FOR LOST EARNINGS: IS IT JUSTIFIED?

The courts and judges have often been criticized for failing adequately to implement the law's professed commitment to the principle of full compensation, but even if this accusation (which we examine further below) is justified, it seems desirable to re-examine the commitment itself. If there is a serious disparity between the theory and the practice of the law, it is surely necessary to examine the basis of the theory with some care: it may be found that the right solution to adjust the theory to make it fit the practice, rather than vice versa.

Apart from the issue of 'windfalls' which we have just mentioned, there are two problems which deserve detailed examination. The first is *why* should different accident victims be compensated for the same type of injury on a different scale which varies according to their previous level of earnings? If two people suffer identical permanent disabilities, but one was formerly earning £7,000 a year and the other was earning £15,000 a year, what justification is there for compensating the latter at a higher rate than the former? Or, still more striking perhaps, if these two people are killed in similar accidents, what justification is there for compensating their widows at different rates? This is, essentially, the problem of the earnings-related principle. The second question is whether it is sensible, or desirable to attempt to replace every penny of a lost income rather than some proportion of it. This is the hundred per cent principle. We take these two principles in turn.

The earnings-related principle

The advantage of earnings-related benefits over flat-rate benefits is that they enable an accident victim to maintain an approximation to his former standard of living. In these days, when so many people have long-term commitments such as mortgages, hire-purchase instalments and so forth, real hardship can be caused by a sudden and substantial drop in income. Moreover, flat-rate benefits have the disadvantage that a single figure has to be selected for all earners, and it is almost inevitable that a low figure will be inadequate for many to maintain their commitments, while a higher figure will result in over-compensation for lower earners. Nevertheless, there are real problems of equity in supporting the earnings-related principle, and these require some consideration.

The social security system, as we shall see more fully later, is still largely based on flat-rate benefits, though there are some earnings-related benefits. But it is important to observe that earnings-related benefits are only payable on the contributory principle. In general, benefits are the same for all, and the reasons behind this are understandable, though now often thought to be out of date. Whatever obligations may rest on the State to see that its citizens do not want for the necessities of life, or even to see that they have a reasonable standard of living, it is not obvious that the State owes any obligation to maintain disabled persons (or the dependants of deceased persons) for the rest of their lives at the standard of living which they had previously enjoyed – at any rate, it is not obvious that this is equitable regardless of how the compensation is paid for. In a competitive and still partly market-oriented society the £15,000 a year person receives, while he is working, a higher salary than the £7,000 a year person presumably because he is thought to provide more valuable services than the latter. But once he has ceased to work this justification is no longer open. It is not easy to justify a system under which many taxpayers would have to support a non-working disabled person, or the dependants of a deceased person, at a standard of living higher than their own. The only way in which this could be supported would be by arguing that the higher income taxes paid by the wealthier person while he is working justify a right to greater compensation when he is unable to work. This argument has proved acceptable in New Zealand,[45] but it remains to be seen whether it would be acceptable in this country. Hitherto, most of those who have discussed this question have suggested that the answer would be No. Thus, it has been said that 'No society can justify on actuarial or ethical grounds the financing of earnings-related benefits by means of flat rate contributions or through the Exchequer [i.e. general income taxes].[46]

On the other hand, there is no objection to paying some or even full compensation for lost earnings on an insurance principle; that is, in accordance with premiums actually paid. If our £15,000 a year person chooses to spend a substantial part of his income in insuring his life so that his widow may enjoy the same standard of living after his death as before, that is his privilege; and the same is true (though much less likely to happen in practice) if he insures himself against the risk of disability or chronic disease. But in practice we know that insurance against the risk of serious disease or accident is not very common even among the relatively well-to-do, and is certainly very rare among working-class people. This partly explains the introduction of earnings-related social security benefits for the sick and disabled. Short term benefits for the sick and disabled (statutory sick pay) is payable at three different rates. However, those earning less than £38 per week (in 1986) are not entitled to statutory sick pay; and earnings of more than £74.50 per week do not count for the purposes of calculating the level of benefit. It should be stressed that the higher benefits are paid for in that social security contributions are also earnings-related. Earnings-related benefits are not financed out of general taxes. People living on higher incomes now also receive more compensation for long-term sickness and disablement than those on lower incomes. To be sure, the acceptance of this principle has so far been confined to a small sphere of practical operation. At present it concerns itself with the person earning between £1,976 and £14,820 a year, but there is a case for a substantial extension of the principle of earnings-related benefits. It must be stressed that all this is done on the contributory principle. The £15,000 a year person gets higher social security benefits than the £7,000 a year man, because he pays a higher social security contribution. There is no question of the taxpayer paying for earnings-related benefits.

When we turn to the tort system, however, things are very different. Here we find the only systematic method of compensation which pays (what are in effect) earnings-related benefits without earnings-related contributions. How did this come about? The answer is that the tort system operates, in practice, in conjunction with liability insurance and not first-party insurance. A system of liability insurance cannot adjust its premiums according to the income of those to whom compensation will be payable, because when the liability insurance is taken out, nobody knows to whom compensation may become payable under the policy. If we look, for instance, at the road accident field we find that the liability insurance premium is adjusted according to the risk presented by the insured; the only person that the insurance company knows anything about. If he is a high-risk driver (for example a young undergraduate), driving a high-risk car (for example a sports car), living in a high-risk area (such as London), he pays higher premiums. But the premiums will not be adjusted according to the income of the insured, because compensation will never be payable to the insured for loss of *his* income under the policy;[47] indeed, the insured is the one person in the world whose income is irrelevant to the risk undertaken by the insurance company.[48] And the person whose income *is* relevant is the person who may be run over and injured or killed by the insured – and he of course is not identifiable when the insurance is taken out.

On the other hand, since the law does at present provide the compensation which takes account of lost earnings, insurance companies have to consider the likely amounts payable under the policy and adjust the premiums accordingly. In other words the more compensation that is paid for lost earnings, the higher insurance premiums must go, but the incidence is spread among all insured persons and is not borne rateably according to the incomes of those to whom compensation will eventually be paid. If all motor insurance premiums (for personal injury) are thought of as an insurance pool, it can be seen that higher-income groups draw much more out of the pool, but do not pay correspondingly more into the pool. Our £15,000 a year person and our £7,000 a year person will pay the same premium if they present the same type of risk; while if they are the victims of accidents, the former will receive vastly greater compensation in the form of lost earnings than the latter. In addition, of course, a pedestrian stands to gain while not contributing anything at all to the insurance fund. The tort system provides a stark contrast with all other compensation systems in this respect, though on the whole this situation is confined to the road accident problem. The tort system does not in practice compensate people on a large scale for personal injuries except for the victims of road and industrial accidents; and the victims of industrial accidents tend, in general to be members of similar earning groups. Though there are wide variations in wages, they are nothing like those found among road accident victims.

Another consequence of the earnings-related principle is that a widow who was wholly dependent on her husband's earnings, is entitled to be maintained for the rest of her life at a standard of living scarcely below that which she enjoyed while her husband was alive.[49] Even if she is young, childless, and well qualified to work, she need not do so; and if she does, she can invite the court to disregard her earnings in assessing the damages.[50] This is strange indeed, for in the conditions of today women are generally expected to be as capable of earning a living as men, even if they do not generally earn so much; and there seems no reason why a young woman should be maintained for the rest of her life by an award of damages (paid by society in one way or another), simply because her husband was killed through someone's fault. It is also grossly inequitable, in that the principle benefits the idle young wife who is wholly maintained by her husband, while the young working wife who maintains herself will receive little or no compensation.

In other areas of the law the position is quite otherwise. For example, a young childless wife separated (or divorced) from her husband cannot obtain maintenance from him without taking account of her own earning capacity, even where he was the 'guilty' party.[51] And as we shall see later, the national insurance system generally gives no pension to a childless widow unless she is over 40 when her husband dies: if younger, she is expected to earn her own living.

The hundred percent principle

There has never been any question but that tort damages for lost earnings are designed to represent the full amount of the loss. Yet most other compensation systems, especially social security systems (and in other countries, workmen's compensation laws) generally reject the hundred percent principle. Our own social security system as we shall see more fully later, generally pays benefits well below the full amount of lost earnings.[52] It is true that (as also we shall see) in practice this does not prevent injured workmen from sometimes obtaining more in benefits than they have lost in earnings, but this is despite, rather than in accordance with, the principles underlying the legislation. Similarly, the New Zealand Accident Compensation Act provides for benefits of 80% of lost earnings; and the Australian Committee of Inquiry recommended benefits equal to 85% of lost earnings.[53] In America, the National Commission on State Workmen's Compensation laws recommended that benefits should generally be equal to $66\frac{2}{3}\%$ of a workman's normal earnings or with dependants' allowances, not more than 80% of the worker's 'spendable weekly earnings.'[54] Moreover, in most compensation systems there are minimal loss qualifications. Thus, no social security benefits are payable in this country for the first three days' loss of earnings;[55]

no criminal injuries compensation benefits are payable if the compensation would amount to less than £400,[56] and so on.

There are two main reasons for rejecting the hundred percent principle. One is the cost involved, particularly at the lower end. As we have already seen, huge sums can be saved by eliminating entitlement to benefits for the first few days, and these savings can be used to provide benefits to those who now receive none. There is no doubt that the hundred percent principle, as applied in tort law today, is one of the principal factors leading to over-compensation for minor injuries, and under-compensation for more serious cases.[57] The Pearson Commission acknowledged the truth of this, and made some proposals to meet it, though not by attacking the hundred percent principle for lost earnings. What they did propose was that social security benefits should be fully offset against damages for lost earnings,[58] and in practice there is no doubt that this would lead to the loss of any further entitlement in many minor claims where at present social security benefits may come close to, or even exceed the earnings loss. In addition, the Commission proposed to eliminate claims for non-pecuniary loss for the first three months.[59] Between them, these proposals would undoubtedly have the effect of drastically curtailing minor injury claims in tort. Unfortunately, there seems no prospect of these changes being implemented in the near future.

The second ground for rejecting the hundred percent principle is that it deprives the accident victim of all incentive to return to work. Human nature being what is is, there can be no doubt that many injured persons would be content to draw benefits in perpetuity if they suffered no financial loss by doing so. The Australian Committee regarded this as so important that, even though injured workmen in some Australian States are already entitled to full compensation amounting to one hundred percent of lost earnings, the proposed scheme would have withdrawn these rights. It is true, of course, that so long as tort damages are paid in a lump sum, the incentive problem is somewhat different from what it is in a system operating with periodical payments. Once a plaintiff has obtained his damages, there is nothing to discourage him from attempting to return to work since the damages cannot be taken away from him. But the problem is that in the long-drawn-out process of negotiating a settlement of the damages claim, the plaintiff has every incentive to pad out the claim as much as he can. Why should the injured person attempt to return to work, when he expects that every week's lost wages will ultimately inflate the damages he obtains, especially if he is in the meanwhile drawing social security benefits which will not be claimed back once he obtains the damages?

Once again, one observes the strange contrast between different systems. The suggestion that there are good grounds for not adopting the hundred percent principle, almost everywhere accepted outside the tort system, is one which simply cannot be discussed in the context of tort law. Yet it does seem somewhat perverse, when this is already the situation, for reformers to devote much time to proposals which would have the effect of *increasing* the damages awarded in tort cases, as both the Law Commission and the Pearson Commission have recently done.[60] This approach cannot be adequately defended by saying that the proposals assume the continuation of the fault system. Even to assume the continuation of this system does not require that proposals for reform should treat fault-caused injuries as a self contained problem, wholly ignoring all the lessons learnt from other compensation systems. The Pearson Commission, though not recommending abolition of tort rights, insisted that the tort system needed to be more fully integrated with the social security system. One method of integrating them, it might be thought, would be to gradually reduce the gulf between the value of benefits payable under the two systems, and in particular, of course, to reduce those benefits which are based on principles simply not acceptable to the social security system, such as the hundred per cent principle. If the fault system is to continue, then far from increasing damages for fault victims, the rational course might well be to decrease them. This may be an unfashionable suggestion, but it is difficult to see why (for example) tort victims should not forgo lost earnings for the first three days, as social security beneficiaries are required to do; or why tort victims should not have to show loss exceeding £400, as criminal injury victims have to do.

5 FULL COMPENSATION: THE COMMITMENT IN PRACTICE

As has been indicated, there has been some criticism of the general level of awards for loss of earnings, and it has been said that 'grave injustice follows from the present practice of the judges in assessing future financial losses.'[61] Apart from general criticisms about the adequacy of awards, three specific points are often made.[62] First, it is said that judges reduce the awards too much for 'contingencies', i.e. for the possibility that the money would not have been earned even apart from the injury. It is possible to make some reasonable estimate of these contingencies from statistical evidence (e.g. the possibility of becoming unemployed or sick, or of being involved in another accident) and it has been calculated that these would justify reduction of the global loss by some 2–6%, while the courts generally deduct substantially more, perhaps about 10%. Occasionally, a judge has made the mistake of saying that reliance on annuity tables would require him to take into account the contingency that the plaintiff may not live as long as he might be expected to, despite the fact that this contingency is already taken account of when estimates of his expectation of life are drawn from statistical tables.[63]

The second principal complaint is that judges make no attempt to calculate the damages on proper actuarial principles. While actuarial evidence is not technically inadmissible in law, it is not customary to present such evidence in English courts; and the House of Lords has made it clear that the traditional 'multiplier' technique is to be preferred to actuarial methods.[64] The use of actuarial techniques is a highly technical matter, but it will suffice for our purposes simply to state that the criticism made of the courts' assessment of lost earnings, is that they fail to use the best techniques for producing an accurate answer to the question of valuing future losses. It has, indeed, been forcefully argued by an actuary that the 'multiplier' technique is itself an actuarial process, but a somewhat crude and unsophisticated one.[65] No attempt is usually made to assess the probable expectation of life (or the probable working life of the plaintiff) with the assistance of actuarial tables which take into account the plaintiff's age, occupation, place of residence, and so on. But two answers may be made to this objection. The first – which is advanced by many lawyers[66] – is that actuarial evidence is only of use where certain reasonably firm data exist as starting points; in particular, unless the rate of future lost earnings can be assessed with some precision no useful actuarial calculations can be made. But in practice it is often very difficult to make a precise calculation of the rate of future lost earnings: indeed it is often difficult enough to calculate the 'special damages' over a period occurring *before* trial.

Anyone who considers the changes in any trade or any individual life over 10 or 20 years or has had to calculate special damages over a mere three-year period with varying trade union rates and overtime, cannot fail to see where the real uncertainty lies.[67]

Hence, it may be urged, it is the lack of basic data which makes the use of actuarial methods suspect inasmuch as it may give a 'scientific' plausibility to what is little more than a guess. Still, it can be argued that once the annual loss has been assessed, however unreliable the resulting figure is, it is undesirable to compound the error by inadequate actuarial methods.

The second objection to the use of actuarial evidence is that actuarial techniques serve different ends from an award of damages. Actuarial techniques were devised by insurance companies to enable them to calculate life insurance premiums and annuity rates for different classes of persons. The object of this exercise is simply to see that the insurance company collects sufficient money to pay out on its policies and annuities and still make a profit: it is no part of the insurance company's purpose to see that each policy holder is adequately 'compensated' for what he pays. In fact, all policy holders or annuitants will pay 'too much' or 'too little', except for the person who dies at precisely the age which the life tables predict for him. But the courts are not concerned with the 'average' plaintiff. It is true that the use of more sophisticated actuarial techniques would mean that the *total* amount awarded in damages in all personal injury cases would be more likely to be 'correct'; but it would not guarantee that any individual plaintiff would be more likely to receive the 'correct sum'. There is, however, a flaw in this objection because it assumes that when a court speculates on what the future will hold for a plaintiff it can in a meaningful sense predict *his* future. In fact the court's predictions are based on a sort of non-statistical averaging based on the judge's knowledge and experience of what in fact happens to people in general and to persons like the plaintiff in particular. A more important objection to actuarial evidence is that actuaries are concerned primarily with life expectancy and not with the wide range of contingencies relevant to future earnings which the courts consider.

It is generally argued that awards would tend to be higher than they are if actuarial techniques were used, but this assertion has never been rigorously or systematically tested. Such evidence as there is suggests that damages awards tend to be relatively least adequate where the length of time of the expected future loss is very great, although this may be more often a result of a refusal by the courts to make adequate allowance for inflation than of refusal to use actuarial techniques.[68] The Pearson Commission proposed (by a majority) that a 'modified multiplier' method should be adopted which makes some allowance for the effects of inflation and tax rates.[69] The proposals are, however, fearsomely complicated, and it is doubtful in the extreme whether any Lord Chancellor could persuade the judges that they are acceptable. In addition, it has been demonstrated that their chief practical effect would be to greatly increase the damages for lost earnings of very high earners.[70] The one point which does emerge from the Pearson Report, and which may perhaps have some influence on future awards, is that the traditional multiplier method has involved an implicit assumption that plaintiffs will, by sound investment, be able to earn a real[71] rate of return of about 4½% on the capital value of their damages. This figure may be unrealistically high, at least in times of high inflation. In the context of awarding pre-trial interest on damages for non-pecuniary loss, the House of Lords has recently accepted 2% as realistic in conditions of high inflation.[72] On the other hand, recent experience shows that interest rates reflect many factors besides inflation and predicting what future rates will be is extremely difficult. Another factor which helps to keep awards unrealistically low is a general failure to allow for the impact of taxation on the plaintiff's income from his damages award.

A remarkable example of the way in which inflation can gravely undermine the value of lump-sum awards, was given in 1974 by the Australian Committee of Inquiry into the National Rehabilitation and Compensation Scheme.[73] In *Thurston* v. *Todd*[74] a young girl of fifteen suffered dreadful injuries in a motor accident, as a result of which, she was rendered a quadriplegic. The accident occurred in 1963. In 1965 she was awarded damages just short of £120,000, which was an exceptionally high award at that time. Over £50,000 of this sum was intended to cover the cost of future nursing services and medical expenses, on the assumption of a weekly cost of some £70. By 1973 the actual cost of these services had risen so much that the income from the entire award of damages (which had all been prudently invested) was inadequate to pay for the nursing expenses alone – despite the mother's unpaid services for some seven hours each day. Nursing costs alone had nearly doubled in the nine years since the damages were awarded.

But there is another question. Increases in wages and salaries are by no means entirely due to inflation: a real element of improvement is often involved in these increases. Awards of damages for future lost earnings do not take this possibility into account, so that the recipient is wholly or partly shut out from sharing in the general rise in standards of living in the future. Between 1948 and 1982 average earnings increased nearly twentyfold, while retail prices increased about tenfold; so that the average earner increased his standard of living by more than 100% during this period. A permanently disabled person, or a widow who received an award of tort damages for lost earnings at any time since 1945, will thus not have shared in this general increase in national prosperity, even if he or she has been able to keep the real value of the income intact. As we shall see later, there is a major difference in this respect between the tort compensation process and the social security system.

Despite all this, the courts have generally refused to increase damages for future losses of earnings (or future expenses and costs) on the ground of likely future inflation.[75] The justification for this approach is the argument that plaintiffs can counteract the effects of inflation by sound investment strategy. There are several reasons to doubt the validity of this argument, but the courts are probably intimidated by the amount of speculation involved in predicting the rate of future inflation, especially over long periods.

But even if it is accepted that many lump sum awards turn out, because of inflation, to be inadequate to produce as much income as has been lost, it does not follow that the right solution to this problem would be to raise the level of awards. There are several things which must be borne in mind, apart altogether from the difficulty of justifying the whole principle of compensation for lost earnings without corresponding variations in premiums. First, the value of a capital sum over the income which it replaces is not inconsiderable. Apart from the sense of security it may generate[76] it has very tangible economic value, inasmuch as many people are in practice unable to borrow capital at anything like normal commercial interest rates. Thousands of people are unable to buy houses because they cannot borrow money at the commercial market rate for interest; and are forced to live in rented accommodation, often paying in rent more than they would have to pay in the form of mortgage payments on a building society loan – if only they could raise some capital for a deposit. Millions of people also acquire goods on hire purchase terms for which they often pay an effective rate of interest of 30% or more. To people in this situation a large capital sum will be worth considerably more than might appear from the normal commercial rates of interest.

In the second place, it must be remembered that in cases where the plaintiff has suffered large earning losses, substantial awards are made for pain and suffering and other intangible losses mentioned below. It is possible to take the view that these are as irrational or excessive as awards for lost earnings are inadequate, and that the one therefore helps to balance the other (although the House of Lords has not shown itself sympathetic to such an approach). Nor does the argument apply to dependency actions where (apart from damages for bereavement) no award for pain and suffering and such like will usually be available to augment the award for lost earnings, and it is possibly in these cases that the awards appear most inadequate.[77] But even here, there are often countervailing considerations – for example, the fact that life insurance is not counted towards a reduction of damages, and that all social security benefits are ignored in the assessment of damages.

In the third place, there is a great deal of double compensation. We shall look into the full extent of this problem later[78], but here it must be noted that many losses are compensated in full or in part two, or even three, times over.

In the fourth place, the question of priorities, which we have stressed so often, must not be forgotten. If more money is to be pumped into the tort system, the effect will be to increase the comparatively generous provision already made for victims of fault-caused injuries who are fortunate enough to collect tort damages. In the meantime, the thousands of less fortunate victims of natural disease and disability and non-fault caused accidents (not to mention many tort victims who fail to recover damages), receive not a penny in tort compensation; and many of these are also (as we shall see) treated less generously by the social security system than most tort victims.

6 MEDICAL AND OTHER EXPENSES

Since the introduction of the National Health Service most victims of personal injury, of course, enjoy free medical treatment, and no damages can be recovered for medical expenses if no expenses have in fact been incurred. But people are still entitled to seek private medical treatment if they wish, and if they incur expense in doing so, the expense is recoverable as an item of damages in a tort action.[79] In practice, few people would do this,[80] partly because the habits of the people in seeking free treatment are now so ingrained that most people would obtain such treatment without thinking twice about it; but partly also because, in the case of treatment obtained *before* trial, nobody can be sure that the defendant will be held liable. If the plaintiff knew that the defendant's insurers would accept liability he might be tempted to indulge in the comfort of private medical treatment in a private nursing home. But in practice the treatment is urgently required immediately on the occurrence of the injuries, and there can at that stage be no certainty that the defendant's insurers will eventually be made to pay for it. In these circumstances few plaintiffs would take the risk of incurring the expense of private treatment unless they had private medical insurance. But there may sometimes be cases where the treatment extends over a long period of time, and during negotiations the defendants may come to admit liability. In this event the plaintiff may (if he is advised as to his rights) continue his treatment privately.

There will also be cases in which facilities are available under the National Health Service, but some charge is made for their use; or in which the Health Service offers necessities but leaves the individual to pay for trimmings, as for example with fancy spectacle frames. In all these cases, tort victims may be able to claim damages covering 'reasonable costs' for services or articles they have to pay for.

There are also some cases – few in number – in which a plaintiff may be so severely disabled or incapacitated that medical and nursing treatment may be required indefinitely, or indeed for the rest of the plaintiff's life. In these cases the plaintiff is entitled to claim damages for private treatment, for example to employ a private nurse at home or to enable him to reside permanently in a private nursing home or institution. Even if such facilities are provided by the National Health Service or a local authority, the plaintiff is entitled to 'go private'. Yet once the damages are paid over there is no obligation on the plaintiff to expend them as he has said he will. There is nothing to prevent a patient spending the rest of his life in a state hospital or institution after receiving damages on the footing that he will incur the cost of private treatment; but the court may reduce the damages where it feels convinced that the plaintiff will spend substantial periods in a state institution, e.g. where other suitable facilities simply do not exist.[81] On the other hand, local authority residential institutions (as opposed to National Health Service hospitals) have statutory power to charge for the care and maintenance of patients, and if substantial damages are awarded to a plaintiff covering the costs of such care and maintenance, there is no doubt that a charge would be made.[82] Even so, local authority charges are far lower than would be made by private institutions. In *Lim Poh Choo* v. *Camden Health Authority*[83] (referred to previously) the plaintiff was awarded no less than £76,000 for the cost of future care, over a period expected to last many years at a rate of £6,400 per annum. But the cost of maintaining the inmates of local authority institutions (many of whom, of course, do not require the same full time nursing care) in 1977 was £500 to £600 per annum.[84]

It is not at all obvious why, nearly forty years after the beginning of the National Health Service, we should continue to subsidize those who seek private treatment in the way that the tort system does. No doubt private treatment is often desirable. Private nursing at home is better than hospitalization, and a private room in a nursing home is doubtless more comfortable than a public ward in a hospital. If these 'luxuries' were really paid for by negligent defendants, they might be justified. But it is the public who pays in one form or another for these luxuries.[85] And the obvious question arises: why should persons with a tort claim enjoy such public benevolence when others desiring private hospital or nursing care must provide it for themselves? It seems difficult to justify the present position, and the Pearson Commission proposed that in future the expenses of private medical treatment should only be recoverable if it was reasonable on medical grounds for the patient to have private treatment.[86] Such a proposal is unlikely to be adopted by the present government, wishing, as it does, to encourage the private sector of medicine.

Other out of pocket expenses incurred as a result of an accident are recoverable in the same way as medical expenses, for example the cost of fares to attend an out-patient department at a hospital; the cost of special medical appliances, or indeed expenses which have nothing to do with medical costs, such as the cost of doing repairs around the house which the plaintiff is no longer able to do himself, or the cost of alterations to a house necessitated by a permanent disability.[87] The sums awarded for such losses are a significant item in some awards.

7 INTANGIBLE LOSSES

Apart from the quantifiable losses which are, at least in principle, measurable in terms of money, damages are awarded for certain intangible losses, or 'psychic losses' as they have sometimes been called by American writers. Damages for mental distress such as pain, suffering, discomfort, humiliation, indignity, and embarrassment, are awarded under the head of 'pain and suffering'. Damages of this kind differ in some respects from damages for actual disabilities which are usually referred to as damages for 'loss of amenities or loss of faculty'; though in some cases it may be difficult to distinguish between them, as for instance, where a plaintiff has suffered a loss of sexual potency, or is so badly injured as to impair the prospect of marriage.[88] The two kinds of damages may both be recoverable since loss of faculty may be accompanied by pain and suffering, but it is possible to have loss of faculty without any pain or mental distress at all, as in the case of someone who is rendered permanently unconscious, or is reduced to such a degree of imbecility as to be incapable of appreciating his situation. It is also possible to have pain and suffering with no actual disability or loss of faculty. But in most serious cases the two go together. Loss of limbs, paralysis, blindness or deafness, and so on, are unlikely to be inflicted without considerable pain and suffering.

In both cases, of course, the calculation of damages is to a very large extent arbitrary. Something which cannot be measured in money is 'lost', and the award of damages requires some monetary value to be placed on it. There appears to be no way of working out any relationship between the value of money – what it will buy – and damages awarded for pain and suffering, and disabilities. All such damages awards could be multiplied or divided by two overnight and they would be just as defensible or indefensible as they are today.[89]

Lawyers are not the only people who have wrestled with the

problem of valuing pain and suffering, disabilities and loss of amenities, and so on. Economists concerned with cost-benefit analysis have tried to place values on these things, and have also found the problems very hard. Economists normally value things by looking for a 'market price', but there is no 'market' for pain or lost limbs.[90] Some economists have simply accepted the lawyers' figures as evidence of the value placed by society on these intangibles. Others have suggested that the 'value' of an injury is the amount which a person would be prepared to pay to avoid incurring that injury; but it has been pointed out that this may be a gross under-estimate, because the sum a person is prepared to pay to avoid an injury is limited by the amount of money he has got.[91] It has therefore been suggested that the real 'value' of an injury is the amount which a person would be willing to *accept* to incur the injury. Thus, attempts have been made to determine values for life and limb implicit in actual wage rates current in industries with different injury rates.[92] Another approach calculates 'implicit' valuations by assessing the cost of measures to avoid *additional* injury or death. The idea behind this is that the value placed on life and freedom from injury can be assumed to be just short of the amount that would have been spent (but is not) to avoid the injury or death.[93] Some of the valuations produced by these approaches (in the millions of pounds) seem very high to the lawyer. But this is partly because the lawyer's concern with just compensation is very different from the economist's interest in determining how much the members of a group faced with a risk are prepared to accept as an alternative to removal of the risk.[94] For this reason, the economic approaches to the value of life are of limited use to the lawyer.

There is, moreover, the additional difficulty that the value of money differs according to the wealth of the recipient. To a wealthy man an award of £5,000 for a lost leg may be of little moment; a similar sum to a poor man may be untold riches. This problem is peculiar to awards of damages for non-pecuniary loss, because where damages are given for pecuniary loss (with a measurable financial value) the wealth of the recipient is immaterial. In practice, as the wealth of a society increases, so the real value of awards of this kind tends to go up; and it is noticeable that awards for non-pecuniary loss are far higher in the United States than they are in this country or anywhere else in the world. So while the wealth of the individual plaintiff does not affect the level of awards for non-pecuniary loss,[95] the wealth of society as a whole does. This suggests that the process of calculating such awards is not *entirely* arbitrary. It is fair to assume that virtually unanimous agreement could be achieved on the extreme outer limits of what would be regarded as 'reasonable' compensation for the intangible aspects of personal injury: for example, few would think £100 too much or a million pounds too little for the loss of a hand. Presumably an upper limit of a million pounds would be rejected as absurdly high, partly at least because it is so far beyond the sort of capital wealth which most citizens could ever hope to acquire; equally, £100 would be rejected as absurdly low, because to most of us an extra £100 in our wealth would be of little moment. Thus it seems that although the selection of particular sums within such wide limits must be arbitrary, the limits themselves are not entirely arbitrary; they bear some relationship to the sort of sums which people in general may expect to enjoy as personal wealth. It would seem to follow that there should also be some relationship between earnings, and hence damages for loss of earnings, and damages for non-pecuniary loss.

One way of dealing with the arbitrary nature of such awards would be to leave it to the public, in the form of a jury, to decide how much to award in particular cases. This course was regularly followed in England until 1934, and it is still generally adopted in Scotland and Northern Ireland, as well as in the United States, and there is certainly something to be said for this solution.[96] But even if the jury can give us some idea of how our society values certain disabilities, leaving this problem to a jury involves sacrificing something else which is of value – namely a high degree of internal consistency. If we cannot say what a leg or an arm is worth, we can at least say that a leg today is worth the same (in real terms) as a leg tomorrow, and we can also say that an arm must be worth more than a hand; a hand more than a finger; two legs more than one; and so forth. Even here, of course, there is great difficulty. Is an arm worth more than a leg? Is it worse to be totally blind than to lose both legs? Is a hand worth more than a foot? With what can you compare the inability to bear a child? But still, making every allowance for the element of arbitrariness in the whole process of compensating for disabilities, it is possible to have some internal consistency in the process, and such consistency would not be easily attained if the decision was left to a jury. The consistency, such as it is, is at present maintained by leaving the decisions in the hands of a small number of judges who are repeatedly facing the same problem, who can discuss the awards among themselves, who can be put 'right' by the Court of Appeal if they depart too much from the norm. A jury, on the other hand, hears only one case; it knows nothing of the general level of awards in comparable cases; indeed, it is forbidden to tell them, and though this rule could be changed, basic ignorance of the system would remain. In the result, the Court of Appeal decided in 1966 that jury trial would henceforth be permitted only in very special cases[97] – for example where the injuries are of so unusual a kind that the experience of the judges would be of little use.[98]

It must be appreciated that the desire for a measure of consistency in the level of awards is not merely an expression of the belief in equal treatment of like cases as an ultimate value of justice – though this is certainly important. Consistency is also important for the smooth running of the tort system because, as we shall see more fully later, most tort claims are settled by negotiation out of court; and without some consistency in the level of awards, there would be much more difficulty in predicting the outcome of a case and hence more difficulty in negotiating a settlement.[99] And it must be appreciated that a very small decrease in the number of cases which are settled, and a corresponding increase in the number of cases which go to trial, could seriously overload the court system.

Although the courts have now definitely committed themselves to the 'tariff' approach, according to which particular ranges of awards are established for particular disabilities, the problem still remains of fixing these ranges. The Law Commission, in its review of the assessment of damages, came to the conclusion that the fixing of damages for non-pecuniary loss was so arbitrary that no principles could be recommended on which the courts should work. The only question, according to the Law Commission, that needed to be settled was 'who ought to decide'.[100] But this seems to ignore the possibility (or desirability) of trying to relate these damages to other comparable sums, e.g. disability pensions under the industrial injury system.

The Pearson Commission accepted the general basis of most of the present law, though they made one important proposal, namely that no damages for non-pecuniary loss should be awarded unless the loss lasts for a period exceeding three months.[101] As about 95% of those injured in accidents are sufficiently recovered to return to work within three months¹⁰² it is plain that this would have a very dramatic effect on eliminating claims for pain and suffering in minor cases. Moreover, the total saving from this would be very substantial. The insurance survey conducted for the Pearson Commission showed that some two thirds of damages paid out by insurers was for non-pecuniary loss, and that the proportion was highest in small cases.¹⁰³

Subjective factors

The tariff approach is in fact quite recent. It is largely a result of the demise of juries in personal injury actions, which has led judges and appeal courts to stress the value of 'objective' consistency in assessing damages for non-pecuniary loss. However, the courts still profess to compensate the plaintiff for the personal effects of the injuries on him as a unique individual. Clearly, there is potential inconsistency between this personalized approach¹⁰⁴ and the tariff system, but what happens in practice is that the court starts with a tariff figure for the particular injury and then increases or decreases this sum to take account of the personal qualities of the plaintiff. Thus, a plaintiff with a hand injury may recover more if he was an amateur pianist who took much pleasure in his hobby; a woman with a leg injury may recover more if she was formerly keen on dancing and is now unable to dance at all. Here again, we find a fundamental inconsistency between the tort system and the social security system. Only the industrial injuries scheme recognizes loss of faculty or disability as a ground for compensation, and as we shall see, under the scheme the assessment is entirely objective: no personal factors (other than age and sex) are taken into account. Indeed, a Committee reviewing the assessment of disabilities under the Act thought that it would be 'inequitable' to do so¹⁰⁵ and so apparently did the Pearson Commission, despite their acceptance of the common law system.¹⁰⁶ This is doubtless based on the view that everyone places an equal value on, for example, their hand (leaving out of account loss of earnings, which are separately compensated). The case for equality of treatment in this respect seems very strong, but has never been the subject of discussion within the tort system.

One problem which has caused much trouble is that of assessing the damages awardable to a plaintiff who has been reduced to a state comparable to that of a 'vegetable'. Medical science can now keep people with the most devastating injuries alive in a state of complete coma for many months, or even years, with no hope of recovery. In a case of this nature it is hard indeed to see what purpose there can be in awarding lump-sum damages for disabilities or loss of amenities, or even for lost earnings if there are no dependants. There is no question of providing substitute pleasures for those forgone, because the injured party is unable to enjoy any pleasures; nor is there any question of providing a solace for pain, suffering or mental distress, because the victim feels none. Yet, the courts have held that though damages for pain and suffering cannot be awarded, nonetheless, damages for loss of 'amenities' or 'faculties' must be awarded; and these damages run into many thousands of pounds. In *H. West & Son Ltd* v. *Shephard*[107] a majority of the House of Lords, following the majority of the Court of Appeal in *Wise* v. *Kaye*,[108] decided that compensation is awarded for the objective fact of 'loss' in cases of this nature. A person who 'loses' a leg gets compensation for the fact of losing the leg, and a person who is deprived of all the pleasures of life gets compensation for the fact of that deprivation. The lack of consciousness of the deprivation, said the House of Lords, 'cannot' reduce the objective fact of the 'loss'; though consciousness of the deprivation can increase the damages by reason of the mental distress that this would involve.

The result of this approach is that the law draws a very sharp distinction between death and permanent unconsciousness. If a person dies as a result of personal injuries, no damages for loss of amenities will be recoverable in respect of the period after his death even if he has dependants; but if he is reduced to a state of permanent unconsciousness, substantial damages under this head will be awarded even if he has no dependants and the damages will eventually accrue as a windfall to the beneficiaries of his estate. The Pearson Commission recommended that damages for non-pecuniary loss should cease to be recoverable in cases of permanent unconsciousness.[109]

The tariff

In many recent cases, actual figures (or a range of figures, a 'bracket') for specific disabilities have been put forward by the Court of Appeal as the 'norm' which should be awarded for injuries of that type – in the absence of special circumstances. In other cases, it is necessary to deduce the figures from a pattern of decisions. The figures must be treated with caution, because some subjective elements are still taken into account, and because some awards may include damages for loss of expectation of life, now abolished. Moreover, the figures increase steadily as the courts strive to keep pace with inflation. Difficulty also arises because some cases still involve awards of general damages, including damages for lost earnings as well as for pain and disability. In May 1985 the Court of Appeal held that the proper award for pain, suffering and loss of amenities in an average case of tetraplegia (that is, in a case of extremely severe injuries in which the plaintiff is reduced to total helplessness and yet is fully conscious of his position) was £75,000.[110] In 1983 a boy who received severe brain damage when aged 3½ but who would eventually have the insight of a 15-year-old into his condition was awarded £60,000.[111] Coming down to less severe injuries, in 1979 a 20-year-old who was rendered paraplegic and sexually impotent was awarded £35,000;[112] while in 1983 a man who suffered severe permanent and degenerative leg and foot injuries was awarded £25,000.[113] Other awards include about £25,000 for loss of an arm above the elbow, rather less for amputation below the elbow; up to £11,000 for loss of an eye[114] and from £50,000 upwards for total blindness;[115] £10,000 to £15,000 for loss of a hand; £2,500 to £3,500 for complete loss of the sense of smell and double this for loss of the sense of taste as well.[116] Even quite minor injuries (if leaving a permanent disability) such as loss of a fingertip, rate several hundred pounds; and awards have been made of £1,500 for loss of a left index finger and £2,250 for loss of a right index finger. In one case in 1983, £7,500 was awarded for a particularly unpleasant and deforming accident to a thumb.[117] There are many cases of relatively minor injuries (including even such injuries as a broken arm or leg) in which there is ultimately complete recovery and no lost earnings (e.g. because the plaintiff is a child or a housewife), in which awards for pain suffering and temporary loss of faculty are the principal elements in danger. As much as £5,000 may be awarded for severe disfigurement in appropriate cases.

Damages for 'pain and suffering' in the literal sense are not today usually very high in this country, no doubt partly because severe and prolonged pain which cannot be adequately relieved by the medical profession is now rare. It has been suggested that something like £10 or £20 per week for actual pain is the norm, with a ceiling of about £1,000.[118] It is interesting to note that the judicial practice of not awarding very large sums for actual pain and suffering, appears to be supported by the relative unimportance attached to this element of the 'loss' by the disabled and handicapped themselves. In the government social survey of 1971–72, handicapped persons were asked about the things which had most affected them. Far more of them referred to the lack of social contact, the restrictions on their movements and their sense of isolation, than to physical pain and suffering.[119] The more severe the handicap, the less significant does actual pain and suffering seem to be, compared with restriction on movement.[120]

The question has recently been discussed whether there is a case for a legislative tariff to replace the judicial one.[121] It is acknowledged that the tariff would have to be somewhat flexible because experience, both of the tort system and of the industrial injuries system, has shown that very large numbers of injuries cannot be neatly labelled and identified in a tariff schedule. Nevertheless, it has been suggested by some, that a legislative tariff could be useful in giving guidance to the judges as to the appropriate norms or brackets. Both the Law Commission and the Pearson Commission found little support for the idea, and rejected it. There was, however, more support for a legislative maximum and the Pearson Commission only rejected this idea by a single vote. But it seems unlikely that such a maximum would make a great deal of difference unless it were set well below the current figure. The Pearson Commission discussed the possibility of a maximum of only five times the average industrial wage, i.e. about £20,000, and that certainly is well below the present maximum. The Canadian Supreme Court adopted a maximum of $100,000 in 1978.[122]

Some concluding comments may be permitted on the overall desirability of retaining damages for non-pecuniary loss. It will be noticed that except for a person who himself suffers physical injury, damages for non-pecuniary loss will only be awarded for the death of a spouse or unmarried minor child under the 1976 Act. In other circumstances, no damages can be awarded for non-pecuniary loss. This rules out, for instance, any damages for the distress, and even anguish, of parents whose child suffers crippling brain damage and whose total life may thereby be destroyed. Similarly, nothing is recoverable for the death of someone, other than under the 1976 Act. So no damages will be awarded for the death of an adult child who has his own dependants; nothing can be awarded for the death of a 'common law' wife or husband; and a husband or wife cannot recover anything for the effects on themselves, of a serious accident to their spouse. All this is not to suggest that there should be payment of damages for non-pecuniary loss in these situations, but to stress the difficulty of justifying such damages in the cases where they are presently awarded. As we have seen previously, the Pearson Commission discovered that something of the order of two-thirds of all tort payments are attributable to non-pecuniary loss; and much of this sum goes on relatively trivial cases where a complete recovery is made by the victim within a short time. The majority of the Pearson Commission found it 'hard to justify payments for minor or transient non-pecuniary losses', and they went on to say, 'The emphasis in compensation for non-pecuniary loss should in our view be on serious and continuing losses, especially loss of faculty.'[123]

It is, once again, necessary to remember the remarkable disparity in treatment between tort victims who obtain full compensation for their pecuniary losses and damages for non-pecuniary losses as well, and most other classes of victims of accidents and disease who rarely obtain full compensation even for pecuniary losses, let alone anything extra for non-pecuniary losses. The truth would appear to be that there is a penal element underlying damages for non-pecuniary loss, which is wholly inappropriate when damages are normally payable by insurers and not tortfeasors. It is perhaps only in the most serious cases of long-term pain and loss of faculty that there is a good case for damages for non-pecuniary loss.

8 OVERALL MAXIMA

Given the practice of itemization of the different sums of damages awarded under different heads, there has been something of a movement away from any attempt which might formerly have been discernible, to limit the total level of damages for pecuniary and non-pecuniary loss together. The result has been that the size of the largest awards has become very great in recent years. Awards of between £200,000 and £300,000 in the most serious cases are now quite common. The highest award so far seems to have been the figure of

£679,264 awarded to a woman who suffered severe brain damage during a routine operation.[124] She was married 19 days before the operation, which left her incontinent and occasionally violent. Her mental age was reduced to that of a six-year-old and her life expectancy to 55 years. She and her husband were divorced when he could no longer cope with the strain. The award included the cost of a purpose-built bungalow and live-in nursing care. It is not difficult to compare these sums with provision made by the State for those who suffer comparable injuries but are unable to recover damages. Careful investment of such an award would generate an income very much greater than the social security benefits payable even to the most seriously handicapped people. Further, although local authorities make grants for the adaptation of houses to suit the needs of the disabled, the vast majority of these amount to no more than a couple of hundred pounds, and no local authority would pay the cost of a complete and specially designed house for a disabled person.

On the other hand, awards of this size must be viewed in perspective. In the first edition of this book in 1970, it was noted that the maximum awards at that time were between £50,000 and £70,000. Today, they are between £300,000 and £400,000. In that period, retail prices have increased almost five times, so that one would expect the top awards to be in the range of £250,000 to £350,000, as most of them are. These increases have, by and large, been the result of inflation rather than of changes in the law. In the past 15 years, too, average wages have increased much faster than prices, and when an award includes a large element for the cost of care (e.g. the wages of a nurse), increases in line with price inflation may not seem so generous. It is, nevertheless, true that recipients of tort awards are a *very* privileged class of the disabled, and their position has, if anything, improved over the last 15 years relative to that of other disabled persons.

PART THREE
The Tort System in Operation

8
The Plaintiffs

1 ACCIDENT VICTIMS AND TORT CLAIMANTS

Who actually gets tort damages? The Report of the Pearson Commission provides a great deal of information on this vital question, and a certain amount of other research has been done. Many of the figures in the Pearson Report are, of course, estimates but they are based on a thorough study of the data, much of which was itself collected by the Commission.

It is necessary to begin by reminding the reader that only a small proportion of tort claims are actually tried in the courts; and although a substantially larger number reach the stage of being set down for trial, even these form a very small percentage of the total number of claims. The great majority of claims are settled by negotiation and agreement.

Cases reaching trial

In 1974 some 2,203 cases of personal injury and death were actually tried in the courts of the whole of the United Kingdom. In England and Wales alone, the figure was 1,870. Of this figure of 1,870 cases reaching trial and receiving a full hearing, 1,169 were tried in the High Court, and 701 cases in the County Courts.[1] In the High Court, cases of this nature constitute the overwhelming bulk of the work of the Queen's Bench Division. Indeed, the Pearson Commission estimated that nearly 80% of the work of this Division consisted of personal injury actions.[2] In the County Courts, the proportion of personal injury actions is very much lower, and indeed, such actions cannot constitute more than a small part of the business of the County Courts.

TABLE 6
PERSONAL INJURY CASES BY TYPE: SAMPLE OF CASES IN THE QBD IN 1973

Source of injuries	Number	Percentage
Road Accidents	317	48
Industrial accidents	304	46
Miscellaneous:		
Other occupier cases	10	
Playground/school	8	
Obstruction, disrepair of highway	6	
Medical	5	
Boating accidents	4	6
Criminal assaults	3	
Train accidents	2	
Air crash	1	
Faulty product	1	
Dog	1	
Totals	662	100

The Pearson Report does not give a breakdown of these cases which actually received a full hearing to enable us to see what kind of actions they were, other than that they were personal injury actions. But further information on cases actually tried is available from a study conducted by Professor Zander in 1973–4.[3] Zander examined some 660 cases of personal injury claims in the Queen's Bench Division in four large cities in 1973. It is true that, even of these, only a proportion were actually fully heard, the majority being settled.[4] Table 6 sets out the source of these claims. It is, however, worth noting that the proportions set out here were found by Zander to be very different from those relating to the cases actually tried. These cases, totalling 124, were overwhelmingly dominated by industrial injury cases. Indeed, of the 124 contested cases in Zander's example, no fewer than 91% were industrial cases.

Cases set down for trial

Only about a quarter of the cases set down for trial actually receive a full hearing. The pressures to settle are great, even after a case is set down, and many cases are settled, more or less literally at the door of

TABLE 7
CASES SET DOWN FOR TRIAL IN ENGLAND AND WALES, 1974, BY TYPE OF CLAIM

Source of injuries	Number	Percentage
Employers' liability	4,114	53·2
Transport	2,956	38·2
Goods and services	22	0·3
Medical negligence	44	0·6
Occupiers' liability	253	3·3
Other personal injuries	344	4·4
Totals	7,733	100

the court just before the trial is due to begin. A small number are even settled during the course of the trial. In England and Wales some 7,733 cases were set down for trial in 1974, where the claim was for damages for personal injuries or under the Fatal Accidents Act.[5] Most of these claims related to road accidents, or (in general terms) industrial injuries. Some 53% of personal injury cases set down for trial are employer's liability claims, and some 38% are transport claims, the great majority arising out of road accidents. The full figures are contained in Table 7.[6] The figures do not wholly tally with previous estimates that, at the stage of setting down for trial, road accident and industrial accident cases were roughly in equal proportion. And if they are compared with those in Zander's study, referred to above, they throw doubt on the view once held that a higher proportion of road accident cases are settled after setting down for trial. Indeed if, as was formerly thought[7], roughly equal numbers of employers' liability and road accident cases are actually tried, at least in the High Court, it follows that a higher proportion of employers' liability claims must be settled, and not a lower one. But the interpretation of these figures is bedevilled by variations between High Court and County Court, and we do not yet have sufficiently detailed information on the nature of cases actually tried.

All tort claims

The Pearson Commission has, for the first time, given us some reasonably precise estimates of the total numbers of tort claims for

198   THE TORT SYSTEM IN OPERATION

TABLE 8

ANNUAL NUMBERS OF TORT CLAIMS AND PAYMENTS FOR PERSONAL INJURY OR DEATH BY TYPE OF CLAIM
(United Kingdom: estimates in round numbers for 1973)

	Claims		Payments	
	Numbers	Percentages	Numbers	Percentages
Employers' liability				
Injury	114,700	46·0	90,500	42·0
Disease	2,900	1·2	1,700	0·8
Motor vehicle	102,200	40·9	98,300	45·7
Other transport	1,100	0·4	900	0·4
Products and services (excluding medical services)	2,200	0·9	1,700	0·8
Medical services	700	0·2	300	0·1
Occupiers' liability	12,200	4·9	10,800	5·0
Other	14,000	5·6	11,200	5·2
Totals	250,000	100·0	215,400	100·0

personal injury and death, including those which are settled as well as those which are tried. The Commission estimated that every year there are approximately 250,000 such claims, of which about 215,000 are settled (or tried) so as to conclude with some payment to the claimant. The detailed position is set out in Table 8.[8] These figures make very interesting reading. They show that, as had always been suspected, the great mass of personal injury claims arise out of industrial and road accidents, and that there is a small miscellaneous number of claims arising from all other kinds of accidents of some 12% or 13%. Comparing the figures in Table 8 with those in Table 7 suggests that the cases which reach the stage of being set down for trial are not wholly disproportionate to the total number of cases, with the exception of industrial cases. Probably a higher proportion of these cases reach this stage simply because the plaintiffs are assisted by trade unions, and they may therefore be less inclined to settle for inadequate offers or abandon their claims altogether.[9]

It is necessary to remind the reader of some of the other figures from the Pearson Report which were cited in Chapter 1. These show that there are some three million personal injury accidents per year (each involving at least four days off work, or comparable injuries) and that of this large number no more than about 6½% obtain any tort payment at all. The Commission also estimated that about 10½% of those who suffer injuries at work, and about 25% of those injured in road accidents, obtain some tort payment.[10]

These figures, so far as they go, present a staggering contrast with the figures for *all* accidents. If the tort liability system worked as it professes to work, if that is to say, people suffering personal injury or property damage generally recovered damages where this was the fault of someone else, we should in the first place, expect to find claims for damage to *property* as a result of road accidents far exceeding claims for personal injuries. Although no precise figures are available, it has been estimated by the Road Research Laboratory that road accidents causing only property damage are probably *six times* as frequent as those causing personal injuries, however slight. And the figure for private car accidents is estimated to be even higher – some 7·7 times as many as personal injury accidents.[11] In addition, there are accidents causing damage by fire. It is estimated that in 1983 fires caused material damage (excluding loss of production, sales and employment) in excess of £560 million.[12] Even if we confine our attention to personal injury accidents, there are large numbers which scarcely ever figure in the tort scene at all. In particular there are accidents in the home. In 1972 nearly as many people died in accidents at home as in road accidents, and although there are no national statistics about accidents at home causing injury as opposed to death, there is every reason to suppose that these are even more numerous than injuries caused by road accidents;[13] though serious injury so caused is probably less common.[14] The personal injury survey conducted for the Pearson Commission found that 27% of all injuries occurred within the home.[15] Of course nobody can be sure what proportion of accidents in the home is due to fault, or whether this proportion is anything like the proportion of road and industrial accidents which is due to fault. No doubt it is probable that *more* home accidents (and fire accidents) are due to the fault of the victim himself – so there could be no tort liability anyhow. But such evidence as there is suggests that a considerable proportion of home accidents are due to 'fault' at least in the sense that they could have been prevented by due care, or by better buildings, design, etc. For example, one survey estimated that one-third of accidents to young children at home could have been prevented by greater care.[16] And a government inquiry found that the two most common causes of accidents in the home were faulty design and equipment, and in the broadest sense 'human frailty'.[17] The Pearson Commission's estimate that rather under a fifth of home accidents could have been due to somebody else's fault seems somewhat low compared with these findings, but it still amounts to about 5% of all accidental injuries.[18]

It is in fact quite plain from the figures alone – indeed this is already perfectly well known – that whatever tort lawyers may say in the lawbooks, the incidence of actual claims for tort damages is affected by many other factors besides the existence of theoretical liability. In particular, it is affected by the existence of other and more satisfactory forms of compensation, such as personal property or fire insurance. Nobody is likely to bring an action for damage caused by fire when he has a perfectly good and easily settled claim against his own insurance company.[19] Even in personal injury cases, the fact that medical expenses are generally taken care of by the National Health Service, and that many employers will pay wages or salary for a reasonable period of absence from sickness or injury, probably means that many minor cases are never made the subject of a tort claim at all. In the second place, the incidence of tort claims is affected – and profoundly affected – by the possibility of actually enforcing a judgment against the defendant. Unless the defendant is insured, or is some substantial corporation, no tort claim is likely to be made in practice. It is this which places the great majority of home accidents beyond the pale of the law of tort.[20] It is not merely that the person at fault is likely to be a member of the same family as the person injured; this does not prevent damages being awarded and paid to a person injured in a road accident, against a member of the same family. It is the fact that the person at fault in the home is very unlikely to be insured against liability to members of his family; even the comprehensive householders' policy (unlike the comprehensive road traffic policy) excludes this form of liability.

It is well to compare some of the figures shown in Table 8 with those relating to all injuries given in Chapter 1, further details of which are to be found in Volume 2 of the Pearson Report. The comparison shows that although about 42% of tort payments were made in respect of work injuries, such injuries accounted for under 25% of all injuries. Similarly, road-accident victims obtained about 45% of all tort payments, but accounted for under 10% of all accidents. On the other hand, 27% of all the injuries occurred at home, but those in this category received less than 1% of all tort payments. These figures show that it is wrong to think of the tort system as being in practice a fault system; it is really a fault *and insurance* system, because the chances of obtaining damages depend on the availability of insurance just as much as on the existence of fault.

2 CLAIMS CONSCIOUSNESS

But these are not the only factors which affect the incidence of claims. One important and largely unexplored factor is that known to American lawyers as 'claims consciousness'. Some people are more 'claims conscious' than others: they are more prone to think of making a claim than others; furthermore, some types of accidents (e.g. road and work accidents) are doubtless more likely to lead to claims being made than others (e.g. leisure and domestic accidents), because people associate the 'law' more with one type than another. This is not merely a question of lack of means or legal advice. That is another question which we consider below, but there is no doubt that many people who could get legal aid, or who have the assistance of trade unions, simply do not think of making claims at all.[22] Differences in the level of claims consciousness can be extraordinary: one American enquiry found that of 38,000 'products liability' cases in the whole of the United States, 67½% came from the New York metropolitan area alone, 12½% came from Boston and the remaining 20% from the whole of the rest of the country.[23]

A recent national survey in Britain found that only one in three of road accident victims, one in four of work accident victims, and one in fifty of other accidents, consulted a solicitor.[24] It was also found that women are less likely to consider making a claim, or to seek legal advice, than men; that children and the elderly are less likely than those in other age groups to do so; and that those in higher socio-economic groups are less likely to do so than those in lower groups. The Pearson personal injury survey showed that only 11% of those injured thought seriously of making a claim for damages.[25] They also noted that one employer reported large and consistent regional differences in the proportion of accidents which led to claims.[26]

No doubt pure ignorance accounts in many cases for failure even to consider making a claim. Many people think of the law (if at all) as something meted out by magistrates; some are probably altogether unaware of the existence of the civil law as opposed to the criminal law. Important in overcoming ignorance are the activities of bodies, such as unions, which provide certain groups of injury victims with advice immediately after the accident. Claims consciousness may also be greater in relation to accidents which occur in public (and are, therefore, more likely to be witnessed and reported) than in relation to domestic accidents, for example.[27]

It is often assumed that those of low socio-economic status are likely to be less claims conscious than those in higher groups; but the 1984 Harris survey casts doubt on this assumption.[28] In cases where some consideration is given to making a claim, factors such as perceived difficulties in obtaining evidence and fear of legal expenses are important in causing a claim not to be made at all, or to be abandoned once made.[29] Fear of legal expenses might itself, to some extent, be a product of ignorance. The 1984 Harris survey found that even amongst those who consulted a solicitor, only one in four knew of the legal advice scheme and less than one half knew of the legal aid scheme.[30]

Even among the better informed many potential tort claims are probably never made owing to ignorance of the law or of the administration of the law. For instance, who even among the better educated and better informed, would think of pursuing a claim on behalf of his child injured in a road accident by his own negligence, against himself? But since passenger liability insurance is compulsory there is no reason in law why his own child should not recover substantial damages against him which will have to be paid by the insurance company. Such claims are indeed made from time to time, but it seems improbable that many are aware that they can be made. Indeed, some people appear to be unaware of the extent to which a liability insurance company takes over the entire responsibility, financial and otherwise, for a claim; American and Canadian surveys have found that there is sometimes a reluctance to make a claim against a friend, even when he was insured, for instance where the potential claimant was a passenger in a car and was injured through the careless driving of his host. Of course reluctance to make a claim against someone well known as a friend or even, perhaps, a professional or business acquaintance, would not always be overcome by knowledge that there was an insurance company in the background. For example, many people might feel understandably reluctant to make a claim for medical negligence against their own doctor, even though he is likely to be insured.

Then there is probably much higher claims consciousness in connection with road accidents and to a lesser extent, industrial accidents, than in connection with other accidents. For example, few people injured (say) in a private house would think of suing the occupant for negligence, even though this kind of liability may well be covered by a householders' comprehensive insurance policy. A study of home accidents in Bristol in 1976 confirmed the great reluctance of the victims of such accidents to make claims; although there were a number of serious injuries, only one person in this study of over one thousand accidents had actually sought legal advice.[31] And astonishingly few people in this country know of the legal liability of a retail seller for damage or injury caused by defective goods: in 1968 a Consumer Council Survey put the figure at only 22%.[32]

There are, moreover, many people who do not appreciate that a tort claim can be made and settled by negotiation. The public image of the 'law' is confined to what happens in courts – and this is not surprising since the public tends to think of the law as mainly the criminal law, and criminal cases cannot be 'settled' as civil claims are. Also, of course, there is a great deal of publicity about dramatic court cases, but a newspaper item stating that a claim had been settled out of court would be a rarity. Thus many people assume that a tort claim necessarily involves a judicial hearing; and fear of the cost of such a hearing, as well as of the burden of giving evidence, may deter them from making a claim. In industrial cases there is often a real fear of causing trouble to work-mates by requiring them to give evidence against their employer.[33] And finally there is remarkable reluctance to consult solicitors in this country. And contrary to what might at first be expected, this reluctance appears, at least in relation to obtaining compensation for personal injuries, not to be confined to (or even more common amongst) the working class.[34] In the Pearson Commission personal injury survey, a substantial proportion of those injured who sought no legal advice or redress said that this was because they did not want to make a fuss, or that it was too much trouble.[35]

Although the evidence on claims consciousness is slight, there is a sufficient core of established fact to make it certain that the presence and strength of claims consciousness is an important factor in determining the number of potential tort claims which are, in practice, prosecuted. This is not of merely academic interest, for if one of the main purposes of the tort system is to compensate those suffering injury from another's fault, then the system does not work well to the extent that people who have good tort claims do not in fact pursue them. It must, of course, be admitted that this criticism is not confined to the tort system. The social security system does not in practice compensate all those who are entitled to social security benefits. Some are too proud or too ignorant to claim what they are entitled to, and there has been much disquiet about the fact that the very poorest families often appear to be among those.

3 ROAD ACCIDENTS AND INDUSTRIAL ACCIDENTS

The fact that road accidents and industrial accidents dominate the tort system justifies a closer look at the figures relating to these. Until relatively recently, it was generally believed that the great majority of road accident victims recovered some tort compensation. But the findings of empirical surveys, first in America and now in this country, have put a very different complexion on things.

Road accidents

From figures supplied by the Pearson Commission it seems (as already stated) that only about one-quarter of road accident victims eventually obtain any damages. In aggregate terms this means that approximately 100,000 tort claims are made every year as a result of road accidents, for damages for personal injuries or death. In some 96% of cases where claims are made, some payment ensues.[36] It is very probable that the proportion of those who obtain damages is higher in cases where the injuries are more serious. In fatal cases, damages are recovered in about one case in two.[37]

The small proportion of those who recover tort damages in road accidents may surprise some, but it is expained (apart from the element of claims consciousness we have already examined) by two main factors: first, the fault system eliminates a substantial proportion of those injured; and secondly, the insurance system is far from being comprehensive. If we take the fault factor first, we cannot tell from looking at the figures what proportion of accidents were caused by someone's fault, but we can make some reasonable guesses about some types of accident. In 1983 out of a total of 242,876 road accidents involving personal injury, over 43,000 involved *only one vehicle*, and these accidents caused 980 fatalities and over 13,000 serious injury cases.[38] Some of these accidents may have been due to the fault of a third party who was not directly involved in a collision; and some of the victims of single vehicle accidents would have been passengers who might have recovered tort damages against the drivers. But there can be little doubt that the single vehicle accident must account for a good proportion of those road accident victims who receive no tort compensation at all. In this connection it is perhaps significant that in 1983 21% of motor cycle riders and 31% of other vehicle drivers who died in road accidents had blood alcohol levels above the legal limit;[39] it would be surprising if most of these were not at least partly to blame for the accidents in which they died.

Then there are accidents caused by sudden vehicle defect, such as sudden brake or steering failure, or the like. There has been much controversy about the extent to which vehicle defects cause or contribute to road accidents. In 1955 it was estimated that 3·3% of personal injury accidents were partly due to vehicle defects, but Road Research surveys have shown much higher figures. Another study of a sample of accidents found that in 25% of the accidents vehicle defects (or more strictly 'vehicle factors') were a contributory cause.[40] But this figure is probably misleading for the present purposes, since it is very likely that a high proportion of cases in which there is a vehicle defect are attributable to the fault of the owner of the car in not maintaining it properly. In this event there would be tort liability, and although the negligence would not be in driving but in maintaining the vehicle, it would be covered by the normal insurance policy, and is required to be so covered. Even so, there are other research studies suggesting that a significant proportion of motorway accidents occur through tyres bursting, and negligence may be hard to prove in cases of this kind.[41] The latest study by the Transport and Road Research Laboratory suggested that vehicle defects account for about 2½% of accidents, but that the road environment also accounts for about the same proportion.[42] Accidents due to sudden illness or death of the driver, which would also fall outside the tort system unless the driver had reason to know he was susceptible to such attacks, are not common, but have been estimated to account for between 0·1% and 2% of all road accidents.[43]

In addition to accidents which occur without fault on anyone's part, it must also be remembered that there may be many accidents which, though caused by someone's fault, cannot be *proved* to have been so caused. The particular problem of the hit-and-run driver is now largely taken care of by the Motor Insurers' Bureau,[44] but proof that someone was to blame for the accident is still required. If, therefore, there are no witnesses of the accident, and the physical facts (such as the position of the vehicles, etc.) do not themselves amount to evidence of negligence, the plaintiff will fail. In practice, this simple lack of evidence is a very common problem.

We shall look at the insurance system in detail later, but there are many road accidents which are the fault of persons who are not required to be – and usually are not – insured against tort liabilities, such as pedestrians and cyclists. Then there are accidents caused by animals on the roads. In 1958 over 4,000 vehicles were involved in accidents with animals, some 2,700 being dogs and 1,400 other animals. Since 1958 the statistics have been kept in a different form so no firm figures can be given as to animal involvement in accidents; one estimate is that dogs are involved in some 500–700 personal injury accidents per year.[45] Another estimate is a good deal higher, and suggests that about 2,400 road injuries a year are caused by accidents involving dogs.[46] Dog owners are sometimes comprehensively insured, and such insurance covers third-party liability, but it is thought that not many owners would be so covered. Of course it must not be assumed that because a dog is involved in an accident the driver of a vehicle also involved may not be legally at fault, despite the presence of the animal.

Industrial accidents

Although many industrial accidents are required by law to be reported, it is well known that the statistics are patchy and not always very reliable. Moreover, the number of persons injured at work who succeed in recovering any tort damages has, until recently, been largely speculative. But the Pearson Report now enables some much more reliable estimates to be presented. The Report estimates that there are some 1,300 persons killed at work, and about 680,000 injured in every year. In addition, about 40,000 self-employed persons are estimated to suffer some personal injury in the course of their work each year.[47] (Once again, it must be remembered that the Pearson Commission defined an injury as one involving absence from work for four days, or an injury of comparable severity.)

Previous estimates of the proportion of these persons who recover tort compensation have now been confirmed as reasonably accurate by the Pearson Report. Ison estimated that some 10% of industrial accident victims recover some tort damages. This estimate is based on figures obtained by Ison from seventy-seven trade unions representing 78% of workmen who were members of unions having at least 500 members. In 1964 these unions recovered tort damages on behalf of over 26,000 members in respect of industrial accidents. Another survey of trade union legal services estimated that in 1971 unions assisted over 50,000 members to obtain damages for industrial injuries.[48] To this number must be added those who obtain damages without the assistance of a union. A TUC study has estimated that about 16% of union members who obtained industrial injury benefits also recovered some damages.[49] This survey was slightly biased to the larger unions, and it is unlikely that members of smaller unions, and non-unionists, would do as well. The Pearson Commission's own estimate is that 10½% of those injured at work obtain some tort compensation.[50] There is, however, a widespread view that the proportion is much higher in serious injury cases[51] and this is to some degree confirmed by the Pearson Report[52] and more clearly by the 1984 Harris Survey.[53]

It seems clear that the proportion of successful claims is a great deal lower than it is in the case of road accidents.[54] This is on the face of it rather surprising. There are a number of factors which *a priori* might lead one to assume that an industrial injury victim has a greater chance of success in a tort action; for instance, employers are often 'strictly liable'; industrial accidents are probably less likely to occur unwitnessed; trade union advice and assistance is more likely to help the industrial accident victim. The 1984 Harris Survey also found that although about the same proportion of road and work accident victims consider making a claim, a smaller proportion of the latter actually seek legal advice.[55] One might have expected fewer road accident victims either to consider making a claim or to consult a solicitor, if only because many road victims are young children or elderly persons in retirement, who would not suffer lost earnings, whereas an industrial accident victim is by definition a wage or salary earner. It seems that these factors must be outweighed by a number of other factors, for example, the reluctance which employees feel to make claims against their employers; the road accident victim, by contrast, probably feels no reluctance to sue a motorist whom, he thinks was 'at fault'. Possibly, the fact that in road accidents the plaintiff may have suffered damage to a vehicle as well as personal injury makes a claim seem more worthwhile. Such evidence as there is, however, suggests (rather surprisingly) that receipt of sick pay or social security benefits has little effect on the propensity of employees to claim damages; that work accident victims consider making claims almost as frequently as road accident victims (although fewer consult a solicitor);[56] and that 'road accidents in general appear to result in fewer permanent injuries than either work or other accidents do.'[57]

There is little doubt that a considerable proportion of the industrial accidents which do not lead to any claim are nevertheless due to negligence on the part of someone. The annual Reports of the Chief Inspector of Factories used to contain an analysis of the cause of all fatal accidents. The proportion of cases in which some responsibility was attributed to the employer went as high as 61%.[58] Some unions have gone so far as to assert that in industries covered by statutory safety codes compensation could be recovered in as many as 50% of the cases, though often at a very unsatisfactory level.[59] No doubt there are very many quite trivial industrial accidents in which the victim is only away from work for a few days, and it is not thought worth while to make a tort claim – particularly if some wages are still being paid. But it must not be assumed that people do not in fact make claims for relatively small amounts in tort claims – we shall see later that the actual amounts paid over in tort settlements are usually quite small, probably far smaller than most people imagine.

In aggregate terms, the findings of the Pearson Commission suggest that industrial accidents may give rise to some 115,000 claims annually, of which perhaps 90,000 result in some payment of compensation.[60] The average payment (at 1977 prices) was estimated at around £900 for an injury and £10,000 for a fatal case. Total payments for injuries at work through the tort system were estimated at around £69 million, though the British Insurance Association has estimated total employers' liability claims for 1977 (paid and anticipated) at £122 million.⁶¹ Like the road victim, the work accident victim is relatively well treated financially, as compared with other accident victims. On the global estimates of the Pearson Commission for the total cost of provision made for accident victims, it seems that although work injuries account for only about one quarter of all injuries, the financial compensation (tort and social security) devoted to those suffering work injuries is about half of the total.⁶² The position is even more startling when one takes account of administrative costs.⁶³

9
The defendants: part I

In legal theory, the accident victim who wishes to make a tort claim can sue either the person whose negligence actually caused the accident; or, where that person was acting in the course of his employment at the relevant time, he may sue the employer; or he may sue both together. He does not, in law, sue the insurance company which has agreed to indemnify the individual tortfeasor, or the employer, against the tort liability. But if we look at the matter from a more practical and realistic viewpoint, we can, at least for some purposes, class employers who are vicariously liable, together with insurance companies. Both of them may be legally liable for the tort damages in the ultimate result; neither of them is (usually) in any way personally to blame for the accident; both of them act as 'loss distributors' in the sense that they pay the damages out of pooled funds; and the fact that one of them may be sued as a defendant in the first instance, while the other cannot, is a technicality. But even technicalities have practical consequences and there are certainly some circumstances, as we shall see, in which there is an important distinction between the liability of an employer and that of an insurance company. Moreover, although the liability of employers is regarded as a part of the 'law of torts' and is studied as a part of that law, the liability of insurance companies is unfortunately regarded as something standing outside the tort system.

1 THE INDIVIDUAL DEFENDANT

In law, the defendant's wealth or financial ability is usually quite immaterial to his liability.[1] The fact that he is rich is no ground for holding him liable; and the fact that he is poor is no ground for acquitting him from liability. Most people accept this principle of equality before the law regardless of wealth as morally right. But it is possible to argue that practical morality often does, and is right to, take account of a person's wealth. A parent will feel morally obliged to pay his neighbour a pound or two for a window broken by his child; but it is doubtful whether he would feel morally obliged to sell up house and home and impoverish himself and his family, if his child were to blind his neighbour's child with an airgun and find himself held liable for damages of several thousand pounds. A person who loses a book lent him by a friend would not hesitate to pay for the book even if its loss was not his fault; but a person who borrows a friend's car would be very reluctant to pay out the whole value of the car if it was completely wrecked in an accident while he was driving it, and it turned out to be uninsured.

But there are also strong social grounds for not placing crushing legal liabilities on people of modest means. It is true of very many people that their only asset of any real value is the house in which they live – or probably more accurately, the value of the house over and above the value of any mortgage secured by it. To impose a liability on a person which would require him to dispose of his house would plainly cause a great deal of dislocation and misery not only to the person himself but to his family as well. Of course the victim must not be forgotten, and if there is no way of compensating the victim except at the expense of someone who has caused his injuries, we may well feel that justice is on the side of the victim even if the tortfeasor has to sell up house and home to pay for the damages. Even in this situation, however, a case could be made for dropping damages for non pecuniary loss. If the victim's economic losses are made good it would arguably be more harmful to society to require the tortfeasor *personally* to pay substantial damages for intangible losses than it would be for the victim to forgo them. Of course, this leaves open the wider question of whether there are not ways in which we can secure that such compensation is paid without inflicting such burdens on individuals. And in practice this is precisely what happens.

But there are a few gaps in the system which are wide in theory, though rarely exploited in practice. These gaps exist where a person intentionally or negligently causes damage or injury to another, and the tortfeasor is not protected by insurance or backed by an employer. In theory there is nothing to stop the injured party from claiming tort damages against the tortfeasor in such a case. For example, a driver injured in an accident through the negligence of a pedestrian or cyclist may sue him for damages. What would actually happen if the victim tried to bring such an action and enforce recovery against the negligent defendant personally?

The first obstacle in the plaintiff's way could well be difficulty in securing legal aid.[2] Under the Legal Aid Act 1974 a person may be refused legal aid for bringing proceedings 'if in the particular circumstances it appears unreasonable that he should receive it'.[3] And Regulations under the Act provide, in particular, that legal aid is not to be given where the applicant is likely to get no more than a 'trivial advantage'.[4] Furthermore, in its notes for the guidance of applicants the Law Society stresses the responsibility of solicitors and counsel to ensure that the applicant has a good case.[5] Moreover, if the defendant consults a solicitor (which he can now do without any formality under the Legal Aid Act), the simplest and most effective advice he can get is to inform the local committee that he is uninsured and has no money to meet any judgment. On receipt of such information the legal aid certificate may be revoked and the whole proceedings brought to a rapid halt. Even if this does not happen, and the proceedings continue under a Legal Aid certificate, the Legal Aid Fund will have a prior claim on any damages awarded to the plaintiff for the payment of its costs. In a case in 1960[6] a legally aided plaintiff recovered damages and costs against an impecunious and uninsured defendant, who was ordered to pay off the debt at the rate of 10s a week. Since the Legal Aid Fund had a prior claim to these payments to cover its costs, it would have been over ten years before the plaintiff received any benefit from the payments.

If, however, the plaintiff proceeds at his own expense and recovers judgment against the defendant, he will have to consider how to enforce his judgment. Where the defendant has virtually no assets at all, he may simply escape from his liabilities by filing his own petition in bankruptcy. If the judgment exceeds £750 and the defendant can find £100 to pay the costs of a bankruptcy petition, his immediate troubles will be over. The result is that the plaintiff will get no money and will have incurred much trouble and expense. If the defendant owns a house or has other minor assets such as a life insurance policy with a cash surrender value, or a car with some secondhand value, the plaintiff may be in a slightly better position. Bankruptcy of the defendant will enable the plaintiff to lay his hands on some of his property. But even so the plaintiff will be faced with difficulties if, as is likely, the house is mortgaged, for in this event the mortgagee has first claim on the proceeds. Moreover, the plaintiff will have to get the defendant out of the house before it can be sold; this will take time, and if the defendant is recalcitrant, further legal proceedings will be necessary to obtain an order for possession. When all this has been done the mortgagee may insist on making a quick sale (at a price sufficient to cover the mortgage) even though the plaintiff may think a better price could be obtained by waiting.

In theory it is possible in two ways to make an individual pay damages out of his income rather than in the form of a capital sum. The first is to make the tortfeasor bankrupt after obtaining judgment against him, and then to try to get him to pay something out of his income each week or each month to the official receiver or a trustee in bankruptcy. This money can then be used to pay off the person's debtors including the plaintiff accident victim. But in practice this procedure is very hard to work satisfactorily. An undischarged bankrupt is entitled to retain what he needs out of his income to maintain himself and his family, and most people likely to find themselves in this position (i.e. those with no capital assets) are unlikely to have anything much to spare out of their income once they have taken what they need for their maintenance. In any case, even if this procedure worked smoothly, the bankrupt would be entitled to ask for his discharge in due course – long before the debt has been paid off. And on proof that his indebtedness arose from some momentary piece of negligence and that he had co-operated satisfactorily with the official receiver, the court would probably grant him a discharge within a year or eighteen months. Thus, if the judgment were of any substantial sum, the bankrupt would probably escape paying more than a relatively small part of it.

The second way of trying to make the tortfeasor pay out of income is by an 'attachment of earnings order': that is to say, an order requiring the debtor's employer to deduct a specified sum from his wages each week and remit the money to the court office. These orders first became generally available for the enforcement of judgment debts under the Administration of Justice Act 1970, which abolished imprisonment for debt.[7] They had not been an unqualified success in matrimonial cases, where they had been available since 1958; payments were made regularly in only a quarter of the cases in which such orders were made in 1960.[8] Some members of the Payne Committee thought, however, that they would be much more effective for short-term liabilities of a commercial character.[9]

There are many problems in enforcing attachment of earnings orders against a really recalcitrant debtor. Frequent moves and changes of employment may be made. The debtor may simply disappear, and the creditor may have no means of tracing him. The police will not help because this is a civil matter, though it would be different if the debtor were first made bankrupt. But even if all these difficulties are overcome and the defendant complies with the order, the procedure is not a very effective way of compensating the plaintiff. In *Jones* v. *Lloyd*[10] the plaintiff's husband had been killed while a passenger in the defendant's car. The plaintiff recovered judgment for £7,100 against the defendant, who was uninsured, and the court ordered payment at the rate of £10 per month. If regularly paid, this sum would doubtless be better than nothing; and indeed it represented an order for periodical payments which (as we saw earlier) has been advocated by some as an improvement on lump-sum damages. But the payment of £10 per month never actually gave the plaintiff what she was held entitled to, since it represented a payment of interest alone of under 2%, while a judgment debt at that date carried statutory interest at 4%.[11] Thus the defendant's indebtedness to the plaintiff would be increasing all the time, despite his payments, and he would never repay the capital at all. Thus it is not in the least surprising that few claims are brought against individual defendants. The difficulties in the way of enforcing a judgment by periodical payments are in practice enormous. On the whole this seems no bad thing. It is questionable whether justice is served by requiring a defendant to shoulder the burden of paying a certain amount a week out of his income for the indefinite future.[12]

More affluent defendants

It may be said that we have underestimated the chances of enforcing a judgment for a capital sum against an individual defendant. No doubt many people have some capital – for instance a life insurance policy with a surrender value, or savings in a building society or bank. And a tiny percentage of people own really significant capital investments. Furthermore it would be a mistake to think that all or most tort claims are for huge sums. As we shall see later, a very large proportion of tort claims are in practice settled for modest amounts of less than £1,000, and there must be many people who could raise a sum of this amount without bankruptcy or even serious financial strain.[13] Yet despite this it seems that claims are rarely made against or paid by individual defendants, except in one type of case. Where a modest amount of damage is done in a road accident and the claim is of the order of £80 or £100 – which usually means that the claim is for property damage only – the defendant may prefer to pay himself rather than ask his insurance company to pay. If he is required to pay an excess of £50 or £100 under his policy, and he has a valuable no-claims bonus, then it will often suit him to pay a claim of such an amount himself. But in personal injury cases there seem to be few cases in which individual defendants are asked to pay tort claims, even where these are of amounts which they could often afford to pay.

The reasons for this are by no means obvious. Probably several factors contribute to this result. First, people who do have capital (and so are able to pay) are perhaps more likely to be *insured* against less obvious risks of personal injury – for example to have a comprehensive householder's policy covering risks to visitors, or a comprehensive liability policy covering liability for damage done by a dog or a child. Secondly, the most serious injuries tend to be caused by machines; and the most common kind of machine is the motor vehicle, which is required to be insured. Other kinds of machines, and also injury-causing processes, are likely to be owned or operated by employers or corporations anyhow. There are of course, many household accidents but obviously no claim is going to be made in most of these cases because they will usually involve members of the same family; and even householders' comprehensive policies, unlike motorists' comprehensive policies, exclude liability within the family. Thirdly, if the defendant is neither insured nor backed by an employer, the plaintiff's solicitor (if he consults one) will very probably advise the plaintiff that it is pointless to proceed.

But whatever the reason, the fact remains that very few individual tortfeasors pay tort damages. In the Michigan Survey it was found that fewer than 3% of the plaintiffs received any tort payment from the individual tortfeasors.[14] The Pearson Commission were unable to provide any estimate of the number or proportion of tort claims which are made against individuals,[15] but it must be very small indeed, probably only a fraction of one percent. It is well to ponder these facts, for though they are well known to most lawyers, the legal system as a whole still appears to be based on the assumption that tort damages are generally paid by tortfeasors. Judges reason in this way – at least openly in court – and even law reform proposals are often based on the same assumption. For anyone who has studied the legal system as it appears in the books and the law reports, it is indeed hard to grasp the significance of these facts and to get used to thinking about the system as it operates in practice. Wholly new perspectives are required, and the moral foundations of the whole compensation system need to be thought out afresh. Even the Pearson Report seems open to criticism for not appreciating this adequately. Despite the wealth of statistics in Volume 2 about the extent of the insurance system, much of Volume 1 reads as though tortfeasors still paid damages themselves.

2 EMPLOYERS AND CORPORATIONS

If an individual tortfeasor carries liability insurance then he will be worth suing. But otherwise claiming against a private individual will usually be a waste of time and money. But in many cases the plaintiff may be able to fasten liability on some financially substantial corporate body such as a company, a local authority, a nationalized industry or a government department. Some very large bodies tend to act as 'self-insurers', which means that in practice they do not insure at all because their activities are so large that, over a period of years, they would probably pay out more in insurance premiums than they would have to pay out in tort damages. At first sight this may seem surprising, but it follows from the fact that insurance costs money to administer and that insurance companies hope to make a profit; with the result that what is paid out by insurance companies is very much less than what is paid in in the form of premiums. Thus, if a thousand small coal-mining companies, each of whom found it profitable to insure, are combined into one large enterprise, that enterprise may find that the total amount paid out in premiums exceeds the total amount of receipts. Of course, if the enterprise acts as a self-insurer it will have to face the additional cost of processing claims itself, whereas this would be one of the services rendered by an insurance company, but even this does not prevent self-insurance being an economic proposition for a large enterprise. Mere size, however, is not the sole consideration. Another factor is the ease with which the enterprise in question can raise money in the event of its being required to meet a very large loss. A small local authority may find it profitable not to insure, whereas a small company with an income of the same size might not be able to take the risk, the difference being that in the event of a catastrophic loss the local authority has a ready source of revenue in its rating powers (and this means that it can also borrow more easily) whereas a company might be forced into liquidation by a similar loss. The result is that the Crown, some of the biggest local authorities and nationalized industries do not generally insure against legal liabilities, or indeed against other losses (such as losses to their property). Business concerns, on the other hand, do generally insure, and since 1969 all employers (subject to a few statutory exceptions) have been required to insure against tort liability to their own employees.[16] So far as personal injuries are concerned, the Pearson Commission estimated that organizations carrying their own risks met about 12% of all tort claims, and paid about 6% of total tort payments in 1973.[17] The result of all this is that a person injured by negligence often has two substantial 'defendants' who may be able to meet his claim: the employer of the party at fault, or the employer's insurance company.

So far as the law of torts is concerned, the liability of an employer or corporation is said to be of two distinct kinds. First, it may be vicarious liability, that is to say, liability imposed on the employer simply because the damage was the result of a tort committed by a servant acting in the course of his employment. Secondly, the liability may be 'personal' in the sense that the employer or corporation is itself responsible, regardless of whether any identifiable servant was responsible. The distinction, however, appears to have little practical importance; and it may well be that cases tend to be classified as vicarious or personal according as whether the damage was done by misfeasance or nonfeasance. In the former case, there is usually no difficulty in identifying a particular employee as responsible; in the case of nonfeasance, however, it may be that no one person is responsible. Indeed, the gravamen of the complaint may be that the corporation has not nominated anybody as the person responsible for taking the precautions that were neglected on the occasion in question. We may therefore commit the solecism of speaking of 'vicarious liability' as covering both these species of legal liability.

Ever since the doctrine of vicarious liability came into the law around the year 1700 it has been steadily expanded by the courts in two principal directions: the categories of persons for whose torts such liability is recognized has been enlarged;[18] and the kinds of act for which vicarious liability can be imposed have been extended.[19] And there can be no doubt that in doing this the courts have been profoundly influenced by the fact that imposing vicarious liability was a satisfactory way of securing the payment of compensation to an injured plaintiff, without imposing crushing liabilities on a negligent tortfeasor. Thus, whereas the doctrine of vicarious liability was originally only used to render an employer liable for the acts of menial servants under his direct 'control', it came in course of time to cover all skilled and professional employees, however attenuated the control possessed by the employer. Moreover, there was also a steady increase in the number of situations in which an employer was held liable for the acts of 'an independent contractor'. The independent contractor was originally treated as outside the scope of vicarious liability and there were sound policy reasons for this, although they were never openly admitted, and perhaps the judges were only unconsciously influenced by them. The main reason why the courts imposed vicarious liability – the fact that the employer of labour was usually an organization better able to carry the risk of loss or damage than the injured plaintiff – did not necessarily apply to the employer of an independent contractor. In one sense, the 'employer' of an independent contractor included every individual who engaged a company to perform some service for him; the individual client who engaged a builder to build a house; the individual who hired a coach and driver; even perhaps the traveller who purchased a railway ticket and travelled by train.

But in course of time it became apparent that there were many circumstances in which refusal to impose vicarious liability for the damage done by an independent contractor meant leaving the injured plaintiff uncompensated altogether, even though by means of such liability compensation could be secured for him without imposing crushing burdens on anyone. This happened, in particular, wherever the independent contractor was a small business enterprise employed by a larger organization. Instead of being a large building contractor employed by an individual client, the independent contractor might be a small businessman employed by a local authority; instead of being a large concern renting vehicles with drivers to individuals, the independent contractor might be a single individual lorry owner who hires the lorry with his services as driver to a large company; instead of being a railway company which carries the public, the independent contractor might be the one man car-hire firm which rents cars to a substantial company. In cases of this kind the independent contractor might well himself be an inadequate risk bearer, at least in cases, which were not uncommon fifty years ago, and are still not uncommon today among certain classes of small business enterprise, where the contractor has no liability insurance beyond what the law requires. On the other hand, the person who engages the services of the independent contractor, far from being a private uninsured individual, is often a substantial corporation itself. Thus, the tendency to extend vicarious liability to cover the acts of an independent contractor began, and has continued to the present day.

But it may be objected that there is a danger that in our anxiety to compensate the plaintiff we will create a rule which works well where the contractor is a small businessman and the employer a large enterprise, but badly when the contractor is a large enterprise and the employer a small businessman or private individual. In fact this danger has not been realized, and the explanation is probably that a plaintiff offered two potential defendants, one of whom can easily bear the liability and one who cannot, will unhesitatingly direct his ammunition at the former. In other words, if both employer *and* contractor are liable, and one is a large organization and the other is not, the plaintiff will sue the former whether that party is the employer or the contractor. If both are small organizations and neither is able to bear the liability, the chances are that the unfortunate plaintiff will simply go uncompensated. If both are large organizations, then the law may have to decide which is the more appropriate body to bear the loss, and this raises a number of new and interesting questions which we look at in a later chapter, but at least there will be no difficulty in the plaintiff obtaining his compensation.

One lesson which might be deduced from all this is that multiplication of possible defendants often does good, and rarely does harm. The more possible defendants there are in law, the greater is the chance that one of them will be able to compensate the plaintiff, or will be insured; whereas if none is in this position no great damage is done because several impecunious defendants can no more be ruined than one. We must not, however, forget the possibility that the defendant may not be so impecunious as to be unable to pay the damages at all, but may only be able to do so at the price of ruin (if he is an individual) or bankruptcy (if it is a company). The former possibility we considered when dealing with the individual defendant. The latter possibility must now be faced. Certainly it is possible that a company may occasionally be forced into liquidation by tort claims which it is unable to meet, but, as we have seen, companies are much more likely than private individuals to be aware of the need to insure, and in practice companies which do not take out such insurance are probably very small firms, which are in much the same position as individuals. The social impact of the liquidation of such companies is much the same as that of the bankruptcy of an individual.

The other major respect in which the doctrine of vicarious liability has been extended is of less importance to the theme of this book since it has little to do with personal injuries. Vicarious liability started by being liability for negligence causing physical damage; and it is only by a long series of slow steps that it has been extended to cases of fraud and theft causing economic loss, and also to wilfully inflicted physical injury. This last type of liability – e.g. for assaults committed in connection with a person's employment, such as where a garage attendant knocked down a customer who he thought was trying to leave without paying,[20] or where a bar attendant threw a glass at someone misbehaving himself[21] – formerly raised an issue solely between the employer and the injured plaintiff. The question of policy was whether the plaintiff's claim for compensation was sufficiently pressing to be met out of the employer's funds (or his insurers' funds) when the damage was the result of deliberate and perhaps unreasonable action by the employee. But since the introduction of the Criminal Injuries Compensation Scheme the issue in cases of this kind is rather a different one. For today there would be no doubt that the person injured by a deliberate criminal assault would recover compensation, if not from the tortfeasor or his employer or the employer's insurer, then from the Criminal Injuries Compensation Board. The question, therefore, is not whether the plaintiff should recover compensation, but who should pay for it; the taxpayer, or the employer (or insurer) of the tortfeasor? This raises issues which we deal with later.[22]

Quite apart from the fact that vicarious liability may help to provide the plaintiff with a defendant who can afford to pay compensation, it also has certain other advantages for him. The most important of these is that it may enable the plaintiff to get compensation even where he is unable to identify the individual tortfeasor responsible for the damage. A person may be run over by a van bearing the name 'Bloggs Bakery', and the plaintiff can make a claim against Bloggs Bakery even though he cannot identify the driver or the registration number of the van. A person who is injured while unconscious on the operating table of a hospital may have no idea who was responsible for his injury, but if all those who might have been responsible are employees of the same hospital authority he can sue the authority, and it is immaterial that he cannot identify any particular tortfeasor.[23] Or a person may be injured in a factory by the negligence of a workmate who cannot be identified; again vicarious liability can be imposed. On the other hand, it is a requirement of the imposition of vicarious liability that *some* employee of the defendant must have committed a tort against the plaintiff. This means that a plaintiff who seeks to obtain compensation from an employer must establish two things: first, that a tort was committed against him by an employee of the defendant; and secondly, that the defendant is vicariously liable for that person. The process is thus a double-barrelled one, similar to that involved in liability insurance (is the insured liable and does his insurance policy cover his liability?), and quite different from that involved for example, in the case of first party insurance (where the only question is whether the insurance policy covers the victim's loss). But the similarity to liability insurance is not a complete one, for an additional problem arises with liability insurance which has no analogy in vicarious liability. In liability insurance cases it may sometimes be necessary to devise means to ensure that the money paid by the insurance company is not intercepted and retained by the insured tortfeasor or his creditors. No corresponding problem arises in the case of vicarious liability because here there is no question of the money ever passing through the tortfeasor's hands at all. The employer is not indemnifying the employee against his liability; he is directly liable himself.

This leads on to another point. A tortfeasor who has liability insurance is himself protected by that insurance: the insurer cannot recover from the insured the damages paid. In cases of vicarious liability, however, there is nothing in law to prevent the employer who has paid damages because of his employee's tort from recovering those damages from the tortfeasor himself. Indeed the employee is legally liable to repay these damages to the employer, just as he is legally liable to pay the damages to the injured plaintiff in the first instance.[24] But in practice, he is not likely to be called on to pay them to the employer any more than to the plaintiff.[25] This point is pursued later when we look at the whole subject of subrogation and its attendant problems.[26]

10
The defendants: part II

1 INSURERS

We have already referred many times to the fact that in the modern tort system the great majority of personal injury claims are made against someone who is insured against legal liability, and indeed, that one major factor which determines whether such a claim is likely to be made at all is the existence of a possible defendant who is insured. The vast majority of personal injury claims arise out of circumstances in which third party insurance is compulsory by law, and the Pearson Commission estimated that 88% of the number of claims, and 94% of the amounts paid in personal injury cases, were cases dealt with by insurers.[1] Moreover, even in those cases not dealt with by insurance companies, the great majority are handled by large corporations or public authorities who act effectively as self-insurers. For most practical purposes, these bodies can be treated as though they were also insurers.

The effect of this is that in most situations the insurance company is the only body with a real stake in a tort claim, and therefore such claims are almost always handled throughout by the insurance company rather than by the individual person who committed the tort. In practice, the great majority of tort claims are settled by agreement between the claimant (with or without legal advice) and the insurance company concerned, and only a tiny handful ever see the inside of a court. And of this tiny handful, only a very small fraction ever get to an appellate court where issues of 'law', as opposed to issues of 'fact', are likely to be discussed. But the conventional way of learning about the law of torts is to concentrate almost exclusively on that small fraction of cases which go to courts of appeal.

To stress the importance of out-of-court settlements and of studying the way they are negotiated, the behaviour of insurance adjusters and the amounts agreed in settlements, is not to deny that what happens in appeal courts is a central and important part of the tort system. Naturally, the way in which settlements are negotiated is profoundly influenced by what happens in courts; settlements are arrived at because of what the parties think would happen if their case ever got into court. Nevertheless, the process of settling claims by negotiation has as much right to be regarded as part of the tort system as the process of settling claims by trial.

In a small number of cases, liability for personal injuries can sometimes be imposed on a secondary insurer, that is an insurer who has not himself directly insured against third party personal injury risks. Such cases may arise where, for example, a plaintiff sues a firm of solicitors as a result of whose negligence (commonly in neglecting to issue proceedings in time) he has failed to recover damages for personal injury. A claim of this kind will be handled by the solicitors' insurers, and if the negligence is clear enough, the claim will come to be treated very much as though it were an ordinary personal injury action.[2] Similar claims may occasionally be made against other defendants, such as an insurance broker through whose negligence a policy has expired; here too, the broker's insurer may take over the claim in the same way.[3]

In this chapter, it is proposed to look rather more closely at the impact of the insurance process on the tort scene. First, it is necessary to enquire into the nature of liability insurance and to compare it with other forms of insurance; secondly, we will consider the impact which liability insurance has had on the law itself. Then we will examine the administrative methods by which tort claims are in practice processed by insurance companies and the Motor Insurers' Bureau. Finally we will discuss some particular problems of liability insurance.

2 THE NATURE OF LIABILITY INSURANCE

Looked at from the point of view of the insured and the insurer, liability insurance does not differ greatly from most other forms of insurance. It is, like other forms of insurance, an agreement whereby, in consideration of a premium, the insurer agrees to indemnify the insured against a loss – in this case, certain types of legal liability. On the face of it, the purpose of this type of insurance – as of all others – is to protect the insured against some contingency against which it is impossible for him to guard adequately by other means. It is, therefore, the insured who pays the cost of the insurance, since he gets the benefit of it. Furthermore, anybody injured or damaged by the insured has no concern with the fact that there is, or may be, an insurance company in the background: the injured person must make his claim against the insured in the ordinary way. The policy is intended to benefit the insured and not the injured party, so the injured party has no direct claim against the insurer. Nor is there any question of the insurance company 'being generous' or paying damages under the policy for the benefit of a claimant who cannot establish a claim in law against the insured. Moreover, since the policy is procured by the insured and is an ordinary contract between the insured and the insurer, it is governed by the ordinary principles of the law of contract. So, for instance, if the insured has obtained the policy by fraud or misrepresentation or if he has failed to comply with the conditions of the policy, the insurance company should not be liable.

But when liability insurance ceases to be viewed as a protective device for a small number of prudent persons and becomes part of a system designed to secure compensation to many injured accident victims, the whole perspective changes. It is no longer the case that liability insurance is always or generally taken out for the protection of the insured. Insurance against liability to third parties is compulsory under the Road Traffic Act not for the protection of drivers, but for the protection of their victims. Many drivers are so lacking in capital assets that they are virtually judgment-proof in practice. Such drivers do not really need protection against liability; and even if they do, their need for protection is certainly not so great that it would have justified Parliament, on paternalistic grounds, in forcing them to insure. Indeed, it is quite plain from various provisions of the compulsory insurance system as we shall see shortly, that Parliament had in mind the protection of victims and not drivers.

This fundamental shift in the purpose for which liability insurance is taken out tends to upset the whole complex system of tort law and liability insurance. Instead of tort law being the primary vehicle for ensuring payment of compensation to accident victims, with liability insurance as an ancillary device to protect the insured, insurance becomes the primary medium for the payment of compensation, and tort law becomes a subsidiary part of the process. As we have previously seen, one of the chief reasons why the great mass of personal injury claims arise out of road accidents and industrial injuries is that insurance is nearly always available in these cases. Indeed, it has been said that 'tort liability can ... be regarded as a means of inducing those who may cause losses to others to procure insurance in their favour by compelling them to pay for the losses themselves if they fail to procure such insurance.'[4] This approach reduces tort law to the level of a mere sanction for failing to insure, and an unnecessary one at that, having regard to the already existing sanction of the criminal law. Moreover, it is a much less effective sanction, as is obvious from the number of motorists who did not buy passenger insurance before it became compulsory in 1971. Nevertheless, it can hardly be doubted that this is a truer perspective of the relative functions of tort law and liability insurance than the more obvious lawyer's approach of treating tort law as paramount and liability insurance as a protective device for the insured. But if this is so, certain difficulties at once become apparent. First, why should the protection of insurance cover be restricted to these cases in which the victim's injuries are the result of actions of someone liable in law? Secondly, as a compensation mechanism tort liability and liability insurance – whereby everybody is in effect insuring for the protection of everybody else – is a vastly more complicated and irrational system than first party accident insurance, whereby everybody can insure for his own benefit directly without the interposition of tort liability at all.

It may help to appreciate the significance of these considerations if we pause for a moment to compare liability insurance with what we have called in this book 'first party insurance'. The risks which are covered by tort liability insurance could also be, and to a certain extent in fact are, covered by first party insurance. For example, a person who has a comprehensive insurance policy on his car is insuring not only against his legal liability should a claim be made against him, but also against the risk of any damage to his car arising from any of the possibilities specified in the policy. Since one of these will be the possibility of the car being damaged in an accident caused by the negligence of another driver, this risk may be covered twice over. The owner of the car may claim either under his own insurance policy, or he may make a tort claim against the other driver which will be met by that driver's insurance company, assuming that *that* driver carries an insurance policy which covers him against legal liability for damage to property. If both drivers carry comprehensive insurance policies then the risk of damage to either car by the negligence of the driver of the other is covered twice.

It will also be seen that the protection afforded by the tort claim and the tortfeasor's liability insurance is much less extensive than the protection afforded by a person's first party insurance. Liability insurance can only protect where there is legal liability, and this, as we saw in Part 2, generally means that the insured must have been at fault. Of course the more 'strict' tort liability is, the nearer liability insurance approaches to first party insurance, until it eventually reaches the point at which it is evidently nothing more than first party insurance purchased by one person for the benefit of others.[5] This is largely the position with regard to liability arising from nuclear hazards. Tort liability here is (by Statute) so strict that in effect the owner of a nuclear installation is simply required to provide first party insurance for everybody else.

But however strict the liability, it is still the case that the insured must be found, and must (if necessary) be proved to have been liable. And *in general*, fault must still be proved. But a person may damage or destroy his property in many ways besides being involved in an accident which is due to the fault of someone else who carries liability insurance. For example, a car may be damaged in a way not due to the fault of anyone or it may be damaged in an accident due to the fault of someone who does not stop and cannot be traced; or of someone who carries no liability insurance, such as a pedestrian or a cyclist. The average motorist, who has invested several thousand pounds in a car, is clearly unwilling to run these risks, but is willing to buy insurance to protect himself against them. On the other hand, although the motorist's first party insurance covers so many more risks than the tort liability insurance of the other party, it is true that the motorist will generally be better off if he can claim against the other party and, through him, against his insurer, rather than claim against his own insurer.

In practice, however, there is a very important difference between personal injury and damage to a car or other property, namely that people do not generally insure themselves against the risk of personal injury. Although a person's most valuable asset is usually his own earning power, very few people in this country insure against loss of, or damage to, this asset. In the case of people of modest means this is understandable because they are already compulsorily insured under the State's social security system which gives them a substantial degree of protection. But even people whose standard of living is a good deal higher than could be enjoyed on social security benefits rarely insure themselves against injury; and so if they are injured tort law and liability insurance may be their only method of obtaining really substantial compensation. It is not simply a question of preferring to claim against the other party to save a no-claims bonus: it is a choice between tort liability and liability insurance, or no compensation at all other than social security payments. If personal income-loss and disability insurance were as common as comprehensive insurance for cars, tort claims for personal injury would probably decline enormously in number and importance;[6] moreover, people would be compensated for personal injury even if it occurred without anybody's fault, just as at present they are compensated under comprehensive insurance policies for damage to their cars even though caused without anybody's fault. If personal insurance became the normal method of financing compensation for personal injuries, the premium would be related to the value of what is at stake (i.e. the earning capacity of the insured). Thus, just as the person with the more valuable car pays more for comprehensive insurance (though not for third party insurance, because a more valuable car is no more likely to damage another than a less valuable car), so the person with higher earning capacity would have to pay more to insure his earning capacity.

One major difference between liability insurance and first party insurance is that the former, to be truly effective, may have to be taken out for an unlimited sum. In the case of some kinds of damage to property (e.g. oil pollution by tankers) the potential liability may be so great that insurers are not prepared to grant unlimited cover. Where a person takes out his own first party insurance, however, this problem does not arise, because the insurer's maximum liability will have a definite ceiling which can be agreed in advance, or will be fixed by the value of the property.

Another major difference between liability insurance and first party insurance, is that a liability insurance system is affected by the law relating to contributory negligence. Since contributory negligence reduces the liability of the tortfeasor, and the insurance company is only bound to indemnify the tortfeasor against his legal liability, it follows that the money actually payable by the insurance company under a liability policy will be reduced by the contributory negligence of the injured party. Most forms of first party insurance do not work in this way, because people wish to protect themselves against the risk of their own negligence as well as against the risk of other people's negligence; and also the risk of pure accident. When a person insures his house against fire, or his car against 'all risks', he does not expect his compensation to be reduced if he is partly, or even wholly to blame, for any resultant loss. It is true that some insurance policies may require the insured to take 'all reasonable care' or all 'reasonable precautions' against the occurrence of the risk, and may even specify certain precautions which must be taken, but it is usually only in extreme cases that conditions of this kind prevent an insured person from recovering compensation under his own insurance policy.[7] Where both liability and first party insurance cover the same risks, as in the case of a comprehensive motor policy, the effect of contributory negligence can, in theory, be extremely complicated. For instance, suppose that A and B are involved in a collision for which both are partly to blame, and that both cars, which are comprehensively insured, are damaged. In law A can recover from B and through B, from his insurers, for the damage to A's car to the extent that B is to blame for the accident; and from his own insurer in respect of the balance of his loss (less any excess which A pays himself). Similarly with B, who can recover part of the compensation from his own insurers and part from A's insurers. In practice, this would be so wasteful and complex a procedure that the insurers prefer to avoid it, if they can, by 'knock for knock' agreements. Under these agreements insurers agree, in effect, to convert comprehensive insurance policies, so far as they relate to damage to the vehicles themselves, from liability *and* first party insurance, into first party insurance exclusively. Thus A's insurer pays A for the damage to A's car, and B's insurer pays B for the damage to his car; this saves much trouble and expense. In any particular case, the effect of the 'knock for knock' agreement may be less advantageous to one insurer than the other; for example, if A is largely to blame for the accident and the damage to B's car is more serious than the damage to A's car, then the effect of the 'knock for knock' agreement is that A's insurer gets off much more lightly than he would have done otherwise, while B's insurer comes off much worse. But insurers know that in the long run these advantages and disadvantages are likely to iron themselves out as between large insurers, and that if they stick to the letter of the law they themselves (and hence their customers) will bear the cost of adjusting the compensation according to the degree of fault of the parties.[8]

We can see, then, that liability insurance is a much more cumbersome form of insurance than personal insurance. It involves three parties (the victim, the insured and the insurer) rather than two (the insured and the insurer), and it involves two legal issues (the insured's liability to the victim, and the validity and extent of coverage of the policy) rather than one (validity and extent of coverage of the policy). Moreover, in practice, the issue of legal liability of an insured is much more likely to raise difficult problems of proof and adjudication than the issue of coverage under a policy. The latter may sometimes be an issue, but in the great majority of cases of first party insurance no problem at all arises about whether the risk falls within the cover granted by the policy. On the other hand, it is only too common that questions do arise about the legal liability of an insured under a liability policy. It is much more difficult to decide if a person has been at fault than to decide if a loss is covered by a particular policy.

3 FIRST PARTY INSURANCE FOR THE BENEFIT OF OTHERS

There is one important species of insurance which is something of a cross between first party and liability insurance. If a person, for instance a warehouse keeper, a carrier, a repairer, or the like, – a 'bailee' in legal terms – has in his possession valuable goods belonging to other persons, it is quite possible that the parties will wish to take out some insurance beyond that provided by property and liability insurance. Liability insurance would not normally satisfy the bailor because it would only protect him if the goods were lost or damaged in circumstances in which the bailee was liable in tort; and the latter would only be liable if he was at fault in some way. So if the goods are stolen despite all precautions, or if they are struck by lightning, or burnt despite all fire alarms, there will be no tort liability and therefore, no insurance compensation. On the other hand the *bailee* would not be protected by the normal form of property insurance taken out by the bailor, because this kind of insurance does not prevent the bailor from suing the bailee in tort (although it does prevent him from recovering *both* types of compensation).[9] How is this situation to be dealt with? One possibility is for the bailee to exclude his normal tort liability by *contract*, i.e. to persuade the bailor to agree that the bailee is not to be liable for loss or damage to the goods. Unfortunately this, although possible, is a dangerous course because in practice the courts frown on this kind of exclusion and the bailee may find himself held liable on some spurious and distorted reading of the exclusion clause. There is also the possibility of such a clause being void under the provisions of the Unfair Contract Terms Act 1977, designed to prevent the use of unreasonable exclusion clauses in certain classes of contract.

The second way of meeting the problem is for the bailee himself to take out property insurance for the full value of the goods, partly in his own interest (i.e. protecting whatever interest he has in the goods) and partly in trust for the owner of the goods.[10] Under this form of insurance either bailor or bailee may claim against the insurance company, and tort liability once again drops out of the picture.

Nothing corresponding to this type of insurance exists in the case of injury to the person. In fact the law places great obstacles in the way of taking out insurance against bodily injury directly for the benefit of another person, as opposed to taking out much more cumbersome liability insurance. In practice, few people would wish to insure *other persons* directly against such risks, but an employer may well wish to insure his own employees. However, it seems almost as if the law wished to discourage employers from doing this. In the first place, the doctrine of privity of contract means that formidable (if not insurmountable) difficulties are placed in the way of such an insurance being legally enforceable by the employee against the insurance company.[11] Thus, if the employer wishes to protect his employees against risks of bodily injury, including those for which legal liability would not arise, the insurance policy he takes out may be unenforceable in law. In the second place, if the employer does take out such an insurance policy and the insurance company (as may be anticipated) does not take any technical point about privity of contract, but pays under the policy, the payment may be disregarded in any subsequent action at law against the employer. This will certainly be the case where the employee is killed and his dependants receive the insurance money, for it is now explicitly provided by law that any insurance policies are to be disregarded in an action under the Fatal Accidents Acts.[12] It is perhaps not clear whether the same result would follow if the workman were only injured and not killed, but it seems probable that it would. And, thirdly, if the employer attempts to meet the absurdity of this position by inviting his employees to give up their common law rights in return for better rights under some insurance scheme which would cover them even for injury or death not caused by fault, it will be found that this course is actually prohibited by law.[13] The result of all this is that in the one area in which direct insurance against bodily injury and death by one person for the benefit of another might have been expected, the law has discouraged the possibility so strongly that, in practice, no real alternative usually exists to liability insurance on the one hand, and first-party insurance on the other. However, there are some cases in which such insurance may be found despite these difficulties, e.g. an athletic club may insure its members against the risk of personal accident.

4 THE IMPACT OF LIABILITY INSURANCE ON THE LAW

We have already seen that in practice the great bulk of tort compensation for personal injuries and death is paid for by insurance companies under liability policies. The question which this raises is whether this has had any impact on the actual law itself. Have the relevant rules of law been modified to take account of the fact that the damages will be paid by an insurer and not by the tortfeasor personally? This is not an easy question to answer, and it may perhaps help if we disentangle a number of separate issues. In the first place, there is the question whether the existence or non-existence of liability insurance is likely to affect a decision in any given case. The second question is whether the general practice of insuring against certain types of legal liability has affected the rules of law or procedure in cases of that general type; and this second question must itself be approached with care, because the answer may differ according to whether we are looking at common law rules, statutory rules, or even 'extra legal' rules not generally enforceable in the courts.

Effect of insurance in the particular case

With regard to the first question, it seems reasonably clear that the presence or absence of liability insurance in any given case is not a material factor in deciding whether the plaintiff or the defendant is entitled to judgment. Indeed, when a case is tried by a jury, it used to be a firm rule in cases tried by jury that the jury was not to be informed that the defendant was insured.[14] This rule probably does not apply to trial of an action before a judge alone,[15] but in any event, 'It is now assumed by judges, and it cannot be doubted by juries, that every defendant is insured, at any rate against third party traffic risks.'[16] Empirical evidence, so far as it goes, suggests that a jury is not more likely to find for a plaintiff merely because it has been disclosed that the defendant is insured.[17] And as to trial by judges, it has been vigorously asserted that the judge must disregard the possibility that the defendant is insured. In *Davie* v. *New Merton Board Mills*, an action by a workman against his employer, Viscount Simonds said:

It was at one time suggested ... that the House should take into consideration the fact that possibly or even probably the employer would, but the workman would not, be covered by insurance, and for that reason should be the more ready to fasten on the employer liability for an accident due neither to his or to his workman's carelessness. I will only say that this is not a consideration to which your Lordships should give any weight at all in your determination of the rights and obligations of the parties. . . . It is not the function of a court of law to fasten on the fortuitous circumstances of insurance to impose a greater burden on the employer than would otherwise lie on him.[18]

It has been suggested that the best reason for rejecting as irrelevant the fact that the defendant is or is not covered by insurance in any given case is that any other rule would make it impossible to fix premium rates for liability insurance.[19] In fact this does not seem to be so. Liability insurance rates are fixed by insurers in the light of past experience as to the number of incidents covered by the policy for which legal liability is likely to be incurred. If liability itself actually turned on whether insurance existed, the extent of such insurance would merely be one more matter relevant to the assessment of the risk. In practice, the presence of liability insurance is often a necessary (though not a sufficient) condition of a claim being prosecuted at all; and it would therefore make no difference to the assessment of the risk if the law were to confine liability to cases in which liability insurance existed. But it would, of course, discourage this form of insurance very severely, for not many people would willingly pay premiums to cover a risk for which they would not be liable if they did not insure.

However, as we have seen, English courts do not generally allow the presence or absence of insurance to affect tort liability. But although the decision on the issue of liability is not likely to be affected by the existence of insurance, it is possible that the level of damages may be affected. In America empirical studies suggest that a jury is likely to award higher damages against an insured defendant.[20] No similar studies exist with regard to the position in England, and the situations are not really comparable. Jury trials of cases of personal injury are now extremely rare in this country; and damage awards by judges in England are much more stereotyped than jury awards in America. Moreover, since judges now assume that the defendant is insured in nearly all cases, it is doubtful if awards would be inflated by actual knowledge of insurance; perhaps actual knowledge that the defendant is uninsured may occasionally act as a brake on large awards, but it seems improbable that this happens often, if at all.[21] Just as the possibility of the defendant having liability insurance in the particular circumstances is ignored, so also, the possibility of the *plaintiff* having first party insurance in the particular circumstances is irrelevant. In a personal injury case, the established rule is that the plaintiff is permitted to keep his insurance money *and* recover damages in addition.[22] In a property damage case (where first party insurance is more common), the insurance company takes over the plaintiff's tort rights by subrogation.

Effect of practice of insurance on the law generally: cases of possible influence

When we turn to consider the effect of the practice of insurance on the law generally, however, the position is very different. There can be little doubt that the actual development of common-law rules has been influenced by the growing prevalence of liability insurance. This is not the kind of thing that can be demonstrated by empirical evidence, but one can at least point to cases in which judges have denied that any hardship is being done to a defendant by observing that it was open to the defendant to insure himself against liability. As long ago as 1778, Lord Mansfield justified the imposition of vicarious liability on a sheriff for the acts of his officer by observing that it was possible, and common, for a sheriff to protect himself against such liability by stipulating for an employee's fidelity bond[23] – in effect the earliest species of liability insurance. And in 1912 Lord Macnaghten said very much the same thing in leading case on the vicarious liability of solicitors for the frauds of their servants.[24]

Moreover, the level of damages in personal injury cases today is explicable only on the basis that judges are influenced by the widespread presence of insurance. It can hardly be supposed that judges would habitually award thousands of pounds in damages without a thought for the effect of such awards on the defendant, if they did not appreciate that the damages would not be paid by the defendants themselves.[25] In recent times some judges have warned that the fact that damages are paid by insurance companies is no reason for assuming that their magnitude does not matter. In one or two cases, it has been suggested that if damages become too large premiums may become so high that some business concerns will suffer financially,[26] or alternatively, that insurance companies may go bankrupt,[27] as indeed a number have done in the past twenty-five years. Insofar as these warnings remind lawyers that damages have to be paid by an insurance company, and that insurance companies have to collect their premiums from the public, they may serve a salutary purpose. But the arguments themselves are quite untenable. In the first place, properly regulated insurance companies should not go bankrupt because damage awards are high. Premiums are fixed partly by reference to the level of awards made by the courts; if awards go up, then premiums must go up too, but unless awards are suddenly doubled overnight without warning, no insurance company should be in trouble merely as a result of the high level of awards (as opposed to sudden extensions of legal liability). It is true that there have been a large number of failures amongst insurance companies operating in the road traffic business, but it seems clear that the explanation of these failures was that the companies were not properly conducted, and the way to deal with this sort of problem is by means of the controls now available in the Insurance Companies Act 1974, and not by artificially pegging the level of awards below their proper level. The second argument, viz. that if premiums become too high business will suffer, is equally suspect, although the position does need to be watched. Premiums form a very small part of the costs of most businesses, and injury costs would have to reach astronomical proportions before premium rates caused serious financial trouble to most businesses. It is true that in America, the proliferation of medical malpractice and products' liability claims is giving rise to serious concern because of the costs of insurance. Some doctors, for instance, are turning away from the high-risk specialist branches of medicine, and some small companies are said to have been driven out of business through their inability to meet products' liability premiums. But damages awards are *very* much higher in America than here, and Americans as a group are very much more litigious than the British. Moreover, there is an argument for saying, at least in some contexts, that if an industry cannot afford to pay adequate compensation for injuries it inflicts it should go out of business.

Another respect in which liability insurance may have affected the law of torts concerns the procedural rules regarding set-off of judgments on claims and counterclaims. For example, in *Smith* v. *W. H. Smith and Son Ltd*[28] two cars were damaged in a collision, caused (as was held) by the fault of both drivers in equal proportions. One car was damaged to the extent ot £58.76 and the other to the extent of £58.35. In such a case it might be thought that the obvious course would be to dismiss both claim and counterclaim, and this is what the county court judge did. But it will be seen that to set-off claim against counterclaim (or dismiss both) means that each party bears his loss himself. However, to give judgment for the plaintiff against the defendant for half of his loss, and for the defendant against the plaintiff for half of *his* loss does not produce this result if the parties carry liability insurance. Indeed the insurance companies will have to pay the sums for which judgment is given, and each party will bear only half of his own loss. Clearly, in some cases this may be of very great importance. If two motorists seriously injure each other in an accident, and each suffers 'losses' of, say, £10,000, then, if both are equally to blame, and each is entitled to judgment against the other for £5,000, each will actually receive this sum from the other's insurers. If the claim and the counterclaim were set off, however, neither party would receive anything at all. In the result, it was decided in the *Smith* case that the proper course was to give judgment for the plaintiff on the claim, and judgment for the defendant on the counterclaim; but not a word was said in the judgment of the court about the effect of insurance on the issue. The decision was based on the unfairness which would arise from set-off as a result of technical rules about costs. It is impossible to say whether the court was influenced by the insurance considerations.

Another type of case in which courts seem to pay attention to insurance arises where machinery is hired with a driver; it is often the practice to require the hirer to indemnify the owner for any damage done, even if the driver is responsible for the damage. At one time, a clause of this kind would have been thought so unreasonable that it would have been construed, if at all possible, so as to avoid this result. But today this is less likely, as the courts are now more aware of the fact that a clause of this kind is merely an indication that insurance is the responsibility of the hirer and not the owner.[29] Indeed, the action may well be brought by the hirer's insurers, as subrogees.

A recent property-damage case which suggests that the court may have been influenced by insurance practices (both liability and first party) is *Hobbs* v. *Marlowe*.[30] The plaintiff's car was damaged in an accident for which the defendant was responsible. Both parties were comprehensively insured. The damage amounted to £237, but in addition the plaintiff incurred further expenses of £63 from hiring a replacement while his car was out of action. The plaintiff's insurer paid him £227 (the amount of the damage less an excess of £10), leaving the plaintiff £73 out of pocket. He sought the assistance of the AA with a view to suing the defendant for this sum. The AA's solicitors knew that if the action was brought for that sum, they would not be awarded costs because of the new County Court rules that costs would not be given for claims under £75 (now £500). They therefore launched proceedings on behalf of the plaintiff for the whole sum of £300. They knew, of course, that the plaintiff would have to refund the £227 paid by his insurers out of this sum. Moreover, because the two insurance companies had a knock-for-knock agreement between them, the plaintiff's insurer would have been obliged to repay this sum to the defendant's insurer. The defendant's insurer, in turn, would have to repay this sum to the defendant under the terms of their comprehensive policy. Thus, as to the £227, the money would travel in a complete circle, starting with the defendant, and ending up with him, to no apparent purpose. The House of Lords held that this did not deprive the plaintiff of his legal title to sue for the whole sum, including the £227; to that extent they upheld the well established law that a first party insurance policy does not affect the rights of the plaintiff against the tortfeasor, even though those rights can only be exercised for the benefit of the insurer who pays under the policy. On the other hand they went on to hold that the County Court judge was entitled to deprive the plaintiff's solicitors of their costs, on the ground that there was no real justification for bringing an action for £300 rather than for £73. To that extent, the decision seems to take account of the realities of the insurance factor and even the knock-for-knock agreement. In general terms, the result seems welcome, because knock-for-knock agreements undoubtedly help to reduce insurance costs to motorists, and if actions of this kind are encouraged the overall result is almost bound to be an increase of cost to motorists. The fact is that a motorist who wishes to claim for an excess (or for some uninsured loss) against another driver is indulging in an expensive luxury. It would be far better for him to take out more comprehensive cover.

So it seems probable, though it is incapable of demonstration, that the prevalence of liability insurance has had an influence on the common law. And probably, though this also cannot be demonstrated, the expansion of liability for negligence which has steadily been going on during the past hundred years, and particularly since the turn of the century, is also partly due to the fact that insurance enables judges to give effect to their desire to compensate a plaintiff without imposing hardship on the defendant. So also it has sometimes been asserted that the standard of care required in the law of negligence has been tightened up over the years, and that this is in part due to the prevalence of liability insurance.[31] The tendency to 'objectivize' the standard of care, and to ignore the personal characteristics of the defendant, which has gathered force during the past fifty years or so, may also have been influenced by insurance considerations. Since the defendant is not going to pay the damages personally, judges may be (consciously or unconsciously) more concerned with the hardship to the plaintiff and less with the defendant and may, therefore, be more willing to find a defendant negligent even though he has not done anything morally culpable.

Again it is hardly possible to demonstrate the truth of suggestions of this kind,[32] but certainly the different treatment accorded to plaintiffs and defendants does seem to confirm them. The fact that more subjective considerations are taken into account in deciding questions of contributory negligence than in deciding questions of negligence, and that venial acts of carelessness in the stress of a factory may be disregarded when contributory negligence, but not negligence, is in question,[33] suggests that liability insurance is exerting an influence on these questions. The same seems to be true of cases in which a trivial act of negligence has resulted fortuitously in serious personal injury. The fact that the courts nearly always 'bend' the law in the direction of the plaintiff in such cases can hardly be pure coincidence.[34]

At one point (especially in America) some went so far as to suggest that as a result of the prevalence of liability insurance injured plaintiffs could, in practice, nearly always be sure of collecting tort damages against an insured or substantial corporate defendant. Probably because a very high proportion of those who get as far as consulting a lawyer do in fact receive some tort compenstion,[35] the belief began to take root in legal circles that the fault principle was in practice being replaced by something very like strict liability, and that most accident victims received some compensation. The empirical studies of the past twenty-five years have proved this belief to be totally unfounded. It is quite clear from this evidence that large numbers of accident victims, especially those not injured on the road or at work, receive nothing at all by way of tort compensation, and that many others receive compensation for only a small proportion of their losses. It is also evident that the fault principle is one major reason for this state of affairs.[36] Thus, it is quite wrong to assume that the spread of liability insurance has in practice supplanted the fault principle.

Effect of practice of insurance: cases where insurance ignored

Moreover, there is no sign that any really deep seated shifts are taking place in the law of torts such as might have been expected if the judges wished to rebuild the law on the foundations of the liability insurance system. Had it been openly acknowledged that tort damges are paid by liability insurers, that this system has come to stay, and that it is a good system on which tort law can be based, one might have expected the courts to start looking for the defendant who is most strategically based to carry such insurance and to worry less about his 'fault'. Quite apart from the fact that this might well have led to stricter liability, it might also have led to much wider use of the notion of vicarious liability. For instance, a passenger in a car negligently opens the door and causes an accident in which a passing cyclist is injured. The person most strategically placed to carry insurance is obviously the driver, and most comprehensive insurance policies actually provide cover against the passenger's liability though this, too, is not legally enforceable by the passenger owing to the privity doctrine. A way of encouraging motorists regularly to carry such insurance would be to make the driver liable for the negligence of the passenger – but he is not.[37] Or again, suppose that a child allowed by its parent to have an airgun causes injury to another person by his negligence. Such accidents fall within the criminal injuries compensation scheme, but only if the conduct is reckless or deliberate and not if the child is merely negligent. The parent, too, is only liable in tort if he was at fault in failing to instruct or supervise his child properly, yet he is clearly the right person to insure against damage caused by his children. The same is true of damage caused by animals, and particularly dogs. The animal owner is strategically placed to insure – dog liability insurance could even be combined with dog licences for the payment of some small premium – yet the liability of animal owners has not been modified to take account of liability insurance. Similarly, where personal injury accidents occur at sporting events (e.g. motor races) there is clearly a case for holding the organizers liable regardless of fault, because they can be expected to insure against the risks. But here again the courts have failed to move away from the fault principle, and the spread of liability insurance has had little impact on the law.[38]

There are many particular areas of law and procedure in which it is plain that the courts turn a blind eye to the practice of insurance. First, and most obviously, the plaintiff must still find and, if necessary, sue a defendant who is liable according to the common law of torts. This may sometimes cause serious inconvenience. For example, negotiations for a settlement may be carried on for months between the plaintiff's solicitors and the defendant's insurers, but if the negotiations break down the plaintiff must then actually find the defendant and serve a writ or summons on him. Unfortunately, it sometimes happens that during the negotiatons the defendant has moved without leaving a new address, or has gone abroad (as where he was a foreign tourist) or has even died. But still the plaintiff must commence proceedings by service of a writ or summons on the defendant or his representatives unless the court exceptionally dispenses with this requirement.

The separation of the real and the nominal defendant can also lead to other inconveniences. An extraordinary comedy of errors was revealed in *Re Harvest Lane Motor Bodies*,[39] in which the plaintiff's husband had been killed in an accident by an employee of the defendant company. The company was insured and when the plaintiff's solicitors made a claim for damages, it was referred to the insurers who negotiated for some time with the plaintiff's solicitors. In due course the negotiations broke down, a writ was issued, pleadings delivered and various interlocutory applications were disposed of in which the company was represented by counsel instructed by the insurer's solicitors. In the meantime, and quite unknown to the plaintiff's or the insurer's solicitors, the defendant company had become defunct, and some two years after the issue of the writ, the Registrar of Companies had struck the company off the register under section 353 of the Companies Act. From one point of view this did not matter at all. The real dispute was between the plaintiff and the insurers, and the defendants were of no importance to the case. But from a legal point of view it mattered a great deal. An injured victim cannot sue the tortfeasor's liability insurance company: he must sue the tortfeasor. It was therefore necessary for the plaintiff to apply to the court to restore the defendant company to the register, simply in order that it could play its role as nominal defendant in the action for damages. Fortunately, the court was able to accede to the plaintiff's request.

A similar sort of problem may arise where one spouse is injured in a road accident due to the negligence of the other spouse, who is killed in the same accident. If the surviving spouse wishes to claim damages against the insurance company, the nominal defendant must be the representative of the other's estate – his executors or administrators. But the surviving spouse will often be the executor or administrator. However, serious legal difficulties would arise if the surviving spouse were both plaintiff and nominal defendant, and it is therefore necessary to obtain a special grant of representation in such circumstances by which a third party is appointed administrator for the sole purpose of being defendant in the proceedings which the spouse wishes to bring.[40]

Another kind of difficulty arising from the court's unwillingness to recognize the effect of liability insurance is to be found in the decision of *Lister* v. *Romford Ice and Cold Storage Co. Ltd*.[41] In this case the House of Lords decided that an employee who negligently injures another employee in the course of his employment, and who thereby renders his employer vicariously liable to compensate the injured employee, is himself liable to indemnify the employer against this liability. This liability arises from the fact that the empoyee has been guilty of a breach of contract in negligently injuring the other employee. On the face of it the decision seems sensible; but when it is appreciated that the employer was insured against the liability, that the damages were paid by the insurance company, and that the proceedings in the name of the employer and against the negligent employee were effectively brought by and for the benefit of the insurance company, the whole process begins to look grotesque. But – and we shall see that this is typical of the way the English legal system tries to come to terms with liability insurance – the decision has proved of little practical importance, because insurers have generally agreed that they will not take proceedings of this nature without the consent of the employer.[42] And in a recent case not falling within the terms of this agreement the Court of Appeal has come very close to refusing to follow the *Lister* case.[43]

Two more recent illustrations of the courts' unwillingness to be influenced by insurance practice in developing the law are to be found in the decisions of the House of Lords in *Chaplin* v. *Boys*,[44] and *Davies* v. *Taylor (No. 2)*.[45] The first case involved a problem in the conflict of laws; the plaintiff was injured in a road accident in Malta (whose law did not recognize claims for pain and suffering) but he brought proceedings in England. The question was whether he could recover damages for pain and suffering according to English law, and the House of Lords ultimately held that he could. But nowhere in the lengthy judgments, nor in the vast academic literature to which it has given rise, was the insurance question raised. Yet perhaps the strongest argument against allowing such a claim is that in all probability the defendant's third party insurance was taken out in Malta, and the premium fixed according to Maltese law. It seems difficult to justify a decision which can result in an insurance company being held liable to pay damages vastly higher than those on the basis of which the premium is fixed.

The second case involved a question under the Legal Aid Act. Under this Act the court may, in certain circumstances, order the costs of a successful defendant to be paid out of the legal aid fund where the action was brought by a legally aided plaintiff. In *Davies* v. *Taylor (No. 2)* it was held that the defendant's costs were 'costs incurred by him' in the proceedings and so payable out of the fund, although in fact the defendant's insurance company was legally bound to indemnify him against the costs. But to treat this as a mere 'indemnity' is wholly unreal. The defendant would never in fact have paid or even incurred the costs. The result of the decision is that, in cases of this nature, the question is treated as though the choice is between making the defendant pay for the costs on the one hand, and making the legal aid fund pay for them on the other. But in reality, the question is whether the defendant's insurer or the legal aid fund is the more appropriate party to bear these costs.

The importance of insurance: statutory modifications of the law

When we turn to consider the extent to which liability insurance has led to statutory modifications of the common law of torts, there is no doubt that we can trace many important statutes back to the influence of liability insurance in one form or another. The Law Reform (Miscellaneous Provisions) Act 1934, for instance, which enabled proceedings to be brought against the estate of a tortfeasor, was a direct consequence of the fact that negligent defendants killed in road accidents were now insured. The Law Reform (Contributory Negligence) Act 1945 also owed much to the fact that, with the spread of liability insurance, it no longer seemed reasonable to deprive a plaintiff of all right to damages merely because he had been negligent. The abolition of the doctrine of common employment by the Law Reform (Personal Injuries) Act 1948 was at least partly due to the complete change which the practice of employers' liability insurance had produced in the legal treatment of industrial accidents. And certainly the Law Reform (Husband and Wife) Act 1962, which enabled husbands and wives to sue each other in tort, was largely due to the feeling that it was unfair that a spouse was the one person who could not claim damages from an insurance company in the event of injury in a road accident through the negligence of the other spouse. Similarly, under the Congenital Disabilities (Civil Liability) Act 1976 it is provided that a child who suffers pre-natal injury shall not be able to sue its mother for negligence, except where the injuries were the result of a motor accident for which the mother was responsible.

But above all, the compulsory insurance system now laid down in the Road Traffic Act 1972 recognizes over and over again the fact that liability insurance is a method of compensating accident victims, and cannot be treated as though it were merely a device for protecting a tortfeasor against legal liability. One of the principal concerns of the Road Traffic Act is that matters arising under the contract of insurance between the insured and the insurer should not be allowed to defeat the claims of the accident victim. Thus, for instance, if the insured obtains his policy by fraud or misrepresentation, the insurer's normal legal right to avoid a contract is severely restricted by s. 149 of the Road Traffic Act. And if the insured breaks some condition stipulated in the policy relating, for example, to the condition of the vehicle or the driver (e.g. that the vehicle must not be driven in an unroadworthy condition, or that the driver must not drive while drunk) this does not affect the rights of the accident victim; although the insured may be under a liability to indemnify the insurer against the damages which the insurer has to pay. Similarly, a failure by the insured to comply with a condition of the policy as to anything occurring *after* an accident, e.g. that he must give notice to the insurers within a stipulated time, etc, does not affect a third party accident victim. In fact, as we shall see shortly, the provisions of the Road Traffic Act are in practice supplemented by the extra legal liability of the Motor Insurers' Bureau, which renders even less effective many stipulations in insurance policies so far as concerns the accident victim.

In addition the Road Traffic Act acknowledges that the accident victim has a direct legal claim against the insurer, even though this claim cannot be enforced by legal action unless, and until, the plaintiff has secured judgment against the tortfeasor. Now that personal injury actions are so rarely tried by juries, and judges are well aware that defendants are insured in practice, there seems no real reason why it should not be possible to add the insurance company as a defendant to any action in which it may be liable to indemnify the nominal defendant. Indeed, it is a general procedural rule that a person who is being sued in an action may himself bring third party proceedings against any person liable to indemnify him, and that those proceedings may be tried together with the main dispute. When jury trials were still common and it was not permissible to tell the jury that the defendant was insured, it was naturally felt undesirable that the insurance company should be openly made a party to the proceedings, but it is perhaps surprising that today it is still not the practice to do so.

The effect of liability insurance is also clear in s. 150 of the Road Traffic Act and the Third Parties (Rights against Insurers) Act 1930, both of which concern the possibility of bankruptcy on the part of the defendant. Normally it is not permissible to take legal proceedings against a person who has been adjudicated bankrupt or against a company in process of liquidation; such claims must be made to the trustee in bankruptcy or the liquidator who will pay a dividend out of the bankrupt's assets. But if there is an insurance company standing behind the bankrupt this process can be bypassed under s. 150 of the Road Traffic Act and the plaintiff can recover from the insurer in the normal way. Difficulty, however, did not stop there, because if the plaintiff sued the tortfeasor to judgment and the tortfeasor was unable to pay the damages personally, the accident victim could originally do nothing to prevent the tortfeasor going bankrupt *after* the judgment. As a result the insurance money would have been claimed by the trustee in bankruptcy or the liquidator, and the accident victim (whose injuries were the sole reason for the payment of the insurance money) would have had to submit a proof for his claim and rest content with a share of the insurance money along with all the other creditors.[46] This was put right by the Act of 1930 so that if the tortfeasor becomes bankrupt, his rights against the insurance company pass to the accident victim who can sue the insurers direct. This once again recognizes that the purpose of liability insurance is to protect the accident victim and not the insured.

Further recognition of the crucial role of liability insurance is found in the Legal Aid Scheme, which takes great pains to prevent an insured tortfeasor from securing legal aid as a *defendant*; since the practice whereby insurers conduct an insured tortfeasor's defence was already established when the legal aid scheme started in 1949, Parliament was clearly disinclined to throw these costs onto the taxpayer and thereby relieve the insurance companies.[47] Yet, remarkably enough, Parliament did just this when it created the National Health Service only one year before the legal aid scheme. Medical costs arising from road accidents are by and large borne by the taxpayer and not by insurance companies and their premium payers.[48] Another notable example of Parliament ignoring insurance is provided by the Occupiers' Liability Acts. In particular, the problem of the liability of a property owner for the negligence of an independent contractor is treated in the traditional common law manner as depending on whether the occupier was in any way at fault, e.g. in selecting an incompetent contractor, or failing to provide adequate supervision. But recognition that the occupier is the person best placed to insure against personal injuries taking place on his premises, and that contractors may be impecunious or may become impossible to trace or identify, might have led to a different result, at least in the case of business as opposed to private premises. Much the same criticism could be levelled against the Animals Act 1971 which pays insufficient attention to possible extensions of liability insurance. On the other hand it is interesting and encouraging to note that the Unfair Contract Terms Act 1977 requires the courts to have regard to the availability of insurance (among other factors) in deciding whether certain types of exclusion clauses are reasonable.[49]

One final example may be given of the complex inter-relation between statute law, liability insurance and judicial decisions. Under s. 143 of the Road Traffic Act, which lays down the basic requirements of the compulsory insurance system on the roads, it is an offence to 'cause or permit' a motor vehicle to be used on a road if it is not insured against third party risks as required by the Act. In *Monk* v. *Warbey*,[50] the Court of Appeal held that a person who is guilty of a breach of this section may be liable to an action for breach of statutory duty, at the suit of an injured party who is unable to obtain compensation from the negligent driver. It is possible that the person sued in such an action would himself have to pay the damages out of his own pocket, but it is much more likely that the action would enable the accident victim to obtain compensation from the defendant's insurance company. The sort of case which the action is designed to deal with, occurs where the owner of a car allows someone else to drive it in circumstances in which that person is not covered by insurance. In this situation, the decision in *Monk* v. *Warbey* renders the owner of the car liable, and therefore in practice may place his insurance company at risk. Whether or not the owner's insurance company is liable in this case depends largely on the terms of the policy, but the normal policy indemnifies the owner in respect of liability arising out of the use of a specified vehicle on the road, and liability under *Monk* v. *Warbey* would seem to fall within these words. Thus the effect of this case is that even where a policy does not cover any person driving a car with the owner's permission (as most private policies do) such cover is, in effect, compulsorily written into the policy – though insurers may have a theoretical right of recourse against the insured after they have paid the damages. However, the importance of the case has been greatly reduced by the creation of the Motor Insurers' Bureau.

5 THE MOTOR INSURERS' BUREAU

The Motor Insurers' Bureau was set up by the insurance industry in 1946 under pressure from the then Ministry of Transport. It is a limited liability company whose members are all insurance companies engaged in road traffic insurance in the United Kingdom. It was set up in order to provide some redress for those injured in road accidents by the negligence of uninsured defendants. Since the Road Traffic Act 1974 all authorized insurers are required to become members of the MIB, and thus to share in its cost. The current position is regulated by an agreement with the Secretary of State for the Environment dated 22 November 1972, under which the MIB – as it is usually called – undertakes to meet any unsatisfied judgment in respect of a liability required to be insured against under the Road Traffic Act. Certain conditions must be fulfilled, but the only one of any importance is that the claimant must have informed the MIB of the proceedings in question within seven days of their commencement. In practice, the MIB does not require the case to be fought to judgment but acts precisely as an insurance company would, negotiating with the claimant or his solicitor over the claim; but if no settlement is arrived at, the MIB normally defends the proceedings on behalf of, and by agreement with, the uninsured defendant.

In practice there are three types of cases in which the MIB may be made liable. First, where an identified uninsured motorist was responsible for the accident the MIB simply acts as though it were an ordinary insurance company. The second type of case occurs where the motorist responsible is identified and an insurance policy was in force at the material time but the insurer is not legally liable under that policy. For example, the policy may have been obtained by fraud or misrepresentation, or the insured may have been guilty of a breach of a condition of the policy. The Road Traffic Act does not permit an insurer to escape all liability to an accident victim in these circumstances simply by repudiating the policy, but it is possible to take certain formal steps to escape liability in such cases. The practice in these circumstances (under a 'Domestic Agreement' between the MIB and its members) is for the insurer to deal with the case as though the policy were a valid one in law. Thus the procedure laid down in the Road Traffic Act for enabling an insurer to avoid liability to an accident victim where the policy was obtained by fraud or misrepresentation or where there has been a breach of condition, has been rendered obsolete. Moreover, the effect of the Domestic Agreement goes beyond the Road Traffic Act in that it provides for the case where the insurer is not liable at law simply because the policy does not cover the liability at all – for example where the insurance is limited to use of the vehicle for domestic purposes and it was being used for business purposes at the time of the accident. In these circumstances, the strict legal position is that the accident victim is completely without redress, but the result of the Domestic Agreement is that the insurer will not be permitted to raise the question.

The third type of case (now covered by an agreement dated 22 November 1972 and a minor amending agreement dated 7 December 1977) is one in which the accident victim is injured by a 'hit and run' driver, that is by a driver who remains unidentified. This type of case caused great difficulty because the MIB operates basically as a liability insurer and, as we have seen, liability insurance requires the plaintiff to find and sue some identifiable defendant. Even if the MIB were legally liable to accident victims under its agreement with the Ministry (and we shall see that it is not), it could still not be sued in this sort of case because its liability is that of an insurer. Although pressure was often brought on the MIB to accept liability in 'hit and run' cases it was reluctant to do so because it claimed that, in the absence of a defendant, and therefore of the possibility of a trial, the MIB could not contest the plaintiff's allegations on the issue of negligence or the amount of the damages claimed by him. Yet in some ways the arguments for holding the MIB liable are strongest in this type of case. In the other two types of cases the MIB, and thus the insurance industry, is accepting a liability for which no premium has been paid; but if the 'hit and run' driver was insured with a member of the MIB then a premium would have been paid. The 1946 Agreement did not impose liability for this type of case, but the MIB did agree in some cases to make an ex gratia payment; but this too was regarded as unfair, because the plaintiff was unable to obtain a judicial ruling on the amount of damages to which he was entitled. The position was severely criticized in *Adams* v. *Andrews*,[51] and pressure on the MIB was maintained by the *Justice* Report on the Trial of Motor Accident Cases in 1966.[52] Eventually, in 1968, agreement was reached between the MIB and the then Ministry of Transport whereby the MIB undertook to accept liability where no defendant could be traced.[53] Under the current procedure the MIB will investigate claims in such cases and will, if satisfied that the claimant was injured in circumstances in which insurance is compulsory under the Road Traffic Act, offer compensation assessed on normal common law principles. If the claimant refuses to accept the MIB's decision he may appeal to an arbitrator appointed by the MIB from a panel of Queen's Counsel maintained for this purpose. The arbitrator's fee is normally paid by the MIB, but the claimant is required to agree to give the arbitrator power to order him to pay part or all of the fee if he thinks there were no reasonable grounds for the appeal. Not everyone is satisfied with this procedure, and attempts to circumvent it and bring proceedings in court have been tried, though without success.[54] In principle, no doubt, there is something to be said for the view that a claimant should be able to have his claim tried in the ordinary courts, like the victims of all other road accidents. On the other hand, it is hard to take seriously a claim 'in principle' in this area where principle is so manifestly lacking in the overall situation. What right has a claimant to demand a judicial hearing when (for example) criminal injury claimants are compelled to pursue their claims against the Criminal Injuries Compensation Board and have no right to a judicial hearing?

It will be apparent from what we have said that the MIB is only liable where insurance is required under the Road Traffic Act. The MIB is not liable in respect of damage to property,[55] nor in respect of personal injury arising from an accident not caused on a public road.[56] The MIB is not liable for injuries to the person driving the car at the time of the accident even if the injuries are attributable to the negligence of the owner (e.g. in failing to warn the driver that the vehicle's brakes were faulty) and even if the driver is driving the vehicle at the request and for the benefit of the owner.[57] And of course, the MIB is only liable where the accident was caused by negligence. Since compulsory insurance against liability to passengers was introduced the MIB has covered such cases as well, but there are special clauses designed to prevent recovery in some such cases, e.g. where two thieves steal a car and the driver causes injury to his colleague.[58]

The MIB is, in many respects, an extraordinarily anomalous institution which operates partly within and partly outside the legal system. In the first place, the right of an accident victim to claim against the MIB is unenforceable in strict law by the accident victim himself. The obligations of the MIB are not statutory but arise under a contract with the Secretary of State, and this contract cannot be enforced by the accident victim because of the doctrine of privity of contract; although in practice courts do award declarations that the plaintiff is entitled to recover from the MIB. In theory, no doubt, if the MIB broke its agreement the Ministry might be able to get an order of specific performance requiring the MIB to comply with the agreement.[59] In practice, however, it is almost unthinkable that the MIB would violate this agreement, and if it did so there is not much doubt that the whole scheme – or some alternative – would be put onto a statutory footing.

The result is that the MIB simply does not take the privity of contract point and behaves as though it were legally liable to accident victims. A victim who sues the MIB will not be met by the clearly good plea in law that he is not a party to the contract of 1972, but by some alternative plea (which may be good or bad) such as a denial that he was injured by negligence; or that he was injured in circumstances in which insurance is compulsory under the Road Traffic Act; or (if liability is admitted) that the damages claimed are excessive. As we have seen, it is not possible to adopt this course where no identifiable defendant can be found, but arbitration, as the next best thing to judicial decision, is now possible.

Like liability insurance itself, the existence of the MIB may cast a shadow over proceedings in court, but is rarely taken account of in the legal process except where it is directly involved. For instance, the offence of driving a motor vehicle while uninsured is still treated by the courts in precisely the same way as when it was first created in 1930. Yet the existence of the MIB has changed the character of the offence altogether; instead of being an offence which involves the risk of depriving accident victims of compensation, it is now an offence more in the nature of tax evasion. Another example of the courts simply ignoring the existence of the MIB is to be found in the decision in *Corfield* v. *Groves*,[60] where it was held that the action under *Monk* v. *Warbey* for permitting an uninsured person to drive in breach of the Road Traffic Act was unaffected by the fact that the MIB would meet any judgment against the uninsured driver.

On the other hand, a recent decision of the Court of Appeal suggests that a more realistic approach to the existence of the MIB may be taken in the future. In *Gurtner* v. *Circuit*[61] the MIB applied to be made a party to an action brought by a road accident victim. The plaintiff in this case had been injured in an accident by a motorist who was insured, but the insurance company was never discovered and the driver had gone abroad and could not be traced. In such circumstances, it is possible for the plaintiff to obtain leave for 'substituted service' of a writ and then to obtain judgment by default against the defendant for damages to be assessed. The difficulty is that, unless the MIB are then made parties to the case, there is nobody in a position to appear and contest the plaintiff's claim when the damages come to be assessed. The Court of Appeal decided in these circumstances that the MIB should be made party to the case. The court made an attempt to bring the MIB within the law, as it were, by stressing that the MIB did have a legal obligation – albeit an obligation only enforceable by the Minister of Transport – to meet any judgment awarded to the plaintiff, and accordingly that the MIB had sufficient 'interest' in the case to be made party thereto. On the other hand, in *Albert* v. *MIB*[62] Lord Dilhorne protested at the anomalous situation in which the courts, who are the judges of legal rights and duties, are required to give judgment against a person who is not liable in law.

One final comment may be made on the situation which arises under the new procedure agreed in 1968, under which the MIB accepts liability even though no defendant can be identified. Here, the defendant is eliminated entirely from the scene, and the issue of compensating the plaintiff is adjudicated upon without the defendant being a party to the proceedings, or present, or even identified. The purpose of the insurance in this situation is simply and unequivocally the compensation of the claimant, and not the protection of an insured tortfeasor. Nevertheless, the claimant must still show that his injuries were the result of a tort committed by the unidentified driver. This restriction seems quite out of place when the purpose of the insurance is so clearly to compensate the victim.

6 SOME PROBLEMS OF LIABILITY INSURANCE

Insurance against legal liability, especially for personal injury and death, involves a number of problems which do not affect other types of insurance. To understand these problems, it is necessary to know something of how liability insurance premiums are fixed. In principle, premiums are calculated on the basis of an estimate of the amount of claims, plus the administrative costs of collecting the premiums and processing the claims. Allowance is then made for the insurer's profit, and also for income which the insurer expects to earn on investment. It is the calculation of the cost of claims which causes particular difficulties in relation to liability insurance. The cost of claims is a function of three main variables, namely, the number of accidents and injuries for which policyholders are held liable, the severity of the injuries, and the level of damages awards. In the case of road and industrial accidents, the first two variables do not present great problems. Given previous experience from which the insurer can judge trends in accident numbers and severity of injuries, a competent insurance company can make reasonably sound estimates for the future. Of course, even the best managed company can be caught out by a sudden, unexpected change in the trends, but large fluctuations in these variables, in the case of road and industrial accidents, are rare.

Estimating these variables can, however, present much greater problems in the case of liability for diseases. An employer, for example, may be held liable to pay damages to employees who contract diseases as a result of exposure to dangerous working conditions. Many diseases take some time to develop, and in some cases symptoms may not be noticeable for 20 or 30 years after exposure. Employers and insurers generally may not become aware of the risk of disease until after the first successful claims are made. Even if they do become aware sooner, and insurers start charging premiums to cover such liability, it may be extremely difficult for them to fix premiums at adequate rates because of lack of past experience. In such circumstances, insurers may be faced with a large number of claims over a short period of time in respect of which no, or only inadequate, premiums have been collected. Reports from the United States indicate that this sort of problem has arisen in relation to claims based on exposure to asbestos, and that the financial stability of a number of insurance companies is being threatened as a result.

The third variable – the amount of damages awards – can also cause considerable difficulties in two ways. First, the size of awards is partly a function of the rules governing assessment of damages. If the rules are changed without warning in such a way as considerably to increase the level of awards, this can upset insurers' calculations significantly. This problem is exacerbated by the fact that, even though changes in the law are not, in strict theory, retrospective, they may be so in effect. For example, when section 4 of the Law Reform (Miscellaneous Provisions) Act 1971 greatly increased the entitlement to damages of widows in Fatal Accident Act claims, the Act came into force one month after it was passed. It thus became applicable to all trials, and hence to all settlements, after that date, even though insurance premiums, out of which those damages had to be paid, were calculated several years previously when the law was different. Similarly, when the law relating to interest on awards of damages for personal injuries was changed in 1969, the effect was a substantial increase in the aggregate amounts which insurance companies had to pay. But these increases took effect long before insurers were able to allow for them by increases in premium rates. Another relevant example of a change in the law was the introduction in 1979 of damages for loss of earnings in the 'lost years'.

The second source of difficulty in estimating the third variable is inflation. This effects most components in damages awards – compensation for loss of earnings and for costs (such as medical and hospital expenses) resulting from the injuries are affected quite directly; and damages for non-pecuniary loss are now increased more or less in line with inflation. Inflation causes most difficulty when the rates of increase of wages and prices vary erratically from year to year, for this makes predicting the size of future awards almost impossible. But even when, as in the last few years, the pattern of inflation has settled down somewhat, predicting future rates is always a risky activity. And yet it is essential when, say in autumn 1986, an insurer is calculating premiums for 1987, to calculate them in the light of expected damages in 1987. But the position is worse, even, than this, because of the length of time it takes to settle many personal injury claims. The premiums collected in 1987 must be adequate to pay all claims based on liabilities arising in 1987, even though a substantial proportion of these claims will not be settled for 2, 3, or 4 years, and a small number (probably of the larger claims) will still be outstanding in 5, 6 or 7 years. When the claims are finally paid, they will be paid in the light of wages and prices at that time, just as a court assesses damages in the light of wages and prices at the date of judgment. So an insurer, to be safe, may have to estimate inflation rates up to 8 years into the future. Even in times of relatively stable currency values, this is a daunting task. And because liability insurance is a competitive business, it is not easy for the insurer to play safe and fix premiums on the assumption of very large increases in earnings rates and costs over the next three or four years. If he does this, he may find himself greatly undercut by other companies who assume a much lower rate of inflation. If, on the other hand, the insurer underestimates the rate of inflation he can expect catastrophic losses.

It must also be appreciated that an insurer cannot easily recoup next year's losses from higher premiums in the following years. State, or social insurance, which operates on 'pay as you go' principles can do this easily enough; the State can compel next year's premium payers to pay enough money to cover the cost of this year's accidents, and so on, as a result of its coercive powers. But private insurance companies have no coercive powers. They have to pay for this year's accidents out of this year's premiums, and if those premiums prove inadequate they cannot be certain that they can ever recoup those losses. A private insurance company which tried to recoup its losses in this way would find itself charging uncompetitive rates against a new insurer unburdened with previous losses. In any event, it is quite contrary to recognized accounting principles to attempt to throw part of the cost of this year's accidents on to next year's premiums. An insurance company cannot be treated as solvent unless it has put aside reserves adequate to meet all its estimated liabilities.

The worst effects of insurance company failures (and it seems clear that some of the failures of motor insurers in the 1950s and 1960s were, in part, the result of inflationary pressures) are now dealt with by the Policyholders Protection Act 1975. But it is important to be aware of the difficulties, so that the position of insurers is not made unnecessarily precarious.

It is therefore clear that even with the present system for the assessment of damages in lump sums, insurers face great problems. These would be magnified many times if they were required to pay damages in the form of periodical payments, which could be adjusted upwards to take account of inflation; and it would plainly be absurd to have a system of periodical payments if they could not be so adjusted. Insurance companies cannot guarantee that periodical payments they have to pay can be adjusted to meet future rates of inflation, as became clear during the many years of discussion about the nation's future retirement pension schemes. In the result, the Pearson Commission accepted that some kind of State guarantee would be needed for this purpose. We have earlier explained that so few annual cases would fall into this scheme (perhaps 600 cases per annum) that it is doubtful if any scheme of tort periodical payments would really be worth while. A far simpler solution would be to require awards of damages exceeding a certain figure to be paid over to the DHSS, who could then be required to pay a pension calculated according to some appropriate formula; the pension would then share in the annual uprating that all DHSS pensions and allowances now receive.

11
The administration of the tort system

1 THE IMPORTANCE OF SETTLEMENTS

The vast majority of tort claims are settled by negotiation and eventual agreement between the claimant and the defendant, or, in practice, the defendant's insurers. Only a very small proportion are ever disposed of by judgment of a court. On the other hand, in a larger number of cases the plaintiff gets as far as commencing proceedings by issuing a writ or summons. From there onwards cases continue to be settled, so that out of all the cases in which proceedings are commenced, many are settled even before the first serious step in the process is undertaken, i.e. before a statement of claim is delivered; others are settled at later stages of the pre-trial procedures, and a substantial number are settled (more or less literally) at the door of the court.

The Pearson Commission estimated from its various surveys that 86% of cases are settled without writ or summons being used; 11% are settled after the issue of writ or summons but before the case is set down for trial, 2% are settled after setting down, and 1% are settled at the door of the court or during the trial, or are actually disposed of by trial.[1] Many other surveys and studies confirm the general pattern of these figures.[2] These figures demonstrate that the tort system is administered very largely by insurance adjustors on one hand, and solicitors on the other hand. In the great majority of cases the process is not in the hands of judges. On the Pearson Commission figures, it seems that the judges actually handle some 2,000 cases per year, while a further 200,000 are settled without trial. It thus seems that the whole of the tort system could be regarded as an administrative process designed to compensate accident victims in which a right of 'appeal' is given to the courts of law. Looked at from this point of view, the system may be said to resemble the national insurance system more closely than might be thought at first sight. Here again, the system is run by an administrative process in which there is a right of appeal to various tribunals established under the Acts. But there are important differences apart from the obvious fact that the 'appellate' tribunals for the tort system are the ordinary courts, and for the national insurance system they are the special statutory tribunals. In particular, the national insurance administration is in the hands of the State and is run by civil servants under the head of a political Minister. On the other hand, the tort administrative machine is in private hands. One consequence of this is that the object of the administrators who run the national insurance system is (or, at any rate, should be) to see that every claimant gets what he is legally entitled to receive; and the purpose of the appeal procedure is to put right mistakes. But in the tort system, the administrators are not concerned to see that the claimant gets his legal dues: the insurance adjustors who run the tort system are primarily concerned to settle cases for the lowest figure which they can induce the claimant to accept. The Winn Committee acknowledged that the parties do not really want a 'fair' settlement but a 'favourable' one.[3] In these circumstances, the right of 'appeal' to the courts is not so much a mechanism to put right the mistakes of the adjudicators, but a weapon to induce the administrators to behave reasonably. This is why such a large proportion of cases in which proceedings are commenced, or even in which preparations are made for trial, are never tried, and this is why a former Chief Justice of Ontario has said that 'the judicial process is being used for other than judicial purposes. . . . It is being used as a threat to bring about an adjustment rather than as a means of adjudication.'[4]

2 OBTAINING LEGAL ASSISTANCE

There is nothing to prevent an individual claimant or plaintiff attempting to negotiate a settlement on his own behalf, and a certain number of claimants do so. But in this event the negotiations will be conducted by experts on one side and a complete novice on the other, and those with direct experience of the system assert that the less reputable insurance companies may take advantage of the individual claimant.[5] In these circumstances, settlements may well be reached which are seriously inadequate, and it has been suggested that there should be a power to review settlements so reached within, say, twelve months.[6] Settlements on behalf of children require the approval of the court in any event, and very few have the necessary skill or expertise to bring a case before the court for approval without legal advice; it is also unlikely that such approval would be given, unless the court were satisfied that the amount had been regarded as satifactory by experienced solicitors or counsel.

A small number of cases are settled with the assistance of unqualified advisers known as 'claims assessors' or 'claims negotiators'. These persons have no offical standing and cannot represent a plaintiff in litigation, nor can they instruct counsel or a solicitor; indeed it is an offence for a solicitor to act on the recommendation of such a person. This means that the claims negotiator's bargaining position is extremely weak since he cannot threaten legal proceedings or even proceed to the stage of issuing a writ, without abandoning the control of the case and with it the prospects of obtaining any remuneration, since he normally expects to receive his remuneration out of any damages which may be awarded. Anybody who negotiates a settlement with the assistance of a person of this kind therefore runs a serious risk that he will receive less than if he were assisted by a professionally qualified lawyer.

The great majority of claims, however, and especially those involving large amounts, are probably made with the assistance either of a trade union or a properly qualified solicitor. Very large numbers of claims for damages arising out of industrial accidents are handled by trade unions. A questionnaire addressed to unions with a membership of over 500 found that in 1964 seventy-seven unions recovered damages on behalf of 26,105 injured persons, totalling over £11 million.[7] More recently it has been estimated that unions obtain damages on behalf of some 50,000 injured members every year.[8] Many of the larger unions do not confine their assistance to industrial accidents; some assist with road accidents occurring while travelling to and from work; other assist with all road accidents; others decide whether to assist in each case individually. There are also variations in the practice of the unions as regards the securing of legal assistance. Some unions simply pass the case on to solicitors; others handle the case in the first instance themselves, but pass it on to solicitors if litigation becomes necessary, or even if the case raises particular difficulty; others make preliminary investigations into the facts, and send the case on to solicitors only if they think there is any prospect of success in a common law claim. In all cases, the expense is borne by the union and the claimant has no need to provide money.

If the claimant has no union to assist him, he may consult a solicitor. Contrary to general belief, no financial outlay by the claimant is normally required if he uses the services of a solicitor to negotiate a settlement, although occasionally a sum on account of costs may be requested in advance. Quite apart from the possibility of legal aid – which we consider below – most solicitors will accept instructions to negotiate a settlement on the basis that their own remuneration is to come out of the compensation ultimately obtained from the insurers. If negotiations are successful, the normal practice[9] is for the insurers to pay the solicitors their cost in addition to the amount offered in settlement. This has the advantage from the plaintiff's point of view that he knows the sum offered will reach him intact,[10] whereas if he had to pay his solicitor's costs out of it, he might not know precisely how much the offer was worth to him. On the other hand, this process has the disadvantage that the solicitor may be tempted to advise the client to accept an inadequate sum, simply because if no settlement is reached the solicitor may be out of pocket. If no settlement is reached, and no proceedings are begun, so that the claim is simply abandoned, most solicitors will not claim for their services against the client, though many will expect to be reimbursed at least for their out-of-pocket expenses. Since the great majority of cases[11] in which solicitors are instructed are concluded with *some* payment by way of settlement, it is clear that the question of costs is not a serious problem. No doubt there are a number of cases in which it is plain from the outset that the claim is hopeless, and in this event the only cost incurred will have been the initial interview with the solicitor. And the cost of this interview will be met by the legal aid fund if the plaintiff satisfies the statutory means test.[12] It is also possible to have an interview with a solicitor at a cost of £5 or less for up to half an hour under the 'fixed fee interview scheme', which was specially introduced to allay the fears of those who were reluctant to consult solicitors for fear of the cost.[13] The Professional and Public Relations Committee of the Law Society also produces a leaflet for use by solicitors which offers a free interview with a solicitor in connection with an accident claim.

If legal proceedings are commenced, legal aid will often be necessary unless the claim is being handled by a trade union. Legal aid is granted by the local area committee of the Law Society, in the form of a 'legal aid certificate', where they are satisifed that there are reasonable grounds for bringing proceedings. And legal assistance (under the 'green form' scheme) is available (up to £50 without prior authorization) for the purposes of negotiating a settlement[14], though as we have seen this is not usually necessary. Very often legal aid will be needed, not so much because it is anticipated that the case actually will be litigated, but to show the insurers that the plaintiff 'means business' as it were. As we shall see, some of the less reputable insurers will not take a claim very seriously unless and until the plaintiff makes it clear that the claim will be vigorously prosecuted. And, so long as no legal aid has been obtained, the insurers may be content to fight a waiting battle since they know that, although solicitors will negotiate without legal aid, they will not initiate proceedings without legal aid.

Nevertheless, in practice it is clear that the majority of cases are settled without legal aid. Of 422 cases covered by Ison's survey,[15] 322 were concluded without legal aid or trade union assistance. Zander's study of cases in the High Court in 1973–74 showed a much higher proportion of legal aid cases, 158 with legal aid as against 142 without;[16] but these were all cases which had reached a more advanced stage in the litigation process, while Ison's study included many cases settled by solicitors without issuing proceedings at all. The Pearson Report found that even among cases which went to trial, only 20% of plaintiffs had legal aid.[17] One interesting point to emerge from Zander's study is that the proportion of legally aided cases is much higher outside the main two classes of industrial and road accident cases, and this was confirmed by the Pearson Commission.[18] This may well be due to the reluctance of solicitors to take on less common claims without legal aid, and it illustrates how, once again, those who suffer injury at work or on the road are more fortunately placed than those who suffer injury elsewhere.

There are income limits on the availability of legal aid. Full legal aid (that is, without any contribution on the part of the applicant) is available to those with 'disposable' incomes below £2,255 p.a. and 'disposable' capital resources below £3,000. It should be noted, however, that 'disposable' income is much less than gross income. For example a married couple with two children, a 'disposable' income of £2,050 might represent a gross income of £8,215.[19] Legal aid with some contribution from the applicant (on a sliding scale) is available to those whose 'disposable' income does not exceed £5,415, and whose 'disposable' capital does not exceed £4,710.

An alternative to legal aid is provided by the community law centres, of which there were about fifty in 1984. The centres are staffed by salaried solicitors, and are funded by a mixture of charitable and government (central and local) grants. Most of the centres are in deprived areas of large cities, and provide their services free. Under an agreement with the Law Society, they do not handle personal injury claims exceeding County Court Scale 2 (presently £3,000).[20] There are also some private forms of 'legal aid'. Insurance against the risk of incurring legal costs is available through the motoring organizations, the AA and the RAC, and from some insurance companies. Assistance in making and defending claims is also offered by the motoring organizations and, sometimes, by employers as a fringe benefit for senior employees.

3 THE COURSE OF NEGOTIATIONS[21]

Where the claim is handled by an experienced union official, or by a solicitor, the normal practice is for the solicitor (as for convenience we shall assume him to be) to write to the potential defendant asking him to pass the letter on to his insurers, or to write direct to the insurers, asking them whether they admit liability for the accident. Few, if any, insurers would admit liability at this stage, whatever the circumstances. The most common practice is for the insurer to write a stock letter denying liability, but asking on what ground it is suggested that the defendant was negligent.[22] At this stage, if he has not done so before, the plaintiff's solicitor may be obliged to start collecting evidence in the form of statements, medical reports, and so on. In the case of a road accident, he will write and ask for a copy of the police report and of witnesses' statements. There was at one time much difficulty over the statements of witnesses made to the police, but the Home Office now requests all police authorities to supply such statements as a matter of course at the request of parties involved in litigation or civil claims. In the case of industrial accidents, attempts have been made to persuade the relevant Ministry to supply copies of factory inspectors' reports in the same way, but so far these have been resisted.[23] It has been argued that a factory inspector, unlike a policeman, rarely has any firsthand evidence which would be of assistance in litigation, since most of his knowledge of the accident is derived from hearsay statements.[24] But the collection of the evidence is not likely to be assiduously pursued until it is clear that no satisfactory settlement is likely to be reached.

When some evidence has been collected, negotiations for a settlement may continue. The plaintiff's solicitor may disclose some of his evidence suggesting that there was negligence by the defendant, and also some evidence as to the extent of the plaintiff's injuries. But neither side is usually at all anxious to disclose everything they know. There is a good deal of bluff and counter bluff in the whole process, and both sides are conscious that if negotiations fail the case may eventually come into court. In that event, each party feels it would be desirable to have some useful evidence up his sleeve which can be produced with devastating effect at the last moment – perhaps just before the case comes on, or even at the trial itself.[25] The result is that both parties spend a good deal of time skirmishing rather than actually trying to reach agreement. Part of the objective is to force the other party to disclose his hand, without having to disclose one's own.[26] This enables the party who succeeds at this tactic to assess the outcome of a trial more accurately than his opponent and therefore, eventually, to secure a more favourable settlement. If, for instance, the insurers know that the plaintiff's case is a weak one standing on its own, but they also know, and manage to conceal, the fact that there are serious weakness in their own case, they may be able to secure a much lower settlement than if the full facts were known to the plaintiff's solicitor.

Sometimes, especially in road accident cases, the course of negotiations may be greatly affected, if not actually determined, by criminal proceedings taken in a magistrate's court; or in fatal accident cases, by a coroner's inquest.[27] Although in legal theory the outcome of a civil case is largely unaffected by what may have been decided by magistrates or a coroner, in practice, these proceedings may be of the greatest importance. It is not merely the result of the case which matters, but the evidence which emerges, the witnesses who appear, and the way in which they give their evidence. In a simple road accident case, for instance, in which the only question is which of two motorists was responsible for a collision, the prosecution of one of the motorists for careless or dangerous driving may provide something like a dress rehearsal of a civil action. Naturally, therefore, insurers usually wish to represent the defendant if he is prosecuted for an offence as a result of the accident from which the claim arises; and insurance policies usually provide that the insurer will provide proper legal representation for the conduct of the defence in any such proceedings.

Sometimes the dispute will be largely, if not entirely, about the amount of damages. Where the issue of liability is so clear that it is plainly incontestable, the insurers may simply dispute the figure the plaintiff claims on the ground that it is excessive. In such a case it is sometimes necessary to wait and see how the plaintiff's injuries develop so that medical prognosis may become more certain. This, as we shall see, tends to contribute to the delay of negotiating settlements. Where there is a possibility of a finding of contributory negligence if the case goes to trial, much of the negotiations may involve trying to agree on some percentage deduction to be made from the figure agreed upon for damages.[28]

After the initial inquiries, claims and polite refusals in this delicate minuet, there will often be a meeting between the plaintiff's solicitor and the insurer's adjuster. Here, while there will still often be no admission of liability, some exploratory discussion of figures may be conducted. Standard tactics well known to serious bargainers will be employed. For example, the solicitor may, in response to an offer, reply that his client is a difficult man to deal with and he is unlikely to accept the sum proposed. Similarly, the solicitor may try to obtain an admission of liability, for example by refusing to disclose medical reports unless there is such an admission.

We have so far been outlining the procedure in a relatively simple case where everything runs reasonably smoothly. Unfortunately, there are many cases where this does not happen. There may, for instance, be great difficulty about obtaining the evidence. Witnesses may be reluctant to make statements, which is hardly surprising in view of the way they are treated by the legal system. In a case a few years ago in which counsel complained of the reluctance of a witness to give evidence, Cantley J. expostulated:

Why on earth should anyone want to be a witness? If you are a witness you will probably be notified by telegram on the day before you are required. You may have to drop everything and go to a distant court – and you may have to find your own way there. When you get there you are usually placed in a room with a stone floor and a wooden bench with a window about fourteen feet above where you are sitting. You sit there, perhaps for hours, while nothing happens. You have nothing to read, and probably no one to talk to. Suddenly, a policeman puts his head round the door and shouts out your name. You come into court like a bull into an arena.

You pick up the Testament to make your oath, and at once someone tells you that you have got it in the wrong hand. You give your evidence and someone suggests you are a liar. I cannot think why anyone should want to go to court as a witness.[29]

Difficulties in obtaining witnesses will be less frequent now that copies of statements given to the police can be supplied to the plaintiff's solicitors. But, of course, witnesses who could have given statements to the police may have disappeared before the police arrived on the scene. Although it is possible to subpoena a witness to compel him to appear and give evidence in court, this tends to be impracticable in most cases. For one thing, witnesses may simply melt away even before they have given their names and addresses, and there is no practical (or legal) way of detaining them. In any event, few solicitors or counsel would be willing to take the risk of calling a witness 'blind', that is without having a 'proof' or statement which the witness has made and which gives some idea of what he may be expected to say in evidence.

In some cases the plaintiff's lack of evidence may be even more desperate. In industrial accident cases, for instance, physical evidence may just get lost.[30] Allegedly defective equipment may disappear after an accident, and there will be no way of proving whether it was defective or not. The plaintiff is helped in some cases by s.33(1) of the Supreme Court Act 1981 under which the court can make orders allowing the plaintiff to inspect, photograph, take samples of, preserve or detain relevant premises or machinery. If the threat of obtaining such an order induces insurers to be more reasonable, it will no doubt serve a useful purpose; but these statutory provisions are only likely to help a plaintiff where the cause of the accident is broadly known, but evidence is required to prove it. They are unlikely to help a plaintiff very much where the cause of the accident is completely unknown. Under section 33(2) of the 1981 Act, the court may order discovery of documents in advance of proceedings in certain circumstances, and such an order may bring to light information which will help the parties to settle.

A plaintiff who cannot prove precisely how his injuries were caused may in some cases be assisted by the 'doctrine' of *res ipsa loquitur*. Under this doctrine, the courts have sometimes been prepared to infer negligence from the fact of the accident itself, or even to throw a burden of proof wholly on to the defendant. The practical impact of this doctrine is, however, unclear.

In any event, many difficulties remain. In the construction industry, which is responsible for a disproportionate number of industrial accidents, the scene of the accident may change rapidly as work progresses, and within a matter of weeks, if not days, the whole site may become unrecognizable. Road accidents also bring similar difficulties. The *Justice* Report on the Trial of Motor Accident Cases gave this example.[31]

In fatal cases, where it may be a motor cyclist has been killed, and his widow is endeavouring to claim damages under the Fatal Accidents Acts, she and her advisers can be completely ignorant of the cause of the accident, and they have to do their best to spell out of the physical circumstances found by those who came on the scene after the tragedy, the positions of the vehicles, the marks on the road, and what may have been said and overheard by witnesses, some evidence of what happened and by whose fault. In such cases there is no duty upon the insurers or their solicitors to go out of their way to provide evidence. They may make an offer ex gratia, perhaps genuinely out of sympathy, perhaps hoping to stifle further inquiry, and it is sometimes difficult for the widows' advisers to decide whether to accept such an offer or to proceed in the dark in the hope that further evidence will emerge at the trial....

As this quotation shows, reputable insurers will on occasion offer some *ex gratia* payment where it is evident that the plaintiff's chances of success are virtually nil. But unfortunately not all insurers are like this. Some insurers, it has been said, are 'disinclined to negotiate until they smell a whiff of powder'.[32] Unless it is clear that the plaintiff is in a position to start proceedings – which usually means he must first obtain legal aid or have trade-union assistance – some companies deny all liability. Other insurers indulge in still more disreputable tactics, such as the following:

> In reply to an initial letter they will say that the matter is being investigated and that they will write in due course. It takes three or four letters to evoke any further response. They then say that their investigations are almost completed. Further pressure elicits the eventual reply that the file has been passed to their legal department and its return is awaited. Then the file is reported lost, and the claimant's solicitor is asked for copies of the correspondence. When they finally start dealing with the claim, it will be by asking that a pair of trousers be sent to them for their inspection in order to see whether they are repairable or suggesting that if a car has been off the road for two months for repairs there should be a set-off because it will not have depreciated. After this protracted correspondence they either refuse to pay anything or offer a derisory sum in settlement in a letter of three lines which does not explain how the sum has been arrived at. Sometimes a cheque for this sum is sent, although the solicitor has not indicated his acceptance of the sum.[33]

Solicitors and trade-union officials told the Winn Committee that in some cases they found the attitude of these insurance companies so impossible, that they refused to see them or have any negotiations with them.[34] The fact that interest on damages in personal injury cases is now generally required to be awarded[35] may have reduced the extent of these abuses. But tactics of this kind may still be adopted, simply in the hope of persuading the plaintiff to settle for an inadequate figure.

The settlement process is very much a matter of bargaining, and it is bargaining of a difficult and expensive character. As economists would say, the case involves a bilateral monopoly, since the plaintiff has to 'sell' his claim to only one potential buyer – the insurer – and the insurer has to 'buy' the claim from only one potential seller – the plaintiff. Thus the plaintiff cannot, as it were, 'shop around' to get good value for his claim. And it is obviously in the defendants' interest to try to persuade the plaintiff to take less than they might really feel his claim is worth because, by insisting that an offer is the furthest they are prepared to go, they may succeed in bluffing their way to a favourable settlement. In practice, rejection of an insurer's offer commonly leads to a second increased offer being made,[36] and in some cases the process can be repeated several times. Indeed, it has been said that 'As a general rule it is safe to say that the first offer will not be the final offer.[37] On the other hand, the 1984 Harris survey found that the first offer was accepted in about two-thirds of cases where an out-of-court settlement was reached. The difficulty and uncertainties of litigation and fear of lengthy further negotiations are, no doubt, potent factors in explaining the high level of acceptance of first offers.[38] The victim is at a great psychological disadvantage: the emotional stress generated by having been injured, and then by having to engage in disagreeable haggling, often produces a desire to settle as quickly as possible, even if at an unreasonably low figure. The insurer, who is experienced in the process and not emotionally involved, can afford to 'sit it out'.[39]

4 WHEN NEGOTIATIONS BREAK DOWN

It is no part of the purpose of this book to trace the course of procedure in a High Court or a County Court action, a subject which is fully dealt with in existing legal literature. But it is important to appreciate that the course of negotiations for a settlement, and the amount of a settlement which is likely to be ultimately agreed upon, is profoundly influenced by what would happen if negotiations broke down and the claim were actually litigated. The cost of such an action, and who would pay it, are in this respect of paramount importance. There is surprisingly little hard data about the cost of personal injury claims, one of the problems being that if settled cases are taken into account, much depends upon the stage reached before a settlement was agreed. The Pearson Report found that the most nearly representative figure for average costs for settled cases was that of £196 derived from a Law Society study in 1975.[40] Yet the Pearson insurance survey shows that in 1973 average fees paid by insurers in settling claims were only £89.[41] On the other hand, Zander's study showed that for contested cases which actually went to trial, the average costs were over £1,000 for each party.[42] These figures related to cases in which the costs were taxed in 1974, and would presumably need to be more than doubled to reflect current costs. Zander's figures relate to the High Court only. Costs in the county court would be considerably less, and might in a simple case be as little as £200 or £300 for each party, but could easily amount to £400 or more for each party. The normal rule in English litigation is that the party who loses the case pays the other party's costs as well as his own, but in practice, at least in personal injury cases, this rule tends to be rather one-sided today, since an unsuccessful plaintiff rarely pays the defendant's costs[43] while an unsuccessful defendant (or insurer) is required to pay the plaintiff's costs. If matters stood there, the fear of having to pay costs would exert much more pressure to settle on insurers than on plaintiffs. But matters do not stand there.

If negotiations break down but the insurers are prepared to make an offer, or have made an offer which the plaintiff has declined, the insurers may wait for the plaintiff to commence proceedings, and they may then promptly make a 'payment into court'. This amounts to a formal offer, without strings attached, which the plaintiff may accept at any stage before the case actually goes to trial.[44] In the case of High Court actions the money is paid into the Law Courts Branch of the Bank of England,[45] and if the plaintiff accepts it, it is paid out to his solicitors immediately and the proceedings will be terminated. There is, however, a catch in this procedure from the plaintiff's point of view, namely that if the plaintiff declines to accept the sum paid in, and if he is eventually awarded *less* than the amount paid in, he will be ordered to pay all the defendants' costs from the date of payment in.[46] From the insurers' point of view this may seem perfectly reasonable. If the plaintiff declines the sum paid in and is later awarded less than that amount, this suggests that he was asking for too much and that he was being unreasonable in persisting with his case. If he had chosen to accept the sum paid in, the insurers would not have incurred any more costs, and since the judgment demonstrates that the payment-in was sufficient to meet the claim, it seems unreasonable that the insurers should have to pay their own costs from then on. But from the plaintiff's point of view, the procedure is perhaps less reasonable. It will be noted that he will have the double burden of paying all his own costs *and* the insurers' costs from the date of payment-in; and if he is legally aided, both sets of costs will come out of the damages.[47] In many cases these costs will make a substantial dent in the damages, and in some cases they will absorb the damages altogether, leaving the plaintiff with nothing at all even though he has been adjudged entitled to damages.[48] Moreover, the basic assumption underlying this procedure, namely that the plaintiff must have been unreasonable to continue the case after the payment-in, is not necessarily true.

In many cases the damages are extremely difficult to assess, as we have seen already, and an experienced counsel may be unable to advise the plaintiff whether the amount paid in is likely to be exceeded if the case goes to trial.[49] It is easy to be out by a few hundred pounds, particularly if there is any possibility of a finding of contributory negligence. Moreover, judges themselves realize that the final figure awarded by them may not be a precise computation of the plaintiff's losses. One judge, for instance, once refused to apply the normal rule as to costs where the amount paid in exceeded the amount of damages awarded, on the ground that he had at one time been minded to award more;[50] and another judge did the same where the damages awarded were exactly the same as the amount paid in, on the ground that the damages had been 'rounded down'.[51] But in both cases the Court of Appeal held that there was no justification for departing from the normal rule, which though theoretically resting in the discretion of the judge, is in practice rigidly applied.

Perhaps the most unjust aspect of this procedure is that the rule as to costs is applied even where the greater part of the costs are incurred in the dispute on liability which is won by the plaintiff and only a small part of the costs are incurred on the damages issue.[52] Thus, for instance, if the insurers pay into court (say) £3,000 and the plaintiff declines the offer, the insurers are still free to contest the whole case and to argue that they are not liable at all, e.g. because there was no fault on the defendant's part. The trial may take three days, of which two and a half may be spent on the issue of liability which the judge finds in favour of the plaintiff, and half a day on damages, the judge finally awarding perhaps £2,800. Yet the plaintiff would still have to pay the insurers' costs from the date of payment-in, although the greater part of these costs have been wasted, not simply because the plaintiff unreasonably persisted in his case, but also because the insurers persisted in denying liability. Another particularly hard type of case arises where proceedings are brought on behalf of a minor after the court has refused to approve a settlement on the ground that the amount is too low. Even in this type of case the plaintiff has to pay the defendants' costs if the sum ultimately awarded is less than the payment-in. The Winn Committee recommended changes in the law relating to payment-in, but the more recent Cantley Working Party felt that there was no real alternative to the present system.[53]

It is important to appreciate that the result of applying this rule as to costs is not merely to cause hardship in a handful of cases in which the plaintiff persists in an action and is eventually awarded less than the amount of payment-in. The primary importance of the rule lies in the great pressure which it brings to bear on a plaintiff to induce him to settle for an amount which he and his advisers may think is inadequate. Especially where the amounts at issue are relatively small, e.g. where the plaintiff is asking for (say) £800 and the insurers offer £500, the plaintiff is virtually required either to indulge in the age-old gamble of 'double or quits', or to accept the offer.[54] Zander's study in 1975 suggests that a case is more likely to be settled if there is a payment-in; indeed, 90% of payments-in were accepted. 'These findings', it has been said, 'suggest that although payments-in may encourage a settlement to be made they do so by reducing the sum acceptable to the plaintiff, rather than by encouraging the defendant to make a "proper" offer.'[55]

On the other hand, the position is rather different with very small claims. If the plaintiff's claim is for £300 or even less, the pressure on the defendant to settle is very much greater than the pressure on the plaintiff, simply because (as we have seen) a successful plaintiff recovers costs, while a successful defendant rarely does so. Hence, when the claim is small in relation to the costs of legal services and of litigation the claim has a substantial nuisance value, so that however poor the plaintiff's chances of winning a court case may be it will often pay the defendant to settle rather than to fight. Plaintiff's solicitors know this, as do insurers, and the knowledge can be exploited by the former; this is no reflection on solicitors, because a solicitor is under a duty to his client to extract the most favourable settlement possible. This means that in practice few cases are totally worthless so long as there is at least some room for argument about fault.

It is not, of course, suggested that litigation is preferable to settlements. Indeed, it is quite clear that the legal system could not possibly cope with personal injury actions if another two or three per cent of the claims were tried instead of settled. But it is clear that if there is pressure on parties to settle because of the way the system works in practice, this is likely to produce a state of affairs in which the amounts of compensation actually paid bear little relation to what the law of torts – in theory – requires to be paid. And when we come shortly to examine the evidence as to the size of settlements, we shall find that this is indeed so.

5 THE TIME TAKEN TO ACHIEVE A SETTLEMENT

Quite apart from delay in cases which are eventually litigated, the process of negotiation takes a considerable amount of time even in cases which are settled. These delays are mostly inherent in the process and it is difficult to see that much can be done about them. In 1967 the Winn Committee devoted a great deal of attention to the problem of delay in litigation.[56] Although the committee also acknowledged the quantitative importance of settlements,[57] their proposals for mitigating delay did not affect settlements. Nor did the committee pay sufficient attention to the fact that much delay in starting proceedings is simply due to the fact that negotiations for a settlement may go on for a considerable time before it becomes clear that no settlement acceptable to both parties is likely to be forthcoming.

As a result of the Committee's Report, provision was made under the Rules of the Supreme Court for interim payments to be ordered in certain types of case, e.g. where liability is plain but there are two or more defendants arguing as to the proper allocation of liability between themselves. The existence of such a power may, in a few cases, encourage a plaintiff to litigate rather than accept an inadequate settlement out of fear that if he does not, it may be years before he gets anything. More recently, the High Court has been given the power to make provisional awards of damages in cases where prognosis of the plaintiff's future medical condition is difficult.[58] In some cases, this may discourage insurers from delaying until the plaintiff's medical condition settles down. But these provisions have not made, and are unlikely to make, any significant impact on delays, especially in settlements.

Since 1970 it has become the practice to award interest on judgments in personal injury claims. One purpose of this change was to provide a financial inducement to early settlements by insurers. There is little evidence yet as to whether this result is being achieved, but there are grounds for thinking the inducement is unlikely to have much effect.[59] One other attempt to deal with the problem of delay deserves a mention. In a series of cases culminating in *Allen* v. *Sir Alfred McAlpine*[60] in 1968, the Court of Appeal decided that it had a general power to strike-out an action on the ground of inordinate and inexcusable delay, even where the plaintiff was not technically in default under the Rules of the Supreme Court. It was hoped that vigorous use of this procedure might help to reduce delays, in particular because a plaintiff whose action was thus struck-out might well have a strong prima facie case of negligence against his solicitors. However, the striking-out procedure ran into difficulties. In *Birkett* v. *James*[61] the House of Lords held that the power to strike-out could not be exercised where the ordinary limitation period had not yet expired; because in that case the plaintiff would simply be able to begin a new action by issuing a fresh writ, and the probability was that the striking-out would thus probably lead to yet more delay.[62]

The Pearson Report has now provided us with a good deal of information about delays, both in cases which are dealt with by the courts and in cases which are settled. As to the former group, the Commission found that in 1974 the average time between the date of the injury and the date of disposal of the claim was 36 months.[63] However, things were much worse in the High Court (where all serious claims must be heard) than in the County Courts. In the High Court, the average time between injury and disposal of the claim was 43 months in London and 41 months in the provinces; in the County Courts the figure was 21 months. More recent estimates suggest a slight improvement on these figures of about 6 months. The figures, however, conceal the wide variations between the simplest and the most lengthy cases. The Cantley Working Party report shows that, among cases in which a High Court writ was issued in 1977, the average time from injury to disposal was 45 months, and no fewer than 122 cases (out of a total number of 5,701) *were still undisposed of eight years after the injury.*[64]

As for settled cases, according to the insurance survey conducted for the Pearson Commission, nearly half of all claims are disposed of within twelve months, though it is plain that these must be the less serious cases because they only account for under a quarter of the total payments. By the end of two years from the injury over 80% of claims have been settled; but nearly 5% take up to four years, and nearly 1% (some 2,000 cases a year) are still unsettled after five years.[65] These findings generally confirm the pattern found by other less comprehensive studies.[66] Furthermore, the larger the settlement, the longer it takes to negotiate. The Pearson Commission's insurance survey found that 96% of payments under £500 were made within two years, but only 42% of payments over £10,000 were made within this time.[67] And in the most serious cases of all, where payments over £25,000 were ultimately made, only 27% were settled within two years. In exceptional circumstances, settlements may take many years. One of the causes which led to the establishment of the Pearson Royal Commission was the realization that many of the thalidomide cases were still unsettled after ten years.

There are two main reasons for delay, and they are both inherent in the tort system. First, in cases of more serious injury, a longer time must generally elapse before a firm medical prognosis as to the effects of the injuries can be given;[68] because tort settlements are normally in the form of a once-for-all lump sum, it is often in the interests of both plaintiffs and defendants to delay final agreement until the plaintiff's medical condition has stabilized. Secondly, when more is at stake, the haggling is prone to be more prolonged and vigorous. This is the result of the fact that the aim of the insurer in the settlement process is to pay not what the plaintiff needs, but as little as possible. Moreover, in very small cases the cost of prolonged negotiation outweighs the value of the claim, and this results in claims being paid more promptly. But it is a sombre thought, and no credit to the tort system, that the more serious a person's injuries the longer he has to wait for his compensation. If it were not for the social security system, which enables a man to live while the settlement process meanders along its way, it is quite plain that the tort system would have collapsed long ago. Compensation for lost earnings is needed when the earnings are lost, not three years later. No doubt there is room for improvement in present procedures, but it seems unlikely that much can be done to reduce the time taken to try personal injury cases, or even to settle them. The problems are inherent in the system. The Lord Chancellor's Department is currently conducting a major study *inter alia* of delays in personal injury actions, but it remains to be seen whether useful reforms will result.

6 THE AMOUNT OF COMPENSATION

In Part 2 we devoted a good deal of space to the rules of legal liability and the principles on which damages for personal injuries are assessed by the courts. Now that we have seen how settlements are arrived at in practice, it will be appreciated that in cases which are settled the legal principles laid down by the courts do not by themselves determine how much, if anything, will be recovered. Naturally, the law relating both to liability and the assessment of damages plays an important part in influencing the parties to a settlement. But the actual result is arrived at in a very different way: the object of a settlement is not to arrive at the result which a judge would probably arrive at according to the established legal principles.

In the first place, when a case is tried in court, the judge is the arbiter who actually decides whether there is a legal liability; whether the defendant was negligent, owed a duty of care to the plaintiff, and was the cause of his injuries; whether the plaintiff was guilty of contributory negligence; and if so, how the responsibility is to be apportioned. But when a case is settled by negotiation these things are never finally determined at all. There is merely a greater or lesser probability that, if the case were litigated, the judge would decide in this or in that way. Accordingly, it often happens in practice that the damages are discounted to a greater or lesser degree according to the parties' estimates of the probabilities. If the plaintiff's case is extremely strong, and there is good evidence of negligence but no evidence of contributory negligence, the case may be settled on the basis of full compensation; but where there is any doubt about the facts, the damages are likely to be discounted by some percentage.[69] A settlement is a business bargain in which the plaintiff sells his claim to a private buyer for what he can get, and the buyer buys for as little as he has to pay. Since the plaintiff is often willing to sacrifice some part of even a good claim in order to eliminate the risk that the action may fail altogether (which can never be wholly ignored), and in order to expedite the actual receipt of the money, an insurer would be foolish to settle for more than about 80% of the probable damages unless the case is a very clear one.

Where the plaintiff's claim is less strong, and there is also the possibility of an adverse finding on contributory negligence, the probable damages may be discounted quite heavily – perhaps a half or a third may come off for the chance that the defendant will not be found at fault at all, and more for the possibility of contributory negligence. In the result, the parties may be thinking in terms of a settlement of 30% of the damages which a court would probably award. The settlement arrived at in the thalidomide cases illustrates this procedure very well, although there was no question of contributory negligence. Because of doubts about proving negligence against the defendants and also about the validity of the claim as a matter of law,[70] the plaintiffs were advised by their counsel to accept a settlement of 40% of the appropriate damages, and this was approved as a fair and reasonable settlement by the court. According to the Pearson Commission findings, over a quarter of cases settled with insurers are disposed of on the basis of partial liability only, that is, on the basis that the plaintiff must have been guilty of contributory negligence.[71]

There is also good ground for believing that plaintiffs tend to recover a larger proportion of what they have 'lost' in cases of minor injury. This has been fully demonstrated in American and Canadian surveys.[72] The Pearson Report, though it does not provide the same full statistics on this particular issue, points in the same general direction. For instance, it is clear from the Pearson findings that the proportion of a settlement which is attributable to non-pecuniary loss is much higher in small claims. Indeed, for claims of up to £5,000 (in 1973) over two-thirds, and in many minor cases over 70% was for non-pecuniary loss. For larger claims, the proportion attributable to non-pecuniary loss drops to around 50%.[73] Sums paid for non-pecuniary loss are important because they help to make good inadequacy in the amounts paid for pecuniary loss as a result of discounting for the risks of litigation and for contributory negligence. The Pearson figures suggest that the inadequacy is made good to a greater extent in less serious cases.

The result of all this, is that in cases which are disposed of by settlement – and this probably means about 99% of all claims – the principles of law laid down by the courts do not alone determine whether and how much compensation will be paid. There is no doubt that the settlement process leads to awards of compensation which are nearly always higher (in many cases) or lower (in more serious cases) than would be awarded in the courts. As Professor Conard and his colleagues at Michigan put it: 'The statistics confirm what every lawyer and adjustor knows – that questions about negligence, proof, the defendant's ability to pay, and the client's desire for an end of litigation, lead to compromises of claims at levels which correspond to no theory of legal right.'[74]

These criticisms of the settlement process usually stimulate demands for reform of that process, so as to improve the position of the plaintiff. But it must always be borne in mind that the plaintiff with a tort claim is already in a very privileged position compared with the great majority of the injured and the disabled. Thus, it is possible to make criticisms of the settlement process not with a view to its improvement but with a view to its abolition.

PART FOUR
Other Compensation Systems

12
First party insurance

1 THE TYPES OF FIRST PARTY INSURANCE

We referred in an earlier chapter to the term 'first party insurance' as a convenient term to use, despite that this is not a technical term used by insurers. The principal types of first party insurance in use today are life insurance, personal accident insurance (including medical insurance), fire insurance and comprehensive motor insurance; permanent health insurance (which insures income) is still relatively unusual. It is not the purpose of this book to delve into the law relating to insurance, which is a complex and very technical branch of the law of contract. The purpose, rather, is to look at these kinds of insurance in order to place the other systems of compensation for accident and disease in their true perspective, and to compare first party insurance with tort law as a method of securing such compensation.

Nearly all accident risks can be covered by first party insurance of one kind or another. Loss of, or damage to, property can be – and commonly is – covered by fairly comprehensive insurance policies; though there are always exceptions of some potential width, such as those excluding loss due to war, riot and so on. On the other hand, insurance covering the risk of personal injury is much less common and relatively expensive to obtain; and it often excludes injury from many specified risks, such as mountain climbing, or other hazardous sports. Life insurance is the widest form of insurance cover for risks of this kind, since it usually covers death from any cause except (in some cases) sane suicide.

The published figures of the total amount of insurance done in these various fields show that life insurance is far and away the most popular form of insurance in the modern world. In 1975 some 79% of households were paying for some life insurance[1] and total premium income in 1984 for life insurances, annuities and pensions was over £12,000 million.[2] In 1976 there were some 18·5 million ordinary life policies in force, with an average sum assured of £3,865, and over 85 million industrial life policies in force with an average sum assured of £111.[3] The popularity of life insurance is partly attributable to the fact that this type of insurance is used as a form of investment and not merely as a protection against risks; but also partly to the fact that premiums for this type of insurance are low. The administrative cost of life insurance is minimal for a number of reasons stated by Ison: '... the characteristics of death facilitate the administration of life assurance on a voluntary and individual basis, for death is inevitable, non-recurring, readily ascertainable when it occurs, is something which the assured is generally anxious to avoid as long as possible, and is a matter of public record and inquiry.'[4] There is therefore little scope for fraud or abuse on the part of those claiming life insurance benefits; and little expense or complexity involved in ensuring that the benefits are indeed payable because the event insured against has actually occurred.

Motor and fire insurance are also very big business. Motor (net) premium income in the UK in 1983 amounted to £1,810 million and fire and general accident premiums to some £3,271 million.[5] The bulk of this last figure is attributable to accident insurance; perhaps between one third and one quarter was attributable to fire insurance.

Personal accident insurance is very much less significant. In 1983 UK companies had premium receipts of £391 million, of which an unknown proportion is attributable to business in this country. People rarely think of insuring themselves against disability which prevents them earning a living for weeks or months or even permanently; or even partial disability, which may deprive a person of some of the pleasures of life, such as the ability to drive or dance or play games, or which may inflict chronic pain and discomfort on him. People whose whole living depends on some particular ability sometimes have substantial personal accident insurance; for instance, a musician may insure his hands, a footballer his legs, a film star her facial appearance. But otherwise this kind of insurance is not very often entered into on a substantial scale. There are, however, many comprehensive motor insurance policies which contain a small element of such insurance, e.g. cover up to £500 for loss of two limbs or such like. And similar cover is sometimes included in other special *ad hoc* types of insurance, such as holiday insurance. Most personal accident insurance is of short duration, often being taken out to cover only a particular event or risk.

To be distinguished from this form of insurance is permanent health insurance, which is designed to insure an income where the insured suffers long-term sickness or disability. This kind of insurance is still relatively insignificant compared to life insurance – premiums were only £112 million in 1984 – and it is largely confined to the self-employed, who have no employer's sick-pay schemes to tide them over periods of sickness or injury. But some employers actually take out insurance of this kind to cover their own sick-pay schemes. There is no doubt that the relative lack of success of permanent health insurance is partly due to the fact that it is much more expensive than most forms of insurance. A person may insure his house against fire for 20 or 30 pence per hundred pounds; he may insure his car, if he is a good risk and has the maximum no claims bonus, for £5 per hundred pounds; but insuring an income of £1,000 per annum would cost a person of 30 about £30 per year in premiums, though this could be reduced quite substantially if cover was not required for the first three or six months of sickness or disability. In terms of the maximum coverage obtained this is not so great, but it is nevertheless a substantial amount to pay out in view of the very slight nature of the risk that a person may become disabled for a long period.[6]

One specialized form of first party accident or sickness insurance has flourished, however. Medical insurance has been steadily growing in importance for some years, despite the existence of the National Health Service. This sort of insurance is not primarily meant to cover ordinary general practitioners attendance (though even this is available) but is principally intended to cover hospital treatment and surgery. The largest institution dealing with this form of insurance is the British United Provident Association, generally known as BUPA, which provides cover for over three million people and offers a wide variety of benefits according to the amount of premium which the member wishes to pay; and there are a number of other provident associations providing a similar service.

In addition, a fair amount of accident or sickness insurance is transacted by friendly societies and trade unions. Most of these bodies pay trivial benefits of only £1 or £2 per week, but some of them are substantial organizations paying significant amounts by way of sickness benefit, e.g. in the £20–£30 range. However, the average amounts received by injured claimants from these sources in 1973 was only £20.[7]

Not every risk which is protected against by the tort system is insurable in practice. For instance, it is hardly possible to protect oneself by insurance against bereavement as such. It is true that a person may insure his life for an amount which is much greater than his income would warrant, so that if he dies prematurely his widow or children may to some extent be compensated in money for the loss of the man as well as for the loss of his income; but few people are likely to take such considerations into account in deciding how much life insurance to buy. Moreover, where young children are concerned, insurance against bereavement is totally prohibited by law. The Industrial Assurance and Friendly Societies Act 1948 prohibits any life insurance on the life of a child under the age of ten which provides for any benefit other than the return of the premiums. This Act is a reminder of the grisly fact that in some circumstances life insurance on the life of a young child might be a temptation to murder, or at least neglect.

War risks are excluded from most insurance policies as a matter of course. Today it has become customary for the State itself to take on the business of providing war damage insurance and of compensating those who suffer personal injury, and the dependants of those killed, as a result of enemy action. Other uninsurable risks are also taken care of by special means. For instance riot damage, which is normally excluded from insurances policies, may be covered by other forms of compensation. In the case of personal injury, it would today probably fall within the criminal injuries compensation scheme; in the case of damage to property, compensation may be payable under the Riot (Damages) Act 1886. And damage done by nuclear installations is the subject of a quite unique set of legal rules and insurance practices, designed to spread the cost of all such risks as widely as possible, while retaining the compensation process in private hands.

2   FIRST PARTY INSURANCE COMPARED WITH
    TORT LIABILITY

First party insurance differs from tort compensation in many important ways, most notably in being almost entirely optional. Nobody has to insure his life or his person, his earning capacity or his property, with any private insurance company. And if he does so, he can choose the amount of coverage he gets. Moreover, it is an area in which there is real freedom of choice, and a good deal of competition in price. In a society which is still to some extent based on the virtues of individual freedom of choice, all this must be counted a satisfactory feature of a method of securing compensation for loss. But it may be questioned whether some degree of compulsion would not be a good thing, even in the area of damage to property. We have had occasion to mention that insurance against fire damage to houses in many cases compulsory in practice, because building societies and other mortgagees require the property to be fully insured against such risks to protect their security. But mortgages are eventually paid off, and insurance policies may then be allowed to lapse. Grave hardship would obviously be caused to most people if their houses were destroyed or seriously damaged by fire, where they have allowed this to happen. No doubt the stalwart champions of individual free choice will accept this, and simply blame the feckless few who have not maintained their policies. But on balance, this may well be an area in which compulsion would do more good than harm.

When one turns to consider other forms of personal loss or damage to property, there is clearly no case for compulsory insurance. If a person wishes to run the risk of damage or destruction to his car there is no reason why he should not be allowed to do so. A person is allowed to risk his earnings on a horse or the football pools; and he is free to spend it on frivolities or junk. Moreover, nobody who runs a motor vehicle can be unaware of the requirement of compulsory third party liability insurance, and this means that the motorist is almost certain to be made aware of the choice between comprehensive cover and liability cover alone.

The problem of insuring against lost income is rather a different one, simply because the State, via compulsory social security, now plays such a large role in this field. This means that the great majority of people in Britain do not think of the possibility or desirability of insuring against such loss privately. But here again, there is something to be said for the mixed system in which the State takes care of those less able to take care of themselves, while others can supplement the State provision with private insurance if they wish. Social security benefits, as we shall see in detail later, provide reasonable compensation for short term income losses for a person with an income below, or close to average earnings, particularly if he is a married man with two or three dependent children. But the middle-class person earning two or three times average earnings would certainly feel the pinch very soon if he was reduced to living on the state benefits. And if this was a serious threat for the middle-class person, permanent health insurance to safeguard earnings would probably have become much more widespread than it has. In fact, however, most middle-class people are relatively well protected against short-term income losses by occupational sick-pay schemes, so that it is really only the long-term sickness or disability or injury which calls for private insurance protection. And this has still not really caught on very successfully, perhaps partly because such insurance is relatively expensive, and partly because the risk is such a remote one that most people fail to appreciate it, or are prepared to run it. There are signs that some employers are now beginning to take out this form of insurance for their employees, to cover the gap between sick-pay and occupational pension schemes which may take over if the employee is permanently retired on grounds of health.[8]

A second major contrast with the tort system is the fact that in the case of first party insurance the method of compensation normally depends on what has been lost. Thus, loss of a capital asset (e.g. destruction of a house or car) will be met by payment of a lump sum; whereas loss of income, under a policy insuring such loss, will normally be met by periodical payments if the loss continues long enough to makes this desirable. There is, moreover, more scope for correcting mistakes in the case of personal insurance than under the tort system. We have seen how tort damages must be assessed once-and-for-all, and how this may lead to over- or under-compensation if things do not turn out as anticipated. In the case of first party insurance, it is possible to guard against this to some extent. For instance, it is possible to provide by contract that disability payments payable only for permanent disability are to be repayable if the disability should turn out not to be permanent,[9] though this is one area in which the correction of mistakes is probably undesirable.[10] At one time, workmen's compensation payments for disability were liable to be reduced if the person showed signs of recovery, and this gave rise to such misgivings that the modern industrial injuries system distinguishes firmly between payment of compensation for lost earnings (which will be reduced if earning capacity improves), and compensation for disability which, once finally assessed, generally remains unalterable even if it proves to have been over-generous.

Another way in which subsequent events can be taken into account after payment of personal insurance is found in contracts of insurance against the risk of loss or theft of goods. If a person insures a valuable piece of jewellery against loss or theft, and payment is made under the policy, this usually has the effect of transferring the legal title to the jewellery from the owners to the insurers. If, therefore, it turns up again later, the insurance company can claim it, and the former owner cannot keep both the insurance money and the article insured. In most cases, the article will be offered back to the owner on condition that the policy money is repaid.

A third point of difference between tort compensation and first party insurance is that the latter often does not offer 'full compensation'. The extent of coverage is usually optional, but there are many types of insurance in which the standard policy requires the insured to bear part of the loss himself. This is a very common feature of the motor insurance policy, but it is also found in householders' policies (at least for some risks, though not necessarily all) and permanent health policies – which do not usually cover the first month or three or six months of lost income, and normally limit the income loss insured against to three-quarters of the insured's normal earnings. One reason for this is to reduce the risk of fraud, especially in permanent health policies insuring against lost income. But another reason is that small claims cost a disproportionate amount to process and since they are so much more likely to occur, they are also much more expensive to insure against. We have already seen that minor injuries and illnesses are much more common than more serious ones. The result is that the cost of insuring against the first part of a loss is very much greater than the cost of insuring against the rest of a loss. So, for instance, the cost of insuring against income loss from sickness is greatly reduced if cover is not required for the first three or six months of illness; and the cost of motor comprehensive policies are very much less if the insured agrees to bear the first part of a loss himself. Indeed, in many cases the extra cost of full coverage would be so great that insurance companies are not prepared to grant it at all. Under the tort system of course, this is not so. We have already examined the tort system's commitment to the principle of full compensation, and it only remains here to point out that this commitment is not necessarily in the public interest. Since tort compensation is itself nearly always paid for by insurance money, and this is itself paid for by the public, a reduction in the cost of the tort system, and hence of premiums to the public, might result if tort claims excluded liability for the first part of a loss – corresponding to the 'excess' in a first party motor policy. However, this is not possible so long as the tort system entitles anyone to claim damages, even for the most trivial injuries (and even though they may cause no pecuniary loss), and so long as compulsory insurance requirements exist for motor and industrial injuries.

Another major difference between tort compensation and first party insurance compensation is the fact that contributory negligence is normally immaterial under an insurance claim. As we have seen already, when a person protects his house or car by insurance he is buying protection against the risk of his own negligence, as well as the risk of loss or damage by other means. Insurance policies often require the insured to take reasonable care to prevent the insured event occurring, and the construction placed on such clauses by the courts is illuminating. Normally, a person is regarded as liable in law for the negligence of his servants in the course of their employment, and in most contracts a clause requiring someone to take reasonable care would be construed without any hesitation as covering negligence of his servants as well as his own lack of care. But in insurance contracts the courts have construed these clauses much more narrowly so that, in effect, they do not cover casual negligence by a servant, but only a total failure in organization or system of work for which some higher-grade employees must be responsible.[11] Clearly, this is because an employer who takes out an insurance policy is guarding against the risk of negligence on the part of his own employees, as much as the risk of negligence by third parties or the risk of pure accident. On the other hand, many insurance policies exclude liability for losses arising from specified events which are akin to 'contributory negligence' – e.g. driving while drunk in the case of a comprehensive motor policy.

Wilful acts which bring about the event insured against are of course not covered. A person who deliberately smashes up his car or sets fire to his house can obviously not claim under his policy; the main reason for this is simply that claims of this kind are almost certain to be fraudulent. A person is unlikely to set fire to his house and then claim against his insurance policy, unless the policy was for very much more than the house is worth. Where there is no fraud – as often in the case of suicide under life policies – liability is usually accepted. A person does not normally commit suicide simply to provide a large sum of money for his dependants. Moreover, suicide is a cause of death which is reflected in the mortality tables on which premiums are based.

On the other hand, problems frequently arise in cases of first party insurance, which are very similar to the causal problems which so often arise in tort cases. If an insurance policy gives cover against certain risks it may obviously be necessary to ascertain whether the event which has occurred is within the risk. This is especially the case where policies are limited to events occurring in special places, at special times or in special ways. For instance, if goods are covered 'whilst temporarily housed during the course of transit', are they covered while awaiting loading?[12] If goods are covered while 'in store' are they covered when packed in lift vans and placed in an enclosed yard at a depository?[13] If marine insurance against damage caused by 'warlike operations' is given, does this cover damage done to cargo which has come adrift in heavy seas, but which is damaged because the vessel continues zigzagging at high speed for fear of attack by enemy submarines?[14] Problems like these frequently arise in insurance cases, and are treated by the courts in much the same way as problems concerned with 'cause' in the law of torts.

There is, however, a major difference between these problems and causal problems in tort cases. As we have seen already, in causal problems the courts are compelled to choose between two sets of causal principles – those supplied by the usages of ordinary speech, and those supplied by independent considerations of policy – and in general they have chosen the former. In the case of insurance contracts, however, there can be no doubt that the standards of ordinary speech are in almost all cases the correct ones to apply. This is because there are generally no independent policy considerations which would dictate whether a loss should be treated as within the cover provided by a certain kind of insurance; and accordingly, the only question is what sort of risk did the parties contemplate when they took out the policy? And the answer to this question can only be derived from the meaning which would normally attach to the wording of the policy. Occasionally, however, policy considerations may have something to say on this issue, because in some cases the real issue is which of two insurance companies, or which of two compensation systems, should, or is required by law to, bear the loss. And in some cases, the desire to punish wrongdoing or reward the heroic may be relevant in an insurance case, very much as in a tort case. For instance, if a person rushed into a burning house to save a child's life and he died in the fire, would this be 'accidental death' within the meaning of an insurance policy, or could it be contended that the man had 'caused' his own death?[15]

Like the tort system, first party insurance in theory offers compensation for financial loss as well as compensation for some kinds of personal disability. But, with the exception of life assurance, which may be for a sum much greater than the assured's earning capacity would warrant, non-pecuniary loss insurance is very limited indeed. Apart from a small number of policies which provide a very limited cover for personal disabilities – usually a maximum of £1,000 – this kind of first party insurance is of negligible importance in practice. All other first party insurance is 'indemnity insurance', which means that it is a very firm principle that the insured is not to profit by his insurance. He recovers his loss – or so much of it as is insured – and not a penny more. This principle is most commonly and stringently applied in cases of property damage insurance. It is immaterial that the maximum insurance coverage provided for in the policy is in excess of the loss, as is commonly the case where a car is damaged beyond repair in a motor accident. In such a case, the insurer's only liability is to pay the value of the car at the time of its destruction. In the case of cars, for which there is an extensive second-hand market, this no doubt works reasonably enough. The existence of this market means that the value of the destroyed vehicle can be ascertained within reasonably narrow margins, and also that the insured can, if he wishes, replace his vehicle with another very similar to it. But this method of compensation does not always work so satisfactorily with personal belongings or property of a different kind. If a person loses his baggage on holiday, or if his house is burnt down and all the contents are destroyed, the insurance company's legal obligations are limited to providing compensation for the 'value' of what has been lost, and unless the contract specifically states otherwise this value is taken as the secondhand value. This rule, which probably originated with marine insurance on ships and cargoes and may have been perfectly satisfactory for businessmen, does not work well for the consumer. The second-hand value of personal belongings such as clothes and furniture is extremely small these days, and compensation at this level is simply not good enough for most people. If the whole contents of a house are destroyed in a fire, it is quite possible that the compensation on a second-hand value basis would be barely adequate to refurnish one room and reclothe one member of the family. Of course, compensation at a 'new' rate increases the temptation for fraud, since it means giving compensation of a greater value than what has been lost. Nevertheless, 'new for old' house contents insurance is now widely available at reasonable rates.

Of course, compensation for property damage in the tort system is also subject to the same principle that the owner recovers the value at the time of the loss or destruction; and the value is taken to mean the second-hand value.

Compensation for lost profit arising from the damage or destruction of profit-earning property is also available under both the tort system and under personal insurance, and the assessment of compensation would follow similar lines in the two cases. But, as we have seen already, there is a fundamental difference in approach with regard to consequential, or purely financial loss which does not follow from physical damage to property owned by the person suffering the loss. This kind of loss is now regularly covered by special types of insurance policy which are available to cover a wide variety of risks which would probably not normally be protected by the tort system, for example, loss of profits arising from damage done to the premises of a customer or a supplier. But there are limits to the cover which insurers are willing to provide for loss of profits. For example, insurers have not so far agreed to provide cover for lost profits suffered by seaside hotel proprietors as a result of disasters such as that of the grounding of the Torrey Canyon in 1967, when many miles of English beaches were polluted with oil.[16] Tort proceedings were brought and settled by the Crown against the shipowners in this case, but the claim was limited to the cost of repairing the damage done, and not to loss of profits by hotel proprietors. Compensation may be forthcoming from the International Oil Pollution Compensation Fund, which administers large funds.

If liability insurance has so far had little impact on the rules of law administered by the courts, this relatively novel kind of insurance cover appears to be still almost entirely unknown to traditional minded lawyers. For example, much time has been spent by academic lawyers in discussing the liability of a tenant to pay rent for a house which has been destroyed by fire, with little apparent appreciation of the fact that loss of rents is usually taken care of by insurance.[17] In another field, it is now possible to buy insurance to cover inability to keep up mortgage repayments as a result of accident, sickness, unemployment or redundancy. However, the premiums are high and the cover lasts for only a relatively short time (say 12 months).

It is worth adding a few words on the absence of any serious first party insurance for non-pecuniary loss in personal injury cases. As we have mentioned, there are certain personal accident policies which do provide for some limited sums, usually on a fixed tariff scale, for injuries such as loss of an eye or a limb, and which clearly do correspond to a sort of first party insurance for loss of amenity. But these forms of cover are normally appendages to other forms of insurance, and in any event, they do not appear to be spreading, or even holding their own. It is reasonable to suggest that there is little public demand for insurance for pain and suffering or loss of amenity. And this is really not very surprising: monetary compensation is not a great deal of consolation for an actual loss of amenity. Yet it will be noted how the tort system, with its liability insurance system behind it, means that the public are in practice compelled to buy this kind of insurance for each other, even though, given the choice, few buy it for themselves. This must surely raise further doubts about the desirability of retaining damages for non-pecuniary loss in the tort system.

13
Criminal injuries

1 THE JUSTIFICATION FOR THE SCHEME

The victims of criminal assault, or other criminal attack causing personal injury, have, of course, a claim in tort against the criminal, but in the great majority of cases the claim is of no practical utility. In their Third Report, the Criminal Injuries Compensation Board reported that they had noted the number of cases in which offenders would be worth suing, and found them to number 17, i.e. 0·7% of the cases which had then come before the Board[1]. By the time of their Seventh Report, the number had dropped to 6 out of nearly 6,000 cases, i.e. about 0·1%.[2]

In one respect, criminal victims have an advantage over the normal accident victim in that they may receive some compensation under the order of a criminal court. Under section 35 of the Powers of Criminal Courts Act 1973 (as amended by s. 67 of the Criminal Justice Act 1982), a Magistrates Court may award up to £1,000[3] compensation for personal injury or damage to property in a criminal case, and other criminal courts may award an unlimited sum. These powers are designed to be a summary remedy for use in simple cases. It has been stressed that the victim of a criminal assault has his normal tort remedy by way of civil proceedings, and should be left to pursue that remedy in serious or complicated cases.[4] Long-term orders for compensation, which may take years to pay off, are generally discouraged.[5] The government recently launched a number of pilot schemes under which an offender may secure a lighter sentence or a caution if he agrees, in negotiation with the victim, to provide some reparation.[6]

Awards by the Criminal Injuries Compensation Board are reduced by the amount of any payment received under a compensation order. In 1984–5 applicants received a total of £130,196 (under 1,527 orders) before the Board's award was made, and a further £63,245 was received by the Board after its award had been made.[7] Thus a total of £193,441 was received under such orders in 1984–5. In addition, applicants are required to repay the Board out of any damages or settlement they receive, but in recent years the Board's reports have not stated how much was recovered in this way. In 1984–5 the Board itself paid out £35,293,451 in compensation.[8] Thus criminals are probably paying less than one per cent of the costs of injuries they cause.

Of course all victims of crime may obtain compensation from other compensation systems. Personal injuries may be covered by the social security system, or occasionally, by personal accident insurance; fatal cases may leave a widow with life insurance and widow's benefits under social security. Loss of property from criminal activity is, of course, more likely to be covered by private insurance.[9] And just occasionally, tort liability may be effectively established against someone other than the offender himself. For instance, the offender's employer may be liable in cases of fraud, and even, though rarely, in case of personal injury. Such liability will not often be established, because criminal assaults and similar violent conduct will not often be regarded as within 'the course of employment' of the offender (so as to render his employer vicariously liable), though this may happen occasionally.[10] Personal tort liability may also occasionally be effectively imposed on the victim's employer, for example where it is alleged that the employer had exposed the victim to unnecessary risk of criminal attack, e.g. by sending a young girl to the bank to collect wages for a company's employees.[11]

Nevertheless, it is clear that until the criminal injuries compensation scheme was set up in 1964,[12] most victims of criminal attack received little compensation for personal injuries other than that normally available through the social security system. Many regarded this as inadequate, partly because of public sympathy for the occasional victim of an especially vicious crime, and partly because the social security system offers no compensation for disability as such, except to those injured at work. The effect of this is that elderly retired people, housewives and young children who are not working, and who suffer injuries very rarely receive anything at all from the social security system. Nevertheless, the idea of selecting yet another group of unfortunates for special treatment is not easily defensible, and it is hard to believe that the government would have regarded the scheme with much favour if it had not been of relatively small quantitative significance, and therefore very cheap compared with most other claims for compensation which are made on the State.

The discussions which led up to the scheme reveal an extraordinary intellectual confusion. The Home Office working party which first looked into the matter, for instance, rejected the idea that the State should assume the burden of compensating victims of criminal violence on the grounds that the State had a duty to protect its citizens; this was a 'fallacious and dangerous doctrine', because the State could not possibly protect its citizens from attack at all times and all places, and because, in any event, if there was such a duty it would be impossible to confine it to personal injury as opposed to damage to property.[13] The committee went on to say that they could find no 'constitutional or social principle on which State compensation could be justified', but they nevertheless thought that compensation could be based on the more 'practical' ground that 'although the welfare state helps the victims of many kinds of misfortune, it does nothing for the victims of crimes of violence, as such.'[14] Accordingly, although there was no 'bounden duty'[15] to compensate these victims, the principle could be accepted.

It is not easy to know what to make of all this. The committee never really came to grips with the crucial issue, which is not whether victims of criminal violence ought to be compensated by the State, but whether there are any grounds for compensating such victims other than by the normal processes of the welfare state. This question was only touched on in passing, by pointing out that the welfare state did nothing for the victims of crimes of violence 'as such' – but why this should matter, provided it does *something* for them, is impossible to see. Perhaps the Working Party were influenced by the belief that the benefits provided by the welfare state were inadequate. But if social security benefits are inadequate, the right solution is to increase them; and if less money were devoted to special categories of unfortunates, it might be possible without much, if any, increased cost, to make benefits generally quite adequate. Abolition of special compensation schemes (including, of course, the tort system) would plainly only be contemplated as part of a reform package; and one component of that package would be to redistribute in a more equitable manner many of the benefits that now go to victims in particular groups.

The arguments for special treatment for the victims of crime were listed by a *Justice* Report as follows:[16]

First, the analogy with war injuries and riot damage was regarded as strong. The State has always accepted the obligation to provide for the victims of war injury and the dependants of those killed in war. And riot damage is, in some cases at least, provided for by the State under the Riot (Damages) Act 1886.

Secondly, the State exhorts the citizen to protect his property against theft but discourages the citizen from carrying weapons to protect his property or his person.

Third, the citizen is under a duty to assist the State, e.g. by going to the assistance of a policeman effecting an arrest or suppressing violence, and he may be deterred from doing so by the absence of compensation for injury.

Fourth, neglect of interests of the victims of crime has made it more difficult to follow an enlightened penal policy because every demand for better treatment for criminals is met by complaints that society is looking after the criminal better than the victim.

Fifth, the State having prohibited the victim from taking the law into his own hands to obtain redress, should provide him with an effective alternative.

Sixth, offenders are often imprisoned for long periods and so the State deprives the victim of any chance of effective redress against the offender.

These arguments are not very convincing. The last is simply untrue in most cases: in 1984, for instance, out of nearly 48,000 persons convicted on indictment of violence against the person in England and Wales, only about 8,000 received immediate custodial sentence, while over 20,000 were fined. About 7,600 were ordered to pay compensation.[17] The fifth argument would justify requiring the State to provide compensation for many accidents for which nobody is to blame; the fourth, in effect, is an argument based on the political need to divert society's irrational demands for retribution against offenders;[18] the third is an appeal to our emotions in a 'hard case' of heroism going unrewarded. Of course, injury arising from heroism elicits admiration, sympathy and demands for compensation; but is the demand any greater where the heroism takes the form of trying to arrest a dangerous criminal rather than (say) trying to rescue a child from a burning house or a climber trapped on a mountainside? The second argument ignores the fact that citizens gain more than they lose by laws prohibiting them from carrying weapons to protect themselves; and the first depends on a doubtful analogy between victims of crime and victims of war injury. The analogy of riot damages is not of practical importance, because compensation for personal injury is not awarded under the 1886 Act.

A more convincing argument is that the risk of injury from criminal attack is so remote that it would be impractical to insure against that risk and no other: the premium required would be so small as to make an insurance system impractical. Even a State insurance system would require less than four pence a week as a contribution. There is, therefore, something to be said for the view that the whole population should be regarded as insured by the State, and the compensation paid for by taxation.[19] But this still fails to answer the really critical question, which is why *this* kind of injury should be singled out for special treatment by the State. It is not possible to justify compensation for injuries merely by pleading that such compensation is needed by those suffering the injury, or that hardship is caused if there is no compensation. That is true of most victims of personal injury.

A similar absence of rational argument is found in the debates in parliament which preceeded the establishment of the scheme. Thus, Lord Shawcross did not feel it necessary or useful to attempt to justify the case for compensation 'by an elaborate theoretical or philosophical speculation as to why the State should intervene in a matter of this kind'.[20] It was enough to rely on the 'public instinct'. Lord Dilhorne, speaking on behalf of the government, rejected the notion that the State was 'liable', but regarded the scheme as an extension of our 'welfare system'.[21] Since nobody suggested that the State was legally liable, this was tantamount to asserting that the State was not morally liable, but nevertheless his Lordship thought that the 'welfare system' (which is obviously based on the moral ideas of our society) should be extended to cover it. Others justified the scheme by asserting that society was 'responsible' for much crime because of the laxity of its moral code and the failure to bring up its young as good citizens rather than criminals.[22] Only Lady Wootton protested that the attempt to assess people's needs by reference to the question of fault was 'illogical and uncivilized'.[23] The debate in the Commons followed much the same form, though with even less attempt to justify the scheme, and with universal self-congratulation on a good job well done.

One particular piece of sophistry which this intellectual confusion produced was the suggestion that the compensation should be awarded *ex gratia*, not as of right; and this suggestion was eventually incorporated in the scheme propounded by the government. Although, in a technical sense, payments are *ex gratia* because they do not have legislative backing (the scheme is 'purely administrative'), in another, and more realistic sense, the denial of a 'right' to compensation was quite meaningless, because the board administering the scheme has no discretion to refuse claims except within the terms of the scheme itself; and the payment of compensation – though not legally enforceable – follows automatically once the board has determined that it should be awarded. So it has been held that decisions of the Board can be challenged in judicial review proceedings on the ground that they do not comply with the terms of the scheme.[24] The Report of the Working Party which reviewed the scheme (and which is further discussed below) acknowledged the reality of the situation: omission of the term *ex gratia* would have no practical effect.[25]

In 1973 a Working Party was appointed to review the working of the scheme with a view to putting it onto a statutory footing. This Working Party was appointed more or less simultaneously with the Pearson Royal Commission, whose terms of reference also included compensation for personal injuries. The Working Party report was published in 1978, shortly before the Pearson Report. The report merely reiterated the views of the earlier Working Party of 1964 that the public feels a sense of responsibility for, and sympathy with, the innocent victim, and 'it is right' that this feeling should find practical expression in the provision of compensation by the community. The Pearson Commission, after referring to some of the above criticisms, as made in the second edition of this book, simply asserted that compensation for criminal injuries was 'morally justified as in some measure salving the nations's conscience at its inability to preserve law and order', and insisted that 'it is right that there should be reasonable provision for the victims of crime.'[26] However, the

Pearson Commission made no attempt to explain why 'reasonable provision' should mean provision according to scales of tort damages. It could be argued with some justification that tort levels of damages are not 'reasonable provision' but exceptionally generous provision. And it is odd that the Pearson Commission should have used the argument that compensation for the victims of crime 'salves the nation's conscience at its inability to preserve law and order', for this argument has always been repudiated by governments and previous working parties. The Commission's only recommendation was that the scheme should be looked at again, in light of the proposals on damages in tort.

The upshot is that the criminal injuries scheme is likely to be with us for the immediate future. In 1984 the government appointed another working party to make recommendations for putting the scheme on a statutory footing.

2 THE SCOPE OF THE SCHEME[27]

The scheme provides for the payment of compensation to persons who have sustained

> personal injury directly attributable (a) to a crime of violence (including arson and poisoning) or (b) to the apprehension or attempted apprehension of an offender or suspected offender or to the prevention or attempted prevention of an offence or to the giving of help to any constable who is engaged in any such activity.[28]

The scheme also provides for payment to the dependents of those killed in the same fashion.

Crime of violence

Confused thinking about the justification for the scheme has, not surprisingly, generated difficulty in defining its scope. Originally, the scheme did not use the words 'crime of violence'. It was believed that it would be sufficient to refer to injuries 'directly attributable to' an offence, on the assumption that, unless the offence was one of violence, it would not lead to personal injury. Of course, this is not so. For instance, offences under the Factories Acts or the Food and Drugs Acts can easily lead to personal injuries, but are not the kind of offences Parliament had in mind when approving the scheme.

Therefore, both the Board[29] and a Divisional Court of the Queen's Bench Division[30] have held them to fall outside the scheme.

The guidelines to the operation of the scheme (known as the Statement) specify that crimes involving violence to the person are only covered if the injuries are inflicted intentionally or recklessly (in the technical sense in which these words are used in the criminal law). Behaviour which is merely careless, even if grossly so, does not constitute a crime of violence. For example, in one case,[31] a man was injured by flying glass when a snowball was thrown at his kitchen window. The application for compensation was rejected on the basis that there was no evidence that the snowball had been thrown with the intention of causing damage. In fact, it appeared that children were in the habit of playing near the house, and it was likely that the snowball had been thrown in the course of a game.

Particular difficulty has arisen in relation to suicide. In *R v. CICB, ex parte Clowes*[32] a policeman was injured by a gas explosion in a house where he had been investigating a gas leak. The occupier of the house had committed suicide by breaking off the end of the gas pipe and allowing gas to escape. A Divisional Court held that the offence of unlawfully damaging the property of another[33] was not a crime of violence because it was concerned with damage to property, not with violence to the person. But the court also held that the offence of unlawfully damaging property with the intention thereby of endangering life, or recklessly as to whether life would thereby be endangered,[34] did constitute a crime of violence. But the Board considered that the deceased had not acted intentionally or recklessly to cause injury to another, and that the only thing present in his mind was a desire to take his own life.

R v. CICB, ex parte Webb[35] concerned train drivers who suffered anxiety and depression after their trains struck people who had deliberately thrown themselves onto the railway line in front of the train.[36] This constituted the offence of unlawfully endangering the safety of railway passengers.[37] The Court of Appeal held that this was not a crime of violence; that it was for the Board to decide whether particular crimes were crimes of violence; and that the words 'crime of violence' ought to be given the meaning the reasonable and literate man would give them. The fact that the commission of a crime carries with it the danger of violent injury to another (in such a case as this, for example, by derailment of the train) does not make it a crime of violence. Although most crimes of violence involve the infliction or threat of force, some might not. It is the *nature* of a crime, not its consequences, which determines whether it is a 'crime of violence'.

The Board clearly does not enjoy its task of interpreting the words 'crime of violence'; it has recently said that the job would tax 'the ingenuity of the participants in a moot'.[38] Certainly, it seems very difficult to construct any rational argument in favour of the State assuming a special responsibility to compensate those, and only those, who suffer injury as the result of a crime of violence defined in the above terms. Nevertheless, the recent European Convention on the Compensation of Victims of Violent Crimes is limited to 'intentional crimes of violence'.[39]

Injuries caused by children and mentally unstable persons gave the Board particular difficulty at first. Unsoundness of mind can excuse a person from criminal responsibility; and in England a child under 10 (8 in Scotland) is treated as incapable of committing a crime. In such cases it could not be easily said that the victim's injuries were attributable to a crime. This problem was specifically foreseen in the debates in Parliament[40], but the original terms of the scheme did not deal with it, and not until later was the scheme amended to provide that compensation could be paid even though the offender was immune from responsibility because of youth or insanity. On the face of it, this amendment seems difficult to reconcile with the notion of a crime of violence which we examined above. But in practice, the Board has interpreted the provision in a complex way which seems designed to achieve some reconciliation. The Board considers, in each case, whether the child (or insane person) has committed an act which would constitute a crime of violence but for the offender's age (or insanity). The Statement says that '[m]uch may turn upon whether the child knew that what he was doing was wrong but nevertheless went on to do it'.[41] So, for example, in one case a child of six cut a girl of twelve on the leg, leaving a slight scar. The Board was satisfied that he had 'guilty knowledge' and awarded £300.[42] In another case a child suffered an eye injury as a result of a blow from a boy of five; the Board was satisfied that the act was deliberate and compensation was awarded.[43] But in another case, a woman struck in the eye by a dart from an air pistol fired by a two-year-old was refused compensation.[44] In yet another case a nurse was injured when a 13-year-old mentally subnormal child, whom she was nursing, butted her in the face with its head. The claim was rejected on the basis that the injury was accidental.[45] This approach to the problem is extremely unsatisfactory. In the case of children and insane persons, the distinction between intentional and accidental injury is extremely elusive, because in many cases it will be unclear whether the offender was capable of forming a criminal intent. This is exactly why the law gives immunity, and so for the Board to inquire into the offender's mental state seems pointless. It is the lack of a reasoned justification for the scheme which has generated this uncertainty and complexity in dealing with such cases. Why should compensation be paid to a person intentionally injured by a young child, but not to a person accidentally injured, when there is no legal liability in either case? Either both should be compensated, or neither.

Accidental injuries[45]

Despite the emphasis on the offender's state of mind discussed above, it is, nevertheless, possible in certain cases to recover compensation under the scheme for accidental injuries (in the sense of injuries not caused intentionally or recklessly). In cases of arson, accidental injuries suffered while escaping from, or fighting, or rescuing people from, a fire are covered, provided the fire was started intentionally or recklessly. Also, accidental injuries suffered while engaged in law-enforcement activities (arresting or attempting to arrest an offender or suspected offender, preventing or attempting to prevent an offence, or assisting a constable) are covered provided that, at the time of the injuries, the victim was taking an exceptional risk which was justified in all the circumstances. It does not matter what the immediate cause of the injuries was, provided the Board is prepared to treat them as directly attributable to the law-enforcement activity. Nor need the victim be the person performing the law-enforcement act – he may, for example, be an innocent bystander knocked down by the person so engaged.[46]

The Statement goes to considerable length to define (by example) 'exceptional risk'.[47] The examples are designed to exclude cases where, for instance, a person trips over while running after an offender,[48] or falls while climbing over an obstacle,[49] or where a police car is involved in an accident on the way to the scene of a suspected crime where speed is not of the essence.[50]

Despite this limitation, however, it is difficult to appreciate the justification for the inclusion of such cases in the scheme, given that if the victim is a policeman,[51] he will be covered by the industrial injuries scheme (by virtue of being an employed worker); and if he is an ordinary citizen, he will be entitled in the normal way to social security benefits. The rationale for awarding compensation in such cases must be very different from the original aim of the scheme which was, essentially, to compensate the victims of intentional violence. One of the problems is that the relationship between the criminal injuries compensation scheme and other compensation schemes has never been properly thought out. Although social security benefits, tort damages, and compensation received under compensation orders are all set off against awards under the scheme, no systematic attempt has ever been made to justify awarding compensation under the scheme (which may be greater than that available from other sources) when alternative sources of compensation exist.

A related issue arose in a recent case[52] in which a man deliberately drove his car at another man, seriously injuring him. The House of Lords held that the Motor Insurers' Bureau was liable to pay damages because the defendant was not insured, as required by the Road Traffic Act. Although the criminal injuries scheme does not, in general, cover injuries attributable to traffic offences, it does include cases of deliberate injury resulting from the use of motor vehicles. The MIB argued that the plaintiff ought to have brought his claim under the scheme, and not under the MIB agreement. But the House held that he had a choice between the two schemes, and was entitled to choose the MIB alternative, which the House considered to be more advantageous to him than the criminal injuries scheme. The House seems to have ignored the fact that the Board does not make awards in such cases where compensation is available from the MIB or under an insurance policy.[53] On the other hand, where the driver is untraced, the relevant MIB agreement excludes deliberate running down, and here the Board would consider making an award.[54] This sort of issue is bound to arise so long as there exists a variety of compensation schemes with overlapping rules of entitlement. The only way of eliminating such problems is to adopt a unified scheme based on the claimant's need rather than the cause of injuries.

Exclusions

As we have just seen, the scheme excludes from its scope injuries resulting from traffic offences, except where the injuries are due to a deliberate attempt to run the victim down, or where they are directly attributable to law-enforcement activities. The reason for this exclusion is that there are usually other means of ensuring that adequate compensation is paid in these cases. Another important exclusion relates to violence within the family. There is no doubt that a high proportion of criminal assaults are committed within the family circle. In 1963, McClintock[55] found that as many as 30·8% of criminal assaults were 'domestic', although he included within this category quarrels between neighbours, and not merely assaults on members of the same family. Subsequent research suggests that perhaps 15% of indictable crimes of violence occur within the family group.[56] Where the victim and the person responsible for the injuries were living in the same household at the time the injuries were inflicted, several conditions have to be satisfied before compensation is payable. These conditions are designed to serve a number of ends. The first is to exclude relatively petty cases; so the injuries must be such as to justify an award of at least £500 (in other cases under the scheme the figure is £400). The second aim is to exclude cases of collusion between victim and offender; so, normally, the offender must have been prosecuted. And if offender and victim are both adults, they must be no longer living together at the time of the application. Furthermore, the Board will not award compensation where it appears that the offender might benefit from it. It may be noted that the tort system does not object to compensation being given, even though the tortfeasor might benefit from it. Indeed, the Law Reform (Husband and Wife) Act 1962 was enacted to enable a spouse to obtain damages from the other spouse's insurers in the case of injuries in road accidents, though there is clearly a difference between paying compensation to a spouse in such a case, and paying it where the other spouse has been guilty of a criminal assault on his partner. Benefiting the 'guilty party' in the former case is not so undesirable as in the latter. It may also be noted that the exclusion of assaults to members of the same family means that this compensation system falls into line with the tort system, which also, in practice, excludes compensation for injuries occurring within the home.

The third aim of the exclusion is to protect child applicants. For example, awarding a child compensation in respect of the act of a parent may only have the effect of making relations between the parents themselves, and between the parents and the child, even more strained, especially if they continue to live as a family. A violent parent may well try to extract the compensation from the child. So the Board will only award compensation to 'battered children' if it is satisfied that this would not be against the interests of the child.

Although one naturally feels sympathy for children who suffer as a result of criminal violence, the scheme does create considerable anomalies. Suppose a man murders his wife and is sent to gaol for many years. His children will be entitled to substantial compensation from the scheme for loss of their mother's services and income. But is it really obvious that there is a rational justification for awarding such compensation when none is awarded to a child who is, say, orphaned through the death of both parents without anyone's fault? And if fault is the essential element, it is evident that death or injury of one spouse in an accident in the home caused by the *negligence* of the other (for which, in practice, a child is highly unlikely to receive any tort compensation) is less worthy of sympathy and compensation?

3 COMPARISON BETWEEN THE SCHEME AND TORT LIABILITY

Mental distress and nervous shock

The scheme has raised problems about mental distress caused by shock, very similar to those which have arisen in tort cases, and the Board has solved them in a similar way.[57] Thus, an elderly woman who suffered a heart attack as a result of witnessing an armed raid at her place of work was compensated,[58] but no award was made to a woman who suffered depression as a result of *being told* that her daughter had been sexually assaulted.[59]

Contributory negligence

Paragraph 6(c) of the 1979 version of the scheme gives the Board a wide discretion to consider whether, because of the conduct of the victim of the crime (before, during or after the offence), or of his character and way of life, it is inappropriate that he should be granted a full award, or any award at all. This is similar to the notion of contributory negligence in that it involves looking at the conduct of the victim, but it is much wider because it involves an assessment of responsibility for many different kinds of conduct. For instance, the victim of a sexual offence may be regarded as partly 'responsible' if she has run risks for her own safety, such as accepting a lift from a stranger late at night.[60] The fact that the compensation is being paid by the State and not the offender obviously plays an important part in a decision of this sort, for if the woman were to sue the offender personally, it is hard to imagine a court reducing the damages in a case of this kind. As between the victim and the offender, the responsibility is evidently that of the offender; but as between the victim and the State, the victim's own conduct becomes of great importance. In another recent case a drug dealer attacked by an irate customer was denied compensation because his injuries were said to have arisen from his drug dealing activities.[61]

Similar problems have arisen where the victim has been injured in a fight with the offender. Where the applicant for compensation is himself the aggressor, or is provocative, or agrees to fight, or is a party to a quarrel which develops into a fight, or attempts to revenge himself on the assailant, the Board's practice is to make no award at all.[62] It seems that a similar result might now be reached at common law as a result of the decision in *Murphy* v. *Culhane*.[63] It was here held that if a person initiates a serious assault on another, and then gets more than he bargained for, he may be met by pleas of *volenti non fit injuria* illegality or, in an appropriate case, contributory negligence. But a trivial assault which is met by savage retaliation may still entitle the victim to full damages at common law,[64] although the Board might in such a case make some reduction in the award.[65] Here again, the difference in result may be justified if in one case the State is paying, and in the other case, the tortfeasor himself is paying. But the law of torts does not distinguish between a tort action in which the damages will be paid by the tortfeasor and one in which they will be paid by someone else, e.g. an employer. Insurers would rarely be responsible for payment of damages in this sort of case because few liability policies would cover criminal assault.[66]

Other cases of fights are dealt with by the Board according to their 'merits'; for example, no award is usually made in cases of 'gang fights',[67] though reduced awards were made where the assailant uses a weapon in the course of a fair fight with fists, or a man fighting with fists is knocked to the ground by his opponents' friends and then kicked as he lies on the ground.[68] The Board has recently said that it takes a 'realistic attitude' to fights, so as to avoid just compensating the loser or the one with the more serious injuries.[69] In a number of recent cases awards have been denied or reduced on the ground that the applicant was injured in a fight precipitated partly by glue-sniffing in which the applicant had participated.[70]

In *R v. CICB, ex parte Ince*[71] the Court of Appeal said that the court should not think of the provision relating to the applicant's conduct in terms of the doctrine of contributory negligence. This is partly because, as we have seen, the Board can take into account a much wider range of factors than are included within the concept of contributory negligence. But also, both at common law and under the scheme, mere negligence, when weighed against a violent intentional assault, may rightly be disregarded as immaterial. But, as we have also seen, in a number of cases accidental injuries are covered by the scheme. It is not clear why it is wrong to think in terms of contributory negligence in such cases. Even so, the cases in which awards can be made for accidental injuries tend to involve 'emergency' situations, such as fire-fighting or law-enforcement; in such cases the common law tends to take a rather lenient attitude towards mere negligence on the part of the plaintiff.

There is a third way in which the provisions of the scheme concerning the applicant's conduct differ from the rules of contributory negligence at common law. At common law there must be a causal link between the plaintiff's negligence and his injuries. Thus, a plaintiff who carelessly sits on a dangerous wall will recover full damages if he is negligently injured by a stray bullet from a careless hunter.[72] In criminal injury compensation cases, the problem of deciding what sort of conduct is to be treated as relevant to a subsequent criminal attack is difficult. For instance, a man is carrying on an adulterous association with a married woman, and is assaulted or beaten up by the woman's husband;[73] or the applicant was drinking in a low-grade public house, flashing his money around, and is subsequently robbed while in a drunken condition;[74] or is solicited by a prostitute and then beaten up by her associates.[75] Cases of this sort at first caused much disagreement amongst Board members, but it is now clear than even a rather tenuous connection between the applicant's former conduct and his injuries will bar compensation.

In *R v. CICB, ex parte Thompstone*[76] the Court of Appeal held that the Board can, at its discretion, reduce or withhold compensation on account of an applicant's character or way of life even if these in no direct way led or contributed to his injuries. In this case the applicants had a history of convictions for crimes of dishonesty and, in one case, of violence. But the court also said that even where the Board takes account of conduct of the applicant before, during or after the events giving rise to the claim, it may not be necessary to establish a causal link between such conduct and the injuries. In other words, under the scheme an applicant can be penalized simply because the Board considers that he is 'not the sort of person' to whom state funded compensation ought to be given. This goes much further than the common law defence of illegality, which requires a clear causal link between the illegality as such and the injuries. The only analogous rule at common law is that in *Burns* v. *Edman*[77] to the effect that damages will not be awarded under the Fatal Accidents Act to the extent that the deceased maintained his dependants out of the proceeds of crime. This frankly moralistic element in the scheme makes it even more difficult to discern a rational policy underpinning it, especially since the Statement says that immorality as such will not be taken into account unless it constituted provocation to the assailant.

The undeserving applicant may sometimes be penalized in another way, because if, for instance, he has been an idler refusing to work and content to live on social security benefits, he will receive nothing for lost earnings. Thus, a blinded applicant who had lived on social security benefits for seven years and refused to maintain his own family during that time, was awarded £5,000 for pain and suffering (and presumably loss of faculty), but nothing for lost earnings.[78] Yet other examples of undeserving cases have come before the Board. For instance, where A assaults B, and then sometime later B returns the visit and assaults A. Contrary to previous practice,[79] no award is now likely to be made to either party in such a case.

The assessment of compensation

The compensation awarded under the scheme is, in general, assessed according to the same rules (including statutory rules) as govern the award of damages by the courts in claims for personal injury and death, but there are certain important exceptions to this principle. In the first place, there is a minimum placed on the scheme, in the interests of economy; the injury must be one for which at least £400 in compensation would be awarded (£500 in the case of family violence).[80] The limit is applied to the award after deduction of social security benefits, but other deductions are ignored so that, in practice, awards of less than £400 (or £500) can be made. The Home Affairs Committee thinks that this limit is too high.[81] It has been objected that the minimum limit on awards does not achieve its objective of economy, because a claim may still have to be investigated to discover if there has been loss exceeding the lower limit,[82] but this fails to take account of the fact that the limit probably discourages a large number of small claims. As we saw earlier, all the evidence suggests that trivial injuries and losses are vastly more common than more serious injuries and losses. This is also borne out by the Osgoode Hall Study (of 1968) into losses arising from crimes of violence in Toronto, which showed over 28% of the victims of crimes of violence with out-of-pocket losses of under $100 and (since 44% had no out of pocket losses at all) an equal percentage with losses exceeding this figure.[83] Of course, this does not take into account the non-pecuniary 'loss' for pain and suffering and disability, but on the other hand, in many cases it includes an item for medical expenses – which would not normally arise in this country. There can, therefore, be little doubt that the minimum of £400 does effectively exclude many claims.

There is also an upper limit on awards for *net* loss of earnings, namely twice *gross* average industrial earnings at the date of assessment. In 1985 gross average industrial earnings[84] were about £170, which means that the scheme provides no compensation for net loss of earnings exceeding about £17,680 per annum. This maximum is probably not aimed at keeping the cost of the scheme down. The number of potential applicants whose net earnings are more than £17,680 must be very small indeed. The real reason for the limitation is that it was thought to be inequitable to have widely varying awards for similar injuries because of wide variations in earnings, given that the scheme is financed by the taxpayer, and not according to an insurance principle under which those earning more pay higher contributions. The ethical problems involved in the earnings-related principal have already been discussed.[85]

Similar problems have occurred to those raised by the 'human vegetable' cases at common law. Awards of £30,000 and even £40,000 have been made in cases of severe brain damage where the next of kin would be the real beneficiaries because the victim himself could not benefit from the award.[86] Occasionally the Board issues guidelines for particular types of case. The latest figures (in the Twentieth Report), which apply to cases of young applicants, include £12,000 for the loss of an eye, and £1,200 for the loss of two upper front teeth. A large facial scar rates £4,500 for a male and £7,000 for a female. Rape of a young woman leading to no serious physical or psychological damage attracts compensation of £2,750. Each case is considered on its own facts in the light of these guidelines.

In fatal cases the compensation is again assessed along the same lines as in proceedings under the Fatal Accidents Act (with the same limitation on high earnings), but no compensation (other than for funeral expenses) is payable for the benefit of the deceased's estate.[87] However, under the Fatal Accidents Act a common law spouse is eligible for an award under certain circumstances, whereas under the scheme he or she is not so entitled. An award for bereavement may be made.

One other, and very important distinction between the assessment of damages at common law and compensation paid under the scheme, relates to the problem of double compensation. Under the scheme, compensation is reduced much more readily than it is at common law because of the existence of alternative forms of compensation.[88]

The great majority of awards are for relatively small sums. In 1984–5, 51·8% were for sums under £800 and 83·6% for under £2,000. But there were 860 (4·4%) awards exceeding £5,000, and the highest awards in recent years have been between £130,000 and £140,000; in 1984–5 an award of over £300,000 was made to a victim who was permanently paralysed as a result of his injuries.

Administration[89]

It is when we turn to the administrative machinery of the scheme that we find major departures from the normal processes of the common law. In the first place, the scheme is administered by a Board with the assistance of a legally qualified staff. The applications are dealt with in the first instance by a single member of the Board, after a preliminary sifting by the Board's staff, but there is a right (in the nature of an appeal) to a hearing before three members of the Board; and the single member may himself refer the case for a hearing if he finds it one of particular difficulty. This procedure is unique in the compensation systems in operation in this country.[90] It excludes the adversary process, so that the object of the administrators and the single member who first deal with a claim is to try to make awards as they would be made by the full Board under the scheme, and not to try to 'settle' them for the lowest possible figure. Thus the process differs dramatically from that by which the tort system is administered. On the other hand, it is administered by lawyers, and every case is dealt with by a lawyer from the outset, and in this way the system also differs from the way in which the social security system is administered. This is inevitable, so long as the basis of the scheme involves the assessment of damages along common law lines, and not the payment of compensation in accordance with a fixed tariff or schedule as with social security, for while payments of this latter kind can be dealt with perfectly adequately by unqualified clerical staff, the assessment of damages along common law lines can obviously only be done by someone familiar with this process, such as an insurance adjuster or a lawyer. This means that the cost of administration is a good deal higher than the cost of administering social security, though very much lower than the cost of administering the tort system, as we shall see later.

The second principal difference between the administration of the scheme and the tort process, is that under the scheme it is possible to make interim awards in the first instance, and postpone the making of a final award until certain unknowns are clarified. This power is widely used, and is found by the Board to be very useful, in particular in two types of case:[91] first, where the medical prognosis is still uncertain when the claim is first made; and secondly, where an industrial injury pension is likely to be payable but the amount of the disability has not yet been assessed – this being a benefit which must be deducted from the compensation. This helps to avoid the problems of the once-for-all lump sum award in the common-law cases. In 1984–5 over 3,000 interim awards were made.[92]

Because of the relatively streamlined procedure, and thanks also to the extensive use of the interim awards, the Board is also able to operate far more quickly than insurance companies. In 1984–5, about 32% of claims were dealt with by a final or interim award within six months of application, and 75% within twelve months. But delays have increased in recent years because increases in applications have not been fully matched by staff increases.[93]

Since the Board is not a legal court, legal aid is not available under the Legal Aid Act for the prosecution of a case before the Board. But legal advice could now be obtained to assist in making an application, or to help decide if an appeal is worthwhile. In any event, it seems that many solicitors are willing to act for a claimant on the understanding that their remuneration is to come out of any compensation awarded; though no 'costs' will be awarded,[94] and therefore the entire cost of legal assistance will come out of the compensation. In 1980, the last year for which statistics were kept, 34% of applicants were represented by solicitors in respect of the decision by the single member of the Board, while 19% were represented by a trade union representative. The rest appeared in person. In 46% of cases in which there was a hearing before three members of the Board, the applicant was represented by a solicitor, while in 14% of cases he was represented by a barrister, and in 5% of cases by a trade union representative. The latest report of the Board says that things have not changed much in this respect. Because the decision process is not adversarial, representation is less critical than in proceedings before an ordinary court.

If a hearing before three members is asked for, the Board instructs one of its own legally qualified staff to appear before it as 'advocate for the Board', and his duties are to present all the facts and arguments to the Board which they may find helpful, whether they are favourable or unfavourable to the claimant.[95] Nevertheless, it is somewhat disturbing to note that those who are represented at hearings enjoy a success rate of between 70% and 85%, while those who are unrepresented have a success rate of only 43%.[96] The explanation may be partly that unrepresented claimants are more likely to ask for a hearing, in circumstances where a represented applicant would not – because, for instance, it is plain to a lawyer that the chances of success are minimal. But it would be surprising if the presence of a legally qualified advocate made no difference to the chances of success. However, this problem is not unique to the criminal injuries scheme: the legal aid scheme does not apply to tribunals generally, and there is no immediate likelihood of any change.

At first there was a good deal of criticism of the level of awards, which were said by many to fall short of the amounts which would be awarded in comparable cases at common law, and lists of cases allegedly supporting this complaint were drawn up and published.[97] On the other hand, the Board repeatedly declared[98] that their only object was to make awards comparable to those which would be awarded by common law courts, and since they are experienced lawyers and are plainly trying conscientiously to carry out the scheme, it is hard to know what to make of the complaints. Possibly, they are in part due to a failure to appreciate the very great difference made by the extent of the deductions required to be made under the scheme, as opposed to the deductions made at common law. For example, in 1982 the highest award was made to a man aged 24 who was seriously paralysed, and was in need of nursing care and a specially adapted house. He suffered partial loss of earnings. The award of £136,500 was arrived at after deduction of social security benefits payable for the rest of the applicant's life. When the value of such benefits is added to the award, it becomes very substantial, and comparable with all but the very highest common law awards.

Another difference in the administrative process relates to appeals. Unlike the Court of Appeal sitting in common law cases, the Board is willing to make very small adjustments to the amounts awarded. Partly for this reason, appeals on the issue of the amount of the award were successful in 82·6% of cases in 1983–4. The Board explains this surprising figure by saying that in most successful appeals additional evidence is available to the Board to which the single member did not have access.[99]

Claims consciousness

Ever since it was started in 1964, the Board has been conscious that the level of claims has been a good deal lower than might have been expected merely by looking at the figures for crimes of violence against the person. But the Board has tried to publicize its operations and they are now certainly well known to the legal profession, and to most trade unions. The number of applications received in 1984–5 was 34,890 and it is still increasing every year. But this figure is less than a third of the crimes of violence recorded by the police in 1984.[100] However, many victims of violent crime suffer little or no injury. According to McClintock's findings, at least 75% of them were back at work within a week, about 12% were off work for 10 days, and less than 2% suffered permanent disability.[101] Moreover, a large number of those who suffer injury incur no financial loss, as the Osgoode Hall Study discovered. In addition to all this, the exclusion of crimes of violence between members of the same household cuts out a very large proportion of potential claimants. It is difficult to say whether there are still significant numbers of potential claimants who are unaware of their rights under the scheme, but who fail to claim.

14
The common law and the welfare state

1 WORKMEN'S COMPENSATION AND NATIONAL INSURANCE

Although the origins of the modern social security system have been traced back to the poor law of the Elizabethan age, it is sufficient for most purposes to look no further back than 1897, when the first Workmen's Compensation Act was passed. Workmen's compensation was pioneered in England,[1] from where it has since spread throughout the Commonwealth and the United States, and it may be taken as a convenient bridge between the tort system and the general social security system operating today. This is partly because it grew out of the deficiencies of the tort system, and partly because it is still much nearer to the tort system in many of its concepts than other parts of the social security system.

When trade unions began to wield increasing power towards the end of the last century they became particularly concerned at the high accident rate in industry, and at the fact that the victims of industrial accidents were usually left with nothing except poor or charitable relief to live on. The tort system rarely provided any compensation to the victim of an industrial injury at that time because of the three doctrinal defences which the courts had evolved for the protection of employers – namely the doctrine of common employment, denying liability for the negligence of a fellow worker; the doctrine of contributory negligence, denying liability where the workman was partly responsible for his injuries; and the doctrine of *volenti non fit injuria*, which (as then interpreted) denied liability for injuries occurring from a known and obvious risk. During the last twenty years of the nineteenth century the courts and the legislature gradually began the slow task of modifying these principles. In 1880, Parliament passed the Employer's Liability Act, which cut down the availability of the doctrine of common employment as a defence to the employer in an ordinary action at common law, though restricting the damages recoverable in such a case to three years' loss of earnings. The courts responded by curtailing the availability of the defence of *volenti non fit injuria* in *Smith* v. *Baker & Co. Ltd*[2] in 1891. Between 1878 when the Factory and Workshop Acts were consolidated, and 1901, a stream of new factory legislation emerged, even from a generally Conservative parliament not particularly devoted to social reform.[3] The courts also responded here by creating the action for breach of statutory duty in *Groves* v. *Wimborne* in 1898.[4]

But these developments were dwarfed in significance by the enactment of the Workmen's Compensation Act of 1897. This Act was Joseph Chamberlain's answer to Liberal attempts to extend the workman's common law rights by further erosion of the doctrine of common employment. Chamberlain had denounced the Liberals' Employers Liability Bill of 1893 (which had proposed such an extension) as illogical. With remarkable insight, Chamberlain pointed out that once personal liability was replaced by vicarious liability the law had already abandoned the principle of liability for fault. Consequently he urged that the only logical course was to jettison the fault principle entirely and proceed on the insurance principle of covering workmen for *all* work-connected accidents.[5] The result was that the Act of 1897 broke away entirely from the basic common law principle that liability must be based on fault, and conferred on a workman (or his dependants) a right to compensation for any accident 'arising out of and in the course of his employment'. In effect, this Act treated workmen as insured against such risks, although employers were not themselves compelled to insure against their new statutory liability. In practice, however, most employers did insure against this liability, and indeed, the new and fast growing liability insurance industry obtained a tremendous fillip from this species of liability.[6] The Act did not follow the common law in providing 'full compensation' for the injury required to be compensated, for it accepted the idea that industrial risks should be shared between employers and employees. Hence, compensation was to be assessed on the basis that the employee was to bear half the loss, and the employer the other half. This was a somewhat unreal approach; as with the modern law of contributory negligence, it simply meant that the employee received much less compensation than he would have earned if not injured, while the cost borne by the employer was passed on (at least so far as the competitive position of the industry made it possible) to the consumers of the products or services provided by the industry. Over the years, legislation gradually ate into the principle of leaving half the loss on the employee, and by 1940 it was possible for compensation to be as much as seven-eighths of the earnings lost in some cases, though the equal division of the risk remained in principle.[7]

But although in these two ways Workmen's Compensation broke away from the common law principles governing compensation for injury, in other important respects the new remedy was cast in the traditional mould. For example, something very like contributory negligence remained a defence to the employer under the Act, in that compensation was denied if the accident was due to the workman's 'serious and wilful default'. This defence was excluded in cases of serious and permanent disablement, and in fatal cases, by the amending Act of 1906, but it was still possible in some circumstances to deny compensation for an accident caused by the workman's fault (even though not serious and wilful) on the ground that his conduct took him out of the 'sphere of his employment', so that the resulting accident was held not to arise 'out of and in the course of his employment'.

The administrative process of workmen's compensation law was also almost identical with that of the tort system. This was not the original intention, which had been that compensation should be assessed in a swift and informal manner, and that disputes should be resolved by arbitration. It was, however, provided that in the event of failure to agree on an arbitrator, the county court judge should act as such; and provision was made for appeals on a point of law. In practice, what happened was that disputed cases went to the county court as a matter of form, and many cases were taken on appeal to the Court of Appeal and even the House of Lords. Moreover, even in cases which were settled, the adversary procedure which still dominates the settlement of tort claims today, was paramount.

Hence, the objective of the employer (or rather his insurer) was always to force a settlement for the lowest possible figure, and to use his greater bargaining power to do so; the threat to carry cases to appeal was obviously a good deal more powerful then than it is today under the tort process, partly because trade unions were not so wealthy then as they are now, and were less willing to bear the heavy costs of frequent appeals; and partly because (with no other social security payments to fall back on) an injured person, or his dependants, simply could not afford to wait while a case slowly meandered through the legal process from court to court.

Another respect in which workmen's compensation followed the common law of torts, was in giving complete freedom to the parties to settle the claim by the award of a lump sum. Although the Act did envisage and provide for the award of compensation by periodical weekly payments to take the place of lost wages, and so provide a regular income to the victim, it did not prevent the employer (or his insurer) and the employee from agreeing to settle the case by payment of a lump sum; and in fact the insurance companies preferred to dispose of claims in this way, and often put pressure on accident victims to accept lump sums.[8]

Although, as we have said, the 1897 Act introduced the idea that the workman should be (in effect) treated as insured against industrial risks, there also remained in the system something not very different from the causal principles applied in common law claims for negligence. The formula that the injury must arise 'out of and in the course of the employment' meant that the employment must not only be a cause-in-fact of the accident, but also that there must be some relationship between the employment and the injury similar to that embodied in the common law notions of cause-in-law. One particular difficulty to which this gave rise was that of industrial disease. If this was to be treated in the same way as industrial accident, great difficulties would often have arisen in dealing with the cause-in-fact problem. Medical science could not then (and indeed still cannot now) always provide answers to questions about the causes of diseases, and if such questions were left to be treated in each case many problems of proof, and inconsistency in decisions, would have arisen. The solution eventually adopted was to include only those industrial diseases which could definitely be shown by medical science to be caused by certain types of work (for example, pneumoconiosis), but this too had difficulties. Since workmen's compensation was payable by the employer, it followed that a person who became disabled by an industrial disease which had been slowly wearing away his lungs over a period of many years, might get all his compensation from the employer with whom he was working when he eventually became disabled.

Two final points of similarity between workmen's compensation and the tort system may be mentioned. The first was that the cost fell entirely on the employer. Although the system was more like an insurance system than the traditional fault based system, it was (like the modern law of torts with liability insurance behind it) a system under which the workman was insured by, and at the expense of, the employer. No contributions or premiums were exacted from the employee, nor indeed would it have been easy to justify such an exaction so long as the compensation was professedly designed to compensate to such a limited extent. But although the law did not exact contributions from employees, the economic facts of life may well have led to such exactions in practice. If the law places financial burdens on an employer, it is obviously quite possible that the employer will pay smaller wages than he might have otherwise done. Whether this happens, and if so, the extent to which it happens, is hardly ascertainable, and in any event depends upon the competitive position of the employer in question. During the 1930s when unemployment was endemic and wages depressed, it cannot be doubted that in real terms workmen's compensation was very largely being paid for by workmen themselves, in lower wages.

The second remaining similarity between workmen's compensation and tort, was that both dealt with partial incapacity as well as total incapacity; injury leading to some loss of earnings because the workman could no longer perform the same work was catered for. This later became a source of grievance, because if the workman slowly recovered his full earning capacity, or if by strenuous efforts he succeeded in earning what he earned before his injury, the compensation (if paid periodically) might be reduced or stopped altogether.

The second major contribution to the foundations of the modern social security system was Lloyd George's National Insurance Act of 1911. While the Workmen's Compensation Act was concerned to fill in the gaps left by the common law, this Act dealt with areas in which the common law had simply not concerned itself at all; that is, with income loss arising from sickness (and unemployment) rather than with work injuries. The Act represented a major departure in many ways. First, it was a national insurance system, established and administered by the State; the private insurance companies were not brought within the scope of the system at all, although friendly and provident societies were used as agencies to assist in administering the system on behalf of the State. This meant, among other things, that the adversary procedure which formed so prominent a part of the workmen's compensation system, with its common law links, played no part in the new system. Those responsible for administering the system were required to decide what benefits an applicant was entitled to according to the law, and to see that he received them. Secondly, the Act brought employer, employee, and the State itself, into partnership in the insurance system – or putting it more bluntly, the worknan's insurance was paid for partly by himself, partly by the employer, and partly by the taxpayer.

Thirdly, the insurance being national, was also compulsory, and the premiums were flat-rate contributions which did not generally depend on the nature of the risk. So also, the benefits payable were not variable according to earnings, as were tort damages and workmen's compensation, but were at flat rates. This was a vital difference, because it meant that the national insurance system was not so much concerned with replacing what had been lost – with 'compensation' in its more obvious sense – but with the meeting of basic subsistence needs. And this fact was also demonstrated by the provisions made in 1921 for the payment, in the case of unemployment (but not sickness) benefit, of allowances for adult and child dependants. A system, like the tort system, which professes to compensate in full for lost income, can clearly not increase its compensation merely because a man has dependants. Workmen's compensation, while starting out like the tort system as a means of compensating for lost income, moved closer to the National Insurance system in 1940 when child allowances began to be paid under the emergency war legislation.

But if the National Insurance Act was concerned with meeting need rather than with replacing lost income, it was never intended to provide sufficient to maintain those who were dependent on it. It would have been quite contrary to the liberal spirit of the time for the State to take over completely the obligation to maintain the sick, the injured, or the disabled. The object of the Act was rather to assist the industrious and thrifty working man who had a regular occupation, by supplementing his own savings and the private insurance schemes operated by trade unions and friendly societies.

In course of time these two pillars of the social security system – workmen's compensation and national insurance – became exceedingly complex. At the same time, other forms of national insurance, principally against unemployment and medical expenses, and pension schemes for the retired as well as for widows – all of which lie outside the scope of this book – grew in importance as well as in complexity. The depression which started in 1929 went a long way towards destroying the insurance basis of the national unemployment insurance system, because it became impossible to maintain two million unemployed out of the contributions which the system levied. And, on the other hand, when the war brought the new problems of persistent inflation, this helped to destroy the insurance basis of all the other national insurance schemes as well as the workmen's compensation system. For, as the value of money dropped, the long-term injured and sick and disabled could no longer survive on the benefits geared to contributions paid many years earlier with money worth very much more. So again the State was forced to underpin the social security system with various supplements during the war. Thus, by 1942, matters were ripe for the Beveridge Report which was published in that year.

2 THE BEVERIDGE REPORT AND THE 1946 ACTS

Beveridge cut through the complex structure of the system as it then was, to propose a new stream-lined system based on six fundamental principles. These were: a flat rate of subsistence benefit; a flat rate of contribution; the unification of administrative responsibility; the adequacy of benefits; comprehensiveness; and classification[9] (by which Beveridge meant the provision of different treatment according to the different needs of various classes of people).[10] The system of national insurance against sickness was not to be greatly changed, though Beveridge was concerned finally to abandon the idea that such insurance was only intended to supplement the worker's own savings. But apart from this, Beveridge's main recommendations here were simply to make the scheme comprehensive so as to cover the whole working population, including the self-employed and the middle classes. Otherwise, the 1911 scheme remained in essence undisturbed. Insurance was to continue on a flat-rate basis, geared to need rather than to what had been lost; but dependants' allowances were now to be paid in sickness as well as unemployment; contributions were to come from the employer, the employee and the State, as before.

But when Beveridge turned his attention to workmen's compensation, he found a system which was becoming increasingly unpopular with employees and trade unions.[11] While acknowledging that it had been the pioneer system of social security in Britain, Beveridge condemned it as based on 'a wrong principle and dominated by a wrong outlook'.[12] In language which could be applied to the whole tort system he added:

> It allows claims to be settled by bargaining between unequal parties, permits payment of socially wasteful lump sums instead of pensions in cases of serious incapacity . . . and over part of the field, large in the numbers covered, though not in the proportion of total compensation paid, it relies on expensive private insurance.[13]

He therefore had no hesitation in proposing the integration of the workmen's compensation system with the national insurance system.

We have already seen that the workmen's compensation system was in various ways much closer to the tort system than to the national insurance system, and the question which faced Beveridge at this point was, therefore, whether workmen's compensation should now be finally cut loose altogether from the tort system or whether it should retain certain special features, despite its merger with national insurance. Beveridge recognized that in principle there was a good deal to be said for a complete unification of the two systems.

If the matter were now being considered in a clear field, it might well be argued that the general principle of a flat rate of compensation for interruption of earnings adopted for all other forms of interruption, should be applied also without reserve or qualification to the results of industrial accident and disease, leaving those who felt the need for greater security by voluntary insurance to provide an addition to the flat rate subsistence guaranteed by the State. If a workman loses his leg in an accident, his needs are the same whether the accident occurred in a factory or in the street; if he is killed, the needs of his widow and other dependants are the same, however the death occurred. Acceptance of this argument and adoption of a flat rate of compensation for disability, however caused, would avoid the anomaly of treating equal needs differently and the administrative and legal difficulties of defining just what injuries were to be treated as arising out of and in the course of employment. Interpretation of these words has been a fruitful cause of disputes in the past; whatever words are chosen difficulties and anomalies are bound to arise. A complete solution is to be found only in a completely unified scheme for disability without demarcation by the cause of disability.[14]

Despite these arguments, Beveridge decided to retain a separate and more favourable scheme for industrial injuries, and gave three main reasons for this course.[15] First, some work is especially dangerous, and it is desirable that men should not be discouraged from entering such employment because of the risks involved. Secondly, a man injured while at work, is injured 'whilst working under orders', which is not generally true of sickness and disease. And third, only if special provision was made for industrial injury would it be possible, as Beveridge wanted, to limit the employer's liability at common law to actions for which he was 'morally and in fact' responsible. Few people today would find these arguments very convincing,[16] although in 1968 a Minister told the House of Commons that the government believed that 'there would be very strong opposition to any suggestion that preference for the industrially and war disabled was wrong.'[17] The fact that work is more dangerous hardly seems a good reason for compensating injuries more generously: the fact that a man injured at work was 'under orders' is merely an indication that he has not voluntarily chosen to incur a risk, but this is also true of the sick and naturally disabled.[18] And the fate of Beveridge's third argument is somewhat ironical, for special provision for the industrially injured was in fact treated as a signal for greatly increased liability for common law damages (as we shall see)[19] and not, as Beveridge himself hoped, as a ground for confining common law actions within very narrow limits. The Pearson Commission adopted a somewhat peculiar stance on the issue. On the one hand, they appeared to condemn the industrial preference (in principle) as unjustified; but on the other hand, they ended up by recommending (in effect) that the industrial injuries scheme should be extended, with modifications, to road accident victims.[20] As we shall see in the concluding chapter, the problem of reform is much influenced by the extent to which preferences of this nature tend to be treated as 'vested rights' which cannot be abrogated. Yet, in reality, the rights are only vested for those who have already become entitled to benefits, and certainly no reform is likely to remove or whittle away rights which are vested in that sense. The present extent of the industrial preference will be made clear in Chapters 15 and 16.

Despite Beveridge's decision to recommend special treatment for the industrially injured, he was determined to bring them within the general principles which he laid down for national insurance as a whole. Workmen's compensation was to become part of the State national insurance system; the private insurance companies, and the adversary process of settlement and litigation, were to go. The system was to be financed by contributions from employer, employee and State in the same way as national insurance, and payments were to be made by way of periodical weekly sums, as with national insurance, and not by way of lump sums as was permitted in workmen's compensation. In some respects, however, Beveridge proposed certain special features for the industrial injury system which were more like those drawn from workmen's compensation. For one thing, he wanted earnings-related pensions for long term disablement cases:[21] this was rejected by the government, who were imbued even more than Beveridge himself with the flat-rate philosophy.[22] Secondly, he wanted to impose a 'special levy' on industries with particularly bad accident records;[23] this too was rejected by the government,[24] principally because of the opposition of the trade unions.

In any case, Beveridge did not propose drastically different benefits for the industrially injured and other cases. His conclusion in favour of special treatment for industrial injury cases was in fact limited to cases where death occurred or disability was prolonged;[25] he proposed that for the first thirteen weeks off work the benefits payable should be the same, whatever the cause. The government, while professing to accept Beveridge's proposals, actually stood his scheme on its head in this respect; for they retained the distinction between industrial injury and other cases, but proposed that different treatment should be accorded them throughout, and not merely after the first thirteen weeks off work. As the government itself acknowledged, this change meant preferential treatment for *all* industrial injury cases, instead of the mere 10% of industrially injured who are away from work for more than 13 weeks.[26]

In one major respect, the government not only rejected Beveridge's proposals, but in a sense drew their inspiration from the tort system rather than workmen's compensation or national insurance. This was in relation to the new disablement benefits; where Beveridge had proposed earnings-related payments, the government decided on disability pensions and gratuities for the disability 'as such', quite irrespective of lost earnings. These payments, therefore, resemble the common law idea of compensation for 'loss of faculty', rather than any national insurance payment for lost income. One of the main reasons for reverting here to a tort idea, was that great indignation had been felt by workmen at the workmen's compensation principle, whereby payments for partial incapacity were liable to be reduced if the workman later began to earn substantially more again.[27]

Another interesting feature of the government's review of the Beveridge proposals was the firm rejection of lump sum compensation for lost income, though payment of lump sums for disabilities in minor cases was accepted.[28]

3 DEVELOPMENTS SINCE 1946

The main outlines of the National Insurance Act 1946 and the National Insurance (Industrial Injuries) Act 1946 (now consolidated in the Social Security Act 1975) have remained intact, together with the family allowance system and the national health service, both of which were regarded by Beveridge as essential parts of the new social security system. There have been many minor changes in the conditions of entitlement to benefits and in the other details of the schemes, and regular increases both in the level of benefits and of contributions have been one result of the inflationary period since 1946. But it would be a mistake to assume that increased benefits are the result of inflation alone. Benefits have increased much faster than prices, and in some years, increased even faster than wages, so that there was a real increase in the value of the payments.[29] Between 1948 and 1977, prices increased by about five times, earnings by about ten times, and social security benefits about twelve times. This was particularly important to the long term disabled or the chronically sick, for it meant that they were enabled to improve their standard of living along with the rest of the community. In 1974 the government went further, by placing on the statute book a commitment to review the levels of national insurance benefits annually, and to increase them sufficiently to keep pace with the general level of earnings;[30] but in 1979 the Conservative Government altered this to a commitment to increase benefits in line with prices.[31] Since then the government has pursued a policy of reducing the cost of social security provision and transferring parts of it into the private sector.

There have been four major areas of change in the social security system since Beveridge's day. First was the introduction of earnings-related payments. These were introduced in 1961 in connection with retirement pensions; in 1966 they were extended on a limited scale to sickness and unemployment benefits, as well as to industrial injury benefits; and in 1975 national insurance contributions became earnings-related, subject to upper and lower limits. Under the Social Security Act 1975, a new long term earnings-related scheme was introduced (effectively beginning in 1979) which will (if it matures) provide earnings-related additions to retirement pensions, as well as to long term contributory invalidity pensions. The scheme will only come into operation gradually, and will not be fully operative for 20 years. In the interim, long term benefits will continue to be basically flat rate, and the earnings-related addition will be fairly small. It will amount to 1¼% for each year from 1979 (reaching a maximum of 25% after 20 years) of a person's average earnings between a set minimum and a set maximum, at present £38 per week and £285 per week. The amounts will be uprated each year to take account of inflation. Although this change was grafted onto the existing system with a minimum of structural alteration, it represented an enormous shift in the philosophy of the national insurance system as a whole. Beveridge was opposed to earnings-related additions: he thought that the state had done its duty when it had provided a subsistence income for all its citizens who were unable to provide their own; protection above this level on a compulsory basis was an unjustifiable interference with the freedom of the individual to spend his money as he chose.[32] If individuals wanted more than basic benefits, they could provide them for themselves by means of private insurance. Introduction of the earnings-related principle was partly a product of increased affluence, and partly of a popular desire to reflect wage differentials in benefits, especially since many poorer people would not be able to afford to buy earnings-related additions in the private market.

In the last few years the earnings-related principle has had a rather strange history. Earnings-related additions to short term benefits were abolished as from 1982; but statutory sick pay, which has now completely replaced short term sickness benefit and industrial injury benefit, is earnings-related (although subject to a very low earnings ceiling of £74.50 per week). At the time of writing the fate of the earnings-related pension scheme (SERPS) is in doubt. In its 1985 Green Paper on Social Security Reform, the government announced its intention to phase out SERPS,[33] but it now appears to be having second thoughts in the face of widespread protest. Opposition to the earnings-related principle has been based partly on a reassertion of ideas like Beveridge's, and partly on a desire to reduce public spending and 'roll back the frontiers of the state'.

The extent to which social security benefits are earnings-related has important ramifications for the tort system, which is, of course, fully earnings-related. Complete abolition of tort as a means of compensating for personal injuries is unlikely to be politically attractive if social security benefits for disabled people are flat rate. We will return to this point later.

The second major change has been the gradual establishment of principles to deal with inflation on a regular basis. As mentioned above, in 1974 a statutory duty was created to raise social security benefits each year in line with the average rate of wage increases. The Conservative government altered this in 1979 to a duty to ensure that benefits keep pace with prices. The efficacy of the obligation has also been impaired in a number of other ways.[34]

The third major change in the social security system has been the gradual improvement of the provision for the disabled, and especially the long-term disabled. During recent years, the disabled have been an active lobby group in Parliament and they have secured many legislative improvements in their position. In particular, the introduction of the attendance allowance, the non-contributory invalidity pension, and the mobility allowance, are all major movements in this direction. It is interesting to note, that the attendance allowance and the mobility allowance are designed to cover additional expenses incurred by disabled people, and thus differ from other benefits which have traditionally been designed, either to provide an income, or (as in the case of disablement benefits) to compensate for loss of faculty.

In this respect, the social security system has thus come to recognize what common lawyers have traditionally regarded as an additional head of damage in a personal injury claim, namely expenses incurred, or likely to be incurred, as a result of the injury. It is also interesting to note that in recent common law cases, this head of damage appears to have been growing in significance, so it seems that social security and tort are marching in step in this respect.

The fourth principal change in the social security system since Beveridge's day has been the gradual erosion of the contributory principle. Except in relation to earnings-related additions to retirement and long-term invalidity pensions, the relationship between benefits and contributions has become attenuated. Many of the new benefits are wholly non-contributory, and there are also (somewhat less valuable) non-contributory benefits available for those who do not satisfy the contribution conditions for other benefits. Further, as we will see, there are no contribution conditions for the receipt of industrial injury benefits – this is one aspect of the industrial preference.

The social security system continues to be highly complex, and much of the legislation is difficult to understand. Comprehensive reform seems as far away as ever.

15
The industrial injuries system

1 THE SCOPE OF THE SYSTEM

The industrial injuries scheme[1] covers, as workmen's compensation did before it, all accidental injuries arising 'out of and in the course of employment'. The first requirement of the scheme is that the victim should have been an 'employed earner' which, in the vast majority of cases, means employed under a contract of service;[2] the system does not extend to the self-employed. There appears to be little justification for this, except for some suggestion that it would be impossible to detect abuse or fraud where a person was self-employed. For instance, a small independent shop-keeper might be tempted to allege that he fell and broke his leg in his shop instead of in his living quarters behind the shop, and it would be impossible to detect the fraud since there would be no employer present to verify the allegation.[3] However, if the 'small independent shop-keeper' converts his business into a limited company (as so many do today), there is nothing to prevent him in law being employed by his own company,[4] and he will then be insured under the industrial injuries scheme. The Pearson Committee recommended that the scheme should be extended to cover the self-employed, with any necessary modifications.[5]

The problem of defining an accident 'arising out of and in the course of employment' is an extremely difficult one. It gave rise to countless cases under the workmen's compensation system, and many cases raise the same problem today, though they are not now dealt with by the courts. This difficulty is inherent in the system; it has nothing to do with the 'meaning' of the words 'out of and in the course of employment'. The difficulty is inherent in the concept of insurance against special 'employment' risks. Because there is no clear and sound policy reason for distinguishing between employment risks and non-employment risks, it is almost impossible to construct a satisfactory criterion for distinguishing accidental injury within the scheme from accidental injury outside the scheme; this generates many borderline cases.

The result was that, despite universal dissatisfaction with the difficulties caused by his formula under the Workmen's Compensation Acts, it was retained when the National Insurance (Industrial Injuries Act) 1946 was passed, subject to reversal of a number of specific decisions under the old scheme which had been felt to be particularly hard. For instance, the Act reversed the decision of the House of Lords in *St Helen's Colliery Ltd* v. *Hewitson*,[6] that a man travelling to a coalmine in a train provided by his employers was not in the course of his employment unless he was required to travel on the train, even though there was no other practical way of getting to work.[7] But even the present law distinguishes between an injury occurring to a person travelling in a bus or train provided by or by arrangement with his employer, and injury occurring to a person travelling by public transport or his own transport. It has been a persistent source of complaint by the trade unions that injuries incurred while travelling to and from work are not covered by the industrial injuries system.[8] By a single vote, the Pearson Commission recommended that the industrial injury scheme should be extended to cover commuting accidents,[9] but in the debate in the House of Commons on 17 November 1979, Mr Patrick Jenkin found this an eccentric proposal which few would support.[10] Given that different treatment for different classes of accident is to remain with us in the immediate future, the question to be asked is whether accidents on the way to and from work should be treated in the same way as other work accidents, or in the same way as other transport accidents. There is no easy answer to this question.

There is a difference between the requirement that the accident should arise 'in the course of' the employment, and that the accident should arise 'out of' the employment. The former normally indicates that a person is doing his work when he is injured; the latter indicates that the injury must have arisen out of a risk peculiar to the employment. For instance, a person working at the workshop bench is in the course of his employment; but if he suffers injury from an assault by an escaped prisoner who has wandered into the factory, the injury will not have arisen 'out of' the employment – unless the employment in some way adds to the risk of such injury, as e.g. if the factory were part of the prison. It has been the law since 1946 that where a person is injured in the course of his employment, the injury is presumed in the absence of contrary evidence to have arisen out of the employment.[11] This provision may be useful where a fatal accident occurs and there is no evidence as to how the accident occurred. In addition, the legislation provides for certain special risks to be treated as though they arose 'out of' the employment. Subject to certain provisions as to the insured's own responsibility for the accident,[12] injury to a person in the course of his employment is now within the industrial injury system if it arises out of 'sky-larking' by his workmates; or as a result of the 'behaviour or presence' of an animal (including a bird, fish or insect); or is the result of being struck by any object or by lightning. So, for instance, if a man takes his dog to work with him and the dog bites his workmate while the latter is at work, this is an industrial injury. Or if a workman is struck by lightning or stung by a bee while at work, this also is an industrial injury. This provision was introduced in 1961 to deal with types of situation in which claimants had previously been denied benefit, but it is hard to see that there is any intelligible policy behind these extensions of the scheme, unless it is merely the feeling that the place where accidents occur is a more important criterion for compensation than the way in which they occur. Possibly it is thought that an accident which occurs on the factory floor should always be within the system (unless the workman has 'taken himself out of his employment' by doing something quite unconnected with his work), no matter how the injury arises. Certainly we appear to have got very close to a point where an accident arising in the course of the employment will almost inevitably fall within the system, and be treated as having arisen 'out of' the employment. This makes it difficult to justify having a special scheme for work-caused accidents.[13] But these provisions have, at least, had a good practical effect: a Commissioner has commented that the 'out of' requirement now gives little trouble.[14]

It is possible, though not very common, for injuries to arise 'out of' the employment, but to a person who is not 'in the course' of the employment. A person who, while taking a prolonged and unauthorized break to drink tea or smoke a cigarette, is injured by a risk arising 'out of' the employment, may be held not to have been in the course of employment.[15] In this kind of situation, the 'course of employment' formula really involves a resuscitation of the 'fault' idea, in a form not very different from that of 'contributory negligence'. The old Workmen's Compensation Acts excluded liability for an injury arising out of the person's own 'serious and wilful default', and although the Government in 1944 declared that a similar provision would be retained in the new industrial injuries scheme,[16] no such provision was included in the 1946 Act. There is, however, a provision dealing with the analogous question which a common lawyer would classify as involving a 'mitigation of damages' point. Under section 90 (1) of the 1975 Act, for instance, a workman is under a duty not to behave in a manner calculated to retard his recovery, and regulations under the Act provide that an insured person may be required to submit to medical treatment. The maximum penalty for a failure to comply with these duties is forfeiture of six weeks' benefit. Furthermore, the proviso to the 1961 extensions of the scheme discussed above, although not strictly involving the concept of contributory negligence, certainly introduces a fault element. The fault idea, although out of place in a social security system, dies hard. Perceived administrative difficulties may have been as important as theoretical objections in preventing the wider introduction of fault ideas into the scheme.[17]

2 ACCIDENTS AND DISEASES

An 'accident' is to be distinguished from a 'process' which is continuous over a period of time.[18] Basically the distinction is between 'accidental injury' and 'disease', and the reason for continuing to draw such a distinction is the difficulty of deciding, especially in relation to diseases common in the population at large, whether, in any particular case, the disease was contracted as a result of the employment. Under the industrial injuries scheme all accidental injuries arising out of, and in the course of, employment, are insured against; but diseases are not insured against, unless they are 'prescribed' by the Minister.[19] This means that when it becomes possible for doctors to assert with some confidence that there is a causal connection between a certain disease and a certain type of employment, the Minister can declare by regulations made under the Act that the disease is to be a 'prescribed' disease under the Act. Any person employed in the relevant occupation who then contracts the disease is treated in the same way – subject to certain exceptions – as a person suffering accidental injury in the course of his employment. It sometimes seems to take the DHSS an unconscionable time to declare a disease to be a prescribed disease, and the standard of proof required to convince the Department seems very high.[20] Common law actions, brought as test cases, have sometimes been a useful way to obtain a public hearing on the causation of industrial disease.

In 1981 the Industrial Injuries Advisory Council recommended a new system (to supplement that of prescribing particular diseases) under which, except in relation to certain diseases such as lung cancer and coronary conditions, the causes of which are much disputed, and which are common in the population at large, it would be open to a worker to claim benefit in relation to any disease which he could prove he contracted as a result of his employment.[21] The government has said that this proposal will not be implemented.[22]

But although most diseases do not fall within the system unless they are prescribed diseases; the accident part of the scheme does cover diseases caused by a single event or series of separate incidents (as opposed to a continuous process).[23] For instance, a worker may suffer a heart attack while trying to lift a heavy object. Inclusion of such cases in the scheme seems to be the result of sympathy more than logic. The anomaly in such a case is that the incident may have acted merely as a trigger; the worker may have been liable to collapse of a heart attack at any moment from any cause, and only if it happens while he is at work and doing part of his job is the result treated as within the system. The only difference between this sort of case and the case of a disease which falls firmly outside the scheme unless prescribed, is that in this case it is possible to point to some specific event or series of events which have produced the result. In some cases, where disease is contracted as a result of a *special* risk arising from the employment, the result seems less anomalous; as for instance, where a student nurse catches polio from a patient.[24] Another difficulty is that the distinction between a series of separate incidents and a continuous process is very difficult to draw, and produces some hard cases, such as that of injury to a hand by constant use of a pneumatic drill,[25] in which the claimant's injury is held not to have been caused by an accident, but is not a prescribed disease either.

Finally, it should be noted that the term 'accident' as used in the industrial injuries scheme means something like 'separate incident' as opposed to 'continuous process'. It does not mean an event which was 'accidental' in the everyday sense. Thus, injuries inflicted deliberately in an assault may be accidental within the meaning of the system,[26] as, for instance, where a man is attacked by robbers while carrying out his duties under his employment. In such cases there is a complete overlap between the industrial injuries system and the criminal injuries sytem, though double compensation is not generally permitted. But since the cost of the two systems falls on different parties, it is necessary to ask which is the more appropriate body to pay for such injuries. This we discuss later.[27]

The accident part of the scheme is, merely in numerical terms, very much more important than the disease part. For example, in 1983 there were 139,000 claims for disablement benefit as a result of industrial accidents, but only 5,000 as a result of diseases.[28] In 1982/3 there were 340,000 certified spells of incapacity (for the purposes of injury benefit – now replaced by statutory sick pay) as a result of accidents, but only 5,000 as a result of diseases.[29] In 1983 there were 8,597 disablement benefit appeals to Medical Appeal Tribunals in accident cases, but only 240 in disease cases.[30] The reason for this disparity is not that industrial diseases are a less frequent source of incapacity than industrial accidents. The converse is, indeed, probably the case. But many diseases which may result from working conditions are not prescribed; and even in relation to prescribed diseases, it is probably the case that many workers do not claim because they are less likely to attribute a disease to their working conditions than an accident. One reason for this is that we tend to see diseases as being the result of 'natural causes', perhaps because they *are* often partly the result of individual predisposition or of voluntary action (such as smoking) by the sufferer himself; or of environmental factors to which everyone is subject. A second reason is that much remains unknown about the causation of diseases.

3 BENEFITS: SHORT-TERM INCAPACITY

The law relating to the benefits provided under the industrial injuries system is today every bit as complicated as the law relating to the assessment of damages at common law, though it is a much more precise and rigid system, in which specific sums are laid down as the appropriate payments for particular cases. We may for convenience divide the benefits into three main classes, namely short-term benefits, long-term benefits, and benefits for widows and dependants. However it must be appreciated that this classification cuts across another important distinction namely that between benefits for lost earnings and benefits for disabilities as such. It should be stressed at the outset that there are no 'contribution conditions' for benefits under the industrial injury scheme. A person injured on his first day at work is entitled to the benefits provided. Moreover, provided a worker is an 'employed earner' he is covered by the scheme whether or not he is liable to make national insurance contributions.

As is generally the case with social security benefits, nothing is payable for the first three days of incapacity.[31] This rule performs a function similar to that of the 'excess' in first party insurance, and eliminates a large number of very small claims which would cost a great deal in aggregate and generate wholly disproportionate administrative expense. Until recently, victims of industrial injury received short-term injury benefit for the first 26 weeks of disablement, and victims of non-industrial incapacity received sickness benefit for this period. The former was paid at a higher rate than the latter, and this was part of the industrial preference. In 1983 injury benefit was replaced, for the first 8 weeks of disability, by statutory sick pay,[32] which was payable by the employer (who could claim complete reimbursement from the DHSS) at the same rate to victims of both industrial and non-industrial incapacity. To this extent, the industrial preference was abolished. In 1985 entitlement to statutory sick pay was extended to the first 28 weeks of disability,[33] thus completely removing the industrial preference in relation to short-term benefits. But the industrial victim is still better off, in that entitlement to long-term disability benefits arises after 13 weeks, whereas for victims of non-industrial disability, no long-term benefits become payable until after 28 weeks of incapacity. The replacement of sickness[34] and injury benefits by statutory sick pay has 'privatized' the administration (but not the funding) of short-term benefits.

The rates of statutory sick pay are earnings-related: for the year ending April 1987 they were £46·75 for those earning £74·50 or more; £39·20 for those earning between £55·50 and £74·49; and £31·60 for those earning between £35·50 (the lower earnings limit) and £55·49. There are no increases for dependants. Statutory sick pay is taxable,[35] and deductions are made in respect of national insurance contributions. This will not, however, significantly affect the lowest paid, who are liable for little or no tax; and there is a lower earnings limit on liability for national insurance contributions of £38.

If one considers statutory sick pay in isolation, it seems unlikely that very many, if any, persons injured at work would be better off on benefits than at work. Indeed, given that the highest rate of statutory sick pay is £46·75 (1986–7), the great majority of workers would be very much worse off receiving benefits rather than their ordinary wages. In the year to April 1985, average weekly earnings for all workers were £171; only 10% of the workforce were earning less than £88·30 per week. Some 10% were earning more than £269·90 per week. But of course in many cases statutory sick pay will not be the only income coming into the home: in many families both spouses work. This does not mean that they have surplus cash or savings to tide them over a difficult period, although it does mean that the proportional drop in total net family income as a result of one spouse receiving only social security benefits will be less than in the case of a one-earner household.

The position of higher paid workers is, on the other hand, not as bad as the rates of statutory sick pay might suggest. In the first place, the higher one's earnings, the greater the amount of tax saved during periods of non-earning (in other words, the proportion of gross income which is a net loss declines as the income becomes larger). Secondly, a large proportion of higher paid workers belong to voluntary occupational sick pay schemes which, for short periods of absence from work, provide full income replacement. Indeed, under many such schemes employees were, in the past, entitled to receive full sick pay without deduction of short-term social security benefits. However it is likely, following the introduction of the statutory sick pay system, that under most schemes statutory sick pay will be deducted from occupational sick pay. It should also be remembered that many employers of higher paid employees simply pay full wages during short periods of illness.

The common law, of course, in theory aims to replace net loss of earnings precisely, and for short periods of incapacity this aim can be achieved without too much difficulty. The main advantage which social security benefits have over tort damages is that the former are paid more or less immediately, and periodically, whereas tort damages will be paid in a lump sum, and usually many months, or even years, after the injury is suffered. Tort also provides damages for short-term non-pecuniary loss, and such damages tend to be a larger proportion of the total award in less serious than in more serious cases. By contrast, disablement benefits (for loss of faculty) do not become payable under the industrial injuries scheme until 13 weeks after the injury.

4 BENEFITS: LONG-TERM INCAPACITY

Long-term incapacity (i.e. for periods exceeding thirteen weeks) which arises from industrial injury is today treated in a very complex way which is not so very different from the common law method of assessing damages. It is in this area that the industrially injured are privileged when compared with those suffering from non-industrial accidents, or from natural diseases, or congenital disability.

Broadly speaking, the industrial injuries system now provides for disablement pensions for long-term incapacity where the disability is a major one, and for disablement gratuities where the disability is not so serious. The amount of the pension or gratuity is related to overall maxima laid down in the Act – in 1986–7, £63.20 per week for a pension, and £4,200 for a gratuity; but subject to these maxima, the amount payable in any individual case depends on the degree of disability. This is assessed in percentages according to guidelines laid down in Schedule 8 to the Social Security Act 1975, and with the assistance of a 'tariff' laid down in Schedule 2 of the Industrial Injuries (Benefit) Regulations 1982, for specific types of disability. The fundamental principle is that the assessment must be based on all disabilities 'to which the claimant may be expected, having regard to his physical and mental condition at the date of the assessment, to be subject ... as compared with a person of the same age and sex whose physical and mental condition is normal.'[36] The assessment is almost wholly objective,[37] and completely ignores the personal characteristics of the claimant; what particular pleasures he may have lost, what particular hobbies he may no longer be able to pursue, and so forth. 'The assessment shall be made without reference to the particular circumstances of the claimant other than age, sex and physical and mental condition.'[38] This contrasts with the common law approach which, though steadily moving towards greater objectivity in assessment for loss of amenities, is still partly subjective in approach. A departmental committee which examined the principles of assessment under the Act in 1965 rejected the introduction of subjective factors which (they thought) 'apart from being impossible to quantify, would clearly have no place in the determination of equitable and consistent assessments.'[39] The Pearson Commission, not uncharacteristically, endorsed the objective approach of the industrial injuries scheme, the subjective approach of common law damages awards, and the argument that compensation schemes should be more fully integrated in the future.[40]

Apart from this particular issue, there has been some criticism of the principles on which disabilities are assessed. It has, for instance, been complained that too little attention is paid to the functional effect of the disablement.[41] What actually does the disability prevent the person from doing? The fact that no distinction is drawn between loss of right and left hand is perhaps illustrative of this point. The committee already mentioned thought that there was no ground for drawing such a distinction, and added that it is generally found that the non-dominant hand can quite easily replace the other after loss,[42] though they did not even mention the difficulty of learning to write with the non-dominant hand.

The 'tariff' in the Benefit Regulations is not, and is not intended to be, exhaustive, nor, in fact, is it rigidly binding in any given case. It merely prescribes the percentage assessment appropriate to certain kinds of disability, where no special features present themselves. Schedules of this kind are in widespread use throughout the world, but they have given rise to much dissatisfaction.[43] This is partly because they often appear very arbitrary and partly because the main difficulties in the assessment of disabilities are associated with less readily identifiable handicaps. Low back injuries, for example, are very common and notoriously difficult to assess. No schedule is likely to help much in such cases. Moreover, the assessment of disabilities in percentages gives the misleading impression that it is possible to make comparisons across the whole field of disability in precise terms. A Report of the Industrial Injuries Advisory Council on Occupational Deafness[44] gives some idea of how exceedingly difficult it is in practice, even in relation to a single disability, to measure disablement in percentage terms. Attempts have recently been made to work out more objective methods of measuring disabilities, by allocating points to a simple series of tests to be done by the subject. The American Medical Association has produced a *Guide to the Evaluation of Permanent Impairment* (1971), which so impressed the Australian Committee of Enquiry that they recommended its adoption for the purpose of their scheme.[45]

Table 9 contains a number of cases extracted from Schedule 2 of the Benefit Regulations, together with the pension or gratuity appropriate to that degree of disablement. If the assessment is 20% or above, a pension is awarded, while if the disablement is 19% or below, a gratuity is payable, except in certain cases of industrial disease where a pension is payable even for an assessment of under 20%. Pensions are based on assessments in multiples of ten, so that a 26% disability rates a 30% pension and so on; gratuities are however assessed by single percentages. Here again, as so often, the more serious cases seem to be relatively worse-treated than the less serious. The gratuity for a 19% disability is only ten times that for a 1% disability. Yet, if anything, it might be thought the position should be reversed. A disability of 1% or 2% is so trivial that it is unlikely to have any effect on a person's life style; a 19% disability may be a real handicap. Moreover, the same criticism can be made of the higher level figures. It is dubious whether one can really say that a 100% disablement should only be worth five times the compensation awardable for a 20% disablement. Once a person is assessed as more than 70% disabled (or thereabouts) it is likely that the incapacity will have a serious effect on the whole life of the disabled person, and also of his family. It may also be noted that there are very few cases of disablement at the 100% rate, so that it would cost relatively little to increase the proportion payable at the top end of the scale, even at the expense of a decrease at the lower end.

TABLE 9
DEGREE OF DISABLEMENT AND AMOUNT OF PENSION OR GRATUITY ATTRIBUTABLE TO CERTAIN INJURIES

Description of injury	Degree of disablement	Amount of pension or gratuity	
Loss of both hands or amputation at higher sites	100%	Pension £63·20	p.w.
Loss of a hand and a foot	100%	,, ,,	,,
Loss of sight to such an extent as to render the claimant unable to perform any work for which eyesight is essential	100%	,, ,,	,,
Very severe facial disfigurement	100%	,, ,,	,,
Absolute deafness	100%	,, ,,	,,
Loss of a hand, or of the thumb and four fingers of one hand	60%	,, £37·92	,,
Loss of thumb	30%	,, £18·96	,,
Loss of two fingers on one hand	20%	,, £12·64	,,
Amputation of both feet	90%	,, £56·88	,,
Loss of one eye	40%	,, £25·28	,,
Loss of vision of one eye, without complications or disfigurement of the eyeball	30%	,, £18·96	,,
Loss of whole index finger	14%	Gratuity £3,150	
Amputation of tip of little finger without loss of bone	2%	,, £630	

It will be seen that even a maximum 100% disablement by no means represents complete helplessness; many blind men are capable of leading full and enjoyable lives, and very severe facial disfigurement may not incapacitate for employment at all. If 100% disabilities do not represent complete helplessness, what about the cases which are in fact reduced to complete helplessness? The answer is that such cases are taken care of by a number of special allowances. In particular, a 'constant attendance allowance' is paid for cases of 100% disablement where the injured person requires continuous attendance; this allowance is normally £25·30 per week but may be £50·60 per week for exceptionally handicapped cases.[46] There is also a further 'exceptionally severe disablement allowance' for the worst cases in which constant attendance is permanently required, and this is payable at the rate of £25·30 per week.[47] Very few people receive these allowances.[48]

The 'tariff' laid down in the Benefit Regulations may be a little misleading, in that it is mostly confined to cases of permanent disability. But most disabilities are not permanent. A person may be temporarily blinded, but may recover his sight in due course; a person may lose the use of a limb for a period, but recover some or all ability to use it eventually; in fact about 70% of disablement pensions last for under five years, and 30% last for only six months.[49] These cases are met by the administrative procedure which enables 'provisional' assessments to be made in the first instance where this is necessary. If the assessment is for 20% or above, a pension is payable, which may then be terminated or reduced when the final assessment is made, if there is partial or complete recovery. Once a permanent assessment is made, however, the pension cannot be reduced, although it can be increased if there is any unforeseen aggravation which would justify an increase assessment at a later date. In the case of an assessment below 20%, for which a gratuity is payable, the Act provides for the maximum gratuity if the disability lasts, or is expected to last, for at least seven years. Thus a 19% disability for seven years rates a gratuity of £4,200. If the disability lasts for less than seven years then the gratuity is reduced proportionately. Here again, it is possible to make provisional or final assessments, so that the gratuity may be paid in more than one sum.

Since the benefits for the more serious cases are awarded in the form of a pension, it is obviously difficult to draw any direct comparison between the value of these benefits, and the sort of amounts which would be awarded by way of common law damages for similar disabilities (ignoring, in both cases, the question of lost earnings). But Table 10 on p. 340 attempts to provide some basis of comparison, by showing the value of a disablement pension capitalized at a 2% discount rate, for varying periods. A discount rate of 2% may seem unrealistically low (thereby possibly making the capital value of the pensions seem higher than they really are), but this is the figure thought appropriate by the Pearson Commission, to take account of inflation and true interest rates.[50] As the value of disablement pensions is now more or less inflation-proofed through annual up-ratings, the capital needed to provide an equivalent income is correspondingly greater.

TABLE 10
VALUE OF DISABLEMENT PENSIONS CAPITALIZED AT 2% FOR VARYING PERIODS

Period of years	20% pension	30% pension	40% pension	50% pension	60% pension	70% pension	80% pension	90% pension	100% pension
5	£ 3,095	£ 4,643	£ 6,217	£ 7,739	£ 9,287	£10,835	£12,383	£13,931	£15,478
10	£ 5,902	£ 8,835	£11,804	£14,755	£17,707	£20,658	£23,609	£26,560	£29,511
15	£ 8,439	£12,659	£16,878	£21,098	£25,318	£29,538	£33,757	£37,977	£42,197
20	£10,746	£16,119	£12,493	£26,866	£32,239	£37,612	£42,986	£48,359	£53,732
30	£14,716	£22,074	£49,432	£36,791	£44,149	£51,507	£58,865	£66,264	£73,582
40	£17,976	£26,964	£35,953	£44,941	£53,929	£62,918	£71,906	£80,894	£89,883

The figures for 100% disablement are somewhat misleading because they ignore the constant attendance allowance and the exceptionally severe disablement allowance, but a better idea of the comparative level of common law awards and disability pensions can be obtained by concentrating on the other assessments. For example, we now know that up to £11,000 is awarded at common law for loss of an eye (no difference apparently being drawn between loss of vision and loss of the eyeball), whereas for loss of vision alone, there would normally be about 30% assessment under the industrial injuries scheme. It is clear from Table 10 that the value of the disablement pension is considerably less than the common law figure at ages exceeding about 60, but much higher at younger ages. Loss of a leg, which at common law would rate up to £25,000, would normally amount to a 50% disability for a below the knee amputation and 70% to 80% for an above the knee amputation, depending on the length of the stump left. Here again the disability pension is worth less for an older person but very much more for a younger one. Coming to the gratuities we find, for instance, loss of the whole index finger assessed at 14%, which today would carry a gratuity of £3,150, again probably rather more than the sum which would be awarded at common law. It appears from these comparisons that the relative value of disablement pensions has increased in comparison with common law damages over the past few years. In the first edition of this book, published in 1970, it was estimated that the disablement pensions were on average worth about two-thirds to three-fifths of damages for pain and suffering. Today, they are often higher than the value of common law awards. If we take the maximum figure of £90,000 as representing the value of a 100% disablement pension to a young man of 20 or 25, then the figure is somewhat more than the maximum awards for non-pecuniary loss at common law; moreover, 100% pensions are awarded in many cases where damages at common law would not be at anything like the highest point.

The disablement pension or gratuity is not intended to be an award for lost earnings, and it is therefore payable even though there is no loss of earnings.[51] But other allowances are payable in addition where there is an income loss. Since entitlement to disablement benefit arises 13 weeks after injury, and statutory sick pay is payable for the first 28 weeks of incapacity, there is an overlap between these two benefits. If the injuries are so serious that the claimant is permanently incapacitated for work, he will normally be entitled to the ordinary invalidity pension and allowances in the same way as the person suffering from chronic illness. These long-term benefits become payable after 28 weeks, when statutory sick pay ceases to be payable. Victims of industrial injuries do not have to meet the contribution conditions for invalidity benefit[52] – another instance of the industrial preference. This means that in order to compare the position of the most severely disabled cases at common law and under the industrial injury scheme, we must consider the maximum benefits payable under all these heads from the 29th week after injury. For a married man with two children, the maximum (in 1986–7) was £261·15 per week, made up as follows:

	£
100% disablement pension	63.20
Allowance for spouse	23.25
Allowance for two dependent children (including child benefit)	30.30
Invalidity benefit or unemployability supplement	38.70
Invalidity allowance or increase to unemployability supplement (maximum)	8.15
Constant attendance allowance (maximum)	50.60
Exceptionally severe disablement allowance	25.30
Mobility allowance	21.65
	261.15

The earnings-related addition to long-term benefits introduced by the Social Security Pensions Act 1975 is now also payable. It will be many years before this amounts to very much; the maximum (in terms of 1986–7 prices) will eventually be £61.75 per week. But the amount of any such addition is deducted from the invalidity allowance (or age-related increase to the unemployability supplement) so that, in effect, the beneficiary receives only the greater of the two. So it is ignored here. It is not possible to give a precise capital value for a pension of this kind because the children's allowances will cease in due course, and also because a person so exceptionally disabled may well have a reduced expectation of life. But if this is not the case, it is clear that for a young man of 30 the capital value of these benefits would exceed £300,000. For an older man, especially if he had no dependent children, the capital value might be in the region of £150,000. There is no doubt that some common law damage awards for the most severe injury cases are more than this, but it must also be remembered that the highest common law awards (those between £350,000 and £400,000) are nearly always given to people with very high earnings, much higher than those likely to be encountered when dealing with industrial injuries.

There are in any event two reasons why comparisons between the value of industrial injury benefits and tort damages are somewhat misleading. In the first place, long-term injury and disablement benefits are not generally taxable. Therefore, in order to compare the maximum benefits payable under the industrial injury scheme of £261 per week (for a married man with two children) with the value of a common law damages award, this sum should be 'grossed up'; and it is then found to be worth more than £19,000 per annum, rather than the tax free £13,579 which is actually paid. This adds another 25% or so to the value of the pension. And secondly, as we have already seen, the pensions are more or less inflation-proofed, by virtue of a statutory duty to increase them each year by not less than the annual rate of price increases.[53] (The figures in Table 10 already take account of this element). When these factors are taken into account, it seems clear that industrial injury benefits are now as valuable as common law awards whenever long-term incapacity is in question. One has only to consider the possible case of a young man of (say) 25 who suffered a serious permanent disability in 1955, to appreciate the value of the regular increases in social security benefits. Such a person would be better off today if he had been awarded a disability pension, than if he had obtained damages at the rates prevailing in 1955. A person required to choose between them might well be advised to choose the industrial injury benefits; in fact no choice is necessary for, subject to some deductions, both are claimable where the requirements of both sets of laws are satisfied.

Special hardship allowance

Cases of permanent and total incapacity for work are, fortunately, rare. Much more common is permanent or long-term disability which does not prevent a person from working altogether, but does reduce his earning capacity. In this event, a misleadingly named 'special hardship allowance' is payable.[54] The maximum payment is at present £25.28 per week, and most recipients receive the maximum.[55] The allowance is payable with a disability pension, or following payment of a gratuity, but the allowance and the pension together may not exceed the amount of a 100% pension. Despite the fact that the allowance is designed to replace earnings, it is payable for life, not just until retirement age.

Special hardship allowance is payable where a person is incapable of following his regular occupation or of 'employment of an equivalent standard which is suitable in his case'. The application of these provisions has given rise to much difficulty and there are many disputes about entitlement to this allowance. In 1965, for example, the Court of Appeal held that a man reduced to working at a lower paid job was entitled to the allowance, although in another town that lower paid job would actually bring him a higher wage than he had formerly earned.[56] In another decision in 1971 the Court of Appeal held[57] that a person who was only able to earn money at a lower *rate* than in his former occupation was not entitled to special hardship allowance when in fact by working much longer hours, he was able to match his former earnings. The former Chief Commissioner has stigmatized this decision as completely unjust,[58] but it remains the law.

A person in receipt of a disablement pension, with or without special hardship allowance, is also entitled, if he subsequently falls sick and is away from work, to the appropriate sickness or invalidity benefits and additions.

The special hardship allowance has played a much larger role in the industrial injuries scheme than was probably originally envisaged. In 1973 over 140,000 such allowances were being paid. Unfortunately, it is widely agreed that it is one of the least satisfactory parts of the whole social security system. It has generated high administrative costs and a complex case law.[59] In its 1981 White Paper on Reform of the Industrial Injuries Scheme, the government proposed replacing the allowance with a new benefit entitled 'reduced earnings allowance', payable at a maximum rate equal to a 100% disability pension. Payment would cease at retiring age. Proposals were also made to ameliorate difficulties in assessing the amount payable.[60]

Earnings-related additions[61]

As we have previously noted, the Social Security Pensions Act 1975 introduced earnings-related additions to the basic flat-rate long-term benefits. Before this there was (except for the special hardship allowance) no earnings-related component in the long-term benefits, and all benefits and allowances were paid according to the degree of disability irrespective of income. The Pearson Commission recommended[62] – without giving any reasons – that for those injured at work, the provisions of the Pensions Act should be accelerated so that earnings-related benefits were payable immediately, in full, as though 20 years of service under the Act had already been performed. It is difficult to see why the victims of work injuries who are, as the Commission itself noted, already much better catered for than most other victims, should receive this further advantage.

Even when the Pensions Act is fully operative, the earnings-related component will not be very large compared with all the other benefits and allowances payable under the industrial injuries system. It will provide for an earnings-related addition of 25% of the average earnings of the claimant over the previous 20 years (adjusted to take account of inflation) between a threshold and a ceiling, which in 1986–7 were set at £38 and £285. Thus the earnings-related component, at its maximum, will amount to one quarter of the difference between £38 and £285, or £61·75 in 1986–7 prices. Even with the earnings-related addition, social security benefits for long-term income loss fall far short of the principle to which tort law is committed, of replacing lost earnings in full. Moreover, it will also be observed that under the Pensions Act of 1975 a person has to *earn* his earnings-related pension, which he does at the rate of 1¼% per annum. This compares oddly with the tort system under which a person is entitled to damages for lost future earnings which he has never enjoyed at all, for example, because he is permanently disabled before he reaches working age. It is not intuitively apparent that the tort system is more equitable than the new social security pensions scheme on this point.

At the time of writing, the fate of the earnings-related pension scheme (SERPS) is unclear. In its 1985 Green Paper the government announced its intention to discontinue the earnings-related component of the state retirement pension scheme, but no proposals were made in relation to the earnings-related component of invalidity pensions. The proposals have met with widespread and vociferous opposition. The main motives for the proposals are the desire to reduce public spending and to further the aim of transferring welfare provision from the public to the private sector. But the move could also be justified in terms of a very different political philosophy, by saying that funds ought to be channelled into the provision of satisfactory levels of flat-rate benefits, so as to provide as generously as possible for the basic *needs* of all welfare recipients. At all events, the more the social security system is based on flat-rate benefits, the greater the contrast with the tort system, which is fully earnings-related.

5 BENEFITS FOR WIDOWS

A woman whose husband dies as a result of an industrial accident or a prescribed disease is entitled to a widow's pension. As in the case of non-industrial death special provision is quite reasonably made for the first six months of widowhood, and indeed, in both cases the amount is now the same – in 1986–7, £54·20 per week – though the industrial injury widow receives her allowance more or less automatically, while other widows will only receive theirs if certain contribution conditions are satisfied. In addition, allowances are payable for dependent children, at a rate amounting now to £15·15 per child (including child benefit).

At the end of the first 26 weeks of widowhood, the widow's pension falls to £39.25 if, *inter alia*, the widow has dependent children (the 'widowed mother's allowance') or if she was over 50 years of age when her husband died. She will still receive allowances for her dependent children; and the earnings-related addition[63] will gradually become payable. If she had dependent children and was over 40 years of age when they ceased to be dependent on her, she will still receive a pension at this rate. In other cases, the widow receives a pension of £11·61 per week. Here, therefore, as with common law damages, a young childless widow is entitled to permanent compensation, irrespective of her ability to earn a living. The Pearson Commission recommended[64] that pensions in this last category should gradually be phased out, though not taken away from widows already in receipt of them. This recommendation is sensible. There seems no reason why a young, childless widow, aged perhaps 25 or 30, should expect to receive a State pension for life (or until remarriage), and the amount itself is merely a token payment. In certain circumstances industrial widowers are entitled to a pension, but the conditions are so stringent that in 1980 only *one* was being paid. The rules bristle with examples of sex discrimination, and provide another instance of the industrial preference, as no such pension is available to non-industrial widowers.[65]

On remarriage the widow's pension comes to an end, but she is entitled to a gratuity by way of 'widow's dowry' of one year's pension, i.e. at the current rates, £2,041. In order to prevent evasion of this, a widow's pension is not payable for any period while she is living with a man as her husband. This is the much disliked 'cohabitation rule', but the 'widow's dowry' provision makes the rule less important here than elsewhere.[66] When the widow remarries, children's allowances cease to be payable (although entitlement to child benefit continues). Widows' benefits are taxable as income, but of course on their own they will not attract any tax as they will be below the tax threshold. Only if the widow has other income, earned or unearned, will she in practice have to pay tax on these benefits.

These provisions form a striking contrast to the treatment of widows under the Fatal Accidents Acts. In an action under these Acts, the widow is (as we have seen) entitled to full compensation irrespective of her age, or whether she is capable of work,[67] or whether she has dependent children (though if she has, they too will be entitled to damages). Moreover, the industrial injury system does not have to guess whether a woman is likely to remarry or not. Benefits can be, and are, paid on the basis that the woman is dependent on the State; if she ceases to be so dependent as a result of remarriage then the position changes and the benefits come to an end; apart from the widow's dowry and the children's reduced allowances. So far as the children's allowances are concerned, the common law is based on much the same idea, but in a much more crude and haphazard way. If a widow has actually remarried when her case comes on for trial, or is likely to do so very shortly, damages for the children are still given, though at a reduced rate. The courts do take into account that the widow's second husband may have assumed the burden of maintaining her children, but they also take into account that he may not be so generous with them as he would be with his own children.[68]

The 'cohabitation rule', as mentioned above, is much disliked because of the intrusions into privacy which it may involve. But every official inquiry into the rule has supported the rule in principle.[69] The simple basis for the rule is that it would be inequitable to treat a widow who marries less favourably than a woman who cohabits with a man without marrying him. Short of paying widow's pensions without regard to remarriage at all, there seems no other solution to this problem. And while it is true that Fatal Accidents Acts damages are now paid regardless of remarriage, that deplorable precedent is not one to be followed. However, as we have already observed, the 'widow's dowry' provision makes the cohabitation rule somewhat less offensive in the case of industrial widows than in other cases.

The result of these differences in approach is that it is not easy to make meaningful comparisons between the value of the industrial injury benefits for a widow and damages awarded to a widow under the Fatal Accidents Acts. Both the industrial injury system and tort law now generally treat widows more favourably than any other class of accident victim. Moreover, the favourable treatment becomes even more marked when a widow is entitled to both sets of benefits, for they are then both payable in full with no deductions. Until 1971, it was probably true to say that social security provisions for widows (with the prospect of annual increases in benefits) were generally more valuable than common law damages. This is clearly no longer so for young widows without children, who may now receive enormous awards of damages, but would be entitled to little in the way of social security benefits. In its 1985 Green Paper the government announced its intention to restructure widow's benefits. The main proposals involve replacing the allowance for the first six months with a lump sum payment (initially £1,000), and raising the age at which a widow qualifies for a higher rate pension to 55. These proposals apply to industrial as well as non-industrial widows.

6 ADMINISTRATION[70]

The industrial injury system is based, in the great majority of cases, on a simple administrative process. Claims are submitted (usually by post, on the reverse side of a medical certificate) to the local office of the Department of Health and Social Security, and are decided in the first instance by an insurance officer who is a civil servant. In most cases, the only evidence needed to support the claim will be a medical certificate that the applicant is unfit for work, and confirmation from the employer that the accident arose out of and in the course of the applicant's employment. However, there are many complexities in the administrative process which affect a relatively small proportion of cases, though these are still large in total number.

Broadly, the legislation divides the final decisions on questions arising under the Act into three classes.[71] Questions relating to contributions, (e.g. whether a man was an employed earner or a self-employed earner) are generally determined by the Secretary of State, which in practice means the legal advisers of the DHSS. These matters relate principally to the financing of the whole system, and are not dealt with here. Other decisions are entrusted to medical tribunals and the 'statutory' authorities. The Act draws a firm line between purely medical questions, which are entrusted to the medical authorities constituted under the Act, and legal questions, which are entrusted to administrative tribunals.

There are two principal questions entrusted to the medical authorities; whether a particular disability was due to the relevant accident, and the assessment of degrees of disability for the purpose of disablement pensions and gratuities. The questions are usually entrusted in the first instance to a single adjudicating medical practitioner, but appeal may be taken from the decision of such a practitioner to one of the twelve medical appeal tribunals,[72] usually consisting of two medical practitioners of consultant status and chaired by a qualified lawyer of at least seven years' standing. Appeals may be brought either by the claimant or by the Minister, and the appeal tribunal may confirm, reverse or vary the Board's decision in whole or in part.[73] There has been some criticism of these Medical Appeal Tribunals, mainly (it seems) because appellants often feel that due consideration has not been given to their cases.[74] This is probably because the medical members tend to make up their minds on the appellant's medical record, so that the decision often appears to have been taken before he even enters the room. It seems to be the principal function of the chairman of the Tribunal to maintain the procedural proprieties, and try to ensure that justice is seen to be done. There have been many applications to the courts for *certiorari* to quash decisions of Medical Appeal Tribunals, though surprisingly there is some doubt about the applicability of the rules of natural justice.[75]

All other matters – and in particular those relating to entitlement to benefits – are dealt with in the first instance by an adjudication officer,[76] from whom an appeal lies to one of the local social security appeal tribunals.[77] These tribunals normally consists of three members; two are drawn from a panel composed of persons who have knowledge or experience of conditions in the area, and who are representative of persons living or working in the area, and chosen after consultation with 'appropriate' organizations or persons.[78] The third member must be a qualified lawyer of at least five years' standing. The officers and tribunals are often referred to as the 'statutory authorities'.

The Social Security Commissioner hears appeals from both the Medical Appeal Tribunals and the statutory authorities,[79] so that the whole administrative process is a self-contained one, providing for appeals on both medical and legal questions, and avoiding as far as possible appeals to the courts; though review in the High Court by way of *certiorari* is not completely ruled out.

The Social Security and Medical Appeal tribunals differ fundamentally from ordinary common law courts. They do not follow an adversary procedure,[80] and the purpose of all parties before these tribunals is to see that the applicant receives what the law entitles him to receive, no less and no more. Even critics acknowledge that, on the whole, the scheme is administered so as to give the claimant the benefit of any doubt.[81] The purpose of the Tribunals and of the adjudication officer who 'represents' the DHSS before them thus differs from the purpose of those responsible for a common law settlement.[82] Tribunals work a good deal faster than ordinary courts. There may be seven cases dealt with in the course of half a day,[83] and the period between the rejection of a claim by the insurance officer and a hearing before a local appeal tribunal, is not more than two or three months.[84] If appeal is taken to a Commissioner there will be further delays, but no more than twelve months is likely to elapse between beginning and end of the whole case, even in this event.[85] This may seem a long time, but is very much shorter than the time an ordinary case before a common law court is likely to take, even without allowing for appeals. A few years ago a PEP Survey found that only 7% of a sample of families had any cause to complain of delays in securing social security benefits.[86] There is no doubt that this figure would compare most favourably with any corresponding figure which might be drawn from a sample of litigants.[87] Nevertheless, complacency is not desirable, and there are complaints that the initial decision of the insurance officer often takes far too long.[88]

The actual procedure before social security and medical appeal tribunals is very different from that of a Court; 'the proceedings are conducted around a table in a most informal way'.[89] Legal representation is rare, though claimants are often assisted by a trade union official who may be very knowledgeable.[90] Legal aid is not available for these tribunals, although the amount at stake may 'far exceed the limits of the county court's jurisdiction, or the size of many high court awards',[91] and the law involved may be complex.

The normal rules of evidence do not apply to these tribunals, so that hearsay evidence and documentary evidence may be relied on to an extent not permissible in an ordinary court.[92] The tribunals sit in public, but in fact the press never attend and the public seldom.[93] No oral judgment is pronounced by these tribunals; the claimant is simply informed of the result in writing at a later date. In many cases, neither the claimant nor the insurance officer is present, and the tribunal decides entirely on the basis of documentary evidence and submissions made in writing by the insurance officer. Naturally, the members of these tribunals acquire a familiarity with the subject matter, which helps to speed the whole process up. It would not be necessary for counsel to spend half a day outlining the most elementary principles of the industrial injury system, as happened when a recent case was taken to the House of Lords.[94] A substantial proportion of appeals to local appeal tribunals end in favour of the claimant. For instance, in 1975, about one-third of the appeals on industrial injury benefit ended in the claimant's favour.

Proceedings before a Commissioner are a little more formal.[95] There are now thirteen Commissioners and a Chief Commissioner (all of whom are qualified barristers or solicitors of at least ten years' standing), and in cases of special difficulty they may sit as a tribunal of three. Legal representation before a Commissioner or a tribunal of Commissioners is not uncommon; and a full reasoned judgment is often given by the Commissioner. Some of the decisions of the Commissioners are also reported by the DHSS, so that the whole process is a little more like that of a court. But these specialist tribunals still have many advantages, not least in simplicity of procedure. Nothing like the 'White Book' governs the procedure before a Commissioner. 'There is no provision for cross-appeals, nor for anything in the nature of pleadings or particulars or interlocutory proceedings except requests for oral hearings. There is no provision for discovery of documents. The rules governing the admissibility of evidence do not apply.'[96]

The Frank Committee on Administrative Tribunals and Inquiries took a good look at these tribunals, and on the whole liked what it saw. The tribunals, the committee reported, have the advantage over the courts of 'cheapness, accessibility, freedom from technicality, expedition and expert knowledge of their subject.'[97] Subsequent writings and research have in general endorsed these conclusions.[98] However, some see in the recent structural reforms (which, amongst other things, amalgamated the old industrial injuries local appeal tribunals with the old supplementary benefits appeal tribunals, and laid down that the chairman should be a lawyer) an undesirable move to increased judicialization and legalism in the social security system.[99] And there have been some complaints about appellate procedures.[100] Some have suggested that lack of assistance and legal representation is the basic problem.[101] Many of those appearing before tribunals are almost completely inarticulate, and are unable to put any sort of case, even assuming they understand the point at issue. Indeed, the complexity of the rules themselves makes it difficult for anyone to understand the issues. The Royal Commission on Legal Services (1979) recommended that legal aid be made available for claimants before tribunals[102] – at the moment only legal advice is available. But some would see such a move as part of a slide into legalism. At all events, it may be that the problems are less acute in industrial injury cases.[103]

Despite these doubts raised by the lack of legal aid, the industrial injury system is basically sound though, of course, this does not involve endorsement of the principle of preferential treatment for those injured at work. If comparison is made between the administration of the industrial injury system, and administration of the tort system, it will be seen that the former system avoids most of the unsatisfactory features of the latter to which we drew attention earlier. For instance, awards are not generally in the form of a lump sum. Statutory sick pay is paid weekly, and so are disablement pensions and widow's pensions. Only the less serious disabilities are dealt with by lump sums, although it must be admitted that many more cases today are dealt with in this way than when the scheme was first inaugurated. In 1951 a quarter of the initial awards were gratuities and the rest were pensions: today the position is reversed, with gratutities being awarded in about 90% of the cases.[104] However, the maximum gratuity is only £4,200 which falls a long way below the sort of awards paid out by ways of damages, and the average gratuity is likely to be a sum within the experience of most recipients. Moreover, it is not even possible for a recipient to be tempted to choose a capital sum rather than a pension. In one case, where the claimant's disability was assessed at 20%, he asked the medical appeal tribunal to reduce this to 19% so that he could receive a gratuity rather than a pension; the tribunal acceded to his request, but their decision was reversed by the Commissioner.[105] Any temptation to 'sell' the pension to a financial institution, or to borrow on the strength of it, is also guarded against by the provision that benefits are not assignable.[106] The contrast between this paternalism, and the willingness of the tort system to trust a recipient with thousands of pounds in damages, is quite remarkable.

Another difference between the industrial injury system and the tort system lies in the fact-finding process. It will be recalled that one of the problems in the tort system is that the injured plaintiff might be unable to find the evidence to support his claim: in the industrial injury system this difficulty is overcome by regulations requiring an employer to investigate the circumstances of an accident, and to furnish the DHSS with relevant information. Another difficulty of the tort system – that memories might fade with the lapse of time – is taken care of, in part at least, in the industrial injury system, by section 107 of the 1975 Act which enables an immediate decision to be arrived at and recorded, on the question whether an accident was an industrial accident, i.e. arose out of and in the course of the claimant's employment. Equally, the procedure for medical determination of medical questions seems more satisfactory than the common law procedure, which often means that a person goes from doctor to doctor hoping to find one whose prognosis justifies higher damages.[107]

Another major difficulty in the tort system we saw to be that of guessing the future – how serious the injuries will be, what is the prognosis, how long will the disabilities last, what loss of earnings will result, and so on. Under the industrial injury system guesses are unnecessary. Provisional assessments may be made which are open to review. Disability assessments may be increased even after a final assessment, if there is any unforeseeable aggravation. Special hardship allowance (for loss of earnings) may be granted for a limited period with the chance of renewal. Widows' pensions are payable in full but terminate on remarriage. On the other hand, the fact that pensions cannot be reduced as a result of an unforeseen improvement after a final assessment, avoids any feeling that a man may be penalized for making particularly great efforts to rehabilitate himself and overcome his handicaps.

It is hard to believe that anyone could make a dispassionate review of the tort system and the industrial injury system, without coming to the firm conclusion that on almost every count the latter is the superior and more up to date model of compensation system. This does not mean, of course, that the system is beyond criticism, and there is doubtless room for much improvement. For example, benefits for partial loss of earnings are meagre, and disablement pensions are still weighted too heavily to less severe injuries. But before these and other improvements are carried out, a much higher priority must be the integration of the whole social security system. The continuation of the present privileged position of the industrially injured is indefensible.

16
Social security: sickness and other benefits

When we attempted in Chapter 1 to look at the issues in perspective, we pointed out that incapacity and disability was much more commonly due to natural causes than to human causes; and we also mentioned that the law generally treated cases of disabilities caused by human activity more generously. All this is as true of the social security system as of all other parts of the compensation process. Far more people are away from work, and suffer a loss of earnings, as a result of sickness due to natural causes than as a result of injuries or diseases caused by human activity. Most of the persons suffering long-term disabilities are the victims of naturally caused diseases or congenital conditions, and not accidents. Most widows are not widowed by accident. Yet the social security benefits for long-term non-industrial disability (which cover most of those suffering from natural disabilities) are less generous than the benefits payable under the industrial injury system, both in terms of the sums payable and of the conditions of entitlement; though the differential has been narrowed in the past few years. It would be beyond the scope of this book to deal in great detail with the non-industrial injury side of the social security system, but the principal points of comparison must be brought out.

1 BENEFITS FOR SICKNESS AND INVALIDITY

Unlike the industrial injury benefits, those payable under the ordinary social security system have in the past all been subject to 'contribution conditions'. A person is not entitled to benefits unless he has paid the necessary number of contributions; or (it may be) he is entitled to benefits at a reduced rate when he has paid some, but not the full number, of contributions. So far as sickness benefit and invalidity benefit are concerned, these conditions are not onerous; they will normally be satisfied by relatively small earnings for one or two years.[1] But some people are never employable at all: those who are born with mental or physical handicaps which prevent them from ever working, will never pay any contributions, and will thus never be entitled to sickness or invalidity benefit. For such people the only provision for many years was supplementary benefit. But in recent years, a number of non-contributory benefits have been introduced which are slowly but substantially improving the position of the long-term disabled. These benefits are considered further below.

As noted in Chapter 15, short-term benefits for non-industrial sickness and disability are now the same as those for industrial injury.[2] Statutory sick pay is payable for the first 28 weeks of incapacity at a rate (in 1986–7) of £46.75 for persons earning more than £74.50 per week; £39.20 for those earning between £55.50 and £74.49; and £31.60 for those earning between £38 and £55.49. There are no allowances for dependants, but child benefit remains payable. The DHSS publishes figures showing the average earnings of male manual workers and net income (after tax and social security contributions) compared with sickness benefit (now replaced, for most workers, by statutory sick pay).[3] These show that since 1972 the proportion of net earnings replaced by sickness benefit has fallen dramatically. Thus, in 1972, the proportion of income replaced was 48.1% for a single person, 59.6% for a married couple and 66.7% for a married couple with two children. In 1983 it was 22.4% for a single person, 34.4% for a married couple and 41% for a married couple with two children. The abolition of the earnings-related addition in 1982 resulted in a large drop. The reduction in the relative value of sickness benefit is the result of deliberate government policy, not only to save money but also to 'restore the incentive to work' (despite record levels of unemployment). Under the new statutory sick pay scheme the position in this respect will not be significantly different.

Long-term benefits under the industrial injuries scheme are more generous than those for non-industrial disability. No disablement benefits or gratuities of any kind are payable to the non-industrially disabled. Victims of industrial injury receive these in addition to the invalidity benefits available to victims of non-industrial disablement. Furthermore, as we shall see, it is only victims of industrial injury who can claim a benefit for partial loss of earnings (the special hardship allowance), or the exceptionally severe disablement allowance (an addition, for serious cases, to the disablement pension). The attendance allowance paid to victims of industrial injury is also higher than that paid to the victims of non-industrial disablement.

But even for the non-industrially disabled, long-term benefits are higher than short-term benefits. Although the highest rate of statutory sick pay is greater than the invalidity pension, its recipients receive no increases for dependants. Further, the invalidity allowance is, of course, only payable to the long-term disabled. Moreover, assuming that the State earnings-related pension scheme remains in place, the position of the long-term disabled will gradually improve even further. This policy of favouring the long-term disabled recognizes the fact that prolonged incapacity and loss of income raise many problems which a family does not encounter in cases of short-term incapacity. Many items of household expenditure (such as new clothes, items of household equipment and household repairs and maintenance) can be deferred for a few weeks or even months without great hardship in a family where an adequate income is normally and regularly available. But after six months or more, the shortage of money is likely to become more acute, and the needs of the long-term disabled are clearly much greater. The invalidity pension in 1986 is £38·70 per week, plus allowances for dependants – £23·25 per week for an adult and £15·15 per week (including child benefit) for a child. In addition, an invalidity allowance is payable for those who first become entitled to the invalidity pension while still relatively young. There are three rates of allowance – the highest rate is for persons who were under 40 when they first became incapacitated; the middle rate is for persons under 50 at that date; and the lowest rate for those under 60 (55 for women) at that date. These benefits are now £8·15, £5·20 and £2·60 respectively. Thus, a married man with two children who is entitled to invalidity pension and allowance would (in 1986) receive £100·40, £97·45 or £94·85, depending on his age when he first became entitled to the pension. In addition, the earnings-related addition is now payable, but since 1985 the amount of any such addition is deducted from the invalidity allowance so that, in effect, the recipient receives only the greater of the two.

As mentioned earlier, there is also a non-contributory severe disablement allowance (which replaces the non-contributory invalidity pension) of £23·25 (in 1986), which carries the same dependent child allowance as the contributory pension (£8·05 in 1986), but a lower rate of adult dependent allowance (£13·90 in 1986). The criteria of entitlement single out those disabled from birth or during childhood and the seriously disabled. It must be said that the distinction between the contributory and the non-contributory pension is hard to justify in principle: the contribution conditions are so easily satisfied that a person who has worked for only two or three years may become entitled to the contributory pension for life. Yet if he has not worked at all, the lower rate pension is payable for life.

Attendance allowance

Mention has also been made of the fact that no disablement pensions or gratuities are available for the non-industrially injured and the sick, nor until quite recently were any other special benefits. But the National Insurance Act 1970 took one other significant step to improving the position of the severely disabled (and, incidently, to narrowing the differential between the treatment of the industrially injured and other disabled people) by introducing an attendance allowance. This allowance is only payable in respect of those disabled persons who are so severely disabled that they require frequent or continual attention or supervision through the day, or prolonged or repeated attention or continual supervision through the night.[4] Where both day and night time attendance is required, the rate of benefit is (in 1986) £30·95 per week, and where only day or night time attendance is required, the rate is £20·65 per week. These rates are significantly lower than those payable in respect of the industrially injured, where the maximum is normally £25·30 per week; but in cases of exceptionally severe disablement an additional £25·30 per week may be payable. There are no contribution conditions for the non-industrial attendance allowance which, in this respect also, narrows the difference between the benefits payable under the industrial injuries scheme and the ordinary social security benefits. In 1983 there were nearly 350,000 persons in receipt of the non-industrial attendance allowance; whereas in 1977 (figures are not regularly published) only about 3,000 constant attendance allowances were being paid under the industrial injuries scheme (at the much higher rates prevailing under that scheme).[5] The Pearson Commission recommended that the industrial allowances should gradually be phased out,[6] and it is difficult to disagree with this proposal. No doubt vested rights, as always, will be preserved, but the continuance of this massive differential for the future seems quite unjustifiable.

Invalid care allowance

Yet another new allowance of importance to the injured and disabled is the invalid care allowance, first introduced in 1975.[7] This allowance is payable to a person who is substantially engaged (fulltime) in caring for a close relative, who is himself or herself in receipt of an attendance allowance or a constant attendance allowance. However, the allowance is not payable to a wife living with or being maintained by her husband or to a woman residing with a man as her husband. This allowance is fixed at the same rate as the non-contributory severe disablement allowance (in 1986, £23·25) and also carries entitlement to dependants' allowances in appropriate cases.

Mobility allowance

Finally, mention needs to be made of the new mobility allowance, first introduced in 1975 and being gradually phased in, for claimants in different age groups. This allowance has a long history which dates back to the period after the First World War when the special invalid vehicles were first supplied to some of the war disabled. In recent years, similar vehicles were also provided for certain classes of disabled persons under the National Health Service, and in some cases, small cars were provided; alternatively, those entitled to the invalid carriages were able to opt for a cash allowance (from 1972). But the position was in many respects unsatisfactory, mainly because the invalid carriages had to be driven by the invalid himself since they were single-seat vehicles. Anyone who was too disabled to drive himself was, therefore, ineligible for this form of assistance. Also, many complained that the vehicles were unsafe. The Government eventually commissioned Lady Sharp to inquire into the question as a whole. The Sharp report proposed that the invalid carriages should be replaced by small cars, but with narrower criteria of eligibility,[8] but this was rejected by the Government. Eventually, the present scheme was proposed; and it was later decided to phase out the invalid carriages altogether.

The position at present, is that a flat-rate mobility allowance of (in 1986) £21·65 per week is payable to any person (in the age groups so far covered) who is so physically disabled that he is unable, or virtually unable, to walk but is capable of benefiting from greater mobility. Thus the allowance would not be payable to a person who is in a vegetative state, or to anyone else who is so mentally affected by his injuries that he could not benefit from an occasional outing. It will also be paid to anyone presently entitled to an invalid carriage, on giving up the vehicle. Over 275,000 persons were receiving a mobility allowance in 1983.[9] The mobility allowance is, of course, a relatively modest sum, but it reflects a widely felt need among the disabled. Many recent surveys have uncovered the fact that the inability to get out of a house, and visit friends or relatives, or even to enjoy the air and a change of scene, is one of the most keenly felt deprivations. On the other hand, to maintain a vehicle or hire a vehicle for the occasion, is a costly exercise. So the mobility allowance – like the new attendance allowance – reflects a move by the social security system towards covering, in a modest and limited way, out-of-pocket expenses which are the result of a disability. In this respect, as we previously mentioned, the social security system shows signs of movement towards doing something which the tort system has done for a long time.

Partial loss of earnings

Ordinary sickness and invalidity benefits are not available to people with minor disabilities which cause partial loss of earnings because they cannot earn at the same rate or at the same job as formerly. If this were due to an industrial injury, some disability pension or gratuity, however small, would become payable, and the claimant could then also claim special hardship allowance for his partial loss of earnings. Similarly the tort system compensates for all loss of earnings, partial as well as total, provided only there is a tort and liability can actually be enforced against someone with adequate purse strings. But ordinary social security benefits provide no assistance (other than child benefit and family income supplement) to people actually engaged in full-time employment. This, therefore, represents one of the principal ways in which industrial injury benefits are still much more generous than ordinary social security benefits. The existence of disablement gratuities and pensions, of course, is the other principal advantage of the industrially injured.

2 BENEFITS FOR WIDOWS

A widow is also treated less generously when her husband's death was not due to an industrial accident. For the first 26 weeks there is no difference. In both cases the widow will receive an allowance of £54·20 per week, together with children's allowances for dependent children at £15·15 per child (including child benefit). And at the end of the first 26 weeks, if there are dependent children, the benefits are largely the same, except that the industrial widowed mother's allowance is £39·25 per week instead of £38·70. This 55p differential has been frozen for many years, and is not increased when benefits are up-rated annually. But if there are no dependent children the legal position of the two types of widow is rather different after the first 26 weeks. In that event, the widow receives an ordinary pension of £38·70 if she is over 50. If the widow is between 40 and 50 when her husband dies or when her children cease to be dependent, the industrial widow gets the full pension but the non-industrial widow only receives a proportion of the ordinary pension depending on her age.[10] If she was under 40 when her husband died the industrial widow gets £11·61 per week and the non-industrial widow nothing. The refusal to pay pensions to widows, irrespective of age and need, goes back to Beveridge himself. He took the firm view that a young childless widow should not expect to be maintained by the State. 'If she is able to work, she should work.'[11] Provision for widows, irrespective of age and need, was a matter for private life insurance which is, of course, very widespread indeed, though by no means always on a scale sufficient to provide an income for life.

As we have seen, tort law compensates a widow for the loss of her husband despite the fact that she was young and childless and quite capable of earning her own living; and the State itself will do the same where the widow's husband dies as a result of criminal violence. Indeed, it is quite possible for a widow under 40 to receive an industrial widow's pension of £11·61 a week *and* tort damages or criminal injuries compensation.[12] Yet the non-industrial widow under 40 receives nothing after the first six months of widowhood.

There is another difference between the position of the industrial and the non-industrial widow. If the industrial widow remarries she receives a capital gratuity as a 'widow's dowry', but a non-industrial widow who remarries forfeits her widowed mother's allowance completely and the same applies to cohabitation.[13]

Like sickness and invalidity benefits, but unlike industrial injury benefits, widows benefits for non-industrial widows are subject to contribution conditions. These conditions are again not onerous, but they are enough to exclude from benefits an estimated 100 to 200 young widows with children every year.[14] However, in general, the social security treatment of widows is very favourable, particularly as there is no earnings rule for these benefits. A widow capable of full-time employment can expect to have a total income which is only fractionally less than a family in which the husband earns an average wage, and she has of course one less mouth to feed.[15]

Finally, we noted in Chapter 15 that the government has announced its intention to replace the widows' allowance with a lump sum payment, to increase the age at which the full pension cuts out to 55 and to increase the age at which the pension ceases to be payable to 45.

3 SUPPLEMENTARY BENEFITS

When Beveridge first put forward his proposals in 1942 he intended that the levels of benefit payable under the national insurance system (whether for industrial or non-industrial cases) should not be less than was thought necessary for subsistence. It was also appreciated that national assistance (as it was first called) would still be needed in some cases where there was no entitlement to the benefits payable under the National Insurance Act. But Beveridge was determined to maintain the insurance element in national insurance – the idea that people are paying for their benefits – and he therefore felt it necessary that national assistance should be made 'less desirable'[16] than national insurance: he proposed to achieve this by making it subject to a means test. But Beveridge clearly thought national assistance would become a fringe area of social security dealing with a small number of special cases.

As things have developed, matters have taken a very different course from that envisaged by Beveridge. For supplementary benefits are not, and never have been, conceived by successive governments as merely filling in the gaps for those who fail to qualify for the ordinary benefit, but as an addition to the ordinary benefits to bring them up to subsistence level. Ordinary sickness benefits were in fact from the very beginning below the rates required for subsistence at the standard fixed by the National Assistance Board, and the Supplementary Benefits Commission. However, the improvements in the legislative provisions for the sick and the disabled now make it more probable that, for the long-term disabled anyway, the original intentions behind the scheme are being fulfilled and that supplementary benefits are likely to be relied on mainly where the contribution conditions are not satisfied in full.

At the end of 1984, out of more than 4·2 million regular recipients of weekly supplementary benefits, about 1·7 million were retirement pensioners; about another 1·7 million were unemployed and about half a million were heads of one-parent families.[17] There were then nearly 240,000 sick and disabled recipients of supplementary benefits, of whom about two-thirds were not in receipt of national insurance benefits.[18] Judging from these figures, it would seem that nearly 160,000 sick or disabled fail to satisfy the national insurance contributions at all, while some 83,000 do receive national insurance benefits but for some reason the benefits are inadequate to their needs, e.g. because the contribution conditions of other benefits are only partially satisfied. Of the former group of 160,000 not in receipt of national insurance benefits, it seems probable that a large proportion have been disabled from birth or early childhood, and many may be people incapable of any employment because of mental handicap or illness. The new non-contributory severe disablement allowance will help to reduce the number of these persons on supplementary benefits.

In recent years significant changes have occurred in some of these figures. In particular, the introduction of various new benefits and allowances for the disabled has cut almost in half the number of those in receipt of contributory benefits who are still also in need of supplementary benefits.[19] Only a small proportion of those who draw contributory benefits for sickness and invalidity (well under 10%) now also draw supplementary benefits; and, because of the industrial preference, it is likely that of these a smaller proportion are people disabled at work than people disabled from other causes. Moreover, the total proportion receiving supplementary benefits is likely to fall if the earnings-related pension scheme is retained. By contrast, the abolition of earnings-related additions to short-term benefits has probably had an effect in the opposite direction. Furthermore, the position remains very different for those who have never worked, and so do not meet the contribution conditions for non-industrial benefits and earnings-related benefits. The non-contributory severe disablement allowance helps, but it is still at too low a level to preclude the need for supplementary benefits in many cases. It is long-term government policy to reduce the reliance of the disabled on supplementary benefit, but this would be expensive and is, therefore, unlikely to be achieved easily.[20]

It is no part of our purpose to explore at length the significance of this aspect of the social security system, but there are at least two points which are of particular relevance to the theme of this work. The first of these is that the requirement of proof of need is one way of preventing over-compensation for a loss. If a person recovers very large damages, for example, from an insurance company, he will find himself unable to claim supplementary benefits. Or again, if a person is privately insured against the risk which overtakes him, supplementary benefits may be unavailable for him. Moreover, even casual earnings by a person incapable of full-time employment will go to reduce his supplementary benefits, unless they are below £4 per week (this figure has not been increased for some years).[21] Yet in other areas there is a great deal of double compensation for the same loss. The person with large tort damages can still claim all other national insurance benefits; the widow can recover tort damages for loss of her husband even though she now goes out to work, and (since the earnings rule for widows was abolished) she can even retain her widow's pension and allowances for dependants, although she is earning an adequate income. These problems form the subject of Chapter 18.

The second point is that the more widespread reliance on supplementary benefits has still further undermined the insurance principle in the whole social security system. Supplementary benefits are paid according to need, and they are paid entirely out of the Exchequer from money raised from the taxpayer. So long as this was intended to be a minor gap-filling exercise it was natural that this should be so, but with supplementary benefits being used on a large scale to top up the ordinary national insurance benefits, it is now clear that social security is an income-redistribution device as much as an insurance system. And the existence of non-contributory benefits reinforces this point. This matter is considered further in Chapter 21.

4 ADMINISTRATION

Considerations of space forbid any detailed account of the way in which the social security system is administered. It is enough to note that, in 1984, the administration of the national insurance and supplementary benefits schemes was rationalized. All claims for benefits under these schemes are initially dealt with by an adjudication officer. The first tier of the appeal structure are the Social Security Appeal Tribunals, which deal with appeals under both schemes; the second appellate tier remains the Social Security Commissioners. The Attendance Allowance Board[22] still deals with medical questions relevant to the award of attendance allowances; but it has been much criticized, partly because it is not clear whether it is meant to be a tribunal exercising adjudicative functions, or a specialist medical authority.

In 1980 the supplementary benefits scheme was radically overhauled, and a great deal of the discretionary element in the scheme was removed by the enactment of detailed regulations governing the entitlement to various benefits. In consequence, the role of the Supplementary Benefits Commission of issuing guidelines as to the exercise of discretion has become largely defunct, and the Commission's place has been taken by the new Social Security Advisory Committee, which gives advice on most social security benefits (but not on industrial injuries benefits, which are the responsibility of the Industrial Injuries Advisory Council). Under this new system the appellate functions of the Social Security Appeals Tribunals and the Social Security Commissioners will, no doubt, gain increasing importance in defining the legal entitlements of applicants for supplementary benefits.

Important criticisms of the new system include the fact that the regulations are extremely complex and difficult to understand;[23] and that discretion has not been expelled from the system, but just relocated in those responsible for drafting the regulations. The government has recently announced its intention to overhaul the system yet again. The current pattern of basic rates of benefit supplemented by additions to meet specific needs will be replaced by a simpler system of basic means-tested income support supplemented by a discretionary Social Fund to meet extraordinary cases and emergencies. The Housing Benefits Scheme, which is administered by local authorities, will be integrated with the new supplementary benefits system.

5 THE PROBLEM OF FRAUD AND ABUSE

There has been a good deal of discussion about the abuse of the social security system,[24] and it is worth devoting some attention to the matter. It is plainly impossible to administer anything as immense as the existing social security system without a certain amount of abuse and sheer fraud. Over 20 million benefits and allowances are paid every week by the DHSS. But solid evidence on the scale of the problem is lacking. The government has stated that in 1980–81, £170 million was saved through the detection of fraud, but it is impossible to estimate the extent of undetected abuse. An investigating team in 1981 estimated that the proportion of those claiming unemployment or supplementary benefits while they (or, in the case of supplementary benefits, their spouses) were working, was 8%.[25] Fraud is, to some extent, harder to perpetrate and easier to detect in the case of benefits, entitlement to which depends on physical disability. There may also be problems of employer fraud. For example, under the statutory sick pay scheme it is for the employer to decide what evidence of sickness will be required, and this might encourage a dishonest employer, in times when business is slack, to lay off unwanted employees, claim they are sick, and receive reimbursement of 'sick pay' from the DHSS. In recent years governments have increased the numbers of staff dealing with alleged fraud and abuse, and the present government plans to deploy yet more staff to this task.

The Fisher Committee identified six principal types of abuse of social security benefits.[26] First, the failure to disclose earnings where means tested benefits are claimed; second, misrepresentations relating to incapacity for work, and the cause of such incapacity; third, voluntary unemployment; fourth, cohabitation and 'fictitious desertions'; fifth, itinerant frauds; and sixth, failure to report changes in the maintenance of dependants where dependants' allowances are being paid. Of these, I have already discussed the cohabitation rule,[27] and the problems of unemployment and itinerant frauds are not relevant to the subject matter of this work. Undoubtedly, the main problem relating to abuse in connection with the injured and the sick concern the malingerer, or the person who claims to have suffered an industrial injury when he has really suffered a non-industrial injury. The latter is, of course, sheer fraud, but arises naturally from the privileged position of the industrially injured. If the whole social security system were integrated with similar benefits for all, this problem would largely be eliminated.[28]

Misrepresentations relating to capacity for work remain an acute problem.[29] The present position is that the DHSS relies heavily on medical certification for evidence of incapacity (with which the malingerer soon becomes familiar) where objective symptoms are not apparent. Where a patient complains of headaches, sleeplessness, muscular pain, backache, nausea, nervousness and so on, the doctor is often unable to verify the patient's story. Either the doctor must, in effect, accuse the patient of lying, or he must certify the patient to be incapable of work. Doctors do not like to acuse their patients of lying, and in the normal doctor-patient relationship the patient has no incentive to lie, so there is a natural tendency for the doctor to accept the patient's complaints as genuine. The medical profession does not like the duty of certifying incapacity for the purpose of the social security legislation, but the Fisher Committee found there was little alternative. The Committee did consider the possibility of allowing claimants to produce unverified claims for short periods of incapacity, but came to the conclusion that the dangers were too great.[30] There are, in any event, certain check procedures, such as requiring the claimant to be medically examined by regional officers of the DHSS, and the number of patients who fail to turn up for these examinations suggests that this is a fairly effective control. Other special checks are used where a claimant has a history of repeated short-term claims.[31]

On the other hand, there are dangers in attempting to tighten the procedures too much. An over vigorous anti-abuse policy can easily result in sick and disabled people being driven back to work before they really feel fit. And there are certain cases where the problem may be seen as one of malingering when it is in fact something quite different. It has, for instance, been suggested that many cases of long-term low back injuries have the appearance of malingering. Frequently, this kind of injury, especially when suffered by a man of middle age used to heavy manual labour, seems to lead to virtual permanent incapacity for work, although the objective medical symptoms seem slight. One possible reason for this is that the kind of person who tends to suffer this sort of injury is the person of poor education and literacy who has spent all his life in manual labour, mostly of a heavy kind. If his injuries render him unfit for this type of work, he may have neither the education nor the experience for any other kind of work, and may find himself permanently unemployable.[32] It is clearly important that the social security system does not allow such cases to slip between the unemployment and the sickness benefit provisions.

It may be worth concluding this section by briefly comparing the effectiveness of tort law and social security in guarding against abuse. Unfortunately, there is very little data on this question, though some generalizations can probably be safely made. In some cases, and especially the most serious cases, the adversary procedures of the law probably operate as a very effective control over fraud and abuse. When every claim is scrutinized with a jaundiced eye by an insurer who is going to pay the claim himself, and when the insurer himself has a medical report (as he normally has in serious cases), it is reasonable to suppose that few serious cases of abuse escape undetected. On the other hand, this is not true of minor claims. As we have already seen, because of the disproportionate cost of fighting many minor claims, the insurer may often agree to pay some small sum without serious examination of the case at all. Moreover, as we have already suggested, it is possible for anti-abuse measures to be too vigorous. Because of the plaintiff's need to prove fault on the part of the defendant in a tort case, possibly some fraudulent claims are prevented; but a great many more perfectly genuine claims are prevented too. There are also some respects in which tort law may be more liable to encourage the malingerer. In particular, the fact that loss of earnings can be recovered in full in claims for damages, is thought by many to be a serious disincentive to a prompt return to work by a person who may think he has a good claim. This is one reason why (as we have already seen) no social security system normally guarantees full compensation for lost earnings.

17
Other forms of assistance

We have now completed the survey of the more regular and usual methods provided by the law for compensating those who suffer personal injury or disability as a result of accidents or disease. But in practice, there are many other ways in which the victims of accidents and disease may receive some assistance from private or public sources, and a comprehensive survey of compensation methods and sources must take these into account.

1 THE TAXATION SYSTEM

The tax system as a whole is not, of course, designed to compensate people, but aspects of it do provide some compensation, in one way or another, for the victims of accidents and disease. In the years after the Second World War, social security beneficiaries benefited from the fact that many social security benefits were not taxable. But in recent years more and more benefits have been brought into the tax system, so that now all the major benefits are subject to tax. The policy of paying benefits free of tax was undesirable because it benefited the better-off (who pay higher taxes) disproportionately.

There are a number of special tax reliefs for the disabled. For example a registered blind person receives an allowance to £360 to set against his taxable income.[1] Similarly, a person who maintains a disabled relative of himself or his spouse is entitled to a deduction from his taxable income.[2] There are also a large number of minor statutory reliefs of one sort or another for the disabled, and especially the blind. For instance, rating relief is available for disabled persons under an Act of 1978;[3] vehicle maintenance grants for the disabled are not taxable;[4] and dog licences are available free for the blind.[5] Travel concessions on public transport can be given to blind and disabled persons.[6]

It is easy to understand the way in which concessions like these tend to be granted. It is simple for an MP to court popularity by tabling an amendment to some taxing Bill to give relief to the disabled, and difficult for a Minister to refuse. 'Taxing the sick' is not a position which any Minister wishes to defend. Nevertheless, these haphazard concessions are scarcely defensible as part of a rational system of compensating the disabled and sick. For one thing, they tend to be concentrated in certain special cases. The blind are always a 'popular' group for relief, but many other disabled people receive less valuable, or no compensation, of this kind.[7] In the second place, income tax reliefs benefit only the better-off – they do not help those who are able to earn little, if anything at all, and so pay no income tax.[8] Another objection to these special tax concessions is that they make no allowance for the fact that other compensation methods may exist. A person disabled in circumstances in which a tort claim lies, can get full compensation in law for his disablement, and will still be entitled to all these concessions.

Taxation, or rather the absence of it, is also indirectly relevant to compensation for injuries in that many charities deriving their funds from donations and subscriptions and legacies, are exempt from income tax. The relief of the disabled, and persons in similar classes, is recognized as a charitable purpose in the technical legal sense, and the tax relief for a body of this kind is of very considerable value. In one sense, this form of tax relief makes little difference to the ultimate burden which falls on the public, since if charities were taxed, and were therefore able to do less themselves to help the disabled and the sick and the injured, a correspondingly heavier burden would fall on the taxpayer. Thus, what the taxpayer surrenders in the form of tax reliefs, he may be saved in social security expenditure. But it does mean that rather more is devoted to relief and assistance of a kind which might not be possible under the welfare state; and it also means that the large amount of voluntary work which is done is not completely starved of funds. To the extent that the tax reliefs encourage voluntary work which might otherwise not be forthcoming, the taxpayer gets a good bargain by granting these reliefs. But since some forms of disability are so much better endowed by charity than others, the question does arise whether it is equitable to enlarge this differential by tax reliefs. On the one hand, it could be said that the differential should be narrowed, and that if charities had to pay tax, the tax paid by the wealthier charities could then be partly devoted to the relief of less popular charitable causes. On the other hand, it might be argued that this would be essentially an undemocratic procedure, since it would mean overriding the deliberate choice of the public to favour, by their free donations and subscriptions, some charities over others.

2 SICK PAY AND OTHER EMPLOYMENT BENEFITS[9]

So far we have normally assumed that a person who is unable to work through injury or illness will have no income during this period, and that some method of compensating him for this lost income must be found. This is a very unrealistic assumption in modern circumstances. Many people are employed on terms which entitle them to wages or salary even when they are away sick. Indeed, it has even been held that there is an implied term in a contract of employment that the employee is entitled to wages when away sick, unless the contract clearly specifies otherwise.[10] This decision is, perhaps, open to criticism in law, and is in any event itself somewhat unrealistic in that entitlement to sick pay is in practice regulated more by the custom of an employer than by 'implied terms' in law. Nevertheless, it is clear that many people receive sick pay from their employers when off work. The Pearson Commission concluded that about half of those injured by accidents who suffer some loss of pay, receive some sick pay from their employers, and that in aggregate, these sums total about £125 million per annum; which is about five eighths of the estimated total tort payments each year.[11]

In 1981 it was estimated that some 90% of employees participate in some form of voluntary (or 'occupational') sick pay scheme.[12] According to a 1985 survey by the Social Security Policy Inspectorate,[13] public employees and office and managerial staff are more likely to receive occupational sick pay than those working in industrial, construction or transport fields; larger firms are more likely to have a scheme than smaller firms; and lower-paid employees are less likely to receive occupational sick pay than well-paid ones.

The fact that some sick pay scheme exists does not mean that full wages (still less full earnings) are automatically payable for all and every period of sickness. There are very wide variations in the conditions of entitlement and the amounts payable, and there are also wide variations between the practices of different industries. In some cases, full pay without any deductions is granted; in other cases, full pay less the value of social security benefits is granted; in some cases half pay is granted, with or without deduction of benefits; in others a small flat-rate payment is made: often a waiting period of up to four days is prescribed. A qualifying period of service with the employer is also often required. It was clear from a 1974 survey of occupational sick pay schemes[14] that a significant number of workpeople were actually making a profit when they were sick or injured, because their employers paid them in full, with no deduction for social security benefits; others deducted half the value of the benefits. There are also wide variations in the length of time for which sick pay is payable; frequently the period is discretionary, which presumably means the employer will go on paying until he feels that it is necessary for him to give the employee notice of dismissal.

The public sector has, on the whole, set a good example in this area.[15] The civil service pays white collar staff up to six months sick pay at full rates and a further six months at half rates, subject to maximum of twelve months sick leave in any four years. On full pay, social security benefits are deducted, but at half pay they are not. All manual workers employed by the civil service are also covered by sick pay schemes which pay up to thirteen weeks full wages in twelve months, and rather more for workers with five years service. Most manual workers in the public sector are entitled to six months sick pay at full rates and another six months at half rates; but these rates are based on basic wages and disregard overtime, shift premiums, bonuses, etc.[16] Nationalized industries now all have sick pay schemes for their manual workers, though some are not very generous. For example, a miner is only entitled to sick pay after one year's service, and only reaches maximum entitlement after ten years' service.[17] Even then, the first seven days of absence is unpaid.[18]

Where a person is so severely injured or disabled or sick that he is forced to retire prematurely from employment, he may be entitled to some pension under an occupational pension scheme.[19] In 1979 over half of all employees belonged to such a scheme. In both the public and the private sector, accrued pension rights are normally unaffected by premature retirement for sickness or ill health and are payable as of right. Indeed, a large proportion of those who are members of such schemes would get enhanced pension rights if they had to retire on grounds of ill-health, i.e. these pension schemes contain what is, in effect, an element of disability insurance. In the public sector, five years service now usually qualified for such benefits, and most private schemes are at least as generous. Some schemes provide benefits which vary with the degree of incapacity. For example, about two-thirds of a million private sector employees are in schemes which provide higher benefits for very serious disability. The injured employee would be entitled to these additional payments in addition to industrial injury benefits.

In the 1970s there was a dramatic increase in the provision for widows under pension schemes. In 1971, only 39% of male members of pension schemes had an entitlement to a widow's pension, should they die in service; but by 1979 the combined figure for the public and private sector was 94%. Widow's pensions are calculated in a variety of ways, but in many cases the amount paid is quite small.

There is no doubt that these occupational sick pay and retirement schemes are growing in number and importance, and the introduction of the statutory sick pay scheme in 1983, and its extension in 1985, show some recognition of this. Under this scheme, employers are required to pay a minimum amount (which replaces sickness benefit) for the first 28 weeks of absence from work. The employer is entitled to 100% reimbursement from the DHSS of the sums so paid. The main aim of this reform was to reduce DHSS administrative costs, but it may also have the effect of reducing the number of employees who receive occupational sick pay without deduction of statutory sick pay. The 1985 survey mentioned above came across no employer who paid statutory sick pay in addition to occupational sick pay, when the latter was equivalent to the normal rate of pay.

3   AD HOC GOVERNMENT SCHEMES

In recent years, the political pressure exerted by various lobby groups on behalf of the disabled has been substantial, and on a number of occasions the Government has been moved to offer financial assistance in a variety of forms, to particular groups. For example, in 1974 the Government provided £100 million to assist the National Coal Board to arrive at an agreement with the trade unions concerned as to a special compensation scheme covering a number of miners suffering from pneumoconiosis.[20] In the same year the Government made an altogether unprecedented grant of assistance to the special charitable trust set up as part of the settlement of the claims of the thalidomide children. When the terms of the settlement were negotiated between the parents and the Distillers company, the parents (despite the best legal advice) were apparently unaware that income from the trust fund, if regularly paid to the children concerned, would be subject to ordinary income tax. The income of the trust itself was exempt, as the trust was a charity; but the income of the children was not exempt because there is no general provision for the income of disabled persons to be free from tax liability. When the parents discovered this fact they appealed to the Government, which decided to waive the tax liability. Subsequently, it was found that this would produce too many anomalies, the Government therefore made a once-for-all grant to the charity in lieu of waiving the children's tax liability. There are, of course, many such trusts in existence for the benefit of disabled people in various classes, and the ordinary tax laws apply to them all.

Other ad hoc schemes of governmental assistance include the special vaccine damage payments, which we discussed earlier. And shortly before the 1979 general election a political scene of almost Gilbertian hilarity was being performed concerning the case of the Welsh quarrymen. These unfortunate men were former workers in a number of Welsh slate quarries, whose employers had gone out of business by the time symptoms of lung disease became apparent. They were, of course, eligible for the usual industrial injury benefits, but in the absence of employers to sue they were unable to obtain damages in tort. Their claim to special treatment was considered and rejected by the Pearson Commission,[21] on the ground that any decision in their favour would have to be applied to anyone in a comparable position. This would have meant the State assuming the obligation to pay damages to anyone unable to sue because the defendant had gone out of business, or possibly, become insolvent. The Commission felt that it was not possible to justify introducing such a principle into the law. Nevertheless, in the few hectic weeks before the vote of confidence which brought down Mr Callaghan's Government in 1979, these Welsh quarrymen played a major political role. The reason for this was that the Government sought to obtain the support of the independent Welsh Nationalist members of parliament by offering special treatment for the quarrymen. Press reports suggested that the Conservative party had privately matched the Government's offer of special treatment. In due course these pledges were redeemed by the passing of the Pneumoconiosis etc. (Workers Compensation) Act 1979 providing for lump-sum payments to those concerned.

This somewhat sordid story illustrates what can happen when 'ad hockery' is substituted for principle, especially on such a delicate issue as the treatment of the disabled. It is always easy to make an impassioned emotional plea for special treatment of one select group for this or that reason; but all the disabled are entitled to equal sympathy and equal support from the State, and ad hoc treatment of special groups can only lead to the abandonment of all rationality in policy. In the end, the disabled whose friends are strongest, or who can shout loudest, will secure the most governmental support if this is how policies are to be chosen.

4 THE SOCIAL SERVICES

This country has an immensely elaborate system of social services which provides assistance to those in need of it in connection with employment, education, housing, health and a variety of subsidiary matters. Most of these services are provided by local authorities in pursuance of statutory powers and duties under Part III of the National Assistance Act 1948, the Local Authority Social Services Act 1970, the Chronically Sick and Disabled Persons Act 1970, and the Housing (Homeless Persons) Act 1977. Few involve the payment of cash benefits, though they are not the less valuable for that. Indeed, many of the beneficiaries of these services are more in need of assistance than money.[22] These social services are little known to lawyers, and in one sense this is just as well. They are not administered by lawyers but by social and welfare workers employed and organized by the local authorities. Nevertheless, no comprehensive inquiry into the methods of compensation available for the victim of accident or disease can ignore these services, for they often perform the same function as other compensation systems.[23] Moreover, they cost money – taxpayers' or ratepayers' money – and it is hardly possible to ensure that this money is well spent unless the social services are integrated as far as possible with compensation systems which provide cash benefits. In addition, an important issue is raised as to the most appropriate way of compensating people for lost incomes or disabilities. Does society at present strike the right balance between compensation in cash and compensation in community benefits? It is hardly possible in a book of this nature to do more than touch on some of the social services insofar as they are of special relevance to the subject matter of this book, and to consider some of these issues.

There has been a good deal of public and parliamentary interest recently in relation to these local authority services. Under the Local Authority Social Services Act 1970 (which implemented the recommendations of the Seebohm Report), every local authority specified in the Act is now required to have a social services committee and a director of social services to co-ordinate and oversee their statutory responsibilities. Under the Chronically Sick and Disabled Persons Act 1970, special responsibilities have been imposed on local authorities in relation to welfare services for the long-term sick and disabled. Section 1 of the Act requires local authorities to take the initiative in tracing those in need of assistance and in publicizing its welfare services, and section 2 requires local authorities to provide a wide-range of welfare services to any person in need of them. And the Housing (Homeless Persons) Act 1977 actually imposes a duty on local authorities, in certain circumstances, to provide some form of accommodation for those who are homeless; rather surprisingly, this duty has recently been held to be enforceable by way of an action for breach of statutory duty by a homeless person who alleges that the Act has been violated.[24] It remains to be seen whether this will prove an effective remedy in practice.

Employment

The social security system is designed, among other things, to provide an income for a person who is incapable of working and so earning his own income. The common law of torts, as it operates at present, also provides compensation on a large scale for income lost as a result of fault-caused injuries and disablement. And payments of cash to those with no income or means of providing one is clearly necessary, and will always be necessary for many cases; but for those with long-term disabilities cash benefits for lost income are very much a second best. Both from a humanitarian[25] and an economic point of view, much the best solution is to try to assist a man to overcome his disabilities to an extent which enables him to become capable of work once more.[26] And, if this is not possible, another alternative may lie in special steps to help the disabled to secure employment in special conditions which take account of their disabilities. Some of these objectives could be met by payments of money, but many of them can be met much more efficiently by special facilities provided by the State. And to some extent this is already done.

For many years now the rehabilitation of the disabled has been treated as a matter of great importance, both in the interests of disabled persons and of society as a whole, which will have to maintain them if they cannot maintain themselves.[27] Special provision was first made to assist in the rehabilitation and employment of the disabled during the First World War, and these services, which were increased during the last war, have become an established part of the social services. The primary purpose, where at all possible, is to rehabilitate a disabled or sick person so that he is capable of returning to normal employment. This objective is pursued in a variety of ways, but principally through the Employment Rehabilitation Centres[28] and the so-called 'Skillcentres'. The Employment Rehabilitation Centres are provided by the Manpower Services Commission and their aim is to 'restore the rehabilitee's confidence in his ability to return to work, to toughen him up physically, to assess his capabilities for various kinds of work, and to advise him, where a change of job is desirable, on the choice of a new occupation or on a suitable form of training.'[29] The Centres are equipped with workshops, gymnasium, garden, schoolroom and accommodation for administration. Most of them are not residential, but accommodation is provided in lodgings for those whose homes are too far away to enable them to come in daily. Maintenance grants are payable to people undergoing these courses which are higher than unemployment or sickness benefit, though lower than a full wage. The courses are free, and during a year over 16,000 persons pass through them. Of these, a fair proportion obtain employment within a short period.[30] Skillcentres are primarily designed to provide vocational training for healthy people who failed to acquire skills when young or have been made redundant or possess obsolete skills. But they also provide training for about 4,000 disabled people. Training is free and a maintenance allowance is paid.

Special facilities also exist for the placing of disabled people in employment and a register is maintained of disabled persons seeking work under the Disabled Persons (Employment) Act 1944. Assistance for this purpose is provided by Jobcentres which are required to have disablement resettlement officers. There are about 550 disablement resettlement officers. The Disabled Persons (Employment) Act 1944 imposes an obligation on an employer of more than 20 people to recruit at least 3% of his labour force from persons on the Disabled Persons' Registers maintained by Jobcentres. Only if no disabled person is available for the job may the employer offer it to another worker. This duty, however, appears to be honoured as much in the breach as in the observance, by public as well as by private employers. In 1981, the Manpower Services Commission estimated that the level of compliance was only 1·5%.[31] The Act also enables the Minister to designate certain types of employment as specially suitable for the disabled, and it is illegal for an employer to employ a non-disabled person in such a capacity unless no disabled person is available. At present there are only two types of job designated under the Act, namely lift attendant and car park attendant, and the Piercy Committee recommended that no new categories should be added but that, if more employment facilities were required for the disabled, this should be achieved by increasing the quota above the present 3%.[32] It is clear that there are considerable practical difficulties in finding employment for seriously disabled people, and the efforts of disablement resettlement officers are not always successful.[33]

Social assistance of different kinds is also available to persons who are so severely handicapped that they could not find employment in open competition in the labour market. In 1984 grants totalling some £60 million were made by the government to local authority and private undertakings which provided employment in sheltered factories and workshops for some 14,750 disabled people. Remploy Ltd, for example, is a non-profit making company employing about 8,750 disabled people in 94 factories. About 40% of these employees suffer from mental and nervous handicap. In 1981/2 Remploy received a subsidy from public funds of some £45.6 million,[34] or about

£5,300 for each disabled employee of the company; the Piercy Committee recognized that 'Remploy is operating a social service for the disabled'.[35] This subsidy is, however, offset by receipts of tax, national insurance contributions and VAT revenue, which would not be received if Remploy did not exist. Rates of pay in sheltered workshops are about 70% of the going rate in the outside world (this rate reflects the lower productivity of disabled people, and was agreed with the appropriate unions).

The importance of these employment opportunities for disabled people must, however, be kept in perspective. In 1984 there were some 420,000 disabled persons registered as substantially disabled for work; and since many do not register, this figure is an underestimate. In March 1985 there were 92,300 disabled persons registered at Jobcentres as seeking employment, of whom a very high proportion are unlikely to obtain jobs. Unemployment amongst disabled and handicapped people who are willing and able to work is probably considerably higher than amongst the ordinary working population.

For the most severely handicapped of all, those who are permanently housebound or bedridden, and for whom employment outside the home is impossible, some form of home employment scheme may be possible. Assistance is usually necessary in trying to devise suitable work and in helping to find a market for products made by the disabled. Unfortunately, not much progress has been made in this area, because the practical difficulties have proved insuperable.[36]

Mobility

We have already discussed the mobility allowance paid to the disabled. The DHSS has also set up a charitable trust, called Motability, which is designed to assist immobile people by providing small cars for them, and to help them obtain value from their mobility allowance. But lack of mobility is another problem which cannot be entirely overcome with money. A disabled person needs to be able to get about by himself; he needs to be able to park his car, if he has one, near enough to a building to get into it; he may need special entrances or lifts suitable for a wheelchair, and so on. Public expenditure of money to overcome difficulties of this kind for disabled people generally is surely a higher priority than compensation for disabilities as such. Some progress has been made in these ways, and impetus was given by the Chronically Sick and Disabled Persons Act 1970. This

Act imposes obligations on those responsible for buildings and premises open to the public to provide special parking facilities and public conveniences for the disabled. A disabled person's badge can be issued under this Act to disabled drivers, and this gives them certain parking privileges. Those responsible for building schools or university buildings are required to make provision for the needs of the disabled. It has been held that duties under this Act are not enforceable by action in the courts.[37]

Housing and residential accommodation

Local authorities have power under the National Assistance Act to make grants to disabled persons to cover the cost of conversions or adaptations to a house, necessitated by the disability; and section 2 of the Chronically Sick and Disabled Persons Act 1970 requires them to make such grants where they are satisfied that they are necessary. Though a recent survey found that half of those severely disabled had benefited from this facility, it has been said that there is still scope for a 'massive expansion of activity here'.[38] Lady Sharp also found that 'nothing like enough has been done to see that disabled people have [suitable] homes'.[39] There is evidence that about half of those severely handicapped need rehousing altogether, because of inaccessibility of toilets, or because they are unable to get upstairs and have to sleep in their sitting-room.[40]

Local authorities also have a duty[41] to provide residential accommodation for persons who by reason of age or infirmity or other circumstances are in need of care and attention not otherwise available, as well as urgently needed temporary accommodation arising from unforeseeable circumstances.[42] This latter power was originally intended primarily to cater for those suddenly rendered homeless by fire or flood or other similar disasters, and to this extent this social service may be regarded as performing a function similar to that of ordinary private property insurance. But in practice, the power has had to be used mainly to assist those who are rendered homeless simply by being ejected from their home for one reason or another. Residential accommodation for more permanent residents is very largely for the old, but in 1973 there were over 11,000 physical and mentally handicapped persons under 65 being looked after in such institutions.[43] Some of these homes are run by voluntary organizations with the assistance of grants from local authorities.[44]

Other social services

There are many other social services which lie on the extreme fringe of the subject matter of this book, and which it is impossible to discuss fully here. But some mention, however brief, should be made of the more important of these because their very existence is a continual reminder of society's needs to strike a balance between compensation in cash and in kind.[45] For example, there are day nurseries (not nursery schools) provided by local authorities which are largely designed to enable widows or deserted or unmarried mothers with young children to go out to work and so to maintain themselves. These nurseries provide places for some 30,000 children (including handicapped children), more than half of them from one-parent families.[46] Home-helps are provided by local authorities (often at a charge) mostly for the benefit of the elderly and the chronically sick, but also for the disabled and handicapped (55,000 such persons under 65 were being helped in this way in 1980). A home help is sometimes also available to those who are in need of temporary assistance at home because of sudden illness or injury to a mother with young children. Local authority day-centres provide some social, recreational and also health and educational facilities for the old and the disabled.[47] Home teachers visit blind people in their homes and teach them to read braille. There are provisions for a home-laundry service in some areas, and for the 'meals on wheels' services, primarily for the old but also for the disabled. There are special schools for the physically and mentally handicapped. All of these personal social services are vitally important in improving the quality of life of the disabled.[48]

Voluntary agencies play an important part in providing, or supplementing, public provision of personal social services to the disabled. For example, special holiday houses for the disabled are almost all provided by voluntary agencies. The role of voluntary agencies is becoming more and more important as a result of government pressure on local authorities to reduce spending, and also because, as a matter of political ideology, the Conservative government believes in encouraging the voluntary sector, and that social welfare provision should be a matter for partnership between the public and private sectors.[49] There are statutory provisions under which grants can be made by local authorities and health authorities to voluntary agencies for the provision of relevant services.

Social services of this sort seem far removed from the law of torts, but the connection between them is in fact closer than appears. For example, a widow with a young child may be compensated by an award of damages for the death of her husband on the supposition that she cannot work. But a more satisfactory arrangement may be to provide day nurseries where she can leave her children while she works. Damages for disability may be awarded to a single tort victim, but an alternative may be to provide facilities available to all disabled persons. From the point of view of society, which has to foot the bill in either case, there can be little doubt that provision of better social services is often a far more economic way of helping the disabled to live fuller and more satisfying lives. An award of £150,000 or more may be made to a badly disabled person to enable him to spend the rest of his life in a private institution, but this money would go in some way to building a local authority home which would provide residential accommodation for half a dozen disabled persons. Even in simpler and more modest situations, social services are a much more efficient way of coping with many problems. For instance, a woman is injured in an accident and is temporarily unable to run her home and look after her children. Tort law may give her, and her husband, damages months or years after the event, in the form of a lump sum. Social services may provide her family there and then with home helps to enable them to get over the immediate emergency. On the other hand, there are some areas in which tort law shows up gaps in the social services. A man whose wife is killed in an accident, leaving young children to be cared for, may recover substantial damages at law if negligence can be proved. But social security benefits are not normally payable to a widower on account of his spouse's death, and large numbers of children are taken into local authority homes where there is no mother to look after them at home.[50] Unfortunately, the social services are the Cinderella of the welfare state. Heavily overburdened, desperately short of money, unable to recruit staff at the wages offered, the social services retain to some extent the stigma of pauperism and charity.[51] Unfortunately, too, the social services are the victims of conflicting policies. On the one hand, the government wants to contain public spending and to encourage the private sector. There is also a strain of liberal ideology which prefers to give cash assistance and leave it to the individual recipient to decide how to spend it (the tort system, of necessity, embodies such a philosophy). On the other hand, for example, in 1983 a provision was enacted extending the powers of health authorities to make grants to local authorities and voluntary organizations which provide social services.[52] This is part of a policy to enable people who do not need to be in hospital to be moved into the community.

… PART FIVE
The Overall Picture

18
A plethora of systems

1 THE INTER-RELATION OF THE SYSTEMS

Now that the survey of current compensation systems in operation in this country is complete, it is time to take stock and consider the overall position. Two questions suggest themselves immediately. The first is the inter-relation between the systems. The second is the basis of the distinctions drawn according to the *cause* of the event giving rise to the claim for compensation: existing systems are largely based on fundamental distinctions between natural and human causes on the one hand, and between fault caused and non-fault caused injuries on the other. These distinctions we reserve for the next two chapters. In this chapter we propose to examine the overlaps and gaps existing in the present systems, and the ways in which the various systems fit together.

Where a person has a claim to compensation which can prima facie be met by compensation from more than one system, two principal alternatives present themselves. First, he may be compensated by both systems, so that in the result he receives more compensation than each system alone deems him entitled to receive. Secondly, he may be compensated only once, and in this case it is necessary to decide which system is to provide the compensation. But matters do not stop here, for even if compensation is to be paid only once, it may be provided by one system alone, or by two or more systems in various proportions; or it may be provided in full by one system to start with, and that system may then be able to recover part or all of the cost from another system. Perhaps the most remarkable thing about this complicated pattern is that each compensation system is largely left to work out its own relationship with each other system. So system A may decide to share a cost with system B, but may be willing to shoulder the whole cost as against system C, while attempting to place the whole of a cost on system D. It will be seen that this could raise acute problems where two systems do not agree as to how they are to allocate a cost as between themselves, though on the whole, these questions are usually settled without great practical difficulty.

Where a person receives compensation from two or more sources he may receive more in total than is necessary to achieve the purpose of the compensation. Such overcompensation, which is referred to here as 'double compensation', appears prima facie to be a wasteful use of public resources. Although there are some circumstances – which are discussed below – in which double compensation may appear unobjectionable, as where the victim has 'paid for' the right to compensation, it seems a reasonable starting point to assume that double compensation for some has a very low priority as compared with full compensation for all. In general, this approach was emphatically endorsed by the Pearson Commission.[1]

We have so far spoken of 'compensation systems' as though these could all be treated as self-contained bodies of law (or non-legal rules), but even this oversimplifies the actual position because each compensation 'system' may itself be composed of various sub-divisions, and indeed in some cases it is purely a matter of choice whether different methods of compensation can be dignified with the name of a separate 'system' at all. For example, is a means-tested rent rebate scheme operated by a local authority a compensation 'system' for the indigent? In general, one would probably answer this in the negative, but in the case of a tenant who is poor enough to qualify under the means-test because he is unemployable as a result of accident or sickness, the relationship between the rent rebate scheme and other compensation systems obviously presents a problem.

On the whole, it is not surprising to find that each distinct compensation system, so far as it is possible to separate them into distinct systems, sets its face against any element of double compensation within its own confines. For example, the tort system will not give damages for the same injury more than once. Thus, if a person is injured in an accident caused by the negligence of two or more tortfeasors, he may recover his damages from them in any proportions he can, but he cannot recover in total more than the amount of the award. Slightly more difficult, is the case where the result of the tort is to confer a right of action on a person while he is alive, but a separate right on his dependants after his death. But here again, the law does not permit double compensation, since no claim will be available for the dependants if the person has enforced his own claim during his lifetime.[2]

The social security system also sets its face against double compensation within its own confines. Beveridge himself enunciated the firm principle that nobody should have the same need met more than once, and this principle has been accepted ever since. A person who is unemployed and becomes sick cannot claim unemployment benefit and sickness benefit. A person can claim both invalidity benefit and disablement benefit, but that is because the former is designed to replace his lost income while the latter is compensation for the disability as such, and is not intended to be for lost income.

Personal insurance also generally refuses to pay more than once for the same loss. Insurance, which is designed to replace something with measurable financial value – indemnity insurance – can never be claimed for more than the amount lost. For instance, a person may be covered by two separate policies, each of which professes to offer him full compensation, yet he is not, by law, entitled to claim more than one indemnity. Prima facie each insurer will have to bear half the loss in this situation.[3] The position is, however, different with non-measurable losses. For instance, life insurance or personal accident insurance against disability alone, unlike indemnity insurance, is cumulative and is not limited by the notional amount of any 'loss'. The amount must be largely notional because of course it is not measurable in financial terms. But this is true also of damages for disability at common law, yet the position here is different. The courts have never said that merely because damages for disability are not properly measurable it follows that a person can recover such damages in full from several tortfeasors. No doubt this is partly because the courts have attempted to fix a 'proper' sum to award as damages for disabilities, even though they are fully conscious of the difficulties of doing so, and therefore it is felt that to give more than one set of damages would in some sense be to award 'too much'. But a better reason for distinguishing between these situations is that in tort liability, the cost is being borne by other parties, while in the case of personal insurance, the insured is paying for the insurance himself. He is left to choose the amount of insurance he wants to buy, and he pays premiums accordingly.

The main difficulties to be examined in this chapter concern the way in which different systems fit together, rather than the way in which each system treats the problem of double compensation within its own confines. We consider first those cases in which double compensation is ruled out, and where the question is how to choose which system should bear the loss, and whether that system which first pays should have any redress against another in due course.

2 THE CHOICE OF COMPENSATION SYSTEMS

If there was any rational pattern to the various compensation systems as a whole, it might have been possible to construct a 'hierarchy' of systems under which a person should be compensated by system A, if that were possible, and if not, he should then be relegated to systems B, C and D in turn. But this is not how things have developed. In fact, each system by and large decides whether it is willing to shoulder a burden, irrespective of other compensation available, or of whether it wishes to push the burden onto another system, or of whether it is willing to share the burden. But the whole process is one of almost unbelievable complexity. Let us look first at some of the simpler cases.

First, the social security system is, in general, willing to shoulder its burdens irrespective of the existence of any other compensation system. Tort damages, private insurance, criminal injury compensation, and sick pay from the employer, may all be available, but still social security remains payable for industrial injuries and sickness leading to absence from work. But this is not true with regard to supplementary benefit, which is only paid on proof of need. There are also a number of other cases where social security benefits are not payable, because other compensation is available. For example, unemployment benefit is not payable to a person who receives wages in lieu of notice on dismissal.

The social security system does not generally attempt to pass any of the burden on, having once assumed the liability.[4] A person who suffers industrial injury (say) as a result of the negligence of an employer, will receive his social security benefits from the DHSS, which has no right of recoupment from the negligent employer. The possibility of giving such a right of recoupment was considered by the Monckton Committee in 1946,[5] but was rejected by them for eminently good reasons. Such a right would be a species of what lawyers call 'subrogation', that is a right conferred on A as a result of his having met an obligation which was 'really' B's. Subrogation is, as we shall see, recognized in some parts of the law, as one way in which a compensation system which is liable in the first instance, may pass its liability onto someone else in the final result. It is subject to many disadvantages in modern conditions, and has probably largely outlived its usefulness.

Voluntary sick-pay schemes are usually less willing than the social security system to shoulder burdens, irrespective of the existence of other sources of compensation. Since the social security payments for sickness are available whether or not wages are paid, most employers naturally feel it to be a waste of money to pay *full* wages to a person off sick, even though they may be willing to pay something. Most sick-pay schemes (as we have seen) therefore provide that the value of benefits will be deducted from sick pay.[6] The trend to deduct social security benefits from sick pay has no doubt been greatly accelerated by the introduction of statutory sick pay payable by the employer.

It is, however, less usual to take account of tort damages when sick pay is granted. This is partly for the purely practical reason that it may be months or years before a penny is recovered in tort damages, and in the meantime the person must live. It is also probable that a claim for tort damages is simply not considered as a sufficiently common event to make it worthwhile to make special provision for this in a sick-pay scheme. But it is apparently permissible to make provision whereby the employer may 'advance' wages as a 'loan' to a person injured in an accident giving rise to a tort claim, and the injured person may then be under an obligation to repay the employer, if and when he recovers damages for lost earnings.[7] It will be seen that this is simply an elaborate device to throw the cost of wages for an injured servant onto the tortfeasor (and hence liability insurers) rather than the employer. In practice, the main issue here is whether employers or motorists should pay for lost wages arising from road accidents, and it might have been thought that this was a policy question of sufficient importance to be settled by the law in one way or another, and not left to be determined by the terms of a sick-pay scheme drawn up by a particular employer with his own interests in mind. In general the cost is borne by motorists to the extent that fault can be proved, and it might therefore be thought that there was no reason why an employer who organized a sick-pay scheme should not be entitled to insist that wages lost through negligent driving should still be borne by motorists, rather than by himself. But it is doubtful if this is really sound policy, because the advantage to the employer must be small: it can only be in a small proportion of cases that sick pay can be recouped in this way, while the general administrative cost of recoupment is high, since it involves reliance on the tort system.[8]

First party insurance is, in some ways, similar to 'sick pay' since it is a matter of private contract, and therefore insurers are free to try to throw losses onto other compensation systems if they wish, by the terms of their insurance policies. For example, a personal accident policy could stipulate that there is to be no liability if compensation is obtained from other sources, but in fact insurance companies do not generally attempt to do this. They are mainly concerned with preventing the insured recovering for the same loss under more than one policy; they also have various subrogation rights, which we shall examine shortly.

In some cases a virtual stalemate can be arrived at between two compensation systems, each declining to meet a claim because it knows that the other system must then step in and do so. Difficulties of this kind were contemplated by the drafters of the Legal Aid scheme. When this was first introduced there seem to have been fears that insured motorists might obtain legal aid for the *defence* of proceedings, which were formerly and customarily handled by their insurers. It was accordingly provided in the legal aid scheme that (in effect) legal aid would be given if necessary in such a case, but the legal aid fund would then be subrogated to the insured's right to an indemnity in respect of the costs of the proceedings.[9] There were also fears that trade unions might prefer to withdraw from the business of assisting their members in personal injury cases, and it is therefore also provided by regulations that legal aid will be refused where the applicant is a member of an organization from which he has a 'reasonable expectation' of obtaining help.[10] There is clearly room here for a game of bluff and counter bluff.[11]

Another example is provided by a recent case[12] in which the MIB sought to argue that a plaintiff, injured by a defendant who deliberately used his car (which was uninsured) to run him down, ought to have sought compensation from the Criminal Injuries Compensation Board rather than from the MIB, even though the latter was, as the House of Lords held, liable under its agreement with the government in cases of deliberate running down. In this type of case, the CICB does not normally award compensation precisely because the MIB agreement covers it. The House of Lords, without adverting to this fact, held that the CICB and the MIB scheme were not mutually exclusive, and that the plaintiff could choose to proceed under whichever scheme was more favourable to him. Thus stalemate was avoided, but the basic issue of which compensation scheme *ought* to have borne the loss was not tackled.

Demarcation disputes

The mere fact of having different systems generates the need to spend time deciding which is the appropriate system to bear the loss. For example, entitlement to damages requires proof of negligence; entitlement to industrial injury benefits requires proof that the accident arose 'out of and in the course of employment'; entitlement to criminal injuries compensation requires proof (with a few special exceptions) that a crime of violence has been committed. Each of these (and other) criteria of entitlement tend to produce troublesome borderline cases, the allocation of which to the 'appropriate' compensation system absorbs a disproportionate amount of administrative effort and cost. The more systems there are, the more borderline cases there will be; and the more demarcation disputes will have to be solved. Such disputes appear even more futile when it is remembered that the ultimate burden of most compensation systems is borne by the public. One of the undoubted attractions of an integrated approach to the question of compensation is that it would eliminate so many of these troublesome questions.

3 SUBROGATION

Where two persons are legally under a liability to compensate a third party for some loss, and as between these two, one is under a 'primary' liability and the other is only 'secondarily' liable, the latter is normally entitled, if he pays the compensation, to be 'subrogated' to the claims of the third party as against the person primarily liable.

Now, as we have seen, in the tort system, tort liability is still treated as a 'primary' liability, while insurance is still treated as an ancillary or secondary feature of the system. Therefore a tortfeasor can sometimes be sued, not merely by the victim of the tort, but by other compensation systems which have indemnified him against the loss. For example, if a person insures his house against fire and the house is burned down as a result of the negligence of a tortfeasor, the owner of the house will probably and wisely claim from his insurers, but they are then subrogated to his claim against the tortfeasor. In practice, insurers would rarely make a claim in this sort of situation because the tortfeasor would probably not himself be insured against the liability, so they would recover little, if anything, for their pains. But it may happen that the tortfeasor is also insured, as in the familiar case of two motorists, both comprehensively insured, who collide as a result of their combined negligence. Here each motorist can claim against his own insurer for the damage to his vehicle; each insurer is then subrogated to the claims of its insured against the other driver, and each insurer is therefore entitled to pass onto the other insurer the cost of the claim by its own insured.[13] It is clear why insurers prefer to ignore these subrogation rights and have knock-for-knock agreements.

Another instance of subrogation is to be found in the case of a servant whose negligent conduct has caused his employer to be held liable to a third party; if the employer was insured, the 'primary' liability is treated as resting on the servant, and the insurer is subrogated to the employer's claim against the servant.[14]

Outside the insurance area, subrogation plays little part as between compensation systems. The social security system does not use it at all in the personal injuries area, although it is used in connection with the somewhat analogous (but different) problems concerning deserted wives.[15] If a husband refuses to maintain his wife and she is forced to apply for supplementary benefits to maintain herself, the Commission has statutory powers to sue the husband.[16] And neither the Criminal Injuries Compensation Board nor the MIB can claim subrogation rights, since neither are strictly liable in law for the payments they make.[17]

We have also seen how the Legal Aid Fund has, in theory, certain subrogation rights against insurers who have undertaken to render legal aid to an insured. A similar species of subrogation is recognized

A plethora of systems 395

in connection with the cost of the National Health Service. Since the State is now under an obligation to provide its citizens with free medical treatment, it could be argued that it ought to have subrogation rights in respect of the cost of the treatment against any person (such as a tortfeasor) legally liable to the patient for that cost. In fact, the Road Traffic Act provides for a statutory right in lieu of, and very much less valuable than, the right of subrogation; and then the principal right is conferred against insurers only, and not against tortfeasors. Under Section 154 of the Road Traffic Act 1972 an insurer who pays damages in respect of a person injured or killed in a road accident, whom he knows to have received treatment in a hospital, is liable to pay to the hospital the cost of expenses reasonably incurred, not exceeding £1,777 for in-patient treatment and £177·70 for out-patient treatment. Under Section 155, a doctor who has treated a patient for injuries as a result of a road accident may recover £13·32 from the person using the car.

From time to time suggestions have been made for a wider use of subrogation – or something akin to it, if not called by the same name – in the compensation process. For example, the Law Reform Committee once proposed that an employer who pays wages to a person injured as a result of a tort should be subrogated to his rights against the tortfeasor.[18] Again, when the criminal injuries scheme was under consideration, it was suggested that the State should have subrogation rights against the criminal.[19] The Winn Committee on personal injury litigation[20] put forward for consideration a scheme under which the State should pay some, or all, of the damages which a road accident victim may be able to recover in subsequent litigation, and may then recoup itself by taking proceedings against the tortfeasor. And the Society of Labour Lawyers once advocated a similar scheme for industrial injuries.[21]

Nevertheless, it is confidently suggested that any serious study of the problem must lead inevitably to the conclusion that subrogation, far from being a device which ought to be extended, should on the contrary, generally be confined within the narrowest possible limits, and in most cases, abolished altogether.[22] From a practical point of view, cases in which subrogation is possible may be divided into two classes: first, where compensation is met by one system, and an attempt is then made to pass the cost onto another system; and secondly, where an attempt is made to pass the cost on to some individual. In the first type of case, the objection to subrogation is principally that it is pointless if the most appropriate compensation system already bears the cost of the loss; while if this is not the case, the proper course is to change the law so that the most appropriate compensation system bears the cost in the first instance. Subrogation is a particularly futile device where the State is concerned because the State has other and easier means at hand for raising money if it wants – namely the taxation system, or some form of compulsory national insurance. It would, for example, be extraordinarily cumbersome for the State to pay compensation to road accident victims, and then sue tortfeasors (by way of subrogation) in the courts just in order to collect damages from the insurance companies which are themselves raising the money in the form of premiums from motorists. Far and away the simplest and cheapest method of achieving the same result would be for the State to collect what is necessary from motorists in the form of tax in the first place, and then redistribute this to victims of road accidents. By these means, all court proceedings and all insurance company costs would be bypassed, but the same ultimate objective could be attained.

In the second kind of case, where an attempt is made to pass on the cost of some loss from a compensation system to a private individual, the principal objection is precisely the same as the objection against making individuals pay tort damages, namely that it is not practicable nor, in the majority of cases, is it just or in the public interest. Since one of the principal objects of any compensation system should be to spread a loss among a large number of people so that the cost does not fall too heavily on any individual, a loss, once passed on to a party well able to spread it, ought not to be shifted again to a party unable to spread it effectively. Further, there are special problems in connection with the State, for if the State pursues subrogation proceedings against an individual, the process begins to look very similar to the infliction of penalties for crime. It is not the point to object that the State's purpose would be to recoup itself the compensation which it has paid to a third party and not to inflict a penalty, for from the individual dependant's point of view what matters is the effect of the proceedings, not their purpose. All this was seen very clearly when subrogation was considered in connection with the criminal injuries scheme, for it was then pointed out that if the State tried to enforce subrogation rights against the criminal it would appear to be duplicating any criminal proceedings by further civil proceedings in which the man could be 'fined' again.[23]

Moreover, subrogation is expensive. Shifting losses around costs a great deal of money because it involves collecting money from one source, deciding how to allocate it by some process, and then distributing it to those to whom it has been decided to allocate it.[24] Subrogation adds another stage in which yet another collection of funds is made from other sources. A classic example of the fatuity of subrogation is provided by the statutory rights given to hospitals to recover from insurers in respect of the cost of medical treatment given to road accident victims. The amount collected is much less than 100% of the costs to the National Health Service of motor accidents, and the costs of collection are undoubtedly high in relation to the sums involved.[25] If it is desired to make motorists pay a great part of these costs,[26] it would be far simpler and cheaper for the State to impose a levy on insurance companies or an additional tax on motorists, which could then be used to help pay for the National Health Service.[27] This is what is done in the case of industrial accidents, for part of the national insurance contributions paid by employers and employees goes towards the cost of the National Health Service, and this part may be regarded as a levy on industry to cover *inter alia* the medical costs of industrial accidents. In 1976 the Government decided to levy a charge on motor insurance premiums to defray the full National Health Service cost of road accidents, but after lengthy discussions with the insurance industry, the proposals were abandoned as impractical.

Insurance companies, who are the main beneficiaries of the doctrine of subrogation in the law, realize that it is not generally a very useful device. The knock-for-knock agreement represents an abandonment of subrogation rights, and more generally insurers would probably be well content to drop all subrogation rights as between themselves. They are also (it seems) not inclined to take subrogation proceedings against individuals. In one particular instance – the case of the servant who renders his master liable in damages, and is in law liable to recoup the employer's insurers – the insurance industry has voluntarily abandoned the right of subrogation by an extra-legal agreement.[28] Of course, given the existing law, insurers cannot always be expected to pass up the opportunity of recouping a large loss from another insurer. Perhaps they are more likely to take subrogation proceedings against large non-insurers such as the Crown. In some countries subrogation is severely limited by law; for example, in Denmark, a person who has insured his property against accidental damage, has no tort action against a person who damages it, and hence the insurers have no subrogation rights.[29] Other Scandinavian countries permit a tort action, but the insurance proceeds are deducted from tort damages and once again there are no subrogation rights.[30] In a recent decision the Court of Appeal has shown willingness to curtail the field of operation of the doctrine of subrogation.[31] It is generally thought that the subrogation rights of insurers are not of substantial economic value,[32] though their subrogation rights against each other may be of some importance in the case of fire and marine insurance.

4 TORT DAMAGES AND OTHER COMPENSATION

The most difficult problems in this field concern the interrelation of the tort system with other compensation systems, and there is no doubt that the conjunction of tort damages and compensation from other sources can create the most glaring instances of overcompensation. The essential question is one of basic policy: how far is it right that a person should be compensated from more than one source for the same loss? Like most policy issues, this one is capable of being discussed in rational terms, but also in the irrational conceptual language which still, unfortunately, is often to be found in the judgments of the courts.

Let us first mention, only to dismiss, three of the approaches which lawyers have traditionally taken when faced with issues of this kind.[33] The first is that other forms of compensation should be ignored if they are 'collateral' or come from a 'collateral source'. If taken literally, this presumably means that benefits deriving from a source other than the defendant himself should all be ignored, while benefits coming from the defendant should be taken into account. But no such extreme view has ever been accepted by the courts, though they have (until very recently) continued to refer to 'collateral' benefits and 'collateral' sources. Once the literal meaning of these words is departed from, a judge who is trying to decide whether another source of compensation is 'collateral' will get no assistance from the word itself, and will therefore be forced to decide the issue as one of policy. Precisely the same considerations apply to the second conceptual technique, which is to ask whether the injury occasioned by the tort was the *causa causans* of the receipt of the compensation, or merely a *causa sine qua non*.[34] Our discussion of causal concepts should suffice to demonstrate that this distinction is of little, if any, use as a basis for decision. Although we have seen that it is possible to use the standards of ordinary speech to determine questions of causation when we are trying to determine responsibility for an event, this is an area in which the ordinary people do sometimes use causal language to ascribe responsibility for events, they are extremely unlikely to use causal language to explain the relationship between an injury and the receipt of compensation. Ordinary speech provides no answer to the question whether (for example) an injury, rather than the payment of insurance premiums, can properly be said to be the 'cause' of the compensation payable by the insurance company.

The third approach is based on the assumption that tortfeasors actually pay tort damages and that therefore the reduction of tort damages because of compensation received from another source will 'benefit' the tortfeasor. Why, it is asked, should this outside source of compensation 'benefit' the tortfeasor rather than the victim? But once it is appreciated that in only a handful of cases does the tortfeasor (at least if he is an individual) pay anything at all, the argument collapses. On the whole, this argument now tends to receive short shrift in the courts, not so much on the ground that tortfeasors do not pay damages, but because it is essentially an argument in favour of penal damages. If the plaintiff is already adequately compensated, then obliging a defendant to pay money to the plaintiff for the same loss on the ground that the defendant should not get the 'benefit' of the other compensation, is merely to penalize the defendant. And on the whole this is now unfashionable.

If we put these arguments on one side, it is suggested that the principal policy considerations are these. First, insofar as compensation from different systems comes from the same source, there should in general be compensation once, and once only, in respect of one need or loss.[35] This is particularly important when the source from which the compensation comes is the public. Taxpayers' and public money should not be wasted by overcompensating some accident victims, particularly when so many other deserving cases (such as victims of disease) receive much less. But in modern conditions, 'public money' is not just money which is actually collected by the State in the form of tax or social security contributions. Tort damages too are, for all practical purposes, paid out of public money, since they are mostly paid out of road traffic and employers' liability insurance premiums which are paid for by virtually the whole public and which have to be paid by law.

Secondly, much depends on what the compensation is *for*. If it is intended to replace something (like a lost income) with a measurable financial value, then there can be little justification for paying compensation more than once from more than one source. If, on the other hand, the compensation is for something with no measurable financial value such as pain and suffering, the argument against double compensation is less strong: since nobody can say what value we should put on pain and suffering it cannot be said that a person has been overcompensated by receiving money from more than one source. This is why there is no subrogation in non-indemnity insurance: since the insurance is not to protect against a loss of measurable financial value there appears to be no reason why the insured should not recover several times over. This argument also appealed to the dissenting minority on the Monckton Committee,[36] who thought that full tort damages and social security payments should be payable to the accident victim because compensation for disabilities could never be excessive. On the whole this does not seem convincing,[37] particularly when the assessment of what is an appropriate sum to pay for the disability is arrived at independently by each compensation system on the assumption that that will be the only compensation payable.

A third policy consideration is whether the people financing one or other of the sources of compensation *want* the recipient to have compensation twice over. This is particularly relevant with charitable donations; for example, the donors of the money which formed the Aberfan Disaster Fund presumably intended the beneficiaries to receive some benefit in addition to their legal claims, and this may be a good reason for refusing to deduct the value of such donations from tort damages. But even this case is not as simple as it may seem, for the donors probably never give a thought (in most cases) to the fact that the beneficiaries may have additional legal rights to other sources of compensation; indeed, it is not unknown for the appeal for donations to be launched in terms which prevent the money being fully expended, because of the compensation obtained from other sources.[38] Another difficulty about giving effect to the intention of the donor to provide *additional* help is that donors are not always donating their own money. Charitable donations often derive in large part from companies who are dispensing largesse ultimately out of the pockets of the shareholders, the employees and the consumers of the company's products. In such cases the public may feel entitled to some say in determining whether (despite the intention of the donor) double compensation should be permitted. For example, many employees who are off work receive full wages or salary plus social security benefits. The employer may be regarded in some sense as making such payments out of 'charity', because he is not usually under any legal obligation to do this and he presumably makes these payments with the intention that his employee should enjoy full salary or wages and the state benefits at the same time. But it does not follow that this is a sensible or satisfactory arrangement from the public point of view; the public cannot very well force the employer *not* to pay full wages when the employee is sick, but it could refuse to pay the employee social security benefits so long as he is paid his wages in full.

A fourth, and more difficult, argument which has played an important role in some cases is that double compensation is less objectionable if the recipient has in some sense 'paid for' the compensation. Thus in *Parry* v. *Cleaver*,[39] Lord Reid thought that the real justification for allowing an accident victim to receive tort damages unaffected by the amount of any personal accident insurance payments was that the plaintiff had 'paid for' the accident insurance and should therefore receive the benefits of his premiums. And the same sort of argument was also used to justify deduction of only part of the value of social security benefits from tort damages.[40] Now in some cases there is no doubt that if a man 'pays for' his insurance benefits he should be allowed to insure for as much as he wants, and so to receive in compensation more than he has lost. A person may, for instance, take out as much life insurance as he likes, and there can be no policy objections to this. But there are many reasons why it does not always dispose of the difficulties to say that a person has 'paid for' his compensation. First, there are circumstances in which to allow 'double compensation' may be a serious temptation to fraud. For example, a person is not generally allowed to recover the value of damaged property twice over, even if he has insured it twice over and 'paid for' the insurance with two lots of premiums. Secondly, the most difficult questions usually arise in connection with tort damages and other forms of compensation, and although the insured may have 'paid for' the other compensation – typically insurance – he will not have 'paid for' the tort damages in any meaningful sense.

A fifth policy consideration concerns the administrative cost of avoiding duplication of compensation. If the amount it costs to weed out those cases in which duplication is likely to occur is greater than the value of the duplicated compensation itself, then this would be a good reason for allowing double compensation. This may be why social security benefits are payable to those who receive sick pay, and why employers for their part also do not always deduct the value of these benefits. Prima facie it would seem that compensation from an uncommon source should be ignored in assessing compensation from other sources, because the cost of dealing with it as a special case may well outweigh anything saved. Moreover, the additional cost to the public will be small. For instance, personal accident insurance against income loss and disabilities is still relatively unusual, so that even if this form of insurance benefit is disregarded in the assessment of tort damages, the total cost of personal accident insurance *and* tort liability insurance will only be marginally affected. The position would, however, change if this form of insurance became common because the degree of overcompensation would become great and much of the amount spent by individuals buying both personal accident and tort liability insurance would be unnecessary. Similarly, if the law provided that a car owner could recover tort damages for negligently caused damage to his car *and* compensation from his own insurance company as well, the combined cost of both types of insurance, and therefore of comprehensive policies which comprise the two, would increase considerably; it is true that in return for this increased cost there would be an additional benefit in the coverage granted, but few people would willingly buy that coverage if they had the choice not to do so. It may, therefore, be sound policy for several reasons to disregard unusual and subsidiary forms of compensation, while taking more common ones into account.

Let us now consider how the law actually deals with these questions.

Tort damages and sick pay

This is an area in which the law is surprisingly uncertain, for the decisions are few and not very clear.[41] Until the decision of the House of Lords in *Parry* v. *Cleaver*, it was generally thought that the position was as follows. First, if the employer is bound by contract or statute to pay the employee wages while he is away from work through sickness, then the employee has not 'lost' any income and cannot recover it in damages. Secondly, if the employer is not so bound but pays nonetheless, then this is a 'charitable' payment which is not to be deducted from the damages, unless the employer is also the defendant, as he normally will be in an industrial accident case. There was thus thought to be an important practical distinction between road accident cases and industrial accident cases. Thirdly, if the employer, while not bound to pay the wages, pays them in the form of a 'loan' subject to an undertaking to repay them out of any tort damages which may be recovered, then again there will be no deduction.[42] It is, however, possible that one result of *Parry* v. *Cleaver* has been to abrogate the distinction between the first two cases. Thus, it appears that any sick pay should now be deducted even if it is paid voluntarily by the employer.

Tort damages and personal insurance

It has always been a firm principle that in cases of property damage the owner cannot recover both tort damages and private insurance. However, he is not technically precluded from suing in tort even if he has collected from his insurers; rather the insurers are subrogated to the insured's rights, and the tort claim can thus only be prosecuted for the benefit of the insurers. In practice, as we have seen, this does not often happen, and in any event it remains true to say that the property owner cannot, after collecting the insurance money, sue for his own benefit.

In the case of personal accident insurance, however, the position has been otherwise ever since the decision in *Bradburn* v. GWR[43] in 1874, where it was held that tort damages should be recovered in full by the victim. Furthermore, there is no question of subrogation here, for personal accident insurance is not 'indemnity' insurance, i.e. it is not insurance designed to protect against a measurable identifiable loss. This decision may have been influenced by the rarity of personal accident insurance at that time, and also by the special circumstances of the case: the defendants were a railway company and railway companies tried to induce the public to protect themselves against risk by buying personal accident insurance.

Unfortunately, the difference between personal insurance on the one hand and sick pay on the other has produced acute difficulty in the case of occupational pensions which are payable to a person prematurely retired as a result of a tort caused accident. A pension of this kind obviously partakes of the nature of sick pay, and also of the nature of accident insurance. This was the difficulty facing the House of Lords in *Parry* v. *Cleaver*, in which it was decided by a bare majority that the value of the pension should not be deducted from the tort damages.[44]

One particular anomaly produced by the present set of rules is that private insurance, even if taken out and paid for by some third party, seems to fall within the same principle. Thus, if an employer buys permanent health insurance for the benefit of his employees, and the employee sues the employer for damages, it seems that the money payable under the policy is not deductible from the damages. The employer thus pays twice over. The Pearson Commission recommended no change here, apparently not thinking of this possibility.[45]

Tort damages and charitable or discretionary payments

Payments made to the accident victim by a person who is under no legal obligation to make them are generally ignored.[46] This explains why it was thought until *Parry* v. *Cleaver* that sick pay which the employer is not bound to pay is normally to be ignored. Also payments in the nature of charitable donations are ignored. In 1964 it was held that payments of national assistance should not be deducted from tort damages, on the ground that they were discretionary;[47] but (as we have seen) under the Social Security Act 1976 there is now an entitlement to supplementary benefits, and it has been held that these benefits must be deducted in full from damages.[48] Similarly, payment of disability pensions to persons suffering accidental injury while serving in the armed forces (unlike the industrial injury benefits which they may otherwise resemble) is discretionary, and it is the practice of the Ministry to deduct something from these pensions where tort damages are later recovered by the victim.[49] Accordingly, the courts themselves make no deduction in assessing tort damages for the same injuries.[50] Why there should be this difference between service and industrial injury pensions passes comprehension. No deduction from damages is made for the value of services gratuitously rendered to an injured person by relatives or friends; furthermore, the damages will include a sum to enable the victim to pay for the services.[51] Nor is the value of free public health care deducted, except that if the plaintiff saves living expenses by being looked after in a public institution, the value of such savings are deducted from damages for loss of earnings.[52]

Tort damages and social security benefits

We saw in an earlier chapter that Beveridge used as one justification for retaining special treatment for industrial injuries the argument that only if this were done would it be possible to restrict liability at common law in industrial injury cases. However, Beveridge did not fully go into this question in his report and he recommended that a special committee should be set up to inquire into the whole question of 'alternative remedies'. Accordingly, a committee (consisting principally of lawyers) was set up under the chairmanship of Sir Walter Monckton.[53] The committee decided, quite naturally, that social security payments should be unaffected by the possibility of tort damages, if only because it is obviously necessary to pay these benefits at once and not to wait and see whether any damages may be recovered. Having then rejected the idea of subrogating the State to the victim's claims against the tortfeasor, the committee was faced with the question whether tort damages assessments should be affected by the social security benefits: in other words, should the principle of *Bradburn* v. *GWR* apply to the national insurance system? The committee thought that there was a fundamental difference in principle between voluntary insurance (such as that involved in the *Bradburn* case) and compulsory national insurance, which was more like a tax, because there was no question of rewarding thrift in the case of the State benefits.[54] There can be no doubt of the good sense of the conclusion, though the arguments are not in all respects the most convincing that could have been advanced.[55] The strongest argument against duplication is that tort damages, no less than social security payments, are paid for by the public, and there is no rational justification for paying double compensation for the same loss at the public's expense.[56] In the end the committee recommended that the value of national insurance benefits should be deducted in full from tort damages.

In fact, the settlement finally enacted [57] was far more favourable to injury victims (and especially industrial injury victims) than the committee had recommended. Instead of providing for full deduction of the value of social security benefits, the Law Reform (Personal Injuries) Act 1948 provided for deduction from damages for personal injuries of half the value of certain benefits received, or likely to be received, during a period of five years. *No* benefits are deducted under the Fatal Accidents Act 1976. The rules about benefits other than those mentioned in the Act are not uniform. Attendance and mobility allowance are not deducted;[58] but supplementary benefits,[59] and unemployment benefits,[60] actually received before the date of judgment, are. As for future benefits, a court might well consider that the amount, if any, likely to be received was too speculative to calculate, and so should be ignored.

The justification for reducing the deduction to half of the value of the benefits listed in the 1948 statute was that in the industrial injury system the employee was paying nearly half the cost (five-twelfths) and that, therefore, he was entitled to receive half the benefits as of right and without affecting his tort claim. But this justification will not stand examination for a moment.[61] First, it was only in the case of industrial injuries that five-twelfths of the cost was paid by employees, yet the half-deduction rule was applied to all benefits. Secondly, even in the industrial injury system the idea that workmen are paying for their own benefits is quite fallacious, because the fact that contribution rates are not risk-related means that workers in some occupations are being heavily subsidized by workers in others. The extent of this subsidy can be gauged from the fact that in 1972 there were over 250,000 reported factory accidents among some seven million employees, while in the same period there were only 18,000 reported accidents in shops and offices and railway premises among a similar number of employees.

There also appears to be no justification for the five year limitation;[62] although, in fact, few industrial injury victims receive benefits for longer than five years, it simply means that where common law damages are at their highest, the amount of duplication is greatest. This parliamentary compromise was partly justified on the ground that general damages were awarded in a global sum, so that it was not possible to isolate the amount awarded for loss of earnings as opposed to loss of amenities. Of course, this is no longer so since *Jefford* v. *Gee*[63], and the element of duplication in the compensation processes is thus much more obvious today than it was in 1948.[64] The result of all this is that the deduction is usually nowhere near the full value of the benefits, and is often a rather trivial sum. A typical illustration of how this works in practice is provided by a case in 1960[65], in which the plaintiff received a disablement gratuity of £210 and industrial injury benefits of £61, totalling £271. The amount deducted from his damages came to only £45. With more substantial cases the element of duplication can be very large. For example, a person who lost the sight of an eye in an industrial accident might collect £11,000 in tort damages, from which would be deducted half the value of a disablement pension of £18·75 for five years. The capitalized value of such a pension for a man of 40 to 50 is today over £15,000, but the amount deducted from the tort damages on account of it would only be about £4,590. So this man would receive from the public his weekly pension plus over £6,000 damages for precisely the same loss.

In the case of widows the position is perhaps even stranger, for no deductions of any kind are made, and on the whole widows with dependent children appear to be treated more favourably than any other group under the social security system. An industrial widow with two dependent children would receive £69·55 per week in social security benefits, a pension which may have a capital value in excess of £80,000 or £90,000; if her husband was killed in a tort-caused accident she would probably recover in addition a similar sum in damages. Life insurance is also ignored in a Fatal Accident Act case, even if it has been bought by the employer, and the man was killed in an industrial accident.

The principal beneficiaries of double compensation are those who are entitled to industrial injury benefits, because of all the victims of accident and disease, these are treated most generously by both the tort system and by the social security system; though other accident victims may do better in other ways, e.g. in receiving full wages or salary while away injured, in addition to sickness benefits and tort damages, and possibly personal insurance. When Beveridge was drawing up his proposals, and even when the Monckton Committee was deliberating, actions for damages in industrial cases were not very common,[66] and it is clear that even the Monckton Committee thought they would not be of great importance. Nobody foresaw at that date the extent to which such actions would increase.[67] In a period of continuous inflation, and generally rather strained industrial relations, employers have preferred not to make an issue of this but simply to pass the cost of rising employers' liability premiums onto the public.

Apart from social security benefits, we saw in Chapter 17 there are many other welfare benefits of which injured persons might be able to take the benefit. None of these are taken account of directly by the tort system so that, for instance, a disabled person may recover the cost of adapting his house to suit his disabled conditions, both as an item of tort damages and in the form of a grant from his local authority. Of course, if the local authority knew that some part of the damages was given for this item they might refuse a grant, but the chances are that even the victim himself will not understand precisely how the damages are made up; still less is it probable that the local authority would come to know of it. Similarly, a person disabled in an accident might attend a government training or rehabilitation centre and receive an allowance while so doing. This is not deductible from damages, though it takes the place of social security benefits which are partially deductible.

The Pearson Commission recommended fundamental changes in the law here.[68] One of their principal recommendations was that there should be 'full co-ordination' of tort and social security, and that the value of social security benefits should be deductible in full from damage awards; each type of benefit (income-loss, loss of faculty, or out-of-pocket expenses) would be offset in full against the corresponding item in the award of damages. There is no doubt that if this were implemented it would make a significant difference to the law, as well as the practice: for instance, many minor claims would scarcely be worth pursuing if social security benefits were deductible in full.

We have also seen how (following the recommendations of the Monckton Committee, though, it seems, contrary to Beveridge's own inclinations)[69] the National Health Service is ignored in assessment of tort damages, so that a person may have private medical treatment and charge this to the tortfeasor (and hence the insurance industry and the premium payers). If he is a member of an organization which covers the cost of private medical treatment, this too will be ignored in the assessment of tort damages, so that he will have private treatment and may recover the cost of this twice over.[70] Here too, the Pearson Commission recommended major change. The costs of private medical treatment would only be recoverable, under their proposals, if it was *medically* reasonable to incur them.[71] If an injured person saves living expenses by being maintained at public expense in a public institution the value of these savings will now be deducted from damages for loss of earnings (if any).[72] This may encourage the use of private hospital facilities.

5 CRIMINAL INJURIES AND OTHER COMPENSATION

When the Criminal Injuries Board was set up, the government was clearly determined to avoid duplicating compensation, and the scheme therefore explicitly required the Board to deduct the value of compensation obtainable from public funds from any award.[73] Thus, the value of social security benefits is deducted in full. Moreover, recipients of awards are required to undertake to repay any award if they subsequently recover any tort damages from the person responsible for their injuries, so that there is no chance of duplication between tort damages and criminal injuries compensation.[74] But, like the tort system, the scheme did not require the Board to deduct the value of private pensions, and this caused something of a public furore in the case of the widow of one of the three London policemen who were shot and killed in 1966. When the widow applied to the board for compensation it was found that the value of her social security benefits, together with her pension under the Police Regulations (which was also payable from public funds, and so deductible), actually exceeded the amount she could have recovered as common law damages; and accordingly no award was made to her at all. This case caused a public outcry, and the point was made that if the widow had been paid a private pension and not a police pension, she would have received compensation in full from both sources.

This case led to some very anomalous amendments to the scheme, but, after further amendments, the scheme now provides that all pensions are deductible.[75] If the pension is not taxable, its whole value is deducted; if it is taxable, half its value is deducted. This latter rule is rather generous, but may to some extent compensate for the fact that the pension may have been contributory.

19
An appraisal of the fault principle

1 THE DOMINANCE OF THE FAULT PRINCIPLE

The concept of fault dominates existing compensation systems. Although it has virtually no place in personal insurance, or in the social security system, it underlies almost the entire law of torts. And for many years the principal developments which have taken place in compensation systems – outside the social security sphere – have all been directed towards extending entitlement to compensation as a result of fault, and towards trying to ensure that people so entitled do in fact receive their compensation. These developments have included the system of compulsory third party insurance for road traffic victims (including, more recently, passengers) and of compulsory insurance by employers for liability to their employees; the Law Reform Act of 1934 allowing actions to be brought against the estate of a deceased negligent person; the creation of the Motor Insurers' Bureau which was designed to fill the gap in the compulsory insurance system caused by those who failed to insure in accordance with the legal requirements; the MIB also later accepted liability in some hit-and-run cases and in cases where the party at fault was insured but the insurer became insolvent.

There has also been other legislation extending throughout the torts field, such as the Contributory Negligence Act of 1945 which allowed a negligent victim to recover some damages despite his negligence; the Personal Injuries Act of 1948 which abolished the doctrine of common employment and enabled a servant to sue his employer where he suffered injury as the result of the fault of a fellow-servant; and the Occupiers' Liability Acts of 1957 and 1984 which, among other things, simplified the law making the occupier of premises liable for fault. The House of Lords decision in *Read* v. *Lyons*[1] gave the severest setback for a century to attempts to extend the circumstances in which liability *without* fault would be imposed by the law of torts.

Outside the law of torts there have been similar developments, the most notable of which was the creation of the criminal injuries compensation scheme, where again, entitlement to compensation depends on proof that someone was at 'fault' – in the sense that he committed a criminal act against the claimant.

Plainly, then, the idea of fault as a criterion of compensation has had a powerful influence on the minds of people generally and of lawyers in particular. In the early years of this century, writers on the law of torts such as Sir John Salmond, whose works were to have much influence with later generations of judges, strove to reduce the whole law of torts to a set of moral principles, around the concept of fault. That liability should be based on fault and on nothing but fault was a shibboleth which acquired a tremendous influence, and its effect can still be seen in the opinions of the judges in *Read* v. *Lyons* in 1947, and even in the first *Wagon Mound* decision in 1961[2] In the United States the idea that liability should be based on fault and fault alone came to have such a status that in 1913 the New York Court of Appeals declared a Workmen's Compensation Act to be unconstitutional, because it required an employer to make compensation to workmen injured without any fault on his part.

Even today, it probably remains true that many people, including quite possibly a majority of the legal profession, have become so attuned to the concept of fault as the principal criterion for determining entitlement to compensation, that they would be prepared to defend the principle. Even proposals for schemes of 'strict' liability (e.g. products liability) usually contain numerous concessions to the fault principle. But in modern conditions it leaves a great deal to be desired, as will be shown. It is first necessary to define more closely what we mean by the fault principle. Traditionally, the principle has had two aspects: it has generally been used as both a sufficient and a necessary test of liability to pay tort damages. That is to say, the principle asserts, first, that it is just that a person who causes loss or damage to another by his fault should be required to compensate that other; and second, that it is just that a person who causes loss or damage to another without fault should *not* be required to compensate that other.

But we must remember that the fault principle, as it operates in the common law, also requires us to take account of the fault of the plaintiff, or the fault of the person who causes himself loss or injury. We must then, expand the first proposition to cover this case, somewhat as follows: it is just that a person who causes loss or damage, *whether to himself or another*, should bear the burden of that loss or damage to the extent that it was caused by his fault. But the second proposition gives us more difficulty, because the whole essence of the fault system involves different treatment for the person who causes loss and for the victim of that loss. To treat fault as a necessary condition of legal liability – 'no liability without fault' – means that a person who causes loss without fault should not be required to pay for it. But it also and necessarily means that the person to whom the loss is caused will have to bear the burden himself.[3] We have therefore a different rule for plaintiff and defendant; the plaintiff, but not the defendant, must bear the burden of loss or injury caused without his fault. The rule used to be the same if both were at fault, but this is no longer so under the modern contributory negligence rule.

Our second proposition must, then, remain unqualified. So we end up with the fault principle standing for the two following propositions: first, that it is just that a person who causes loss or damage whether to himself or another, should bear the burden of that loss or damage, to the extent that it was caused by his fault, second, that it is just that a person who causes loss or damage to another without fault should not be required to compensate that other.

In assessing the soundness of these propositions it is necessary to appreciate that we are concerned here with corrective, and therefore relative, justice. We are starting with the hypothesis of loss or damage, and trying to decide who should bear that loss as between the victim and the person who caused the loss; or as between the victim and society; or as between the person who caused the loss and society. The fault principle concentrates on the first relationship: if the causer of the loss was at fault, the plaintiff is entitled to compensation, otherwise not. By concentrating on the immediate parties concerned, the fault principle creates what may be an agonizing dilemma: either the plaintiff must be left to bear the loss, although he was in no way to blame for what happened; or the loss must be placed on the defendant's shoulders, whatever the consequences may be for him. Treating the fault principle as a sufficient condition of liability is sometimes very hard on the defendant because, for instance, the fault principle pays no attention to the degree of the defendant's fault (unless the plaintiff was also at fault); nor in general does it pay any attention to the defendant's means; nor to the question whether the defendant's behaviour was morally culpable as well as legally 'negligent'. As between a plaintiff and a defendant, it is perhaps understandable that the fault principle should ignore considerations of this kind, notwithstanding the hardship to the defendant, if the only alternative is to leave the loss on the plaintiff.

But the fault principle also attempts to answer the question: 'When should we compensate a plaintiff?' by looking exclusively at the conduct of the defendant. It treats fault as a necessary ground for making a defendant pay, and therefore as a ground for compensating the plaintiff. But although fault may sometimes be a good reason for taking money away from a defendant, it is much less satisfactory as a condition of giving money to a plaintiff. From the plaintiff's point of view, the fact that the loss or damage was due to the fault of another is immaterial. Treating fault as a necessary condition of liability, therefore, makes the fault principle sometimes appear very hard on a plaintiff: it involves denial of redress to the person suffering loss or damage merely because it has not been caused by the fault of another; this remains the case however meritorious the plaintiff's own behaviour may have been; and whatever risks (if 'reasonable') were taken at his expense. Here again by concentrating on the relationship between plaintiff and defendant it is understandable that the fault principle should often leave a meritorious plaintiff without compensation – if the only alternative is to burden an equally innocent defendant with the loss.

In both types of case, the fault principle only produces results which can be regarded as 'just' if attention is focused exclusively on the relationship between plaintiff and defendant, and no attention is paid to the possibility of the loss being borne by society itself, or some large section of society; and even as between the parties themselves, the justice of the fault principle is sometimes open to question. The remainder of this chapter takes the form of an indictment of the fault principle which attempts to enlarge on these points. The first three counts are largely concerned with cases in which great hardship can be caused to a defendant by the fault principle, and which suggest that fault as a sufficient condition of liability leaves much to be desired; the second three counts are concerned mainly with cases in which it appears particularly hard not to recompense a plaintiff for loss or damage, and are therefore an attack on fault as a necessary condition for compensating a plaintiff.

2 AN INDICTMENT OF THE FAULT PRINCIPLE

Count 1: the compensation payable bears no relation to the degree of fault

Fault is like a magic talisman; once it is established, all shall be given to the injured party. It is generally immaterial whether the fault was gross and the consequences trivial, or whether the fault trivial and the consequences catastrophic. Some degree of fault on the part of someone justifies full compensation to the plaintiff provided he was not at all to blame himself. Yet we know very well that the consequences of a negligent action are often out of all proportion to the fault which gave rise to it. A piece of momentary thoughtlessness on the road may cost someone his life, with incalculable loss to his wife and children. But similar acts of thoughtlessness may be committed by scores of others every day with no such disastrous consequences. It has been estimated that for every accident on the roads there are 122 near misses,[4] and an American study found in a test under normal driving situations in Washington, D.C., that even 'good' drivers committed an average of nine driving errors of four different types in every five minutes.[5] Yet in this country, only some 4% of drivers are involved in a personal injury accident in any one year, so that the average car driver may expect to be involved in such an accident only once in twenty-five years.[6] Thus, it seems that whether an act of negligence ends up in the accident statistics or as a near miss is almost pure chance: it has little correlation with the defendant's culpability. It is true that there is some evidence for asserting that in road accident cases there is a slight correlation between accident involvement and driving ability. Road Research Laboratory Reports have found for instance, that there were significant differences between the driving ability of two groups of fifty drivers, the members of one group all having been convicted of careless or dangerous driving.[7] Consequently, it is going too far to say that accident involvement is entirely a question of bad luck; careless drivers are more likely to have accidents than careful drivers. Moreover, it may well be that many road accidents, and perhaps the more serious accidents, are the result of obviously serious and undeniably culpable acts of carelessness such as driving while intoxicated or speeding. Nevertheless, it is a matter of everyday observation and experience that the most shocking pieces of carelessness are constantly committed with no ill-consequences to anyone.

Even as between the plaintiff and the defendant, doubts are often felt about the justice of imposing liability on a defendant for the most catastrophic consequences of a negligent act; we have already seen how various attempts have been made to limit the defendant's liability in extreme cases by invoking causal or risk principles, or simply by denying liability for unforeseeable consequences. On the other hand, if justice between plaintiff and defendant demands that liability be imposed on defendants however extreme the consequences, and however trifling the negligence, then it may be felt unjust that the defendant be left to bear this bill, as between himself and society. Since he may be no more culpable than many others, since he may only have done what others are constantly doing, it seems inequitable that he alone should be required to bear this burden while others go free.

Count 2: the compensation payable bears no relation to the means of the defendant

If it were seriously contended that the fault principle required the party at fault to pay compensation for the damage he has caused, it could be objected that any such requirement which took no account of the means of the party at fault might be very unjust. No criminal court would think of imposing a fine for culpable conduct of the amounts which civil courts award as damages every day, without serious enquiry into the ability of the defendant to pay. The fact that the civil courts do so is justified by saying that the 'purpose' of the civil law is to compensate and not to punish. But the 'purpose' of the law is irrelevant to the defendant if he is made to pay the damages. What matters to him is the effect of the law, not its 'purpose'. So far as the defendant is concerned, the deprivation of money which is imposed on him by order of the court is precisely as painful and punitive, whether the 'purpose' of the judge was to punish the defendant or to compensate the plaintiff, or even to earn a bribe.[8]

Let us for a moment remind ourselves of what would actually happen if the party at fault were actually required personally to pay compensation for the damage he has inflicted. Where the damages were of any appreciable amount, say over £500, any attempt to require the party at fault personally to pay the damages would in most cases impose on him a most crippling burden. In many cases the damages could only be extracted by turning the defendant and his family out of their home – since in many cases the house is the only asset of any realizable value which a person has. And in many cases such a requirement would also involve imposing an obligation to make payments over a prolonged period of time. When we recollect that all this may be done as a result of some venial act of negligence, the justice of the course is surely open to question.

No doubt if there is no other way in which the plaintiff can be compensated, and if the plaintiff is reduced to penury, we may feel impelled to force the defendant to pay the compensation; though even as between plaintiff and defendant it is by no means obvious that justice demands that we ignore the defendant's capacity to pay.[9] But if the plaintiff can be compensated by other means, it is often recognized that it would in fact be unjust to compel the negligent party to pay for the damage that he has caused, out of his own pocket. It is also sometimes recognized that to make a tortfeasor actually pay damages would be to punish his family as much as himself, and that justice does not necessarily demand that, as between the tortfeasor's family and the injured person the latter should be given a prior claim.[10]

Count 3: the fault principle is not a moral principle because a defendant may be negligent without being morally culpable and vice versa

If the fault principle has any justification at all, it must be that it rests on some ultimate moral principle which would be generally acceptable in society today. It certainly can claim no support on more practical grounds, such as convenience, efficiency, speed or cheapness of operation. What, then, is this moral principle on which it must rest? It can only be that, as between two parties, one of whom is morally innocent, and one of whom is morally guilty, that party who is morally guilty should pay for any damage or loss for which he is responsible. Now we have already seen that the law evidently does not take this moral principle seriously, for if it did, it would presumably prohibit liability insurance, vicarious liability and other loss distribution devices whereby the burden is shifted from the party actually at fault. We must now observe that the law's concept of fault is itself not easy to rest entirely on a moral basis. This is partly because the law takes an objective view of fault and ignores the personal qualities of the persons involved, and partly because the law's concept of negligence does not require that the defendant should have had any consciousness of moral wrongdoing, or even of the risk he was creating or the dangerousness of his conduct.

The objective definition of fault

Negligence, as we have seen, is defined as the failure to take reasonable care; the care which the reasonable man would have taken to avoid risks, which the reasonable man would have foreseen. It does not matter that the defendant is not a 'reasonable man' but is clumsy or stupid or forgetful or has bad judgment. It does not matter that he is inexperienced or young or old or (probably) even that he is handicapped or disabled. It does not generally matter that the defendant could not personally have foreseen the risk, or avoided the accident.

In most such cases, nobody doubts that the law takes a sensible course in holding the plaintiff entitled to compensation, even though the party at fault was not morally to blame by a subjective standard. Even the most convinced moralists, those who have wholeheartedly supported the principle of no liability without fault, have also subscribed wholeheartedly to the objective definition of fault. The objective standard was developed during the very period in which the fault principle came to hold such complete sway over the law. And the reason usually given for this approach is that the injury to the plaintiff is the same whether the defendant could or could not personally have avoided the accident. So, for instance, Mr Justice Holmes declared, in a celebrated passage:

If, for instance, a man is born hasty and awkward, is always having accidents and hurting himself or his neighbours, no doubt his congenital defects will be allowed for in the courts of Heaven, but his slips are no less troublesome to his neighbours than if they sprang from guilty neglect. His neighbours accordingly require him, at his proper peril, to come up to their standard, and the courts which they establish decline to take his personal equation into account.[11]

It is strange that judges and lawyers could reason thus far without perceiving that the damage or injury to the plaintiff is the same whether or not there has been fault at all, even as objectively defined by the law. If the only reason for adopting an objective standard of fault is that when damage is done the plaintiff has been hurt and deserves to be compensated whether or not there has been subjective fault, it is hard to see why it does not also follow that a plaintiff should be compensated whether or not there is fault at all, in any sense of the word.

It is possible that lawyers have been partly, if unconsciously, influenced in their approach to this problem by the ambiguities in the word 'reasonable'. We do not have much sympathy with a man who is, by definition, not a reasonable man. Similarly, it sounds perfectly just and moral to say that people must behave 'reasonably' and if they fail to do so they must compensate those injured by the failure. But all this is just to play about with the word 'reasonable' and its many meanings. If we take a concrete case in which the issue is squarely faced, we may have more sympathy with the defendant.

Suppose, for instance, we are faced with a situation in which an inexperienced (though legally qualified) driver has caused an accident as a result of failing to appreciate something which a more experienced driver would have appreciated, for example, he has misjudged the speed of an approaching vehicle. We know, because it has been statistically demonstrated, that inexperienced drivers do have more accidents than experienced drivers:[12] it has, for example, been estimated that motor cyclists have twice as many accidents in their first six months as drivers than in their second six months.[13] Now here we would probably be much more hesitant about saying that the driver's conduct was 'unreasonable'. No doubt we might still say that in a sense, he 'could have helped it' and need not have placed himself in a position in which the misjudgment was capable of causing an accident, and that in that sense he was morally to blame. But still, drivers must learn to drive somewhere, and they must acquire experience of driving on the roads amidst traffic, and to expect them to display the same skill and judgment as experienced drivers is to expect them to do something which we know from the evidence they are not capable of doing as a class, though individuals may be capable of doing it.

If we take a still more extreme case where we would not think of classing the defendant's conduct as 'unreasonable', for example, where an accident has occurred because the defendant was physically handicapped or disabled, even the law begins to have doubts. Suppose a one-eyed driver is involved in an accident which a two-eyed driver could have avoided by use of reasonable care, but which the one-eyed driver was unable to avoid (e.g. because he did not observe the danger until it was too late), it is uncertain whether the defendant's conduct would be stigmatized as negligent. And the law is even more doubtful where extreme youth is concerned. Is a child of 15 or 10 years of age bound to display the same degree of care as an adult?[14] In the case of children the problem rarely arises, because young children are not often sued for negligence, though there can surely be no doubt that a 17-year-old motor cyclist would be allowed no indulgence on account of his youth, any more than on account of his inexperience.

Cases of this kind raise an acute problem for the law as it operates at present. If we think of the law as designed to regulate the conduct of people to whom it is addressed, it seems unreasonable to treat as negligence something which a person could not avoid because of his physical condition. On the other hand, if we think that the main purpose of the law is to compensate injured persons it seems less reasonable to demand moral fault as a precondition of liability. It is plain, then, that the law is constantly being faced with a dilemma here. The more 'moral' the fault principle becomes, the more refined and subjective it is made, the more often will the compensation objective of the law be defeated. Equally, the more often the compensation purpose of the law is treated as paramount, the more 'objective' and crude will the moral principle applied by the law become.

This uncertainty about the aims of the law has led in practice to the drawing of an extraordinary distinction between physical and mental incapacity. A man who is seized with a sudden incapacitating physical illness while driving a car cannot be expected to drive as though he was in perfect health, and is therefore not negligent,[15] so his victims will go uncompensated. But the driver who is struck by sudden paralysing insanity is merely mentally incapacitated, and so may be treated as negligent:[16] his victims, therefore, get compensation.

It must not be thought, however, that in practice these problems give rise to frequent difficulty in the courts. Only in a case of really gross abnormality would a court be likely to consider the question at all, e.g. where the defendant is actually physically disabled, or where he is suddenly taken ill while driving a vehicle. In most cases, the courts do not stop to consider whether the particular defendant *could* have avoided the accident, but merely whether he *ought* to have avoided it. Nevertheless, this discussion casts further doubt on the fault principle's claim to be a moral principle. Conduct which the law condemns as negligence is often not conduct which would be regarded as morally blameworthy.

Negligence and error[17]

The fault principle recognizes the distinction between negligence and error, or mistake. Not every mistake constitutes fault, because even reasonable men can make mistakes. But in practice it is often found that the line between negligence and mistake gets blurred and may even disappear altogether in common situations. It is true that there are some particular cases where the courts are insistent that not every mistake is to be treated as negligence, for instance, when they are dealing with allegations of medical negligence. And it may also be true that, when they are dealing with questions of contributory negligence, the courts are apt to insist that not every mistake should be treated as grounds for reducing the plaintiff's damages. But in other cases courts often appear to assume that the reasonable man never makes a mistake. On the road, for instance, almost any driving error is apt to be treated as negligence without argument, even though it is well known (as we have seen) that virtually all drivers commit driving errors every few minutes. And in other situations it often happens that acts of casual or momentary carelessness can be treated as negligence, even though most of us regularly commit such acts without thinking ourselves to be guilty of moral fault.

Collective liability

So far we have been looking at the morality of the fault principle in cases in which it is possible to identify the parties responsible for what has happened with relative ease. But there is another type of case, where responsibility is sought to be imposed on large groups of people in the form of companies, local authorities, government departments and the like, in which, if anything, the moral content of the fault principle becomes even more attenuated. Suppose it is sought to impose liability on some corporation for a failure to appreciate and guard against a danger which ought to have been guarded against. As often as not, the complaint is that there has been some failure of organization, some failure in the system, which has led to there being no person charged with the responsibility of foreseeing and preventing the accident which has occurred. Now, failures of organization and system may be due to negligence on the part of those whose business it is to organize and plan the system, but the idea of personal moral responsibility often seems out of place in such cases. Consider a case like *Carmarthenshire County Council* v. *Lewis*.[18] In this case, a little child wandered out of a nursery school maintained by the defendants, down a lane, through a gate and on to a busy road, where a lorry driver, trying to avoid the child, crashed into a tree and was killed. The Court of Appeal held that the child's teacher was negligent for failing to keep sufficient observation on him, but the House of Lords exonerated the teacher from the charge of negligence, while still holding the defendants liable. 'They' (that is, the County Council) were negligent. 'They' should not have allowed an unlocked gate at the end of a lane near a nursery school bordering a busy road. But who actually was 'at fault'? Was it every councillor who ought to have proposed a resolution at a meeting of the council for the appointment of someone whose duty it was to prevent such accidents? Or the town clerk? Or the head-teacher of the school? Possibly some attempt could have been made to answer these questions in this case, but this would not always be a useful or meaningful exercise in cases of this kind.

Perhaps an even more remarkable example of this sort of 'negligence without individual fault' is provided by the Report of the Public Inquiry into the disaster at the Hixon railway crossing in 1968.[19] This inquiry revealed that the new automatic half-barrier crossings being installed at many level crossings (in place of the old manual crossings) gave a bare twenty-four seconds warning of the approach of a train which might be travelling at 80 mph; and it also discovered that certain very large slow-moving vehicles carrying special loads for which Ministry of Transport approval was necessary, would take longer than twenty-four seconds to cross. But the remarkable thing was that not one person either in British Railways, or in the Ministry of Transport had connected these two facts so as to appreciate the very real danger arising from them. This was not a question of ignorance, stupidity, or mental incapacity. Here were a number of highly responsible officials, intelligent and experienced men who did not foresee a danger which, in hindsight, seems to stare one in the face. The Under-Secretary of the Ministry of Transport explained this failure at the Inquiry as a failure of imagination:

'I think,' he said, 'the two pieces of knowledge, the knowledge of the half-barrier working, and the knowledge of the exceptional loads, had to come together in one person's mind and he would have to see the connection between them. That is what could have happened really anywhere in the Ministry, or indeed in quite a lot of other places. But that linking, and that, as it were, flash of the imagination, did not happen.'[20]

Any lawyer considering the evidence contained in this report would probably have said that the railway authorities and the Ministry were guilty of negligence as the law understands that term, yet Mr E. B. Gibbens Q.C., who conducted the inquiry, obviously felt very reluctant to condemn anyone as having been guilty of culpable or blameworthy conduct for failing to appreciate this danger. He stated in his report, that he felt it was odious 'to criticize anyone unfavourably for having failed to foresee a danger when many intelligent minds and experienced and talented people have conscientiously considered the same problem before the danger manifested itself, yet failed to appreciate it.'[21] In the result, Mr Gibbens decided to adopt a subjective test of negligence 'lest able men of integrity be unfairly blamed for incompetence.'[22]

It seems significant that when the issue is whether an injured plaintiff is to be compensated, as it would be in an action of negligence, a judge would not hesitate to make a finding of negligence in such circumstances, but when questions of compensation are not in issue, as they were not in this inquiry, there are hesitations about condemning 'able men of integrity' for negligence.[23]

Moral culpability without negligence

So far we have been discussing cases of negligence which may not involve any moral culpability. The converse is less likely, but there is one striking sort of case which (as we have already seen) does raise the possibility, namely where the defendant has been guilty of an omission. We have previously discussed this question, and it remains only to notice here that this is one further difficulty in the way of equating negligence with moral culpability.[24]

The fault principle and popular morality

In all these ways, then, there is a gap between notions of legal responsibility and of moral responsibility. But there is reason to question the idea that even in general terms the fault principle is based on popular morality. Recent research[25] suggests that personal injury victims do not always think that being responsible for an accident entails moral culpability or that either of these things entails an obligation to pay compensation; nor, conversely, that absence of moral responsibility entails an absence of obligation to pay damages. It seems that whether an injured person thinks that someone else should pay depends much more on what he knows of what the law says about when compensation is payable than on independent ideas of morality and fault. So, for example, in the industrial context where employers have for a long time been subject to liability in certain circumstances regardless of fault, injured workers are quite likely to think that their employer ought to pay without basing that judgment on an attribution of fault.

In relation to accidents in the home, it seems that injured persons are very unlikely to attribute fault and even less likely to think that they ought to be compensated. It is arguable that this has little to do with morality and more to do with a desire not to disrupt harmonious domestic relations by the aggressive act of litigating; and perhaps with a realization that since the party responsible will rarely be insured litigation would be pointless. In brief, it may well be that for many victims of personal injury, thinking that someone is responsible for injuries is neither a sufficient nor a necessary condition for thinking that that person ought to pay compensation for the injuries.

It does not follow from this that the fault principle is not defensible as a principle, but only that it may not be defensible on the ground that it is based on popular conceptions of who ought to pay.

Count 4: the fault principle pays insufficient attention to the conduct or needs of the plaintiff

The fourth count of the indictment against the fault principle, is based on the fact that the law pays insufficient attention to the conduct of the plaintiff. If no defendant can be found who was to some extent at fault for the plaintiff's injury or loss, the plaintiff will not be compensated under the fault principle. In this event, it is immaterial whether the plaintiff injured himself in a drunken stupor; was driving his car with a slight degree of negligence; was indulging in some perfectly ordinary activity with all due care; or was engaged in a heroic attempt at rescuing someone in great peril, at risk to his own life. Let it not be thought that in practice it is always immaterial how a plaintiff was behaving. Judges are human and are not uninfluenced by the 'merits' of a case. Where, for instance, a person has been killed in a heroic attempt to rescue another, judges will strain every nerve to find someone at fault if they possibly can — which is what happened, for instance, in *Videan* v. *British Transport Commission*,[26] in which a stationmaster sacrificed his own life in a heroic (and successful) attempt to save the life of his young child. Conversely, a person injured as a result of a piece of utter folly on his own part would find a judge somewhat unreceptive if he tried to convince him that another person was partly responsible for his injuries — which is just what happened, for instance in *I.C.I. Ltd* v. *Shatwell*,[27] in which a coal miner blew himself up by testing a shot without taking shelter, and tried to pin part of the blame on his colleague. But it is to be noticed that, when courts take account of the plaintiff's conduct in this way, they do so in spite of the fault principle and not because of it.

The law's refusal to compensate (let alone reward) heroic rescuers, except where the fortuitous fact of negligence on another's part can be proved, runs counter to the accepted moral feelings of the public at large. The public's tendency to respond to charitable appeals in cases of loss and injury arising from disasters and accidents of various kinds, is often most marked where the victims of the disaster have themselves behaved with special heroism. The case of the Penlea lifeboat disaster in 1982 provides a noteworthy example. Popular morality is concerned with the merits of the victim's conduct as well as with the question of whether the injuries were caused by anyone's fault.

Although the courts pay no attention to the fact that the plaintiff may have been doing something specially meritorious, they do, through the doctrine of contributory negligence, pay some attention to fault on the part of the plaintiff. And this presumably rests on some moral notion similar to that which underlies the requirement that a man at fault pay compensation. But we have seen before how the treatment of contributory negligence as a relative doctrine requires the courts to compare the plaintiff's degree of fault with the defendant's; and how this leads to results which, however justifiable as between plaintiff and defendant, appear indefensible in a wider context. To give no compensation to a wholly innocent plaintiff because he was injured without fault on the part of a defendant, while giving part compensation to another plaintiff who may have been 80% to blame for his own injuries because someone else was partly to blame, though justifiable in terms of the fault principle, seems quite inequitable when it is remembered that in most cases of fault it is not the defendant who will pay but an insurer and, ultimately, the public at large. Why should fault on the part of the defendant be a precondition of an award of compensation when it is not the defendant who will pay the compensation?

It would, in theory, be possible to construct a compensation system based on the fault of the plaintiff alone, if that were felt to be desirable. A claim against a government compensation fund could be admitted wherever a person was injured without fault on his part, even if no defendant at fault could be found; and reduced compensation could be given to a plaintiff who was partly to blame, if that were felt to be just. This would also be a 'fault' system, and perhaps a more moral system (though it would be open to the same objections as the present doctrine of contributory negligence).[28] But it is not the fault system we have now.

In addition to paying too little attention to the plaintiff's conduct, the fault principle largely ignores the plaintiff's needs – just as it ignores the defendant's capacity to pay. Here again, this may be just as between plaintiff and defendant, although even this is open to doubt in some cases. For example, it is by no means obvious that justice requires a working man to pay an annuity to a young childless widow whose husband he has killed (say) by negligent driving.[29] But even if this is thought to be just, the position may once again change where it is not the defendant personally who is to pay the damages. As between the widow and the public, it seems difficult to say that justice requires compensation for the death of the husband without considering the widow's needs.

Count 5: justice may require payment of compensation without fault[30]

Neither in law nor in morality is fault the *only* ground on which a person may be required to compensate another, although in the sphere with which we are mainly dealing the law at least generally recognizes no other. But there are other branches of the law in which the liability to make compensation does not depend on fault, for example the law of property and the law of restitution. It is a commonplace of property law that the owner of property is generally entitled to recover it, or compensation in lieu, even from a bona fide purchaser for value. A man who in all good faith buys a car from a thief will have to give up the car or compensate the owner. Similarly, in the law of restitution, for example where a person has been overpaid by mistake, he will be required to restore the money he has received. No question of fault arises in this sort of case; we do not necessarily condemn as culpable or blameworthy what the defendant has done. But we require him to make compensation on other grounds. The main such ground is that if the compensation were not paid, the defendant would be unjustifiably enriched at the expense of the plaintiff. The defendant would have gained and the plaintiff been deprived, without justification. This sort of argument for no-fault liability may at first sight appear to have little place in the field of accidental damage to person or property, because in such circumstances there is rarely any 'gain' in an obvious or tangible sense to the defendant. But this depends on what we mean by 'gain'. Let us look for a moment at a leading American case in the law of torts, *Vincent* v. *Lake Erie Transportation Co.*,[31] which illustrates in dramatic form the struggle between the no-liability-without-fault concept and other moral grounds for requiring compensation to be paid.

In this case the plaintiffs were the owners of a dock in which the defendant shipowner's vessel was anchored. A storm was threatening and both parties were anxious for the safety of their property, the plaintiffs for their dock and the defendant for his ship. The defendant was requested to remove his ship, but he declined to do so as he feared that damage would be done to it in the storm. The result was that the vessel remained at anchor, and in the ensuing storm the vessel was repeatedly hurled against the dock and the dock was damaged. The question was whether the plaintiffs were entitled to compensation for the damage. In technical legal concepts, the defendant had committed a 'trespass' to the dock, and the question was whether it was a defence to an action for trespass that the defendant had acted out of 'unavoidable necessity', here the 'necessity' arising from the need to save property. The court conceded that perhaps the defendant would not be considered morally culpable, or blameworthy. A man whose property is in jeopardy may not be thought of as acting wrongly if he tries to save it, even at the expense of creating a risk of loss to someone else. Naturally, the case would have been even stronger if the defendant had been actuated by a desire to save lives. For instance, it is plain that a shipowner who discharges oil into the sea is not regarded as 'negligent' if this is done in order to lighten the vessel and save the lives of those on board, provided that this is not itself the result of a danger created by negligence.[32] But in *Vincent* v. *Lake Erie* the court did not rest content with exonerating the defendant from moral blame. It was not, said the judges, just a question of whether the defendant had acted wrongly. If a person chooses to save his own property at the expense of risk to someone else's property, we might not regard the defendant's conduct as blameworthy, but we might nevertheless think he ought to pay for the privilege he has enjoyed. Even if life is at stake, and the need to save life is regarded as an overriding value justifying the infliction of all sorts of damage on others, would fairness not require compensation to be paid?

The idea that compensation ought to be paid even though the person paying it is not morally culpable is well established in public law contexts. If a government authority compulsorily acquires private land in order to build a road or a school few would regard this as in any way morally reprehensible (assuming, as we can for the sake of the argument, that the power to acquire has been exercised wisely and reasonably), but most people would think it only fair that the deprived landowner should be paid compensation for his loss. The payment of such compensation is usually provided for by statute. The common law recognized an obligation on the Crown to pay compensation to the owners of property destroyed in the course of battle[33] or in order to prevent it falling into enemy hands in wartime[34] completely regardless of whether the destruction of the property was wrongful or not. Again under the Land Compensation Act 1973 landowners whose land is injuriously affected, for example by noise or vibration caused by an airport or motorway built near their land, are entitled to compensation even if the disturbance is the result of perfectly lawful and publicly authorized works.

In the case of both compulsory seizure of property[35] and injurious affection[36] the older common law *did* concern itself with whether the taking or disturbance was wrongful or not, but the modern position is that since the public generally benefits from the taking or the project which causes the disturbance, it is only fair that those who suffer should be compensated out of public funds.

This idea that it can be fair to require compensation to be paid even in the absence of wrongful conduct plays very little part in private law. Even the principle of *Vincent* v. *Lake Erie* would probably not be followed in England; so that a person may lawfully inflict damage on his neighbour if this is necessary to save his own property – at least where the amount of damage done is not disproportionate to what has been saved.[37] Much more importantly for our purposes, the whole law of negligence rests on the idea that compensation need only be paid when someone has done something wrong. Admittedly, in a negligence action we cannot usually say that the defendant has been unjustly enriched at the expense of the plaintiff. But we can say, as in *Vincent* v. *Lake Erie*, that the defendant has 'gained' or furthered his own ends by taking a risk at the expense of the plaintiff. This can be illustrated by two examples.

In *Bolton* v. *Stone*,[38] the cricket club case to which we have referred several times before, the House of Lords held that the club had not acted unreasonably in not building a higher fence around their ground because the risk of a ball escaping was very remote. Thus the club benefited by not having to spend money on a higher fence, but at the cost of a risk of injury to the plaintiff and others. In such circumstances one might think that it would be fair for the club to pay compensation to the plaintiff even though their actions were not negligent. Or take the case of the installation by British Railways of automatic half-barrier level crossings which was the subject of investigation at the Public Inquiry into the Hixon crossing rail crash. The inquiry found that these half barriers were not as safe as the manned gates they replaced.[39] The reason for installing the new barriers despite this was that they save time and money. British Railways estimated that they would save £2 million a year by installing automatic barriers at all level crossings; and such barriers are much quicker in their operation than the old ones, thus reducing delays to people using the crossings. So, the installation of the barriers benefited certain people but created risks of injury for others. If the benefits are thought to outweigh the disadvantages, it seems only fair that those who benefit should compensate those who are injured, regardless of whether installation of the barriers was in some sense negligent or blameworthy.

The point becomes even clearer when the impact of insurance is taken into account. In a situation such as that in *Bolton* v. *Stone*, for example, the law would not *require* the club to build a fence even if it were held liable for escaping balls. It would be open to the club simply to insure against the risk of liability and, except in cases where the risk of balls escaping was quite high, this course would usually be cheaper than building a new fence.[40] But once the issue is reduced to terms of who should insure against a particular risk it seems clear that it might be fair for a person to do so even if he is not at fault in creating the risk.

Count 6: fault is an unsatisfactory criterion for liability because of the difficulties caused in adjudicating on it

The sixth count against the fault principle is based largely, if not entirely, on the practical difficulties to which adjudication on fault gives rise. There are, perhaps, two distinguishable aspects of this problem. The first, which has been the source of most of the discussion and controversy, concentrates on the practical problems of proof. The second, which we touch on later, concerns the difficulties involved in concentrating too much on one specific case to the exclusion of statistical and other evidence about accidents of the kind in question.

So far as the first question is concerned, the argument against the fault principle runs something like this. In many accidents these days – and particularly those with which we are mainly concerned, that is road and factory accidents – the events which cause the injury occur in a very brief period of time, often a matter of a fraction of a second. Adjudication on the fault issue requires witnesses to be able to recall accurately what occurred in that fraction of a second, if we are to have any confidence that the findings of a court correspond with what actually happened. Similarly, if the case is settled by negotiation, the fault system requires the parties' advisers to be able to assess with reasonable confidence the likelihood that a court will find fault from the evidence of the witnesses. The inaccuracies in the observations even of eye witnesses have often been demonstrated by experiment, and may occur even in highly intelligent and experienced observers. To the inaccuracies of observation must be added the difficulties produced by long delays before cases are actually tried, in cases which go to trial. Even in cases which are settled, some of the statements of the witnesses, which will be relied on by the parties' advisers in assessing the likelihood of success of the action, may not be taken until many months or even years after the event.

If the witnesses are mistaken, or if the version of some witnesses conflicts with that of others, what chances are there of ever reaching a correct conclusion? Most practitioners are confident that in the overwhelming majority of the cases which come to trial the courts are able to arrive at the truth as between the contentions of the parties,[41] but others are much less confident. A former Lord Chief Justice has drawn attention to the 'limited and dangerous doctrine that you can always tell by a witness's demeanour whether he is telling the truth',[42] and one book estimates that the chances of the court finding the facts correctly may well be no more than 50%.[43] In those relatively rare cases in which one accident gives rise to more than one legal trial, it is by no means unknown for different judges to arrive at completely different conclusions as to the party to blame.[44]

It may be said that all this is an attack on legal procedure rather than on the fault system, and that however defective our procedure may be there is not much we can do about it since the defects stem from the fallibility of human beings, whether witnesses, barristers or judges. This is partly true, but it is not the whole truth. Obviously, the legal trial is a fallible piece of machinery for ascertaining the truth, but if the object of the exercise cannot be achieved in other ways then we must have legal trials, fallible though they may be. But this part of the argument against the fault system stems not so much from the inherent fallibility of the legal trial, but from doubts as to its suitability for the purposes for which it is being used. If it were indeed true that courts only arrived at a true view of the facts in 50% of personal injury cases because they could not correctly decide questions of fault, this would be a strong argument indeed for deciding that fault was an unsatisfactory criterion by which to determine if compensation should be given.

But whether or not the courts arrive at the correct conclusion in cases which actually arrive in court, the number of these cases is, as we have emphasized, quantitatively insignificant beside the great mass that get settled by negotiation. If courts make mistakes, how much more likely is it that insurance adjusters make mistakes? They frequently have only the witnesses' statements to go by, and one experienced Queen's Counsel has said that 'more often than not' the evidence a witness gives in court differs substantially from that in his statements, even before he has been cross-examined.[45] In addition to all this, we must never forget that in a not insubstantial number of cases the evidence is simply unavailable at all, and 'real' evidence (i.e. objects) may disappear.

Lawyers have for long been well aware of difficulties of this nature in the legal process, but it has recently been suggested that it is a mistake to over-emphasize the problems raised by the difficulty of proving fault in practice. At a conference in Illinois in 1967 on the problem of road accidents, the vice-president and general counsel of a leading insurance company challenged the idea that it is often very difficult to know how accidents have happened, or who was at fault.[46] He asserted that:

a large proportion of all automobile accidents are uncomplicated events in which the fault determination is very easy and that many of the more complex accidents can be accurately analysed by people trained to do such work on the basis of the physical facts even when the impressions of the witnesses are confused. The final position of the cars, the tyre marks, the location and extent of the damage, frequently established very clearly how the accident happened and who was at fault.[47]

He went on to say that a sample of 352 cases analysed for the purpose from the files of the company had produced the following result:

Policyholder clearly at fault	201 cases or 57·1% of all the sample
Claimant clearly at fault	125 cases or 35·5% of all the sample
Doubtful cases	26 cases or 7·4% of all the sample

Figures of this kind may be accepted, so far as they go. But they make no allowance for cases in which no claim was made at all,

An appraisal of the fault principle 433

because the injured party realized or was advised that a claim was hopeless in the absence of witnesses; nor do they preclude the possibility that the claims adjusters were simply mistaken in their views, even in cases which they thought were 'clear', because of the absence of relevant evidence which would have affected their decision. Moreover, they do not give any indication of the trouble and cost necessary to arrive at a decision on fault, even if the ultimate decision may be clear. Evidence, photographs, witnesses' statements, policy reports and so on, all have to be collected and examined by skilled personnel. The cost of all this is very great.

But we must now go on to the second aspect of this problem, which has not received so much attention in discussions of this nature. It may be true that if we concentrate exclusively on the behaviour of the principal parties involved in an accident, we can in a reasonable proportion of cases arrive at a workable conclusion on fault. But this exercise can often be misleading, because it omits to take account of factors which would not always, or indeed often, be thought to be responsible for accidents. Study of accident causes on a broader scale, such as is made by statisticians, rather than study of the causes of *this* accident, such as is made by lawyers, often throws an entirely different light on matters. The point is well put in the following extract from a volume on road safety published by the Stationery Office in 1963:

The statistician does not think so much of the individual accident and its causes, but of the probability of accidents and whatever may affect this probability. Now such things as the width of a street, its curvature or gradient, the quality of its surface, the flow of traffic and its speed, all influence the probability of an accident in a street. Such things, since they influence the probability of accidents and therefore the number of accidents, should appear in the statistical picture of factors important in accident causation. Add a foot to the width of a road and a certain number of accidents will in the long run be eliminated or provoked. When individual accidents are studied and 'causes' sought it is not, in general, these factors that will be cited. Then only the unusual or abnormal are usually noticed: not the width of the road but only whether it narrows suddenly, not the visibility allowed by the size and shape of the car's windows but only the obstruction caused by pennants or a dangling doll. Ignoring the normal gives rise to a tendency to ascribe most accidents to human factors such as error or carelessness, since it is usually possible to believe that there would have been no such accident if someone had acted differently.[48]

It may be objected that a lawyer cannot look at a problem in the same way as a statistician; that any attempt to do so would lead rapidly to a deterministic view that nobody is really to blame for anything that happens at all; that statistics show that such and such a number of accidents will occur in such and such ways, and that if one is involved in an accident one is not really to blame at all but is merely fulfilling one's predestined fate as a potential statistic. And that this conclusion, however hard it may be to refute from a logical and philosophical standpoint, is simply unacceptable to the lawyer for purely practical reasons. All this may be true, but it is possible without going to such extremes to assert that the statistician's facts and figures do often throw doubt on the meaningfulness of the lawyer's notions of fault and cause. The more that the significance in the cause of road accidents of factors other than driver behaviour is appreciated, the less does the notion of fault appear to make sense. Let us illustrate.

In recent years much research has been done on the skidding-proneness of various types of road surface, and it is now known that skidding accidents can be greatly reduced by altering the surface of the roads, in places which are particularly likely to cause such accidents.[49] For instance, a survey[50] was made of fifty-five skidding accident sites with an average length of a quarter of a mile, before and after the sites were treated with a non-skid surface. The results were as follows:

	Before	After
Total number of accidents at the 55 sites:	723	130
Average number of accidents per year per site:	6	1

Who, one wonders, was primarily to blame, or at fault, for those 723 accidents which occurred before the sites were treated?[51] And suppose that lack of funds had held up the treatment at other sites, and skidding accidents had continued to occur there, who would really be to blame for them? Or suppose that the local authority prefers to spend its income on building a new school, rather than treating the skid-prone sites, who would be to blame for the accidents that would inevitably occur? Or indeed, suppose that it is simply not appreciated that the road surface is contributing to the accidents so substantially, as in the case of the one and a half mile stretch of road which accounted for sixty-four skidding accidents in three and a half years, before it was noticed that something was wrong?[52] Consider also the case of the motorist who tries to reduce speed as he approaches a roundabout, skids and crashes into the bollard in the centre of the road. Who can doubt that if this case ever came into court the motorist would be found entirely responsible for causing the accident by his negligence? Yet this sort of accident is so common at some roundabouts that it is actually cheaper to treat the road with a non-skid surface than to replace the bollards every time they are damaged.[53] If this is not done, who is more at fault? The motorist or the highway authority?

Many other illustrations could be made of the point. A motorist crashes into the car in front of him while driving at night, although that car has its lights on. Who is to blame? Evidently the driver of the rear car. But suppose we discover that cars as old as the front vehicle are six times as likely as other cars to be involved in accidents of this kind, because their lights are less satisfactory: would we still so confidently say that the driver of the rear car was to blame? A motorist fails to see, or understand the meaning of a road signs, and an accident ensues. Who is to blame? Obviously the motorist. But is it still so obvious when we know that many motorists, even when under observation and consciously trying to be at their most attentive, still fail to observe some road signs?[54] Or when we know that only a small fraction of motorists know what some signs mean?[55]

Then there are still wider considerations which emerge from statistics. A child playing ball with another child in the street is run over and killed. Whose fault is it? Plainly the child's own fault. But when we know that children who come from poor homes and have nowhere to play are more likely to be involved in road accidents than other children, are we still so confident of our conclusion?[56] Do we not begin to think that the organization of society may have some responsibility in the matter?

All serious research into the causes of road accidents shows that accidents can generally be prevented more easily by improved road engineering and improved vehicle design, than by punishing or deterring bad drivers or exhorting them to drive more safely.[57] A pre-war estimate reckoned that some three-fifths of all road accidents could be prevented by the removal of ordinary road defects;[58] and there is no doubt from the figures both in this country and abroad that motorways have far lower accident figures than other roads. Yet ordinary road defects are still visible on all sides; and the motorway mileage is still quite small. If society chooses to spend its money on other things than improved roads, is the 'negligent' motorist, rather than society as a whole, really responsible for accidents? We also know that vehicle design contributes greatly to the damage caused by accidents. Here the motor manufacturer bears the primary responsibility, but society as a whole cannot escape all responsibility. The manufacturers tell us that vehicle design is responsive to public tastes, and if dangerous features in vehicles are still incorporated it is because the public likes them, or because the public will not pay for their elimination.[59]

The fact that in the road accident field the fault system has hitherto been directed almost exclusively at motorists does not mean that it may not in the future be used against motor manufacturers – and highway authorities as well. We have already seen how, in this country, actions alleging negligence in design as opposed to execution are very unusual, but in the United States they have become commonplace, and no doubt this development could spread to this country. Moreover, highway authorities may find themselves facing all sorts of new liabilities, especially since the Highways Act of 1961, which abolished their immunity from liability for nonfeasance.[60]

But all this makes little difference to the central point. Certainly, the fault system could be a lot less crude; certainly, we could start bringing negligent design within its scope; and in the result we might even succeed in shifting (at least in the first instance) quite a lot of the cost of road accidents to motor manufacturers and highway authorities. But the central point we have been making is that the fault principle leads us to seize on a number of limited and relatively obvious accident-causing factors, and to blame the party responsible for these as having been 'negligent'. This whole process looks a lot less rational when we move away from the particular accident in question and survey the whole field. From this new vantage point, many accident victims who go uncompensated because there does not appear to have been any individual negligent defendant, may be thought to have a good claim against society.

20
The distinction between human and natural causes[1]

Concentrating on the tort system naturally emphasizes the distinction between injuries, diseases and disabilities caused by fault and those not so caused, on which so much of the tort system hinges. But looking at compensation systems as a whole, the distinction between injuries, diseases and disabilities caused by human action and those caused by natural events is just as striking. A man loses a leg as a result of human action: he may receive damages, or a disability pension. But another man loses a leg through disease not caused by man, and he will receive no damages, though he may receive sickness benefit under the social security system. A baby is born blind because its mother had rubella during pregnancy: he will probably receive nothing in the way of damages, though he will have the benefit of the welfare state's provision for the blind, such as special educational facilities. But another young child loses an eye when a playmate throws a piece of glass at him, and compensation may be obtainable from the Criminal Injuries Compensation Board. Does anything underlie these distinctions? Are they entirely haphazard and irrational, or is there some explanation for them? The question is not merely of academic interest, for reform of the whole compensation process, which many think is bound to come eventually, is going to raise the question whether injuries caused by human acts and activities on the one hand, and by natural causes on the other, should be treated in the same way. So long as the personal responsibility of some individual (if nominal) defendant is insisted on as a condition of entitlement to compensation, it naturally follows that only injuries which are caused by man will (in general) be compensated. But when we get to the stage – as we already have with the industrial injuries system, and (in practice if not in theory) with the tort system – in which the compensation is paid by the public in one way or another, and not by any individual, the justification for distinguishing between man-caused and natural disability or disease becomes less obvious.

1 SOCIETY'S 'RESPONSIBILITY' FOR HUMAN CAUSES

One possible answer to this is to say that in some sense society is 'responsible' for man-caused injuries, diseases and disabilities in a way in which it is not 'responsible' for naturally caused conditions because the former are, while the latter are not, caused by people, or by the organization of society in certain ways. But this rationale does not explain why many diseases which are in some sense attributable to human activities, are still treated less favourably for compensation purposes than accidental injury. For instance, much bronchitis is caused by industrial smog, much cancer is caused by smoking, and countless diseases are spread by the fact that people are brought into contact with one another in public transport and work places, as a result of the way in which society organizes itself. Indeed, it is no longer true to say that society is not 'responsible' for congenital malformations. In the first place, badly deformed babies (e.g. those suffering from spina bifida) who would probably have died in infancy not long ago are now kept alive; it is surely wrong for society to do this without accepting the responsibility which that entails. But secondly, because babies with congenital malformations are now sometimes curable, they can survive to grow up and reproduce – thus passing on genetic malformations to a new generation, for which society is even more responsible.[2]

In any event, the question remains, in what sense is society 'responsible' for man-caused disabilities? This cannot mean that society is responsible for making good the consequences, i.e. is under any obligation to compensate for such injuries, for this would be to beg the very question at issue. Society may also regard itself as 'responsible' for those disabled by natural causes, in the sense that it regards itself as obliged to maintain them at a reasonable standard of living, but it would involve circular reasoning to justify different treatment of different classes by pointing out that society 'accepts responsibility' for them in varying degrees.

Another possible meaning to society's 'responsibility' for man-caused disabilities is that society is 'at fault' or 'to blame' for man-caused disabilities in a way in which it is not responsible for disability from natural causes. But this too is a difficult argument to sustain, since it involves constructing criteria by which the 'fault' of society can be determined, and when this is done, it is apt to be found that we have moved away from the concept of 'fault' which we apply to individuals, to some quite different concept. Thus, we might, for instance, take the view that society is 'responsible', in the sense of being 'at fault', with respect to most road accidents. A judgment of this nature uses quite different criteria from those involved in a legal finding of negligence in an individual case. The suggestion here is that society is somehow partly to blame for the whole state of affairs – that people in their capacities as judges, magistrates, legislators, jurymen, organs of public opinion, highway authorities, and so on, pay insufficient attention to the 'massacre on the roads'. But this suggestion depends on the view that when people, in these various capacities, take decisions which may have some bearing on the road accident situation, they place 'too high' a value on the advantages of motor traffic at a certain speed, etc. and 'too little' weight on the value of the lives and limbs which are being jeopardized. This is itself a value judgment which may not appear to be so wholly different from that involved in a legal finding of negligence. But there is in fact an important difference: a finding of negligence normally imports that the negligent party has paid too much attention to his *own* interests (to the value of the activity being pursued, the cost of precautions, etc). But society's decisions are in theory the decisions of a majority of people, and in a democratic society the majority are (it is usually assumed) entitled within certain limits, to pay greater attention to their own interests than to those of the minority. Thus, while it may be perfectly intelligible to criticize society's decisions (or governmental decisions, etc.) it is not easy to apply to these decisions the criteria of fault which we apply to an individual under the law today.

There would moreover be great difficulties in trying to construct criteria whereby society could be adjudged to be 'at fault' in permitting certain types of accident to take place. While the individual critic may adopt different values from those adopted by society, and use his values to criticize society, it is not easy to see how society could itself provide criteria by which it can pass judgement on itself. The criteria would, of course, have to be passed into law by the legislature which is itself society's principal spokesman, and would have to have the support of the government which is society's principal henchman. Thus the government and Parliament would be in the somewhat remarkable position of having to propose and enact various policies, while at the same time suggesting criteria whereby these policies might be found faulty. It is an entertaining but somewhat unreal picture.

Another possible meaning of the 'responsibility' of society for man-caused disabilities is perhaps to be found in the concept of cause. Rejecting the notion that society can be sensibly treated as 'at fault' for allowing accidents to occur, it may nevertheless be urged that society 'causes' them to occur in a way which is not true of disabilities caused by natural events. But to suggest that society 'causes' certain disabilities is simply another way of saying that people cause them, and this raises all over again the criteria by which it is to be determined whether one thing can be said to be the cause of another. Insofar as disabilities are caused by somebody's fault we may readily say that they are caused by people, but insofar as they are not caused by anybody's fault, by what criteria are we to say that they have been caused by people? Moreover, it must be recollected that according to the normal usages of speech a person may be said to have caused something by an omission, if it was his duty to avoid the result. Insofar as society could avoid or minimize the effects of natural causes by taking steps within its capacity, but which it finds it expedient not to take, e.g. because it prefers to spend the money on submarines or travelling to the moon, it would be perfectly sensible to say that society is the cause of those effects, just as much as it is the cause of man-caused injuries. Some may find the notion of fault so embedded in the notion of cause that they will find this argument hard to accept; to many it will seem obvious that society 'causes' disabilities caused by people in a sense in which it does not 'cause' disabilities caused by operation of nature. But even to people who take this view, there must still be a large gulf between admitting that society 'causes' disabilities caused by human action and finding in this a justification for more generous treatment by society of the victims of man-caused injuries compared with the victims of disabilities from natural causes. To say that one individual who 'causes' an injury ought for that reason to make compensation to the victim is a difficult proposition to maintain when causation is divorced entirely from fault; to say that society ought to make compensation for the injuries 'it' causes is even more difficult, since it involves accepting responsibility by society for the acts of all its individual members, i.e. some people are to be charged with paying compensation for the acts of others. There may well be, indeed, almost certainly are, ample and good reasons why society *should* make compensation to victims of man-caused disabilities, but these do not depend on the fact that such disabilities are 'caused' by some members of society, and cannot therefore be used to justify different treatment for those disabled by human actions and those disabled by natural causes.

2 PROTECTING REASONABLE EXPECTATIONS

One of the important aims of a compensation system is to minimize the hardships which arise out of the disappointment of reasonable expectations, in particular the expectation of regular future income. It might be thought that one of the reasons why the law distinguishes between human and natural causes is that human causes of disability tend to strike more suddenly and with little warning, whereas natural causes tend to operate more slowly, thus giving the victim more time to adjust his affairs and lifestyle to cope with the disability. However, on examination, this argument has very little force. It is true that being seriously injured or killed in a road accident, for example, is a sudden misfortune; but by no means all traumatic injuries are caused by human actions; (even less are they all caused by anyone's fault, and yet the tort system compensates on the basis of fault). It is also true that some diseases have a gradually disabling effect, but others do not; and a person afflicted with a gradual disease is not necessarily better able, because the disease is gradual, to take steps to ameliorate the misfortune it brings in its wake. Besides, the nature of the disease as either sudden or gradual in effect is not related to whether it is caused by man or by nature.

Perhaps one factor which influences our attitude to whether disabilities from particular causes deserve compensation is the relative frequency of disability from that cause. Serious long-term disability (such as is apt seriously to disappoint expectations) caused by human activities is relatively rare in our society, and so we feel that those unfortunate enough to suffer from it ought to be compensated because they have probably planned their lives and entered commitments on the reasonable assumption that they will not be seriously disabled in this way. Thanks to advances in medical science, serious or prolonged disease and premature death resulting from natural causes are also relatively uncommon today, and people tend to plan their lives on the basis that these misfortunes will not befall them. This might encourage us to feel that compensation is as due here as in the case of man-caused disability.

This would suggest that any argument which justifies compensation on the basis of disappointment of expectations should focus not on the suddenness of the disability but on its relative frequency and the extent to which people ought reasonably to guard against the risk of disability by personal insurance.

3 EGALITARIANISM AND THE PROBLEM OF DRAWING THE LINE

There is another reason why, as medical science has advanced, and prolonged disease and premature death have ceased to be normal hazards in our society, it has become less easy to maintain the distinction between man-caused and natural disabilities, and less easy for people to accept these misfortunes when they occur. When sickness and death from natural causes are liable to strike anyone at any time, the individual victim is more likely to accept his lot, partly at least because there are so many others who share it. To ask for compensation for such misfortunes is to ask for preferential treatment; it is to ask to be treated differently from many others who suffer similar misfortunes. But when these risks become much less normal, and strike so few, the individual victim is likely to feel more aggrieved. To the misfortune itself, there is now added the additional grievance of unfairness. To ask for compensation in this new situation is not to ask for special or preferential treatment at all; it is to ask merely that the *status quo* which was disturbed by the unusual risk should be, so far as it is possible, restored. It is to ask that the consequences of such misfortunes should, as far as possible, be spread equally among large numbers, rather than left to lie where chance has placed them. It is, in effect, one of the facets of an egalitarian society that people come to feel a sense of inequity in the chance distribution of misfortune. When compensation is paid to assuage such feelings of unfair disadvantage, it promotes ideas of social equality.

The idea of 'distributing losses', which is examined in more detail later (and which is as relevant to man-caused losses as to losses from natural causes) owes a good deal to egalitarian ideas, at least where it has been the result of conscious decision, and perhaps even where it has merely grown up as it has done in the tort-cum-liability insurance field. The justice of loss distribution owes something to the feeling that 'we are all in this together', that when misfortune strikes fortuitously and unequally the inequality it creates can be partly removed by the payment of compensation. This is perhaps nowhere more vividly illustrated than by the adoption of the principle of State compensation for war property damage during the Second World War. Sir Winston Churchill explained the genesis of the war damage scheme in his history of the war in the following terms:

Another time I visited Ramsgate. An air raid came upon us, and I was conducted into their big tunnel, where quite large numbers of people lived permanently. When we came out after a quarter of an hour, we looked at the still-smoking damage. A small hotel had been hit. Nobody had been hurt, but the place had been reduced to a litter of crockery, utensils and splintered furniture. The proprietor, his wife and the cooks and waitresses were in tears. Where was their home? Where was their livelihood? Here is a privilege of power. I formed an immediate resolve. On the way back in my train I dictated a letter to the Chancellor of the Exchequer laying down the principle that all damage from the fire of the enemy must be a charge upon the State and compensation be paid in full and at once. Thus the burden would not fall alone on those whose homes or business premises were hit, but would be borne evenly on the shoulders of the nation.[3]

Here, in the usual moving Churchillian language, the justice of treating war damage as a charge on the State is clearly rested on the notion of equality. Few would disagree with the justice of these sentiments. The question is how far this principle can be extended.

The difficulty is, of course, the same as the one that has faced all egalitarian political philosophies. People are not born equal, and they do not grow up equal. They have different physiques, different strengths, different intellects, different health. How far is the equalization process to go? If egalitarianism requires us to compensate one person for earning less than another because he is ill or has suffered an accident, why does it not require us to compensate one person who earns less than another because he is less intelligent or less strong? If egalitarianism requires us to compensate a person with a congenital disability, why does it not require us to compensate a person who is less attractive or has a deficient personality? There is no final and ultimate answer to these questions. The fact is that in a society such as ours much has already been done to even out the inequalities between people which derive from the natural inequalities of man, though this is principally done by taxation and the redistribution of income, rather than by any of the compensation systems which form the subject matter of this book. Whether there is still too much inequality is simply a matter of political judgment, on which one opinion may be as good as another. But what can at least be said is that as one moves away from compensating only for man-caused disabilities towards compensating also for disabilities from natural causes, these problems of drawing lines between misfortunes for which society should compensate and those which the victim must bear himself become much more obvious.

Compensating for income loss resulting from naturally caused sickness – as the social security system does, if rather ungenerously for long-term cases – seems no more difficult to justify than compensating for income loss due to man-caused injury; but compensating for disabilities as such, or for pain and suffering or mental distress, in the case of naturally caused disabilities, could certainly raise some delicate questions. For example, the industrial injuries system (and of course the tort system) compensates for facial disfigurement, irrespective of actual disability or loss of earning power. But if it were thought right to do away with the distinction between man-caused and naturally caused disabilities, how could one justifiably distinguish between disfigurement from illness and mere ugliness or unattractiveness? And again the distinction between disabilities on the basis of cause enables a line to be drawn between disabilities due to normal ageing and similar disabilities caused by man; but could we justifiably distinguish between similar disabilities due to normal ageing and premature (but naturally caused) ageing? The industrial injuries system has already met this difficulty to some extent, by providing that the criteria of disability should be the extent of deviation from the objective norm, judged by the 'normal' person of the same age and sex.[4] Thus no attempt is made to 'compensate' for disabilities due to old age, although in theory this could sometimes occur in part, as for instance, where a less than usually healthy man of sixty suffers an industrial injury which only partially disables him. This person's disability would be measured by reference to what the normal person of sixty could do without the disability, and not by reference to what *he* could do before the disability, so that in the result he may be partly compensated for the fact that he was less than normally healthy even before the accident. Conversely, an unusually strong and active person may suffer a minor accidental injury which reduces him to the level of a normal person of sixty; he will (in theory) have a nil assessment, though he has plainly suffered a disability. Clearly, difficulties would arise if it were sought to compensate for natural disabilities by the sort of provisions already in the industrial injuries scheme.

All this is not to suggest that difficulties of this nature are insurmountable, or that they provide an adequate justification for maintaining the distinction between disabilities based on cause in the fundamental place which it occupies in today's compensation systems. It is merely intended to demonstrate that this distinction has, in a sense, been a natural stopping place in the development of compensation systems. It may be that the time has come to abandon this stopping place. It would not, however, follow from the abandonment of *this* stopping place that it would be indefensible to distinguish between disabilities due to age, and those due to sickness; or between disfigurement arising from sickness and from natural unprepossessiveness.[5] Fifteen or twenty years ago such an abandonment seemed possible and even likely in some countries, but it seems a very dim prospect today when even the movement to abolish the distinction based on fault between man-caused disabilities has lost much of its steam.

4 DRAWING THE LINE IN PRACTICE

The examples just given show that even if the distinction between human and natural causes was abandoned because unjustifiable as a matter of justice and theory, we would still want to distinguish between different types of natural disadvantage and rule out compensation for some disadvantages. At the end of the day it might not be possible to draw and justify such distinctions on any more precise basis than that the notions of human individuality and personal responsibility require people to cope themselves with (or to compensate themselves for) certain types of differences between human beings which disadvantage some people compared with others. Few, if any, advocates of egalitarianism see this notion as justifying or requiring the elimination of all differences between individuals. Such distinctions are bound, however, to appear to some extent *ad hoc* and arbitrary.

Once the practical job of drawing lines is undertaken, however, there is one fact which shows clearly that drawing the line between human and natural causes is extremely difficult to justify. It has recently been demonstrated that by far the largest class of disabilities is that attributable to diseases and illnesses (as opposed to traumatic accidents). It has, however, also been pointed out that in practice it is very costly and extraordinarily difficult to determine whether particular diseases and cases of disease are the result of human or natural causes. If proper attention were paid to the compensation of victims of diseases, the distinction between human and natural causes would have to be abandoned.[6]

21
The cost of compensation and who pays it

To complete our overall review of the compensation systems in use today we must now turn to an aspect of the matter which we have so far only briefly touched upon. Compensation has to be paid for, and the questions considered in this chapter concern the different ways in which the different systems are paid for, and the cost of the systems themselves. Fortunately, one result of the Pearson Commission is that we now have a great deal of information relevant to the question of costs.

In considering this question of cost, it is necessary to bear in mind that there are two quite different types of costs, namely private costs and social costs. The main function of compensation systems is to transfer money from some persons to others; the sums so transferred are a cost to those who have to pay them, but they are not a social cost. They do not reduce society's resources as a whole. In economic terms, they are transfer payments, and not real costs. So far as these transfer payments are concerned, the questions of interest concern the total value of the payments and the way the burden is distributed. In the context of compensation for personal injuries, social costs are, in essence, the administrative costs of making transfer payments. Administrative costs are real costs to society because they are the measure of the administrative resources consumed in making the transfer payments. Deciding how much ought to be paid out in compensation is basically a matter of social policy, a matter of justice and fairness as between those in need of compensation, on the one hand, and those who will provide it (either directly or indirectly) on the other. But the level of administrative costs of a compensation scheme, and the ratio of those costs to transfer payments, has nothing to do with justice, but is relevant to efficiency. The lower the administrative costs of a system, both in total and as a proportion of compensation paid out, the more efficient the system is *as a compensation system*. As we shall see, some compensation systems are much more expensive to administer, both absolutely and relatively, than others. Higher relative costs can be justified only if the system in question delivers benefits other than, and additional to, the amount of compensation paid out.

One other preliminary point deserves mention. In the past, the law of torts has not been treated as a matter of substantial *public* concern. Although, as we have seen, the compulsory insurance system for motor and industrial accidents means that the public as a whole is largely compelled to pay for the tort system, there has been little attempt to assess legal reforms in the light of their cost. Changes in the law may be made by the courts with minimum attention to considerations of policy, and with virtually no opportunity for public debate and discussion. Law reform Bills which alter the rules of liability in tort are presented without any indication of their financial implications. A Bill which makes some change, however minor, in the social security system would have an explanatory memorandum showing the financial implications of the proposals, what new money will be needed and how it will be raised; but Bills to alter the law of torts do not give any indication of the repercussions they may have on insurance premiums, what the total cost will be, and how it will be distributed among premium payers, or others. This can cause considerable difficulties for insurance companies, who often find their liabilities increased by changes in the law of which inadequate notice has been given. For example, the changes in the law and practice relating to awards of interest on damages greatly increased total insurers' liabilities, but it was a long time before premiums caught up with these increased liabilities.

One notable exception to the failure to consider financial implications is provided by the discussions about the extension of strict liability for defective products, in which considerable attention has been paid to the costs of the proposals to manufacturers, and of their effect on insurance premiums.

1 THE COST OF TORT COMPENSATION

The Pearson Commission estimated that in the years 1971–76 total tort payments (at 1977 prices) averaged some £202 million per annum, of which £69 million (about 34%) went on industrial accidents, and £118 million went on road accidents.[1] In terms of 1987 price levels the figures would need to be increased by about 100%. However, as will be apparent from what has been indicated previously, the total *cost* of the system is nearly *double* the amounts paid out because the tort liability insurance system is staggeringly expensive to operate. The Pearson Commission estimated that the administrative cost of making the annual payments of £202 million (referred to above) averaged some £175 million during this same period, 1971–76 (again in terms of 1977 prices). This aggregate figure includes legal costs paid by the insurers and self-insurers to claimants in settlements (as well, of course, as those awarded in cases tried); legal costs paid by insurers and self-insurers to their own legal advisers; other disbursements paid by insurers and self-insurers to claimants (for example, to cover the cost of medical reports); and the general administrative costs of the insurers, or in the case of self-insurers, of their claims departments. These aggregate figures mean that the administrative expenses of the system as a whole amount to about 85% of the value of the sums paid out, or about 45% of the total of compensation and operating costs.[2] So (if we ignore investment income) we can say that about 55p of the premium £ is paid out to injured victims, and 45p is swallowed up in administration.

As we shall see later, no other compensation system is anything like as expensive to operate as the tort system. The social security systems, for instance, run at a cost of about 11% of the total amounts paid out.[3] The great expense of the tort system seems to be largely due to two principal factors; first, the very large sums paid in commission brokerage and advertising by most insurance companies, which make the cost of 'selling' insurance extremely high; and secondly, the whole settlement process, which requires a detailed examination of the causes of every accident which gives rise to a claim. This process is very expensive, not because of the high cost of litigation, which only affects a small minority of claims, but for several other reasons. First, the tort system means that an attempt must be made to ascertain who, if anyone, was at fault for the accident, and this requires a certain amount of expertise, as well as expense in the process of interviewing witnesses, taking statements and so on. Secondly, it requires an assessment of the amount of compensation to be paid, which involves a careful inquiry into the consequences of the accident with all that this means in the way of medical reports, and so on. And finally, it must be remembered that the adversary system means that this whole process is duplicated, since *both* parties will be employing advisers to make the same inquiries, about the causes and consequences of the accident. This duplication itself accounts for a considerable proportion of the total cost. Even the Pearson Report does not, for all its wealth of figures, give a detailed breakdown of the estimated overall administrative cost of £175 million per annum. But the Commission estimated that fees (i.e. costs) paid by insurers amounted to about 20% of compensation payments.[4] As compensation payments totalled £202 million, this means that fees paid to claimants must have totalled about £40 million.[5] If we assume that insurers had similar costs of their own in dealing with the claim itself, this would account for about £80 million of the estimated total of £175 million. The balance must have been accounted for by policy costs and general overheads. Clearly then, a major part of the total cost of the system consists of legal costs. And it is the nature of the system which renders these legal costs necessary, because it is almost indispensable for a person claiming damages to have the assistance of a solicitor. Other forms of insurance do not usually have this result. A person claiming for damage to his own car under a comprehensive policy would very rarely need to consult a solicitor. Yet many such claims are more substantial than many damages claims.

Who pays for all this? So far, we have contented ourselves with the general answer that the 'public' pays. But it is now necessary to delve a little further into this question to see how the burden of payment is distributed. It will be seen at once that there is a major difference between road and industrial accidents in this respect. In the case of industrial injuries the cost is in the first instance paid for by employers, mostly in the form of premiums for employers' liability insurance. These premiums are, of course, business expenses, like all other insurance premiums paid for by businesses, and are therefore deductible for tax purposes. This means that in one sense part of the cost is borne by the taxpayer. The rest of the burden is distributed by employers in the same way in which they distribute all their costs –

which means that it is impossible to say *how* it is distributed. All one can say is that the cost is spread over all those who are interested in the goods or services produced by industry, that is to say, the employees, the shareholders and the consumers. If a wholly new burden is placed on employers for the first time, and all other things remain equal, it may be possible to say how the employer has absorbed this new cost; for example, he may have reduced the dividend available for distribution; or he may have increased costs and so passed the burden onto the consumer; or (though he is unlikely these days actually to reduce wages) he may pay a lower wage increase than he would otherwise have done, and in this way pass the increased cost onto his employees. But in practice it is not usually possible to see precisely how the cost is passed on; moreover, the way the burden falls may change from time to time in a particular business as the competitive position of that business changes, and as profits rise or fall. Thus all one can say is that the cost of legal liability for industrial accidents is paid for partly by shareholders, partly by employees, partly by consumers and partly by taxpayers.[6]

It will be appreciated that employers' liability insurance means that the cost of injuries in one business will be paid for partly out of premiums received from other businesses. A business would have to be very large indeed before it paid entirely for its own injuries and once it reached this stage it would cease to be economical to insure at all. As between different classes of businesses, insurance rates are principally adjusted according to the risk which they present. An industry with a higher accident rate will have to pay a higher premium than an industry with a low accident rate. Hence consumers, employees and shareholders of high accident rate industries will pay rather more; though the differences are in most cases likely to be so small when spread among these groups that they will not be perceptible at all. As between different enterprises within a single industry, the scope for variation according to risk is limited by a number of technical considerations. Although it might be thought that an employer with a 'bad accident rate' would have to pay a higher premium than an employer with a 'good' rate, the extent of such variations of premium rating is in fact quite restricted. The principal limiting factor is that it is actuarially unsound to base premiums on the past record of an employer unless the firm is one of some substantial size.[7] In America, some 80% of all firms are too small to be experience rated and the same is probably true of this country.[8]

In the case of road accidents, the cost, though still largely spread by means of liability insurance, is spread in different ways. Part of it – namely that part which is attributable to commercial vehicles, or vehicles owned by public or local authorities – is distributed in a way similar to that applicable to industrial accidents, except that with public vehicles the cost falls on the taxpayer or the ratepayer. But about four-fifths of the vehicles on the road today (over 16½ million out of some 20 million) are cars and motor cycles, as opposed to commercial vehicles, and most of them are privately owned; so insurance costs in this area cannot be distributed beyond the vehicle owner. The car owner pays for his own insurance – with no tax relief – and cannot spread the cost any further. Moreover, as between car owners, the cost is distributed by insurers principally according to the accident causing potential of the owner. We have already seen that road traffic liability insurance compensates road accident victims according to their incomes, but that premiums cannot be calculated according to this criterion. In this respect, again there are differences between road traffic insurance and industrial injury insurance, although the legal framework of tort and liability insurance applicable to these two situations is broadly the same. In industrial injury cases the cost is paid by a very *wide* class, consisting of employees, shareholders and consumers for the benefit, generally speaking, of only one segment of that class, namely employees. In road traffic insurance the cost is largely borne by a *narrow* class, namely the private motorist, for the benefit, generally speaking, of a very wide class, namely all road users including pedestrians and cyclists, as well as motorists themselves.

As between different motorists the burden is generally distributed, as we have seen, according to the accident causing potential of the motorist. In practice, insurers usually classify motorists according to certain factors which have been shown to be statistically significant in accident involvements; in particular according to age, claims record, place of residence and type of vehicle. This means that a person who is a member of a high-risk group pays a larger premium than a person who is a member of a low-risk group, despite the fact that the former may in fact be a more responsible and careful driver than the latter. So long as this form of compensation is organized around liability insurance, and so long as liability insurance is itself based on competitive market principles, this is presumably inevitable, but it should not be thought that it is necessarily the most equitable way of distributing the costs of road accidents.[9] It is just possible that *all* the members of a certain group or classification are more likely to have accidents than all other motorists, but it is more likely that only a proportion are likely to have more accidents, and everybody else in the group is paying more because of that particular sub-group. No doubt one answer to this is further sub-classification by insurers of high-risk and low-risk groups, but there are two reasons why this may not be a satisfactory answer. A practical reason is that increased sub-classification would be expensive and complex to administer.[10] However, the end of the motor 'tariff' in 1969 has led to increased competition among insurers and greater experimentation with different schemes and different rating factors. Some of the changes (such as those involving greater discrimination against the young) may well have some accident prevention consequences.[11]

But objections to sharing costs in the way in which liability insurance does so, would remain, however much sub-classification was achieved. The fact of the matter is that the whole principle of insurance involves a pooling of risks; the cost of road accidents is to be shared among all who take part in the activity of motoring. To make some people pay more than others because they are members of a higher risk group, is to make some people pay more because they are *more likely* to have accidents, although they may not in fact do so. And to say that a person is *more likely* to have an accident does not mean (at least to an insurance company) that he is a worse driver; it means that he has certain characteristics which are statistically associated with a higher accident rate, which in turn means that people with those characteristics have more accidents than people without them. It may be more economically efficient, but it is not necessarily more equitable that the cost of road accidents should be distributed in this way. And if these arguments are not felt to be convincing, the reader may care to ask himself whether he would agree that other road accident costs which are not at present borne by road traffic insurance at all, such as police or National Heath Service costs, should be distributed in the same way?

Another feature of the way in which private insurance distributes costs is worthy of consideration. Insurance companies, who are in business to make money, may find it pays them to subsidize one group at the expense of another. They may find, for instance, that the premiums chargeable to young drivers on strictly statistical principles are so high that few young drivers would be able to afford them at all. Insurers may then be tempted to undercharge young drivers, and to compensate for this by overcharging older drivers. Again, this may be thought inevitable in the context of a free enterprise insurance, but it will be seen that if there is any virtue in the allocation of costs by the free market system in the first instance, this adjustment of it by the insurers themselves involves an element of subsidy, or income redistribution. And the question may be raised whether this sort of income redistribution is an appropriate job for insurance companies, more particularly when it is done in private and in secret by companies who are not accountable to the public. In fact, the disappearance of the 'tariff' may well mean an end to this sort of subsidization, because it probably cannot survive in a more competitive market. For instance, subsidization of the young driver by the older driver will collapse if some insurers are free to offer more tempting terms to the older driver; and if the older driver is not burdened with a subsidy in favour of the younger one, he *can* be offered better terms. It seems very probable that this is just what has been happening since the old 'tariff' system was abandoned, for it seems that the differential between the better risks and the worse risks has greatly increased. But this itself may not prove such a satisfactory conclusion in the long run, for American experience shows that if the insurance market is genuinely and highly competitive, insurers become more and more keen to secure the low-risk customer and less and less prepared to take on the high-risk customer. Hence, the gap between the lowest and the highest premiums will tend to rise until the highest premiums may reach formidable proportions. And this, as we have suggested, may be felt inequitable by the members of some of these high-risk groups.

There are also the costs of accidents caused by uninsured motorists to be considered. As we have seen, the MIB meets liability in cases of this kind today, as well as in other similar cases, such as where a person is injured by a 'hit and run' driver. The MIB collects its income from its constituent members, who are themselves insurers engaged in road traffic business in the United Kingdom, and all such insurers are now required to be members of the MIB. This has the curious result that the large numbers of disqualified motorists who still drive but cannot get insurance are having their insurance paid for them by other motorists who are insured with members of the MIB.[12]

It must be remembered, however, that by no means the entire cost of all industrial and road injuries is paid by insurance companies and their premium payers. To start with, in the case of injuries not caused by anyone's fault, or injuries for which the victim is partly to blame (and so for which he receives only partial compensation), the cost may be borne partly by the plaintiff himself. But part of it, at least, is likely to be met in other ways, such as by the social security system, or the social services, or even by friends and family. The same is often true even in the case of fault-caused injuries. We have seen that the difficulties of proving fault, and the operation of the rules governing assessment of damages, and certain features of the settlement process, have the effect, in very many cases, that an injured person receives no tort compensation at all, or an amount inadequate to meet his needs fully.

2 COSTS NOT PAID THROUGH THE TORT SYSTEM

The cost of social services

The cost of social services falls predominantly on the taxpayer or ratepayer. For example, the cost of medical treatment for injuries and diseases falls mainly on the National Health Service, which is largely paid for by the taxpayer. This is so regardless of whether the injury or disease was due to anyone's fault, and regardless of whether the victim recovers any tort compensation. About 10% of the cost is borne by the NHS component in the national insurance contribution exacted from all employed persons; nominally, the major part of this is born by the employee and only a small part by the employer, but we have seen how difficult it is to say how employer/employee costs are really distributed. We have also seen that under sections 154–156 of the Road Traffic Act 1972, vehicle users and road traffic insurers are liable to make some payment to a hospital rendering medical services to the victim of a road accident, but the costs of collection are large (about 25%) and the proceeds trifling. National Health Service costs attributable to motor accidents were about £50 million in 1976, but the amount collected under these statutory provisions in 1981–2 was only about £3.8 million.[13] The total cost to the Health Service of accidents and industrial diseases was estimated by the Pearson Commission to be over £500 million per annum (at 1977 prices).[14] Obviously, only a small fraction of this amount is borne directly by those responsible for the injuries and diseases.

Then again there are legal aid costs which are borne by the public directly, and which are to some extent attributable to road and industrial injuries. But the amount involved here is small, because the great majority of legally aided actions are 'successful' and in the case of personal injury or fatal accidents actions, this means that the costs will be paid by the defendants, rather than by the Legal Aid Fund.[15] The only costs borne by the fund are those in which a plaintiff is unsuccessful, and such cases are uncommon. As we have seen, there may also occasionally be cases in which the plaintiff recovers judgement for a sum less than that paid into court by the defendants, and in this event the plaintiff may be required to pay both sets of costs. Even in these circumstances no burden will fall on the Legal Aid Fund, unless the damages awarded to the plaintiff are inadequate to pay the costs, and this is unlikely to occur, because if the amount at stake is small in comparison with the probable costs it would be difficult for the plaintiff to turn down a reasonable 'payment in'. If he did so, his legal aid certificate might well be revoked. The total cost of legal aid in civil cases in 1983–4 was over £71 million, of which more than half was attributable to matrimonial proceedings. Total payments to solicitors and counsel for non-matrimonial civil cases in 1983–4 were some £38.4 million.[16] Other legal aid costs, amounting in all to close on £2 million per annum (in 1974), are paid for by trade unions.[17]

Then there are other social services paid for by taxpayers or ratepayers, such as the police, rehabilitation units, local authority welfare services and so on. Part of the costs of these services are certainly attributable to road and industrial injuries, and these again are not directly contributed to by premium payers. The Pearson Commission made some (fairly rough) estimates of the total cost to the community of injury, industrial disease and death from either of these causes.[18] They estimated the cost of the total compensation payments, from all sources, at around £827 million per annum (in

1977 prices). This includes administrative costs. In addition, they estimated the cost of other public provision, in the form of the NHS, personal social services and other miscellaneous services, at £625 million per annum. The greater part of this massive aggregate attributable to fault-caused injuries is externalized, and not paid directly by those responsible for the accidents or diseases or their insurers. Prior to the availability of the Pearson statistics, it was estimated that in 1970 42% of the cost of road accidents and 76% of the cost of industrial accidents were borne by 'external' sources, i.e. the social security system, the NHS, private insurance and sick pay arrangements.[19]

It would be a mistake, however, to assume that because road traffic premium payers do not directly contribute to external costs of this nature, therefore motorists are not 'paying their way'. Motorists are already extremely heavily taxed as a class,[20] and by far the simplest way to make motorists contribute to the National Health Service or other costly social services is to tax the motorist (or motor insurance companies) and pay for the social services with the proceeds. Since this is exactly what is already being done, there is no justification for suggestions that the motorist is 'not paying' for road accident medical costs; although conversely this is no conclusive answer against taxing the motorist more heavily still, if this is felt to be politically desirable. Precisely similar considerations apply to the cost of industrial accidents. Even if industry does not directly pay the full cost, it no doubt contributes handsomely in the form of taxation to the costs which are externalized.

The cost of the social security system

The social security system is vastly more expensive than the tort system, but it provides many benefits (such as retirement pensions) which are quite different from anything provided by the tort system. However, even the cost to the social security system of maintaining the sick, the injured and the dependants of those who die from injury or disease, is more than the cost of the whole tort system. On the Pearson Commission estimates, it seems that tort payments to the injured (and dependents of those killed) total about £202 million per annun (at 1977) prices. But as the administrative costs of the social security system are only a fraction of those of the tort system, the differences in the amounts paid out are very much greater than the differences in total cost estimated by the Pearson Commission at £377 million for tort and £468 million for social security.

The largest component of social security payments in respect of injury and death consists of benefits paid under the industrial injuries scheme in respect of injuries at work: £259 million per annum (1977 prices), at an administrative cost of some £28 million, or about 12% of the benefits paid.[21] Although the industrial injury fund no longer has an independent existence, the method of financing contributory social security benefits in general has remained, in essence, unchanged since they were introduced, the cost being shared between employers, employees and the state (or the taxpayer). Employees pay contributions amounting to between 5% and 9% of their gross wages, subject to lower and upper earnings limits. Employers pay between 5% and 10·45% of such wages, but their contributions are not subject to any upper wages limit. In each case the percentage is less if the employee contracts out of the State earnings-related pension scheme (SERPS). It is difficult to assess how the burden of contributions is actually discharged. Although formally the employer's and the employee's contributions must be paid by them respectively, it cannot be doubted that the total cost of all contributions is taken into account when decisions have to be made about wage scales, prices and dividends. The Exchequer (that is, in effect, the taxpayer) contributes an amount equal to 11% of all other contributions used to finance contributory benefits. Non-contributory benefits are paid in full by the Treasury.

Although the industrial injuries system is still popularly treated as a species of national insurance, the insurance element in the system is minimal. In the first place, there are (as we have seen) no 'contribution conditions'; every employed person in the country is entitled to the same benefits, irrespective of contributions paid. In the second place, the principle of 'pooling of risks' which has always been so prominent a feature of national insurance has here been carried to its ultimate conclusion.[22] This principle of pooling of risks means that all employers and all employees pay contributions at the same rate irrespective of the nature of their occupations, and therefore of the risks which are involved. The pooling of risks was natural, and indeed inevitable, in the case of ordinary national health and sickness insurance, and also perhaps in unemployment insurance. There were obviously sound reasons for not adjusting premiums according to the risk in the case of health or sickness insurance, when these were first introduced. Quite apart from the administrative complexity of adjusting premiums according to the health of those concerned, the net result of doing so would have been that those in the most serious need – those with chronically poor health – would either have been required to pay premiums so prohibitive that they could not have afforded them, or alternatively would have been offered benefits so derisory that they would have been no use. It was therefore clear that national insurance involved as a logical corollary an element of subsidy or income redistribution. The only question was, where was the subsidy to come from? One answer was that the better risks should subsidize the worse risks, that those in robust health would receive less in benefits than they would have been actuarially entitled to on strict insurance principles, while those in poor health would receive more. But this answer would have meant confining the element of income redistribution to the smallest limits. It would moreover, have meant ignoring the taxpayer who was the most obvious source of wealth if there was to be any redistribution of income. Accordingly, it became a well-established feature of national insurance from the very beginning that contributions were not to vary according to the risk, and also that the cost should be borne in part by the Exchequer.

When the industrial injuries system was being designed by Beveridge he gave some thought to the question whether the fixed-rate principle should also be applied here.[23] In this area there was not the same necessity to maintain the fixed-rate principle; the rate could have been made to vary (as did the rates for workmen's compensation insurance which industrial injuries was replacing) with the extent of the risk, or the accident rate of the industry in question. But the trade unions – and particularly the Mineworkers' Federation – were strongly opposed to variable premiums. They thought that miners' wages were depressed by the cost of mining accidents, and they argued that nearly all industries were dependent on coal and so ought to pay their share of the cost of coal mining accidents through flat-rate premiums. They do not appear to have appreciated that the price of coal itself included some item representing the cost of coal mining accidents, and that industries dependent on coal were already contributing in this way to the cost of coal mining accidents.

Beveridge in principle accepted the arguments of the Mineworkers' Federation though he wished to impose a 'special levy' on particularly high-accident-rate industries, primarily for its accident preventive value. The government was unimpressed by the suggestion that higher premiums deterred accidents, rejected the 'special levy' and therefore adopted the uniform fixed rate for all industrial injuries insurance.[24] One has only to look at the figures (for 1972) comparing the accident rate in factories (250,000 per 7 million employees) with the accident rate in shops, offices and railway premises (about 18,000 per 8 million employees) to get some indication of the extent of the subsidy involved in this fixed-rate principle. On actuarial principles it is clear that premiums for factory workers would on average have to be nearly doubled, while premiums for office workers could be reduced to a minute fraction of their present level.[25] There is, of course, nothing wrong or objectionable in principle to a subsidy of this nature, but what is objectionable is to allow the system to masquerade as an insurance system when it is nothing of the kind. This emphasis on insurance also leads to the belief that those who receive the more valuable benefits provided by the industrial injuries system over those provided by ordinary national insurance, have in some sense 'paid for' the extra benefits they have received. This is not so. Every employed person (except the anomalously placed self-employed) pays the same rate of contribution, but only those who are injured at work receive the more generous treatment of the industrial injuries system. The Robens Committee called for an urgent re-examination of the fixed-rate principle[26], but a majority of the Pearson Commission reaffirmed it, mainly on the ground that the cost of risk-related contributions would outweigh the benefits. Because the issue has now become closely linked with arguments about industrial safety, further consideration of the point is deferred till later.[27]

A third respect in which the industrial injuries system does not work on insurance principles is that while social security contributions are earnings-related, industrial injury benefits are not (with the exception of statutory sick pay; and the theoretical exception of the special hardship allowance, which, in the vast majority of cases, is paid at the maximum rate). So the system embodies an element of income redistribution. Perhaps the major respect in which the social security system is based on insurance principles is that in respect of some benefits (but by no means all; and not in respect of industrial injury benefits), certain conditions, relating to the amount of contributions paid, have to be satisfied before the benefit is payable.[28]

But even here, the contribution conditions are not usually actuarially determined. On the whole, then, the social security system is, in very many respects, based not on insurance principles, but on welfare principles. This is most obviously true of benefits – notably supplementary benefits – entitlement to which is not subject to contribution conditions, and which are not funded by contributions, but entirely by taxation.

We have seen that the administrative cost of the industrial injuries system is about 12% of the amounts paid out in benefits. This is very much less than the administrative cost of the tort system, but it is still substantially more expensive than the rest of the social security system, which operates at a cost ratio of about 6.25%.[29] One reason for this difference is presumably that there are more issues to be decided in an industrial injury case – in particular, whether an accident was an industrial accident, the degree of resulting disability, and whether there is a partial loss of earnings.[30] It will be observed that the very same questions may also have to be decided in a tort case, and the cost of making both decisions will often be borne by the public.[31] Another reason for the extra cost of industrial injuries insurance is possibly that there are more appeals in these cases. In 1983 there were over 2,500 appeals to Local Appeal Tribunals (now Social Security Appeal Tribunals) in injury benefit and disablement benefit claims, and 253 appeals to the National Insurance Commissioners (now the Social Security Commissioners) in injury benefit claims. At the same time there were 3043 sickness benefit appeals to LATs and 81 appeals to the Commissioners. Yet total sickness benefit claims outnumber those for injury benefit many times over. The reason why there are proportionately more appeals in industrial injury cases is no doubt partly due to the greater complexity of the system; but partly it is almost certainly the result of trade union assistance to claimants, and a willingness to provide representation on appeals.

3 THE COST OF CRIMINAL INJURIES COMPENSATION

The criminal injuries compensation system is on a modest scale compared with the other systems operating today. In the first full year of operation the scheme cost just over £400,000 and by 1984–5 the cost had climbed to almost £40 million. Since 1974–5 the number of new applications received by the Board each year has more than doubled, and the number of awards has risen from about 9,000 to about 20,000. In 1976–7 almost £10 million was paid in compensation and by 1984–5 this had risen to more than £35 million.

The administrative costs of the scheme were at first very steady at between 8% and 9% of the amount of awards paid out, and in 1984–5 they were 10·6%.[32] Although the scheme requires (like the tort system) an analysis of the circumstances of each case to ascertain the cause and gravity of the injuries, it is very much cheaper than the tort system to operate. In the first place, it eliminates the cost of raising the money to pay for the compensation, or more accurately, it disregards these costs, which are treated as a part of the costs of the taxation system. Of course, the cost of raising the money is a very substantial item in the tort system because of the high costs of insurance brokerage and advertising. In the second place, the criminal injuries system is cheaper than the tort system because it eliminates the adversary process, and therefore involves only one set of costs rather than two. The costs of claimants who are represented are not paid by the Board because the Board does not award 'costs' as a court does. Hence, the cost of legal advice and representation does not fall on the public; but compensation awards are therefore correspondingly less than tort damage awards.

The whole cost of the scheme falls on the taxpayer, though it is in some respects a mistake to look at the scheme in isolation from other compensation systems. It is by no means true that the whole cost of criminal injuries is met by the scheme. As we have seen, social security benefits are deducted in full from awards under the scheme. There are also some cases – though they are not likely to be frequent – in which tort damages can be obtained for criminal injuries. The main reason why the scheme is financed by taxation and not by any form of insurance is simply that the risk of being injured by criminal attack is so small that the cost of administration would be out of all proportion to the size of the premium which it would be necessary to levy. The Home Office Working Party found that even one (old) penny a week would be excessive,[33] and today a levy of 4p a week would more than cover the cost of the scheme.

One feature of the scheme, which may be thought to bear on the question of financing of the scheme, is that a proportion of claimants receive injuries from an assault or attack which is in some sense related to their occupation. For example, police officers, security guards, barmen, wages clerks, bus conductors and post office workers are all peculiarly vulnerable to criminal attack. In the Board's Second Annual Report, they noted that one-third of the claimants were in occupations directly relevant to the offence in question, and of those, nearly half were police officers.[34] In recent years, however, the proportion of awards which were made to policemen has fallen and was only 3·4% in 1983–4. It could be argued that employers ought to be made responsible for compensation awards where the offence is related to the occupation. Why should the taxpayer pay for criminal assaults on barmen or wages clerks? It could be argued that assaults of this kind should be a charge on the business in question.[35] But in practice, this would probably raise more problems than it would solve. And in any event, a substantial proportion of those whose occupations are relevant to the offence are public officials of one sort or another – policemen, post office employees, public transport employees and so on.

PART SIX
Objectives

22
The meaning and purposes of compensation

Most of us are content to take the notion of compensation for injuries or losses as a starting point, without pausing to enquire too closely into *why* we should compensate people for these or other misfortunes. But the operation of the existing systems of compensation is so extraordinarily arbitrary and haphazard that it is worth devoting some time to a serious enquiry into what we mean by 'compensation', and what purposes we hope to achieve in awarding compensation. Does the existing order after all rest on some peculiar and undefined concepts of justice, are there intuitive feelings common to most of us about when it is just to pay compensation which explain the existing arrangements in the law? Or is the existing order in truth just a jumble of unjustifiable irrationalities, born of political compromises and historical anomalies which no one has had the courage to uproot?

1   SOME PRELIMINARY QUESTIONS

The popular sense of justice
Among the great difficulties which face us in attempting to answer these questions is the fact that nobody can be really sure what the popular sense of justice, assuming that there is such a thing, does in fact demand.[1] Does the man in the street really think that it is just to

pay very large compensation to people injured due to the fault of some other person, and to pay very little compensation to persons who suffer injury, disease or disablement from natural causes or accidents not due to anyone's fault? Does he think it is right to award damages for pain and suffering? Or for death of a young child? Does he think it right to award more compensation to people injured at work than those injured at home? The answer is that we do not generally know what the popular sense of justice demands. Attempts have, it is true, sometimes been made to ascertain popular views and attitudes by survey questionnaires, but the results are not particularly helpful. For example, one writer concludes that 'there seems to be rather little evidence that when asked, people actually do express consensus support for a fault-based compensation system.'[2] Individual attitudes seem to depend to a considerable extent on whether the person questioned has suffered personal injuries and made or attempted to make a claim.

The Michigan Survey and the Ontario Survey both found that an overwhelming proportion of those questioned were in favour of damages being awarded for pain and suffering; but when it is appreciated that those questioned were themselves recent victims of road accidents, what is surprising is not the majority of affirmative replies, but the substantial minority of those who did not favour such awards – some 20% in the Michigan Survey[3] and around 30% in the Ontario Survey.[4] Another American survey devoted to pain and suffering, found widespread misunderstanding about the way damages are calculated, and about the likelihood of receiving damages for pain and suffering.[5] In England we also have the evidence of a former trade union claims official that people injured in industrial accidents sometimes 'can hardly be convinced' that they are entitled to claim disablement benefit, even though they have suffered no loss of earnings.[6] On the other hand, some recent public debates (for example, concerning the thalidomide cases) suggest that there is a real demand for substantial damages, not necessarily limited to a pecuniary loss. However, if people were asked whether they would be willing to pay premiums sufficient to cover compensation for pain and suffering, it is not at all certain that they would answer in the same sort of way.

Such evidence does not really take us very far in deciding what the popular sense of justice demands, still less does it tell us what variations there may be between different countries. There is, too, a further difficulty. It is very hard to say how far a person's views about justice are themselves conditioned by his contact with compensation systems – either in the form of direct contact, or vicariously through what he reads in newspapers or sees on television or hears from his colleagues and friends. We have already noted evidence to the affect that the attitudes of personal injury victims to questions of fault, responsibility and compensation are heavily influenced by what they know of the relevant legal rules.[7] More generally, there is probably a good deal of reaction and interaction between the law itself and general ideas of justice and equity.

Even when Parliament – one of whose functions is presumably to represent the popular sense of justice – finds time to discuss some aspects of the compensation systems, the discussion is apt to be distorted by the very fact that it will be on *some aspect* of the systems, and not on the whole range of systems. The debates on the criminal injuries compensation scheme illustrates the defect of this sort of selectivity only too well. Asked to approve a scheme for compensating the victims of crimes of violence, both houses gave a hearty and virtually unanimous approval; but Parliament never had the opportunity of saying (for instance) that victims of crimes deserved compensation, but their claims did not rank higher (say) than those of an accident victim who had received social security benefits from the State.

But there is also a further question. Even if we are satisfied that the compensation systems existing at present conform to the popular sense of justice, we are still entitled to ask for rational justification of those systems. The man in the street, it must be admitted, is hardly sophisticated enough to appreciate the many sides to the problems of compensation, nor has he the time to study the detailed implications of these systems. It may be enough for him to say that he 'feels it is just', without trying to analyse his feelings or justify them; but it should not be, and cannot be, enough for anyone seriously concerned with the legal system, whether as a student, teacher, practitioner, judge, administrator or legislator.

Two sides to a compensation system

As we turn then to a consideration of the purposes which a compensation system serves, the first thing that strikes us is the fact that compensation is a two-sided process. We take money away from one person, or one group of persons (which may be the whole body of taxpayers), and give it to another. To justify a particular compensation system, therefore, we may need to enquire why the burden of paying compensation is imposed on a particular person or group of persons, as well as why we want to compensate the recipient. In general, these are two separate questions and can be approached separately. There is nothing absurd or irrational in asking, first, whether a person should be compensated for such and such a misfortune, and secondly, if so, who should pay that compensation. The payment to the recipient is the natural starting point, because that is usually our ultimate objective; the collection of the money from those on whom we impose the burden is merely the means by which we fulfil our objective. We raise the money in order to be able to pay the compensation.

But there are at least two reasons why the questions we have posed cannot be entirely separated. In the first place, there are some circumstances in which our normal order of reasoning may be reversed, that is, in which we may give people compensation partly at least because we want to take the money away from somebody else in order to punish him. Whenever punitive damages are awarded in a tort case – a rare event nowadays – we are not taking the money from the defendant in order to give it to the plaintiff, we are giving some money to the plaintiff because we want to punish the defendant. In a case of this kind we cannot separate the two questions we have put, because until we know who is going to pay the compensation, we cannot rationally decide how much to give the plaintiff. So far as the actual law is concerned, this problem raises practical difficulties in at least two classes of cases. First, where a person commits a tort in circumstances in which punitive damages could be awarded against him, and it is sought to render someone such as his employer, vicariously liable for these damages, obviously difficulties arise.[8] If the purpose of the damages is purely retributive – to make the wrongdoer smart – there could be no justification for making the employer pay the punitive damages; but if the purpose is partly deterrent, a stronger case could be made for doing so. The law itself seems uncertain on the issue. The second type of case which raises difficulty is where the wrongdoer is insured against the liability. Should the insurance company be liable to pay the punitive damages?

Here again the answer is not entirely certain, but there seems less ground for fastening the liability on the insurer than on an employer – indeed, there seems *no* rational purpose at all in doing so. Not only is there no point in seeking retribution against the insurer nor even in trying to deter him, but the punitive purpose of the award against the actual wrongdoer will be lost if he can shift the liability to the insurance company.

The second reason why these questions cannot be kept entirely separate, though not dissimilar to the first, is much more important since it goes to the root of a very large part of our compensation system today. The fact is that even where we do not wish to *punish*, our decisions as to what misfortunes should be compensable, and by how much, are apt to be profoundly influenced by the question whether the party likely to pay the compensation was in some sense to blame for the misfortune. For example, if we ask whether persons injured in accidents should receive compensation for pain and suffering, the answer may very well depend on who is to pay the compensation. If it is to be paid by a person who was seriously to blame for the accident, we are more likely to feel that such damages should be awarded; whereas if it is to be paid by the taxpayer, or some large group of persons in no way responsible for the accident, we may feel less sure of the justice of this course.[9]

It is apparent then that we cannot wholly forget who pays for the compensation when we are enquiring what misfortunes should be compensable, and how great the compensation should be. Nevertheless, in the great majority of cases it would seem more profitable to look at the purpose of paying compensation to the victim of the misfortune, without worrying about who is going to pay for it, because we know very well that in the long run the overwhelming bulk of the compensation paid out is going to come from such a large group of persons as to render any relationship between them and the victim completely impersonal. Thus, we know that compensation for injuries incurred in road accidents is, in the long run, paid for by the premium payers of all the vehicles on the roads; that compensation for industrial accidents is paid for by all those who participate in the industry as consumers, workers or shareholders; that sickness and unemployment benefits are paid for by all those insured under the Social Security Acts, as well as by the taxpayers generally, and so on. While recognizing then, that special considerations may need to govern the case where the person paying the compensation was actually to blame for the misfortune in question, we ought to be able to enquire into the rational objectives of a compensation system without concerning ourselves in the ordinary case about who is going to pay.

The wealth of society

There is, however, one further qualification which needs to be made to what we have said. There can be no doubt that the types of misfortune which a society is willing to treat as compensable, and the amount of compensation to be awarded, will to a not insubstantial extent depend on the wealth of that society. A very poor society, in which people die of starvation or malnutrition and many live in conditions of great need, is unlikely to pay or provide for compensation for misfortunes which may appear trivial by comparison with the daily life of suffering millions, but which would be a serious tragedy in a wealthier society. There are higher priorities in the demands made on the available resources of such a society than paying compensation for misfortune; and in any event, the people in such a society may not feel the same need for protection from these misfortunes in the face of other and more serious conditions.

Even in a modern western state, money for compensation systems is severely limited. Even a relatively affluent society is not willing, it seems, to make great sacrifices to help those afflicted by injury, disease or disablement. It will not let them starve, to be sure, but it does not in general seem too concerned with whether they have a fair share of the good things of life. All the more reason then for seeing that our various compensation systems work sensibly and justly as between those similarly afflicted.

2 COMPENSATION

We return, then, to the question with which we started this chapter. What is compensation for? What objectives does a compensation system have? What indeed, *is* compensation? It seems that the notion of compensation embraces at least three distinct ideas. Sometimes, compensation is granted as an equivalent for what has been lost; sometimes, it is granted as a substitute or solace for what has been lost; and sometimes it is granted not because of what has been lost, but because of what the victim has never had in comparison with others in a similar situation. Let us take these ideas in turn and elaborate on them.

Compensation as an equivalent for what has been lost

This is the simplest and most straightforward case (which we may call 'equivalence compensation'), but even here we can distinguish at least three types of case according to the kind of 'loss'. First, a person may 'lose' (in the sense of being physically deprived of) money or other valuable property which can be replaced with money. A person's car is wrecked in an accident and he wants compensation to enable him to buy an equivalent car, or his house is destroyed by fire and he must rebuild or buy a new house. In this type of case the purpose of compensation seems self-evident – we are simply restoring what has been taken away; we are restoring the *status quo*.

The second type of equivalence compensation is designed to compensate, not for physical deprivation of property, but for costs which are incurred by the victim. These may take varied forms, from medical expenses to the cost of hospital visits or the cost of modifying a house to make it easier for the victim to live in. They all involve financial losses incurred as a result of some misfortune – illness, injury, death – and here again compensation is a complete equivalent to what has been lost. If it is desired to make compensation of this kind, the most efficient way of doing so is to spare the victim the need to make the payments at all, as is done in the case of most medical expenses incurred under the National Health Service. Free medical treatment has become so much an accepted part of our way of life in this country that we now scarcely think of it as a form of compensation at all.

The third type of equivalence compensation is compensation for lost expectations, chiefly the expectation of being able to earn in the future. When a person is sick, or injured or disabled, so that he is unable to work, or when a person is killed or dies leaving dependants who would have been maintained by his earnings, compensation for lost income will be needed. It will be noticed that this form of compensation differs from compensation for an actual deprivation. For this reason it is sometimes said that what the law compensates for is not lost earnings but lost capacity to earn.[10] In many cases the best evidence available of this capacity is evidence of what the plaintiff was earning before he was incapacitated. But in some cases (e.g. children) the court has to speculate on what the plaintiff's capacity would have enabled him to earn had he not been injured.

We have already noted that it is difficult to justify payment of compensation for lost earnings on the basis of the individual's past earnings unless those with higher earnings are expected to contribute more to the fund from which compensation is to be paid. It is also difficult to justify paying compensation for loss of earning capacity to persons who have never contributed to the fund. But, so long as we have a tort system in which compensation for pecuniary loss is based on past earnings or future earning capacity and which is supported by liability insurance in a competitive insurance market, there are only two alternatives with regard to lost earnings. Either we pay a flat rate for lost earnings to all victims regardless of their past earnings or future earning capacity, or we retain the present system in which those who suffer higher income losses receive higher compensation without having paid higher premiums. There is no way of making the higher income groups pay higher premiums for the risk within the present framework.[11]

Substitute and solace compensation

In the second type of case, compensation is awarded not as an equivalent but as a substitute or solace for what has been lost. Since it is almost impossible in any modern legal system to award compensation in any form other than money, it follows that giving compensation for 'losses' which cannot be replaced by money (such as pain and suffering or loss of amenity) must have a different purpose from that involved in giving compensation for things that can be replaced by money. The object here cannot be to replace what has been lost by some equivalent, but to enable the victim to obtain a substitute source of satisfaction or pleasure, or alternatively to comfort him (provide him with solace) for what has happened. This type of compensation is most commonly associated with bodily injury (although damages for inconvenience and mental distress are increasingly being awarded in cases involving claims arising out of property damage or financial loss).

Other compensation systems usually ignore this type of compensation altogether. Extra sickness benefits are not awarded for the loss of amenity under the Social Security Act; personal accident insurance policies (rare enough themselves) are usually limited to medical expenses or income losses; and though small disability payments are often made under comprehensive road traffic insurance policies, they rarely exceed £500 for severe disablement, with lesser sums for other cases.

Examples of substitute compensation are easy to imagine. The man who is blinded and can no longer watch television may be enabled to buy a gramophone and a collection of records, to give him an alternative form of pleasure. The man who loses a leg and can no longer go for a country walk may be enabled to buy a car, and savour the pleasures of the countryside in a different way. It might be thought that this type of compensation requires much greater justification than the types of compensation we have previously discussed. There is, for one thing, the difficulty of fixing the level of compensation. What is a reasonable substitute for a pleasure forgone? How can one measure the amount of pleasure or happiness a person derives from this or that activity? Is one to make some financial estimate of the subjective value to the victim of various forms of activity, or is one to look at objective costs? Does one deduct from the value of the pleasure forgone the cost which would have been required to obtain it?

In some cases, for example where a person loses the sense of smell, it is difficult to think of anything which would count as a substitute. Even where some substitute pleasures can be given, it is bound to be only partial. So compensation for lost amenities is often wholly or partly solace for what has been lost. Damages for pain and suffering also provide solace, although in theory they, too, compensate for losses. The tort system, and to a lesser extent the Criminal Injuries Compensation Scheme, are the only compensation systems operating today which provide such compensation. In only one situation does the law explicitly award damages as a solace, namely when it awards damages for bereavement under the Fatal Accidents Act.

Solace compensation, it might be thought, is even harder to justify than substitute compensation. If such compensation were actually paid by the tortfeasor himself it might be supportable on grounds of fairness. But when it is realized that such compensation will usually be paid out of insurance premiums and so, ultimately, by the public, one is forced to ask whether there are not other claims on society's resources which deserve priority. This point applies to both substitute and solace compensation, but more so to the latter. It is hard to justify compensation for mental distress and deprivation of pleasure when many of the injured receive little or no compensation even for income losses.

Equalization compensation

We have already suggested in an earlier chapter that there are circumstances in which the payment of compensation is based on a notion of egalitarianism. Especially when a person's need for compensation is the result of natural causes, our desire to compensate arises out of a desire to equalize the position of the disadvantaged person with that of normal people. This sort of egalitarianism underpins the welfare state, but it is not a notion with which the common law has concerned itself. The law of torts embodies ideas of corrective justice (i.e. it is concerned with making good disturbances of the status quo), whereas egalitarianism is a variety of distributive justice (i.e. it concerns how the resources of society should be distributed amongst its members). The modern compensation debate is based largely on ideas of distributive justice.

3 THE DISTRIBUTION OF LOSSES AND THE ALLOCATION OF RISKS

As the popularity of the fault principle has waned among academic lawyers, they have begun to suggest that the law is primarily concerned with the 'distribution of losses' or the 'allocation of risks'. The question which it is necessary to examine in this section is how far the distribution of losses and the allocation of risks may be said to be objectives of the law, and how much assistance they provide in formulating a rational basis for the compensation process.

The distribution of losses

To suggest that the law is concerned with the distribution of losses begs at least three important questions. The first is how we are to define 'loss'. The present approach seems to assume that 'losses' are easily recognized things which exist or occur outside the law, and that the law merely provides some remedy for a loss after it has occurred. Of course this is not so. It is the law itself which defines what is meant by 'loss'. For example, it is only recently that the law has recognized that a housewife who is rendered incapable of doing housework has herself suffered a loss for which damages may be awarded; again, the loss caused by bereavement was recognized for the first time in 1982. A striking example is provided by the need of an injured person to be nursed; if a relative or friend does the nursing gratuitously, the law treats the victim as having suffered a loss (assessed as the reasonable value of the nursing services) for which damages can be awarded; but if he is nursed free in a National Health institution, no damages are awarded for the value of the nursing. It is not, therefore, possible to define what is meant by 'loss' – all one can do is to describe the losses for which the law provides compensation.

A second important question which is begged by simply speaking of the goal of the law as loss distribution is how we are to value losses. We have seen, for example, that the law adopts the 'full compensation' and 'one hundred per cent' principles in relation to pecuniary losses, and a crude tariff system for the assessment of non-pecuniary losses. On the other hand, for example, social security systems never compensate for income losses in full. A different type of valuation issue arises in relation to compensation for loss of ability to do housekeeping or for gratuitous nursing services. Suppose the housekeeper or nurse gives up a job or forgoes the opportunity of working in order to keep house or nurse. Should the services be valued at what it would cost someone to perform them, or at what the person doing them could have earned at work? The law of torts has not committed itself to either of these measures of value, but awards what, in the particular case, the court considers to be the 'reasonable value' of the services.

The third and most fundamental question which is begged by speaking of loss distribution as the goal of a compensation system is whether it is 'loss' for which the injured person *should* be compensated. The idea that losses should be compensated for is to some extent a corollary of the fault principle and of the individualistic nature of tort law. Social security systems tend to be much more concerned with meeting basic *needs* by means of flat-rate benefits and very limited compensation for non-pecuniary losses. The idea that losses should not always be compensated for has been the subject of some debate in the tort system: it will be recalled that in *Lim Poh Choo*, which we have mentioned frequently, Lord Denning argued unsuccessfully that a plaintiff in a state of (almost) total incapacity who has no dependants should not be awarded damages for loss of income in addition to adequate damages for the cost of care because, in effect, the plaintiff does not need and cannot use them, and they would be simply a windfall to his relatives.

Compensation for loss can be said to involve shifting the loss from one person to another. But where the loss is not of money or money's worth (e.g. pain and suffering), the process of making some person compensate the victim for the misfortune is very inaccurately described as 'shifting the loss'. Losses of this kind *cannot* be shifted from one person to another in any meaningful sense. It may be possible to minimize pain and suffering, e.g. by medical treatment, and it may be possible to make someone else pay for this medical treatment, and this may, perhaps, be regarded as 'shifting a loss'; but when all has been done to minimize the pain and suffering by medical means, any residual pain and suffering cannot be shifted at all. It remains with the victim, no matter what compensation is paid to him by other parties.

The shifting of a loss – or making one person compensate another for some misfortune – involves an alteration of the status quo and so it involves administrative expense. Therefore (it is usually asserted), the onus is on those who wish to shift a loss to justify the shift. Unless there is some good reason for shifting a loss, it should be left to lie where it falls. The law of torts attempts to justify the shifting of losses by reference to the fault principle, but we have already seen that this principle is not easily defensible by rational argument. Modern tort lawyers have searched for something to put in its place, and some of them have found their answer in the idea of 'loss distribution'. The law does not, in general, merely *shift* a loss from one person to another; it normally *distributes* that loss over a large number of people, and over some period of time. It is true that this distribution is not normally achieved by rules which would be regarded as part of the law of torts, except where the defendant is a corporate body, but the combined effect of tort law and liability insurance is, in practice, to distribute losses among a large group of people, and over a period of time.

There is no doubt that the distribution of losses is itself an important and usually desirable result of the legal process. Losses which may be crushing if imposed on an individual can be borne easily when distributed over a wide class of people; this is clearly in the interests of those who are themselves at risk, as well as of society as a whole. There is also a great gain in security and peace of mind when the fear of crushing losses from sudden disaster is displaced by knowledge that the loss will be spread. All this is perfectly true, but to advocate loss distribution as an end in itself invites as an obvious retort: *loss distribution among whom?*[12] There are many ways in which losses can be distributed – or, which is merely saying the same thing in another way – there are many ways in which money can be raised from members of the public. The law of torts, interwoven as it is with liability insurance, provides one way, or rather two principal ways, for we have seen how the costs of industrial accidents is distributed differently from the cost of road accidents. First party insurance provides another way; and we have seen that there are very important differences between the way in which losses are distributed when they are borne by first party insurance on the one hand, and liability insurance on the other. In particular, premiums in first party insurance are levied according to the amount of coverage desired, whereas in liability insurance, premiums are fixed by the accident causing potential of the insured. Social security provides still another way of distributing losses, with its mixture of insurance and income redistribution, while supplementary benefits represent the ultimate in loss distribution – namely distribution among all taxpayers. But these are by no means the only ways of distributing losses. All sorts of permutations and combinations are possible. For example, compensation for road accidents could be financed by a fund contributed to solely by motorists, but by flat-rate contributions instead of by the present variable insurance premiums; or it could be financed by a special tax on petrol, so that (in general) motorists who use the roads more would pay more; or the fund could be contributed to by all road users, including cyclists and pedestrians – though this would be so nearly co-incident with the entire population that it would be tantamount to an ordinary tax. Or again, a special levy could be imposed on motor manufacturers and perhaps also on highway authorities, which could be paid into the fund. Much would no doubt depend on how compensation was to be assessed. If it involved paying variable compensation for income losses, it might be thought equitable to make people pay contributions to the fund according to their income. Alternatively the whole process could be financed out of general taxation, and no special tax imposed for the purpose.

Because there are so many ways of distributing losses, it cannot be said that loss distribution as such is a rational and desirable goal of the law. Any loss distribution system must be judged according to the way it distributes particular losses. For example, few would find acceptable a system which distributed the costs of road accidents entirely amongst non-motorists or the costs of smoking-induced cancer entirely amongst non-smokers. Two things about the tort system seem clear, however. The first is that loss spreading cannot be the sole purpose or justification of the tort system, because both in theory and in practice it allows recovery for only a small proportion of personal injury losses. Secondly, it seems clear that there are much cheaper and more efficient ways of distributing the losses the tort system does deal with than the present combination of liability rules and liability insurance.

Equitable loss distribution

How, then, are we to choose between methods of loss distribution? Or, to put the question differently, how ought a system of loss compensation to be funded? There seem to be three broad options: first party loss insurance (whether private or State-run (national insurance)), which spreads the loss amongst potential victims, third party liability insurance, which spreads the loss amongst those likely to inflict it; and general taxation. Each of these mechanisms can be used alone or in combination with other methods. Just as important as the method of funding is the question of whether the compensation paid out on the one hand, and the contributions to the fund on the other, are to be the same for all beneficiaries or contributors (i.e. flat rate) or variable in some way (i.e. income related). A third important question which cuts across the first two is whether losses ought to be distributed by free market mechanisms (which would make people pay for what they enjoy and for the losses they cause), or by State-run schemes, or by a mixture of the two. State-run schemes can be used to achieve other ends in addition to loss distribution, such as income redistribution in favour of the poor.

Efficient loss-distribution

Another criterion relevant to choosing between methods of distribution is efficiency. There are many aspects to the question of efficiency. First, there is the administrative cost of the process, and here, as we have seen, the social security system wins hands down with administrative costs of about 6% for sickness benefits and supplementary benefits, to about 12% for the industrial injuries system. The criminal injuries compensation system, too, can hardly be seriously faulted on the cost issue, since its administrative cost runs at about 11% of the sums paid out. The tort system, on the other hand, as we have also seen, runs at an administrative cost of about 85% or more of sums paid out. The comparisons are slightly misleading because a large part of the cost of the tort system is attributable to the cost of collecting the money, while the cost of collecting social security payments is almost entirely borne by employers, and does not figure in the direct cost actually borne by the National Insurance Fund, though it is a social cost borne in the long run by society. But even making all due allowances for this, it is clear that, on cost alone, the tort system is extremely inefficient.

Other aspects of efficiency must also be considered, for example, the prevalence of fraud or abuse, the extent to which the compensation system in fact meets the needs they profess to meet, and the speed with which they do so. Most of these questions we have already considered at some length in discussing the detailed provisions of the various systems, and in general the verdict must plainly go to the social security system. The principal defect of the social security system lies in the inadequacy of some of the benefits, and in particular those for long-term incapacity for people suffering from non-industrial injury or from disease, or from congenital disability. There is no doubt that tort damages are a more adequate compensation for those with large incomes, though only a small proportion of victims receive damages. Possibly, the tort system is also more efficient in guarding against fraud and abuse.[13] But in almost every other respect the tort system is inferior to social security as a means of compensating the victims of personal injury and incapacity.

The allocation of risks

Lawyers have sometimes urged that the 'real' purpose of the law is not so much to decide whether one person has caused injury to another by his fault, or whether one person should compensate another for a wrong, but merely to allocate the risk of the occurrence of certain events between various parties. This sort of language seems particularly suitable to cases of strict liability in the law of tort, and to many areas of the law of compensation outside the tort system, such as the industrial injuries scheme. For example, the basis of the principle in *Rylands* v. *Fletcher* is that a person who collects dangerous substances on his land should bear the risk of their escape whether or not the escape was his fault.

It was in the field of workmen's compensation that the idea of risk-allocation first made a powerful impact. It was felt to be unjust that the whole burden of accidents should lie on the injured workman, and that it was immaterial that the accidents were or were not caused by fault. These risks were felt to be risks of the business.[14] Similarly, the vicarious liability of an enterprise for the wrong of its servants has for many years been justified by invoking the idea that the employer should take the risk of his servants damaging others.[15]

It is obvious that simply to say that the law is concerned with allocating risks does not answer the important question of how particular risks ought to be allocated or why certain risk are allocated in a particular way. Why, for instance, does an injured pedestrian on the road take the risk of a non-fault caused accident, rather than a motorist? Or, conversely, suppose that we think – as many do – that the risk should lie on the motorist, we are still faced with the question, why? Doubtless some will feel impatient with such questions. It is obvious, they will say, that certain risks should be on certain people. Common sense, or the instinctive sense of justice, is a sufficient answer to this question. For instance, in a case like *Dunne* v. *NW Gas Board*,[16] where the plaintiff was injured as a result of an explosion of gas from a fractured main, it seems obvious to many that the risk of the accident should have been on the gas board, whether or not negligence was proved. Nevertheless, it is not very satisfactory to abandon the search for rational objectives in the law, and be forced to rely on common sense or the instinctive sense of justice as a guide for practical decision.

When an attempt is made to analyse some of these common sense ideas about risk distribution, there appears to lie at the root of many of them the notion that a person who has 'created' a risk should be made to bear the cost of the risk; and when efforts are made to explain on what bases it can be said that a person has 'created' a risk, it will usually be found that causal concepts are dominant. A gas board whose leaking pipes lead to an explosion is thought to have 'caused' the destruction of the plaintiff's house, and so to have 'created' the risk of such damage. But (if fault is ruled out as a hypothesis) there is no greater reason for saying the destruction of the house was 'caused' by the presence of the gas pipes than by the presence of the house itself. And if the house was built after the pipes were laid, it will be apparent that there is no more reason for saying the risk was 'created' by the gas board than by the house owner. If we are to justify allocation of risk to one party or the other we need some better criterion. One possible approach is to impose liability on the party in the better position to minimize the risk, so as to give him an incentive to do so. Another approach would be to ask which party would be in a better position to distribute the loss caused if the risk materialized. So, as with loss distribution as a goal of the law, risk allocation as such is not an adequate objective. A scheme of risk allocation must be judged according to *how* the risks are allocated.

There are other functions besides loss distribution and risk allocation which a compensation system might perform. In the next chapter we will consider whether a desire for retribution or vindication provides a legitimate goal for a compensation system. In Chapter 24 we will consider the role of compensation rules in preventing injuries and deterring injury-causing behaviour.

23
Retribution and vindication

1 RETRIBUTION

It is no longer fashionable to regard retribution as a legitimate objective of a penal system. The desire to seek vengeance, to punish because we want to inflict pain or suffering, is nowadays generally felt to be a primitive instinct which should be kept in check in a civilized society. If this is so in the penal system, the declared purpose of which is to catch and punish malefactors, how much more must it be the case with a system of compensation which is not, on the face of it, concerned with punishing wrongdoing.

Certainly this is the 'conventional wisdom' of the law of torts, the purpose of which was emphatically said to be compensatory and not punitive by the House of Lords in *Rookes* v. *Barnard*[1] and the decision and general approach of that case were reaffirmed by the House in *Broome* v. *Cassell*.[2] In the former case Lord Devlin, with the concurrence of all the other judges, held that unless there was express statutory authority, punitive damages could be awarded in only two situations: first, where the defendant being in a position of public authority was guilty of arbitrary, oppressive or unconstitutional conduct; and secondly, where the defendant has made a profit out of his wrongdoing which exceeds the loss to the plaintiff. In neither of these situations, however, need the award of damages be seen as primarily retributive. In the second type of situation the damages could be seen as preventing the defendant being unjustly enriched at the expense of the plaintiff; in the first type of case they could be seen as designed to deter abuse of power by public officials. We will return to the deterrent function of tort law later.

There are, however, certain other situations in which the law of torts might be seen as performing a retributive function. First, it seems that retribution does play a part in certain types of tort case in which the plaintiff recovers damages although he has suffered no real financial or bodily injury, but has merely been subjected to outrage, humiliation or indignity by the defendant. It is perhaps still doubtful whether it is an actionable tort wilfully or intentionally to inflict outrage or indignity on a plaintiff (though it is certainly so in the United States),[3] but even in England such conduct would be actionable where the defendant has been guilty of conduct which can be classified under one of the traditional heads of common law torts, such as fraud,[4] assault (or more strictly, battery) or libel. So, for example, if a person commits a battery by spitting at another, it is inconceivable that a judge would send the plaintiff away with nothing but nominal damages, Lord Devlin notwithstanding. To be sure a plaintiff would not be awarded enormous damages for such conduct, but he might easily collect £100 or something of that sort. It is implausible to regard such an award as performing a purely deterrent function: in such a case the plaintiff would almost certainly bring his action with the purpose of making the defendant pay, of making him smart and suffer for what he has done. Another part of the law of torts which may be seen as performing a retributive function is the tort of defamation, although in theory this tort is designed to compensate the plaintiff for 'loss of reputation'.

It is unlikely that retribution is often a factor in personal injury actions, although damages for bereavement get close to being punitive (in theory they are meant to provide solace). Because damages for personal injuries aim to be compensatory, it is perhaps more accurate to describe the aim of the law not as retribution but as fairness or corrective justice – the law aims to restore and redress the balance of fairness or justice which the defendant has upset by his negligence or by creating a risk of injury. This aim is distinguishable from retribution because, as we saw in Chapter 19, justice and fairness can require the payment of compensation even in the absence of fault. And even where the defendant was at fault, the compensatory principle of damages prevents the tort action from being seen as retributive in a strict sense. Neither retribution nor corrective justice are served by compensation systems which do not involve an individual victim suing an individual defendant for monetary compensation.

2 VINDICATION OR SATISFACTION

When a person is involved in a dispute with another who he thinks has done wrong, and when that other refuses to admit that he has done wrong (and sometimes even when he does admit it), it may be a great satisfaction to the former to know that he has the right to summon the latter before one of Her Majesty's judges for a public confrontation in which the latter may be branded as in the wrong. It has been suggested, for example, that victims of adverse drug reactions who receive substantial compensation paid voluntarily by a drug company may still not feel satisfied because the company has got away with simply paying a sum of money.[5] This desire for an 'official' decision to settle a dispute or an argument, a decision which will finally put an end to excuses, evasions and prevarication, sometimes extends to the public at large. Frequently, this demand is met by setting up public inquiries of one kind or another, such as the public inquiry into the disaster at Aberfan in 1966, in which 116 children and 28 adults lost their lives as a result of the collapse of a coal tip on to their school. Here the National Coal Board and various public officials were plainly in the 'dock', in the sense that the parents of the dead children, and indeed the whole village of Aberfan (which had complained about the coal tips for years), had a passionate desire to have a public confrontation with the Coal Board and these officials before an impartial judge who would finally determine whether anyone, and if so who, was responsible for the disaster. There is no other explanation of why the tribunal should have taken so much trouble in its report to pronounce on the 'blameworthiness' of various parties, when the issue of legal liability was regarded as incontestable, and was in fact not contested.

This sort of inquiry, it will be noted, is not a decision-making body. Its objects are merely to ascertain facts and, sometimes, to ascribe responsibility for them. It does not award damages or grant any other legal remedy, though doubtless its findings would usually be accepted for the purposes of negotiating a settlement of claims arising from the facts inquired into. But it is plain that this is not always felt to be a necessary adjunct of the process. The desire for the public confrontation, the opportunity to state one's case in public before impartial judges, the desire for a public judgment in which one is vindicated and another person condemned, all this is often sufficient in itself.

Clearly, public vindication of this sort is not provided at all by compensation systems such as personal insurance and social security, in which entitlement to compensation does not depend on establishing wrongdoing, where the compensation is sought from and paid by persons in no way responsible for the loss suffered, and where entitlement to compensation is determined by an administrative process conducted in private. Even in the case of the Criminal Injuries Board, which follows semi-judicial procedure, the hearings are in private and the wrongdoer is not represented.

The tort system, based as it is on the notion of fault and on the public adversarial trial, does offer some scope for public vindication. This is clearly so when, for example, a court awards damages against a bully or thug who has beaten up the plaintiff. But even an ordinary finding of negligence may give satisfaction to an injured person. It has also been suggested that tort law can play a role as a public grievance mechanism similar to an Ombudsman,[6] especially in cases against public authorities or large corporations (such as drug companies) whose actions have caused widespread damage or injury to many people (e.g. the thalidomide tragedy or the Bhopal chemical disaster). In such cases a tort action may serve as much to establish responsibility and to vindicate feelings of outrage and grief as to obtain compensation. It is true that statutory public inquiries are often held into major disasters such as aircraft or railway crashes; but the great attraction of tort law for the citizen is that he can set the system in motion himself and does not have to wait for the government to act. If the tort system of compensation for personal injuries were ever abolished entirely, it might be thought desirable to institute some procedure for citizen-initiated inquiries of this type.

It must be noted, however, that the capacity of the tort system to provide vindication is limited by the fact that in most cases the real defendant is a liability insurer and the purpose of the action is chiefly to unlock the door to the insurance fund; and also by the fact that the vast majority of tort claims are settled out of court, in private, by administrative processes and without formal admission of liability. Furthermore, it is apparent that the law does not set a very high value on vindication: if the defendant offers sufficient compensation to the plaintiff by way of settlement of his claim but the plaintiff rejects the offer and insists on his day in court, not because he finds the offer insufficient but simply out of a desire for public vindication, he will, in the majority of cases, have to pay the costs of the hearing.

24
Deterrence and prevention

One of the major suggested functions of personal injuries compensation law is deterrence of potentially injury-causing conduct and the prevention of injury-causing incidents such as accidents. A distinction is sometimes drawn between specific and general deterrence. Specific deterrence involves the direct prohibition or regulation of dangerous conduct or activities (by means of statutes or regulations, for example) in order to reduce the number of injuries and injury-causing incidents. General deterrence involves the use of compensation rules to provide indirect incentives to people to behave safely – the general idea is that the prospect of having to pay damages for injuries caused by particular conduct will deter people from engaging in conduct of that type.

The idea of general deterrence can be given a more or less precise interpretation. The less precise version says that by establishing rules and standards of conduct and by attaching the sanction of damages (or, in the case of plaintiffs, a reduction of damages) for failure to satisfy those standards and rules, the law can provide incentives to safe conduct. This version also sees the law as performing an educational function. The more precise interpretation, which is based on economic principles, says, broadly, that if the cost of injuries inflicted by an activity are required by law to be paid by those who engage in that activity, then they will take precautions to prevent inflicting injuries, provided the cost of precautions is less than the cost of the injuries (i.e. the damages they have to pay); and that in this way the optimum or efficient level of precautions (and, conversely, of injuries) will be reached. This version is sometimes called 'market deterrence', but more commonly 'general deterrence', and in what follows the term 'general deterrence' will normally be used to refer to the more precise version.

In this chapter we will be primarily concerned with the two versions of general deterrence, because they are about the way compensation systems can be used to promote safety. But it should be noted that compensation systems are not the only, or even the most important, means of deterrence and injury prevention. In the two main fields in which personal injuries are compensatable by common law damages, that is road accidents and industrial injuries, other methods are at least as important. On the road, reliance is placed on a combination of criminal penalties – fines for careless, dangerous and drunken driving, and disqualification from driving; and improved road and vehicle design. In the case of industrial injuries, reliance is placed on the criminal law and on education and publicity. On the other hand, it may be that compensation law is more effective as a deterrent in the latter case than in the former, because in these cases the defendant will very often be a business concern, and business concerns are probably more sensitive to the incentives which tort law provides than are individuals. This will be discussed in greater detail later.

1 RULES AND STANDARDS OF BEHAVIOUR

The less precise version of general deterrence has two aspects: first, that of deterring people from conduct which may injure others, and secondly that of deterring people from conduct which may injure themselves.

Causing injury to others

It is fairly evident that no compensation system can be any use as a deterrent against causing injury to others, unless it is based on a connection between the person who causes the accident and the person who pays compensation. A State social security system will not deter people from causing injury to others. Under this sort of system the compensation is paid by the whole nation as insured persons and taxpayers, and the burden on any individual does not increase because he has caused an accident, the victim of which is qualified for social security benefits. Similarly, with first party insurance as a method of compensation: nobody is going to be deterred from setting fire to another person's house by the thought that that person will receive compensation from his own insurance company. The only type of compensation system which can operate in any way as a deterrent is a system like the tort system, in which one of the conditions of legal liability is that the defendant's conduct caused, or at least contributed to, the accident. If we make a person pay for the damage or injury which he causes to others, then he may try to cause less damage or injury. But the effectiveness of the tort system as a deterrent depends on two main factors.

The ability to avoid accidents

First, it depends on the ability of the potential tortfeasor to take steps in advance to prevent the damage or injury occurring. One aspect of this issue was discussed in Chapter 19, where we pointed out that in concentrating on the parties to the action, the law tends to ignore other factors which may be responsible for accidents in many cases, such as the state of roads. Clearly the deterrent value of tort law is thrown into grave doubt if the courts regularly ignore important causes of injuries.

Another factor is whether intentional conduct is involved in the tort in question. There is no doubt that it is much easier to deter intentional conduct by the threat of a tort action for damages than it is to deter negligent conduct. The tort action is certainly a more effective deterrent, for instance, in preventing a surgeon operating on a patient without his consent, than it is in preventing the surgeon from making a negligent mistake in the course of the operation. Also there is no reason to doubt that the law of torts is a very important factor in deterring newspapers from publishing much which could be defamatory. Newspaper proprietors can and do take steps to eliminate defamatory matter (such as getting lawyers to read doubtful items before they are published), and they do this because it is cheaper than paying the heavy damages which juries tend to award against them in defamation actions.

The effectiveness of tort actions or, indeed, any legal sanction to deter non-intentional conduct is much more doubtful. Road and industrial accidents, with which the tort system is in practice chiefly concerned, are often caused by failure of observation and perception, by faulty judgment, by lack of basic skills and many other factors which are not readily responsive to any type of deterrent. If a person has not perceived that there is danger in a certain course of conduct, he will not be deterred from embarking on that conduct by any threat of penalties for doing something dangerous. However high the penalty may be for failing to stop at a stop sign, a motorist is not going to be induced to stop by a stop sign which he has not seen – even if he ought to have seen it. Furthermore, given that the negligent driver puts himself as well as others at risk by his carelessness, it is unlikely, if he is not deterred by fear for his own safety, that he will be deterred by the prospect of having to pay a fine or damages.[1]

This does not mean that we can never deter people from negligent conduct by threats of penalties or even of tort liability. We may not be able to deter a drunk from dangerous driving once he has got behind the wheel, but we may be able to deter him from getting behind the wheel while he is drunk, or from getting drunk when he knows that he is going to drive. We cannot induce a driver to stop by a stop sign which he has not seen, but we can try to bring pressure on him to look for stop signs rather more carefully. People can be encouraged not to speed. Tort liability may also have some deterrent effect where the potential defendant is a business concern and will weigh the relative costs of paying damages and preventing injuries; and where the injuries are caused by defective products or premises or by unsafe working conditions which can be made safer by conscious design.

But even so there are serious limitations on the effectiveness of deterrence as a means of preventing injuries. Trying to deter people from dangerous conduct by bringing pressure to bear before they get themselves into the dangerous situation is only effective to the extent that people recognize dangerous situations. Take, for instance, the drunken driver. Before the law prohibited driving with more than a specified level of alcohol in the blood, the law of torts and its exhortation to take care did very little to deter drunk-driving because people did not recognize that even a moderate amount of alcohol can so affect a person's skill and judgment as a driver as to very substantially increase the risk of his being involved in an accident.[2] Even now breach of the drunk-driving laws is common because people still do not fully realize the risks involved.

More difficult still are cases in which motorists are simply ignorant of accident-causing factors. For instance, one common cause of road accidents is the night-time driver who runs into the vehicle in front of him because he has not seen it early enough to be able to stop. Trying to apply deterrence at the accident stage itself is clearly useless; if the driver has not *seen* the vehicle in front, no threats are going to affect him. But in this situation it is not much use trying to deter the motorist at an early stage either, for this would only work if motorists generally knew that this sort of accident was a serious risk of night-time driving, and they do not appear to do so.

Two lessons may be drawn from these facts. First, in order to reduce accidents and injuries it is necessary to study their causes very carefully. It is not enough simply to take road conditions and vehicle qualities as given, and assume that all accidents are 'caused' by careless or negligent conduct – even if it is true that most accidents could be avoided by greater care. The fact is that 'If we try to find out why a particular accident occurred, we can seldom pinpoint a single cause. Nearly always, it might have been prevented if any one of a variety of things about the road, the vehicles, or the people involved had been different.'[3] When the statistics are carefully examined, it may be found that deterring people from negligent conduct is not always or usually the easiest, cheapest or simplest way to avoid a certain type of accident. For example, the most effective way of preventing accidents of the type referred to in the previous paragraph may be to require the rear end of vehicles to be better lit.

The second lesson is that if we are to take deterrence seriously, we must give people detailed guidance as to how to behave. General exhortations to drive with care are useless: nearly every motorist thinks he does drive with great care already,[4] though 'many drivers are much less skilled than they think'.[5] But tell the motorist that he is not to cross the double white line, and there is a reasonable chance he will obey this specific direction. A general exhortation to drive at a speed which is reasonable in all the circumstances of the case is less effective than an imposed speed limit.[6] General directions to drive with reasonable care or consideration for others are not very helpful at a roundabout, compared to specific instructions to give way to drivers already on the roundabout. Indeed, one writer on the subject of road accidents has convincingly argued that a prime cause of accidents is the 'ambiguous' situations in which drivers often find themselves, i.e. situations in which it is not entirely clear what is required of them.[7]

The common law of torts does not in general give detailed guidance to people as to the precautions they should adopt to avoid injuries and damage. The only guidance it gives is the general requirement to take reasonable care according to all the circumstances of the case, but what is reasonable care will only be decided by the courts *after* an injury has occurred. Indeed, even then the court will often avoid trying to lay down what would have been reasonable care or what would not have been reasonable care, let alone lay down guidance for future conduct; courts are frequently content to say that in *this* case, the actual care taken was or was not reasonable. The courts take this approach because of the view that the exact circumstances of the particular case are crucial in deciding how the defendant ought reasonably to have behaved. As a method of telling people how to regulate their lives or their conduct, this is clearly of very little use.

Despite all that we have said, however, it would be a mistake to conclude that even the common law of negligence can never be used as a means of regulating people's conduct and preventing accidents and injuries. There are undoubtedly some situations in which the same kind of risk recurs continuously in what are, in all relevant essentials, similar circumstances; and in a case of this kind, a decision of a High Court Judge, or still more, the Court of Appeal, as to what is or is not negligent conduct, could well be taken in practice as laying down a standard of conduct which should be followed. For example, it is hard to imagine any reason why the thickness of the glass in glass-panelled doors in local authority schools should vary from one school to another. When, therefore, Veale J. decided in *Reffell* v. *Surrey County Council*[8] that it was negligent of the local authority to use untoughened glass only one-eighth of an inch thick instead of toughened glass because of the risk of accidents to the pupils, it is not surprising that this decision should have been treated as laying down a rule that the glass in such doors should be toughened in all local authority schools; and that some local authorities should have proceeded to act on that rule by changing the glass in schools where it did not conform to the rule. Similarly, when the House of Lords held in *Morris* v. *West Hartlepool Steam Navigation Co.*[9] that the risk of a seaman falling into the hold of a ship was so obvious that it was negligent not to provide some sort of protective fencing, even though this had never been the practice of shipowners, this decision may well have been treated by shipowners as itself being a rule to be complied with. Yet there was no obligation on shipowners to take this course. It would have been no crime to continue as before. The only sanction would be the near certainty[10] that in the event of other similar accidents they would have to pay out damages for negligence. If the cost of erecting some protective barrier were so great that it was likely to exceed the total damages that would probably have to be paid out for accidents so caused, a shipowner might very well decide to do nothing, though a series of like accidents, with public denunciation of its conduct from the bench, might eventually make it change its position.

It may be that the law of negligence is most effective as a regulator of conduct in cases where it is least desirable that standards of conduct *should* be laid down by the courts. For example, public bodies are very likely to act upon adverse findings of negligence by courts; and yet, for example, the funds necessary to replace glass doors in schools may have to be found at the expense of better facilities in local hospitals. The concentration in a civil trial on a single incident may exclude these wider policy issues.

Counter-productiveness of compensation systems

There is no doubt that tort law is counter-productive with respect to safety and injury prevention in certain areas, and most notably in the industrial accidents area. This subject was discussed at some length by the Robens Committee on Safety and Health at Work. The Committee recorded that they had received many representations to the effect that:

> the present system of civil actions for damages for industrial accidents, whatever its other merits or demerits, has an inhibiting and distorting effect on the work of making and enforcing regulations to prevent accidents, and indeed, on the accident prevention effort generally.[11]

The main problem appears to be that the industrial safety legislation is very rarely the subject of any criminal proceedings, and that, in practice, the main role of the legislation is to support claims for damages for breach of statutory duty. Thus, when such legislation is being drafted and when it is being interpreted in the courts, it is nearly always the compensation aspect which comes into question. The fact that the primary purpose of the legislation is safety tends to get overlooked.

The second way in which tort law tends to be counter-productive concerns the immediate aftermath of an industrial accident. Because of the possibility that a claim for damages will result, it is often very difficult to investigate an accident with a view to discovering how it was caused and to preventing a recurrence if at all possible. The employers (acting under some constraint because of the terms of their insurance policy) will be reluctant to discuss the cause of the accident, lest they may make remarks which can be construed as an admission of negligence or breach of statutory duty. The injured person's workmates, likewise, may be reluctant to discuss the case, lest they prejudice their colleague's claim for damages. And nobody wishes to take remedial measures before the claim is settled for fear that this too may be interpreted as an admission that adequate precautions were not taken before.[12]

Another area where tort law may well be counter-productive is that of medical negligence. It is widely said that in America, where malpractice actions are now very common, doctors are encouraged to practise 'defensive medicine', that is to say they prescribe treatment or medical tests, not for truly therapeutic reasons, but to safeguard themselves from possible legal liability. Even in England, it has been said that a doctor may be tempted not to use a particular form of treatment because it carries a small risk; if the risk eventuates, the doctor may be blamed or even held liable, while if the treatment is not used, the ill consequences will be laid at the door of the disease and not the doctor.[13]

The incidence of payment

There is no doubt that the prevalence of liability insurance greatly reduces the deterrent potentiality of tort law. It is absurd to suppose that a motorist who is not deterred from doing something foolish by fear for his own safety or that of his family, nor by fear of the criminal law, nor by fear of being disqualified, is going to be deterred by the fear of being sued in a tort action in which the damages will be paid by his insurance company. The only financial stake that the motorist has in all this is any excess he may be required to pay under the insurance policy (such as the first £50 of any claim), and the loss of his no-claim bonus. We would not suggest these are wholly negligible or derisory sums to many motorists, but there is no real evidence that fear of loss of an excess, or a no-claim bonus, has any significant effect on accidents[14] – though it may well have a real effect on claims.

It has sometimes been suggested that motorists should not be permitted to protect themselves by unlimited liability insurance, that they should for instance, be required to pay up to £100 (or £500 or even £1,000 in serious cases) without recourse to liability insurance.[15] But to jeopardize the accident victim's chances of actually receiving his compensation would be a high price to pay for the additional deterrent value of such a scheme. Moreover, if the threat of having to pay large sums of money is really a valuable deterrent against dangerous driving, then a more satisfactory way of enforcing payment would be by use of the criminal law. For one thing, this would not involve the risk that the victim might not receive his compensation; and for another thing, use of the criminal law would obviate the unequal treatment of equally culpable motorists where one has injured a victim and the other has not. A more sophisticated version of the scheme is that liability insurance should continue as at present with the victim assured of his compensation, but the insurer should be required, or permitted, to claim the designated sum from the insured after the victim has been paid off. In France, a law of 1978 permits insurance companies to claim re-imbursement of damages paid out as the result of the negligence of a motorist who was drunk at the time of the accident. But this scheme also has grave disadvantages, not the least being that neither insurer nor insured would have any interest in enforcing the payment; even the insurer would find it simpler to raise the level of his premiums generally, than to try to extract indemnities from individual motorists. In any event, if sums are to be extracted from the motorist as a quasi-fine after the victim is paid, this appears a more appropriate task for the criminal law, with its recognized procedural safeguards for an accused.

In industrial accident cases the problem is similar, if not entirely the same. Here also, liability insurance is now compulsory; which means that the immediate financial consequences of an accident are never felt by the employer. It is, perhaps, an indication of the general attitude to tort law as an accident prevention measure that there was no serious opposition to the introduction of compulsory insurance in the Act of 1969. The effectiveness of liability insurance in accident prevention is examined later.[16]

It is true that employers shoulder considerable indirect or incidental costs arising from accidents, such as the disturbance and loss of time, the need to shut off machinery or plant, and so on, all of which has been estimated to cost more than half the actual accident costs themselves.[17] These are not covered by insurance[18] but here again, these costs are simply absorbed or passed on to the consumer to the extent that the industry is able to do this. The costs simply do not hit any individuals sufficiently hard to provide the incentive to take accident avoidance measures.

The conclusion must be that, even in the industrial field, the role of tort law as a deterrent must be a very limited one, so long as the primary aim of tort law remains the compensation of the injured.

Avoiding injury to oneself

If the utility of compensation law as a deterrent against causing injury to others must be so doubtful, how much more doubtful must be its effectiveness in deterring injury to the actor himself. The only way in which we could hope to do this would be by refusing compensation – or full compensation – to a person indulging in an activity of which we disapproved, or indulging in any activity without taking sufficient care for himself. We could, for instance, refuse compensation to people injured through the fault of others, if they were engaged in serious crime at the time they were injured. This might conceivably have *some* deterrent value. But it is unlikely that such a threat would be a significant additional deterrent beside the threat of imprisonment.

The law does, of course, through the doctrine of contributory negligence, offer some incentive to people to take care of themselves, but it seems unlikely that it is very effective in promoting safety. If a person's instinct for self preservation does not deter him from dangerous conduct, then it is unlikely that a denial of monetary or other assistance will do so. If people are not deterred from smoking by knowledge of the health risks, then it is unlikely that they would be deterred by a refusal of treatment under the NHS for cancer contracted from smoking. Similarly, it seems unlikely that a person will be induced to have an operation which is medically advisable by threats to deprive him of damages if he fails to have it.[19] A person who fails to have recommended medical treatment because of some irrational phobia is surely not going to respond to inducements and threats concerning the award of damages in a totally rational manner.

The case of failure to wear a seatbelt is somewhat more complex. As we saw earlier, the common law does treat failure to wear a seatbelt as contributory negligence, and a plaintiff's damages may be reduced on this ground. However, research has shown that during the period 1973–80 only about 30% of drivers and front seat passengers wore seatbelts, despite the risk of receiving reduced damages if injured while not wearing a seatbelt. But in 1983 when, subject to limited exceptions, it became a criminal offence for a driver or front seat passenger not to wear a seat belt if provided, the compliance rate rose to 95% for cars and over 80% for vans.[20] This dramatic change is, no doubt, partly attributable to the greater deterrent effectiveness of the criminal over the civil law; partly to the fact that the new provision was much better publicized and known than the common law rule; and partly because of the confirmed efficacy of seatbelts in reducing injuries – it is estimated that there are now some 20–25% fewer fatal and serious injuries to drivers and front seat passengers than there would have been without compulsory belt-wearing.[21] Without the widespread compliance induced by the new law, these figures could never have been assembled.

Not surprisingly, then, most compensation systems in force today make little or no attempt to deter people from causing loss or injury to themselves. The doctrine of contributory negligence, which reduces the amount of compensation payable to injured plaintiffs on account of their own fault, cannot seriously be justified as a means of deterring people from conduct likely to injure themselves. It must stand or fall with the rest of the fault system as a moral principle.

2 ACCIDENT PREVENTION VIA INSURANCE[22]

If insurance tends to remove what deterrent value the law – or the risk of injury or damage – may possess, there remains the possibility that insurers may themselves contribute something in lieu. In principle, there is no doubt that this is possible. Insurance can, and perhaps does, contribute something to loss prevention in two distinct ways. First, insurers may themselves attempt to take direct steps to minimize the losses against which they insure. And secondly, the premium rating system adopted by insurers may encourage other parties to take steps to minimize losses.

Direct action by insurers to minimize losses

Insurance involves a pooling of risks and an insurer – or *a fortiori* a combination of insurers – may find it worth while to take steps to reduce or eliminate risks which no individual risk-bearer would find profitable. It is of some interest to note, for example, that fire brigades in England were originally established and maintained by insurers.[23] Until 1832 the only fire brigades in London were maintained by individual insurers; in that year all the insurers formed one brigade. Not until 1865 was responsibility for fire fighting transferred to the local authority. Now clearly – in the absence of public interference – the institution of fire brigades could only come about from a pooling of risks. No individual householder could find it profitable to maintain his own fire brigade, because the risk of his house being burned down is far less than the cost of a fire brigade. But the risk of one house out of 10,000 being burned down is not so small, and if those risks are pooled with an insurer it becomes profitable for the insurer to maintain fire brigades.

There are other applications of this idea. Insurers maintain inspectors to survey plant, equipment and premises, and to advise the insured how to minimize risks and avoid losses. In this country insurers have traditionally played their largest loss minimization role in connection with engineering and fire insurance.[24] For example, they maintain a 'salvage corps' whose task it is to save and realize property involved in fires; and they also maintain (in conjunction with the fire brigade authorities) a joint fire research organization which investigates fire causation and prevention. And no insurer would take on any significant fire risk without a proper survey of the premises. Similar surveys are also carried out by employers' liability insurers, who may be able to persuade the employer to eliminate hazards, or may even require various safeguards to be taken before the risk is accepted.[25]

But it will be noticed that if the pooling of risks with insurers makes it worthwhile for them to undertake loss prevention, pooling of risks by the whole populace is more efficacious still. Fire brigades maintained by insurers are better than no fire brigades at all; but fire brigades maintained by the State are better still. Advice and assistance in preventing industrial accidents may be rendered by insurers, who have a wider experience to draw on than a single insured, but this advice and assistance can probably be better rendered by a government inspectorate who have unrivalled information, statistics and the fruits of research at their disposal.

In fact, inspectors employed by the liability insurance companies are today largely duplicating the work of the factory and other official inspectorates. The factory inspectorate are just as much concerned with accident prevention as the insurance inspectors, and demands that the former should be more concerned with enforcement of the law by prosecution were emphatically rejected by the Robens Committee.[26] It is, moreover, clear from the Robens Report that in modern industrial conditions there is a need for specialization in the skills of inspectors, who must be able to cover an enormous range of industries.[27] This makes it unlikely that insurers can maintain sufficiently large staffs with the necessary skills to rival the official inspectorate. It is possible that in the past the insurers' inspectors have sometimes been able to obtain results from employers because of the techniques of persuasion at their disposal, *viz.* threats of higher premiums or total refusal of cover. But the latter threat is now one which insurers find difficult to use with an existing customer (because, as a result of the requirement of compulsory insurance, such a refusal of cover can close the business down), and the Safety and Health at Work Act 1974 now gives official inspectors equally effective powers. Under the Act an inspector may serve a 'prohibition notice' or an 'improvement notice' on an employer requiring improvements to be carried out, or prohibiting the use of some plant or machinery.

In any event, the scope for direct loss prevention activity by insurers is limited by a number of factors. First, such activities have to be paid for out of premium income, and the return on them is not always immediately apparent. This means that an insurer who chooses to cut down or even eliminate expenditure on such activities can probably undercut other insurers in a competitive market. Unless insurers can undertake this sort of activity jointly (which does happen to a significant degree in the fire insurance industry) not much can be achieved; and joint activity is now less easy, since it is always liable to produce complaints of restrictive practices and price fixing, and consequent reference to the Monopolies Commission (as indeed happened with the fire insurers).

Second, the incentive on the insurer to minimize losses is, in the last analysis, small. For if some new accident prevention device on the road or in industry led to a large cut in the cost of accidents, the insurers would immediately come under pressure to reduce their premiums. Conversely, if accident rates go up because of insufficient attention to accident prevention, insurers can and do increase their premium rates. This has led to a somewhat curious situation, as the managing director of a large insurer has pointed out:

> Run an expensive accident-prevention service, reduce the losses, show a profit: result, over-high expense ratio, good profit, public criticism. Run the account without providing service at all: result, low expense ration, high loss ratio, underwriting loss, public commiseration on the difficulties of the time.[28]

The result of all this is that although insurers are, in practice, well placed to play a large role in accident prevention if they want to, there is little incentive for them to do so. Even in the United States, where insurance companies have played an important role in promoting safety in industry, they have not generally done much, if anything, to further accident prevention on the roads.[29] One notable illustration is the failure of the insurance industry to force motor manufacturers to install seat belts in cars once it became clear that they could play a major role in reducing the gravity of injuries: action in this field had to be left (both in America and in this country) to legislative control.

Use of premium rating system for loss minimization

Insurance companies can, in principle, devise premium rating structures that encourage the insured himself to minimize the risk of accidents, and to reduce the cost of those accidents that do occur. For example, fire insurers can and do offer very different rates for the insurance of buildings which have adequate sprinkler installations. The premium for unsprinklered risks is commonly five or six times that for sprinklered risks of the same character.[30] Clearly, this provides an incentive for the installation of sprinkler systems.

But in the area with which this book is mainly concerned, that is with third party personal injury insurance on the roads and in industry, it has been much more difficult to devise a premium structure which has a significant effect on accident costs and rates.[31] So far as concerns road accidents, the general picture is well enough known. Premiums depend on a variety of factors which have been associated with high claims experience in the past, particularly age and claims experience. Usage, vehicle characteristics and area of garaging, are also major factors used in premium fixing. The elaborate no-claim bonus system now operated by most insurers means that a person with a history of accidents (or at least of claims) will pay substantially more for motor insurance than a person who has the maximum discount after several years without a claim on his policy. Unfortunately, there are substantial grounds for believing that the whole premium rating structure of motor insurance is based on a hotchpotch of irrationalities, mythologies and traditional practices, rather than (as many people think) on any scientific or statistical basis.[32] The full explanation of this would require a volume in itself, but it is enough here to point to one major weakness in the whole system. Personal injury road accidents are (as we have seen) rare events for the individual motorist, though property damage only accidents are far more common. Probably only some 3 to 4% of drivers are involved in a personal injury road accident each year, whereas six or seven times this number may be involved in property damage accidents. The consequence is that the claims record of the insured which largely determines the size of his premium is, in most cases, a claims record based on property damage accidents only; but this claims record also determines the size of that part of his premium which is required for third party personal injury risks.[33] This would not matter, of course, if there was any evidence of a real correlation between involvement in property damage accidents and involvement in personal injury accidents, but there is no such evidence. And it certainly would be unsafe to assume that this must be so *a priori*, because a large proportion of property damage accidents consist of little more than dents and scratches unlikely to cause personal injury to anyone.

Another problem is that, in the last analysis, most studies show that a high proportion of accidents are indeed just that, namely accidents, and are produced by a combination of relatively fortuitous events. They are thus random events and cannot be linked to driver behaviour. Except for the factors of youth and inexperience, there is no firm evidence showing any significant correlation between past accident experience and likely future accident experience, all other things being equal.[34] But even if we ignore the deficiencies in the premium rating system, it is very difficult to believe that fear of loss of a no-claims discount plays a significant role in making drivers drive more carefully.[35]

With regard to industrial injuries, the position is more complex. As we have seen, the national insurance industrial injuries system operates with premiums which do not vary with risk, and therefore have no effect on injury rates, or injury prevention. The employers' liability system for damages, however, operates according to the usual market principle, under which employers who present higher risks pay higher premiums. However, it must be appreciated that the great majority of employers pay premium rates which are determined by the average experience of employers in that class of business, and not by reference to their own experience. The principal reason for this, is that the employer's own past experience is not a sufficiently certain indication of his likely future experience unless he employs a substantial number of workmen. In the United States, an employer's experience for workmen's compensation insurance is not regarded as fully 'credible' (that is, sufficiently reliable to form the basis for the *entire* premium) unless the firm employs 2,500 workmen.[36] Below this, the employer's experience may still be taken into account, but the premium will partly be determined by reference to his experience, and partly by reference to the general experience of that class of industry. But even this is not possible for small firms whose experience is likely to be very unreliable statistically speaking. In Britain insurers do not work to a formula in the same way that American insurers do, and in evaluating a firm's experience they exercise a degree of judgment and discretion not used in America. But even here it is still impractical to take account of a firm's own experience unless it employs at least 100 workmen, and the firm would not be fully rated on its own experience unless it employed a great many more than this – perhaps 500 employees or more. This rules out the great majority of employers, because over 96% of all firms in manufacturing industry have a workforce of under 500.[37] However, the rest of the firms in manufacturing industry employ on aggregate about 50% of the country's total manufacturing workforce, so this does not demonstrate that experience rating is unimportant.

But there are other problems about experience-rating which undoubtedly tend to reduce its value for loss prevention purposes, though it is not possible to go into these in any detail here. Some of the main problems are the following.[38] First, it is not simple to define what is meant by the 'experience' of a firm: does this mean the number, or the cost of the accidents and injuries that have occurred; should the experience take account of 'costs' which are not paid by the employer's insurer, such as NHS costs (and if so, how are these to be estimated?); what is to be done with one very large claim which could distort the employer's claims experience for years, and so on. Secondly, there is the time-lag problem. Experience rating is always based on conditions which are to a greater or lesser extent out of date. For example, a firm's premium in 1987 must be fixed sometime in 1986, and must therefore be based on the experience of 1985 and earlier years. One year's experience is unreliable statistically, so a 'moving average' of three years' experience is usually used, but this means that the premium for 1987 will depend in part on the experience of 1983. During this period, many relevant factors may have altered the reliability of that previous experience as a guide to likely future experience. Thirdly, the total cost of employers' liability insurance is relatively low when compared with the employer's total wage bill on the one hand, or his total insurance costs (and especially his fire insurance costs) on the other. It would not be uncommon for an insurer to refrain from imposing a justified addition to an employer's liability insurance premium, because (for example) of the insurer's desire to retain the fire insurance account. Fourthly, premium variation is virtually unknown in relation to clerical and office staff, where the risks of injury are very small compared with those for manual or manufacturing staff, but there are nevertheless many thousands of accidents among such employees every year.

It is not easy to summarize the position, but it seems fair to say that it is unlikely that experience rating for employers' liability insurance has a very significant effect in reducing or minimizing accident costs.[39] On the other hand, it may well have some effect, and it does not seem justifiable to discard this possible method of helping to reduce accident costs, unless the arguments against it outweigh any possible advantages. It is true that its introduction into the industrial injuries system would add some additional complexity into the financing of that system; but the total number of establishments that could be sensibly experience rated is quite small. There are only about 3,000 manufacturing establishments in the whole UK which employ more than 500 persons each, and experience rating for this number would seem worth preserving. Whether or not tort liability remains for industrial injury cases, therefore, it is suggested that the industrial injuries legislation should introduce experience rating, at least for firms of this size in the first instance; the system could be extended to smaller firms in due course if the results seemed to justify it. However, the Pearson Commission rejected this proposal, mainly because of the complexity it would entail, though it is not clear that they really asked the vital question, namely whether the complexity would outweigh the benefits it would bring.

The case for extending the system of classified-rating (as opposed to experience-rating) into the industrial injury legislation is a different one. As the Pearson Report shows, accident rates vary widely; from as little as 4 per 1,000 employees per annum (for insurance, banking, etc.) to as many as 198 per 1,000 employees per annum (for mining, quarrying, etc.).[40] The case for a differential rating system among these employers depends partly on equity (why should industries with widely different accident rates pay the same accident costs?), and partly on resource allocation arguments (each industry should pay its own costs). It is to this latter question that the following sections are devoted.

3   GENERAL DETERRENCE[41]

As we have already noted, general deterrence ideas are based on economic theory about how free markets work. Proponents of general deterrence argue that the tort system of compensation is preferable to non-market systems, such as social security, because it performs the valuable incidental service of deterring dangerous behaviour and thus reducing injuries and losses. The following discussion is based on the work of Guido Calabresi, the originator and one of the leading exponents of the idea of general deterrence.

The price mechanism and the minimization of injury costs

Microeconomic theory is based on the hypothesis that in conditions of 'perfect competition' society would produce precisely those goods and services which the consumer wanted, in the quantities in which he wanted them, and that this ideal – the 'optimum allocation of resources' – is attainable through the use of the price mechanism. According to classical economic theory, a competitive economy naturally tends to bring the supply and demand for goods and services into equilibrium. If demand is greater than supply, the price will tend to rise, and producers will find it profitable to produce more of that product to meet the increased demand. The price will then stabilize, and if too much of the product is produced it will eventually start to fall again. This in turn will lead to rather fewer of the goods being produced, the price will rise again and so on. In due course, a state of equilibrium is reached at which the consumer gets what he wants at the prices he is prepared to pay. In short, the lower the price of a commodity, the higher, other things being equal, the demand for it, and vice versa.

When supply and demand are in balance, the price of a commodity accurately reflects the cost of producing it. If the price of a commodity is too low because it does not accurately reflect the cost of production, demand for the commodity will be too high and resources will be used in producing it which, if it were properly priced, would be used to produce something else which people wanted more.

One of the costs of producing a commodity is the cost of raw materials. Another is the cost of harm, injury or damage caused by the commodity or the process of producing it. Both need to be reflected in the price if the use of resources is to be optimized. Suppose, for example, that two firms are producing almost identical products, but that firm A uses more expensive raw materials than firm B, with no corresponding gain in the utility or appeal of the product. The result is that of firm A's product will be more expensive than firm B's, and firm B's will be bought in preference to firm A's. Hence, the unnecessary use of a more expensive raw material will be brought to an end. Now suppose that both firms use the same raw material but a different process of manufacture. A's process is unfortunately apt to cause a certain number of injuries to workers. Again, it is desirable that the price of A's product should reflect the cost of the injuries to workers, but it will only do this if the *cost is shifted* from the workers to A, perhaps in the form of higher wages for workers at risk of injury. If this does not happen, A, who is using a more costly method of manufacture (in that it causes injuries), will be able to sell his product at the same price as B. He will, therefore, be able to compete with B on equal terms instead of being squeezed out by competition. It would not be difficult to take the matter a stage further. For instance, suppose that A's process is quicker than B's and therefore, in this respect, cheaper. If the cost of the injuries is not reflected in the price of A's products, A may be able in fact to sell his product at a lower price than B's. It will then be B who is squeezed out by competition, with a consequential misallocation of resources.

In theory, if the market is working perfectly such cost shifting (which internalizes the costs of an activity to that activity) would occur naturally and without the need of local intervention – provided, of course, that a relevant market exists. For example, injury costs of road accidents attributable to defective car design might be shifted by the market to car manufacturers; but there is no market mechanism for shifting to negligent drivers the costs of accidents attributable to bad driving. But even where there is a relevant market, markets often do not work perfectly for a number of reasons, and so legal rules are often needed to shift losses onto the activity which caused them.

By thus ensuring that the prices of commodities reflect the cost of damage done, the market mechanism (or the law, if there is no market, or if the market is not working properly to internalize costs to the activity which causes them) can regulate the amount of damage done. It should be noted, however, that not every change in the level of damage brought about by the operation of the market will be a reduction. One of the points stressed by Calabresi is that the ultimate objective of the law must be not the mere reduction of accident costs (which includes the costs of damage and injuries), but the reduction of the sum total of accident costs and accident prevention costs. If the cost of maintaining a certain level of damage were found to be higher than the cost of the damage itself, the operation of a perfect market would reduce expenditure on damage prevention and allow damage to increase.

The attraction of the use of the market mechanism is that by this means society's decisions may be taken by the cumulative choice of individuals, each of whom is free to decide how much an activity is worth to him, and not by collective decisions which may be contrary to the wishes of the majority and will in any event simply override minority views. Calabresi does not suggest that every decision in relation to accident-causing activities can be left to market choices. Many of these decisions will be made by legislative, or other collective choices. But there is undoubtedly an attraction in the use of the market mechanism in certain situations. A number of simple illustrations may be in order. One simple case, where market considerations operate to some extent, concerns accidents which cause damage to motor vehicles, but without the complication of personal injury. Insofar as vehicle damage is paid for out of the owner's comprehensive insurance policy, market considerations are operative. This is because (as we have seen) the average repair costs of vehicles involved in accidents are largely what determines the comprehensive premium rate for different classes of vehicle. Insofar as the average repair cost for similar vehicles may be different, that difference will be reflected in the insurance premium, and may influence the buyer. He will not necessarily buy the vehicle with the cheaper insurance rate, because he may think the advantages of the other vehicle outweigh this differential, but at least he has to face the question whether those advantages are worth the additional insurance costs. In marginal situations he will buy the car with cheaper insurance and so contribute to a reduction in accident costs. Unfortunately, there is good ground for thinking that these differences in premiums due to average repair costs are more than outweighed by the elaborate no-claims discount system – and this rests on much less sure foundations.

A similar situation arises with regard to fire insurance on commercial premises. A firm may install sprinklers and thereby get a huge reduction in its fire insurance premium; or it may choose to pay the higher premium and not install sprinklers. Provided that the cost of installing sprinklers is, in the long run, less than the saving in premiums[42] it obviously becomes economic to install sprinklers – and less fire damage will be done.

The working of general deterrence has been summarized by Professor Calabresi as follows:

If we can determine the costs of accidents and allocate them to the activities which cause them, the prices of activities will reflect their accident costs, and people in deciding whether or not to engage in particular activities will be influenced by the accident costs each activity involves. They will be influenced without having to think about it, for the accident costs will simply be a part of the price which will affect whether they buy one product or engage in one activity rather than another. If insurance charges for teenage drivers accurately reflected the accident costs such driving causes regardless of fault – and if teenagers have to carry insurance – the price of a car to a teenager will be the price of a jalopy plus the price of the premium. At that price some may still decide to drive (the price is worth it to them) but others will walk, and use the money saved in other ways. The effect will be that individuals, through the market, will have limited teenage driving because of its accident costs. Similarly, if manufacturers of cars without seat belts were charged the accident costs which resulted from the absence of belts, no federal law would be needed requiring seat belts. A beltless car would save the cost of the belt, but bear the accident costs which resulted; a car with a belt would save on accident costs but bear the cost of putting in a belt. The decision as to whether belts were worth it would be made by buyers of cars in the light of the price of each kind of car. The question of whether safety sells would be given a market answer rather than the purely conjectural one to which we have become accustomed.[43]

What then is the possible scope for applying this notion of general deterrence in dealing with compensation for injury and illness and so forth? The basic idea is that by ensuring that the costs of injury are borne by the activity which causes them, the law can encourage those engaged in that activity to reduce those costs (by reducing injuries and injury-causing events) to a point where any further reduction would cost more than the injury costs themselves. There appear to be two conditions which need to be satisfied for general deterrence to work at all. First, it must be possible to identify the activity or activities which (in a broad sense) cause the injuries or losses; and secondly, these activities must, to some extent at least, be responsive to the price mechanism. Both conditions effectively rule out any possibility of applying general deterrence to many forms of disease. There are no identifiable activities which can be said to cause pneumonia, many forms of cancer, and multitudes of other ailments; and since we cannot trace these diseases to particular activities we naturally cannot affect their incidence by use of the price mechanism. This is by no means true of all diseases, however. There is for instance the obvious case of lung cancer which is significantly attributable to smoking. But this would not be a good candidate for general deterrence measures because the level of smoking would not be substantally affected by increased costs (as is demonstrated every time the taxes on cigarettes and tobacco are raised), unless the increase was so great that it would be politically unacceptable. There are, however, a number of diseases which are now known to be caused by certain industrial conditions, such as excessive quantities of certain kinds of dust. Industrial diseases are particularly in point because the law already equates them with industrial accidents under the industrial injury system. The theory of general deterrence could, in principle, be applied to reducing the incidence and cost of such industrial diseases in a similar way as it applies to industrial accidents.

Let us assume that we are so far sufficiently convinced of the value of general deterrence that we would like to make greater use of it as a basis of compensation law. We are faced at the outset with two major problems. These problems arise from the fact that general deterrence requires us to place the costs of an activity on those taking part in that activity. We now have to decide what *are* the costs of an activity, and how we allocate the costs between several activities when (as is usually the case) a number of different activities are jointly the cause of losses.

The allocation of costs to an activity

The ascertainment of costs: **Purely economic costs can, of course, be ascertained and evaluated relatively simply, but an activity may cause many non-economic losses or benefits which ought to be costed. For instance, an activity may create noise or smoke which is a source of irritation, rather than damage; it may destroy a beautiful view which thousands have admired daily; or it may maim and injure, causing pain and suffering. It may also give pleasure and satisfaction, the value of which may offset some of the costs of the activity.**

Is it possible to place an economic valuation on such losses and benefits? This subject has proved a source of extensive controversy among economists, as it has among lawyers. We have already discussed the legal aspects of the assessment of damages for 'pain and suffering' and we there referred briefly to a number of problems raised by economists in a similar context. On the whole, economists have tended to be more interested in the difficulties of valuing lives rather than disabilities, whereas with lawyers it has usually been the other way round. There is no need to explore this question at length because at the end of the day there is almost universal agreement that, for purposes of cost-benefit analysis, economists must either ignore non-economic losses (and benefits) or place some fairly arbitrary conventional valuation upon them. As Professor Calabresi says:

This is just making the best of a bad situation. Failing to include these losses means that people will drive more than they should; failing to include uncomputable non-economic benefits means that they will drive less than they should. There is no assurance that the two will even out, or more important that they will stand in the same relation to each other with respect to driving and with respect to other activities that compete with driving. But since computing them would, *ex hypothesi*, result in a greater bias than not computing them, this is the best we can do. We can then comfort ourselves in the knowledge that resource allocation even in theory is an exercise in doing the best possible and not achieving perfection.[44]

Allocation of costs to particular activities: We must now face up to a difficulty which we have already encountered in discussing causation, that in practice few losses or costs can be attributed obviously and solely to one 'activity' – indeed the very attempt to define an activity reveals a good many difficulties. Consider, for example, road accidents, and the activities that may be involved in causing them. At first sight, one may be inclined to say that road accidents are obviously caused by motoring and leave it at that. But on reflection it is clear that this is far too simple a view. For one thing, why should we treat motoring as an activity, rather than break it down into various sub-categories, such as driving for pleasure, driving to the pub, driving to work (and indeed to different kinds of work), driving lorries, driving buses and so forth. Secondly, many road accidents involve non-motorists, such as pedestrians, or cyclists. What, if anything, enables us to say that these accidents should be treated as part of the activity of motoring rather than walking or cycling? Indeed, the very use of the word 'activity' is to some extent misleading and question-begging. In terms of 'cause' – as we have seen already – vehicle manufacturers and designers and road makers are just as responsible as motorists for most road accidents. There is a good deal of evidence to suggest that the number and the costs of road accidents could be reduced more effectively by concentrating on road improvements and on vehicle design, than by worrying about the motorist. How then can general deterrence work, unless we have some idea how to allocate the cost of road accidents between these various activities and causes?

This problem of allocating a cost to a particular activity is one that runs right through the whole subject. Take a products liability example: suppose the product in question is itself used in a process of manufacture. For instance, X Ltd makes widgets which are bought by Y Ltd, and used in the process of manufacturing didgets. A certain proportion of widgets explode and cause injuries. Should we regard these costs as chargeable to X or Y? Moreover, every personal injury accident by definition involves a conjunction of at least two factors, namely the injured person and some external factor which 'causes' the injury. To an economist, the presence of the injured person at the time and place he is injured, and his own failure to escape the injury, may be just as real causes of the injury as the external factor. For the purposes of general deterrence, the attribution question is not (as in the law) one of moral responsibility but of ease of avoidance: the person who could best avoid the injury ought to be treated as the cause of the injury, and that person may be the injured person himself. Does it matter from an economic, general deterrence point of view, that the law attributes responsibility for injuries according to criteria different from those used by the economist?

In order to make some attempt at answering this difficult question we must first distinguish two different types of case.

The bargaining case: Let us take first, the case where a certain type of activity in which two groups of people, A and B, are involved, tends to cause harm to B, and the two groups are in a bargaining relationship with each other. The classic illustration concerns legal liability for defective products to the consumers who buy and use these products. Does general deterrence give any guidance in deciding whether losses caused by defective products should be allocated to the maker or the consumer? Now, after what was said earlier about charging the costs of accidents to those who cause them, it will seem at first sight obvious that if general deterrence has any meaning at all, it must be taken as indicating that we should allocate these risks to the manufacturer. But, in fact, some economists argue that it is immaterial, from an accident-prevention point of view, how the losses are allocated by the law, so long as they fall on one party or another in a bargaining relationship. To understand why this is thought to be the case, let us consider first what would happen if the losses *were* allocated to the manufacturer.

If the manufacturer has to bear the costs of accidents in the first place, these costs will become part of the costs of his business and will be borne by the consumers, the employees and the shareholders of the business. The way in which these costs are allocated between these three groups will largely depend on the manufacturer's competitive position. Let us assume for a moment that he is a monopolist in the happy position of having no competitors. Clearly he can add the whole cost to his prices, and the consumers of his product as a group pay in full. Equally, if the risk is allocated to the consumer in the first instance, so that the manufacturer is not legally liable, then (however deplorable the result may be from the point of view of loss distribution) the position will be similar: consumers pay. If the manufacturer is not a monopolist but in a competitive business, market pressures would work towards an optimal allocation of resources, whether the loss was borne by the manufacturer or consumers. If they were borne by the manufacturer, he would be forced to make his product safer to the point where further safety measures would cost more than the accidents which occur without them. If consumers bore the loss in the first instance, they would buy other non-accident causing substitutes, to the point at which the additional cost of those substitutes exceeded the cost of accidents, thereby again forcing the manufacturer of the dangerous product to take the same safety measures to the same extent as before. In the last resort, the extent to which the manufacturer or consumers pay depends not on the incidence of legal liability but on their relative bargaining power.[45]

Thus, at first sight, it seems that general deterrence can give us no guidance in this type of case as to who should be made to bear the loss by law. Whatever the law says, the ultimate result is the same, and in a perfectly operating competitive market optimal allocation of resources results. If the market is not working properly, then if the law allocates the loss to the wrong party, it may never be shifted because the costs of so doing (called transaction costs – these are discussed in the next section) may rule this out. But even if we ignore transaction costs Calabresi has convincingly demonstrated that this is too theoretical an approach and that, in practice, there may be very good general deterrence arguments for placing the risk on one or other party in the first instance.[46] For example, one party may be in a much better position to evaluate the risk of accidents and their probable cost. Usually, in the case of products' liability, that party is the manufacturer. If, therefore, the risk is allocated to him, we may be sure that the cost of this legal liability will be fairly accurately reflected in his prices; with the consequential result that (as before) he will be forced to take steps to reduce the dangerousness of his products to the point at which the cost of further steps would exceed the cost of the accidents still likely to be caused. On the other hand, the consumer in practice may find it impossible to evaluate the risk. So that although in theory we should expect consumers to buy non-accident causing substitutes, even at a greater price than the accident-causing product, this is in practice unlikely to happen except in very special cases.

A second reason for thinking that general deterrence gives guidance as to the allocation of risk, even in a bargaining type case, is that the ability of the two parties to secure cheap insurance may differ. In the case of products' liability, for instance, the manufacturer can clearly secure insurance more easily and cheaply than the consumer. To be weighed against this is the fact that the consumer is in a better position to assess the peculiar risks which need to be covered by insurance which arise from his own personal position (e.g. his income, the size of his family and so on), as well as the fact that the risk may vary between consumers because some may be more vulnerable than others, or more skilful in avoiding the danger of the defective product, and so on. If liability is on the manufacturer, therefore, factors of this kind may tend to increase the cost of insurance, though to such a small extent that in this sort of case it is unlikely to counterbalance the other considerations. In other cases, however, this factor could have considerable importance. If, for example, we are considering whether the law should place the risk of goods being lost at sea on the consignor or the carrier, the fact that the consignor knows more about the goods, how they should be packed, what kind of damage may be incurred and so forth, may make it cheaper for him to insure. And even in an ordinary products' liability case, these arguments may be a good reason for not placing liability on the manufacturer for injury caused to someone (say) who suffers from some special or unusual allergy of which he is aware. For he then becomes the person more easily able to avoid the harm caused by that product – by not using it.

Another important illustration of the 'bargaining case' is the employment situation. Prior to the establishment of workmen's compensation in 1897, economists thought that the introduction of such a system would have no effect on the relative financial position of the parties. If the employer had to pay workmen's compensation premiums he would either have to absorb the cost in full, or would pass all or part of the cost on in the form of lower wages, according to the bargaining power of the parties. It was not thought that workmen's compensation insurance would have any effect on the actual cost of accidents. But in fact the introduction of workmen's compensation laws, placing the risk of work accidents on employers, had a dramatic effect in reducing the number of factory accidents both in this country and elsewhere. This happened partly, at least, because employers are plainly better able to evaluate the risk of accidents, and therefore decide what safety measures will be cheaper than the cost of the accidents they save, and also because employers can insure more cheaply.[47]

The non-bargaining case: The second type of case which needs consideration differs from the first in that the parties are not in a bargaining relationship. For instance, road accident victims are not in a bargaining relation with persons who cause road accidents. There is, therefore, no obvious method by which, if the law places the cost on one group, that group can shift it to another group or, at any rate, substantial transaction costs would be incurred in so shifting it. In this type of case, therefore, the rules of legal liability are of greater importance, and general deterrence might be used to indicate what these rules should be.

Now it should be observed that there are some situations in which, although the parties are not originally in a bargaining situation, they are in a position to strike a bargain after the intervention of the law. This sort of problem, which has been illuminatingly discussed by Professor Coase,[48] is best illustrated by the case which he uses to explain his thesis, *Sturges* v. *Bridgman*.[49] This was an action in nuisance by a doctor against his neighbour, a confectioner, in which the doctor complained that the noise and vibration made by the confectioner's machinery made it impossible for him to use a consulting room which he had built at the bottom of his garden. The court held that the plaintiff, the doctor, was entitled to an injunction to restrain the confectioner from using his machinery so as to prevent the doctor's use of the consulting room, on the ground that this was a serious interference with the plaintiff's use of his own land. The decision is criticized by Professor Coase, on the ground that the real question facing the court in an action of this sort is the economic question, namely which of the services which have to be sacrificed here are more valuable to society? But he also points out that since the parties could have modified the court's ruling by subsequent agreement between themselves, the ruling did not, in fact, greatly matter from the economic point of view. Thus if, for instance, the net value to the confectioner of the use of his machinery was (say) £500 a year, while the net value to the doctor of the use of his consulting room at the end of his garden was (say) £200 a year, it would plainly have been in the interest of both parties for the confectioner to resume using his machinery, and to pay the doctor anything between £200 and £500 a year. In the economic world in which all men are economic men, this is just what would have happened, so that the court's original decision to grant an injunction would not have stopped the confectioner using his machinery. Equally, if the doctor's loss of income from his inability to use his consulting room was £500 a year, and the confectioner's loss from inability to use his machinery was only £200, and the court had refused an injunction, it would have been profitable for the doctor to pay the confectioner anything between £200 and £500 a year not to use the machinery, and it would have been profitable for the confectioner to take it. Thus, once again, there is no misallocation of resources, whatever result the law arrives at. If it places the risk on the party who should bear it in order to optimize the allocation of resources, the risk will remain there, whereas if the law places the risk on the wrong party, the parties will correct the law's mistakes by a bargain. Again, this type of case must now be read subject to Calabresi's points about the relative ability of the parties to assess the risk and insure against it. (In the bargaining case, too, transaction costs may prevent the parties in the bargaining relationship making good a misallocation of costs by the law.)

But there is an additional factor to be considered namely the actual cost of striking the bargain by which the law's misplacing of the risk may be corrected. Here the confectioner and the doctor have to get together, negotiate, and perhaps draw up a contract, which then has to be implemented by regular payments, year by year. Let us vary our hypothetical figures now and assume that the value to the confectioner of his machinery is £500 a year and the value to the doctor of his consulting room is £470 a year. Suppose that the cost of a bargain between the parties is £50. Now, if the court places the burden on the doctor and refuses an injunction there will be a correct allocation of resources, whereas if the court grants the injunction there will be a misallocation, *and in this case the misallocation will not be corrected by a bargain because it will be too expensive to correct it.* In this type of case therefore, the correct placing by the law of the initial liability is of great importance.

Now it may be said that these hypothetical figures are somewhat improbable and that it is unlikely in this sort of case that the cost of bargaining would be very great. This is true, but it is not true of many other situations. For instance, if the law places the risk of road accidents on the wrong parties, or places them in incorrect proportions on various parties, a misallocation of resources will result which it would be prohibitively expensive to correct by bargaining, even if it were practically possible. In theory, no doubt, all motorists could get together and (if too much risk is placed on them) offer to 'bribe' pedestrians to reduce the amount of pedestrianism to such an extent that the cost of accidents would be reduced by rather more than the 'bribe'. But in practice, apart from the obvious impossibility of such a course, the cost would greatly exceed the benefit to either party. Here again, therefore, we must reckon the cost of bargains as an additional factor rendering the correct placing of the risk a matter of some importance for the allocation of resources.

It may well be that the traditional distinction between the bargaining and the non-bargaining case has been overstressed. Apart from Calabresi's approach (which makes the distinction much less important), other arguments have been put forward which (in effect) equate the voluntary assumption of a risk with the bargaining case.[50] For example, it has been suggested that for cost-benefit purposes it is unnecessary to take account of losses arising through voluntarily incurred risks. Since the actor has taken the risk he must be assumed to have decided that the benefit he obtained from his activity was worth more than the risk. This argument is also open to the Calabresi objections – e.g. that the actor may not have been able to evaluate the risk – but in any event, it proves too much. For on this approach, it could be said that all losses are voluntarily incurred (except perhaps by small children), because merely by continuing to live a person shows that he prefers life plus the risk of injury or loss, to a risk-free death.[51]

We have so far done nothing more than demonstrate that the legal allocation of risks both in the bargaining and in the non-bargaining situation is, or may be, of real importance for general deterrence purposes. We must still make some attempt to discover how to allocate these costs between various parties, if this is possible. Some, indeed, have asserted the impossibility of doing this at all, and have concluded that general deterrence is a broken reed.[52] But despite doubts to be expressed later, we need not abandon the general deterrence idea altogether. For some guidance can be given as to how best to allocate risks between joint cost-causers.

First, it should be noted that general deterrence suggests that the 'activities' in question should be broken down into the smallest subcategories which it is worth while to break them down into.[53] We do not want to reduce all motoring, but motoring which causes accidents. Therefore we want to increase the costs of that type of motoring most likely to cause accidents, such as motoring after dark in old sports cars by young men.

Secondly, we must bear in mind the activity which is most likely to be affected by cost considerations. To increase the cost of motoring, or some types of motoring, would certainly have *some* effect on the amount of motoring. To increase the 'cost' of pedestrianism (especially if this increase merely takes the form of refusing damages to the injured pedestrian) is not likely to reduce the amount of walking.

The application of these guide lines may sometimes produce surprising results. It is not always economically desirable that the activity which appears more obviously to be the 'cause' of the risks should be charged with the cost. For example, a factory which contains dangerous chemicals with an explosion risk may seem the right party to be charged with the damage to neighbours arising from explosions. Not only does this seem fair; it seems at first sight to be economically desirable that the factory owners be given incentive to minimize the physical risk by placing the legal risk on them. No doubt this often will be the right solution, but Coase has demonstrated that this is not necessarily so in all situations.[54] There may be cases in which the overall economic position of the community would be improved if the risk was *not* placed on the factory owner. The extreme and obvious illustration of this possibility is where closure of the factory would be entailed by placing the risk on the owner, and the net cost in social welfare is higher than the risk of damage to neighbours. Another illustration may be found in the recent cricket ball case, *Miller* v. *Jackson*,[55] where the plaintiffs complained of the playing of cricket on adjoining land as a result of which the occasional six landed in their garden. It was clear that Mrs Miller was a very sensitive lady who was greatly disturbed by the risk of being hit; in such circumstances, it would probably be better in an economic sense for the plaintiff to sell her house to a less sensitive person than it is to stop the cricket playing altogether. Of course, that may offend ideas of fairness, and it must never be forgotten that at the end of the day economic considerations about efficiency may have to give way to considerations of justice. But where justice is an uncertain guide, economic arguments may determine the issue; and anyway, it is sensible to ask what the price of justice is.

In looking for that activity which is most likely to be influenced by cost considerations or which has, in economists' jargon, a high elasticity of supply or demand, we must beware of the danger of describing activities too broadly.[56] For example, it is quite possible that the activity of dog-owning has a very low elasticity of demand, so that increasing the cost of dog-owning (e.g. by adding some small sum on to the cost of a dog licence to cover the cost of dog-caused accidents) would have virtually no effect on the incidence of dog-owning and therefore would not reduce dog-caused accidents. But we may find it possible to break down the activity of dog-owning into sub-categories – e.g. based on different types of dogs – as between which there may be a high elasticity of demand. Suppose, for instance, it is found that certain types of dog cause more accidents, whether road accidents or others, than other dogs; general deterrence would require us to make the cost of owning the more accident-prone dogs more expensive. And as between different types of dogs it may be that the public demand would be substantially affected by cost considerations.

Quite possibly, the same is true of motoring. It may well be that motoring as a whole has a low elasticity of demand, so that the total amount of motoring does not respond appreciably to increases in the cost of motoring – as is indeed demonstrated by the fact that little change follows from the regular increases in petrol prices. But it does not follow that we could not break motoring down into categories which would be responsive to price variations. Within the activity of motoring we could distinguish driving different types of vehicle, old vehicles, and new ones, vehicles of different colour or power, driving at night and in the day, in the town and in the country, and so on. If the cost of some of these sub-categories of driving were higher than others, we might find that an appreciable difference in driving habits would follow. If, therefore, we could find that certain types of vehicle are more accident prone than others, we could make the cost of driving those vehicles somewhat more expensive.[57] If the vehicle in question is much more accident prone than other vehicles, the point may of course be reached at which we would wish to prohibit use of it altogether, or insist on modifications to its design and construction. But general deterrence could work long before that stage is reached, because we might find that the vehicle is slightly more accident prone than others, but not so seriously as to justify us in prohibiting its use.

Thirdly, we must remember the two factors we considered in the bargaining case, i.e. the importance of deciding who can best evaluate the risks and who can insure most cheaply.

Finally, it should be said that general deterrence requires above all that costs should not be 'externalized', i.e. removed altogether from the activities responsible for them. In other words, if the entire cost of road accidents was removed from motorists and pedestrians and all other parties responsible, and placed on the taxpayer by some new social security scheme, this would be the worst of all possible worlds from the economic point of view. Therefore, failing all else, some practical division of the risk is better than nothing.

Now these criteria may undoubtedly be of some help in deciding where to place the risk of certain activities and certain costs. Certainly, they appear to go a long way to justify placing the cost of industrial accidents on industry, and the cost of fire damage to property on property owners, as, in practice, is largely done today. But it must also be said that the criteria can only be applied with the greatest difficulty to the road accident problem. Most of the criteria we have discussed above would suggest that a large part of the cost of road accidents should be placed on highway authorities and on motor manufacturers. There is no doubt that they would be much more responsive to price considerations than the individual motorist; and there is also no doubt that they are able to evaluate the risks much better than the motorist. A highway authority which knows that an average of ten accidents takes place every year at a certain junction can easily calculate that it would be cheaper to modify the junction than pay for the cost of the accidents. So long as the cost is paid by motorists and their insurance companies the incentive on the highway authority to make improvements of this kind is more limited. (But it must be appreciated that the highway authority is merely the public in another guise – the ratepayer or the taxpayer – so that to place the cost on the highway authority is, to some extent, to externalize it.) Similarly, placing part of the cost on motor manufacturers would probably stimulate safer design, and more research into what safer design actually requires. In this respect the price mechanism could work very well. Manufacturers would soon learn how much it was worth spending on research, and what safety modifications would be worth their cost in terms of reduced accidents, or reduced damage in those accidents which do occur. As between manufacturers and motorists, we have in effect a bargaining situation and therefore the ultimate cost would eventually be divided between manufacturers and motorists according to their relative bargaining strength and so on; but placing it on the manufacturer in the first instance would enable us to get the benefit of his expert skill and research facilities, to the extent that he finds it more economical to try to reduce these costs than to pass them on. Apart, however, from the cost which might be placed on manufacturers and shifted, wholly or in part, to the motorist, some part of the cost would rightly and inescapably be placed on the motorist in the first place, because only he can control the total amount of driving. Moreover, any attempt to discriminate against driving which is shown to be statistically less safe, such as driving by young people or old people, or driving older cars, or sports cars, and so on, involves discriminating between motorists and therefore involves placing part of the cost on them through insurance companies (or some agency) which can so discriminate.

All this may lead readily to the conclusion that the cost of road accidents should be divided between motorists, manufacturers and the public (in the guise of highway authorities), though the manufacturers may be able to shift part of this cost back onto the motorist. But nothing we have said can really give us much help in deciding what proportion of the cost should be allocated among these three groups. Nor is it obvious that highway authorities will respond more readily to financial constraints than to political or other pressures.

General deterrence and the existing systems

In this section we shall be concerned to enquire how far the various methods of compensation for which the law at present provides are in any way affected by considerations of general deterrence.[58]

The tort system: There is no doubt that to some extent the tort system reflects the purposes of general deterrence. To the extent that tort damages are paid through the insurance premiums of those who take part in an activity, that activity is being charged with the cost of the damage which it causes. And to the extent that insurance companies vary their premium rates so as to put the greater burden on those most likely to cause losses or most likely to cause heavy losses, the cause of general deterrence is being furthered. Nobody could seriously suppose that, in developing the law of torts as it operates today, the courts have been consciously influenced by any theories as elaborate and sophisticated as Professor Calabresi's, but it does not follow that there is not some connection between popular and judicial ideas of equity, and some of the assumptions underlying the theory of general deterrence. In particular, there is a close similarity between the widely held notion that it is equitable to make an activity pay for the damage that it causes, and the underlying capitalist assumption of general deterrence that activities should be charged with their own costs. It is quite possible that, historically speaking, the origins both of much modern law – and its associated legal morality – and modern economic theory can be traced back to the intellectual climate of the early nineteenth century. Utilitarian theory and classical economics were then closely associated bodies of ideas, and the law drew inspiration from them both.[59]

It has recently been argued by some proponents of the new law-and-economics school that many of the fundamental principles of tort law do reflect economic efficiency ideas. Thus the negligence formula, as, for example, propounded in the famous Learned Hand calculus,[60] may be seen as based on an economic idea. It is negligent not to avoid a danger where the cost of avoiding it is lower than the probability of its occurrence multiplied by the cost of the damage if the risk occurs.[61] On the other hand, it is not negligent to take a risk where the cost of avoidance is actually greater than the probability of occurrence times the cost of the accident if it happens. Similarly, it has been argued that the doctrine of contributory negligence reflects the same kind of efficiency ideals. If the plaintiff could avoid the accident more cheaply (or more easily) than the defendant, then the doctrine of contributory negligence will deprive him of damages or, at least, reduce his recovery. This helps to deter plaintiffs from taking risks with their own safety where it is cheaper for them to avoid the risks than for others to avoid them. There has been much controversy about the extent to which the detailed rules of the law of negligence and contributory negligence can be said to be efficient,[62] and there has also been controversy about the extent to which strict liability may in some circumstances be more efficient in the economic sense than fault liability. But in a broad sort of way, it does not seem necessary to dissent from the idea that there is some connection between morality and economic efficiency in these areas of law.

But although the tort system does probably further the idea of general deterrence in some respects, it is worth observing that the position is likely to vary widely according to the context. Where legal liability is placed on enterprises (as with fault-caused products' liability, or in the case of damage done by their employees) we are dealing with a group of people who are probably peculiarly price conscious and accident conscious. A well conducted company will, for instance, be aware of the value of taking safety measures which are less costly than the damage they prevent. A company, certainly if it is of any size and is well advised by its accountants, operates at least to some degree in the way that the economists' 'economic man' is expected to operate, although Professor Galbraith has pointed to the many ways in which companies do not, in practice, pursue profit maximization at all costs.[63] The individual man on the other hand, is in a somewhat different position. He does not regularly pay out damages, he is not often involved in accidents, nor is it always possible for him to take safety measures today to avoid accidents tomorrow because he may simply be unable to raise the money today. So, for instance, the motorist who pays for some road accident costs through his premiums makes his payment once a year and then does his best to forget about it till the following year. He probably does not even calculate the cost of motoring in the same way that a company will calculate its costs. The motorist is apt to look at the *marginal* cost of motoring in deciding how much to drive, that is he looks at the cost of each additional mile. Since his overheads consist principally of his licence, his insurance premium and depreciation, the marginal cost is little more than the cost of petrol.[64] Hence, to increase the cost of insurance to the motorist would not necessarily affect greatly the amount of driving which he does, because it merely increases the amount of the annual payment he has to make, while it would in no way change the marginal cost of driving. Of course, in the long run, and over the whole country, some reduction in motoring might be anticipated, but there can be little doubt that the effect of the increased cost would be largely determined by the way in which it is paid. In this respect the individual motorist may differ from a company, which perhaps would tend to look at the *average* rather than the marginal cost. Since the average cost would certainly be increased by increasing insurance premiums, the amount of commercial driving might be more affected by such a move than the amount of private driving. Of course, to increase insurance premiums might push off the road altogether some of the poorest motorists and so reduce motoring and accidents. But even this result assumes that poor motorists will sacrifice motoring rather than something else if costs of motoring go up – a somewhat dubious assumption. Professor Conard and his colleagues concluded that in the case of auto accidents, 'there are no adequate grounds for believing that the proper cost allocation would either reduce accidents nor change the total amount of driving appreciably.'[65]

It must next be pointed out that tort law is only effective in charging one person with the cost of accidents which he causes to others. And the legal concept of 'causation' is not broad enough to include somewhat passive activities (such as merely owning property) within its scope. If gas authorities are legally liable for damage to houses caused by gas explosions then there may be, through tort law and liability insurance, financial pressure on gas authorities to minimize gas explosions. But where is the pressure on house owners to buy or build houses which are not exposed to the risk of gas-caused explosions, or which can withstand such explosions? If a motorist is liable for negligently damaging another vehicle, then tort law and liability insurance may impose constraints which tend to minimize the active damage done by a car in a collision. But what about pressure to build cars which withstand damage, or which better protect the occupants against injury?

To some extent, these problems are taken care of by the very deficiencies in tort law which prevent it from being a very satisfactory mechanism for compensating others. Because tort law does not generally impose liability for non-fault caused accidents, or for accidents in respect of which there has been contributory negligence, every property owner and every person must take into account that he may be injured, or his property damaged, in circumstances in which there is no tort recourse. Consequently there is likely to be pressure, financial and otherwise, to minimize the risk of injury to oneself and one's own property. Precisely *because* gas authorities may not be liable for non-fault caused explosions which damage houses, the house owner may have a financial incentive to buy or build a house which is less susceptible to gas explosions. Precisely *because* damage to a car may well occur where there is no chance of tort recovery, financial incentives may exist to buy cars which are cheaper to repair, and less susceptible to damage. This economic analysis suggests that there is often a case for having both some form of legal (third party) liability for damage to another, and also some form of no-liability (or 'first party liability') for damage suffered by oneself, or one's own property. The problem is to know whether the present division along fault/no fault lines is right: and there is good ground for thinking that it is not.[66] There are too many cases in which an activity does contribute (in a statistical sense) to accident causation, but in which the law's concepts of fault and cause are too narrow, so that one 'causer' of an accident may be charged with too high a proportion of the costs, and another 'causer' with too small a proportion. For example, a person who parks his car in a street undoubtedly creates a risk both to his own car, and to others; this risk is sufficiently obvious to justify a higher comprehensive motor premium for cars regularly garaged in a public road. But in the event of a collision between a moving and parked vehicle, the entire fault, and hence cost of the accident, will nearly always be attributed to the driver of the moving vehicle. The result of this may be that too high a proportion of the cost of such collisions is borne by the third party component of the comprehensive policy, and too little by the first party component. Consequently, there may be a marginal excess in the pressures to produce a car (or a driver) which does less damage to others, and a marginal deficiency in the pressures to produce a car which better resists damage to itself, or to avoid garaging cars in the street.

Apart from this, there is also the important question whether the fault/no fault line is not so expensive to maintain, because of the heavy cost of administration of a fault system, that other, broader divisions of cost between those who 'cause' and those who 'suffer' may not be preferable. Let us take an example from shipping law, about the relative liabilities of shipowners and cargo-owners for damage done to cargoes at sea. The Calabresi analysis suggests that it is desirable that both shipowners and cargo-owners bear part of this cost. If shipowners had no responsibility, ships would be designed to maximize profit to the shipowner without worrying about the extent of cargo-damage. And if the cargo-owner bore no responsibility, the packaging and crating of goods would be neglected as cargo-owners tried to maximize *their* profits. But it does not follow that a division of the responsibility along fault/no fault lines is the appropriate answer. A simple and equal division of the cost of all cargo damage might well achieve broadly similar answers, without the incidental and heavy costs of examining every case in detail. Of course, the division does not need to be equal. If, for instance, it is found that the great majority of the risks to which cargoes are exposed are not under the control of the cargo owner (because, say packaging and crating is ineffective against many of these risks), the cost could be divided by placing two-thirds on shipowners and one-third on cargo owners. On the other hand, it might be argued that 'inherent risks' should in principle be placed on the cargo-owners rather than on the shipowners; so some assessment of how much damage is due to such risks overall may be necessary.

It must next be observed that the tort system underrates the costs to be charged to accident-causing activities in various other ways. For instance, (as we have seen) almost the entire cost of medical services required by tortiously caused injuries is rendered under the National Health Service which is largely paid for by the taxpayers, thus relieving motorists as such of a substantial burden which would otherwise have to be paid for in tort damages, and hence in premiums. Similarly, the cost of police activity following road accidents is not charged to the accident causers, but to the ratepayers. Again, the offsetting of social security benefits against tort damages relieves tortfeasors of some of the social costs of their torts. The general deterrence argument has been used in such contexts to support the case for 'full compensation'.[67] This is no doubt a correct application of the concept, so long as it is not used to beg questions about damages for non-economic loss. Similarly, the general deterrence case for maintaining compensation for 100% of income loss must be weighed against the additional costs that this may create through the disincentive to return to work.

Then again tort damages are intended to compensate for the private loss of the injury victim and his dependants. They do not in any way amount to an assessment of the social loss. The social loss involved in the death of a young unmarried adult for instance, may be high, especially if he has been educated to a high degree at the State's expense. But tort damages for the death of such a person will be very low. If no dependency can be proved, the only damages recoverable will be a small amount in respect of losses suffered between the date of the accident and the date of death (assuming they are different), which clearly bears no relationship to the social loss involved. Moreover, much of the cost of compensating road accident victims is borne by the social security system, sick-pay schemes and other forms of compensation.

Other tort rules: There are some tort rules which do appear to further the policy of general deterrence, and, indeed, which are not always easily explicable on other grounds. Thus the idea that damage is compensatable only if it falls within the 'risk' which a particular rule is designed to guard against[68] is explicable in general deterrence terms. For instance, if we hold that an unlicensed driver is not liable for an accident merely because of lack of a licence, we are in effect refusing, and rightly refusing, to treat that accident as a particular cost of the category of 'unlicensed driving'. In determining that the lack of license was irrelevant to the causes of the accident – as the law would do – we are also determining that the costs of that type of accident cannot be allocated intelligently to that type of activity. Similarly, with some of the rules relating to remoteness. If the consequence of a negligent act is altogether too freakish or unforeseeable so that the law exonerates the negligent party from liability, this may help place the cost on the correct type of activity – correct because it may at least be placed on an activity which more frequently causes that type of damage. For example, suppose that a negligent motorist were to collide with a car in front of him and damage some exceptionally valuable paintings stored in the boot. It is possible that in such a case the courts would hold the loss unforeseeable and therefore refuse to throw on the negligent motorist (and hence on to road traffic insurance premiums) the cost of the damaged paintings. Hence, the owner of the paintings (and his personal accident insurers) would have to bear the cost. This would probably be a sound result from the point of view of general deterrence, because damage to such valuable objects would be so unusual a consequence of negligent driving that it would be pointless to regard it as an incidental risk of negligent driving and to bring pressure to bear on drivers to eliminate the danger. On the other hand, risks of this kind are connected with facts peculiarly within the knowledge of the owner, and imposing the loss on the owner could result in better provision being made for the safe transportation of such property.

The social security system: It is apparent that insofar as the social security system is financed out of general taxation it flies in the face of the precepts of general deterrence. In fact most parts of the social security system are nominally, at least, based on the principles of insurance and are not wholly financed by the taxpayer. But since the rates of insurance are fixed by Parliament, and since they are generally rates which do not vary with the nature of the risk involved, there is little scope for the operation of general deterrence.

The absence of varying premium rates under the industrial injuries scheme, is, however, a somewhat different proposition. It is largely impractical to make ordinary social security contributions vary according to risk. We cannot make the chronic sick pay premiums for sickness benefits according to risk, and there is no reason to suppose that this would have any significant effect on the incidence of sickness if we did. But the cost of industrial injuries, and industrial diseases, could be made to fall more heavily on those industries which present the greater risks. This is what happens with employers' liability insurance, and this is also what happens in most of the world with regard to workmen's compensation. In many ways, this is a key issue for the validity and utility of the concept of general deterrence and it is worth devoting a little attention to the question.

The case for making high risk industries pay higher premiums for industrial injuries insurance is different from the arguments in favour of experience-rating,[69] which relates the employers' premiums to the injury rate of that particular employer, and offers some real incentive to the employer to cut his injury costs. Classification of industries for premium purposes cannot create the same incentive to injury reduction because the injury rate in one enterprise would rarely have any significant effect on the premium rate for the entire industry. The case for such a premium variation is essentially based on general deterrence. If the National Coal Board had to pay industrial injuries premiums which reflected the fact that coal mining was a high risk industry, then the price of coal would more nearly reflect the full costs of the injuries incurred in winning that coal. And when the consumer is making up his mind which kind of fuel to buy he will be able to make his choice on the basis of the real cost of those fuels, including this injury cost component. Because this is not the case, coal is cheaper than it would otherwise be, and the consumer may be encouraged to buy more coal than he would have done otherwise. Oil and gas, on the other hand, do not enoy this element of subsidy (assuming that their accident rate is lower than the coal mining rate) and the consumer therefore buys less oil and gas, and more coal than he would otherwise do. This leads to a misallocation of resources, and the total social cost of injuries is increased.

For the benefit of law students who may not be familiar with economic arguments about allocation of resources, it may make this argument more intelligible if it is based on some hypothetical figures. Assume, for the sake of argument, that coal, gas and oil are competitively priced to the consumer, so that he gets the same amount of energy from each £100 worth of coal, gas or oil. Assume then that coal mining injuries paid for by the industrial injuries scheme amount to 1% of the total cost of coal to the consumer, while gas and oil accidents are only one-tenth of this. The result would then be, that the true social cost of coal costing the consumer £100 would be £101, that is, £100 for the coal and another £1 for the injuries; while the true social cost of £100 of gas or oil would be £100·10. Every time that the consumer chooses to buy £100 worth of coal, rather than of oil or gas, he then costs the community 90p, which he would have spared the community if he had bought oil or gas instead.

There is, of course, no doubt that the whole thing is a great deal more complex than this simple hypothetical example may suggest; and we go on to consider some of the complexities later.[70] But essentially, belief in variable premium rates for industrial injuries insurance depends on acceptance of the economic arguments about allocation of resources. And these arguments, in turn, largely depend on acceptance of the essentials of private enterprise economics. But by no means everyone accepts these essentials. Socialists may prefer to argue that accidents are a social responsibility, that the cost should be borne evenly by the whole nation, and that there is no particular virtue in making high risk industries pay higher premiums. Both the

New Zealand Royal Commission[71] and the Australian Committee of Inquiry[72] took this view. On the other hand, the Robens Committee came down in favour of changing the present flat-rate system of industrial injuries premiums,[73] though it must be said that there are signs of some confusion in all three of these Reports, between experience-rating and classified-rating. The Pearson Commission, as we have seen, decided against any change here, not so much on principle, but simply because they were unconvinced of the economic advantages of this course. Perhaps significantly, the only economist on the Commission, Professor Prest, dissented on this point.

The cost of criminal injuries awarded by the Criminal Injuries Compensation Board is borne entirely by the taxpayer, though even in this field there is some scope for the operation of general deterrence. It would be impractical, though desirable, to charge the activity of taking part in crime with the costs that it generates in the hope of reducing crime,[74] but this does not mean that there is no room for general deterrence in this field. To the extent that some people are engaged in occupations which generate a higher risk of criminal violence, general deterrence could be forwarded by placing extra costs on the employers – and in fact about one-third of the applicants for criminal injury compensation are engaged in such occupations – such as police officers, postmen, wages clerks, night watchmen and so on.

Accident and life insurance: There is some room for the operation of general deterrence when a person insures himself against personal injury, or against property damage, or fire, or insures his own life. By these forms of insurance the costs of various types of losses are spread over those who participate in an activity. Moreover, to the extent that insurance companies charge different rates for different risks, the higher risk activities may be discouraged and the taking of safety precautions may be encouraged. As we have already seen, installation of sprinklers in commercial buildings leads to large reductions in fire insurance premiums; people who engage in hazardous occupations may have to pay higher life insurance premiums, and so forth. In the case of damage by fire, at least, general deterrence probably operates reasonably well, and it seems plain that insurance by the property owner is the most efficient way of reducing the costs of fire damage,[75] but in the other fields the scope for general deterrence is somewhat limited. Insurance companies must sell their wares, and they cannot take into account too many loss causing activities, without raising the cost of certain types of insurance to such a degree as to reduce the total amount of business they do. For example, heavy drinkers and smokers may have a lower expectation of life than abstainers, but the extent to which insurance companies can take these things into account is limited by the premiums that people are willing to pay.

An assessment of the value of general deterrence

Any assessment of the value of general deterrence must start with appreciation of its limitations. The foremost of these is that general deterrence could never be used without regard to other objectives. No modern society could possibly tolerate any and every anti-social activity, even if those taking part in it were prepared to pay for the cost. Some activities must be the subject of outright prohibition: we permit people to drive cars if they pay for the cost of their accidents (their fault caused accidents, at least), but we do not permit them to drive while drunk, however much they may be prepared to pay for the cost of extra accidents they may cause in that state. We charge the factory owner with some part of the cost injuries to his workmen, but if his factory causes intolerable inconvenience and discomfort to the neighbours then we will stop him altogether. So general deterrence can never be considered in isolation, apart from the background of specific deterrence by criminal sanction, and administrative control under regulatory statutes.

In the second place, proponents of general deterrence do not suggest that – even where outright prohibition is not in question – we must always ignore other considerations. We can, for instance, combine some degree of general deterrence with some degree of wealth redistribution, if that is what we wish to achieve. This is, for example, exactly what we are doing at present in the industrial injuries field by not relating contributions to risk. Refusal to adjust premiums to the risk simply means that low-risk industries are subsidizing high-risk industries, and therefore that those who participate in the low-risk industries (whether as consumers, workers or shareholders) are in a sense subsidizing those who participate in high-risk industries.

It will be noticed that the whole concept of general deterrence is in conflict with the concept of loss distribution. The latter notion, as we saw earlier, suggests that losses should be spread over as wide a segment of the population as possible. General deterrence, on the other hand, suggests that losses should be concentrated on those who can best avoid or minimize them. The most extreme form of general deterrence would be to place the *entire* cost of a loss on that person. Clearly, the incentive to avoid or minimize a loss would then be much greater, but equally clearly, this could lead to very serious consequences in the absence of liability insurance. It cannot even be assumed that economically the gains in accident prevention would outweigh the cost in terms of bankrupted tortfeasors.

Is it then possible to reconcile general deterrence and loss distribution at all? The answer is that it is possible, through the medium of insurance with varying premium rates. Insurance operates as a method of distributing losses, and the varying premium rates operate as a form of general deterrence. Thus the combination of the two seems to produce the perfect blend. But now another question arises. How can we be sure that we have in fact the right proportions? How do we know that if (for instance) we put a slightly higher premium on such and such a class, as potentially more likely to cause accidents, we would not achieve a better balance between general deterrence and loss distribution? Or alternatively, that if we put a lower premium on such and such a class, we would not have a better balance?

Professor Calabresi's ingenious answer to this difficulty is to say that this too can be left to the operation of the market mechanism.[76] His point is that insurance companies will (or at least should) vary premium rates to the extent that it is economically profitable for them to do so. If the difference between the accident causing potential of different factors is significant enough to outweigh the additional administrative cost of drawing further distinctions, then the insurance companies in a competitive world can be trusted to draw these distinctions – at least so the argument runs. If, for instance, it is discovered that (as indeed seems to be the case) orange cars are less dangerous than green cars, and that the difference is sufficiently great to be worth acting on, insurance companies will start to reduce premiums for orange cars (or increase them for green ones). If one insurance company does not consider it worth while, another one will do so, and others will then have to follow suit. Unfortunately things do not always work in this way.[77] Although it might *in fact* be profitable for insurance companies to draw further distinctions, they may be reluctant to do so because the additional administrative cost is certain to follow, while the additional benefit from the further sub-category may be somewhat uncertain at the outset. Moreover, insurance companies are not well-known for their competitive vigour – indeed, the interest of society in solvent insurance companies is so great that competitive vigour is not necessarily a good thing in this area, as recent experience in this country shows; to put it at its lowest, the increased risk of insolvency among insurers arising from greater competition would have to be balanced against the gains to the public.

Even as a matter of theory, Calabresi appears to have a greater confidence in the statistical basis of insurance than is justified by the facts. The fact is that (outside the life insurance field) the role played by statistical methodology in premium fixing is surprisingly small. The main reason for this is that insurers have not yet generally identified the effect of individual significant factors on different risks. All that they do is to calculate the appropriate premium rate for all the members of a given class; the consequence is that any multiplication of the number of component factors to be considered, rapidly reduces the size of the class to numbers which are not statistically reliable. For example, a motor insurer with a million policy holders who wanted to calculate the appropriate premium for a motorist with six common characteristics could find himself with a sample of 172, which is obviously not statistically reliable.[78] The result is that premium fixing is a much more arbitrary process, depending on the insurer's judgment, than is commonly thought; equally, the scope for efficient or 'correct' sub-classification is more limited than is commonly thought.

In practice, insurance companies appear to use premium rating for encouraging safety factors or discouraging dangerous activities very differently in different classes of insurance. Even in the case of fire insurance, where they have done a great deal to encourage the installation of sprinklers, we now know that premium reductions have not matched the reduction in risk. Owners of sprinklered premises have thus been subsidizing the owners of non-sprinklered premises, so that there has been inadequate incentive to install sprinklers.[79] It is true that this occurred while there was not a wholly free market, since a 'tariff' existed among many leading insurers. But only the most dedicated believer in the private enterprise system can think that insurers are really concerned to maximize safety precautions by their use of premium fixing methods.[80] In the case of industrial injuries they have done very little (particularly in the case of smaller firms), and in the case of road traffic insurance, virtually nothing.

But even if we were satisfied that insurance companies varied premiums to the most efficient extent possible, the conflict between the purposes of general deterrence and the purposes of loss distribution would become acute in many areas. This is because the further insurance companies go in varying premium rates according to risk, the heavier the premium is bound to be for people who are thought to be serious risks. Losses are not well distributed if (for instance) one person has to pay a premium of £100 per annum, and others pay only £10 or £15 towards the same loss. If the object of the law is to *distribute* the cost of accidents widely, so that too heavy a burden does not fall on any one person, then this objective is being defeated by premium rating. Doubtless, many people will feel almost instinctively that it is perfectly reasonable and equitable that a higher risk person should have to pay a higher premium, but it is suggested that this is largely because of familiarity with the system. But whatever may be thought of the equity of the situation, the fact is that loss distribution is also generally accepted as a legitimate and desirable objective of the legal system, and there is no escaping the fact that premium rating may conflict with the objective of distributing costs widely.

An attempt at empirical verification: In the nature of things, Calabresi's theories do not easily lend themselves to empirical verification or refutation, but in 1972 the American National Commission on State Workmen's Compensation Laws attempted to test his theories in one particular area. The Commission studied the industrial accident levels in States with very different levels of workmen's compensation benefits. On the basis of economic theory, it might have been supposed that in States where the benefits and therefore the premiums were higher, employers would take more care (and spend more money) to minimize accident costs by keeping the accident levels as low as possible. However, no systematic relationship was discovered between accident levels and benefit levels.[81] Even when comparisons were made between States with similar industrial backgrounds, there was no observable correlation between accident levels and benefit levels. For example, Virginia, Georgia and Alabama had similar benefit levels but widely different accident levels; while Pennsylvania and New Jersey had very similar accident levels but vastly different benefit levels. The Commission concluded that the evidence suggests that 'workmen's compensation insurance rates are not the strongest force affecting the frequency of accidents'.[82]

Some presuppositions of general deterrence: We have not so far discussed some basic presuppositions of general deterrence. These basic assumptions have been extensively discussed by economists in the wider context of welfare economics, of which general deterrence really forms part, but for our purpose it will be sufficient to draw attention to three points at which the assumptions necessarily made by general deterrence may appear to have at best a dubious validity.

The first of these assumptions is that in a free society people know what is good for them. There is no criterion for measuring economic efficiency which is not based on the freedom of consumer choice. We have already seen how the price mechanism works in a competitive economy, and we have also seen that attempts to optimize the allocation of resources depend largely on the operation of the price mechanism. But the price mechanism is itself conditioned by consumer preference. If (taxation apart) the market price of twenty cigarettes is equal to the market price of a dozen oranges, then this is because the consumer thinks that twenty cigarettes are worth the same as a dozen oranges. Attempts to improve the allocation of resources accept that in so thinking *the consumer is right*, simply because there is no other assumption that can be put in its place. All discussion of allocation of resources therefore is based on the assumption that what we want to do is to give the consumer as much as we possibly can of what he wants in the amounts in which he wants them.

It does not follow from this that economists are not prepared, like anybody else, to make value judgments asserting that the consumer is wrong in his order of preferences, and that consumer preference should be overridden in this or that field. But when the economist takes this line he is saying, in effect, that economic efficiency is not the only criterion for deciding how a society ought to regulate its affairs. Or alternatively, he is placing different values on the non-economic costs and benefits of some activity from those of the average consumer, and asserting that he prefers his values to those of the consumer. It is important to appreciate that this treatment of consumer preference does not amount to a value judgment that the consumer *is* right, and that consumer preferences *should* always be respected. It is merely an assumption that is made in order to produce a yardstick by which we can measure economic efficiency. To measure something in yards assumes the correctness of the yard as a measure, but does not assume that a better measure might not be the metre.

The second presupposition that is made by general deterrence is that the market is in fact operating smoothly so that consumer preference is correctly reflected in the prices at which goods are sold. It would be a mistake to underestimate the extent to which the price mechanism still operates in our mixed economy, but there are great distortions produced by government decisions to tax or subsidize this or that activity. Besides these distortions the cost of injuries and even diseases pales into insignificance. We have, for instance, commented on the slight misallocation which may result from the fact that there are no variations in the premiums for industrial injury insurance. But the total premium for industrial injury insurance is a minute proportion of the employer's total wage bill, and an insignificant figure beside the employer's tax bill. When the Selective Employment Tax was in existence the rate of the tax (levied on service but not manufacturing industry) was over 25 times that of the industrial injuries premium.

Or again, there is the immense burden of taxation imposed on the motorist in the form of VAT and car tax on vehicles, excise licences on vehicles, and excise duty on petrol, a burden which amounted to over £11,000 million in 1984–5. There is some doubt whether the motorist pays the total social cost of road accidents in insurance premiums at the moment, but even if the entire cost were placed on motorists, it could hardly be more than about £2,400 million per annum.[83] This sounds a large sum, and could certainly lead to a substantial misallocation of resources, but when set against the figure of £11,000 million in annual taxation it begins to look less significant. In the face of figures of this kind it is indeed hard to assert with any confidence that placing more costs on the motorist would lead to an improvement in the allocation of resources, which implies that there is at present 'too much' motoring, because the activity does not pay its full social cost. It might be urged that the £11,000 million tax paid by motorists is not simply intended to finance the losses caused by road accidents, but also goes to the building and maintenance of the roads (£1,500 million in 1984–5), not to mention other general government expenditure. Hence, it could be argued that part of the sums paid by motorists must be disregarded in deciding whether motorists bear the full cost of road accidents. But this really will not convince either, because this argument presupposes that all activities are taxed equally, or at least on a similar basis, and so bear an equal share of general government expenditure; but this assumption is manifestly untrue.

Another fact which should be borne in mind in assessing the value of general deterrence is that a large part of our economy is today not governed solely by price considerations. The public sector of industry does not operate according to the classical theories of free enterprise by seeking to maximize profits, nor is it always exposed to the harsh winds of competition: in this sector, accident prevention, or the minimization of accident costs, is more likely to be achieved by a sense of public responsibility and by humanitarianism, than by market forces. Even in the private sector, it is absurd to suppose that businessmen in fact pursue profit maximization at all costs. Public opinion, as much as competition, restricts the level of profits which may be decently earned over a period of time: if profits seem excessive, public demands for price reductions may in due course become irresistible, quite apart from competition. Conversely, businessmen may also be sufficiently humanitarian to wish to reduce accident costs even at the expense of higher profits. It is thus unrealistic to suppose that accident costs can always or often be best minimized by use of the market mechanism.

Conclusions: Most of the growing literature on this subject is American in origin, and much of it is based on assumptions about private enterprise economics which are not so widely or so strongly held in this country.[84] It is, for example, simply taken for granted in this American literature that there is only one rational way of approaching the problem of safety and accident prevention – namely the market way. It is assumed that an individual, an enterprise and a society can only rationally decide to spend as much on accident prevention as the value of the lives and the injuries saved; indeed, it often seems to be assumed that there is no other criterion at all which can help in deciding whether any given accident prevention expenditure should be undertaken. It is important not to underestimate the value of these economic considerations, and of the proper use of cost-benefit analysis in injury prevention measures, as elsewhere; and it may well be that in this country we often tend to pay insufficient attention to these matters. But the economic way is *not* the only way. It is possible for society to make collective judgments about the degree of risk which is justifiable in industry, on the road and elsewhere, and about the expenditure which is justified in accident prevention measures. No doubt this is sometimes irrational: money is spent in preventing accidents in one field, where a smaller expenditure might save more injuries in another field. Money is spent on safety in industry even though the result is to make that industry's products less competitive with other products. And so on. It is no use pretending that these things do not happen. Society does not always, or consistently, act rationally in these matters. Decisions are taken on political grounds, or on broad grounds of public interest, which bear little relation to immediate cost-benefit equations. Moreover, governments constantly attempt to control the economy in the country by fiscal and monetary measures which (however unsuccessful they seem to be in achieving their objectives) mean that market forces are often irrelevant to policy decisions. We discussed earlier the application of economic theories to the competitive position of coal compared with other fuels. But that theoretical discussion seems to bear little relation to the realities which control policy decisions. Even if the industrial injuries system, for instance, gives some small subsidy to the price of coal, it is not this which will, in the main, decide whether the consumer, or Britain's power stations, or her industries use more coal or gas or oil. These matters are likely to be largely determined by government policy about energy prices, which is itself going to be determined by fundamental political and economic considerations about the availability of Arab oil, the availability of North Sea oil, the relative efficiency of oil and coal-fired power stations, and so on.

Similarly, at the lower levels of decision making, when it has to be decided whether to install some particular accident prevention machinery, for instance, or some fire fighting equipment in a factory or a plant, there are severe limitations to the economic approach. Expenditure on fire prevention equipment in coal mines, for instance,[85] depends for its economic justification on the ability to put a value on the probable cost it saves. But the attempt to place an arithmetic probability value on the chance of a fire breaking out, and then to estimate what damage might be done if it did, appears to strain cost-benefit analysis beyond reasonable bounds. In practice, this kind of decision will often be dependent on the judgment of those responsible.

The American tradition differs from the British in other relevant ways also. One reason why Americans rely so much on economic constraints as regulators of conduct is that they have been so much more free of other restraints. In this country, control and regulation of activities which are dangerous to life and limb have long been provided for by statutes, most of which rely on criminal prohibitions or other forms of regulatory control such as licensing mechanisms. Factory legislation, for instance, has been a governmental responsibility since the last century in this country; the unwillingness of American legislators (until recent times) to enact corresponding legislation, has resulted in much of the function of the British factory inspectors being carried out by insurance inspectors. Similarly, statutory control over the construction and standards of motor vehicles in Britain goes back over forty years, while in America this was an innovation sparked off by Mr Nader's activities. Consumer protection legislation in Britain now gives statutory power to Ministers to lay down standards for preventing the marketing of dangerous products; this function in America is largely performed by the common law of products liability, backed by the constraints of liability insurance costs.

It is considerations such as these which make it improbable that Calabresi's analysis holds many valuable lessons for this country. Although it would be wrong to overlook altogether the broad effect of market deterrence on accidents costs (and Calabresi has certainly rendered a useful service in drawing attention to this), the details of the argument seem to depend too much on forms of 'fine tuning' which are inappropriate to the circumstances. Thus, any suggestion that an elaborate system, placing carefully calculated accident costs attributable to each activity onto that activity, would be justifiable, seems quite unacceptable. Indeed, crude though the tort system itself may be, it is by no means certain that other systems of distributing accident costs would be any improvement from the point of view of general deterrence. As we have seen, tort law does at least have the virtue from this point of view that it places some accident costs on those who cause accidents, and some on those who suffer them. From the point of view of general deterrence this is a reasonable result, even though 'fine tuning' might suggest a much more elaborate way of dividing the costs. The case against tort law, and the case for its replacement, do not depend on considerations of these kinds.

The difficulty of calculating social costs, of evaluating non-economic costs and benefits, of allocating different costs to different activities, and of assessing the effect of general deterrence in face of a market distorted by taxation, are such that general deterrence can usually only operate in a rough and ready way at best. If this is once conceded, then it is not easy to see why – in the field of personal injuries and disease – the loss distribution function should not be undertaken by a social security system paid for out of taxation. Although this could potentially 'externalize' the cost of this type of loss, this result can be avoided because there is no reason why, in raising the taxes needed to pay for it, account should not be taken of general deterrence. Thus the Pearson Commission proposed that their road accident compensation scheme should be financed by a special levy on the price of petrol. Similarly, if it was decided to replace the whole personal injury tort system by social security, it is reasonable to suppose that the taxes needed to pay for it would in part be raised by a levy on motorists.[86] In fixing the amount of this levy, the government would naturally consider whether it wished to increase or reduce the incidence of motoring. Since there could easily be reasons of national policy for either of these courses, such as a desire to stimulate the motor industry, or, conversely to reduce home demand so as to boost exports, the incidence of road accident costs would not be a decisive factor; but it could be taken into account. It would doubtless be objected that a levy of this kind would be a much cruder instrument than the price mechanism of the market, which enables insurers to differentiate between various classes of driver. But the answer to this is really implicit in what we have already said. Since the whole exercise can only proceed on the basis of approximations and guesses anyway, there is little purpose to be served by the use of these supposedly more delicate instruments.

OBJECTIVES

All this is not to say that the concepts underlying general deterrence hold no lessons for us. The fact that we can reduce the costs of certain types of misfortune in society by using the market mechanism is one which should always be borne in mind. Sometimes we will find (as in the case of property fire damage) that general deterrence probably works better than anything we could put in its place. On other occasions we may find that we can reduce the cost of accidents more easily or more efficiently by other methods, and sometimes we may even find it desirable for overall reasons of national policy to allow the accident rate to rise above the level it would reach if the market operated freely.

PART SEVEN
The Future

25
Reform

The main aim of this chapter is to discuss options and prospects for reform of the law concerning compensation for personal injuries. Dissatisfaction with the tort system is widespread in common law countries, not to mention Scandinavia and other countries with different legal systems and traditions. The result has been a stream of proposals for reform, but there is considerable disagreement about what to put in the place of the tort system.[1] Most of the discussion has centred on compensation for injuries resulting from accidents, because this is the area in which the tort system is most widely used and in which, therefore, its deficiencies are most clearly observable. But there are other areas in which tort is even more deficient and where, consequently, the case for reform is even stronger. For example, because of problems relating to time, causation and proof of fault, tort law is very rarely used as a means of compensating the victims of disease.[2]

In the first part of this chapter we will discuss a number of basic issues of principle and policy relevant to reform of the law, and then we will discuss more specifically some of the proposals for reform which have been made in Britain and elsewhere and some compensation schemes which have actually been put into effect.

1   BASIC ISSUES

The fault principle

Most recent reform proposals[3] have involved the abolition of the fault principle to a greater or lesser extent. The reasons for dissatisfaction with the fault principle have already been discussed. The main arguments used in favour of retention of the principle are that it expresses a basic notion of human responsibility and of corrective justice, that it plays an important role in accident prevention, and that, being basically a free-market mechanism, it allocates social resources efficiently.

Such arguments have proved most popular and pervasive in the United States, and seem in the last few years to have put a significant brake on the impetus for reform of personal injuries law. The personal responsibility argument is also currently in favour with politicians (but not with academics) in Britain. The proposals of the Pearson Commission involving abolition of the fault principle have been shelved, and the only proposals which have been given statutory force (in the Administration of Justice Act 1982) are some of those relating to assessment of tort damages. The proposal for periodical payments has not been taken up. The Lord Chancellor has launched a big inquiry into the civil justice system with particular reference, *inter alia*, to personal injuries; but this inquiry will concern itself only with questions of jurisdiction, procedure and court administration, and not with substantive law. Indeed, the Lord Chancellor recently went so far as to say that he had 'given up all hope of removing inconsistencies' in the law relating to personal injuries. The most that can be hoped for from this inquiry, it seems, is some reduction of delays in the tort system.

The economic recession has also slowed down the pace of reform. But given that sooner or later the recession will end, or at least be significantly ameliorated, and that ideological fashions come and go, it seems likely that the patent absurdities and defects of the fault principle will eventually revive the reform movement, even in countries where it is presently most quiescent.[4]

Strict liability or no-fault?
Proposals involving abolition of the fault principle take two basic forms. Some involve its replacement by strict liability, that is liability without proof of intention or negligence. The most important area of proposed strict liability in Britain is products liability.[5] The main impetus for reform in this area was the thalidomide tragedy of the 1960's. The legal aftermath of this affair demonstrated, amongst

other things, the difficulties of proving negligence against manufacturers of drugs in respect of the testing of new products to ensure safety, and of proving a causal link between the alleged negligence and the plaintiff's injuries, especially in the case of injuries to unborn children. One of the main advantages claimed for strict liability over negligence lies in the fact that the plaintiff need not prove fault in order to obtain compensation. In practice, however, most strict liability proposals contain fault elements (such as retention of the defence of contributory negligence; and definition of 'defective product' in terms of a negligence-type test such as objectively defined standards of 'reasonable safety') which reduce their appeal as *reform* measures.

Moreover, strict liability schemes do nothing about two of the major drawbacks of the tort system – the need to prove a causal link between act and injury and the need to find a responsible defendant. In economic terms, strict liability is sometimes said to have the edge on negligence in respect of accident prevention because, by imposing liability for injuries which were unavoidable given knowledge and technology at the time of manufacture, it forces manufacturers to spend more on research and development in the attempt to discover defects in products before they are manufactured in quantity and marketed. But the force of this argument depends on the extent to which liability rules have a significant impact on manufacturers' behaviour, and about this there is considerable dispute.

Reform proposals of the second type – so-called 'no-fault' proposals – eliminate the need both to find a responsible defendant and to prove a causal link between a specific act or omission and the plaintiff's injuries. No-fault schemes concentrate on the plaintiff's injuries rather than on the way the injuries were caused. For example, a no-fault road accident scheme will provide compensation for injuries suffered in a road accident regardless of whether those injuries were caused by another road user or by the injured person himself; and regardless of fault.

However in practice no-fault schemes do not eliminate all problems of proving causation, because such schemes tend to be limited in scope rather than comprehensive. For example, a person claiming no-fault road accident compensation will have to prove that his injuries arose 'out of or in connection with the use of a motor vehicle', or something like that; a person claiming no-fault compensation for drug-related injuries would have to prove that his injuries were the result of the drug and not, for example, of natural causes, which may not be easy because many adverse drug reactions are indistinguishable from other illnesses.[6] The only way of eliminating causal issues entirely is to base entitlement to compensation solely and entirely on the need of the plaintiff for compensation. At present, not even the most extensive no-fault scheme in operation (that in New Zealand) compensates entirely regardless of cause.

There is no discernible principle according to which reform in some areas takes the form of strict liability and in others, no-fault compensation. Legal tradition probably plays a part in some countries;[7] the influence of strong lobby groups has undoubtedly been important in moulding the shape of products liability proposals; and the political and economic environment is extremely important to no-fault reforms, as the fate of the Pearson Commission proposals has shown.

Limited or comprehensive reform?

This book is about personal injuries. But physical disablement is only one type of misfortune which people suffer, and which generates needs for financial support, and it is not necessarily the most important of such misfortunes. Unemployment, for example, is an important source of financial dislocation and need. Some would argue that the basic problem which the State ought to seek to relieve is poverty and financial need, and that to the extent that the disabled suffer, as a result of their disability, from low income, they should be treated in the same way as other poor people. The disabled may well have additional needs generated by their physical condition, and these should be separately met. But so far as provision of income is concerned, the disabled should not be singled out for special treatment.

The obvious course of action required by this line of argument is to leave all victims of personal injuries to rely on the social security system in the same way as others in need. Unfortunately, this apparently simple solution would not really work because the social security system itself is far from perfect in the way that it deals with the disabled; and, perhaps more importantly, the social security system does not dispense benefits solely on the basis of financial need. Not only do different groups of the disabled receive different treatment in respect of exactly the same needs; but different sources of need such as disablement and unemployment are treated differently. In other words, the social security system does not provide a minimum income and uniform provision for those with special physical needs. Before this proposal could be seriously considered, the social security system itself would have to be overhauled. Since this is a matter totally beyond the scope of this book, the rest of the discussion will concentrate purely on reform of the law concerning provision for the physically disabled in general, and victims of personal injury in particular.

The most radical type of reform of the law concerning compensation for personal injuries involves abolishing the tort system entirely and incorporating no-fault compensation for victims of personal injuries into the social security system. According to the most thoroughgoing version of this approach, all those who suffer disabilities (of whatever nature) for which society accepts responsibility should receive financial and other support from the state according to the same criteria of need, regardless of the source or nature of the disabilities. This position, however, only expresses an ideal. The writer of a recent study of disability income systems in Britain concludes that 'reasonably equal treatment of people with equal needs is not a notable feature of the present arrangements whether inside or outside the State schemes' (of compensation).[8] Again, the New Zealand Accident Compensation Scheme, which is often held up as a model for reform of the law of compensation for personal injuries, is very far from the ideal. It covers personal injury by accident, 'medical misadventure', occupational diseases and deafness, and criminal injuries, but not other sources of personal injury;[9] and it treats the victims of personal injury more generously than other social security claimants.[10] Many jurisdictions have no-fault compensation schemes for road and industrial accidents (and, often, some occupational diseases) which provide better benefits for claimants than general social welfare provisions. Various jurisdictions have limited compensation schemes for the victims of violent crimes,[11] vaccination damage,[12] medical experiments,[13] drug injuries[14] and so on. In New South Wales there is even a sporting injuries compensation scheme.[15]

In fact, everywhere the present pattern of reform seems to be to institute limited no-fault schemes to deal with particular classes of injured persons whose claims are pressed by politically powerful groups, or whose light for some reason attracts public attention and sympathy. The basic question raised by this limited and piecemeal approach is how the preference for the groups of injured who are singled out for special treatment under a no-fault scheme (or, in the case of products liability, for example, a strict liability scheme) is to be justified in comparison with the position of less favoured groups of injured persons. It may be that good (or at least popularly acceptable) reasons for treating some groups of the disabled differently from others can be adduced, but serious attempts to do this are very rare. However, it seems that the likely direction of future reform measures is towards limited rather than comprehensive schemes. In New Zealand, early intentions to extend the accident scheme quickly to other sources of personal injury show no signs of being fulfilled; and in Australia the path to comprehensive reform is seen as lying *via* transport accident schemes.

One possible argument in favour of limited schemes is that by focussing on one injury-causing activity (e.g. motoring), the scheme enables the cost of the activity to be fully internalized to that activity. But even in a comprehensive scheme the funding sources could, to some extent, be organized to achieve this objective.[16]

Another important respect in which no-fault schemes are often limited is that even in the area in which they operate (e.g. road accidents) they do not always entirely supersede the tort system, but leave the common law to operate side-by-side with the no-fault scheme. Sometimes tort and no-fault rights run in parallel, with set-off provisions to prevent double recovery. Indeed, we have already seen that under present law in Britain, there are rules determining when and to what extent no-fault, first-party insurance and social security benefits are to be set off against tort damages. The Pearson Commission recommended, as a general principle, that social security benefits should be set off in full against tort damages, but this proposal seems, for the present, to have fallen by the wayside; indeed, in fatal accident cases, the effect of the Administration of Justice Act 1982 is that there is no set-off of social security or other collateral benefits.

Another type of 'dual system' provides for no-fault benefits up to a ceiling, and then tort rights are available to top the compensation up to the level of 'full compensation'. Such dual systems have several disadvantages. First, they require the whole structure of tort law and third party liability insurance, with all its inefficiencies and costly waste, to remain in existence. American experience now shows that schemes which limit rights to sue in tort cut costs much more effectively than schemes containing no such limitation.[17] Secondly, since the no-fault benefits are subject to a ceiling, those who suffer most from the faults of the retained tort system are the long-term seriously disabled, who must rely on the common law to bring their compensation up to an adequate level. Conversely, those best off under a dual system are the less seriously injured, who can expect to receive compensation for most or all of their economic losses under the no-fault scheme, and who also enjoy the option of using the tort system to secure compensation for their non-economic losses. The long-term disabled, by contrast, may have difficulty obtaining adequate compensation even for financial loss, despite using both elements of the dual system. Dual systems, therefore, tend to be costly, to preserve all the flaws of the tort process, and to disadvantage those most in need relative to those less in need.

A case in favour of a dual system might be based on arguments about 'justice'. From this perspective, a dual system has the advantage that it embodies principles *both* of individual and of social responsibility.[18] Thus a dual system might be constructed which would ensure the victim adequate financial support but also allow him to sue the tortfeasor for intangible loss as an expression of the latter's individual responsibility. The desirability of retaining the element of individual responsibility is established, it is said, by the fact that criticism of the fault principle is not directed at the validity or acceptability of the ideals or objectives it embodies, but at the law's inability to achieve those objectives.[19] There may also be a political case in favour of dual systems. In New Zealand, the 'price' of the abolition of tort rights was that benefits under the Accident Compensation Scheme should be broadly commensurate with those in tort, at least so far as financial losses were concerned. The high level of benefits both creates anomalies with other social security benefits and makes the scheme expensive. The expense has probably inhibited the extension of the scheme to disease. The retention of tort might make it possible to introduce a more comprehensive no-fault scheme with relatively low flat-rate benefits. This would give all the disabled a floor of support but also enable those who wished to gain higher tort benefits.

On balance, however, the case for a dual system is not convincing. The fact that the objectives of the tort sytem might be thought desirable does not justify retention of a system which achieves those goals so inefficiently, and in many respects not at all. The political point could be met by a two-tier no-fault system in which relatively low flat-rate benefits were financed by compulsory levies and contributions and higher benefits for those who desired them could be bought by higher voluntary contributions, or by the purchase of insurance in the open market.

The basic policy choice between comprehensive and limited reform is a choice between viewing the position of victims of personal injuries in terms of social welfare, on the one hand, or in terms of legal rights and duties on the other.[20] The first perspective leads to attempts to integrate compensation for personal injury into the social welfare system of compensating for those misfortunes for which the State takes some responsibility. It by no means follows that all victims of misfortune will be treated in the same way by the social welfare system, and that no distinctions will be drawn on the basis of type and source of misfortune. But the comprehensive approach does involve opting for social welfare techniques, and espousing as an ultimate goal an integrated system of social welfare to deal with all cases of 'social misfortune' on the basis of need. The second perspective, on the other hand, tends to start with the existing pattern of legal liability for personal injuries, and to concentrate on improving existing legal mechanisms so that they deliver compensation to more of those for whom it is intended (for example, the 93·5% of accident victims who at present receive no tort compensation). This approach may lead simply to procedural reforms, or to reform of the rules governing assessment of damages, or it may lead to no-fault schemes, such as road accident schemes, designed to use the resources presently poured into compensating personal injury victims more efficiently to provide more victims with tort-type benefits. The two approaches are quite different, and in recent years the second has been much more in evidence than the first.

Preferential treatment
An important feature of the present law, of avowedly limited reform

proposals, and even of proposals and schemes designed by reformers with comprehensive reform as their ultimate goal, is that some groups of victims of disability receive better treatment than others. The extreme egalitarian position would be that the only criterion of compensation should be need, and that like needs should be treated alike whatever their source. But we have seen at various points how, in practice, particular groups receive preferential treatment despite the fact that their needs are no different from those of less favoured groups. We have, for example, noted the industrial preference in the social security system; in Chapter 20 we discussed at length the preferential treatment accorded to the victims of injuries attributable to human as opposed to natural causes. The commitment of tort law to the principle of full compensation and to the hundred percent principle produces a preference in the law for the victims of injuries as opposed to other misfortunes such as unemployment. We have also noted that, in practice, tort law makes it easier for the victim of traumatically caused injuries to recover compensation than for the victim of illness and disease attributable to human causes – what one writer has called the 'accident preference'.[21]

This last preference is also present in the New Zealand accident compensation scheme,[22] and in this context the preference is partly the result of the fact that diseases are a much more common source of physical incapacity than accidents; and so the cost of a scheme which covered the former as well as the latter would be very much greater than that of a scheme covering accidents only. For example, the Australian Committee of Inquiry into a national compensation scheme found that a scheme covering accidents, congenital incapacity and sickness would cost about five times as much as one covering accidents only.[23] On the other hand, this estimate takes no account of the cost of existing schemes which compensate disease victims (such as occupational sick pay and personal insurance) and so does not represent the *additional* cost of a disease scheme.[24] Moreover, the proposed Australian scheme provided high level earnings-related benefits which added considerably to the cost of the scheme. Nevertheless, the argument based on cost is a potent political weapon available against the introduction of comprehensive compensation schemes covering illness and disease as well as accidents. Opposition to the abolition of tort rights tends to be bought off by providing generous benefits, but when applied to the sphere of disease as well as accidents, the high benefits generate new opposition because they make the scheme very expensive. Thus it can be seen that the shape of reform can be influenced as much by political pressures as by rational arguments of principle or policy.[25]

Finally, it is worth noting the point that every proposal or scheme for strict liability (such as strict products liability) or no-fault compensation (such as the criminal injuries compensation scheme) in a limited area creates a preference in favour of some victims of personal injury against others.

The purpose of pointing out that the law, and most reform proposals, contain such preferences is not to show that preferential treatment of selected groups is necessarily unjustifiable. It may be possible to produce more or less convincing arguments in favour of preferential treatment of various groups. The point to make is simply that it is important to recognize and to seek to justify preferential treatment, in order to ensure that any scheme proposed or put into effect gives effect to an acceptable set of priorities for the use of social resources. For example, some good reason might be found for compensating injury victims for financial loss more generously than victims of redundancy, but we should be clear what that reason is before we institute or continue a system which gives effect to that preference.

Assessment of compensation

As we have seen, the tort system seeks in theory to compensate plaintiffs for 100% of their financial losses, and to provide monetary compensation for a wide variety of non-economic losses; it also purports to provide compensation for the full period of the plaintiff's incapacity or the full period during which he suffers loss. In other words, the tort system attempts to restore the plaintiff to the financial position he was in before the injuries were suffered (*restitutio in integrum*). To this end it provides fully earnings-related income replacement ('standard of living' benefits) for earners, and income for some non-earners (e.g. housewives) on the basis of the notional market value of their services; and full compensation for expenses incurred as a result of the injuries. The tort system also provides compensation for the disability itself – pain and suffering and loss of amenities. In order to do all this the tort system of assessment has to be highly individualized, and so is costly and slow.

The features of the tort system of assessment represent a maximum, and reform proposals usually involve some sort of trade-off under which more people are compensated than under the tort system, but at a lower level of benefits. For example, one of the reforms recommended by the Pearson Commission was that no damages ought to be awarded for non-pecuniary loss suffered in the first three months after injury. Since the vast majority of accident victims recover fully in this period, this proposal, if implemented, would remove from the tort system a large number of minor cases, and free considerable resources to compensate the more seriously injured or those who suffer permanent disability but currently receive no, or inadequate, tort damages. Again, social security systems often begin paying income-replacement benefits only after the claimant has been off work for a fixed number of days. One writer has criticized the New Zealand accident compensation scheme for concentrating too heavily on short-term disabilities by paying generous income-related benefits for merely temporary or short-term incapacity.[26]

The common law's willingness to compensate for non-pecuniary losses is usually not shared to the same extent by other compensation systems.[27] The recommendation of the Pearson Commission mentioned above illustrates this. The disability pension available under the industrial injuries scheme is a form of compensation for non-pecuniary loss, but it is peculiar to that scheme and is part of the industrial preference. The unemployed, for example, are not compensated for the pain and anguish of being out of a job for a long time. And when compensation is given for non-pecuniary loss, it is usually calculated on a tariff basis to reduce administrative costs. The major arguments against compensating for disability as such are that when resources are limited (as they always are), it is more important to compensate for pecuniary than for non-pecuniary loss; and that disability is not necessarily related to income loss. For example, a university professor who loses a leg may suffer no income loss, whereas a policeman similarly injured might suffer considerable income loss. The second objection is particularly important when disability is used as a measure of compensation for future pecuniary loss (the main advantage of doing this is that it removes the need to calculate future pecuniary loss which, as we have seen, is a very difficult and speculative operation). But even if compensation for disability is *additional* to compensation for loss of income, the low earner might feel aggrieved if, in addition to receiving earnings-related compensation for lost earnings, the higher earner also receives the same amount as the low earner for his disability.

Non-tort systems of compensation often impose quantum limitations on recovery for pecuniary loss. For example, most social security systems compensate for only a proportion (e.g. 80%) of lost earnings in order to encourage return to work. At the other end of the scale, first party insurance policies often require the insured to bear the first £X, or a certain proportion, of his financial loss, in order to discourage small claims. Strict liability schemes sometimes impose ceilings on the amount individual plaintiffs can recover, and on the aggregate amount which can be recovered from a particular defendant in relation to a particular incident or a particular period of time – such provisions are designed to prevent very risky but socially desirable activities, such as the development and marketing of drugs, from being burdened with such a level of liability that they cease altogether, or are reduced below a socially desirable level.[28]

In relation to income replacement, non-tort systems of compensation are often less committed to providing income-related benefits than is the common law, although many would now subscribe to the view that the state has a vital role to play in providing income-related insurance schemes.[29] The chief reason for this attitude to income-related benefits is that they are regressive in effect (that is, they distribute wealth from the poor to the rich) unless such benefits are funded in a fully income-related way – which may not be politically feasible. In this respect the tort system is highly regressive, because third party liability premiums are not at all related to income, while tort benefits are fully income-related. On the other hand, the fact that the social security system has a significant element of income-relatedness in it shows that earnings-relation is not perceived as being inconsistent even with a social security scheme of compensation. Indeed, income-relation is one of the basic principles of the New Zealand Accident Compensation Scheme. The proposals of the present Government to curtail the earnings-related state pension scheme are based on cost as much as on the ideological consideration that earnings-related benefits ought to be bought by individuals in the private insurance market.

Other expressed objections to income-related benefits are that they divert resources from areas of greatest need, that they make the compensation system too expensive, and that, even if they are progressively funded, they reflect existing inequalities in patterns of remuneration in society.[30]

Another respect in which social security systems restrict entitlement to benefits is by means-testing. If the basis of entitlement is need, then collateral sources of income are relevant. The common law, on the other hand, compensates for losses, and the fact that even though a person's income has been reduced, he is not actually in need, is irrelevant in assessing common law compensation. Benefits under the New Zealand scheme are not means-tested, and this has led one writer to observe that the scheme is not designed to meet need or to help the poor, but to protect against financial inconvenience even people who are in no real sense in need.[31]

A final point to note is that the question of assessment of benefits is separate from that of the basis on which benefits are paid. For example, negligence as the basis of entitlement could be replaced by a strict liability or no-fault regime in a particular area, without tort principles of assessment being abandoned in that area. Thus, compensation under the Criminal Injuries Compensation scheme and under the various proposals for strict products liability is assessed basically on classic tort principles. Indeed, the whole basis on which the New Zealand scheme, and the proposed New South Wales scheme for transport accidents, were designed was that community expectations generated by the principles of assessment at common law ought to be met in the no-fault scheme, by providing benefits broadly commensurate with those available in tort. This approach was taken partly to increase the popular and political acceptability of the reform; and also because it was perceived that the tort system had created 'vested rights'. The argument based on 'vested rights' is a very weak one for a number of reasons. In the first place, very few injured people actually receive tort compensation. Secondly, the rights in question are only 'inchoate' or potential rights to claim and be awarded compensation in the event that an injury is suffered. The use of the word 'vested' tends to conceal this fact. Finally, the 'vested rights' argument, carried to its logical conclusion, would rule out any reform of the law which deprived anyone of a potential right to some benefit or to compensation.

In the result, some of the cost savings which could be achieved by introducing flat-rate benefits and less individualized assessment rules are not realized in schemes which are designed so as to preserve 'vested tort rights'. And, contrary to what might at first be expected, even a commitment to a State-run comprehensive scheme is not always accompanied by a commitment to flat-rate income replacement and abolition of compensation for non-pecuniary losses.

Funding

We have noted several times throughout this book that the question of how a system of compensation is funded can be decided quite separately from the question of what benefits it provides and to whom. So, for example, it is possible to design the benefits side of a system to give effect to some notion of 'just compensation for losses', and to design the funding side to achieve goals such as accident prevention or income redistribution.

A number of basic funding issues deserve mention. The first is a question of approach: one approach is to construct an ideal scheme and estimate its cost, leaving it to politicians to decide whether the cost is worth the benefits. A danger here is that if a scheme is indivisible, and thought too expensive, it may fail completely. To meet this eventuality it may be possible to construct the ideal scheme in steps which could be implemented separately as funds became available. For example, the original intention in New Zealand was eventually to extend the accident compensation scheme to diseases. But the danger in *this* course is that, once the first step has been implemented, the momentum for reform will decrease and the later stages might never be implemented. This sort of global approach tends to be associated with comprehensive reforms which aim to cover areas not previously covered by an effective compensation scheme.

A very different approach involves designing a scheme which seeks to rationalize and make better use of already available resources, and even of present funding mechanisms. For example, the proposed New South Wales no-fault transport accident scheme is seen by its designers as particularly attractive because it would cost no more than the present tort-cum-liability-insurance system, and the funds could be collected in exactly the way they are at present, that is by liability insurers. Such an approach sees the reform task as being to streamline and improve the present system, rather than to look at the issue of injury compensation in terms of wider social issues about the community's responsibility for the injured.

A second major funding issue is whether the scheme is to be State-run or based on the market. The chief importance of this choice is that a market-based system will be funded on the simple principle that a person should pay for the damage he causes (if a liability scheme is in issue), or that a person should insure against his own losses (if a no-fault or first-party insurance scheme is in issue); whereas a State-run scheme can accept this insurance principle or modify it to achieve other social objectives, such as redistribution of income to the poor. So, whereas in a market-based system insurance premiums would ideally be based on a person's injury record (in a no-fault system), or on his safety record (in a liability system),[32] in a State-run system contributions could be based on income in such a way as to be distributionally regressive, neutral or progressive, according to the wishes of the political framers of the scheme.

A third issue is whether the scheme is to be fully-funded, or funded on a pay-as-you-go basis. In a fully-funded scheme the contributions in any one financial year have to be sufficient to cover all claims made in that year in full (even if the claim will be paid out periodically over a period of years, or in one lump sum but not for several years' time). In a pay-as-you-go scheme, contributions in any one year need only be sufficient to cover amounts actually paid out in that year. Thus in a fully-funded scheme, but not in a pay-as-you-go scheme, substantial reserves have to be built up. In theory, premiums under a fully-funded scheme can be lower than under a pay-as-you-go scheme because the reserves can be invested to produce income out of which future payments can be partly met. But when there is significant inflation this advantage is often illusory because returns on investments do not keep pace with inflation.[33]

The choice between these two methods of funding is not unrelated to the last point, because the realities of the private insurance market, and the legal accounting requirements placed on insurance companies, require them to run fully-funded schemes. They cannot deliberately run on a deficit one year and make it up by increased premiums the next year. In other words, only a State-run scheme can be pay-as-you-go. A pay-as-you-go scheme is desirable if benefits for financial losses are to be periodical, at least when inflation rates are high or unpredictable and liable to considerable variation. A system in which security of periodical payments depends on prudent investment of reserves may prove too risky in the long term.

From a general deterrence point of view a fully-funded scheme is, in theory, more efficient than a pay-as-you-go scheme. Under the latter, sums collected this year are used in part to pay for injuries inflicted by activities carried on in the past, whereas under a fully-funded scheme the premiums paid in any one year are sufficient, and only sufficient, to meet obligations arising out of activities carried on in that year. In reality, however, even under a fully-funded scheme new premiums are often used to make up deficits (caused, for example, by inflation) incurred in previous years.

Goals of a compensation system

Many of the issues we have discussed so far in this chapter can only be resolved if the goals of a system of personal injury compensation are made clear. Three main goals can be distinguished: compensation, deterrence (or injury prevention) and fairness (or corrective justice). An important ancillary goal, which is not strictly a goal of a compensation system but is an end which such a system can be used to further, is achieving a particular pattern of social wealth distribution or redistribution.

Compensation is, of course, the principle underlying the assessment of damages in the tort system, but it is, in a sense, a subsidiary goal of the system, in that personal injury attracts compensation in tort only if a responsible defendant can be found to pay it. Thus the tort system focusses primarily on the obligation of the defendant to pay, rather than the entitlement of the plaintiff to be paid compensation. Thus the fundamental goal of the tort system is corrective justice or fairness – in other words, the aim is to redress the balance of fairness or justice between the parties, which has been upset by the tortious behaviour of the defendant. In a negligence regime, that conduct is, of course, carelessness; in a strict liability regime, the appropriate conduct is causing damage by creating a risk of injury which then materializes. As we have seen, there are strong reasons to doubt that the tort system is very effective as a deterrent or accident prevention mechanism, and while modern economic analysts of law see deterrence as the main function and rationale of the tort system, the practical barriers to the fulfilment of the theoretical deterrence function of tort law are so substantial that it is unsatisfactory to attempt to justify the tort system in terms of the goal of deterrence. Finally, as we have noted, the tort system does have important wealth distribution effects, in some areas at least – the fact that third party motor insurance premiums are calculated without reference to the insured's income, while tort damages are income-related, means that the wealthy get much more out of the tort system than they put in relative to the poor.

So far as goals are concerned, there are some important differences between negligence-based and strict liability. In theory, at least, strict liability performs the compensation function better, simply because more people will recover compensation if fault does not have to be proved. As for deterrence, there has been much discussion of the relative efficacy of negligence and strict liability, and of whether strict liability will induce higher levels of safety than negligence liability. There is reason to think that the only respect in which strict liability is superior is that, by placing the costs of injuries not caused by fault on the defendant rather than on the plaintiff, the former might be encouraged to initiate research and development to reduce or eliminate the risks of such accidents. The corrective justice principle underlying strict liability is clearly different from that underlying the fault principle – strict liability is based on the idea that the person who reaps the benefit of engaging in a risky activity ought in fairness to bear the cost of any loss or damage caused by the activity.

In terms of wealth distribution, strict liability-cum-liability insurance could be just as regressive in effect as negligence liability if, for example, liability for motor accidents were strict. But in practice, proposals for strict liability tend to be made in respect of entrepreneurial activities (such as manufacturing); in such cases, the costs of liability will be passed on to consumers in increased prices. This may be regressive if consumption by the poor is equal to or greater than that by the rich, but the amounts involved per consumer will perhaps be so small that this element of distribution in favour of the better-off might be thought by some to be tolerable.

How well do no-fault schemes fulfil the goals stated above? So far as compensation is concerned, the 'success' of any system depends entirely on who is entitled to receive benefits under it, and on the level of benefits. We have already discussed the issue of limited versus comprehensive reforms, and touched on the issue of how close to the tort principles of full and hundred percent compensation no-fault benefits ought to be. Since no-fault schemes are all the result of legislative action, these issues can be decided as a matter of principle and policy. In practice, justification of no-fault schemes always involves being able to compensate more injured persons at no extra cost, or compensating more people by removing conditions of entitlement to compensation other than that of having suffered loss or being in need. A commitment to wide entitlement rules is basic to a commitment to no-fault. Similarly, the wealth-distributional effects of a no-fault scheme can be designed in advance to meet desired political goals; and they depend on the relationship between benefits and contributions.

No-fault schemes are often criticized because of their failure to further the goals of deterrence and corrective justice. Because no-fault systems do not involve an individual causer of injury paying an individual victim of injury, they clearly do not embody the principles of justice and fairness (or further the associated goals of retribution and vindication) which are a feature of the tort system. Rather, no-fault systems embody a principle of *social* justice and *community* responsibility for those in need.

What is the exact basis of the idea of social or community responsibility? The simplest basis is to say that everyone is entitled to a basic standard of living and to have certain basic material needs met, and that inequalities in society are only acceptable once everyone has been brought up to a minimum level of material well-being. This argument, however, will not justify a system which provides earning-related benefits or (perhaps) compensation for non-pecuniary loss; nor a system in which people with like needs are treated differently according to the source of their needs (e.g. a system in which accident victims receive earnings-related benefits but the unemployed receive basic flat-rate benefits).

Another approach (which underlay the Report on which the New Zealand scheme was based) is to argue that because the activity of individuals *in society* is the *cause* of many personal injuries, then society as a whole ought to take responsibility for these injuries. The nature of modern social life, it is said, generates an increasing amount of personal disability, and so society as a whole should bear the financial burden of these disabilities. This approach suffers from serious conceptual difficulties. In the first place, it assumes that for the purposes of society's responsibility to provide compensation, there is a relevant difference between disability caused by human action and disability resulting from natural causes. As was argued in Chapter 20, however, this distinction is not easy to justify, and many would question the idea that society (as opposed to individuals) has any more or less responsibility in the one case than in the other. Secondly, by utilizing the notion of causation, the approach makes it difficult to justify compensating for disabilities the cause of which is not known with any certainty; and it also introduces into the debate many of the ambiguities and value-laden uncertainties of the notion of causation. Thirdly, even if we accept the link between individual causation of disability and social responsibility in the abstract, we might have doubts about its applicability to cases such as disabilities caused by criminal conduct. Many would vigorously deny that social conditions (as opposed to the free choice of the criminal) are the real cause of criminal activity. On the other hand, community responsibility might seem clearer in the case, for example, of victims of government-backed vaccination programmes or volunteers in drug testing programmes, since their injuries are the result of taking part in activities which are specifically designed for the benefit of all. Finally, the notion of social responsibility by itself goes very little way towards determining exactly what society ought to do to help the disabled whose incapacity is society's responsibility. Should benefits be basic flat rate or earnings-related? Should intangible losses be compensated for (do they generate 'needs')?

The choice of justification also has ramifications for the issue of funding. The 'needs' justification might be seen as justifying funding by progressive taxation, whereas the 'causal responsibility' approach might seem more congenial to funding, as far as possible, by levies on disability causing-activities proportional to the risks created by them.

The choice between individual and social responsibility is, of course, of great importance; but it is hardly a valid criticism of either the tort system or of no-fault schemes that they do not embody the fundamental justice ideas of the other. On the other hand, it is valid to ask how well each type of system fulfils the justice goals it sets for itself; and there are, as we have seen, several compelling grounds for believing that the tort system does not give proper effect to the principle of *individual* responsibility embodied in the fault principle. So far as no-fault systems are concerned, the idea of social responsibility is, as we have noted, open to so many interpretations that individual no-fault schemes can only be assessed according to the values of the assessor, and according to how well the system achieves its expressed aims.

As for deterrence, a no-fault system clearly does not perform the function which tort law aims at when it sets up *standards* of conduct. However, this educational function could (and would probably have to) be performed by an agency charged with responsibility for promoting health and safety.[34] There is some evidence that accident rates in New Zealand have increased since the introduction of the Accident Compensation Scheme.[35] But there is no reason *in theory* why a no-fault system should not achieve as much by way of general (or economic) deterrence as the tort system. Contributions to the scheme could be related to the risk of injury created by the contributor on the basis of classification or experience rating.[36] We have seen that there are difficulties both with the general theory of economic incentives, and with classification and experience rating in particular. But these difficulties are no greater in a no-fault system than in the tort system. Indeed, in a no-fault system administered by a central agency, useful statistics could gradually be gathered on which a more sophisticated system of rating could be based.

In New Zealand the accident scheme is funded from three sources: levies on employers and the self employed (for occupational injuries), levies on motor vehicles (for road injuries) and general taxation (for other injuries). The first levy varies with the nature of the activity being carried on, but one commentator thinks that 'even with the variable levy it is clear that much refinement will be necessary if the goals of deterrence are ever to be achieved'.[37] The motor levy varies *only* according to the type of vehicle and not according to the experience of the individual driver or the amount the car is used (a petrol levy would achieve the latter). Furthermore, there can be political obstacles to proper variable rating – in New Zealand the levy on motor cyclists is far too low relative to claims by motor cyclists for compensation, largely because of the strength of the opposition to rate increases.[38] Finally, many accident causing activities are subject to no levies at all, so that such activities receive no economic safety incentives from the scheme.[39] On the other hand, the technical and theoretical difficulties and the administrative cost of precise allocation of costs in correct proportions to activities which cause accidents, would probably mean that only the broadest system of variable rating is justified, given the doubts about the deterrent effect of economic incentives.

It may be apparent from what has been said already that, although a no-fault scheme can be funded in such a way as to meet a variety of social goals, choices between these goals may well be necessary, since it would not be possible to pursue them all simultaneously. In particular, if a no-fault compensation scheme were seen basically as a social security programme to fulfil society's responsibility to the disabled, the most justifiable funding mechanism would be a general progressive tax – and this would be so whether the benefits were basic flat-rate or earnings-related. But this method of funding would involve at least partial abandonment of the deterrence goal, which would require for its fulfilment a set of levies on disability-causing activities which would internalize the costs of disabilities to the activities which caused them. Disabilities not caused by human activities could then still be paid for by general taxation. It may be that a mix of taxation and levies based on risk provides the best possible funding pattern.

Finally, it is worth noting that a major advantage called in aid to justify the change from tort liability to no-fault compensation is that the administrative costs of a no-fault system are usually much less than those of the tort system. For example, the Pearson Commission found that under the tort system the administrative cost of delivering £1 of compensation was 87 pence, while the cost of delivering £1 of social security benefits was only 11 pence. In the year to March 1979 the cost of handling claims in the New Zealand Accident Scheme amounted to about 8% of the benefits paid.[40] It does not follow from this that the tort system is too expensive, because it may be argued that the tort system serves goals and values which by their nature are expensive to secure – for example, the highly individualized nature of the damages assessment process in the tort system is inherently expensive. But since so many people receive no compensation under the tort system, and given that the administrative cost is so substantial, it is necessary to ask very seriously whether the tort system is worth what it costs. It is difficult to answer this question other than negatively.

2 PROPOSALS AND SCHEMES
Road accident schemes

The majority of no-fault schemes so far enacted have been limited to road accidents, although there are quite a few criminal injuries schemes, and some drug injuries schemes. The industrial injuries scheme in this country is, of course, a no-fault social security scheme, but in most countries which have specialized industrial injuries schemes, compensation is given on the basis of strict employer liability funded by compulsory insurance. In American, and most Canadian, jurisdictions, the insurance fund from which no-fault road accident compensation payments are made is operated by the same private insurance companies as offer standard third party liability insurance. In some jurisdictions, such as Victoria and Saskatchewan, the fund is operated by a government insurance agency, but this does not alter the essential nature of the scheme. In systems where the no-fault scheme is financed solely by premiums paid by vehicle owners, claims made by others injured on the road will be third party, not first party, claims (i.e. they will be made against the insurer of the vehicle by which the person was injured).

Traffic accident schemes fall into three broad categories. First, there are 'add-on' schemes, which typically provide limited no fault benefits for pecuniary losses arising from personal injury, but no no-fault benefits for non-pecuniary losses or property damage. Under such schemes the tort action remains intact, but there are provisions requiring no-fault benefits to be set off against tort damages to prevent double recovery. An example of such a scheme is that operating in Victoria, which provides loss of earnings benefits up to $20,800, death benefits to dependents of deceased victims, and compensation for 80% of the reasonable cost of hospital, medical and related services incurred as a result of the accident. The legislation contains provisions designed to prevent double compensation for losses covered by the scheme.

The second type of no-fault scheme can be called the 'modified' scheme. Under modified schemes the no-fault benefits are similar in type to those available under add-on schemes, although sometimes greater in amount. However, the right to sue for tort damages for non-pecuniary loss is abolished in less serious cases. In some jurisdictions, the right to sue in tort in respect of pecuniary losses is not affected, but set-off provisions prevent double recovery; in other jurisdictions, this right is abolished to the extent that the plaintiff is entitled to recover no-fault benefits. Fourteen American states have adopted modified no-fault schemes.[41] In a couple of states, the no-fault scheme gets very close to abolishing tort altogether – no-fault benefits for pecuniary losses are high, and the right to sue in tort is abolished to the extent of these benefits; tort damages for non-pecuniary loss can be recovered only in very serious cases.

The third category of scheme comprises what might be called 'pure' no-fault schemes. Under such schemes the tort action is abolished entirely (or nearly so – in the Northern Territory of Australia the right to sue in tort for non-pecuniary loss survives, but only if compensation for such loss is not claimed under the no-fault scheme). The chief example of a pure scheme is that in New Zealand, which has been in operation since 1974 and covers all accidents, not just road accidents.[42] The New South Wales Law Reform Commission has recently recommended a pure no-fault scheme for that state. In broad terms, modified no-fault schemes are designed to deal with less serious cases on a no-fault basis, and to restrict use of tort to more (or the most) serious cases. Under a pure no-fault scheme, since tort is abolished entirely, the benefits under the no-fault scheme have to be generous enough to provide adequate compensation even in the most serious cases. Thus benefits for loss of earnings tend, subject to certain thresholds and ceilings, to be standard of living benefits; in addition, limited benefits for non-pecuniary loss are usually available on a tariff basis according to the type or degree of disability. The tort concept of full compensation (*restitutio in integrum*) forms the basis of the benefit scales in these schemes.

No-fault schemes generally cover personal injury only, but in a couple of American states there have been signs of a movement to no-fault property damage compensation as well. State-run pure no-fault schemes are unlikely ever to embrace property damage. Pure no-fault schemes tend to place considerable emphasis on rehabilitation as well as compensation, and facilities may be provided for this purpose.[43]

In Britain the road accident scheme proposed by the Pearson Commission does not fall neatly into any of the above categories. The proposal involved an extension of the industrial injuries scheme (itself extended to cover the self-employed) to road accidents – loss of earnings benefits would be less than those available in tort, and compensation for disability would replace damages for non-pecuniary loss. As in the case of industrial injuries, the tort action would not be abolished (thus allowing recovery in serious cases of the difference between no-fault and tort benefits), but benefits obtained under the no-fault system would be set off in full against tort damages. The Commission also recommended that damages for non-pecuniary loss should not be recoverable in tort where the plaintiff completely recovered within three months. The effect of these proposals would be to eliminate many minor tort claims, to transfer the bulk of the remainder to the social security system, and to relegate the tort action to cases of serious and lasting disability, especially those involving high earners. In essence, therefore, the proposals are for a modified no-fault scheme. It seems unlikely that any of these proposals will be implemented in the near future.

Which of the three types of no-fault scheme is to be preferred? We have already noted that dual schemes which retain the tort action wholly or partly appear to suffer from two major disadvantages: they require the retention of the apparatus of third party liability insurance in addition to the new first party insurance mechanism; and, secondly, they subject to the defects of the tort system those most in need – the seriously disabled. This second disadvantage appears even more significant when it is recalled that the tort system tends to overcompensate in minor cases and to undercompensate in serious cases.

At the end of the day the success of any reform depends on how well it eliminates the faults of the old system. The main defects of the tort system which no-fault schemes aim to ameliorate or eliminate are: the high volume of litigation generated by the need to decide complex issues of fault and assessment of damages; the high administrative costs (legal fees and insurance company overheads) of the tort system; the fact that the majority of road accident victims receive no compensation from the tort system, and that of those who do, the less seriously injured tend to be overcompensated while the more seriously injured are often undercompensated; the delay in obtaining compensation; the fact that the dynamics of the settlement process lead many claimants to accept considerably lesser sums than they would be awarded by a court. American research suggests that add-on schemes do very little to eliminate these defects, while modified schemes fare considerably better.[44] If partial abolition of tort can achieve improvements in the above respects, one can be confident that its total abolition improves matters even more.

Another crucial issue is that of cost. Two questions arise: does the no-fault system cost more or less than the old system would have cost for the same period; and is the no-fault system more efficient in the sense that a greater amount of its total cost is paid out in compensation (as opposed to administrative costs) than under tort? As for the first point, reformers usually perceive it to be politically prudent to design a road accident scheme which costs no more than the present tort system, and reform proposals are often accompanied by actuarial calculations and costings to show that this aim has been achieved. The way it is achieved consistently with compensating many more people is by reducing the levels of compensation for lost earnings and for non-pecuniary loss, and by reducing administrative costs. American evidence on the cost of dual systems is equivocal. But it seems quite clear that the administrative costs of a pure no-fault scheme would be dramatically less than the administrative costs of the tort system, so that, provided benefits were not pitched too high, it would not be difficult to compensate many more people at no extra cost. Of course, commitment to no extra expenditure is quite easily satisfied in the road accident sphere because so much is currently spent on compensating victims of road accidents. The extension of no-fault schemes to areas where very few people currently receive tort damages would probably require considerable new expenditure, if benefits greater than basic and generally available social security benefits were to be paid.

Finally, it is worth noting again that limited no-fault schemes, such as road accident schemes, invariably create (or entrench, or extend) a preference for one group of the disabled over others. The justification for limited road accident schemes appears not to be that road accident victims deserve preferential treatment. The catalysts for such limited reform are the fact that the problem of road accidents is an old and easily recognized, not to say glaring, one; and the fact that it has been at the centre of criticism of the tort system because it is a major area of effective tort liability which has not previously been encroached upon by strict liability or social security schemes (as the industrial injuries area has) which have, to some extent, diverted attention from the defects of the tort system. The concentration on road accidents is looking increasingly anachronistic in the light of our growing realization of the role of human activities in producing all sorts of non-traumatic injuries. Moreover, road accident victims are already relatively well catered for by the tort system. If extra money is to be made available for extension of, or improvements in, the social security system, what is the case for injecting this money into those corners where victims already do relatively well? As one MP was moved to comment in the debate on the Pearson Commission Report in 1978: 'The arguments about improvements and alterations to the tort system are irrelevant. They are arguments about the distribution of the icing, when more than 90 per cent of the victims are not getting any of the cake'.[45]

There have been no new road accident schemes in the United States in the last few years, but a new proposal for a pure scheme has just been made in New South Wales. Some reformers still hope that a good limited scheme will eventually be extended in scope and become a comprehensive scheme. But New Zealand experience is not encouraging in this respect. The original hope there was that the comprehensive accident scheme would be extended to cover all injuries; but there is, at present, no sign of this, despite the fact that New Zealand currently has a socialist government, and has long had a strong social welfare tradition.

Other schemes

The variety amongst no-fault road accident schemes is partly the result of the fact that the tort system is much used in this area. This has generated a variety of solutions to the problem of the relationship between tort and no-fault schemes. A similar variety exists in the way industrial injuries are dealt with in different jurisdictions – industrial injuries are, of course, the other main area of effective tort liability. One might have thought that in areas where successful tort actions are much less common, there might be less variety in the approach to the preservation of tort liability; but a recent survey of drug injury compensation schemes shows this not to be the case.[46] The West German scheme is based on strict liability-cum-liability insurance. The Swedish scheme has three components: basic losses are met by social security, and further losses are dealt with by a voluntary (i.e. non-statutory) first party insurance scheme (analogous to the Motor Insurers' Bureau scheme in England), set up by the pharmaceutical manufacturers and importers with major insurance companies; tort liability continues to exist, but all benefits received from social security or the insurance scheme must be set off against tort damages, and neither of these funds has a right of recourse against the tortfeasor. In Japan the tort remedy continues to exist and, indeed, no-fault benefits are not payable if it appears that someone's negligence was responsible for the injury.

The Swedish idea of using private first party insurance to cover top losses rather than basic losses is a flexible one, because it could be combined either with a social security system, offering flat-rate income benefits or earnings-related benefits up to a ceiling; or with a tort system made subject to a damages ceiling – this would utilize the acknowledged fact that the tort system compensates generously for minor injuries, but inadequately for serious cases of large losses.[47]

3 THE WAY AHEAD

In the third edition of this book it was argued that what was needed was a single comprehensive system for assisting the disabled, based on the existing social security system, but with benefits as large as society can afford. In particular, it was suggested that the most practicable and desirable direction of movement was a gradual extension of the industrial injuries scheme, with any necessary modifications, first to all accidents, and ultimately to disease and illness, whether caused by human action or the result of natural causes.

The main argument in favour of such a comprehensive scheme lies in the unfairness produced by lack of integration of the various presently existing schemes for assisting the disabled. Not only is the element of double compensation which overlap of systems creates a waste of resources, but it is indefensible to compensate some people twice over while others go without any compensation at all. For example, how can we justify paying compensation twice over to a person who loses an eye in an industrial accident merely for the disability itself, while we refuse any compensation for the disability itself to a person who is blinded by a disease resulting from natural causes? How can we justify giving social security benefits to people who continue to receive full wages while they are off sick, when the level of long-term sickness benefits is still so low?

Then there is the difficulty of justifying payments made under one system but refused by another. How can we justify giving damages for loss of support to a young childless widow, for example, when the social security system fails to provide any assistance at all to a childless widow under 40 unless she is an industrial widow or unless she is quite destitute or incapable of work. Surely society must decide whether it thinks a widow is entitled to support irrespective of her capacity for work, and regulate its compensation systems accordingly. Finally, there is the whole problem of justifying the various preferences in favour of particular groups of the disabled embodied in the present set-up.

On the other hand, it must be admitted that there are very considerable difficulties facing the sort of comprehensive reform suggested above.[48] The disability income system is extraordinarily complex, and the project of reforming it in a comprehensive way would be very difficult, time-consuming and expensive. The fragmented nature of the proposals made by the Pearson Commission perhaps provides a warning against being too optimistic about the prospects for comprehensive reform. Nevertheless, the fact that a comprehensive accident scheme has been in operation in New Zealand since 1974, and that a national scheme covering disease and illness as well as accidents reached the stage of draft legislation in Australia before being shelved after a change of government shows that, given vision and energy, plus a determination that broad principles should not be swamped by a mass of detail, a comprehensive scheme of assistance for the disabled need not be unattainable.

Another major obstacle in the way of comprehensive reform is the inevitable opposition from special interest groups which, naturally, seek the preservation of schemes, arrangements and preferences which benefit them. One of the important arguments in favour of comprehensive reform is that justice requires that people with similar needs should receive similar assistance. But justice is a very slippery concept, and it is possible to make an argument, based on a more or less plausible concept of justice, to justify many of the preferences for particular groups embodied in the present law. So comprehensive reform requires a firm adherence to a particular notion of social justice, and the political will to disregard the pleas of those who receive special treatment under present arrangements. Recent history does not give much cause for optimism on this score.

A related difficulty is that experience suggests that in a democratic system, large-scale reform is on the whole harder to effect than small-scale or incremental change. This is no doubt one reason why, in the past, pressure groups have been able to secure the enactment of specific preferential schemes (such as that to compensate vaccine-damaged children). Since any reformer must accept the realities of the political process, there may be an argument for aiming at comprehensive reform via limited reform – the development of more and more special schemes might generate pressure for rationalization into a comprehensive scheme; or, alternatively, special schemes might eventually cover virtually the whole field of disablement.

A major argument made against proposals for large-scale reform is that of cost. In the case of some limited reforms, such as no-fault road accident schemes, this objection can be met simply by designing a system which, by effecting various savings and trimming certain benefits slightly, costs no more than the scheme being replaced. But comprehensive reforms will almost certainly require some new money, because it will compensate many disabled persons who receive little or nothing under present arrangements. One of the advantages of reform by extension of a currently existing scheme is that, by choosing a scheme with relatively generous benefits, the end result might be a general upgrading of provision for the disabled. But the danger in this course is that the objection of cost might lead to a general downgrading of benefits in the existing scheme before its coverage is extended. There is, then, a basic dilemma facing the comprehensive reformer – is it better to compensate more people at lower levels, or few people at more generous levels? In the end, a compromise is most likely which involves, for example, compensating the more seriously disabled quite generously, at the cost of relatively low benefits for those with only minor or short-term disabilities – in this way a large number of the disabled receive some assistance, but the more seriously disabled are relatively better catered for.

Crucial to the issue of cost is that of whether the income replacement element of benefits (as opposed to the element designed to meet the special needs of the disabled arising out of their physical condition) is to be flat rate and means tested – that is, designed to provide a level of reasonable subsistence; or earnings-related and regardless of means – that is, designed to compensate for income loss. We have seen that income relation is a basic principle of the New

Zealand accident compensation scheme, and those who support special schemes for disabilities identified by cause (e.g. industrial disabilities) usually argue that the fact that the disabilities in question arose from a particular source justifies compensatory benefits, even if social security benefits generally are flat rate and means tested. Clearly the cost of an income-related scheme will be much greater than that of a flat-rate scheme, and as a matter of principle it is justifiable to ask to what extent it is the obligation of the State to maintain people in their accustomed way of life, as opposed to providing them with a reasonable floor level of support. It is clear that very few would argue that a State-run system should compensate relative to income, however high that income is. But very many reformers would now argue that, up to a certain maximum, benefits ought to be income-related, at least if the income loss lasts for more than a relatively short time (a qualifying period for income-related benefits would save money, and might encourage rehabilitation).

On the other hand, if the demand for income relation were seen as a major obstacle to comprehensive reform, it might be worthwhile giving more thought to some sort of dual system under which flat-rate means-tested benefits at a reasonable level would be available through the social security system, leaving it to individuals to take out private insurance if they wanted benefits above the State-provided level.

A related question concerns the future of tort law. One of the factors which has led reformers to propose earnings-related benefits is that the tort system provides such benefits (in theory at least) whatever the income of the injured person, and in order to defuse opposition to the abolition of tort it has seemed expedient to provide benefits under the new system broadly comparable to those available under tort. This might suggest that at least some, if not most, of the opposition to the introduction of a scheme under which all the disabled received flat-rate income replacement, plus provision for special needs, could be defused by leaving the tort system in existence, so as to provide a source of earnings-related benefits for those who wanted them. Such a proposal would avoid some of the criticisms of dual systems noted earlier. Since all the special needs of the disabled would be met by social security, it could not be argued that those most in need (i.e. the severely disabled) were being relegated to an inferior remedy – their basic needs would be met by the State. It is true that such a dual system would be administratively expensive, but one might expect that the tort system would not be heavily used if the State benefits were reasonable in amount (ideally based on average weekly earnings).

But such a dual system suffers from what is really a fatal disadvantage. The tort system would provide earnings-related benefits for only a proportion of the disabled, as indeed at the moment it only covers a small proportion of the disabled. It would be difficult to justify special treatment for some of the high-earning disabled, when the removal of special treatment is a major justification for comprehensive flat-rate benefits. A much more satisfactory solution would be to abolish tort and leave all high earners to insure themselves for income-related benefits.

Finally, the proposal to use the industrial injuries scheme as the model for comprehensive provision for the disabled runs into the difficulty that the industrial injuries scheme itself is far from flawless. In particular, it is arguable that better provision might have to be made for partial loss of earnings in cases of short-term incapacity. Secondly, it is arguable that provision for compensation for permanent disability, regardless of income loss, is unjustified while so many are without adequate income. Even if there is a genuine public demand for disablement benefits over and above adequate income replacement benefits, there is a strong case for restricting these benefits to serious cases. There is little to be said for disablement benefit in cases of minor injuries (e.g. those assessed at under 10%); it is only where the disability threatens to destroy a person's normal mode of life that the case for such benefits is at all strong. Even so, these points do not amount to a strong argument against considering extension of a modified industrial injuries scheme to all disabilities. The emphasis in such a scheme should be firmly on income replacement and provision for the special needs of the disabled.

Given that the present political and economic climate is uncongenial to comprehensive reform, should lawyers support and press for whatever limited reform (such as a road accident scheme or a drug injuries scheme) seems politically feasible? The answer must be 'yes'. The waste and inefficiencies of the tort system are continuing realities, and there is only so much that tinkering with the tort system can achieve. Even if all we can realistically hope for is that the funds currently tied up in the tort system as it now operates will be better used, this is enough to justify a limited reform, even at the cost of creating or perpetuating anomalies between road accident victims and other social welfare recipients. And in the process the public mind might be sufficiently weaned off the idea of tort rights and onto the notion of no-fault welfare rights, to lead eventually to more comprehensive reform.

4 DAMAGE TO PROPERTY

If the law of torts in regard to personal injuries was completely abolished, the question would arise as to the fate of the law relating to property damage. We have already seen that (except in the very special case of ships) actions for property damage are now in practice almost invariably confined to cases of damage to vehicles (and such like) in road accidents. Outside this sphere, few tort actions are ever brought, and those that are brought are rarely justifiable. The practice of insuring property is so much more widespread than the practice of insuring one's own earning power that no hardship would probably be caused by total abolition of the tort action for damage to property, even if nothing else were put in its place.[49] The deliberate infliction of damage would of course remain a criminal offence, and so would careless and dangerous driving. There is no doubt that this would save a great deal of money for motorists in the long run, since it would be much cheaper for them to insure their own cars against damage than to be compelled to go on carrying personal *and* liability insurance policies, even if they were restricted to property damage. However, it is possible that people would find this inequitable in certain circumstances.[50] For one thing, the fact that comprehensive insurance is not usually full insurance but involves an excess of £50 or so, (not to mention loss of a no-claims bonus) means that a motorist whose car was damage entirely by fault of another might well be dissatisfied if the law gave him no redress against the other, and his own insurance left him £40 or £50 out of pocket.[51] One possible answer to this – though a limited one – would be to make it a regular practice for criminal courts to make awards of compensation of sums of about this order on the conviction of a motorist for a driving offence which caused damage to another vehicle. Alternatively, it might be possible to abolish tort liability for property damage except for (say) the first £50 of damage, and then to prohibit people from insuring against this liability. This would leave the injured property owner with his own insurance in the case of really serious damage, while he would still be able to claim the loss of his excess or no-claims bonus from another motorist at fault, and the fault principle would be given a reality it does not now possess by ensuring that there is no liability in insurance, and that therefore the man at fault actually pays for the damage.

5 THE ROLE OF THE INSURANCE INDUSTRY AND THE LEGAL PROFESSION

If actions for damages for personal injuries were eliminated, a large proportion of the third party liability insurance which is at present undertaken by the insurance industry would come to an end. Although no industry is likely to welcome the disappearance of a substantial amount of business – especially captive business such as third party liability insurance – we have given reasons for thinking that current rates of inflation may be rendering this form of insurance unattractive. In any event, it is suggested that the insurance industry has no real reason to fear changes along the lines here advocated. If some forms of insurance business disappear, insurance companies may be encouraged to develop others more in line with public needs. For example, if tort liability insurance for personal injuries were abolished, it is reasonable to suppose that the development of personal accident insurance and private occupation insurance schemes against income loss for high salary earners would be given a much needed stimulus. In this way, private insurance against loss through sickness or accident could supplement the social security system for the middle classes, in precisely the same way as it is expected to do with regard to retirement pensions.

And if – though this seems less likely to win public acceptance – liability at law for negligent damage to property was also abolished (at least in some spheres), there can be little doubt that there would in consequence be a great expansion of property loss and damage insurance. It is true that the protection afforded the property owner by legal liability of others is limited, and not very valuable in comparison with the much more extensive protection afforded by his own insurance cover; and therefore the elimination of legal liability would not be a particularly good reason for deciding to invest in property insurance, if the property owner had done without it before. But it is to be expected that the psychological effect of a change in the law of this nature would be immense, and insurance companies would be well placed to take advantage of this fact. Indeed, they would have to do so if the change were to have any real propect of success, because the main reason for proposing this change so far as property damage is concerned is the belief that private insurance is a cheaper, simpler and more effective form of protection for the property owner.

Clearly, reform along the lines outlined above would also have profound implications for the legal profession. If it is true, as we have suggested, that some 80% of all litigation in the Queen's Bench Division is personal injury litigation, it is obvious that the transfer of this work to the social security system would have serious implications for the Bar, and, though to a much lesser extent, for the solicitors who do this sort of work. It is important that proposals for reform should grasp this nettle, and not dismiss the problem with an airy reference to 'vested interests'. Clearly, the interests of a few hundred barristers cannot, in the long run, be allowed to determine the shape of the law relating to compensation for personal injuries; law is a social service, and in the long run the interests of the consumers and not the administrators must prevail. Moreover, abolition of tort actions would clearly be a slow process with a long transitional period, if only because of the backlog of old cases waiting to be disposed of when the legislation takes effect. In any event, there is likely to be plenty of other work available for lawyers in the future,[52] and it is fair to add that this may well involve a better use of the available legal talent.

One obvious way in which the effects on the legal profession of eliminating all personal injury litigation could be cushioned would be to make legal aid available for social security tribunals. These tribunals already deal with far more cases than the tort system, and although the average cases probably involves less money than the average tort case, many social cases involve entitlement to long-term benefits whose capital value may be many thousands of pounds. The law relating to these benefits is also becoming extremely complex and yet it is administered in the first instance by non-lawyers, and even the local appeal tribunals rarely have the assistance of legal representatives for the insured. There is a great deal to be said even now for extending legal aid to some cases before these tribunals;

plainly, the case would be stronger if social security benefits become more valuable, and if all personal injury cases are to be dealt with by these tribunals. If, in addition, the provision of legal aid for such cases would help to tide the Bar over a few difficult years, the change might well be rendered politically more palatable.

The danger in this course of development is that social security law will become as dogged by delay, technicality, formality and excessive rigidity as the tort system; and this will open tribunals to the same criticisms as are currently levelled at the courts. If these dangers are to be avoided and the Bar brought effectively into the tribunal process, then it seems certain that some adjustment in the ways in which barristers think and work will become necessary. This adjustment will not be an easy one. The traditions of the Bar may well be hostile to the political philosophy which underlies the social security system and the welfare state. The Bar is a profession for individualists and those who succeed at that profession are, more than most, likely to espouse the virtues of rugged individualism. The Bar's traditions are in tune with the common law of torts, where people are expected to stand on their own feet, assert their own rights, and gamble with offers or payments into court; where people bear with fortitude the necessary delays, learn to accept their fate if no negligence can be proved against a solvent or insured defendant, and can be relied on to deal prudently with damages of many thousands of pounds. These traditions are not in tune with the social security system, which in so many ways is based on an entirely different set of political assumptions. If the Bar is to work within the framework of the social security system, then it must come to terms with that system. This is indeed but one aspect of a problem which has so far been dimly perceived, namely the role of the lawyer in society.

Notes

CHAPTER 1

1 Stapleton, (1985) 5 *Oxford J. Leg. Stud.* 248.
2 Pearson Report, Vol. 1, para. 271.
3 See the Accident Compensation Act 1972 and Accident Compensation (Amendment) Acts (No. 1 and No. 2) 1973. For a summary of the Acts, see Harris, (1974) 37 *Modern Law Review* 361.
4 *Compensation and Rehabilitation in Australia, Report of the National Committee of Inquiry* (Canberra, 1974).
5 By means of a memorandum prepared by Professor Atiyah and subscribed by 33 lawyers, parliamentarians and others. See (1969) 119 *New Law Journal* 653 for the text of the memorandum, and *The Times*, 5 July 1969.
6 See paras. 448–50.
7 Pearson Report, Vol. 2, para. 16.
8 *Ibid*, paras. 16, 22.
9 *Ibid*, Table 57.
10 *Ibid*, para. 27.
11 Cmnd. 9302 (1984).
12 Pearson Report, Table 5.
13 *Social Security Statistics, 1984*, Table 21.10. But the number of assessments has halved since 1966.
14 *Ibid*, Table 21.10.
15 *Ibid*, Table 21.30.
16 *Ibid*, Table 21.34.
17 Pearson Report, Vol. 2, Table 7.
18 *Ibid*, Table 4.
19 *Handicapped and Impaired in Great Britain*, 3 Parts by Amelia Harris and others (HMSO, 1971–2).
20 *Ibid*, Part I, Table 1.
21 *Ibid*. For these categories, see para. 3.3.3.

22 *Ibid*, compiled from Tables 9 and 10. The figures include women aged 60–64 as the survey did not estimate the numbers in this category separately. In 1981, 27,200 persons under 65 were registered under s.29 of the National Assistance Act 1949 as severely handicapped; and 127,100 were registered as severely or appreciably handicapped (*Health and Personal Social Services Statistics for England*, 1981, Table 7.12).
23 Pearson Report, Vol. 2, Table 54.
24 *Handicapped and Impaired in Great Britain*, Part I, para. 6.2.
25 *Ibid*.
26 Figures for England and Wales only. See *DHSS Annual Report 1977* (HMSO, 1978), para. 167.
27 *Health and Personal Social Services Statistics for England*, 1981, Table 7.1; this figure includes short-stay residents.
28 *In-patient Statistics from the Mental Health Inquiry for England 1982* (HMSO, 1985), Tables B8, B9.
29 *Aids for the Disabled* (London, 1968), para. 21.
30 *General Household Survey* (HMSO, 1973), Table 8–11.
31 *Social Security Statistics, 1984*, Table 3.75, shows 361 million days lost in 1982/3 for which sickness and invalidity benefit was paid, but of these, 33.2 million were due to (non-industrial) accidents including poisonings and violence; in addition 9.3 million days were lost through industrial accidents (Table 20.70) and 0.2 million as a result of prescribed diseases.
32 See the *Report of the Australian Committee of Inquiry*, para. 485, pointing out that in Australia the average age of a widow whose husband was killed in an accident was 39, while the average age of a widow whose husband died of natural causes was 51.
33 Pearson Report, Vol. 1, Table 4.
34 *Ibid*, Vol. 2, para. 52.
35 Based on Pearson Report, Vol. 2, Table 158.
36 *Social Security Statistics, 1984*, Table 34.34.
37 TUC *Evidence to the Pearson Commission*, Table 6.
38 Pearson Report, Vol. 2, Table 78.
39 *Ibid*, para. 522.
40 *Harris 1984 Survey*, pp. 86–91.
41 *Social Security Statistics, 1984*, Table 21.34.
42 Criminal Injuries Compensation Board, 20th Report, para. 9.
43 Pearson Report, Vol. 2, para. 522.
44 Criminal Injuries Compensation Board, 14th Report, para. 37.
45 Fisher *Report*, para. 175.
46 *Report of the National Commission on State Workmen's Compensation Laws* (Washington, 1972), Table 3.5.

CHAPTER 2

1 *Davis Contractors v. Fareham U.D.C.* [1950] A.C. 696, at p. 728.
2 See Powell, *The Unreasonableness of the Reasonable Man*, (1957) 10 *Current Legal Problems* 104.

3 *Morris* v. *West Hartlepool Steam Co.* [1956] A.C. 552; *Cavanagh* v. *Ulster Weaving Co.* [1960] A.C. 145.
4 Allen, *Legal Duties* (Oxford, 1931), p. 72. This is, in any event, an extreme statement of the 'subjective' position. Because some element of personal judgment is necessarily inherent in a decision of this kind, it does not follow that in making such a decision a judge is merely stating what *he* thinks; see p. 42.
5 See the *Report of the Public Inquiry into the Accident at Hixon Level Crossing* (1968, Cmd. 3706).
6 See Prosser on *Torts*, 4th edn, pp. 146 *et seq.*
7 *US* v. *Carroll Towing Co.* (1947) 159 F. 2nd. 169.
8 R. A. Posner, *Economic Analysis of Law* (2nd edn, Boston, Toronto, 1977), pp. 122 ff.
9 [1965] A.C. 778.
10 The distinguished mathematician, G. H. Hardy, once wagered 'his fortune till death' to a halfpenny that the sun would rise on the following day.
11 *Bolton* v. *Stone* [1951] A.C. 850.
12 *The Wagon Mound* (No. 2) [1967] 1 A.C. 617.
13 See the Hixon Level Crossing *Report*, para. 265.
14 [1951] A.C. 367.
15 *Research on Road Safety* (HMSO, 1963), pp. 89–90.
16 An attempt is made by Fried, (1969) 82 *Harvard Law Review* 1415. One answer is that the time available for rescue in such circumstances places a very real finite limit on the amount that can be expended.
17 See Chapters 19 and 24.
18 A possible field for empirical research?
19 *Nettleship* v. *Weston* [1971] 2 Q.B. 691.
20 *Roberts* v. *Ramsbottom* [1980] 1 All E.R. 40.
21 *Maynard* v. *Midlands R.H.A.* [1984] 1 W.L.R. 634, 638 G–H.
22 *Scottish Omnibuses* v. *Wyngrove, The Times*, 24 June 1966. It is symptomatic of the treatment of such a case as raising a 'pure question of fact' that it should not even be reported.
23 Stapleton, (1985) 5 *O.J.L.S.* 248, 253.
24 For the same reason there might be objections to allowing actions for damages in respect of faultily designed houses, although it is believed that negligent design accounts for many accidents in the home (8% according to one enquiry: see *Accidents in the Home* (London, 1964), p. 17).
25 *Home Office* v. *Dorset Yacht Co.* [1970] A.C. 1004.
26 Cmnd. 3358, p. 37.
27 See *Schuster* v. *New York* (1958), 154 N.E. 2d. 534, where the police authority were held liable for failure to protect a witness in such a case.
28 *Anns* v. *Merton L.B.C.* [1978] A.C. 728.

CHAPTER 3

1 [1932] A.C. 562.
2 *Anns* v. *Merton L.B.C.* [1978] A.C. 728.

3 See Buckland, (1935) 51 *Law Quarterly Review* 637; *Some Reflections on Jurisprudence* (Cambridge, 1945), pp. 110–15.
4 [1969] 2 Q.B. 412 at p. 426.
5 [1970] A.C. 1004 at p. 1058.
6 For an example of this confusion see *Arenson* v. *Arenson* [1972] 2 All E.R. 939, 948 *per* Brightman J. (reversed on appeal: [1977] A.C. 405).
7 [1970] A.C. 1004.
8 Another doubtful area concerns liability for freak or extraordinary consequences; these are normally dealt with by another 'control device', namely the rules of causation or remoteness – see Chapter 4.
9 [1932] A.C. 562.
10 Prosser on *Torts*, 4th edn, p. 362.
11 See, e.g., Heuston in (1957) 20 *Modern Law Review* 1.
12 There is some difficulty in accepting this view so far as England is concerned. In the mid-nineteenth century, when these restrictions on liability were most severe, England was the wealthiest country in the world, and its industries the most prosperous and powerful in the world. By the end of the century this was no longer the case, and yet it was then that the courts (and Parliament) began to impose increasing liabilities on industry.
13 Until the establishment of the County Courts in 1846 there were only fifteen common law judges for the entire country.
14 In particular, the *Hedley Byrne* case [1964] A.C. 465, *Anns* v. *Merton L.B.C.* [1978] A.C. 728 and *Junior Books Ltd* v. *Veitchi Co. Ltd* [1983] 1 A.C. 520.
15 [1983] 1 A.C. 410.
16 See *Hinz* v. *Berry* [1970] 2 Q.B. 40.
17 *Bourhill* v. *Young* [1943] A.C. 92.
18 Cf. *Boardman* v. *Sanderson* [1964] 1 W.L.R. 1317, with *King* v. *Phillips* [1953] 1 Q.B. 429.
19 [1983] 1 A.C. 410.
20 Cf. *Hambrook* v. *Stokes* [1925] 1 K.B. 141, with *Hinz* v. *Berry* above.
21 *Chadwick* v. *British Railways* [1967] 1 W.L.R. 912.
22 *Dooley* v. *Cammell Laird Ltd* [1951] 1 Lloyd's Rep. 271; Cf. *Mt Isa Mines Ltd* v. *Pusey* [1970] 125 C.L.R. 383.
23 Lords Russell of Killowen, Scarman and Bridge of Harwich.
24 Law Reform (Miscellaneous Provisions) Act 1944 (N.S.W.), s.4.
25 [1964] A.C. 465.
26 *Junior Books Ltd* v. *Veitchi Co. Ltd* [1983] 1 A.C. 520.
27 *Electrochrome Ltd* v. *Welsh Plastics Ltd* [1968] 2 All E.R. 205; *S.C.M. (United Kingdom) Ltd* v. *W. J. Whittall & Son, Ltd* [1971] 1 Q.B. 337; *Spartan Steel & Alloys Ltd* v. *Martin & Co. (Contractors) Ltd* [1973] 1 Q.B. 27.
28 See *Riley on Business Interruption and Consequential Loss Insurances and Claims* (6th edn, David Cloughton ed., London, 1985), Chapter 16.
29 *Ibid*, paras. 350–2.
30 *Caltex Oil (Australia) Pty Ltd* v. *The Dredge 'Willemstad'*, 136 C.L.R. 529 (1975–76).
31 *Rivtow Marine Ltd* v. *Washington Ironworks* [1973] 40 D.L.R. (3d) 530.
32 *Leigh and Sillivan* v. *Aliakmon Shipping Co. Ltd* [1986] 2 W.L.R. 906.
33 Section 1A.

34 Section 1.
35 *Flint* v. *Lovell* [1935] 1 K.B. 354.
36 Administration of Justice Act 1982, s.4(2).
37 Law Comm. No. 56, *Report on Personal Injury Litigation – Assessment of Damages*, 1973, paras. 92–9, 172–80.
38 [1975] 2 All E.R. 1107, 1111.
39 Administration of Justice Act 1982, s.2.
40 *Cunningham* v. *Harrison* [1973] Q.B. 942; *Donnelly* v. *Joyce* [1974] Q.B. 454.
41 For a useful review of some of these problems, see Clarke and Ogus, 'What is a Wife Worth?', 5 *Br. J. Law & Soc.* 1 (1978).
42 Administration of Justice Act 1982, s.2.
43 See p. 403.
44 (1928), 160 N.E. 301.
45 (1978), 83 D.L.R. (3d) 609.
46 *The Guardian*, 1 July 1967.
47 *Deyong* v. *Shenburn* (1946) K.B. 227.
48 For a review of the literature on this question, see Honoré, *International Encyclopaedia of Comparative Law* (Tübingen, The Hague, Paris and New York, 1971), vol. XII, chapter 7, §§25–8.
49 See *Horsley* v. *Maclaren (The Ogopogo)* [1971] 2 Lloyd's Rep. 410, on which this example is based.
50 See generally Hart & Honoré, *Causation in the Law* (Oxford, 2nd edn, 1985), *passim*; Shapo, *The Duty to Act* (Austin, Texas and London, 1977).
51 Also because, in general, clients can sue their professional advisers in either contract or tort: *Midland Bank Trust Co. Ltd* v. *Hett, Stubbs & Kemp* [1979] Ch. 384.
52 *Anns* v. *Merton L.B.C.* [1978] A.C. 728.
53 Private professional practitioners such as doctors are not normally obliged to accept clients and so could not be sued for nonfeasance in refusing to accept a case. But the same may not be true of N.H.S. hospital doctors. If a person is taken to the casualty department of an N.H.S. hospital and the hospital sends him away without treating him, it seems that the hospital may be liable for the negligence of the doctors on duty: *Barnett* v. *Chelsea Hospital* [1968] 1 All E.R. 1068. Public authorities generally may often have duties to take positive action which private citizens similarly placed would not have.
54 *Newton* v. *Edgerley* [1959] 1 W.L.R. 1031.
55 *Hudson* v. *Ridge Manufacturing Co.* [1957] 2 Q.B. 348.
56 See, e.g., *Brown* v. *Roberts* [1965] 1 Q.B. 1, where the claim was rejected on the ground that the owner of the car was not in fact negligent in failing to prevent the passenger opening the door. Some 3,000 to 4,000 accidents a year (about 1·6% of all personal injury road accidents) are caused in this way (see *Research on Road Safety* 1963, HMSO) and such liability is often covered by comprehensive policies even though the driver is not legally liable.
57 *Home Office* v. *Dorset Yacht Co.* [1970] A.C.1004.
58 See *Selfe* v. *Ilford & District Hospital Management Committee*, *The Times*, 26 November 1970.
59 [1967] 1 A.C. 645.
60 [1980] 1 Q.B. 485.

61 Cf. *Fagan* v. *Metropolitan Police Commissioner* [1969] 1 Q.B. 439, a criminal case.
62 An Australian decision supports the imposition of liability: *McKinnon* v. *Burtakowski* [1969] V.R. 899.
63 *The Times*, 13 July 1978.

CHAPTER 4

1 See, e.g., *Caswell* v. *Powell Duffryn Collieries* [1940] A.C. 152.
2 Stapleton, (1985) 5 *O.J.L.S.* 248, 250–2, 267 n. 54.
3 [1972] 3 All E.R. 1008.
4 [1962] 1 All E.R. 623.
5 [1974] 1 All E.R. 262.
6 Weinrib, 'A Step Forward in Factual Causation', 38 *Modern Law Review* 518 (1975).
7 Doubts are expressed later about the effectiveness of tort liabililty as a way of influencing conduct – see p. 490.
8 [1952] 1 D.L.R. 1.
9 See *Kingston* v. *Chicago & N.W. Rly* (1927), 22 N.W. 913.
10 *Baker* v. *Willoughby* (1970) A.C. 476.
11 *Dillon* v. *Twin State Gas & Electric Co.* (1932) 163 A. 111.
12 *Performance Cars Ltd* v. *Abraham* [1961] 3 All E.R. 413 (property damage).
13 [1965] A.C. 75.
14 [1965] A.C. 75 at pp. 112–13 and 165.
15 *Barnett* v. *Chelsea Hospital* [1968] 1 All E.R. 1068; for a development of the idea of liability proportional to the risk for which the defendant is responsible, see Robinson, 68 *Virg. L.R.* 713 (1982).
16 *Jobling* v. *Associated Dairies Ltd* [1982] A.C. 794.
17 See Collingwood, *Proceedings of the Aristotelian Society*, xxxviii, 85 at p. 93, for a famous passage putting this point.
18 *Causation in the Law* (2nd edn., Oxford, 1985).
19 See, e.g., Linden in (1965) 53 *California Law Review* 1098 at 1102, protesting that we cannot discard the notion that in road accidents, 'motoring and not perambulating is the villain of the piece'.
20 Lloyd-Bostock in *Harris 1984 Survey*, ch. 4.
21 *Op. cit.*, p. 5.
22 See, e.g., *Ryan* v. *New York Central Rly Co.* (1866), 35 N.Y. 210.
23 See, e.g., *McDowall* v. *G.W. Rly* [1903] 2 K.B. 331.
24 (1874), L.R. 9 Ex. 125.
25 [1964] 1 Q.B. 518.
26 [1961] A.C. 388.
27 [1921] 3 K.B. 560.
28 See Hart & Honoré, *op. cit.*, pp. 262–7, for a theoretical explanation of this point.
29 E.g. *Smith* v. *Leech Brain & Co. Ltd* [1962] 2 Q.B. 405.
30 E.g. *McKew* v. *Holland and Hannen and Cubbits (Scotland) Ltd* [1969] 3 All E.R. 1621; *Lamb* v. *Camden L.B.C.* [1981] Q.B. 625.
31 For a discussion of the origins of this statute see Ogus, *Vagaries in Liability for the Escape of Fire*, [1969] *Cambridge Law Journal* 104. Ogus rejects the idea that the

development of insurance influenced this statute, but on the seemingly inadequate ground that subrogation was unknown at this time.
32 *Smith* v. *Leech Brain* [1962] 2 Q.B. 405; see also *Warren* v. *Scuttons* (1962) 1 Lloyd's Reports 497.
33 *Sayers* v. *Perrin* (1966) Q.L.R. 89.
34 *Pigney* v. *Pointer's Transport Services Ltd* [1957] 1 W.L.R. 1121; cf. *Brice* v. *Brown* [1984] 1 All E.R. 997.
35 [1974] 2 All E.R. 737. For an extraordinary Australian case where a man was drowned in a suburban road and yet the result was held 'foreseeable', see *Versic* v. *Connors* (1969) 90 W.N. (N.S.W.) (Pt. 1), 33.
36 [1964] 1 Q.B. 518.

CHAPTER 5

1 See, e.g., Bowen L.J. in *Thomas* v. *Quatermain* (1887), 18 Q.B.D. 685, 694, and *Caswell* v. *Powell Duffryn Collieries* [1940] A.C. 152.
2 See Schwartz, 'Contributory and Comparative Negligence: A Reappraisal', 87 *Yale Law Journal* 697 (1978).
3 See *post*, p. 498.
4 See Salmond on *Torts*, 18th edn., pp. 481–3.
5 See, e.g., *Davies* v. *Swan Motor Co.* [1949] 2 K.B. 291, 310; *Stapley* v. *Gypsum Mines* [1953] A.C. 663, 677.
6 [1976] Q.B. 268.
7 *Owens* v. *Brimmell* [1977] Q.B. 859; see Gravells, 'Three Heads of Contributory Negligence', 93 *Law Q. Review* 581 (1977).
8 For some evidence about the role of contributory negligence in settlement of cases, see *Harris 1984 Survey*, pp. 91–2.
9 The point is well made by Tunc, *La Securité Routière* (Paris, 1966), pp. 31–7, and (1965), 14 *International and Comparative Law Quarterly* 1100–1.
10 *Road Accidents Great Britain 1983* (HMSO, 1984), Table 31.
11 Vol. 1, para. 1077.
12 *Staveley Iron & Chemicals Co.* v. *Jones* [1956] A.C. 627.
13 *Waite* v. *North Eastern Rly* (1858) E. B. & E. 719.
14 *The Bernina* (1888) 13 App. Cas. 1; and see too, *Oliver* v. *Birmingham & Midland Omnibus Co.* [1933] 1 K.B. 35.
15 *Franklin* v. *Franklin* (1975) C.L.Y. §811.
16 [1978] Q.B. 543.
17 The Harris Survey found that in 26% of the cases studied in which tort damages were obtained, there was some reduction explicitly on the ground of contributory negligence. For the results of the 1984 survey see *Harris 1984 Survey*, pp. 91–2.
18 Hellner, *Scandinavian Studies in Law* (Stockholm, 1962), 131 at 159, n. 9.
19 Pearson Report, Vol. 2 Table 117.
20 See the Australian Committee of Inquiry Report, paras. 130–1. The proportion of successful actions in which reduction was made for contributory negligence was found to vary from 10% to 28%.
21 See Schwartz, *op. cit.*, supra, n. 2.

22 No precise figures are available for damage-only accidents since there is no obligation that these be reported, but this is the estimate of the Road Research Laboratory, see *The Cost of Road Accidents in Great Britain*, L.R. 79 (HMSO, 1967).
23 *Photo Production Ltd* v. *Securicor Transport Ltd* [1980] A.C. 827; *George Mitchell Ltd* v. *Finney Lock Seeds Ltd* [1983] 2 A.C. 803.
24 *Smith* v. *Baker* [1891] A.C. 325.
25 For a review of some of these cases, see Gordon, (1966) 82 *Law Quarterly Review* 62. Some Australian courts now appear disenchanted with these decisions which have led to strange distinctions being drawn, e.g., *volenti* held inapplicable where plaintiff too drunk to appreciate defendant's drunken state, see *Dodd* v. *McGlashen* [1967] A.L.R. 433.
26 *Owens* v. *Brimmell*, *supra*; see also *Gregory* v. *Kelly* [1978] R.T.R. 426.
27 *ICI Ltd* v. *Shatwell* [1965] A.C. 656.
28 *Murray* v. *Harringay Arena* [1951] 2 K.B. 529.
29 *Wooldridge* v. *Sumner* [1963] 2 Q.B. 43; cf. *Rootes* v. *Shelton* (1967), 116 C.L.R. 383.
30 *Hall* v. *Brooklands Auto Racing Club* [1933] 1 K.B. 205.
31 *Withers* v. *Perry Chain Co.* [1961] 1 W.L.R. 1314.

CHAPTER 6

1 In *Read* v. *Lyons* [1947] A.C. 156, it was indeed doubted whether damage for personal injuries could ever be recovered in an action under this rule, but these doubts have, for the moment (and probably for good) been set at rest by *Perry* v. *Kendricks Transport Ltd* [1956] 1 W.L.R. 85.
2 See e.g. *Leversley* v. *Thomas Firth* [1953] 1 W.L.R. 1206, 1210.
3 See *Annual Report of the Chief Inspector of Factories*, 1967, Cmnd. 3745, p. 23.
4 *Groves* v. *Wimborne* [1898] 2 Q.B. 402.
5 *Phillips* v. *Britannia Hygiene Laundry* [1923] 2 K.B. 832; *Tan Chye Choo* v. *Chong Kew Moi* [1970] 1 All E.R. 266.
6 See the comments of Lord Reid in *Nimmo* v. *Alexander Cowan & Sons* [1968] A.C. 107.
7 See. e.g. Report of Robens Committee on Health and Safety at Work, para. 29: 'the attempt to cover contingency after contingency has resulted in a degree of elaboration, detail and complexity that deters even the most determined reader'.
8 Cmd. 6860; see further as to this Committee, p. 462.
9 [1974] 1 W.L.R. 43, 54–5.
10 See Chapter 8.
11 Moreover, although the manufacturer is not strictly liable directly to the consumer, strict liability may be imposed on him through intermediaries in some cases; see, e.g., *Dodd* v. *Wilson* [1946] 2 All E.R. 691 (veterinary surgeon strictly liable for breach of warranty for defective toxoid inoculated into plaintiff's cattle, but surgeon entitled to indemnity from supplier and supplier from manufacturer).
12 C.f. pp. 55–9.
13 *Mason* v. *Levy Auto Parts Ltd* [1967] 2 Q.B. 530 is the first successful *Rylands* v. *Fletcher* action in England to be reported for many years. The Tribunal of Inquiry into the Aberfan Disaster thought that the Coal Board was liable under the rule for the damage done by the 'escaping' coal tips (1967 H.C. 553) but the Tribunal also

found that the Coal Board officials had been negligent. However, it would occasion no surprise if there were to be a sudden resurgence of strict liability though probably the House of Lords would have to set the trend.
14 *Wringe* v. *Cohen* [1940] 1 K.B. 229.
15 See *Civil Liability for Animals* (Law Comm. No. 13, HMSO, 1967), paras. 36–8.
16 Although the Act overrules the former principle that an employee could not sue in such cases, the effect of s.2(2)(b) and s.6 seems to be to exclude strict liability for injury done by a bull.
17 Chapter 9.
18 Of course 'cause in fact' would remain a necessary condition of liability but no legal system could possibly make cause in fact a sufficient test of legal liability.
19 For a limited proposal of this nature see *Compensation for the Injured* (1971), a Report of a Committee of the Society of Conservative Lawyers, and Professor Atiyah's criticisms in (1971) 34 *Modern Law Review* 432.
20 Liability for Defective Products (Law Comm. No. 82, Cmnd. 6831).
21 Report, Vol. 1, Chapter 22.
22 *Official Journal of the European Communities*, 7 August 1985, L210/29.
23 Report, Vol. 1, para. 1202.
24 *Ibid*, para. 1201. Strict liability is likely to be of limited value to those who suffer diseases rather than traumatic injuries: Stapleton, (1985) 5 *O.J.L.S.* 248, 254.
25 *Ibid*, para. 1186.
26 *Ibid*, Vol. 2, para. 224.
27 *Ibid*, table 47.
28 *Ibid*, Vol. 1, para. 1389.
29 Social Security Act 1985, s.23.
30 See *post*, p. 429.

CHAPTER 7

1 Pearson Report, Vol. 2, paras. 44–45.
2 Very occasionally facts emerge which are somewhat disquieting, e.g., in *King* v. *Spours* (Kemp & Kemp, *The Quantum of Damages*, 11th Suppt., London, 1973) damages were awarded to a man of 25 on the footing that he would live 30 years; in fact he died one month after the trial.
3 See *Seventh Report* of the Board (1971), para. 6(7).
4 Compensation neurosis (variously named) has attracted a considerable medical literature since it was first described by Miller in (1961) 1 *British Medical Journal* 919, 992. There does, however, seem a danger of a mythology growing up which is not supported by actual research. Some recent Australian literature, in particular, suggests that predictions about the disappearance of symptoms after damages are awarded are often not borne out in practice, e.g., Balla, (1970) 1 *Medical Journal of Australia* 355; Cole, (1970) 1 *Medical Journal of Australia* 93. There is also evidence that compensation neurosis is also associated with low-level periodical payments; see, e.g., Ellard, (1970) 1 *Medical Journal of Australia* 349.
5 [1967] 3 All E.R. 608.
6 [1969] 2 All E.R. 949.

7 [1971] A.C. 666.
8 Hansard H.L., Vol. 428, cols. 28–9.
9 The words 'dependency' and 'dependant' are slightly misleading because the Act entitles members of a defined class of persons to recover damages for financial loss suffered by them as a result of the death. Such persons will usually be dependants in the ordinary sense, but not always.
10 [1979] A.C. 566.
11 *Goodburn* v. *Thomas Cotton Ltd* [1968] 1 Q.B. 845; the rule was much older than this case which reaffirmed it.
12 See *Buckley* v. *John Allen & Ford Ltd* [1967] 1 Q.B. 637, and the Winn Committee Report, paras. 378–9.
13 But nobody has ever complained about the 'cattle market' element of valuing the *loss* of marriage prospects of an unmarried girl.
14 See now s.3(3) of the Fatal Accidents Act 1976. The change does not affect claims by men (*Regan* v. *Williamson* [1976] 1 W.L.R. 305) nor the assessment of damages for a child whose father has been killed (*Thompson* v. *Price* [1973] Q.B. 838).
15 *The Times*, 15 May 1974. This was no doubt an exceptional case, but the fact is that many widows, especially young widows, do remarry. In 1982 the remarriage rate for widows aged 20–29 was 90 per thousand, and for those aged 30–34, 77 per thousand. These rates have been falling for some years: *Marriage and Divorce Statistics 1982* (Office of Population Censuses and Surveys, 1985), Table 3.3.c.
16 But see Pearson Report, Vol. 1, paras. 409–17.
17 H.C. Debates, Vol. 958, cols. 771–875.
18 See Trindade & Cane, *The Law of Torts in Australia* (Melbourne, 1985), p. 411.
19 *Regan* v. *Williamson* [1976] 1 W.L.R. 305.
20 *Hay* v. *Hughes* [1975] 1 All E.R. 257.
21 *Regan* v. *Williamson*, supra.
22 See Clarke & Ogus, (1978) 5 *Brit. J. Law & Soc.* 1; Komesar, (1974) 3 *J. Leg. Stud.* 457; Pottick, (1978–9) 50 *U. of Colorado L.R.* 59.
23 13th Report of the Board, para. 27.
24 Vol. 2, Table 89.
25 In Ontario the Workmen's Compensation Board takes a great deal of care before commuting periodical payments to lump sums, to ensure that the money is likely to be wisely used. But in 1973 Professor Atiyah was told that only about half the cases of commutation turned out successfully.
26 See, e.g., *Warren* v. *King* [1963] 3 All E.R. 993n., where the C.A. pressed a girl of 20 to settle an award of £35,000 so that she could not touch the capital until she was 31. But it seems that the court has no power to compel the infant to agree to this course: *Allen* v. *Distillers Co. (Biochemicals) Ltd* [1974] 2 All E.R. 365.
27 *Social Insurance*, Part II (1944, Cmnd. 6551), para. 30.
28 Law Comm. No. 56, paras. 29–30.
29 Pearson Report, Vol. 1, chapter 14.
30 Pearson Report, Vol. 2 Table 122.
31 *Ibid*, Table 109.
32 And the Commission so recommended, Vol. 1 para. 614.
33 Assuming that about half of the amount awarded would be for non-pecuniary loss.
34 Report, Vol. 2, Table 128 shows that, of the total number of tried cases in 1974

(2,313), about one quarter (521) were awarded more than £5,000.
35 [1979] Q.B. 196; [1980] A.C. 174.
36 [1975] Q.B. 262.
37 For another recent illustration, see *Ichard* v. *Frangoulis* [1977] 2 All E.R. 46 (plaintiff injured on holiday entitled to extra compensation for loss of enjoyment of holiday).
38 See Pearson Report, Vol. 2, Table 90.
39 *Watson* v. *Powles* [1968] 1 Q.B. 596.
40 *Jefford* v. *Gee* [1970] 2 Q.B. 130; *Cookson* v. *Knowles* [1979] A.C. 556.
41 *Wright* v. *British Railways Board* [1983] 2 A.C. 773.
42 Street, *Principles of Damages* (London, 1962), pp. 152–3.
43 *Pickett* v. *British Rail Engineering Ltd* [1980] A.C. 136.
44 *Lim Poh Choo* v. *Camden A.H.A.* [1980] A.C. 174.
45 Where the Accident Compensation Act provides for very high rates of earnings-related benefits though not exacting any earnings-related contributions except from the self-employed.
46 *George*, p. 52.
47 Comprehensive policies often provide for some accident payment to the insured himself, but this usually takes the form of a flat-rate benefit, and does not vary according to the income of the insured.
48 It would be a different matter if it were found that there were some correlation between accident involvement and earnings, but this would not affect the point being made in the text, because this would still have nothing to do with the amount of compensation paid to victims.
49 It is quite immaterial that the widow may have a substantial private fortune of her own, unless she lived on her own money rather than on her husband's (*Shiels* v. *Cruickshank* [1953] 1 W.L.R. 533). But then so would it be if the widow claimed national insurance benefits (other than supplementary benefits).
50 *Bishop* v. *Cunard White Star* [1950] P. 240. The doubts expressed in *Cookson* v. *Knowles* [1977] Q.B. 913, seem to relate only to earnings which the plaintiff would not otherwise have been able to make as a result of her services in the home.
51 See Matrimonial and Family Proceedings Act 1984, s.25(2). Despite para. (g), it appears that conduct will be relevant only in exceptional cases.
52 *Post*, p. 333.
53 Para. 343.
54 Pp. 60–4.
55 *Post*, p. 333.
56 *Post*, p. 306.
57 *Post*, p. 275.
58 *Post*, p. 408.
59 *Post*, p. 186.
60 Law Comm. No. 56; Pearson Report, Vol. 1, Chapters 12 and 15.
61 *Justice* Report on *Trial of Motor Accident Cases* (London, 1966), p. 30.
62 See Street, *Principles of Damages* (London, 1962), especially Chapter 5, for details of these criticisms. Much has happened of course since this book was published to render the discussion somewhat out of date.
63 See *Pope* v. *Murphy & Son Ltd* [1961] 1 Q.B. 222. It is unlikely that this mistake would be made today.

64 *Taylor* v. *O'Connor* [1971] A.C. 115; see also *Mitchell* v. *Mulholland* [1972] 1 Q.B. 65.
65 Prevett, (1972) 35 *Modern Law Review* 140, 257.
66 Kemp & Kemp, *The Quantum of Damages* (4th edn, London, 1975), Vol. 1, p. 55.
67 Munkman, *Damages for Personal Injury* (7th edn, London, 1985), p. 56.
68 See Prevett, *op. cit.*, pp. 263–4; Kidner & Richards, (1974) *Economic Journal* 130.
69 Report, Vol. 1, Chapter 15.
70 See the paper by Mr D. R. Harris in *Accident Compensation After Pearson*, eds. Allen, Bourn and Holyoak (London, 1979).
71 I.e. after making allowance for inflation.
72 *Wright* v. *British Railways Board* [1983] 2 A.C. 773.
73 Paras. 149–50.
74 (1966–7) 84 W.N. Pt. 1 (N.S.W) 231.
75 *Mallett* v. *McMonagle* [1970] A.C. 168; *Mitchell* v. *Mulholland* [1971] A.C. 666; *Cookson* v. *Knowles* [1979] A.C. 556.
76 See Little, *A Critique of Welfare Economics*, 2nd edn (Oxford, 1959), p. 62.
77 Street, *op. cit.*, regards awards in these cases as less open to criticism, but the Michigan Automobile Survey found that tort damages were least satisfactory in fatal accident cases: see Conrad, p. 179. See also the *Osgoode Hall Study*, Chapter 4, pp. 25–6.
78 See Chapter 18.
79 This is specifically provided for by the Law Reform (Personal Injuries) Act 1948, following the recommendations of the Monckton Committee, though contrary to Beveridge's views; see p. 465.
80 All 90 of the cases studied in the Harris survey obtained free medical treatment under the NHS; see also *Harris 1984 Survey*, pp. 240–2.
81 *Cunningham* v. *Harrison* [1973] Q.B. 942.
82 See *Lim Poh Choo* v. *Camden Health Authority* [1979] Q.B. 196.
83 *Ibid.*
84 See *Health and Personal Social Services Statistics for England, 1977* (HMSO, 1978), Table 2.11.
85 This point is developed in Chapter 10 and Chapter 21.
86 Pearson Report, Vol. 1, paras. 339–42. See also the views of the Working Party into the criminal injuries compensation scheme, Report, para. 10.7.
87 See *Olsen* v. *Demolition & Construction Co. Ltd* (1957) Kemp & Kemp, *op. cit.*, Vol. 1, p. 361.
88 *Moriarty* v. *McCarthy* [1978] 1 W.L.R. 155.
89 For an analysis of the conceptual basis of such awards, see Ogus, (1972) 35 *Modern Law Review* 1.
90 Although Russell L.J. once offered himself 'for minute bruising any time of day at £5 a time'; see (1965) 62 *Journal of the Chartered Insurance Institute* 213.
91 See Mishan, *The Costs of Economic Growth* (London, 1967), Chapter 5.
92 C. Veljanovski, unpublished Ph.D. thesis, 'Regulating Industrial Accidents – an Economic Analysis of Market and Legal Responses' (York Univ., 1981), Ch. 3; see also A. Martin & G. Psacharopolous, (1982) 90 *J. Polit. Econ.* 827. Some governmental bodies also utilize this methodology: see, e.g., Health and Safety Executive, *Cost-Benefit Assessment of Health and Safety and Pollution Control* (1982, HMSO).

93 See T. Craig Sinclair, *A Cost-Effectiveness Approach to Industrial Safety* (HMSO, 1972, Robens Committee Research Paper). This approach can produce very different valuations for different industries; for example, the author finds that the implicit valuation of a life in the pharmaceutical industry is about 700 times the implicit valuation in agriculture; see *ibid*, Table 12. For a recent review of the economics literature, see M. W. Jones-Lee, *The Value of Life: An Economic Analysis* (London, 1976).
94 Cf. Veljanovski, (1985) 7 *Research in Law and Economics* 41, 51.
95 In *Fletcher* v. *Autocar Ltd*, Diplock L.J. expressly denied that damages for pain and suffering could be affected by the wealth of the plaintiff, but cf. the strange view of Cotton L.J. in *Philips* v. *L. & S. W. Rly* (1879) 5 C.P.D. 280, that a wealthy man might receive less for pain and suffering since he could alleviate his discomfort in other ways not open to the poor man. This dictum would certainly not be followed today. Street, *op. cit.*, p. 12, thinks that some judges award higher sums in practice to wealthier plaintiffs even for disabilities.
96 It appears to be favoured by Street, *op. cit.*, pp. 6–13, but experience of jury awards in Scotland is not very encouraging; see Walker, 84 *Law Quarterly Review* 400.
97 *Ward* v. *James* [1966] 1 Q.B. 273.
98 *Hodges* v. *Harland & Wolff* [1965] 1 W.L.R. 523 (loss of penis).
99 See Winn Committee Report, Minority Report of Mr Thompson, para. 52.
100 Law Comm. No. 56, para. 20.
101 Report, Vol. 1, paras. 382–9.
102 *Ibid*, Table 2.
103 *Ibid*, Vol. 2, Table 107.
104 The most extreme version of the personalised approach is that of Diplock L.J. (dissenting) in *Wise* v. *Kaye* (1962) 1 Q.B. 638, who would have assessed the effect of the injuries on each individual victim's happiness.
105 See p. 336.
106 Pearson Report, Vol. 1, para. 823; compare paras. 379–81.
107 [1964] A.C. 326.
108 [1962] 1 Q.B. 638.
109 Pearson Report, Vol. 1, paras. 393–8.
110 *Housecroft* v. *Burnett* [1986] 1 All E.R. 332.
111 *Allen* v. *Burroughs Machines* [1983] C.L.Y. 994.
112 *Walker* v. *John McLean & Sons Ltd* [1979] 2 All E.R. 965.
113 *Mullarky* v. *Edmund Nuttall* [1983] C.L.Y 996.
114 *Lamb* v. *Durham C.C.* [1983] C.L.Y. 1014.
115 *Miller* v. *Tremberth* [1983] C.L.Y. 1011.
116 *Kearns* v. *Higgs & Hill* (1968) 4 K.I.R. 393 (updated for inflation).
117 *Moody* v. *Newcastle Church High School* [1983] C.L.Y. 1029.
118 *Accidents at work: compensation for all*, Evidence of the Society of Labour Lawyers to the Pearson Royal Commission, 1974, p. 2 (more now if inflation is taken into account).
119 *Handicapped and Impaired in Great Britain* (HMSO, 1971), Pt. 1, Table 179.
120 *Ibid*, Table 182.
121 Law Comm. No. 56, paras. 31–6; Pearson Report, Vol. 1, paras. 377–9.
122 *Thornton* v. *Board of School Trustees* (1978) 83 D.L.R. (3d) 480; *Andrews* v. *Grand and*

Toy Alberta Ltd (1978) 83 D.L.R. (3d) 452.
123 Pearson Report, Vol. 1, para. 384.
124 *Thomas* v. *Wignall, The Times*, 20 December 1985.

CHAPTER 8

1 Pearson Report, Vol. 2, Table 124.
2 *Ibid*, para. 83.
3 *Guardian Gazette*, 25 June 1975, p. 679.
4 In the *Harris 1984 Survey* only 5 out of the 1177 cases in the survey were fully heard; writs were issued in just under 40% of the cases in which an out-of-court settlement was finally reached (p. 112).
5 Pearson Report, Vol. 2, Table 124.
6 Derived from Pearson Report, Vol. 2, Table 125.
7 As a result of a statement in the Winn Committee Report, para. 39.
8 Based on Pearson Report, Vol. 2, Table 11.
9 Cf. *Harris 1984 Survey*, pp. 67–9 on role of trade unions.
10 Pearson Report, Vol. 2, Table 14. Cf. *Harris 1984 Survey*, Table 2.2.
11 These figures are the estimates of the Road Research Laboratory, L.R. 79 (HMSO, 1967).
12 *Insurance Facts and Figures* 1983 (B.I.A.), p. 13.
13 Cf. *Harris 1984 Survey*, Table 2.1.
14 See Table 1 on p. 16; but see *Harris 1984 Survey*, pp. 57–8.
15 Pearson Report, Vol. 2., para. 326.
16 *Accidents in the Home* (London, 1964), p. 8.
17 *Ibid*, p. 16, referring to the Report of the Standing Interdepartmental Committee on Accidents in the Home (HMSO, 1953).
18 Pearson Report, Vol. 2, para. 326.
19 In theory the insurance company could sue the tortfeasor after meeting the claim, under the doctrine of subrogation, but in practice such claims are rarely brought. See p. 403.
20 In *Accidents in the Home*, p. 24, it is pointed out that in the index to Halsbury's Statutes there is a listing for nearly every conceivable kind of accident except accidents in the home.
21 *Harris 1984 Survey*, pp. 69–70.
22 *Harris 1984 Survey* concludes that the group of victims who give no thought to claiming is 'very large': p. 71; see also pp. 49, 61.
23 See Keeton & O'Connell, *After Cars Crash* (Dow-Jones Irwin Inc., 1967), p. 109, a version for the general reader of the same authors' *Basic Protection for the Traffic Victim* (1965).
24 *Harris 1984 Survey*, p. 65.
25 Pearson Report, Vol. 2, para. 389.
26 Pearson Report, Vol. 2, para. 79.
27 *Harris 1984 Survey*, p. 67.
28 *Ibid*, pp. 53, 63, 68.
29 *Ibid*, Tables 2.12, 3.12.

30 *Ibid*, p. 67; many of those who have heard of legal aid are very vague about how to obtain it; see Abel-Smith, Zander and Brooke, *Legal Problems and the Citizen* (London, 1973), pp. 194–5.
31 Burman, Genn and Lyons, 'The Use of Legal Services by Victims of Accidents in the Home – A Pilot Study', 40 *Modern Law Review* 47 (1977).
32 See Diamond, 31 *Modern Law Review* 372.
33 Webb, *Industrial Injuries: a new approach* (evidence of the PO Engineering Union to the Pearson Royal Commission, London, 1974), p. 8.
34 See n. 28 above.
35 Pearson Report, Vol. 2, Table 84.
36 Pearson Report, Vol. 2 paras. 199–201.
37 *Ibid*; Cf. *Harris 1984 Survey*, p. 57, Figs 2.8, 2.9.
38 *Road Accidents Great Britain 1983* (HMSO), Table 18.
39 *Ibid*, Table XXI.
40 See *Research on Road Safety* (HMSO, 1963), and Transport and Road Research Laboratory Reports, L.R. 434 (1972) and L.R. 498 (1972).
41 See L.R. 498 (1972), *supra*.
42 Cited in *ibid*, para. 196.
43 See *Medical Factors and Road Accidents*, Road Research Laboratory Report L.R. 143 (HMSO, 1967). See also *Medical Aspects of Fitness to Drive* (1968, published by the Medical Commission on Accident Prevention); Norman, *Road Traffic Accidents, Epidemiology, Control and Prevention* (WHO, Geneva, 1962).
44 See p. 248.
45 See *Civil Liability for Animals* (Law Comm. No. 13, HMSO, 1967), paras. 36–8.
46 See Pearson Report, Vol. 2 para. 294.
47 *Ibid*, Table 29.
48 Latta and Lewis, (1974) 12 *British Journal of Industrial Relations* 56.
49 Evidence of the TUC to the Pearson Commission (unpublished), para. 96.
50 Pearson Report, Vol. 2, Table 14.
51 Evidence of the TUC to the Pearson Commission, para. 97.
52 Vol. 2, paras. 77–8.
53 *Harris 1984 Survey*, Table 2.8.
54 *Ibid*, Table 2.8: 19% as against 29% for road accidents.
55 *Ibid*, p. 56 and Table 2.12.
56 *Ibid*, Fig. 2.2.
57 *Ibid*, p. 57.
58 See *Manufacturing and Service Industries*, Report of HM Factory Inspectorate 1977, Table F (HMSO, 1978). The conclusions are expressed rather more cautiously than was customary in the older form of Reports.
59 *Accidents at work: compensation for all* (Society of Labour Lawyers, evidence to the Pearson Commission, 1974), p. 7.
60 Pearson Report, Vol. 2, para. 168.
61 *Insurance Facts and Figures* (BIA, London, 1978); the corresponding figure for 1983 was £211·4 million (*ibid*, 1983, p. 13).
62 Pearson Report, Vol. 2, Table 159.
63 *Ibid*.

CHAPTER 9

1 But, as we have seen (p. 91), it is possible that in some circumstances the wealth of the defendant may affect the standard of care required of him.
2 In fact most tort claims are not litigated but settled, and in the majority of cases no legal aid is necessary (see Chapter 11). But a person who wished to sue a private uninsured individual would probably have difficulty in persuading a solicitor to handle the case without legal aid, since the solicitor might otherwise be unable to secure his own remuneration.
3 Legal Aid Act 1974, s.7(5A).
4 Legal Aid (General) Regulations 1980, reg. 30.
5 *Legal Aid Handbook* 1984 (HMSO), pp. 209–30.
6 See Abel-Smith and Stevens, *In Search of Justice* (London, 1968), p. 260.
7 The legislation followed the recommendations of the Payne Committee: Cmnd. 3909, 1969. See now the Attachment of Earnings Act 1971. About 42,600 attachment of earnings orders were made in 1983 (*Judicial Statistics*, 1983, Cmnd. 9370). The number of such orders has been declining for a number of years.
8 Payne Committee Report, Appendix 2.
9 See Cmnd. 3909, para. 602. But substantial tort damages could take years to pay off and, if the statutory interest is also payable, might become a permanent charge on the debtor. This sort of case was not explicitly considered by the Payne Committee.
10 See *The Times*, 22 March 1967. Compulsory insurance for this kind of case was not in force until 1971.
11 The rate of interest has been substantially increased since then. There is some doubt as to whether statutory interest is due where the judgment is made payable by instalments, but this is usually an academic question. Surprisingly, it does not appear to have been settled by the Attachment of Earnings Act 1971.
12 That the courts themselves appear to recognize this is shown by *R* v. *Daly* [1974] 1 All E.R. 290, where a criminal court held that it was undesirable to burden a man with a compensation order which will affect him for many years under (now) the Powers of Criminal Courts Act 1973.
13 The Criminal Injuries Compensation Board has found that only a minute fraction of offenders would normally be worth suing (Third Report, para. 21; Seventh Report, para. 17), but the proportion of negligent tortfeasors with money must be much higher than this.
14 Conard, p. 221.
15 Pearson Report, Vol. 2, para. 61.
16 See the Employers' Liability (Compulsory Insurance) Act 1969.
17 Pearson Report, Vol. 2, Table 119.
18 See Atiyah, *Vicarious Liability in the Law of Torts* (London, 1967), Parts II, III and VII.
19 *Ibid*, Part V.
20 *Warren* v. *Henly's* [1948] 2 All E.R. 935.
21 See *Deaton's Pty Ltd* v. *Flew* [1949], 79 C.L.R. 370; *Pettersson* v. *Royal Oak Hotel Ltd* [1948] N.Z.L.R. 136; *Keppel Bus Co. Ltd* v. *Sa'ad Bin Ahmed* [1974] 2 All E.R. 700.
22 Chapter 21.
23 *Cassidy* v. *Minister of Health* [1951] 2 K.B. 343.

24 *Lister* v. *Romford Ice & Storage Co. Ltd* [1957] A.C. 555.
25 See Atiyah, *op. cit.*, pp. 426–7.
26 See p. 393.

CHAPTER 10

1 Pearson Report, Vol. 2 para. 509.
2 See *Paterson* v. *Chadwick* [1974] 2 All E.R. 772.
3 See *McNealy* v. *Pennine Insurance Co.* [1978] R.T.R. 285.
4 Hellner, *Scandinavian Studies in Law* (Stockholm, 1962), p. 150.
5 Jorgensen, *Scandinavian Studies in Law* (Stockholm, 1963), p. 33.
6 This assumes that (contrary to the present law) the injured party would not be allowed to recover both damages and insurance benefits; as to this element of duplication, see p. 403.
7 A motorist who damages his car by his own careless driving is certainly not precluded from claiming under his comprehensive insurance policy, but a motorist who crams eight adult passengers into a Ford Anglia and thereby loses control of the vehicle may be deprived of his claim: *Clarke* v. *National Insurance Corpn* [1963] 3 All E.R. 375.
8 This is precisely what happened to the V. & G. Insurance Company who thought they could operate more efficiently without the knock-for-knock agreement. This was a major factor in the company's ultimate failure; see the *Report of the Tribunal of Inquiry* (HMSO, 1972).
9 The insurance company is subrogated to the claims of the bailor; see p. 393, as to subrogation.
10 See, e.g., *Hepburn* v. *Tomlinson* [1966] A.C. 451.
11 See *Green* v. *Russell* [1959] 2 Q.B. 226.
12 Fatal Accidents Act, 1976, s.4.
13 Law Reform (Personal Injuries) Act 1948; *Smith* v. *B.E.A.* [1951] 2 K.B. 893.
14 *Gowar* v. *Hales* [1928] 1 K.B. 191. But in *Morey* v. *Woodfield* the trial judge declared that he was not going to be bound by this 'old fashioned rule', and the defendant's counsel does not seem to have thought it worth while to raise this on appeal: [1963] 3 All E.R. 533n.
15 *Harman* v. *Crilly* [1943] 1 K.B. 168.
16 Winn Committee Report, para. 349.
17 Kalven, 'The Jury, the Law and the Personal Injury Damage Award' in (1958), 19 *Ohio State Law Journal* 158, 171.
18 [1959] A.C. 604, 627.
19 Jorgensen, *Scandinavian Studies in Law* (Stockholm, 1963), p. 29.
20 See n. 17.
21 But see *Birch* v. *Thomas* [1972] All E.R. 905 for a case in which knowledge that the defendant was uninsured may possibly have influenced the result in the defendant's favour.
22 See p. 403.
23 *Ackworth* v. *Kempe* (1778) 1 Doug K.B. 40.
24 *Lloyd* v. *Grace Smith & Co.* [1912] A.C. 716.

25 Lord Denning virtually says as much in *Morris* v. *Ford Motor Co.* [1973] 1 Q.B. 792, 798. Lord Denning was particularly prone to bring the insurance issue into the open in discussing points of law.
26 *Heaps* v. *Perrite Ltd* [1937] 2 All E.R. 60, 61; cf. *Lim Poh Choo* v. *Camden AHA* [1979] 1 All E.R. 332, 341 *per* Lord Denning MR (dissenting): the defendant in this case was a self-insurer and Lord Denning was worried about the burden on taxpayers of very large awards against public authorities. While a very large award may create difficulties for a particular authority, the ultimate issue here is how much of society's resources we wish to spend in this way.
27 *Fletcher* v. *Autocar Ltd* [1968] 2 Q.B. 322.
28 [1952] 1 All E.R. 528.
29 See, e.g., *Blake* v. *Richards and Wellington Industries* (1974) K.I.R. 151.
30 [1978] A.C. 16.
31 See, e.g., Jorgensen, *Scandinavian Studies in Law* (Stockholm, 1963), p. 53 *et seq.*
32 But Lord Denning more than once said as much, e.g. in *Nettleship* v. *Weston* [1971] 2 Q.B. 691.
33 See p. 120.
34 See, e.g., *Robinson* v. *Post Office* [1974] 2 All E.R. 737.
35 Some 93% according to Ison's Survey, see Ison, p. 156; cf. *Harris 1984 Survey*, p. 61.
36 In the Michigan Survey it was found that in 68% of the serious injury cases in which no tort compensation was received, the reason for this was that there was no party at fault, or that there was no proof of fault, or that the plaintiff was guilty of contributory negligence (which is still a complete bar to success in most of the United States): see Conard, Table 6–2, p. 210. The *Harris 1984 Survey* found that problems in obtaining evidence and attribution of the injury to the plaintiff's own fault were the two most frequently cited reasons for abandoning claims (Table 3.12), and the second and fourth most frequently cited reasons (respectively) for not claiming at all (Table 2.12).
37 Cf. *Brown* v. *Roberts* [1965] 1 Q.B. 1. In 1972 some 1,243 accidents were caused in this way; see *Road Accidents in Great Britain 1972*, Table 39. More effective than tort law might be a criminal sanction: compulsory insurance would be even better.
38 See, e.g., *Bolton* v. *Stone* [1951] A.C. 850 (cricket); *Wooldridge* v. *Sumner* [1963] 2 Q.B. 43 (show jumping); *White* v. *Blackmore* [1972] 3 All E.R. 158 (motor racing).
39 [1969] 1 Ch. 457. See also *Re Roehampton Swimming Pools* [1968] 1 W.L.R. 1963.
40 See *Re Newsham* [1966] 3 All E.R. 681.
41 [1957] A.C. 555.
42 See Atiyah, *Vicarious Liability* (1967), pp. 426–7.
43 *Morris* v. *Ford Motor Co.* [1973] 1 Q.B. 792.
44 [1971] A.C. 356.
45 [1973] 1 All E.R. 959.
46 *Re Harrington Motor Co. Ltd.* [1928] Ch. 105; *Hood's Trustees* v. *Southern Union* [1928] Ch. 793.
47 See now the Legal Aid Act 1974, s.24. Yet (as seen above, p. 281) in exceptional cases this can now be done, as a result of *Davies* v. *Taylor (No. 2)*.
48 For the limited qualifications to this, see p. 395.
49 See s.11(4) of the Act.
50 [1935] 1 K.B. 75.

51 [1964] 2 Lloyd's Rep. 347.
52 Appendix 3.
53 *Hansard*, 5th Series, H.C. Vol. 770 Written Answers, col. 93. This procedure closely resembles that of the criminal injuries scheme, see p. 357.
54 See *Persson* v. *London Country Buses* [1974] 1 All E.R. 1251; *Clarke* v. *Vedel* [1979] R.T.R. 26.
55 The government has announced its intention to introduce legislation in the 1985–6 session to implement an EC Directive requiring compulsory motor insurance for third party property damage. Most policies in fact already include this cover, but requiring it by law will expose the MIB to liability, and fears have been expressed that large claims may be made for damage to property other than cars; for example, premises abutting the highway.
56 See *Randall* v. *MIB* [1968] 1 W.L.R. 1900, where plaintiff recovered damages when he was injured by a lorry half on and half off a public road. But cf. with this case, criminal injuries case No. H72 where claimant was injured on a private road, and failed to get anything under the criminal injuries scheme, after being turned down by the MIB. Presumably somebody finds this result sensible or the law would be otherwise.
57 *Cooper* v. *MIB* [1985] Q.B. 575.
58 These clauses may be of no or only limited effect: *Gardner* v. *Moore* [1984] A.C. 548, read in conjunction with *Ashton* v. *Turner* [1981] Q.B. 137.
59 *Beswick* v. *Beswick* [1968] A.C. 58; *Gurtner* v. *Circuit* [1968] 2 Q.B. 587.
60 [1950] 1 All E.R. 488.
61 See n. 59.
62 [1972] A.C. 301.

CHAPTER 11

1 Pearson Report, Vol. 2, Table 124.
2 Winn Committee Report, paras. 116–118, 123 and Appendix 8; Ison, *op. cit.*, Appendix C, Table 11; Cantley Working Party on Personal Injury Procedure, esp. Appendix G; Harris 1984 Survey, p. 112.
3 Para. 133.
4 *Canadian Studies in Tort Law* (ed. Linden) (Toronto, 1968), p. 312.
5 Justice *Report on the Trial of Motor Accident Cases*, p. 2.
6 Justice *Report*, p. 3.
7 Ison, Appendix D.
8 Latta and Lewis, (1974) 12 *British Journal of Industrial Relations* 61.
9 Which obtains in about 76% of the cases in which insurers make some payment: Pearson Report, Vol. 2, Table 110.
10 But some solicitors do charge the client in addition to what they receive from the other side: see Ison, pp. 166–7.
11 According to *Harris 1984 Survey*, p. 46, the proportion is 80%.
12 For details, see Legal Aid Act 1974, s.4.
13 Legal Aid Handbook 1984 (HMSO), p. 10.
14 *Ibid*, p. 6.

15 *Op. cit.*, Appendix C, Table 29.
16 *Guardian Gazette*, 25 June 1975, p. 679.
17 Pearson Report, Vol. 2, Table 126; see also *Harris 1984 Survey*, pp. 130–1.
18 *Ibid.*
19 *Legal Aid Handbook 1984*, p. 2 The figures given are those for 1985–6.
20 See Zander, *Legal Services for the Community* (London, 1978), pp. 76–80; Cooper, *Public Legal Services* (1983); White, *The Administration of Justice* (1985), ch. 15.
21 For a sociological study of this process in America, see H. L. Ross, *Settled Out of Court* (Chicago, 1980).
22 Justice *Report on Trial of Motor Accident Cases*, p. 5.
23 Winn Committee Report, Section VII.
24 *Ibid*, Appendix II.
25 *Ibid*, para. 131 *et seq.*
26 Justice *Report*, pp. 9–10.
27 Winn Committee Report, p. 209.
28 See J. Prichard, *Personal Injuries Litigation*, 2nd edn (London, 1978), pp. 23–30.
29 *Daily Telegraph*, 29 November 1968.
30 Winn Committee Report, Appendix 12.
31 Pp. 9–10.
32 *Ibid*, p. 13.
33 Elliot & Street, *Road Accidents* (Harmondsworth, 1968), p. 225.
34 Winn Committee Report, Minority Report of Mr Thompson, para. 20.
35 Supreme Court Act 1981, s.35A; County Courts Act 1959, s.197A.
36 Pearson Report, Vol. 2 para. 402.
37 J. Prichard, *op. cit.*, p. 31.
38 See *Harris 1984 Survey*, pp. 93–112.
39 Phillips and Hawkins, (1976) 39 *Modern Law Review* 497.
40 Pearson Report, Vol. 2, para. 93.
41 *Ibid*, Table 111. There is inconclusive data in the *Harris 1984 Survey*, pp. 128–32.
42 *Guardian Gazette*, 25 June 1975, p. 679.
43 The Legal Aid Fund hardly ever pays the costs of a successful defendant although there is a very limited power to order such payment under the Legal Aid Act 1974, and this power can be exercised for the benefit of an insurer; see *Davies* v. *Taylor (No. 2)* [1973] 1 All E.R. 959. Trade unions sometimes pay costs to a successful defendant where they have acted for the plaintiff, but they have no obligation to do so, and often do not (Ison, *op. cit.*, Appendix C 19). The MIB never claims costs (see Justice *Report*, p. 59). The result is that only the unsuccessful individual plaintiff will usually be ordered to pay costs and these will often prove irrecoverable; moreover in legal aid cases the court is bound to take account of the plaintiff's means in making an order for costs against him.
44 For the position once the trial has begun, see *Gaskins* v. *British Aluminium* [1976] Q.B. 524.
45 No interest is payable on it unless the court orders it to be placed in a deposit or investment account.
46 *Finlay* v. *Rly Executive* [1950] 2 All E.R. 1969.
47 If the case is fought with the assistance of a trade union, the plaintiff will not normally be in any difficulty, because most unions will pay the costs in any event.

Counsel advising on quantum may be specifically instructed to ignore the risk following a payment into court where the union is meeting all costs.
48 In 1983–4 over £2·6 million paid in damages to legally aided plaintiffs in non-matrimonial cases was regained by the Legal Aid Fund to meet costs not recovered from defendants: see 34th Legal Aid Annual Reports (1983–4), p. 116.
49 Justice *Report*, p. 31.
50 *Wagman* v. *Vare Motors* [1959] 1 W.L.R. 853.
51 *McGuckin* v. *Cammell Laird & Co. Ltd* [1962] 1 Lloyd's Reports 635.
52 *Hultquist* v. *Universal Pattern Engineering Co.* [1960] 2 Q.B. 467.
53 Paras. 507–40; see also Law Comm. No. 56, paras. 287–92; Cantley committee, Report, para. 99.
54 The *1984 Harris Survey* found that the first offer was accepted in about two-thirds of cases. On average, second offers were found to be a third to a half higher than first offers; and third offers about a third higher than second offers. But these averages conceal wide variations. For example, in one work-accident case where four offers were made, the amount of the first three offers as a percentage of the fourth was 2, 10 and 60 respectively; in another work-accident case where five offers were made, the percentages were 70, 72, 85 and 97.
55 Phillips and Hawkins, 39 *Modern Law Review* 497, 509 (1976).
56 Section III.
57 Section V.
58 Supreme Court Act 1981, s.32A (inserted 1982, now in force).
59 See Law Comm. No. 56, para. 271.
60 [1968] 2 Q.B. 229.
61 [1978] A.C. 297.
62 See Report of the Working Party, paras, 44–53.
63 Vol. 2, Table 129.
64 Appendix E of the Report of the Working Party.
65 Pearson Report, Vol. 2, Table 17.
66 See the Winn Committee Report, Section IX and Appendix 13; (1967) 117 *New Law J.* 198; Ison, *op. cit.*, Appendix C, pp. 178–80; *Which?*, October 1970; T.U.C. Evidence to the Royal Commission (unpublished), para. 110; *Harris 1984 Survey*, pp. 105–10.
67 Pearson Report, Vol. 2, Table 115. Cf. Ison, *op. cit.*, p. 179; the *Harris 1984 Survey* found a more direct correlation between length of time and degree of residual disability than between time and size of award as such.
68 Yet this difficulty does not arise in fatal cases where delays appear to be no less serious: see the Winn Committee Report, Minority Report of Mr Thompson, para. 59.
69 There are grounds for believing that the size of the discount may depend as much on the experience of the plaintiff's solicitor as on the facts of the case: Abel-Smith, Zander and Brooke, *Legal Problems and the Citizen* (London, 1973), p. 177.
70 Because of the argument that a person cannot owe a duty of care to an unborn child, see p. 63.
71 Pearson Report, Vol. 2, Table 117.
72 Conard, Table 6–14, p. 197; Table 5–13, p. 179; Fig. 5–11, p. 177. The Osgoode Hall Study does not show such dramatic differences between the more and the less

serious cases, though it shows serious under-compensation in the fatal cases (see Chapter IV, Table IV–6). The *Harris 1984 Survey* found that there was no clear correlation between likelihood of obtaining damages at all and degree of residual disability or amount of time off work: pp. 56–8.
73 Vol. 2, Table 108.
74 Conard, p. 199.

CHAPTER 12

1 Pearson Report, Vol. 2, para. 146.
2 *Life Insurance in the U.K.* (BIA, London, 1985).
3 Pearson Report, Vol. 2, para. 148.
4 *Op. cit.*, p. 43.
5 *Insurance Facts and Figures*, 1983 (BIA, London).
6 See *Underwriting Problems of Permanent Health Insurance*, a Report of the Insurance Institute of London, c. 1972.
7 Pearson Report, Vol. 2, para. 153.
8 *Ibid*, para. 144.
9 See *Alder* v. *Moore* [1961] 2 Q.B. 57.
10 See the dissenting judgment of Devlin L.J. in *Alder* v. *Moore* above.
11 See *Woolfall & Rimmer* v. *Moyle* [1942] 1 K.B. 66; but cf. *Liverpool Corpn* v. *T. & H. R. Roberts* [1964] 3 All E.R. 56.
12 *Crowes Transport Ltd* v. *Phoenix Assurance Ltd* [1965] 1 All E.R. 596.
13 *Wulfson* v. *Switzerland General Insurance Co. Ltd* [1940] 3 All E.R. 221.
14 *Liverpool & London War Risks Insurance Association* v. *Ocean Steamship Co. Ltd* [1947] 2 All E.R. 586.
15 See *Trew* v. *Rly Passengers' Assurance Co.* (1861), 6 H. & N. 839, 842.
16 *Riley on Business Interruption and Consequential Loss Insurances and Claims*, 6th edn (1985, Cloughton ed.), para. 337.
17 *Ibid*, paras. 294–6.

CHAPTER 13

1 Para. 21; Fifth Report, para. 11.
2 Para. 17; see also Seventeenth Report, paras. 53–4.
3 See Magistrates Courts Act 1980, s.40.
4 *R* v. *Daly* [1947] 1 All E.R. 290.
5 *Ibid*.
6 *The Times*, 17 September 1985.
7 Twenty-First Report, para. 47.
8 Twenty-First Report, para. 12.
9 It is generally accepted that 'in present economic circumstances a central fund to make public provision for victims of property crime is not practicable': *First Report of the Home Affairs Committee on Compensation and Support for Victims of Crime*, HC 43 (1984–5), paras. 54–59; and Government Reply (Cmnd. 9457, 1985), para. 19.

10 See Atiyah, *Vicarious Liability*, especially at pp. 262 *et seq.*.
11 See *Williams* v. *Grimshaw* (1967) 3 K.I.R. 610; *Houghton* v. *Hackney B.C.* (1961) 3 K.I.R. 615; *Charlton* v. *Forest Printing Ink Co.* [1978] I.R.L.R. 559.
12 The scheme was last revised in 1979.
13 Cmnd. 1406, para. 17.
14 *Ibid*, para. 18.
15 *Ibid*.
16 Report on *Compensation for Victims of Crimes of Violence* (London, 1962).
17 *Criminal Statistics England and Wales 1984* (Cmnd. 9621, HMSO 1985), Table 7.2.
18 However, a more sophisticated version of this argument might be that society often takes risks by being lenient with offenders, e.g. fining them or putting them on probation instead of incarcerating them. This leniency is justified in the interests of society as a whole because even if it pays in only 20% or 30% of the cases it is probably worthwhile. But it does involve risks, and it could be urged that since society as a whole gains from taking these risks, society should compensate those who suffer from the risks. The argument is essentially the same as that put forward on p. 490, in cases of negligence.
19 See the *Osgoode Hall Study (Victims of Crime)*, p. 3. This approach led some to advocate that the State should simply meet judgments obtained by victims of crimes of violence against the offenders in the ordinary courts, but the Working Party pointed out some formidable objections to this course: Cmnd. 1406, paras, 136–40.
20 *Hansard*, 5th Series, H.L. Vol. 245, col. 263.
21 *Hansard*, 5th Series, H.L. Vol. 257, col. 1353.
22 *Hansard*, 5th Series, H.L. Vol. 245, cols 267, 269.
23 *Hansard*, 5th Series, H.L. Vol. 257, col. 1381.
24 *R* v. *CICB, ex parte Lain* [1967] 2 Q.B. 864.
25 *Review of the Criminal Injuries Compensation Scheme: Report of an Interdepartmental Working Party* (HMSO, 1978), para. 5.1.
26 Pearson Report, Vol. 1, paras. 1588, 1591.
27 The current version of the scheme dates from 1979. For a comparative study of the schemes in Britain and Ontario, see Miers, *Responses to Victimization* (1978).
28 Para. 4 of the scheme.
29 Criminal Injuries Compensation Board, First Report, para. 14(3).
30 *R* v. *CICB, ex parte Webb* [1986] Q.B. 184.
31 Sixteenth Report, para. 17.
32 [1977] 1 W.L.R. 1353.
33 Criminal Damage Act 1971, s.1(1).
34 Criminal Damage Act 1971, s.1(2).
35 [1986] 3 W.L.R. 251
36 The Board was holding 100 similar applications in abeyance pending the outcome of this appeal: Twentieth Report, para. 15.
37 Offences Against the Person Act 1861, s.34.
38 Twentieth Report, para. 17.
39 Council of Europe, European Treaty Series No. 116; see also Home Affairs Committee Report, p. 6.
40 *Hansard*, 5th Series, H.L. Vol. 257, col. 1364.

41 Statement, para. 4(H), (J) (insane persons).
42 Third Report, Case H. 36.
43 Case H. 49.
44 Ninth Report, para. 12.
45 In the sense of neither intentionally nor recklessly inflicted.
46 *R* v. *C.I.C.B., ex parte Schofield* [1971] 2 All E.R. 1011.
47 Statement, para. 4(G) and para. 6(L).
48 Case A. 570; Case H.17.
49 Eleventh Report, para. 7.
50 This example probably means that a case such as *R* v. *C.I.C.B., ex parte Ince* [1974] 3 All E.R. 808 would now be excluded from the scheme.
51 In 1984 awards were made to 1,017 policemen injured on duty (3·4% of resolved cases). The number of such awards in 1977–8 was 2,600 (15·9% of resolved cases).
52 *Gardner* v. *Moore* [1984] A.C. 548.
53 Statement, Para. 11.
54 Twentieth Report, para. 32.
55 *Crimes of Violence* (London, 1963) p. 32.
56. See Working Party Report, p. 89.
57 Ninth Report, Appendix F.
58 Eighth Report, para. 7.
59 *Ibid.*
60 Third Report, para. 13. But the Working Party did not think there should be any reduction in this sort of case; see their Report, p. 62.
61 Twentieth Report, para 28.
62 Statement, para. 6(D).
63 [1977] Q.B. 94.
64 *Lane* v. *Holloway* [1968] 1 Q.B. 379.
65 Statement, para. 6(E).
66 It would be 'contrary to public policy' for an insured person to enforce payment under a liability policy for his own benefit where he has been guilty of deliberate criminal conduct, but this does not prevent the policy being enforced for the benefit of an injured third party: *Hardy* v. *MIB* [1964] 2 Q.B. 745. Cf. *Gray* v. *Barr* [1970] 2 Q.B. 626.
67 Even 'gangs' of children, see Ninth Report, para. 12.
68 Fourth Report, para. 11(4)(b); Ninth Report, p. 36.
69 Nineteenth Report, para. 29.
70 Twentieth Report, paras, 45, 46.
71 [1973] 3 All E.R. 808.
72 *Jones* v. *Livox Quarries Ltd* [1952] 2 Q.B. 608.
73 Fourth Report, para. 11(4)(d).
74 *Ibid*, para. 11(4)(e).
75 *Ibid.*
76 [1984] 1 W.L.R. 1234.
77 [1970] 2 Q.B. 541.
78 Fourth Report, para. 14.
79 Third Report, para. 13.
80 Para. 5 of the scheme.

81 Report, para. 50.
82 Samuels, (1967) 17 *University of Toronto Law Journal* 20.
83 *Osgoode Hall Study (Victims of Crime)*, p. 35, Table VIII.
84 In fact, the term 'average industrial earnings' has no strict technical meaning. The nearest equivalent in the statistics published by the Department of Employment is average earnings in manufacturing industry, and that is the figure given here.
85 See p. 000.
86 Seventh Report, para. 13. It seems that the Board may have misinterpreted the law here in awarding the cost of private medical treatment which would probably never have been incurred.
87 Para. 15 of the scheme.
88 See Chapter 18.
89 See Garner, [1967] *Public Law* 323.
90 The nearest analogy is the 'hit and run' road accident case dealt with by the MIB, see p. 00.
91 Third Report, para. 15; Fourth Report, para. 9.
92 Twenty-First Report, para. 3.
93 See Report of Home Affairs Committee, para. 49; but the government's reply was rather negative: para. (4).
94 Travel and subsistence expenses for witnesses are, however, payable if a hearing is held.
95 Second Report, para. 31.
96 Report of the Working Party, p. 75.
97 See 110 *Solicitor's Journal* 970, and 111 *Solicitor's Journal* 481.
98 Third Report, para. 20.
99 Twentieth Report, para. 53.
100 *Criminal Statistics 1984*, Table 2.8.
101 *Op. cit.*, p. 54.

CHAPTER 14

1 That is, among the common law countries. It was, in fact, first started in Germany.
2 [1891] A.C. 325.
3 Factory and Workshops Acts of 1883, 1891, 1895 and 1901; Cotton Cloth Factories Acts of 1889 and 1897.
4 [1898] 2 Q.B. 402.
5 See Hanes, *The First British Workmen's Compensation Act 1897* (Yale, 1968). Chamberlain's arguments against the Bill of 1893 are still well worth reading for their relevance to the current debate about the fault principle.
6 Dinsdale, *History of Accident Insurance in Great Britain* (London, 1954), p. 152.
7 See the Beveridge Report, para. 99 and pp. 216–17, 233.
8 These criticisms were all put very forcefully by Beveridge in his report, paras. 77 *et seq*.
9 Beveridge Report, para. 17 and paras. 303–9.
10 *Ibid*. para. 309.
11 *Ibid*, paras. 93–6.

12 *Ibid*, para. 80.
13 *Ibid*.
14 *Ibid*.
15 *Ibid*, para. 81. See also Pearson Report, Vol. 1, paras. 93–108.
16 For criticisms of Beveridge's arguments, see the Woodhouse Report, paras. 52–4; the Seebohm Report, para. 327; George, p. 184; Matheson (1969) 18 *I.C.L.Q.* 191; see also the views of the BMA and the Medical Commission on Accident Prevention expressed in their evidence to the Robens Committee, vol. 2, p. 63, para. 46 and p. 558. Trade union evidence to the Pearson Commission failed to refer to this question.
17 *Hansard*, 5th Series, H.C. Vol. 751, col. 1396; cf. Vol. 779, col. 128.
18 Beveridge may well have been thinking more of the war disabled who are in a much more real sense injured while 'under orders'.
19 See p. 405.
20 Pearson Report, Vol. 1, paras. 289–91.
21 Report, para. 85.
22 See the Government White Paper, *Social Insurance*, Part II (1944, Cmnd 6551), para. 28.
23 Report, paras. 86–9.
24 Cmnd. 6551, para. 31.
25 Report, para. 85.
26 Cmnd. 6551, para. 26.
27 *Ibid*, para. 29 (iii).
28 *Ibid*, para. 30 (cited, on p. 188).
29 George, p. 211.
30 S.39 of the Social Security Act 1973 originally gave this commitment in terms of *price* levels, but it was altered by the Labour government's National Insurance Act 1974 to a commitment as to *earnings* levels. For some controversy over the precise effect of the section, see *Metzger* v. *DHSS* [1978] 1 W.L.R. 1046.
31 See Ogus & Barendt, pp. 410–12.
32 Beveridge Report, para. 304.
33 Cmnd. 9517.
34 See Ogus & Barendt, p. 410.

CHAPTER 15

1 For a much fuller statement of the law than is possible here, see Ogus & Barendt, Chapter 8. The term 'industrial injury scheme' (or 'system') has been retained here, although there is no longer a separate Act or a separate fund. Industrial injury benefits are now simply a part of the social security system, provided for in the Social Security Act 1975.
2 The Secretary of State has power to include within, or exclude from, the scheme, categories of workers regardless of the strict terms of the definition of 'employed earner': see S.I, 1975/467 as amended.
3 There are suspicions of widespread fraud already, since it is easy for a workman to allege (say) that muscular strain was due to something that happened at work; it is

said that the number of 'industrial injuries' rises disproportionately after a fine weekend in early Spring as a result of gardening by workmen out of condition: *Guardian*, 3 March 1969.
4 *Lee* v. *Lee's Air Farming Ltd* [1961] A.C. 12.
5 Pearson Report, Vol. 1, paras. 851–7.
6 [1924] A.C. 59.
7 See the Social Security Act 1975, s.53, replacing the 1946 Act, s.9.
8 See TUC evidence to the Pearson Royal Commission, paras. 22–5.
9 Pearson Report, Vol. 1, paras. 858–68.
10 Hansard, H.C., Vol. 958, col. 795.
11 Social Security Act 1975, s.50(3).
12 Now s.55(1) of the Social Security Act 1975.
13 Ogus & Barendt, p. 285.
14 See Micklethwait, *The National Insurance Commissioners* (London, 1976), pp. 82–3.
15 *R* v. *Industrial Injuries Commissioner* [1966] 2 Q.B. 31.
16 Cmd. 6551, para. 33 (iv).
17 When the criminal injuries scheme was under consideration it was thought administratively impossible to combine an industrial-injury-type scheme with weekly payments etc., and a provision for reducing benefits on the ground of 'provocation': see Cmnd. 1406, para. 92.
18 *Roberts* v. *Dorothea Slate Quarries* [1948] 2 All E.R. 201, followed by the Tribunal in C.I. 257/49.
19 See s.76 of the Social Security Act 1975.
20 See the TUC evidence to the Pearson Royal Commission, paras. 29–38.
21 Report on Industrial Diseases (1981, Cmnd. 8393), paras. 6–32; Lewis [1983] *J.S.W.L.* 10.
22 52 H.C. Official Report (6th Series), Written Answers, cols. 328–9.
23 See further Ogus & Barendt, pp. 268–70.
24 C.I. 159/50.
25 See Micklethwait, *op. cit.*, p. 82.
26 See, e.g., C.I. 3/48; C.I. 51/49; C.S.I. 63/49.
27 See p. 462.
28 *Social Security Statistics 1984* (HMSO), Table 21.10.
29 *Ibid*, Table 20.44.
30 *Ibid*, Table 21.21.
31 Social Security Act 1975, s.56(5).
32 Social Security and Housing Benefits Act 1982.
33 Social Security Act 1985.
34 Persons who do not qualify for statutory sick pay may be entitled to sickness benefit. The most important group are the self-employed.
35 Because income tax is progressive and calculated on total annual earnings, the exact impact of periods of absence from work on an employee's net annual earnings is a complex matter.
36 Para. 1(a) of Schedule 8 to the 1975 Act.
37 This form of benefit does not deal with lost earnings, which are considered on p. 343, so the objective approach does not preclude some discrimination according to earnings.

38 Para 1(c) of Schedule 8 to the 1975 Act.
39 1965, Cmnd. 1847, para. 14.
40 Pearson Report, Vol. 1, paras. 823, 373–80 and 271 respectively.
41 Townsend, *The Disabled in Society* (London, 1967), p. 7.
42 Cmnd. 1847, para. 29.
43 *Report of the National Commission on State Workmen's Compensation Laws* (Government Printer, Washington, 1972), p. 69.
44 Cmnd. 7266, 1978.
45 Report of the Committee, para. 400.
46 Social Security Act 1975, s.61.
47 Social Security Act 1975, s.63.
48 Pearson Report, Vol. 1, para. 830: less than 3,000.
49 Ibid, Vol. 2, Table 7.
50 Ibid, Vol. 1, para. 690.
51 For the same reason it is payable for life and does not stop at retirement age.
52 Social Security Act 1975, s.50A (inserted 1982).
53 See Ogus & Barendt, pp. 410–13.
54 Social Security Act 1975, s.58. Yet this allowance, too, is payable for life and does not stop at retirement age, see C.I. 1258/49; Micklethwait, *op. cit.*, p. 109.
55 Pearson Report, Vol. 2, para. 101.
56 *R v. Industrial Injuries Commission, ex parte Humphreys* [1965] 3 All E.R. 885.
57 *R v. Industrial Injuries Commissioner, ex parte Mellors* [1971] 2 Q.B. 401.
58 Micklethwait, *op. cit.*, p. 108.
59 Pearson Report, Vol. 1, Annex 6 (by the DHSS), para. 37.
60 See Ogus & Barendt, pp. 319–22.
61 For details, see *ibid*, pp. 220–2.
62 Vol. 1, para. 804.
63 Ogus & Barendt, pp. 233–4.
64 Vol. 1, para. 840.
65 Ogus & Barendt, pp. 334–5.
66 See p. 157.
67 Where the widow is permanently incapable of self-support at the date of the death, she is entitled to the higher rate whether or not she has dependent children.
68 *Reincke v. Gray* [1964] 1 W.L.R. 832. As the court pointed out in this case, the widow's second husband came under a legal obligation to maintain the children once he had accepted them as members of his family.
69 See the *Report* of the Supplementary Benefits Commission to the Secretary of State (HMSO, 1971); the Fisher Committee *Report*, Chapter 13; the Finer Committee Report, paras. 5.266–77; although it is noteworthy that the industrial widower's benefit does not terminate on remarriage and is not suspended on cohabitation.
70 See Farmer, *Tribunals and Government* (London, 1974), Chapter 4.
71 This is a very general account. For a detailed examination of the law, see Ogus & Barendt, Chapters 14 and 15.
72 Social Security Act 1975, s.109(2).
73 *Ibid*, s.109(3).
74 See TUC evidence to the Pearson Royal Commission, paras. 70–3. But the success rate of appellants is about 40%: *Social Security Statistics 1984*, Table 21.21.

75 Ogus & Barendt, pp. 599–600.
76 Social Security Act 1975, s.98. Health and Social Services and Social Security Adjudications Act 1983 (HASSASSA), s.1(1).
77 *Ibid*, s.97; HASSASSA, s.1(2).
78 Health and Social Security Act 1984, s.16.
79 Social Security Act 1975, s.101.
80 *Ex parte Moore* [1965] 1 All E.R. 81.
81 *Accidents at Work: Compensation for All* (Society of Labour Lawyers evidence to the Pearson Commission), p. 2.
82 Which is (as we saw earlier, p. 298) to achieve a 'favourable' rather than a 'fair' settlement.
83 Street, *Justice in the Welfare State* (London, 1968), p. 16.
84 *Ibid*, p. 27.
85 *Ibid*.
86 *Family Needs and the Social Services* (London, 1961), p. 161.
87 One in three of those who obtained damages in the *Which?* survey thought their cases took far too long to settle (*Which?*, October 1970, p. 316). See also Pearson Report, Vol. 2, Table 90.
88 Webb, *Industrial Injuries: a new approach* (London, 1974), p. 4.
89 Street, *Justice in the Welfare State*, p. 17; see also Bell *et al.*, 3 *Journal of Social Policy* 289 (1974) and 4 *Journal of Social Policy* 1 (1975).
90 Street, *Justice in the Welfare State*, p. 16.
91 See Law Society's 17th Annual Report on the Legal Aid Scheme (1967), Appendix B.
92 *Ex parte Moore* [1965] 1 All E.R. 81. It is typical of the English system that nobody appears to be troubled by the fact that this means that either the courts or these tribunals are operating with an unsatisfactory procedure, since the rules of evidence must either be an aid or a hindrance to doing justice.
93 Street, *op. cit.*, p. 16.
94 See the argument of Fisher QC in *R* v. *Deputy Insurance Commissioner* [1967] 1 A.C. 725.
95 See generally Micklethwait, *The National Insurance Commissioners* (London, 1976).
96 *Ibid*, p. 47.
97 (1957) Cmnd. 218, p. 9.
98 Street, *Justice in the Welfare State*, Chapter 1; see also Farmer, *op. cit.*, pp. 111–12; Bell, *op. cit.*
99 Harlow & Rawlings, *Law and Administration* (London, 1984), p. 639.
100 See Zander, (1969) 32 *Modern Law Review* 187; Whitmore, (1970) 33 *Modern Law Review* 481, especially at 484–6.
101 See A. Frost and C. Howard, *Representation and Administrative Tribunals* (London, 1978).
102 Cmnd. 7648, Vol. 1, p. 172.
103 The success rate on appeal to a local tribunal in industrial cases was over 40% in 1983, compared with 18% in unemployment cases and 19% in sickness cases: *Social Security Statistics 1984*, Tables 20.20 and 21.20, 1.20, 3.20 respectively.
104 *Social Security Statistics, 1977*, Table 21.10.
105 R.(I) 6/65.

106 Social Security Act 1975, s.87.
107 For a case on *certiorari* which give some indication of the work of the Medical Tribunals, see *R* v. *National Insurance Commissioner, ex parte Viscusi* [1974] 2 All E.R. 724.

CHAPTER 16

1 For the details, see Ogus & Barendt, pp. 66–72.
2 See p. 333 above.
3 *Social Security Statistics, 1972*, Table 46.5; *Social Security Statistics, 1984*, Table 46.14.
4 Social Security Act 1975, s.35.
5 Pearson Report, Vol. I, para. 830; *Social Security Statistics, 1984*, Table 14.30.
6 Pearson Report, Vol. I, para. 833.
7 Now in Social Security Act 1975, s.37.
8 Lady Sharp's *Report on the Mobility of Physically Disabled People* (HMSO, 1974).
9 *Social Security Statistics, 1984*, Table 15.30.
10 Entitlement to pensions for widows aged between 40 and 50 was first introduced by the National Insurance Act 1970, now the Social Security Act 1975, s.26.
11 Beveridge *Report*, para. 153.
12 See, e.g., criminal injuries case No. A. 345 where a widow of 45 receiving an industrial pension of £1 (which would now be over £10) was awarded £3,500 of taxpayer's money. A widow of 39 whose husband died a natural death, or who was killed in an accident which could not be proved to be the fault of a third party, would receive neither payment at present.
13 See p. 347, for discussion of the cohabitation rule.
14 Finer Committee *Report*, paras. 5.297–5.301.
15 *Ibid*, Figure 5.11.
16 Beveridge *Report*, para. 369.
17 *Social Security Statistics, 1984*, Table 34.34.
18 *Ibid*.
19 See *Social Assistance*, A Review of the Supplementary Benefit Scheme in Great Britain (DHSS, 1978), especially at pp. 13–17.
20 See Social Security Advisory Committee, 2nd Report, 1982/3, Para. 5.30.
21 Similarly, if his wife goes out to work, the dependant's allowance will cease, yet the widow referred to in n. 12 above was entitled to go out to work without forfeiting either her industrial pension or her criminal injuries compensation award.
22 Social Security Act, Schedule II.
23 But see 2nd Report of Social Security Advisory Committee, 1982–3, paras 9.15, 9.16.
24 See generally the Fisher Committee *Report*.
25 DE/DHSS Rayner Scrutiny *Payment of Benefits to Unemployed People* (1981).
26 Para. 129.
27 See p. 347.
28 It is unlikely that such problems will ever be completely eliminated, because there are insuperable problems in treating disability arising from natural causes in the same way as disability arising from human actions.

29 Fisher *Report*, paras. 185–90.
30 In Sweden where this procedure is used, there is apparently a dramatic tendency for patients to recover when a certificate is first required: see Fisher *Report*, Appendix 9, para. 17.
31 Fisher *Report*, Appendix 6.
32 In Ontario, Professor Atiyah heard many complaints of such cases (in 1973) where a workman was assessed at 20% or 30% disabled, but was effectively unemployable.

CHAPTER 17

1 Income and Corporation Taxes Act 1970, s.18.
2 Income and Corporation Taxes Act 1970, s.16.
3 Rating (Disabled Persons) Act 1978.
4 Finance Act 1972, s.70.
5 Dog Licences Act 1959.
6 Transport Act 1968, s.138.
7 Townsend, *The Disabled in Society* (London, 1967), p. 6, points out that mental abnormality is not a disability which attracts public sympathy; the Spastics Society has an income of about £2m per annum, but the National Society for Mentally Handicapped Children, only about £40,000.
8 This was the government's answer in 1967 to pleas for extra tax reliefs for the blind, see *Hansard*, 5th Series, H.C. Vol. 748, col. 815. I am grateful to Mrs M. du Boisson for this reference.
9 This section concerns contractual as opposed to statutory sick pay (discussed in Chapters 15 and 16). Statutory sick pay is really a social security benefit, because while the employer pays it in the first instance, he is entitled to 100% reimbursement from the DHSS.
10 *Orman* v. *Saville Sportswear* [1960] 3 All E.R. 105.
11 Pearson Report, Vol. I, paras. 137–41. See also *Harris 1984 Survey*, Ch. 7.
12 See 13 H.C. Official Report (6th Series), cols. 642–3.
13 *Inquiry into Statutory Sick Pay* (1985).
14 Published in a Report by the DHSS in 1977 (HMSO, London), Table xi.
15 See *New Earnings Survey 1970*, Appendix III.
16 See TUC evidence to the Pearson Royal Commission, para. 85.
17 Lewis and Latta, *Evidence to the Royal Commission on Civil Liability* (unpublished), p. 7.
18 *Ibid*.
19 The information in this and the next paragraph comes from the Report by the Government Actuary on *Occupational Pension Schemes*, Sixth Survey by the Government Actuary (HMSO, 1979).
20 See Pearson Report, Vol. I, paras. 788–91; Coal Industry Act 1975.
21 See Pearson Report, Vol. I, paras. 88–92.
22 Many sociologists believe that benefits in kind are preferable because they cannot be wasted; this is especially true of benefits which are primarily intended for children: see George, *Social Security*, p. 190, but cf. Lady Wootton in *Social Science and Social Pathology* (1959). Most charitable activity these days takes the form of

assistance in kind: see Brenton, *The Voluntary Sector in the British Social Services* (1985), Chs. 1, 2.
23 This was pointed out in the Beveridge *Report*, Appendix 13, para. 15.
24 *Thornton* v. *Kirklees M.B.C.* [1979] 2 All E.R. 349; see also *Cocks* v. *Thanet D.C.* [1983] 2 A.C. 286.
25 Townsend has spoken of the 'near desperation' of those disabled persons below pensionable age who would like paid employment: *The Disabled in Society* (1967), p. 15.
26 Piercy *Report*, para. 26.
27 'The overriding aim is to enable each handicapped person to live a life which is as nearly normal and as full of interest and satisfaction as his disability permits.' – *Health & Welfare, The Development of Community Care* (1963, Cmnd. 1973), para. 109. See also Cornes, *Employment Rehabilitation* (Manpower Services Commission, 1982), Ch. 2, for a fuller account of the aims of the Employment Rehabilitation Service and its failure to fulfil them.
28 Established under the Disabled Persons (Employment) Acts 1944 and 1958.
29 Piercy *Report*, para. 68; Fisher *Report*, para. 254. See Cornes, *op. cit.*, for research into their effectiveness. See also *Employment Rehabilitation* (M.S.C., 1981), Ch. 5.
30 At the time of the Piercy Report it was said that 80% obtained employment in under three months, but more recent research puts the figure much lower (Cornes, *op. cit.*, paras. 9.23–9.28); *Employment Rehabilitation* (M.S.C., 1981), para. 7.9.
31 *Review of the Quota System for Employment of Disabled People* (M.S.C., 1981), pp. 6–7.
32 Piercy *Report*, para. 178.
33 Only 16% of those registered under the 1944 Act thought that being registered had helped them to obtain employment, see *Handicapped and Impaired in Great Britain* (HMSO, 1971), Pt II, para. 8.5. An increasing problem has been unwillingness by disabled people to register: *Review of Quota System* cited in n. 31 above.
34 *Employment Gazette* (Dept of Employment, 1982), pp. 192–5 (Remploy had 8,600 employees in 1982).
35 Piercy *Report*, para. 213.
36 Piercy *Report*, Pt IX.
37 *Wyatt* v. *Hillingdon L.B.C.* (1978) 76 L.G.R. 727.
38 Townsend, *The Disabled in Society* (London, 1967) p. 10.
39 *Report*, para. III.
40 *Handicapped and Impaired in Great Britain*, Pt II, Table 117.
41 Under sections 21–8 of the National Assistance Act 1948 as amended by the Health Services and Public Health Act 1968; see also the Housing (Homeless Persons) Act 1977.
42 *Ibid.*
43 *Health and Personal Services Statistics for England & Wales 1973*, Table 7–2. The Seebohm *Report* was critical of the present position in this field, see para. 332.
44 The power to make cash grants was conferred by the 1968 Act.
45 The range of welfare services is set out in the Seebohm Report, Appendix F.
46 Finer Committee *Report*, paras 8.38 and 8.104–8.109.
47 See *Handicapped and Impaired in Great Britain*, Pt I, para. 20.
48 Seebohm *Report*, para. 334. See *Handicapped and Impaired in Great Britain*, Pt I, Tables 38, 39 and 40, for some data on the use made of these various services.

Notes to pages 381–394   613

49 See generally Brenton, *The Voluntary Sector in the British Social Services* (1985).
50 Finer Committee *Report*, para. 8.45.
51 Townsend, *op. cit.*, p. 13, refers to the 'huge latent demand' for social services which is not at present satisfied. And Willmott, *Consumers' guide to the British Social Services* (Harmondsworth, 1967), says, p. 171, 'In fact almost everywhere "community care" is at present more of a humane idea than a practical reality.'
52 HASSASSA, s. 1.

CHAPTER 18

1 Pearson Report, Vol. 1, chapter 13.
2 See pp. 78–80 above.
3 *Gale* v. *Motor Union Insurance Co. Ltd* [1928] 1 K.B. 359.
4 Except in the 'liable relative cases', i.e. where social security is paid to a deserted wife or unmarried mother because the man responsible has failed to meet his legal obligations; see Finer Committee *Report*, para. 4.176 *et seq.*
5 *Final Report of the Committee on Alternative Remedies* (1946) Cmnd. 6860, paras. 44 *et seq.* See p. 405, as to this committee.
6 And see *Marrison* v. *Bell* [1939] 2 K.B. 187, holding that the receipt of sickness benefits was no ground for displacing the 'implied term' in a contract of employment that a workman is entitled to wages even when away sick. Cf. *Elliot* v. *Liggens* [1902] 2 K.B. 84.
7 Local authority contracts of employment do this, and it is assumed to be effective in law, see *IRC* v. *Hambrook* [1956] 2 Q.B. 641 at pp. 656–7.
8 So far as is known, there is no evidence as to the extent to which recoupment actually takes place. There are probably many cases in which the 'loan' is not repaid although the injured party does recover damages.
9 Though there are now some rare cases where insurers can be awarded costs from the Legal Aid Fund, see p. 243.
10 Legal Aid (General) Regulations 1980, Reg. 31(1).
11 For another example in a different area, see *R.* v. *Barnsley Appeal Tribunal* [1977] 3 All E.R. 1031.
12 *Gardner* v. *Moore* [1984] A.C. 548.
13 But if a person is covered by two separate *liability* policies neither insurer can claim subrogation rights against the other, though either can claim contribution: *Austin* v. *Zurich Insurance Co.* [1945] K.B. 250.
14 *Lister* v. *Romford Ice & Storage Co.* [1957] A.C. 555. But see *Morris* v. *Ford Motor Co.* [1973] 1 Q.B. 792, p. 652 above.
15 The problem is unquestionably different from that concerning accidents because no one can doubt that the State is in general entitled to require a husband to maintain a wife who is unable to maintain herself if he can in fact do so. See the Finer Committee *Report*, para. 4.129.
16 See Finer Committee *Report*, paras 4.85–4.90 and 4.176 *et seq.*
17 The MIB used to obtain subrogation rights against insolvent insurers but this has become obsolete since the Policyholders Protection Act 1975 has taken over responsibility for payments in these cases. The Criminal Injuries Compensation

Board say that the number of cases in which they could usefully sue if they had the power is minimal; see Eighth Report, para. 18.
18 Eleventh Report (Loss of Services etc.) (1963, Cmnd. 2017), para. 5. But the Law Commission has rejected this idea; see Law Comm. No. 56, paras. 146–50. The Pearson Commission also agreed: Vol. 1, para. 446.
19 Justice *Report on Compensation for Victims of Crimes of Violence*, p. 20.
20 Winn Committee *Report*, paras, 107–10 and Appendix 7.
21 *Accidents at Work: Compensation for All*, evidence to the Pearson Committee, 1974.
22 A similar case could be made against the 'contribution' legislation whereby one person held liable in damages may obtain contribution from another who would also be liable. In practice such claims are most likely to be brought by an insurer or other defendant well able to spread a loss against an individual who would have to pay from his own pocket. See James, (1941) 54 *Harvard Law Review* 1156, but cf. *ibid*, 1170. The danger is well illustrated by *McCallion* v. *Dodd* [1966] N.Z.L.R. 710, in which a child injured partly by the negligence of an insured motorist, and partly by the negligence of his own parent, sued the motorist, whose insurers then claimed contribution from the parent. Since the parent could not touch the damages awarded to the child, he might have had to sell up house and home in order to pay the contribution.
23 See Justice *Report on Compensation for Victims of Crimes of Violence*, p. 20. The point was also made in Parliament: Hansard, 5th Series, H.C. Vol. 694, col. 1159.
24 This was the main reason given by the Monckton Committee for rejecting subrogation in favour of the National Insurance Funds: Cmnd. 6860.
25 See p. 455 below.
26 For a contrary view, see p. 000 below.
27 This is advocated in *Social Services for All?*. (London, 1968).
28 See Atiyah, *Vicarious Liability* (London, 1967), pp. 426–7.
29 Hellner, *Scandinavian Studies in Law* (Stockholm, 1962), pp. 140–1.
30 *Ibid*.
31 *Mark Rowlands Ltd* v. *Berni Inns Ltd* [1985] 3 W.L.R. 964. See also Hasson, (1985) 5 *Oxford J. Legal Studies*, 416.
32 Jorgensen, *Scandinavian Studies in Law* (Stockholm, 1963), p. 33; Hasson, *op. cit.*, pp. 421–2.
33 The first two of these arguments may have received their quietus in *Parry* v. *Cleaver* [1970] A.C. 1.
34 See *Payne* v. *Rly Executive* [1952] 1 K.B. 26.
35 'An injured person should not have the same need met twice over' – Beveridge *Report*, para. 260. The principle was also accepted by the Monckton Committee, Cmnd 6850.
36 Para. 53.
37 The argument is less convincing when it is appreciated that the two dissenting members of the Committee were trade union representatives who were thinking principally of the industrially injured. In the result the dissenters have more or less had their way, see p. 406.
38 See, e.g. *Re Gillingham Bus Disaster Fund* [1959] Ch. 62.
39 [1970] A.C. 1.
40 See p. 406.

41 See *Dennis* v. *LPTB* [1948] 1 All E.R. 779; cf. *IRC* v. *Hambrook* [1956] 2 Q.B. 641. See also *Jenner* v. *Allen West & Co.* [1959] 1 W.L.R. 554.
42 See pp. 390–1.
43 L.R. to Ex. I.
44 Above.
45 Pearson Report, Vol. 1, para. 529.
46 *Peacock* v. *Amusements Ltd* [1954] 2 Q.B. 347; *Redpath* v. *Belfast & Co. Down Rly* [1947] N.I. 167.
47 *Foxley* v. *Olton* [1964] 3 All E.R. 248.
48 *Lincoln* v. *Hayman* [1982] 1 W.L.R. 488.
49 See the Pension Appeal Tribunal Act 1943, s.11. For details of the Ministry's practice, see Kemp & Kemp, *The Quantum of Damages*, 1st edn (London 1956), Vol. 112, Appendix VI (not reproduced in 2nd edn).
50 *Carroll* v. *Hooper* [1964] 1 All E.R. 845; *Elstob* v. *Robinson* [1964] 1 All E.R. 848. In *Parry* v. *Cleaver* it was said that the mere fact that a payment was discretionary was not by itself ground for ignoring it in the assessment of damages but only for discounting its value; but where it is known that the ministry will definitely make a deduction from the pension on account of the damages, then it would still be correct not to reduce the damages.
51 *Cunningham* v. *Harrison* [1973] Q.B. 942; *Donnelly* v. *Joyce* [1974] 1 Q.B. 454; *Hay* v. *Hughes* [1975] 1 All E.R. 257.
52 Administration of Justice Act 1982, s.5.
53 The committee issued three reports: (1944), Cmnd. 6580; (1945), Cmnd. 6642; and (1946), Cmnd.6860. The first two reports were concerned with the Law Reform (Contributory Negligence) Act 1945 which was then under consideration.
54 Para. 32. As we have seen the trade union members dissented.
55 The committee thought that full deduction would help to discourage common law actions for damages, though it is unlikely that this would have happened in practice. In fact, of course, actions for damages have increased enormously since 1946 but there has not been full deduction: see p. 406.
56 We have suggested (p. 402) that the rarity of a type of benefit may justify ignoring it; it is thought that the Monckton Committee was wrong in thinking that the vital distinction is between voluntary and compulsory insurance. Insurance of houses against fire, for instance, is not compulsory although very common, but nobody would expect to recover tort damages and insurance moneys as well if his house was burned down by someone's negligence.
57 Law Reform (Personal Injuries) Act 1948. For more detail see Hepple & Matthews, *Tort Cases and Materials*, 3rd edn (London, 1985), pp. 354–5.
58 *Bowker* v. *Rose* [1978] 2 C.L. § 271. Moreover, the deductions (contrary to the Monckton Committee recommendations) are only set off against damages for lost earnings. So, for instance, if there are no lost wages but a pure 'loss of faculty', the injured person may be entitled to both damages and an industrial disablement pension in full.
59 See n. 48 above.
60 *Nabi* v. *British Leyland (UK) Ltd* [1980] 1 All E.R. 667.
61 It was specifically rejected by the Monckton Committee.
62 See *Haste* v. *Sandell Perkins Ltd* [1984] 3 W.L.R. 73.

63 [1970] 2 Q.B. 130.
64 See Williams, (1974) 37 *Modern Law Review*, 281.
65 *Hultquist* v. *Universal Pattern Engineering Co.* [1960] 2 Q.B. 467.
66 The percentage of workmen injured in circumstances giving rise to workmen's compensation who claimed damages was only 0·1 in 1935–7 (a total of 500 cases) and 0·26 in 1941 (see Young, *Industrial Injuries Insurance* (London, 1964), pp. 162–3). A major reason for the paucity of common law claims at this time was that the injured party had to elect between a claim for damages and workmen's compensation.
67 As we have seen, there were in 1973 some 90,000 payments a year, probably representing about 10·5% of all industrially injured persons (see p. 198).
68 Pearson Report, Vol. 1, paras. 467–95.
69 Beveridge *Report*, para. 262. The Monckton Committee thought it was 'inconsistent' to allow people to have private medical treatment but not to claim damages in respect of the cost (para. 56). But there is no inconsistency at all, since the only question is who is to pay for the private treatment – the patient or the public?
70 BUPA tries to avoid this by stipulating that it will not pay for medical expenses which are legally recoverable from a third party. But since in practice the expenses will usually need to be paid long before anything is actually received in damages, BUPA will advance the amount payable by way of 'loan', and the member is expected to repay this when the damages are in fact recovered. But it seems probable that many members nevertheless secure double recovery, and the total amount of repayments obtained by BUPA in this way is negligible. (We are obliged to BUPA for information on this point.)
71 Pearson Report, Vol. 1, para. 342.
72 See n. 52 above.
73 But not compensation obtained from private funds, so insurance paid for by the victim and charity payments are ignored as with tort claims: para. 19 of the Scheme.
74 Para. 21 of the Scheme. There are, apparently, very few cases in which any repayment has been made. One case in which damages of £1,000 were recovered was sufficiently rare to be worthy of special mention, Sixth Report, para. 13.
75 Para. 20 of the Scheme.

CHAPTER 19

1 [1947] A.C. 156.
2 [1961] A.C. 388.
3 Of course other compensation may be available, but one cannot very well defend the shortcomings of the fault principle by pointing to the existence of non-fault compensation.
4 Austin, *Accident Black Spot* (Harmondsworth, 1966), p. 33.
5 *Driver Behaviour and Accident Involvement: Implications for Tort Liability*, pp. 176–180 (Automobile Insurance and Compensation Study; US Government Printer, Washington, 1970).
6 *Research on Road Safety* (HMSO, 1963), p. 4.
7 Reports L.R. 70 (1967) and L.R. 146 (1968); and see also L.R. 395 (1971) and L.R. 449 (1972).

8 Which was why s.11(2) of the Criminal Justice Act 1948 did not allow a court to order reparation to be made to the victim of a crime if it also fined the offender. But the Powers of Criminal Courts Act 1973 shows less sensitivity on this issue.
9 When it comes to the enforcement of a judgment debt, all 'are aware that it is necessary to have regard to the social needs of the debtor': *Report of the Committee on the Enforcement of Judgment Debts* (1969, Cmnd 3909), para. 76.
10 See, e.g., Second Report of the Criminal Injuries Compensation Board, para. 34.
11 *The Common Law* (Boston, 1949), p. 108. Holmes' argument could be strengthened. Morality does not always acquit a person of blame for acts traceable to congenital failings or defects. Adults are expected to take measures to protect others from the adverse consequences of their nature.
12 A survey showed that 6·8% of drivers with over five years experience were involved in single vehicle accidents (i.e. those least likely to be due to the fault of anybody else) while 19·4% of drivers with under six months' experience were involved in such accidents: see *How Fast?* (HMSO, 1968), para. 77. See also Transport and Road Research Laboratory Report, L.R. 567 (1973).
13 Austin, *op. cit.*, p. 60.
14 See *McHale* v. *Watson* (1964) 111 C.L.R. 384.
15 *Waugh* v. *James Allan Ltd* [1964] 2 Lloyd's Reports 1.
16 *Adamson* v. *Motor Vehicle Insurance Trust* (1957) 58 W.A.L.R. 56; *Robert* v. *Ramsbottom* [1980] 1 All E.R. 7. Cf *Buckley* v. *Smith Transport* [1946] 4 D.L.R. 721.
17 See Tunc, 'Fault: A Common Name for Different Misdeeds', 49 *Tulane Law Rev.* 279 (1975).
18 [1955] A.C. 549.
19 1968, Cmnd. 3706.
20 Para. 184 of the Report.
21 Para. 210.
22 *Ibid.*
23 In this respect the Report of the Tribunal into the Aberfan Disaster (H.C. 553, 1967) adopted a somewhat different approach and was very free in condemning the people involved as 'blameworthy'. Perhaps this tribunal was more concerned about the desire of the bereaved parents for 'satisfaction' (see Chapter 23) for it is hard to see what other purpose was served by these findings of 'blameworthiness'.
24 See an exchange of notes in [1974] C.L.J. 52, 241.
25 Lloyd-Bostock in *Harris 1984 Survey*.
26 [1963] 2 Q.B. 650.
27 [1965] A.C. 656.
28 See p. 122.
29 See p. 214.
30 This section owes much to Keeton, 'Conditional Fault in the Law of Torts', (1959) 72 *Harvard Law Review* 401.
31 (1910), 124 N.W. 221.
32 *Southport Corpn* v. *Esso Petroleum* [1956] A.C. 218.
33 This obligation was given statutory force and much compensation has been paid under statute.
34 *Burmah Oil Co.* v. *Lord Advocate* [1965] A.C. 75. This decision was reversed by the War Damage Act 1965 in order to remove the assessment of compensation from the

35 See especially the *Case of Saltpetre* 12 Co. Rep. 12.
36 *Vaughan* v. *Taff Vale Rly* (1860) 5 H & N 679 (nuisance claim); *Hammersmith City Rly* v. *Brand* (1869) L.R. 4 H.L. 171 (claim for compensation under compulsory requisition legislation). Both were cases of vibration and noise caused by railways operating under statutory authority.
37 See *Romney Marsh* v. *Trinity House* (1870), L.R. 5 Ex. 204, a case very similar to *Vincent* v. *Lake Erie*, and *Cape* v. *Sharpe* [1912] 1 K.B. 496.
38 [1951] A.C. 850.
39 1968, Cmnd. 3706. More recent research has found otherwise, however: *Level Crossing Protection* (HMSO, 1978), para. 10.10; but public perceptions do not, apparently, reflect the facts: *ibid*, para. 8.2. See also *Railway Safety 1983* (HMSO, 1984), para. 50.
40 Of course on some particular grounds it might pay to erect a fence rather than to insure, as was presumably the case in *Miller* v. *Jackson* [1977] Q.B. 966.
41 See Justice *Report on the Trial of Motor Accident Cases*, p. 27.
42 See (1965), 18 *Current Legal Problems*, I, 3. See also Harvey, *The Advocate's Devil*, p. III, where the author (a highly respected Queen's Counsel) relates how on one occasion he was flatly disbelieved by a magistrate while giving evidence. 'Nothing brings home to the mind more clearly than an episode of this sort the difference between the story which is true and the story which is likely to be believed.'
43 Elliott & Street, *Road Accidents* (Harmondsworth, 1968), p. 243
44 See, e.g. *Johnson* v. *Cartledge* [1939] 3 All E.R. 654; cf. also the findings of fact in *The Wagon Mound* (No. 1) [1961] A.C. 388, and *The Wagon Mound* (No. 2) [1967] 1 A.C. 617.
45 Harvey, *The Advocate's Devil*, p. 67.
46 *Crisis in Car Insurance*, p. 28 et seq.
47 *Ibid*, p. 28.
48 *Research on Road Safety* (HMSO, 1963), pp. 3–4; see also Leeming, *Road Accidents: Prevent or Punish?* (London, 1969).
49 Leeming, *op. cit.*, p. 58, describes some of the results as 'almost magical'.
50 *Research on Road Safety* (above), p. 498.
51 Leeming, *op. cit.*, forcefully argues that the state of the law itself has been a factor in preventing earlier recognition by highway engineers of the importance of skid-prone surfaces. The law encourages the authorities (police, highway authorities, magistrates) to treat skidding accidents as the 'fault' of the driver and this itself obscures the need for accident prevention measures not directed at the motorist.
52 *Research on Road Safety* (above).
53 *Ibid*, pp. 5–6.
54 See Austin, *Accident Black Spot* (Harmondsworth, 1966), p. 138. Leeming, *op. cit.*, pp. 64–8, gives an example of a road junction which was the scene of many accidents. Over a hundred motorists were prosecuted and fined for failing to halt, etc., before it was realized that the layout of the junction was such that motorists were unable to see the Halt line in the road until it was too late.
55 See the Road Research Laboratory Report L.R. 91.
56 *Research on Road Safety* (above), p. 57.

57 See Leeming, *op. cit.*
58 See Austin, *op. cit.*, chapter 4.
59 But see p. 509, for the view that society has never been given a real choice in this respect.
60 See, e.g., *Bird* v. *Pearce* [1978] R.T.R. 290.

CHAPTER 20

1 In the third edition of this book the discussion in this chapter contained a crucial ambiguity: it discussed the distinction between human and natural causes in terms of the distinction between accidents and diseases, thus assuming, falsely, that all traumatic injuries are caused by man and, more importantly, that all diseases are caused by nature. Recognition of the importance of the category of man-made diseases is due to the work of Dr Jane Stapleton (*Disease and the Compensation Debate* (Oxford, 1986), summarized in (1985) 5 *O.J.L.S.* 248). On the other hand, as she points out, there are important legal differences between accidents and diseases and some of these have been mentioned at appropriate points in this book. Further discussion will be found in Chapter 25.
2 See Chamberlain, *The Safety of the Unborn Child* (Harmondsworth, 1969), pp. 82–3.
3 *The Second World War*, Vol. II (London, 1949), p. 308. It is interesting to note that Churchill pointed out in his speech to the House of Commons introducing the War Damage Bill that the principle of State compensation must be confined to direct loss from enemy action and not indirect loss (e.g., purely pecuniary loss such as loss arising from business failure) 'or we should be opening up a field to which there would be no bounds' – precisely the same sort of language which judges have used to deny a remedy for pecuniary loss in negligence actions. Churchill, of course, was one of the pioneers of social insurance: see *Liberalism and the Social Problem*, 2nd edn (London, 1909), pp. 309, 315–16.
4 See p. 336.
5 The Australian Committee of Inquiry, while proposing one comprehensive compensation scheme for accident, sickness and congenital disabilities, nevertheless retained certain distinctions in the treatment of accidents and sickness.
6 Stapleton, *op. cit.*

CHAPTER 21

1 Pearson Report, Vol. 2, Tables 158 and 159.
2 *Ibid*, Vol. 1, para. 261.
3 *Ibid*, Vol. 2, Table 158.
4 *Ibid*, Vol. 2, para. 526.
5 In fact fees were not paid explicitly in about 25% of cases, but presumably the claimant received a sufficient sum in settlement to pay his own costs in these cases.
6 The extent to which such costs are passed back to employees or forwards to consumers depends largely on whether the costs are unique to the employer in question, or are generally similar through industry. See generally for an analysis of

how these costs are paid, Gregory and Gisser, *Theoretical Aspects of Workmen's Compensation* (Supplemental Studies for the National Commission on State Workmen's Compensation Laws, 1973), Vol. 1, p. 108.
7 See further Atiyah, 'Accident Prevention and Variable Premium Rates for Work-Connected Injuries', 4 *Industrial Law Journal* 1, 89 (1975); but for a rather different view, see Phillips, 'Economic Deterrence and the Prevention of Industrial Accidents', 5 *Industrial Law Journal* 148 (1976).
8 National Commission on State Workmen's Compensation Laws, *Report*, p. 96. It is true that the remaining 20% employ 80% of all workmen, but it is also true that these bigger firms already have much better accident rates: *ibid*, Figure 5.2.
9 The view that this way of distributing costs helps to reduce accident costs is considered in Chapter 24.
10 Moreover, as sub-categories are multiplied, the classes become smaller and less reliable statistically; see p. 534.
11 See N. Doherty, *Insurance Pricing and Loss Prevention* (Westmead, Farnborough, England, 1976), Chapter 6.
12 There is no doubt that there are large numbers of disqualified drivers who still drive regularly, perhaps as many as 20,000; see Elliott & Street, *Road Accidents* (1968), p. 116 *et seq.*
13 Report of NHS Scrutiny Programme, *The Collection of Fees by Health Authorities under the Road Traffic Act 1972* (DHSS, 1985); Pearson Report, Vol. 1, para. 1084. The Government has announced its intention to abolish fees charged to vehicle users but not those charged to insurers. Collection mechanisms are to be improved.
14 *Ibid*, Vol. 2, Table 158.
15 In 1983–4 over £21·2 million was recovered in costs by the Legal Aid Fund; see 34th Legal Aid Annual Reports, p. 116.
16 *Ibid*, p. 115.
17 Lewis and Latta, (1974) 12 *British Journal of Industrial Relations* 56, 64.
18 Pearson Report, Vol. 2, Table 158.
19 Lees and Doherty, *Lloyds Bank Review*, April 1973, p. 20.
20 In 1984–5, motorists paid £11,230 million in taxation (including fuel duty, vehicle excise duty, VAT and car tax). In the same period, total expenditure on construction and maintenance of roads was about £1,500 million. See *Basic Road Statistics* (British Road Federation, 1985).
21 Industrial injury benefits and the administrative costs of the industrial injuries system are no longer separable from National Insurance payments and costs generally. These figures are based on Pearson Report estimates (Vol. 2, Table 158) and *Social Security Statistics 1978*.
22 There is an excellent account of the essential differences between social and private insurance with reference to 'pooling of risks' in Marshall, *Social Policy in the Twentieth Century*, 2nd edn (London, 1967), Chapter 4.
23 Beveridge *Report*, paras 86–9.
24 Cmnd. 6551, para. 30.
25 Common law employers' liability premiums (which do, of course, vary according to the nature of the risk) vary from 3p per £100 of pay-roll for clerical and office staff, to upwards of £4 per £100 of pay-roll for a really high risk industry.
26 Para. 447.

27 See pp. 502–6.
28 See generally Ogus & Barendt, pp. 65–72.
29 In 1983 all social security payments totalled about £12,000 million and expenses about £751 million (*Social Security Statistics 1984*, Tables 44.01, 44.04). The administrative cost has crept up from about 2.5%, reflecting no doubt the increased complexity of the system.
30 There were some 185,000 medical board examinations in 1983: see *Social Security Statistics 1984*, Table 21.09.
31 In R (I) 11/59 the insurance officer rejected the claim on the ground that the claimant's disability arose from natural causes, but in later proceedings at common law the judge held that the disability arose from an industrial accident.
32 See Fourth Report of the Board, para. 3; Fifth Report, para. 3; Ninth Report, para. 6; Twenty-First Report, para. 1.
33 Cmnd. 1406, para. 13(a).
34 Second Report, para. 38.
35 See Chapter 24.

CHAPTER 22

1 For a serious attempt to ascertain popular conceptions of justice in a particular area, see Cohen, Robson and Bates, *Parental Authority: The Community and the Law* (1958), and for an account of the methodology involved, see the article by the same authors in (1955) 8 *Journal of Legal Education* 137.
2 Lloyd-Bostock in *Harris 1984 Survey*, p. 143, referring to U.S. and Canadian surveys; cf. *Ison*, p. 217 (England).
3 Conard, p. 265. See also O'Connell and Simon, *Payment for Pain and Suffering – Who Wants What, When and Why?* (University of Illinois Press, 1972).
4 *Osgoode Hall Study*, Chapter VIII, Section E.
5 O'Connell and Simon, *op. cit.*
6 Bell, *How to Get Industrial Injuries Benefits* (London, 1966), p. 78.
7 Lloyd-Bostock in *Harris 1984 Survey*; see also Genn in same volume, especially pp. 65–70.
8 See Atiyah, *Vicarious Liability*, Chapter 39.
9 The Working Party on Compensation for the Victims of Crimes of Violence expressed grave doubts about the idea of the State paying compensation for non-pecuniary loss except as part of a contributory (sc. insurance) scheme: Cmnd. 1406, para. 48.
10 We might ask why a person should be compensated for loss of earnings when he never has to render the services for which they are payment. The obvious answer is that he has been deprived of the choice whether or not to exercise his earning *capacity*. At the same time it might be argued that the common law's commitment to 100% compensation for lost future earnings is unnecessarily generous, given that the plaintiff will never have to exert himself.
11 It may be noted, however, that this could be substantially achieved were all road traffic insurance handled by one insurer or a State monopoly, even if the tort system remained intact. If the insurer who issues the policy is the same insurer who will pay compensation when the insured himself is injured, then the insured's income can be

taken into account in fixing the premium. Even this will produce some element of 'subsidy' because the car driver under this system will be 'subsidizing' the pedestrian.
12 See Blum & Kalven, *Public Law Perspectives on a Private Law Problem* (1964), 31 *University of Chicago Law Review* 641, published in 1965 as a paperback by Little, Brown & Co.
13 See p. 368.
14 See Atiyah, *Vicarious Liability*, pp. 22–4.
15 *Ibid*.
16 [1964] 2 Q.B. 806.

CHAPTER 23

1 [1964] A.C. 1129.
2 [1972] A.C. 1027.
3 See Prosser on *Torts*, 4th edn, p. 49 *et seq*.
4 *Wilkinson* v. *Downton* [1897] 2 Q.B. 57.
5 Melville and Johnson, *Cured to Death* (Sevenoaks, Kent, 1983), p. 211.
6 See Linden, *Canadian Tort Law*, 2nd end (Toronto, 1977), pp. 20–27.

CHAPTER 24

1 There is evidence that people do learn from accidents independently of whether their conduct was penalized: Sheppard, *Experience of an Accident and its Influence on Driving* (Transport and Road Research Laboratory, Supplementary Report 750, 1982); see also Quimby and Watts, *Human Factors and Driving Performance* (Transport and Road Research Laboratory, Laboratory Report 1004, 1981).
2 The evidence is summarized in the White Paper, *Road Safety Legislation 1965–66*, Cmnd 2859. For a study of the deterrent effect of strict drink-driving laws in Sweden see Snortum and Ross, (1984) 6 *Law and Policy* 5.
3 *Road Safety – A Fresh Approach* (Cmnd 3339, 1967), para. 7. But cf. Pearson Report, Vol. 2, Table 42 summarizing findings of a Road Research Laboratory study that 65% of accidents may be due to human error alone.
4 See, for example, Parry, *Aggression on the Road* (London, 1968), for some examples.
5 See *How Fast?* (MOT 'Green Paper', HMSO, 1968), para. 4.
6 The 30 mph speed limit is not a very effective deterrent, it is true, but that is because its enforcement is so haphazard and arbitrary. There is real evidence that the general 70 mph speed limit has affected driver behaviour (see the Road Research Laboratory Report RRL-6 on the 70 mph speed limit). There is also evidence that newly imposed speed limits are nearly always followed by a reduction in accidents, see *How Fast?* (above, n. 5), paras. 9–10. But though speed limits may influence driver behaviour, this does not necessarily mean that they will always reduce accidents, see Leeming, *Road Accidents: Prevent or Punish?* (London, 1969), pp. 78–81.
7 Austin, *Accident Black Spot* (Harmondsworth, 1966), pp. 68–9.
8 [1964] 1 W.L.R. 358.

9 [1956] A.C. 552.
10 If a similar case were litigated, the decision in the earlier case would technically be of no relevance. But since most cases are settled out of court, such decisions have considerable practical importance in influencing negotiations and settlements.
11 Para. 425.
12 Webb, *Industrial Injuries: A New Approach* (1974), p. 11.
13 See, e.g., Professor Tizard's illustration in Clive Wood (ed.), *The Influence of Litigation on Medical Practice* (London and New York, 1977), p. 128.
14 See p. 503.
15 See Leeming, *op. cit.*, pp. 210–11.
16 See p. 499.
17 Beckingsale estimated these indirect costs at an average of £22 per accident (as against his estimate of £40 for direct liability costs) in 1964. These estimates were based on the results of a survey among a number of members of the Institution of Industrial Safety Officers: see the Redgrave Memorial Lecture 1963 and *Proceedings of the National Safety Study Conference*, 1966, pp. 25–6. See also Robens Committee Report, Appendix 9 and T. Craig Sinclair, *A Cost-Effectiveness Approach to Industrial Safety* (Research paper for the Robens Committee), Table 3, showing huge variations in international estimates of these costs.
18 The standard 'consequential loss' policy does not cover losses following personal injury: see *Riley on Business Interruption and Consequential Loss Insurance and Claims*, 6th edn, ed. Cloughton, (London, 1985), para. 452.
19 See *Morgan v. T. Wall, Ltd* [1974] 1 Lloyd's Rep. 165.
20 *Road Accidents Great Britain 1983* (HMSO, 1984), Table 11.
21 *Ibid*, para. 3.10.
22 See generally, N. Doherty, *op. cit.* (*supra*, p. 620, n. 11).
23 Garnham, *How to Insure* (London, 1962).
24 Sansom, (1965) 62 *Journal of the Chartered Insurance Institute* 97. In France, insurers have opened a laboratory for testing burglar alarms and supervising their manufacture.
25 See the evidence of the BIA to the Robens Committee, published in Vol. 2 of the Report, p. 43 *et seq*.
26 See, as to the present position, Carson, (1970) 33 *Modern Law Review* 396, and as to the Robens Committee recommendations, see Chapter 9 of the Report.
27 Para. 227.
28 Sansom, *loc. cit.*, p. 106.
29 See Keeton & O'Connell, *After Cars Crash* (1968), p. 95. Insurers may be unduly sceptical of their ability to influence vehicle design. See *Report of the British Columbia Royal Commission on Automobile Insurance*, 1968, citing the Swedish experience.
30 See *Report of the Monopolies Commission on Fire Insurance* (HMSO, 1972), para. 106.
31 Atiyah in 4 *Industrial Law Journal* I, 89 (1975). There is American evidence that product liability insurance premiums bear very little relation to the risks associated with the particular insured: Pierce, (1980) 33 *Vanderbilt L.R.* 1281, 1298–1300.
32 Doherty, *op. cit.*, Chapter 6, is more favourable.
33 For this reason, in Australia the third party personal injury premium is fixed by law and does not vary with previous claims experience. Australian insurers strongly oppose the UK practice on this point.

34 Pearson Report, Vol. 2, para. 202.
35 Sansom, *loc cit.*, pp. 107–8.
36 See generally for the data from the US, Vol. III of the *Supplementary Studies to the Report of the National Commission on State Workmen's Compensation Laws*, 1973, especially pp. 27–53 and 240–5.
37 See *Annual Abstract of Statistics*, 1973, Table 156.
38 See 4 *Industrial Law Journal*, 1, 89 (1975).
39 The BIA, in its evidence to the Robens Committee, admitted that 'broadly speaking, the system of employers' liability insurance is not designed to be a major incentive to the adoption of safe working practices', see Robens Report, Vol. 2, p. 55.
40 Pearson Report, Vol. 2, Table 32.
41 See Calabresi, *The Costs of Accidents* (New Haven, Connecticut, 1970) and for his earlier articles, see (1961) 70 *Yale Law Journal* 499; (1965) 78 *Harvard Law Review* 713; (1965) 75 *Yale Law Journal* 216; (1968) XI *Journal of Law and Economics* 67; (1968) 33 *Law and Contemporary Problems* 429. More recent articles are in (1972) 81 *Yale L.J.* 1055 and (1975) 84 *Yale L.J.* 656. For an attack on Calabresi's ideas, see Blum and Kalven, *op. cit.*, and also their rejoinder in (1967) *University of Chicago Law Review* 239. This chapter is very largely an attempt to explain Calabresi's views to the English law student in the context of English legal institutions, with the addition of some critical comments. Since Calabresi began writing on these questions, a considerable literature has grown up concerning the economics of accident law. Among the more intelligible papers are the symposium on product liability in 38 *University of Chicago Law Review* 3 (1970); Schwartz on contributory negligence in 87 *Yale L.J.* 697 (1978). Works specifically for students include Bowles, *Law and the Economy* (Oxford, 1982), Ch. 7; Polinsky, *An Introduction to Law and Economics* (Boston, 1983), Chs. 6 and 7; Posner, *Economic Analysis of Law*, 2nd edn (Boston, 1977), Ch. 6.
42 Unfortunately it has not so far been less, because insurers have not reduced the premiums for sprinklered premises to an extent which is commensurate with the reduction in the risk; consequently, the incentive to install sprinklers has been less than it should have been, which may explain why such installations have not developed as much as might have been expected; see the *Monopolies Commission Report on Fire Insurance* (HMSO, 1972). para. 183; Doherty, *op. cit.*, Chapter 5.
43 *Crisis in Car Insurance*, pp. 243–4.
44 78 *Harvard Law Review*, 713, 724, n. 17.
45 And this itself may depend largely on whether these costs are peculiar to the particular manufacturer, or are common to all the industry.
46 See Mishan, *The Costs of Economic Growth* (London, 1968), p. 64.
47 At least, so it is nowadays usually assumed. But alternative explanations have been proffered, e.g. the relative change in the price of labour compared to capital goods, see *Supplemental Studies for the National Commission on State Workmen's Compensation Laws*, Vol. I, pp. 116–20.
48 In (1960) 3 *Journal of Law and Economics* 1.
49 (1879) 11 Ch.D. 852.
50 See Mishan, (1971) 79 *Journal of Political Economy* 697.
51 Atiyah, 'A Legal Perspective on Recent Contributions to the Valuation of Life' in

The Value of Life and Safety, Jones-Lee (ed.) (Amsterdam, New York, Oxford, 1982), pp. 192–9.
52 This is the conclusion of Blum and Kalven, *op. cit.*
53 As to how this is to be done, see p. 000.
54 *Op. cit.* This is the celebrated 'Coase theorem' which has given rise to considerable literature among economists.
55 [1977] Q.B. 966.
56 The authors are indebted to Professor Calabresi for emphasizing this point, and also for the illustration which follows in the text.
57 This is already reflected to some extent in insurance premiums but these variations tend to be swallowed up by large no-claims discounts.
58 See Conard, pp. 92–7.
59 See generally Atiyah, *The Rise and Fall of Freedom of Contract* (Oxford, 1979).
60 *Supra*, p. 41.
61 See, e.g., Posner, *The Economic Analysis of Law* (2nd edn, 1977).
62 See, e.g., Schwartz, *op. cit.*, n. 41.
63 J. K. Galbraith, *The New Industrial State*, 2nd edn (Harmondsworth, 1969).
64 An Australian economic study of road accidents states that the 'structure and character of motoring costs is a fundamental barrier to rational and conscious care in road use', Troy and Butlin, *The Cost of Collisions* (Melbourne, 1971), p. 128.
65 Conard, p. 127.
66 See especially Calabresi, (1968), 33 *Law and Contemporary Problems*, 429.
67 Williamson, Olson & Ralston, (1967) 34 *Economica* 235.
68 See p. 109.
69 See p. 502.
70 See p. 538.
71 Para. 314.
72 Paras. 495–7.
73 Paras. 426–9 and 447.
74 It has also been suggested that though insurance companies can hardly attempt the moral regeneration of the criminal classes, insurance companies could try to reduce burglary losses by use of varying premium rating for different classes of risk: see Mackie, *The Times Annual Financial and Economic Review of Insurance*, 1 October 1968.
75 See the delightful tongue-in-cheek suggestion that fire damage to property should be remedied by tort liability plus liability insurance in *Dollars, Delay and the Automobile Victim*, pp. vii–xii. But see also p. 526.
76 78 *Harvard Law Review* 733–4.
77 See Kulp, (1950) 15 *Law & Contemporary Problems*, 493, 494.
78 See Hall, (1973) 70 *Journal of the Chartered Insurance Institute*, 79–80.
79 The unreality of some of these economic arguments is partly demonstrated by the fact that despite this, sprinklers have still been installed. Yet in economic terms it must have generally been a waste of money in that the reduction in risk was not matched by a commensurate reduction in premium.
80 See p. 501.
81 *Report*, Figure 5.5.
82 *Ibid*, p. 97.
83 The total social cost of road accidents was estimated to be £2,380 million in 1983:

Road Accidents Great Britain 1983 (HMSO, 1984), para. 8.5.
84 Comparison between the weight placed on economic considerations by the Robens Committee and the Pearson Commission on the one hand, and the American National Commission on State Workmen's Compensation Laws on the other hand, is very revealing.
85 See Robens *Report*, Appendix 9.
86 Which would simply replace the present third-party liability insurance. This has been proposed by the N.S.W. Law Reform Commission.

CHAPTER 25

1 See generally Tunc, *International Encyclopaedia of Comparative Law* (Tubingen, The Hague, Paris and New York, 1971), Vol. XI.
2 Stapleton, (1985) 5 *O.J.L.S.* 248.
3 But certainly not all. One of the most curious features of tort law reform in the last 25 years is the way in which areas such as liability for animals and occupiers' liability have been 'reformed' by being made to rest on the fault principle. This has happened even in jurisdictions, such as Victoria, where no-fault schemes have been introduced in other areas in the same period.
4 See Atiyah, (1980) 54 *Tulane L.R.* 271.
5 Strict products liability is widespread in the United States and has been largely a common law development. The British position was discussed briefly in Chapter 6.
6 Stapleton, *op. cit.*, pp. 250–2, 255–7; Melville and Johnson, *Cured to Death*, p. 211; about 25% of unsuccessful claims made in the first two years of operation of the Swedish no-fault drug injuries scheme failed because of lack of proof of causal link: Fleming, (1982) 30 *Am. J. Comp. L.* 297, 303 n. 37.
7 As in the case of the drug injury compensation scheme in Germany: Fleming, *op. cit.*, p. 300.
8 Brown, *Disability Income*, Vol. 2, (London, 1984), p. 342.
9 See Ison, *Accident Compensation* (1980), pp. 18–19; Palmer, *Compensation for Incapacity* (1980), ch. XV.
10 Rea, (1982) 4 *Auckland U.L.R.* 235; Palmer, *op. cit.*, pp. 322–3.
11 See Chapter 13 above.
12 See p. 147 above.
13 For the British position see *The Times*, 13 May 1985.
14 Fleming, *op. cit.*
15 Sporting Injury Insurance Act 1978.
16 Fleming, *op. cit.*, p. 322.
17 See U.S. Dept of Transportation study, *State No-Fault Automobile Insurance Experience 1971–1977* (U.S. Govt Printer, Washington 1978); J. O'Connell and J. Breck, *Insurance Law J.* 129 (1979).
18 Klar in *Issues in Tort Law* (Steel and Rodgers-Magnet eds, Carswell, Toronto, 1983), p. 18.
19 Klar, *op. cit.*, p. 33.
20 Palmer, *op. cit.*, p. 93.
21 Stapleton, *op. cit.*

22 Ison, *op. cit.*, ch. 2; Palmer, ch. XV.
23 Report, para. 483.
24 Ison, pp. 30–1.
25 Palmer, pp. 204–5, 338.
26 Ison, pp. 31, 74–5, 188.
27 The Pearson Commission estimated that two-thirds of all tort payments are for non-pecuniary loss. Under the New Zealand scheme for the year ended 31 March 1978, compensation for non-pecuniary loss (permanent disability and pain and suffering) amounted to $18.1 million, while total compensation paid was $89.1 million (Palmer, p. 243).
28 Fleming, *op. cit.*, pp. 311–12.
29 Ison, pp. 187–8, 189.
30 Palmer, pp. 322–3.
31 Henderson, (1981) 48 *U. of Chi. L.R.* 781, 788–9.
32 Leaving aside here the complication introduced by the distinction between category rating and experience rating – see pp. 502 and 529 above.
33 Palmer, pp. 338–9. See further on funding method Ison, pp. 135–6.
34 Ison, ch. 8.
35 Klar, *op. cit.*, pp. 37–8.
36 Ison, pp. 124–34.
37 Palmer, p. 367.
38 Palmer, p. 370. On the other hand, cost externalization causes political problems too – opposition from those who perceive themselves to be the subsidizers.
39 Furthermore, the deterrent effect of the levies, especially those on manufacturers, is further diluted because the levies are spread via the price mechanism.
40 Ison, p. 122.
41 Many of the American schemes were inspired by Keeton and O'Connell, *Basic Protection for the Accident Victim – A Blueprint for Reforming Automobile Insurance* (Boston, 1965).
42 There is now quite an extensive literature on this scheme. See particularly Palmer, *op. cit.*; Ison, *op. cit*; Klar, *op. cit*; Gaskins, (1980) 18 *Osgoode Hall L.J.* 238; Henderson, (1981) *U. of Chi. L.R.* 781; Rea, (1982) 4 *Auckland U.L.R.* 235; Harris, (1974) 37 *M.L.R.* 361.
43 Ison, ch. 7; Palmer, pp. 391–9.
44 See n. 17 above; O'Connell, (1977) 56 *Neb. L.R.* 23, *The Law Suit Lottery* (New York, 1979), ch. 8; Henderson, (1977) 56 *Oregon L.R.* 287.
45 Mr Bruce Douglas-Mann, Hansard H.C. Vol. 958, col. 838 (17 November 1978).
46 Fleming, *op. cit.*
47 See Morris and Paul, (1962) 110 *U. Pa. L.R.* 913.
48 See especially Brown, *Disability Income*, Vol. 2, Chs. 12 and 13.
49 Leaving out of account also contracts of bailment (e.g., carriage, warehousing etc.) where accident prevention arguments may still be very relevant.
50 Professor Linden finds it 'paradoxical' to contemplate with equanimity the total abolition of actions for personal injury, but draw back from abolition for property damage, see (1971) 49 *Canadian Bar Review* 148, 151. But the explanation is that we anticipate an adequate and universal replacement for the former action, while only a voluntary replacement for the latter.

51 Moreover, not all vehicles on the road are insured against property damage; and although a motorist who does not take out comprehensive insurance is, in a sense, already running a serious risk voluntarily, this is less true of (say) bicycle owners.
52 See the Justice *Report on Compensation for Victims of Road Traffic Accidents*, para. 174.

INDEX

Abuse
  of social security, 366–8
Accident
  animals, caused by, 139–40, 142, 206
  distinguished from disease, 3–4, 619
  distinguished from negligence, 3
  gas leaks, caused by, 142
  industrial, *see* Industrial accidents
  notion of, 3 *et seq.*
  personal injury and death caused by, 16–17
  prevention, *see* Accident prevention
  risk, not within, 109–11
  road, *see* Road Accidents
  sporting events, at, 131, 240
Accident preference, 553
Accident prevention, 7, 9, 489 *et seq.*
  ability of tortfeasor to prevent accident, 491–5
  actor, deterring injury to, 498–9
  compensation systems not main line of attack, 490
  differences between Britain and US, 540
  effectiveness of tort in, 491
  incidence of payment, 496
  industrial accidents, 495, 497
  liability insurance, effect of, on, 496–8, 499–506
  need for guidance as to permitted behaviour, 493
Actuarial techniques, 177–8
Affirmative duties, *see* Omissions

Animals, accidents caused by, 139–40, 142, 206
Assumption of risk, *see* Volenti non fit injuria
Australian Committee of Inquiry, 14, 553

Bereavement, 76–8, 154–9, 167
Breach of statutory duty, *see* Statutory duty, action for breach of

Cantley Working Party, 269, 272
Care
  duty of, *see* Negligence, standard of care
  contributory negligence, in, 117
  liability insurance, effect of, on, 238–9
  objective, 53, 418
  subjective, 90
Cause
  as basis of compensation systems, 547–8
  distinction between human and natural causes of injury, 437 *et seq.*
  fact, in, 95 *et seq.*
    attributive enquiry, distinguished from, 102 *et seq.*
    burden of proof, 97
    'but for' test, 97
    omissions and, 97–8
    contributory negligence, relation of, to, 117–19

'real' or proximate cause, 102
    et seq.
  generally in tort law, 94 et seq.
  responsibility and, 108
Claims assessors, see Settlements
Claims consciousness
  among consumers, 203
  criminal injury compensation
    scheme, and, 311–12
  generally, 201 et seq.
Collateral benefits
  collateral, meaning of, 398
  conceptual arguments for rule,
    398 et seq.
  Pearson Report, proposals on,
    408
  policy arguments concerning,
    administrative cost, 402
    compensation, purpose of, and,
      400
    intention of person paying, 400
    victim, compensation paid for
      by, 401
    tort damages and
      charitable payments, 400–1,
        404–5
      occupational pensions, 404
      personal insurance, 403–4
      sick pay, 403
      social security benefits,
        405–9
      social services, 408–9
Compensation
  as a goal of compensation
    systems, 467 et seq., 560
  double, see Collateral benefits and
    Double compensation
  faculty, loss of, for, 24, 183 et seq.
  'full', principle of, 162, 169 et seq.
  meaning and purpose of, 467 et
    seq.
    equalization, 476
    'equivalence', 473
    punishment, 469–72
    solace, 475
    substitute, 474

pleasure forgone for, 475
neurosis, 151
see also Compensation, cost of;
  Compensation systems;
  Damages and Settlements
Compensation, cost of
  criminal injuries compensation,
    461–3
  distinction between private and
    social costs, 447–8
  high, reasons for, in tort system,
    adversary system, 450
    commission, 449
    settlement process, 450
  industrial accidents, 450–2
  legal aid, 456
  medical treatment, 455–6, 457
  non-fault caused accidents,
    455
  road accidents, 452
    borne by narrow class, 452
    distributed according to
      accident-causing
      potential, 452
    uninsured motorists,
      attributable to, 454
  social security, 457–61
    administrative costs, 461
    Beveridge proposals for special
      levy, 459
    fixed-rate, contributions, 458–
      60
    industrial injuries, 458 et seq.
  social services, 455–7
  subsidization between activities,
    451
Compensation neurosis, 151
Compensation systems
  choice of, 390 et seq.
  interrelation of systems, 387 et
    seq.
    possibility of stalemate in, 392
  mixed systems in mixed society,
    7 et seq.
  policy questions, relation to, 13
Contract, 73–5, 137–8

see also Undertakings *and* Volenti
non fit injuria
Contributory negligence
  action for breach of statutory
    duty, defence to, 134
  cause, and, 117 *et seq.*
  criminal injuries scheme, 303–6
  deterrent, as, 117, 124–5, 498
  family cases, and, 121–2
  identification, doctrine of, 121
  insurance, relationship with, 120
  last opportunity rule, 117
  penal effects of, 124
  question of fact, treated as, 119
  relative fault, 122
  seat-belt cases, 119, 498–9
  settlements, effect of, on, 124
  strict products liability, and, 145
  test of, more subjective, 119–21
Corporations, liability of, 216 *et seq.*
Cost of compensation, *see*
  Compensation, cost of
Costs, 267 *et seq.*
  payments into court, effect on,
    268
  settlements, effect of, on, 270
Criminal injuries compensation
  scheme, 291 *et seq.*
  administration of, 308–11
    interim awards, 309
    lawyers, by, 308
    legal aid not available, 309–10
    level of awards, criticisms of,
      310–11
    representation at hearings, 310
  assessment of compensation,
    306–8
    damages, similarity to, 306
    exceptions, double
      compensation, 308
    losses below £400, 306–7
    maximum earnings, 307
    no damages for benefit of
      estate, 308
  claims consciousness, 311–12
  cost of, 461–3
  crimes of violence, 297–300
  fraudulent claims, danger of, 302
  justification for, 291 *et seq.*
    intellectual confusion involved
      in, 293 *et seq.*
    parliamentary debates, 295–6
  payments, *ex gratia*, 296
  Pearson Report, and, 296–7
  scope of
    accidental injuries, 300–1
    children, injuries caused by,
      299–300
    exclusions, 301–3
    occupational hazards, 300–1,
      462–3
    suicide, 298
  tort liability, compared to, 303 *et
    seq.*
    contributory negligence, 303–6
    fights, 304–5
  vicarious liability, relation with,
    220

Damage
  extraordinary, 112
  physical, duty of care in relation
    to, 63 *et seq.*
  property, to, 4
  reform of law of, 576–7
  remoteness of, 110 *et seq.*
Damages
  actuarial techniques, 177–8
  amenities, loss of, for, *see under*
    pain and suffering
  defendant, individual, not
    usually paid by, 215
  disabilities, for, *see under* pain and
    suffering
  earnings-related principle, 169–
    73
  Fatal Accidents Acts, under,
    154–9
  general, *see under* special
  household services, for, 159
  inflation, effect of, on, 178
  interest upon, 165–6
  interim awards, 153–4
  lost earnings, for,

INDEX

actuarial techniques, 177–80
'multiplier', 166
lump sum, 159 et seq.
  matrimonial cases contrasted, 158
  periodical payments, difficulties of enforcing, 213, 255
  maximum awards, 191–2
  medical expenses, for, 181 et seq.
  pain and suffering and loss of amenities and faculties, 183 et seq.
    jury assessment of, 185
    objective/subjective elements in damages for, 187–8
    proportion of damages attributable to, 555
    'tariff' approach, 188 et seq.
  periodical payments, 161–2
  settlements, 154, 273 et seq.
  special and general damages, distinction between, 164
  speculation involved in assessing, 150 et seq., 155 et seq.
  tax, effect of, on, 178
  variation of awards after trial, 153–4
  widows, remarriage of, effect on, 156 et seq.
  see also Settlements
Death
  of tortfeasor or victim, effect of on claim in tort, 76–8
Dependency, 78 et seq.
  see also Fatal Accident Acts
Deterrence, see Accident prevention and General deterrence
Disabled, 17–20, 375 et seq.
  see also Social services
Disability benefits, see Social security
Disease
  accident preference, 553
  distinction between accident and, 3–4
  industrial, see Social security
  personal injury and death caused by, 17–20
  special difficulties in compensating for, 96
Distribution of losses, see Loss distribution
Distribution of wealth as a feature of compensation systems, 560
Double compensation, 180, 387 et seq.
  compensation systems individually against, 388
  criminal injuries compensation scheme, not permitted under, 393, 409–10
  Pearson Report on, 408–9
  legal aid, and, 392
  see also Collateral benefits and Subrogation
Double recovery, see Double compensation

Economic loss, 73–5
  family cases, 78–80
Egalitarianism, 442 et seq.
  war damage schemes, influence of, on, 443
Employers
  liability of, 216 et seq.
    assaults, for, 220
    independent contractors, for, 218
    vicarious and personal, 217
  right of recompense against employee, 222
  see also Sick pay
Expectation of life, loss of, 76
Expectations, protection of, 441–2

Fact
  findings of, 95–6
  question of, 35–9
Fairness as a goal of compensation systems, 560
Fatal Accidents Acts, 154 et seq., 163, 167–8; see also Damages
Fault

adjudication on, difficulties of,
    430 et seq.
  in negotiating settlements, 432
  in trial cases, 431
  statistical factors relevant to,
    433 et seq.
conduct of plaintiff ignored,
  425-6
  except in case of contributory
    negligence, 426
degree of, ignored, 415-16
indictment of principle of, 415 et
  seq.
means of defendant ignored,
  416-17
morality of principle of, 417 et
  seq.
  collective liability, cases of,
    422-4
  conflict between compensation
    purpose and, 420
  objective definition of fault,
    418-21
necessary and sufficient test of
  tort liability, 412
needs of plaintiff ignored, 426-7
other grounds for requiring
  payment of compensation,
  484 et seq.
place of, in compensation
  systems, 411 et seq.
plaintiff, of, 413
proof of, see adjudication
Fire, liability for, 90 et seq., 114
Foreseeability, 44 et seq.
  degrees of, 44-5
  and remoteness, 110-12

General deterrence, 506 et seq.
  accident and life insurance, and,
    531-2
  activity causing accidents,
    identification of, 512-13
  as a goal of compensation
    systems, 560
  assessment of value of, 532 et seq.
  cost of activity, allocation of, 511
    et seq.

  bargaining case, 513-16
  non-bargaining case, 516-22
elasticity of supply and demand,
  520
enterprise and individual
  liability, 524
limitations of, 532
loss distribution, conflict with,
  532 et seq.
  premium rating and, 533 et seq.
marginal costs, 524-5
non-economic costs, valuation of,
  511
presuppositions of, 536-8
  taxation, effect of, on, 537
social security system and, 529-
  31
tort system and, 523 et seq.
  costs not charged to activities,
    527
  enterprise and individual
    liability, 524
  non-fault caused accidents, 525

Industrial accidents
  doctrinal defences to tort actions
    for, 313-14
  insurance, effect of, on, 497
  proportion of victims who receive
    damages, 206 et seq.
  statistics of, 16 et seq.
Industrial injuries scheme, see
  Social security
Industrial legislation, 133 et seq.,
  495
Inflation
  damages, effect on, 178 et seq.
  insurance companies and, 253-4
Insurance
  bereavement, against, not
    obtainable, 282
  business losses, against, 75
  companies, see Insurance
    companies
  fire, 91, 280
  first party, 279 et seq.
    compared with tort liability,
      283 et seq.

causal problems, 287
contributory negligence immaterial, 286
correction of mistakes, 284
full compensation often not payable, 285
method of compensation depends on loss, 284
optional, 283
third parties, for benefit of, 230 *et seq.*
relation to other compensation systems, 389, 392
tort damages and, 403
householders', 200
indemnity, 288
liability insurance,
  accident prevention, effect of, on, 499 *et seq.*
  benefit of insured, no longer intended for, 225–6, 244
  comparison with other types of insurance, 226–7
  compulsory system of, 243
  contributory negligence, relationship to, 229
  criminal assualts, not covered by, 304
  general deterrence, and, 532–5
  legal aid, effect of, on, 243
  nature of, 224 *et seq.*
  tort law, impact of, on, 232 *et seq.*
    effect on level of damages, 235–6
    effect on set-off procedure, 236–7
    effect on standard of care, 238–9
    vicarious liability compared to, 221–2
life,
  actuarial techniques, 177
  popularity of, 279–80
medical, 281
motor, *see* Road accidents
national,
  cost of, 457 *et seq.*
  hotchpotch of insurance and welfare principles, 458–61
  and see Social security
personal accident, 280
  disabilities and lost earnings, 283–4
  employers, by, for employees, 231–2
  less signficant than other, 280
permanent health, 281
premium rating, 502 *et seq.*, 532–5
profits, loss of, 75, 289
property, loss of, or damage to, 228, 285, 289
  bailees, by, 230–1
riot damage, 282
risk, reduced to measurable terms by, 430
road traffic, 244–5
self, 216
subrogation, *see* Subrogation
war risks, 282
Insurance companies
  accident prevention, role of, in, 499 *et seq.*
  bankruptcy of, 235–6, 255
  claims settlement, role in, 256 *et seq.*
  control over, 235–6
  inflation and, 253–4
  problems of, 252 *et seq.*
  reform, role of, in, 577 *et seq.*
  solvency of, public interest in, 534
  subrogation, attitude to, 394, 397–8
Intangible losses, *see* Damages *and* Loss
Interim awards, 153–4
Invalidity benefits, 355 *et seq.*

Joint liability, 140–1
Jury
  pain and suffering, role of, in assessing damages for, 185

Index 635

question of fact, 36
Legal aid
  cost of, 456
  criminal injuries compensation scheme, not available for, 309
  figures and statistics, 260–1
  knowledge of, 202
  liability insurance, relation to, 243, 245, 392
  payments in, refusal of, effects of, 268
  proposals for change, 578
  settlements usually made without, 260
  social security tribunals, not available for, 352
  subrogation and, 394
Legal profession, role of, 578–9
Liability insurance, *see* Insurance
Life, value of, 48, 183–4
Litigation, *see* Costs *and* Settlements
Local authorities, liability of, 57–8, 495
Loss
  amenities, of, *see* Damages
  distribution, *see* Loss distribution
  deceased, to estate of, 76 *et seq.*, 155, 167–8
  definition of, 476–7
  economic, 73–5
  faculty, of, *see* Damages
  happiness, of, 187–8
  intangible, 183 *et seq.*
  more and less serious, 23 *et seq.*
  notion of, 476–7
  shifting of, 478
Loss distribution, 476 *et seq.*
  among whom, 479
  desirability of, 479–80
  efficient, 480–1
  equitable, 480
  loss shifting, by, 478
Malpractice claims, *see* Medical negligence
Medical negligence, 496
Mental distress, 69 *et seq.*

Misfeasance, *see* Omissions
Monckton Committee, 400, 405 *et seq.*
Motor Insurers' Bureau, 247 *et seq.*

National insurance, *see* Social security
Negligence
  burden of proof, 96, 97, 265
  custom, 37
  damage not within risk of, 109–11
  design in, 55 *et seq.*
  distinct tort, 33
  duty of care, 60 *et seq.*
    breach of, 35 *et seq.*
    criteria, 39 *et seq.*
    precautions, burden of, 49 *et seq.*
    control of property, 90–2
    control of third parties, 89–90
    expansion of, effect of liability insurance on, 238
    general principle, 61–3
    miscellaneous cases, 65 *et seq.*
    occupiers of land, 68–9
    omissions, 80 *et seq.*
    pecuniary loss, 73–5
    physical damage, 63 *et seq.*
    privity restriction removed, 66–8
    relativity of, 60
    undertakings, 87–8
  economic basis of, 41
  error and, 421
  essential elements of, 34–5
  family claims, 75 *et seq.*
  foreseeability and, 44–7
  operation, in, 55 *et seq.*
  public authorities, of, 57–8, 495
  regulator of conduct, as, 490 *et seq.*
  standard of care, 53 *et seq.*, 417 *et seq.*
  tort law, place of, in, 33
New Zealand compensation system, 173, Ch. 25 *passim*

No fault schemes, 546–8
Nonfeasance, *see* Omissions

Objective standard of care, 53 *et seq.*
Occupiers, liability of, 68–9, 90–2
Omissions
  cause and, 85–6
  control of others, 89–90
  control of property, 90–2
  policy reasons for not imposing liability for, 82–6
  undertakings, 87–8

Pearson Report
  establishment, 15
  estimates on sources and cost of compensation, 16 *et seq.*, 34, 197 *et seq.*, 208, 256–7
  fate of proposals, 546
  industrial preference, on, 321
  integration, proposals for, 13, 408
  road accident proposals, 567–8
Pecuniary loss, *see* Economic loss
Periodical payments, *see* Damages
Personal injury actions, 195 *et seq.*
  see also Litigation; Settlements *and* Trials
Plaintiffs, *see* Tort system
Priorities
  accident and disease, between, 17–20
  systems, between, 13–14
  victims, between, 146, 148, 191, 192, 549–50, 552–4, 569, 572
Premium rating, 502 *et seq.*
Products liability, 144–6
Proximate cause, *see* Cause
Public bodies, liability of, 57–8, 495

Railway accidents, 146–7
Reasonable man, 36–9
Reform
  assessment of damages, 554–8
  comprehensive reform, characteristics of, 548–9
  difficulties facing, 572 *et seq.*
  dual systems of compensation, 550–2
  earnings-related compensation, 556–7
  fault liability, 545–6
  funding of compensation schemes, 558–60
  goals of reform, 560–5
  industrial injuries scheme as a model for reform, 571, 575
  insurance industry, role of, in, 577 *et seq.*
  legal profession, role of, in, 577 *et seq.*
  liability rules, 545–8
  limited reform, 548 *et seq.*
  long-term and seriously disabled, benefits for, 555
  means-tested compensation, 557
  New Zealand compensation system, Ch. 25 *passim*
  'no-fault' schemes,
    characteristics of, 547–8
    costs of, 565
    funding of, 558–60
    justification for, 562–3
  non-pecuniary losses, compensation for, 555–6
  property damage, 576–7
  relationship between tort liability and no-fault compensation, 550–2, 574–5
  road accident schemes, 566 *et seq.*
    advantages of no-fault schemes, 568–9
    British proposals, 567–8
    preferential treatment for road accident victims, 569
    types of, 566–7
  strict liability, 546–7
Remoteness of damage, 110 *et seq.*
  see also Cause
Rescue, 82 *et seq.*, 425
Responsibility
  ascription of, as related to cause, 106, 424–5

Index 637

society, of, for injuries, 438 *et seq.*
Retribution, 484–6
Risk
   allocation, 481–3
   bearer, 143
   see also Negligence
Road accidents
   assumption of risk of, *see Volenti non fit injuria*
   causes of, 105–6, 205–6, 433–6
   design of vehicles and roads, 55
   duty of care, 64
   generally in tort system, 204–6
   learner driver, 54
   level-crossing accidents, 40
   passengers as victims, 205
   skid-prone roads, 434
   reform of law, 566–70

Satisfaction
   compensation systems, as aim of, 486 *et seq.*
Settlements
   amount of, 273 *et seq.*
   bargaining nature of, 266–7
   claims assessors, role of, in, 258
   children, on behalf of, 258
   contributory negligence, effect of, on, 274
   costs system, effect of, on, 268–9 *and see* Costs
   course of negotiations, 261 *et seq.*
   criminal proceedings, effect of, on, 262–3
   damages awards, consistency of, necessary for, 186
   defendant, need to find, 240–1, 248
   delays in, 271 *et seq.*
   disreputable tactics in resisting, 266
   evidence, difficulties in obtaining, 260 *et seq.*
   ex gratia offers, 265
   insurers, practice of, 261 *et seq.*
   judicial process, use of, in obtaining, 257
   legal aid, *see* Legal aid
   payments into court, 268
   payment of solicitors for, 259
   proportion of, 256
   purpose of parties to, 257
   small claims, nuisance value of, 270
   trade unions, role of, in, 202, 258
Sick pay
   occupational, 371 *et seq.*
   statutory, 333–5, 356
Social security
   attendance allowance, 358
   cost of, 457 *et seq.*
   double compensation not generally permitted, 405–8
   earnings-related benefits, 324–5, 342, 345–6, 357–8
   implications for tort system of, 325
   industrial injuries scheme, 327 *et seq.*
      accident distinguished from 'process', 330
      administration of, 348 *et seq.*
      assessment of disabilities, 349
      medical tribunals, 350–1
      Social Security Commissioners, 350, 351–2
      Social Security Appeal Tribunals, 350–1
   benefits, 333 *et seq.*
      long-term incapacity, 335 *et seq.*
      short-term incapacity, 333–5
      tax, effect of, on value of, 334, 343
      widows, for, 346 *et seq.*
      effect of remarriage on, 347
   Beveridge proposals for, 321
   causal problems, 327–30
   course of employment, 327 *et seq.*

638   INDEX

disablement pensions, 335 *et seq.*
   compared to common law awards, 341
   objective assessment of, 336
disease, industrial, 330 *et seq.*
premium rating system, 529 *et seq.*
origins of, Beveridge Report, 319 *et seq.*
   comprehensive nature of proposals, 319–20
   criticisms of workmen's compensation, 320
   proposals for industrial injuries, 321 *et seq.*
scope of, 327 *et seq.*
   accidents arising out of and in course of employment, 327 *et seq.*
   self-employed not covered, 327
   special hardship allowance, 343
   skylarking accidents, 329
invalid care allowance, 359
invalidity benefits, 357
mobility allowance, 359
statutory sick pay 333–5, 356
supplementary benefits, 362 *et seq.*
tariff for assessment of disabilities, 336 *et seq.*
widows' benefits, 346–8, 361–2
see also Workmen's compensation

Social services
day nurseries, 381
employment, 376 *et seq.*
   Employment Rehabilitation Centres, 377
   rehabilitation of disabled, 377
   Remploy, 378
   'skill centres', 377
   quotas, 378
home helps, 381
home teachers, 381
housing, 380
local authorities, provided by, 381
   in association with charities, 381–2
meals on wheels, 381
mobility, 379–80
Standard of care, *see* Care *and* Negligence
Statutory duty, action for breach of, 133 *et seq.*
Strict liability, 133 *et seq.*
   animals, for, 139
   breach of statutory duty, 133 *et seq.*
   contractual duties, 137–8
   nature of, 141–3
   nuisance, 138
   Pearson proposals for, 143–4, 146–7, 148–9
   products liability, 144–6
Subrogation, 393 *et seq.*
   attitude of insurance companies to, 394, 397–8
   criticism of, 395–7
   insurance cases, 394
   Monckton Committee proposals on, 391
   problems relative to State, 396
   proposals for wider use, 395

Taxation
charities, free of, 370
compensation, as method of, 369
disabled, reliefs for, 369–70
social security benefits, effect of, on, 334, 343
Tort system
administration process, can be regarded as, 257
cases set down for trial, 196–7
cases tried, 195–6
claims and payments, 197 *et seq.*
claims consciousness, 201 *et seq.*
cost of, 449 *et seq.*
defendants, individual bankruptcy of, 213
deterrent, as, 489 *et seq.*
difficulty of enforcing judgment against, 212 *et seq.*

Index 639

attachment of earnings
    order, 213–14
  more affluent defendants,
    214 et seq.
  delays, 152, 271 et seq.
  general deterrence, and, 506 et
    seq.
  industrial accidents, 206–9
  road accidents, 204–6
  see also Costs; Damages; Fault;
    Negligence; Settlements
    and Trials
Trials
  delays, 271 et seq.
  figures for, in High Court, 195
  see also Costs

Unborn children, duty of care to,
  63
Undertakings, 87–8

Vaccine damage, 147–9
Vicarious liability, 141, 217 et seq.
  liability for independent
    contractors, 218 et seq.
Vindication, 486 et seq.
Volenti non fit injuria, 126 et seq.
  agreement, as, 126–8
  contributory negligence, and,
    128–30

exclusion clauses and, 127
sporting events, 131
standard of care, and, 130–2

Welfare state, 7 et seq., 313 et seq.
Welsh quarrymen, 374
Widows
  claim by, against husbands'
    estate, 241
  damages for, see Fatal Accidents
    Acts
  remarriage of, 156–8
  social security benefits, see Social
    security
Workmen's compensation
  administration of, 315–16
  allocation of risks, and, 314–16
  American National Commission,
    173, 535
  Beveridge Report, condemned
    by, 320
  causal principles involved in, 316
  contributory negligence as
    defence to claim for, 315
  cost of, 317
  full compensation not payable,
    314
  industrial disease, 316
  origins of, 314
  partial incapacity, 317